Annual Survey
of
African Law

Volume III – 1969

Annual Survey of African Law

Volume III—1969

Edited by

N. N. RUBIN, B.A., LL.B.
*Advocate of the Supreme Court of South Africa
and the High Court of Swaziland*
*Lecturer in African Law, School of Oriental and
African Studies, Institute of Advanced Legal Studies,
University of London*

and

E. COTRAN, LL.B., LL.D., DIP.I.L.
of Lincoln's Inn, Barrister at Law
*Lecturer in African Law, School of Oriental and
African Studies, University of London*

FRANK CASS : LONDON

First published 1973 in Great Britain by
FRANK CASS AND COMPANY LIMITED
67 Great Russell Street, London WC1B 3BT, England

and in United States of America by
FRANK CASS AND COMPANY LIMITED
c/o International Scholarly Book Services, Inc.
P.O. Box 4347, Portland, Oregon 97208

Library of Congress Catalog Card Number 73–23072

ISBN 0 7146 2948 0

Copyright © 1973 N. Rubin and E. Cotran

Printed in Great Britain by
The Garden City Press Limited
Letchworth, Hertfordshire
SG6 1JS

CONTENTS

PART I: COMMONWEALTH AFRICAN COUNTRIES

TABLE OF CASES

A

B

N

O

P

Q

R

* *

PART I

Commonwealth African Countries

CHAPTER 1

GHANA

A. N. Allott

CONSTITUTIONAL LAW

No apology whatsoever need be made to the reader because this chronicle of legal events in Ghana during the year 1969 devotes so much attention to constitutional developments there, since this reflects local pre-occupations with the transition from military to civilian rule. Almost uniquely in Africa there was a planned surrender of power by the ruling military National Liberation Council [N.L.C.] to a constitutionally-elected civilian government; and, what is more important still, the originally announced timetable, which envisaged such a handing over by the end of September 1969, was adhered to despite various intermediate holdups, notably those caused by the slow progress of the Constituent Assembly's deliberations. This body had been charged with the task of debating, framing and enacting a new Republican Constitution for Ghana in the light of the report of the Constitutional Commission designated by the N.L.C. (the appointment of each of these bodies was discussed in detail in the Survey for 1968, q.v.). As the tale of events and achievements is complicated, it may be helpful if the framework is set out as a chronology below:

1957 The Gold Coast and Togoland became independent under the name of Ghana as a monarchy within the Commonwealth, with Dr. Kwame Nkrumah as Prime Minister.

1960 Ghana adopts a Republican Constitution [now referred to as the "First Republic"], with Nkrumah as President.

1966 *7th February*. Nkrumah ousted, the Constitution suspended, and military and police rule substituted. The new government headed by the newly created National Liberation Council.

1966 *September*. A Constitutional Commission appointed.

1968 *January*. Report of Constitutional Commission published.

1968 *30th December*. First meeting of Constituent Assembly. Speaker (R. S. Blay) and Deputy Speaker elected.

1969 *6th January*. Assembly meets with 136 members to begin discussions.
7th February. Proposals of Constitutional Commission adopted as a working basis for discussions.
18th February. N.L.C. issues the Elections and Public Officers

(Disqualification) Decree,[1] which bars 152 persons from public office.

2nd April. General Ankrah dismissed as Chairman of the N.L.C., being replaced by Brigadier Afrifa. Reshuffle of N.L.C.

1st May. Formation of political parties again permitted with coming into effect of the Political Parties Decree.[2] The Decree also banned a further list of functionaries under the Nkrumah régime from holding public office.

2nd May and subsequently. A number of political parties formed and registered under the Decree, notably the Progress Party (P.P.) and the National Alliance of Liberals (N.A.L.), led by Dr. Busia and Mr. Gbedemah respectively.

12th May. First Report of Jiagge Assets Commission. Among those adversely commented on and ordered to make repayment by the N.L.C. is Mr. Gbedemah.[3]

6th June. The People's Popular Party, a new party allegedly containing a large number of ex-C.P.P. supporters and with a generally socialist outlook, banned by the N.L.C. under the Prohibited Organisations Decree, 1969,[4] which also disqualifies persons listed in the Schedule to the Decree "from holding office in, or being founder members, of a political party" (para. 2).

Article 71 of the proposed Constitution is passed by the Constituent Assembly. This Article, which was highly controversial and was vigorously contested by a minority in the Assembly, disqualifies a person from holding public office if adversely commented on by an assets commission of enquiry. Since there had been an adverse finding by the Jiagge Commission against Mr. Gbedemah, his party sees this as a direct personal attack on him.

18th July. Discussions of Constituent Assembly completed with Third Reading of all Articles of the Constitution. At the end of this, the 92nd and final session of the Assembly, the Assembly adjourns *sine die.*

8th August. Party political broadcasts permitted.

13th August. Constituent Assembly meets again. A new motion that the functions of the President should be exercised for the first 5 years by the Chairman and Deputy Chairman of the N.L.C., together with the Chief of Defence Staff, is ruled out of order by the Speaker.

14th August. Constitution formally enacted.

18th August. Dispute as to which body should promulgate the Constitution. The N.L.C. says that this is the function of the Constituent Assembly.

21st August. A new clause in the Constitution, providing that the functions of the President should be exercised for a period not exceeding three years and until the National Assembly should otherwise decide by a Presidential Commission consisting of the Chairman (Brigadier Afrifa), and the Vice-Chairman (Mr. Harlley) of the N.L.C., together with Major-General Ocran (Chief of Defence Staff), was put to the Constituent Assembly and passed by it, by virtue of a special Decree[5] made on 18th August permitting it to re-convene.

22nd August. Constitution promulgated.

29th August. General Election, contested by five registered parties. Landslide victory for Progress Party (led by Dr. Busia) with 105 seats; main opposition party the National Alliance of Liberals (led by Mr. Gbedemah) with 29 seats. Busia invited to form government.

3rd September. Dr. Busia sworn in as Prime Minister.

5th September. Mr. Justice N. A. Ollennu elected Speaker of the National Assembly.

26th September. Hearing of proceedings in High Court to unseat Mr. Gbedemah.

30th September. Inauguration of Second Republic.

1st October. Dissolution of National Liberation Council and Executive Council by the Constitution (Consequential and Transitional Provisions) Decree.[6] This, the final decree of the N.L.C., marks the end of military rule in Ghana.

2nd October. State Opening of Parliament.

This chronicle of events brings out both the early commitment of the military régime to a return to civilian rule, the clearly envisaged timetable for such return, the delays (especially through the dilatory debates of the Constituent Assembly) imposed on the timetable, the uncertainty about the correct machinery for the restoration of constitutional government (cf. the dispute between N.L.C. and Assembly about which body should promulgate the new constitution), the effectiveness of the contribution made by the very detailed investigations and recommendations of the Constitutional Commission to the elaboration of the new constitution, the last-minute afterthought which substituted an interim troika for the President, and the dispute about the position of Mr. Gbedemah which represented the clash between the wish to suppress all vestiges of the old C.P.P. system and its operators on the one hand, and the desire to inaugurate a new plural democratic society of free speech and party organisation on the other.

So far as the content of the Republican Constitution as actually enacted is concerned, this, while based on the draft prepared by the Commission, differed from it in certain important respects. An attempt to reduce the minimum voting age from 21 to 18 was defeated in the Assembly, as were proposals for a bicameral legislature, a Vice-President, and salaries for M.Ps. Among the new features were a National House of Chiefs; substantial change in Article 3 dealing with the defence of democracy; new Article 37A proscribing tribal or religious parties; new Article 13 providing for legislative protection of the family as the unit of society; new Article 21(2) forbidding the depriving of a child or other person in a weak position of medical education, education, etc, "by reason only of any religious or philosophical doctrine or belief"; that a candidate for presidency should be at least 40 years old (rather than 50 as proposed); the composition of the presidential electoral college; the procedure for removal of a president; the composition of the Council of State; the principles upon which Ghana should conduct its international affairs (Article 57); the procedure for selection of the Prime Minister; the effect of a successful no-confidence resolution in the National Assembly; and the appointment of an interim Presidential Commission to exercise the functions of the President.

The main features of the Constitution have already been summarised in the 1968 report;[7] briefly they are: a ceremonial rather than executive president; unicameral parliamentary government with a prime minister responsible to parliament; a Council of State to advise the President; an ombudsman; judicial review by the Supreme Court of the constitutionality of legislation; entrenched fundamental rights. All in all, they represent an attempt to prevent, by the use of the classical devices available in constitutions around the world, the abuse of power by one organ or individual.

The rest of the constitutional story for 1969 can be swiftly told. On 24th November Mr. Gbedemah was declared by the Supreme Court to be disqualified under Article 71(2)(*b*)(ii) of the Constitution from being a Member of Parliament, and his seat in the Keta constituency to which he had been elected was declared vacant. Dr. G. K. Agama was declared Leader of the Parliamentary Opposition in his place.

Among the legislation providing for the machinery of transition to parliamentary rule the most significant were:

the Elections and Public Offices Disqualification Decree,[7a] which disqualified for 10 years a long list of party functionaries and public office-holders under the Nkrumah régime from holding a number of public offices, notably as a member of the Constituent Assembly or National Assembly;
the Prohibited Organisations Decree,[8] which banned the People's Popular Party as contrary to the public good, and disqualified a list of named persons in Part II of the Decree:

> "(*a*) from holding office in, or being founding members, [*sic*] of a political party; and
> (*b*) from election or appointment to or the holding of any office listed in para. 1 of the Elections and Public Offices Disqualifications Decree, 1969 . . .";

the Political Parties Decree,[9] which contained in its Schedule a further list of persons disqualified by reason of their former offices from holding office in, or being founder members of, a political party; the Decree by para. 2 prohibited the formation of tribal or religious parties:

> "2(1) It is hereby prohibited for any political party to be formed on a tribal or religious basis or for any such party to have a name which is intended by the political party to arouse tribal or religious feelings or to employ in connection with its name any words or symbols which are intended by the political party to arouse any such feelings.
> (2) For the purposes of the foregoing sub para., a political party shall be deemed to be formed on a tribal or religious basis if its membership or leadership is restricted to members of any particular community or religious faith or if its structure and mode of operation are not national in character."

and by para. 4 provided that every political party must be registered. Paras. 6, 20 and 22 are of special interest:

> "6. (1) No political party shall be registered under this Decree unless at least three founding members of the political party are ordinarily resident, or registered as voters, in each of the Regions of Ghana.

(2) Not more than six of the founding members of a political party shall belong to any one tribe.

(3) The decision of the Registrar as to whether or not any person belongs to any tribe shall, for the purposes of this paragraph, be final.

"20. (1) Every political party which contravenes any provision of this Decree shall on application by the Attorney-General to the Registrar be declared by the Registrar in addition to any penalty provided under this Decree to be a prohibited organisation.

(2) Where a political party is declared under the foregoing sub paragraph to be a prohibited organisation no person shall:

(*a*) summon a meeting of members or officers of the political party;

(*b*) attend or cause any person to attend any meeting in the capacity of a member or officer of the political party;

(*c*) publish any notice or advertisement relating to any such meeting;

(*d*) invite persons to support the political party;

(*e*) make any contribution or loan to funds held or to be held by or for the benefit of the political party or accept any such contribution or loan; or

(*f*) give any guarantee in respect of such funds as aforesaid.

(3) Upon application being made by the Attorney-General, the High Court may with respect to any political party declared under this paragraph to be a prohibited organisation, make such order as appears to the Court just and equitable for the winding up and dissolving or the disposition of any property or assets held by the political party.

(4) For the purposes of this paragraph officer includes, in relation to any political party, any person taking part in the management or control of the political party or any person holding or purporting to hold a position of management or control therein.

"22. In this Decree, unless the context otherwise requires:

(*a*) political party includes any free association or organisation of persons (whether corporate or unincorporated) one of whose objects is to bring about the election of its candidates to public office or to strive for power by the electoral process and by this means to control or influence the actions of Government; and

(*b*) region, for the purposes of this Decree, includes the administrative area known as Greater Accra."

and the Representation of the People (Amendment) Decree,[10] which modified in some respects the parent Decree.[11]

In the area of public and administrative law there were a number of enactments which overlap into the economic and social fields. Most important was the law affecting aliens. On 19th November the Government announced without warning that all aliens, African and non-African, without residence permits must leave Ghana in 14 days and in any event not later than 2nd December.[12] Large numbers of aliens who failed to comply, including many Nigerians and citizens of other African countries, were arrested by the police and escorted to the frontier. Hundreds of thousands of such aliens, including many born in Ghana, were affected by the order. It is worth noting that the fundamental rights provisions of the new constitution apparently did not avail to prevent this expulsion and consequent deprivation of property and other rights. This, taken with the earlier tightening up by the Government of job reservation for Ghanaians, is symptomatic of the xenophobia currently sweeping West Africa, which has led to the enactment of laws for the expulsion of foreigners or the indigenisation of commerce in many countries.

Also noteworthy is the Public Service Commission Decree,[13] which re-established a Public Service Commission. Among those included in the public service by the Decree (para. 7) are, apart from the Civil Service, members of the Teaching Service, the Prisons Service, and the Fire Service (though the police are excluded). Para. 7(3) explains that:

> "The Teaching Service shall comprise all teachers employed in public institutions".[14]

As the staff of local authorities are incorporated by para. 8(1) in the Civil Service, the role of the Public Service Commission is a wide one. Every public servant is by para. 16 given a right of appeal to the Commission if

> "he is aggrieved by the decision of any authority affecting his employment, promotion, transfer, terms and conditions of service, or any disciplinary matter. . . ."

Wages in the public service are to be periodically reviewed by a Public Service Advisory Board set up by the Public Service Wages and Salaries Decree.[15]

Professions and education

A number of Decrees have regulated different professions or constituted public institutions. Thus the Ghana Institute of Management and Public Administration Decree[16] constituted an institute of that name; the National Museum Decree[17] controls the export of antiquities and the excavation of or search for antiquities, permits any monument to be proclaimed a national monument, and regulates the existing Ghana Museum and Monuments Board.[18] A National Council for Higher Education is established by Decree,[19] the purposes of the Council being similar in many respects to those of the University Grants Committee in England, i.e. to act as a buffer between government and universities and to advise government generally on the financing and development of university institutions in Ghana. The architects' profession is regulated by the Architects Decree,[20] which establishes an Architects Registration Council and restricts practice as an architect to those who are registered under the Decree and hold an annual practising certificate. Similar provision is made in the case of engineers by the Ghana Institution of Engineers Decree,[21] which establishes a Ghana Institution of Engineers to regulate the profession.

Among the constitutional cases calling for comment, by far the most important are those affecting the position of Mr. Gbedemah and his eligibility for membership of Parliament, to which brief reference has already been made. In *Gbedemah* v. *Awoonor-Williams*[22] in the Supreme

Court (Azu Crabbe, Apaloo, Siriboe, Sowah, and Archer, JJ.A.) Mr. Awoonor-Williams, a defeated candidate for the Keta constituency in the General Election of 29th August 1969, sued for a declaration that Mr. Gbedemah, the successful candidate for the constituency, was not qualified to be a member of the National Assembly by virtue of Article 71(2)(*b*)(ii) and (*d*) of the Constitution, which says:

"(2) No person shall be qualified to be a member of the Assembly who . . .
(*b*) has been adjudged or otherwise declared . . .
   (*ii*)   by the report of a Commission of Inquiry to be incompetent to hold public office or that while being a public officer he acquired assets unlawfully, or abused his office or wilfully acted in a manner prejudicial to the interests of the State . . .
(*d*) has had his property confiscated as the result of the findings of a Commission of Inquiry; . . ."

Mr. Gbedemah then in due course, after filing a defence, applied to the Supreme Court to strike out the claim by Mr. Awoonor-Williams, on the ground that the court sitting as the Supreme Court was incompetent to deal with the claim, as this was within the jurisdiction of the High Court. Article 76(1) of the Constitution provides that:

"(1) The High Court of Justice shall have jurisdiction to hear and determine any question whether
(*a*) any person has been validly elected as a member of the National Assembly or the seat of any member has become vacant; or
(*b*) any person has been validly elected as Speaker of the Assembly or, having been so elected, has vacated the office of Speaker."

The Supreme Court rejected the objection to its jurisdiction. It was correct that, to invoke the jurisdiction of the Supreme Court, it had to be shown that the claim was either (i) concerned with the interpretation of the Constitution, or (ii) to enforce a provision of the Constitution, or (iii) to determine whether an enactment was *ultra vires*; and it was also found by the court that in this case no question of interpretation was raised, nor was it a question of an *ultra vires* enactment. Yet, said the Supreme Court, its jurisdiction was not exhausted by Article 2 of the Constitution, and the Supreme Court was not inhibited from suppressing any act or conduct which was calculated to subvert the Constitution itself. In particular, even though one might agree with the applicant Gbedemah that respondent's claim was essentially an election petition to determine who was a Member of Parliament and hence was allocated to the jurisdiction of the High Court, the right to present an election petition to the High Court and the right to apply for enforcement of any provision of the Constitution under Article 106(1) were not mutually exclusive. The Supreme Court accordingly rejected the preliminary objection to its jurisdiction.

The substantive hearing of the plaintiff's claim for (i) a declaration that Mr. Gbedemah was disqualified by virtue of Article 71(2)(*b*)(ii) and (*d*) of the Constitution and (ii) an injunction to restrain him from taking his seat in the National Assembly is reported *sub nom. Awoonor-Williams* v. *Gbedemah*.[23] The basis of plaintiff's claim was that Mr. Gbedemah had been "adjudged or otherwise declared" by the Jiagge Commission to have unlawfully acquired assets and so was disqualified. The Supreme Court spent some time considering whether the finding or report of an assets commission could be taken to have adjudged or declared anything, or whether these terms were terms of art which could refer only to the judgment of a regular court of law. The majority (Azu Crabbe, J.A., dissenting) accepted that "adjudged or declared" could apply to the report of a commission of enquiry.

A second point raised for the defendant was that the Constitution must be taken to have overridden the N.L.C. Decree 129, which took away the right of appeal against the findings of the Jiagge Commission. Again the majority of the court rejected the argument: the Constitution did not retrospectively affect the validity of decrees made under the National Liberation Council, which indeed were saved by Article 126(1)(*d*) of the Constitution as "existing laws".

While giving judgment for the plaintiff, the Supreme Court, *per* Apaloo, J.A., asserted the inherent right of the superior courts to supervise the proceedings of inferior courts and tribunals. The prerogative orders of *certiorari, mandamus* and prohibition would accordingly lie to question the findings of commissions of enquiry, even where there was no statutory or inherent right of appeal from them. The court expressed *obiter* its hope that legislation would, however, be introduced to provide for a right of appeal to the courts for persons adversely reported on by assets commissions.

JUDICIAL AND LEGAL SYSTEM

The composition, constitutional functions and powers of the Supreme Court newly constituted by the 1969 Constitution were fully explored in the two cases concerning Mr. Gbedemah which have just been discussed. A constitutional court is a novelty in Ghana, and clearly its role remains to be defined by the judiciary in interpreting the very wide powers conceded to it by the Constitution, made wider still by the broad view which the Supreme Court's members apparently take of their own functions.

Kwansah XII v. *Rockson & anor*.[24] explored what has been a perennial question under the laws in force in Ghana at different times, namely, the jurisdiction of traditional state councils in chieftaincy matters and the appellate jurisdiction, if any, of the High Court. In the days when native courts, as successors to the customary tribunals, were recognised in Ghana, the policy of the law varied. A "State Council", consisting of a paramount chief with his traditional elders and councillors, was recognised as a body separate from the tribunal of the paramount chief;[25] as indeed it was, both in composition and functions, in Akan customary law. Nevertheless, it was provided by the then applicable Native Administration Ordinance, Section 90 that "a State Council . . . shall have powers corresponding to those of a Paramount Chief's Tribunal" (sub-section (1)), and that "The like appeals shall lie from a State Council as lie from a Paramount Chief's Tribunal" (sub-section (2)).

When the Native Administration Ordinance was replaced in 1944 by a pair of ordinances, the Native Authority (Colony) Ordinance[26] and the Native Courts (Colony) Ordinance,[27] the native courts went one way (under the N.C.C.O.) and the State Councils went the other way (under the N.A.C.O.). The State Councils were given power to determine "any matter of a constitutional nature", but appeal lay to the Provincial Commissioner, and not to a magistrate's court (as from the native courts). In other words, what was a customary constitutional matter was characterised as political in nature, even if the form of proceeding had a judicial flavour. This approach has been preserved in subsequent legislation, the most recent example of which is the Courts Decree, 1966.[28]By the Chieftaincy Act, 1961,[29] Section 41(1), and the Constitution, Article 154(3)(*b*), appeal in a dispute properly cognisable by a Traditional Council lies to the Regional House of Chiefs and not to the High Court, which lacks original or appellate jurisdiction. Hence in the instant case, where plaintiff challenged in the High Court the appointment of first defendant as *mankrado* and also challenged the right of the Ekumfi Traditional Council to hear the dispute Owusu, J., was obliged to hold that he had no jurisdiction.

With the concentration on constitutional matters during the year under review, little legislative activity affecting the judicial and legal system as a whole falls to be reported. The effect of the Constitution itself on the judicial and legal system was, of course, a major one, not only by introducing fundamental rights provisions and other provisions which substantially alter the law which will be applied in future and the manner in which it will be applied, but also by creating a constitutional Supreme Court. The constitutional provisions on the sources of Ghana law are also important and deserve citation here:

"126. (1) The laws of Ghana shall comprise
    (*a*) this Constitution;
    (*b*) enactments made by or under the authority of the Parliament established by this Constitution;
    (*c*) any Orders, Rules and Regulations made by any person or authority pursuant to a power conferred in that behalf by this Constitution;
    (*d*) the existing law; and
    (*e*) the common law.

(2) The common law of Ghana shall comprise the rules of law generally known as the common law, the rules generally known as the doctrines of equity and the rules of customary law including those determined by the Superior Court of Judicature.

(3) For the purposes of this Article, the expression 'customary law' means the rules of law which by custom are applicable to particular communities in Ghana.

(4) The existing law shall, save as otherwise provided in clause (1) of this Article, comprise the written and unwritten laws of Ghana as they existed immediately before the coming into force of this Constitution, and any Decree

or statutory instrument issued or made before that date which is to come into force on or after that date.

(5) Subject to the provisions of this Article, the operation of the existing law after the coming into force of this Constitution shall not be affected by such commencement; and accordingly the existing law shall be construed with such modifications, adaptations, qualifications and exceptions as may be necessary to bring it into conformity with the provisions of this Constitution, or otherwise to give effect to or enable effect to be given to any changes effected by this Constitution."

Two important and difficult points arise from this Article. Firstly, the position of customary law. "Common law", as used in this Article, is given the extended meaning which it already possessed under the Interpretation Act, 1960;[30] i.e. to include the common law in its narrower and normal signification, together with the doctrines of equity and the received English statutes of general application still in force in Ghana. Now, however, a further very substantial extension is made of the term, to include "the rules of customary law including those determined by the Superior Court of Judicature". The 1960 legislation provided that common law should include "rules of customary law included in the common law under any enactment providing for the assimilation of such rules of customary law as are suitable for general application";[31] but no such rules were ever assimilated to the common law by the formal process of assimilation provided. The present provision in Article 126 supersedes all this — not only is there no longer any formal process of "assimilation", but there is not even the necessity for judicial recognition or declaration of the customary law. An important change of wording from the Constitution as proposed by the Constitutional Commission must be noted: draft Article 127(2) contained the phrase, "the rules of customary law *as determined by* [my italics] the Superior Court of Judicature". It is notorious that customary laws are not uniform, and vary from one part of the country to the other; how in these circumstances the customary laws can elegantly be described as "common" law is not apparent.

Equally unclear is the effect of this provision on the choice of law rules contained in the Courts Decree, 1966, para. 64 of which requires a court to decide whether to apply the common law or customary law to a given issue.

The other main item for comment is that, as the *Gbedemah* cases show, the existing laws are not affected by the commencement of the Constitution; on the other hand, Article 126(5) expressly requires the existing law to be construed with such modifications, etc., as may be necessary to bring it into conformity with the Constitution.

One other matter affecting the courts and the judicial system generally, where the Constitution has made a significant contribution, can be reported. Normally in the past, when one constitutional or judicial order has taken over from another, there has been no provision at all on the question of court succession, that is, which court, if any, in the new hierarchy is to be deemed successor to a court in the old hierarchy (bearing the same or a different name). The main interest of this point is in determining how the doctrine of judicial precedent is to operate. The draftsman has on this occasion made full provision for the point. Article 104(2) and (3) provide:

"(2) The Supreme Court may, while treating its own previous decisions as normally binding, depart from a previous decision when it appears right so to do; and all other Courts shall be bound to follow the decisions of the Supreme Court on questions of law.
(3) For the purposes of hearing and determining any matter within its jurisdiction and the amendment, execution or the enforcement of any judgment or order made on any such matter, and for the purposes of any other authority, expressly or by necessary implication given to the Supreme Court by this Constitution or any other law, the Supreme Court shall have all the powers, authority and jurisdiction vested in any Court established by this Constitution or any other law."

And Article 125 provides:

"(1) The High Court of Justice established under the provisions of clause (4) of Article 102 of this Constitution, shall be the successor to the High Court of the Supreme Court of Judicature in being immediately before the coming into force of this Constitution.
(2) The Court of Appeal established under the provisions of clause (4) of Article 102 of this Constitution, shall be the successor to the Court of Appeal of the Supreme Court of Judicature in being immediately before the coming into force of this Constitution; and accordingly the Court of Appeal as established by this Constitution shall be bound to follow the decisions on questions of law binding on the Court of Appeal as it existed immediately before the coming into force of this Constitution.
(3) The Supreme Court shall not be bound to follow the decisions of any other Court."

Dagartey v. *Ekwamu & anor.*[32] dealt with several important issues. Appellant had sued respondents to recover a debt of NC 130. The magistrate dismissed the claim on the ground that the action was barred by the Limitation Act, 1623,[33] being a received English statute of general application, in that the debt had arisen 14 years before the action. The English Limitation Act is admittedly in force in Ghana; but what has been much discussed in the past is the extent to which it applies, especially to cases apparently governed as to substance by customary law.[34]

The learned judge allowed an appeal from this decision, since the Limitation Act, as an English statute of general application, does not apply to a transaction between natives unless the parties to the transaction have previously agreed that it should be governed by English law. Here there was no evidence of any such agreement. Customary law must therefore apply to the exclusion of the Limitation Act. While a statute of general application applies in Ghana as part of the common law, it does not take precedence over customary law, and cannot apply to a transaction governed by customary law.

This decision appears to be in line with the authorities, though *Aradzie* v. *Yandor*[35] held that the Statutes of Limitation apply where parties have used an English method of loan; and the use of a written document[36] or the fact that a party is educated[37] have in the past been effective to cause a court to apply the limitation statutes to a "native".

CRIMINAL LAW

In *Halm* v. *The Republic*[38] the appellant had been sentenced to four months' imprisonment for perjury by the chairman of the Manyo-Plange Commission on a summary trial before the commission on the ground that the appellant had told a lie to the commission. His appeal was allowed by the Court of Appeal because the chairman was held to have prejudged the issue. The court said:

> "It would be safer in all summary proceedings for perjury to follow the procedure set out in the Nigerian case of *Deutsche L. Gesellschaft* v. *Attorney-General* 1 N.L.R. 123 which was approved by the West African Court of Appeal in *Rex* v. *Otubu* (1943) 9 W.A.C.A. 20. If a judge is satisfied that there has been contempt of his court the proper course is to commit the witness for trial upon information when the matter would then be dealt with by 'another tribunal free from any objection of arbitrariness'."

In *Republic* v. *Halm & anor.*[39] a Full Bench of the Court of Appeal reviewed the decision of the Court of Appeal which had allowed the appeal of respondents against their conviction on seven counts of stealing.[40] The court restored the convictions. The three ingredients to sustain a charge of stealing under the Criminal Code, 1960[41] — viz. (i) that the person charged was not the owner of the thing taken; (ii) that he appropriated it; and (iii) that the appropriation was dishonest — had been established in the present case; and it mattered not if Nadeco, whose monies respondents had misappropriated, was merely a trustee of the monies for the beneficial owner, the then President Nkrumah. There was a sufficient interest in the monies on the part of Nadeco, and the court would not imply a constructive trust in favour of Nkrumah: "the principles of equity are not meant to be used blatantly in support of fraud".

Both these cases illustrate the continuing story of the bringing to book of those who were prominent during the Nkrumah era, a process already much discussed in previous surveys in this series. The anomalous character of the hearings by assets commissions of inquiry is a thread running through many of the cases: not a criminal trial, but with effects more far-reaching than many criminal proceedings.

CONTRACT

The so-called "work-and-pay" contract, usually a system of acquiring the use of a commercial motor vehicle by the payment of instalments, is a well-established feature of modern economic life in Ghana. What is not at all clear is the origin of the institution, its exact definition, or its differentiation from hire-purchase transactions and other types of sales by instalments. The Ghana Hire-Purchase Act, 1958,[42] replaced the received English law on the subject of hire-purchase agreements, while the Sale of Goods Act[43] introduced in 1962 now defines and controls both hire-purchase and sales by instalments (*inter alia*).

S. A. Brobbey, in an extremely useful article in the Review of Ghana Law,[44] criticises the Sale of Goods Act for its deficiencies, especially "in that certain types of sale of goods by instalments, such as work-and-pay, are not covered at all . . .". Brobbey defines and explains "work-and-pay" as follows:

"Work and-pay is yet another system of sale by instalments. An agreement for the sale of goods under this system, which is occasionally drawn well-nigh on the same lines as ordinary hire-purchase agreements, sometimes provides that the purchaser pays a deposit which forms part of the purchase price. The parties are however at liberty to dispense with the payment of a deposit. Normally the purchaser takes possession of the goods, which are usually commercial vehicles, and works with them. He then pays by instalments the remaining balance of the purchase price with the proceeds from his user of the vehicle.
More often than not the agreement will authorise the owner to retake possession in the event of the buyer either defaulting in the payment of the instalments or breaching any of the conditions in the agreement, whether fundamental or otherwise. Property in the goods almost invariably remains in the seller until the buyer pays all the purchase price. Insurance and licensing certificates are frequently taken in the name of the seller until the final payment of the last pesewa to the seller when transfer may be effected in the name of the buyer. Quite rarely, some agreements stipulate that the buyer is a co-partner with the owner of the goods. Under such generous agreements, insurance and licensing certificates may be taken in their joint names. In any case, the buyer receives no remuneration from the owner. The owner sometimes restricts the user of the vehicle to a particular locality or for a particular purpose. But short of this, the buyer is given a *carte blanche* as to the user and management of the vehicle."

Work-and-pay agreements can be made orally (unlike hire-purchase agreements); nor is title immediately vested in the buyer (as with a credit sale). Brobbey isolates the two essential factors of the "work-and-pay" contracts as a particular mode of paying by instalments, and the retention by the seller of title until the payment of the final instalment. He rejects Kom's view[45] that the institution is customary or peculiar to Ghana, finding analogues in English law.

This discussion has been largely stimulated by the *Dodoo* v. *Ashittey* dispute, which was tried in the High Court by Archer, J.,[46] went on appeal to the Court of Appeal[46a] sitting as an Ordinary Bench, whose upholding of the High Court's decision has now been reviewed by a Full Bench of the Court of Appeal[47] which ordered a retrial of the case, on the grounds that the learned trial judge failed to make appropriate findings of fact and it was not competent for the Court of Appeal to make its own findings of primary facts in default — this was a function solely of the trial court. The main failure of the trial judge was that he did not thoroughly investigate the principles of the work-and-pay system:

> ". . . at the retrial the party seeking to rely on the system known as 'work-and-pay' must place before the court every essential material to enable the features of the system to be judicially appraised."

The most essential question for resolution was that of the nature of the relationship between the owner and the driver of the vehicle. It is worth noting that the original dispute in this case was not between the owner and the driver, but arose out of a claim by a person for negligence in respect of injuries he suffered as a result of the negligent driving of the vehicle by the second defendant of a vehicle owned by the first defendant.

TORT

One of the main problems of Ghana law is the question of how far a plaintiff may choose his form of action under the common law or customary law respectively, and how far, once he has done so, both the essential ingredients of the claim and the defences available to the defendant are restricted to those associated with the form chosen. *Yanney* v. *Nyamekye*[48] was such a case, involving a claim by plaintiff for the seduction of his niece by the defendant. The English tort of seduction, as introduced into Ghana, is based, at least in theory, on the injury to the master-and-servant relationship between plaintiff and the seduced girl. Although wildly inappropriate in the case of the modern English parent, this basis allows for the extension of the action to those who do not stand in a parental relationship to the seduced girl, as with the uncle in this case. Furthermore, there must have been some loss of services, however minimal, through the seduction. Neither restriction applies to the customary tort of seduction.

Plaintiff here chose to sue under the common law. As the court observed:

> "The right to recover damages in this type of action is available both at common law and in native custom, and so the plaintiff who is native is at liberty to bring either form of action."

The court went on to contrast the requirements of the two forms of action:

> "In the present appeal, the question which arose is this: considering the form of action adopted by the appellant could it be said that she has proved the necessary ingredients as required, namely, the relationship of master and servant and loss of service?
>
> "Proof of these ingredients is essential in an action for seduction at common law, whereas under customary law if a man seduces an unmarried woman of the type in this appeal, he is automatically liable to pay to her or her family damages for the wrong he has done to her and the disgrace brought on to her family. As damages are presumed to have been sustained, whenever an injury is done to the right of a party, the seduction of the appellant's relative may be an invasion of her legal right giving her the right to recover damages without necessarily proving loss of service as is required under common law."

And the court dismissed the appeal, upholding the finding of the learned trial judge that the evidence did not establish that there was a master-and-servant relationship between uncle and niece, or that the niece rendered services to the plaintiff, or that these services had been lost as a result of the seduction.

This case is a fascinating illustration of changing social trends. Under Akan customary law (although neither the ethnic affiliation of the parties nor the relevant customary law is indicated in the report) the dominant relationship was that of maternal uncle and nephew (or niece). In a matrilineal society the uncle and not the father was the legal guardian of a child. All this has now changed, and fathers exert much more control over their children, and are subject to greater legal responsibilities than was the case in the past. The adaptation of English tort law to this differing social structure is thus a matter of some complexity.[49]

Another tort case involving a similar problem of choice of common or customary law was *Attiase* v. *Abobbtey*,[50] in which plaintiff sued defendant for defaming her by alleging that she was a prostitute who used the store she kept for prostitution. The local court of first instance gave judgment for the plaintiff, but this was reversed on appeal by a circuit court, partly on its findings of fact, and partly on the ground that under the common law calling a woman a prostitute who practised prostitution in her store was not actionable *per se*.

The Court of Appeal allowed the appeal, disagreeing with all the conclusions of the circuit court. It was not for the circuit court to reverse the findings of fact of the trial court; the words complained of *were* actionable *per se* under the common law of Ghana, because they implied commission of the offence of keeping a brothel contrary to the Criminal Code; but in any case the circuit court judge was wrong to apply common law in this case, instead of the customary law which had been applied by the local court and argued by all the parties: Courts Decree, para. 64(1). In the customary law of defamation, said the Court of Appeal *per* Ollennu, J., defamatory words are actionable even if they might be rejected under English common law as vulgar abuse. The English Slander of Women Act, 1891, having been enacted after the 1874 reception of English law in Ghana, was not applicable in Ghana; but in effect the same result is achieved by the Ghana courts through reliance on customary law principles.

There was considerable discussion of what are the customary remedies for slander. The *obiter dictum* of Ollennu, J., in *Kwaku* v. *Addo*,[51] to the effect that "native customary remedy for slander is more to penalise than merely to compensate", was not a full statement of the law. There are two remedies for customary slander: (i) an order for retraction and apology, and (ii) an award of pecuniary damages.[52] In the latter case the court may or may not make an order to recant, but generally the mode of recantation should be the same as that by which the defamatory words were originally published. Apology may mitigate the quantum of damages, as the primary object of customary proceedings for slander, even in modern times, is to clear one's name rather than make money.

FAMILY LAW

The tissue of family relationships is often exposed by actions relating to sexual misconduct. One such example, *Yanney* v. *Nyamekye*,[53] which related to seduction and concerned the relationship of uncle and niece, has already been discussed. Another such was *Tepretu* v. *Akpetey*,[54] in which a husband brought an action for "seduction" (meaning adultery) in customary law[55] against defendant, whom he alleged to have had adulterous relations with plaintiff's wife. He averred that the marriage had not been dissolved and that defendant had already admitted adultery by paying the NC 10 adultery fee. At the trial defendant submitted that there was no case to answer, because plaintiff had deserted his wife three years previously and there therefore could have been no seduction. The trial magistrate accepted this submission. The appeal court set aside this judgment, as there was a prima facie case supported by the payment of the NC 10 adultery fee, and a new trial was ordered.

Other cases which concern the family, in the extended lineage sense current in Ghana, are dealt with under PROPERTY and SUCCESSION, *infra*.

PROPERTY

A case which reflected both the predominance in former times of the family in the management and enjoyment of property, and the impact of modern ideas on this predominance, is that of *Quashie* v. *Baidoe*.[56] The case concerned gift of land, and it has long been a principle, at least of Akan customary law, that gifts of land require to be done publicly, and with the knowledge, if not necessarily the consent, of the donor's family, who would otherwise be entitled to succeed to this property if he died intestate. What sort of publicity and what sort of notice to the family are now required is a matter of some contention, but must depend to some extent on the circumstances of each case. In this case there was an alleged gift from father to son (the commonest type of gift in matrilineal areas) of land held by the father on leasehold (in itself an interesting example of the mixture of English and customary institutions). The gift was in the presence of witnesses including the father's paternal cousin. The son also alleged that he gave a thank-offering for the gift of a bottle of whisky and two bottles of soda water.[57] The son built on the land with the aid of his brother, though the father subsequently let these premises to tenants. When the father died, the son took possession of the house. The appellant in this appeal claimed to be successor to the late father's estate, and therefore entitled to the house on the ground that there had not been a valid gift under customary law to the son as alleged.

Both the trial judge in the High Court and the Court of Appeal rejected this claim and upheld the gift, the Court of Appeal holding that the essentials of a valid gift were all present here: intention to make a gift;

transfer; acceptance by the donee; evidence of that acceptance by thank-offering; publicity; notice to donor's family. The following general passages from the court's judgment are of interest in tracing the evolution of individual property and in evidencing the court's approach to these problems in modern times:

"The giving of publicity to transactions involving property and other legal rights has always been the most effective means by which communities without the art of writing have sought to perpetuate the testimony of these transactions. An example may be that of the old practice in England of conveying land by livery of seisin before conveyances in written form became general. Such publicity either to the family or generally in the days gone by was essential for many sound reasons. Time was when the only form of what may be described as self-acquired property was either a farm made on family land or a house built on family land by a member of the family, and before the practice of selling land outright was developed, such self-acquired property might be a farm made or a house built on land, permission to occupy which had been granted by the owner thereof to a stranger. In all these cases the family or the owner of the land concerned had a reversionary interest in the land, and it was not only reasonable but necessary that any disposition of the farm or house be made not only with the consent of the reversioner but also with his concurrence.

"Ownership of land has undergone considerable changes in the past half-century or so, and the concept of absolute ownership of land has developed to a remarkable degree. . . .

"With the rapid development of the concept of absolute ownership in property has also developed a gradual whittling down of the traditional principles of custom relating to the disposition of property by property owners. When a person has acquired an absolute ownership in property, that is one that is not in any manner incumbered by family claim, it sounds unrealistic to require that such an owner, when he is disposing of his property by sale or gift, should do so in the presence of his family. The rationale for any such publication has completely disappeared and the common practice now is that an absolute owner of property is entitled to do with his property as he wishes without any reference to his family. Ollennu, J. (as he then was) expressed correctly the modern view of the law when in *Yeboah* v. *Tse* 3 W.A.L.R. 299 at p. 301, he said:

'According to native custom a man can dispose of his self-acquired property without reference to his family. All that is necessary is that publicity should be given to the transaction, for example, the sale and conveyance must take place in the presence of witnesses, some of whom may be members of his family.'

This proposition is not limited to a sale. It applies to a gift as well.

"Publicity in the traditional manner as a means of perpetuating the testimony of any transaction in property or other legal rights has given way to written conveyances of sale and deeds of gifts. There are still, however, oral transactions and these undoubtedly require some form of procedure whereby the testimony of such transactions can be adequately perpetuated, hence *inter alia* the 'rendering of thanks with a thank-offering' in the presence of witnesses required of a donee who accepts a gift from a donor made orally, but the requirement that the family must necessarily witness the transactions has ceased to have any meaning in present-day Ghanaian society in cases where the property involved is self-acquired property, and has therefore ceased to have any juridical significance."

Republic v. *Chief Inspector of Mines and another, ex parte Kese*[58] was an important case which involved another major aspect of land exploitation in Ghana, viz. the winning of minerals and the law which regulates it. It also concerned the tangled history of the Akim Abuakua stool lands, which had, under the Nkrumah régime and by virtue of the Administration of Lands Act, 1962,[59] been vested in the Government of Ghana. Under the Concessions Ordinance[60] a person who wants to exercise mining rights over land has to obtain (i) a concession to this effect from the landowner; (ii) a certificate of validity from a Concessions Court; (iii) a mining licence from the Chief Inspector of Mines; and (iv) a digging licence under Section 38(2) of the Ordinance. Obtaining each of these certificates or licences depends on having first obtained all the prior grants or licences.

The applicant in this case had a concession agreement and a certificate of validity. He also obtained in 1968 a digging licence in respect of the land from the Chief Inspector of Mines, which expired on 31st December 1968. When he applied to renew the licence, the Chief Inspector, without assigning a reason, on 8th February 1969, declined his application. He accordingly applied for a writ of mandamus to compel the Chief Inspector of Mines and the Chief Lands Officer to issue the necessary licences. The main reason deployed on the respondents' behalf for refusing the application were that the Diamond Mining Corporation was operating in the locality and the applicant had not exhausted all his remedies of appeal.

Anterkyi, J., held that the Chief Lands Officer had no power to cancel the concession agreement between the Government and the applicant; that the reasons given by respondents did not fall within the specified grounds of refusal in the Concessions Ordinance, Section 38(2) proviso; that the Diamond Mining Corporation was apparently a trespasser; that an order of mandamus will not lie to compel an officer of state to do his duty to the state, and so no order would be made against the Chief Lands Officer as a government official; but an order would be made against the Chief Inspector of Mines who had personally refused the application for removal.

Ironically, on the very day that judgment was delivered, 25th April 1969, a new Decree[61] was made and published which empowered the Commissioner responsible for Lands and Mineral Resources to grant mining and digging licences, and the Commissioner duly made an order granting mining and digging licences to the applicant in execution of the concession agreement.

SUCCESSION

Canfor v. *Kpodo*[62] has already troubled the courts;[63] in an earlier hearing Mrs. Canfor, mother of the applicant in the present case, had applied for letters of administration to the estate of her late husband, Sidney Canfor, but the court had granted letters to the present respondent. Now the present applicant, on behalf of herself and the other children of Sidney Canfor, asked for a declaration that they, being the children of deceased in a patrilineal line of succession, were entitled to the beneficial enjoyment of his estate; they also asked for an interim injunction to restrain defendant from intermeddling with deceased's property pending trial of the issue.

Respondent opposed the motion for an interim injunction on the grounds that he had been properly appointed successor to deceased in accordance with Ewe customary law and had in the earlier suit been declared entitled to letters of administration in preference to the applicant and her mother, who were therefore estopped.

It was held by the court that estoppel would not operate to prevent grant of an interim injunction. A successor appointed by the family, if he has no beneficial interest in the property, has the same position as a trustee. The children of deceased were clearly entitled to a beneficial interest, and the beneficiaries accordingly had a remedy in equity. They were *cestuis que trust* with a right which could be protected by the equitable remedy of injunction. An interim injunction was ordered and the High Court registrar was appointed manager and receiver of the estate.

This tangled web of cases was further complicated in *Re Estate of Canfor* (*Deceased*), *Canfor* v. *Kpodo & Anor*, [63a] in the Court of Appeal, which was an appeal from the High Court's decision in the earlier case, already mentioned, in which the widow of the late Mr. Canfor had applied for Letters but had been refused. It was argued for the appellant that the trial judge had been wrong to hold that the Togo marriage was not a monogamous marriage under the Ghana Marriage Ordinance, and that Section 48 of the Ghana Marriage Ordinance, prescribing a special scheme of succession to the estate of those who marry under the Ordinance or "any other enactment relating to marriage", was not applicable to Canfor's succession. A further ground of appeal was the trial judge's finding that under Anlo customary law the family entitled to succeed was the family of the deceased's mother. On all these points the Court of Appeal found for the appellant. The court held that the marriage of deceased in Togo was a monogamous marriage, and that this marriage under Togo law had exactly the characteristics of a marriage under the Marriage Ordinance. So far as the question whether the marriage fell within Section 48's terms was concerned, Akufo-Addo, C.J., for the court, said:

"[The question of whether] the marriage of a Ghanaian celebrated outside Ghana can be assimilated to an Ordinance marriage for the purpose of conferring on a party to the marriage the rights of succession provided by that section [Section 48], and whether these rights can lawfully be conferred on such a party depends on the scope and meaning of the expression 'in accordance with the provisions of this Ordinance or of any other enactment relating to marriage'. . . I am inclined to agree with [the trial judge] that the expression can only refer to a Ghanaian enactment. My reason for so agreeing is that the party seeking to establish that his marriage is a valid monogamous marriage such as conforms with the requirements of the essential validity of a marriage in Ghana must do so by reference to the foreign law under which he contracted the marriage, and in so doing he is not limited, for the purpose of adducing evidence, to an 'enactment' in the foreign country although in proving the foreign law he may refer to an enactment as part of the law of the foreign country. He does this not in conformity with any requirement implicit in the expression 'in accordance with the provisions . . . of any other enactment relating to marriage,' but as part of the evidence by which he is ordinarily required to prove the foreign law.

"The provisions of the Marriage Ordinance fall into two main categories. . . . These are, the provisions which prescribe the formalities of celebration, and those which lay down the requirements of the essential validity of the marriage. The former in accordance with established principles of law can operate only in Ghana. . . . The legislature cannot be presumed to make a law that is wholly impossible of performance, and such would be the law relating to the formalities of marriage if it is contended that a marriage that takes place outside Ghana must conform to these formalities in order to render it capable of being assimilated. As a matter of logical necessity, therefore, the expression 'in accordance with the provisions of this Ordinance' contained in Section 48 can only mean 'in accordance with the provisions of the Ordinance relating to the essential validity of the marriage,' there being no other enactment relating to marriage than the Marriage Ordinance. . . . [This] view . . . is not based on the doctrine that the *lex loci celebrationis* determines the nature of a marriage, that is, whether a marriage is polygamous or monogamous. It is a view which accords with the doctrine that the nature of a marriage is determined by the law of the matrimonial domicile."

The question of the Anlo customary law of succession might appear to have been *obiter* in the circumstances of the case; but the court went on to explain that law as they saw it. It will be remembered that Canfor in fact was Ewe only on his mother's side. Ewe law is patrilineal in character, unlike Akan customary law, upon which most of the customary succession cases in Ghana have been based, and which is essentially matrilineal. The Court of Appeal was willing to accept that Canfor might have acquired "community status" in the Anlo community through his mother's membership of that community; but once it was determined that he was an Anlo man through his mother, succession to his estate would go in accordance with normal Anlo rules, which give "to the children of an Anlo man who dies intestate the entire beneficial interest in their deceased father's estate. . . . The alleged appointment of the second respondent as successor, if he was so appointed, does not operate to vest in him any beneficial interest in the estate."

Atuahene v. *Amofa*[64] was a Court of Appeal case concerning the Akan institution of *samansew* (spelt in the report *samansiw*), which is an oral disposition of property in contemplation of death. In many ways the rules which affect *samansew* are comparable to those controlling customary gifts, which have already been discussed above;[65] and the same sort of modifications has been introduced as a result of modern social developments. It was alleged that the deceased father of appellant had appointed his (deceased's) cousin as his successor, to hold certain farms, now the subject of the dispute, in trust for the children of deceased (the appellant and his brother) until they were of full age, when the cousin was to hand over the farms to the children. The cousin was duly appointed successor by the family after the decease of the father, and held the farms for the children for some years, until respondent, a uterine brother of deceased, claimed that he was the proper person to administer the farms; whereupon the cousin handed the farm over to respondent, who thereafter administered them on behalf of the children. When the appellant and his brothers were of sufficient age, they called on respondent to hand over the farms to them, but he refused. They sued him in the local court and the High Court, but lost, mainly on the ground that the *samansew* had not been proved.

The Court of Appeal held that there was no evidence of an enforceable *samansew*; reiterated that publicity is an essential feature of the making of an oral will, as of a customary gift; and stated that, even more than with a gift *inter vivos*, the presence of members of the family is desirable.

By appointing the cousin "successor", however, the family bound themselves to the terms of the declaration of deceased; the children had been led for more than 20 years to believe that their father had left the property to them. Even the respondent had accepted this. The appointment of the cousin "was in essence an appointment as guardian (or trustee) of the infant children". The appeal was allowed, the children's claim to the property in dispute being upheld.

The Court of Appeal's finding that there was insufficient evidence to support recognition that a *samansew* had been validly made in the instant case depends, of course, on the circumstances of the case, and cannot therefore be challenged. On the other hand, gifts of this kind "in trust" for testator's children are a common feature of the Akan *samansew*, and on the face of it the account of the appellant would appear credible. Both the courts and the customary law have generally set their faces against recognition of appointment by testator of his general successor, as this appointment rests with the family after the decease; but judicial recognition here of what may loosely be called indigenous equity is most welcome.

In *Adjei & others* v. *Bempong*[66] Owusu, J., strongly disapproved of the decision in *Fordwour* v. *Nimo*[67] in so far as it laid down that in Akan customary law a man who marries into a matrilineal family is obliged to shoulder a portion of the funeral debts of the family. The correct rule, said Owusu, J., is that a husband is only required to assist his wife to meet *her* share of her family's funeral debts; and other gifts are not of obligation.

PROCEDURE

Only one bizarre problem requires reporting here. It was posed in *Adanuty & another* v. *Manchie*,[68] presumably another Ewe case. Plaintiffs had refused to attend a customary arbitration before the village chief between themselves and defendant. Thereupon defendant went to a fetish priest and put the plaintiffs into fetish. Plaintiffs brought an action before a magistrate's court against the defendant for putting them into fetish. The magistrate gave judgment for defendant, but ordered him to remove the suit from the fetish for trial by the village chief.

When the case came on appeal to the High Court, Francois, J., had to consider "whether a cause of action could be founded on the defendant's action in bypassing the recognised courts of this land and commencing his action with a complaint to a fetish priest". The cause of action was certainly novel, said the learned judge, but the categories of action are not closed and provided a plaintiff can show sufficient injury to himself the novelty of the action is no bar to its institution. But a fetish priest has no legal power to adjudicate on disputes. In dealing with this matter, the High Court had to take account, said Francois, J., of popular prejudices and the superstitions of the illiterate majority, who believed in the efficacy of fetishes. The question therefore was not whether the fetish was effective, but the effect of the threat on the plaintiff. The appeal was allowed.

CONFLICTS

As with most other African countries, conflicts of law occur at two levels, internal and external (or international). Though in theory separable, in practice the two levels often overlap and interact. Internal conflict cases may make use of private international law categories and methods; external conflicts often refer one to a national law itself containing conflict rules. This was so, for instance, in *Canfor* v. *Kpodo*, already cited,[69] where it was argued at the trial of the case that since the deceased Sidney Canfor belonged to the patrilineal line of succession, his father being an Englishman and his mother an Ewe, the *lex domicilii*, i.e. Ewe law, should apply to his succession.

In the batch of defamation cases which came before the courts, it was the internal conflict aspect that was paramount. In *Attiase* v. *Abobbtey*[70] the factors which influenced the Court of Appeal to hold that customary law was the appropriate law to govern the case were: (i) both parties were subject to customary law, so that the law applicable, in the absence of any contrary intention, was customary law; (ii) counsel for both parties based all their arguments on customary law; (iii) by the Courts Decree, 1966,[71] para. 64(1), rule 6, customary law would have been applicable even if one of the parties had not been a person subject to customary law.[72]

In *Kwabena* v. *Banahene*,[73] the complaint was again of slander. Plaintiff sued for NC 300 damages for "defamation of character" in a District Court Grade II. He was awarded NC 200 damages by the trial magistrate. On appeal, it was argued *inter alia* that the action was under customary law, and that the remedy in customary law was retraction rather than substantial damages. Mensa Boihin, J., held on this point that as no particular law to be applied had been pleaded, the law applicable had to be determined from the nature of the claim and the judgment of the court. The claim was not for an order to recant, and throughout the magistrate applied English law. Hence English law was applicable, and the magistrate was therefore right to award monetary damages.

The argument that the customary law of defamation does not recognise substantial damages as a remedy requires qualification in the light of the Court of Appeal's findings in *Attiase* v. *Abobbtey*, *supra*; but this pair of cases shows the generally unsatisfactory basis upon which it is at present decided in Ghana whether a tort case is to be governed by customary law or the "common law" (i.e. English law). Rule 6 of para. 64(1) is the only and operative guide in these matters; it lays down that:

"Subject to the foregoing rules, an issue should be determined according to the common law unless the plaintiff is subject to any system of customary law and claims to have the issue determined according to that system, when it should be so determined."

It is submitted that the claim by plaintiff to have the case determined by customary law must be explicit; in default of this, the court is bound to apply the common law. Hence in *Kwabena* v. *Banahene* it is respectfully submitted that the final result was right, but that the reason given — that the magistrate at first instance applied English law — does not fall within the terms of Rule 6. Similarly in *Attiase* v. *Abobbtey*, none of the reasons given for applying customary law appear to square with the terms of Rule 6.

LEGAL LITERATURE

This report cannot conclude without a reference to the enormous service now being rendered to the administration and development of the law in Ghana by the regular appearance of *Current Cases*, published on behalf of the General Legal Council, and which produces comprehensive and up-to-date digests of recent decisions. This contribution was complemented by the publication in 1969 of a new *Review of Ghana Law*, edited by Mrs. Janet Daniels and also issued by the General Legal Council. This *Review*, by articles and notes on cases and legislation, attempts to inform the practitioner of developments requiring his attention (though equally useful for the academic student of the law). Its account of the modifications of the draft Constitution by the Constituent Assembly is particularly valuable.

The appearance of volumes I and II of *Reports of Land Cases* decided in the courts of Ghana between 1938 and 1947, and 1948 and 1951, respectively is equally noteworthy. The editor, Dr. G. R. Woodman, has tried to bridge the reporting gap between 1937 (when the Gold Coast Divisional Court Reports end) and 1956 (when the West African Law

Reports began), a gap which has been a major obstacle to the study of Ghana law in a formative period. A third volume, covering the years 1952 to 1955, is promised.

---

1. N.L.C.D. [National Liberation Council Decree] 332.
2. N.L.C.D. 345, as amended by N.L.C.D. 347.
3. By N.L.C.D. 354, made 21st May 1969.
4. N.L.C.D. 358.
5. Constituent Assembly (Amendment) Decree, N.L.C.D. 380.
6. N.L.C.D. 406, made 30th September 1969.
7. At p. 4.
7a. N.L.C.D. 332; made 11th February 1969.
8. N.L.C.D. 358; made 6th June 1969.
9. N.L.C.D. 345; made 28th April 1969; as amended by N.L.C.D. 347.
10. N.L.C.D. 350; made 25th April 1969; and see the Representation of the People (Amendment) (No. 2) Decree, N.L.C.D. 363.
11. N.L.C.D. 255.
12. Aliens Compliance Order.
13. N.L.C.D. 393; made 2nd September 1969.
14. *Quaere* whether this definition is apt to include university teachers.
15. N.L.C.D. 348; made 19th April 1969.
16. N.L.C.D. 381; made 12th August 1969.
17. N.L.C.D. 387; made 29th August 1969.
18. For which see the Ghana Museum and Monuments Ordinance, 1957, No. 20 of 1957, repealed by N.L.C.D. 387, para. 31.
19. N.L.C.D. 401; made 27th September 1969.
20. N.L.C.D. 357; made 21st May 1969.
21. N.L.C.D. 404; made 27th September 1969.
22. (1970) C.C. 12; judgment delivered 30th October 1969.
23. (1970) C.C. 18, S.C.; judgment delivered 8th December 1969.
24. (1969) C.C. 13, H.C., Owusu, J.
25. cf. Native Administration Ordinance, No. 18 of 1927, Part 10 (for the then Colony).
26. No. 21 of 1944.
27. No. 22 of 1944.
28. N.L.C.D. 84.
29. Act 81.
30. C.A. 4.
31. Interpretation Act, Section 17(1).
32. (1970) C.C.1, H.C.; Aboagye, J.
33. I.e. the Statute of Limitations.
34. For a discussion of the point, see my *New Essays in African Law*, 1970, 250–251.
35. (1922) F. Ct. '22, 91.
36. *Amarquaye* v. *Broener* (1898) Ren. 145.
37. *Koney* v. *U.T.C.* (1934) 2 W.A.C.A. 188.
38. (1969) C.C. 96, C.A.
39. (1969) C.C. 155, C.A.
40. See (1967) C.C.85 for the case in the High Court, and comments at *Annual Survey of African Law, 1967*, p. 7.
41. Act 29, Sections 120-124.
42. Act 55 of 1958.
43. Act 137.
44. "Selling by instalments. Part I. The meaning of hire-purchase, credit-sale and work-and-pay", (1970) 2 R.G.L.13.

45. E. D. Kom, "Work-and-pay contracts, and their place in insurance law — an appraisal of *Dodoo* v. *Ashittey* (1965) C.C.6, C.A.", (1967) C.C. vol. 3, p. xi.
46. See (1965) C.C.6.
46a. (1967) C.C. 79.
47. (1969) C.C.157, C.A.; *sub nom., Ashittey & anor.* v. *Dodoo.*
48. (1970) C.C.34, C.A.
49. So Rattray, *Ashanti law and constitution*, 1929, 18, could say that the Roman *patria potestas* is replaced by the Akan "avuncular *potestas*"; and a nephew was *akoa* (loosely translated "slave", but more correctly meaning "person in subjection") to his maternal uncle, who was his *owura* (or "master"). The analogy with medieval English law, *mutatis mutandis*, is striking.
50. (1969) C.C.149, C.A.
51. (1957) 2 W.A.L.R. 306, at p. 311.
52. Approving a decision of Apaloo, J., in *Wankyiwaa* v. *Wereduwaa* [1963] 1 G.L.R. 332 that slander is a civil wrong in customary law redressible by pecuniary award.
53. (1970) C.C. 34, *supra.*
54. (1969) C.C. 88, Francois, J.
55. Although the particular variety of customary law is not stated in the abbreviated report, one must presume that it was Ewe.
56. (1969) C.C. 153, C.A.
57. The giving of a thank-offering (*aseda*) is an essential constituent element in a customary gift.
58. (1969) C.C. 114, Anterkyi, J.
59. Act 123.
60. Cap. 136, 1951 Revision.
61. Minerals Act and Regulations (Amendment) Decree, 1969, N.L.C.D. 344.
62. (1969) C.C. 81, Charles Crabbe, J.
63. See (1968) C.C. 76.
63a. (1969) C.C. 19, C.A.
64. (1969) C.C. 154, C.A.
65. See p. 18 *supra.*
66. (1969) C.C. 161.
67. [1962] 1 G.L.R. 305.
68. (1969) C.C. 84, Francois, J.
69. (1969) C.C. 81; see above, p. 21.
70. (1969) C.C. 149, C.A.; see above, p. 17.
71. N.L.C.D. 84.
72. The court applied *Ampong* v. *Obraa* [1960] G.L.R. 29.
73. (1969) C.C. 112, Mensa Boisin, J.

CHAPTER 2

NIGERIA

A. V. J. Nylander and A. B. Kasunmu

CONSTITUTIONAL LAW AND GOVERNMENT

The year under review is the fourth year of the military administration in Nigeria and the Federal Military Government was still engaged in suppressing the rebellion. The Federal forces continued in their drive to liberate the Eastern States. During the year, the Federal Military Government established the National Commission for Rehabilitation to undertake and co-ordinate relief operations in the war-affected areas[1] and the Lagos State Government set up Committee on Abandoned Properties to take possession of and maintain any abandoned property.[2]

The Western State Government set up a tribunal of inquiry for each group of administrative divisions in the State to inquire whether members of local government staff or other public officers have corruptly or unproperly enriched themselves and if so, the extent of such enrichment.[3] The tribunal of inquiry was set up under powers conferred by the Investigation of Assets (Public Officers and Other Persons) December 1968.

The Interim Common Services Agency continues to operate in respect of the six Northern States.

Legislation

The Supreme Military Council

The appointment by name of Lieutenant-Colonel (now Brigadier) Hassan Usman Katsina as a member of the Supreme Military Council was revoked since he is now a member of the Council by virtue of his appointment as Chief of Staff of the Nigerian Army. The Director of Training and Planning was also removed as a member of the Council but a general provision was added authorising the Head of the Federal Military Government to appoint other members to the Council from time to time.[4]

Statutory Corporations

The appointments of the Chief Executive Officers of statutory corporations are now required to be submitted to, and be approved by, the Federal Executive Council.[5]

The States

The Federal Military Government suspended[6] the operation of Section 3 of the Interim Administration Councils (Amendment) Decree 1967 relative to the South-Eastern and the Rivers States of Nigeria and established a Public Service Commission for each of the two states with powers to review appointments (other than judicial appointments). The provisions of the Constitution of the former Eastern Region of Nigeria as affected by Section 1(5) of the States (Creation and Transitional Provisions) Decree 1967 are to apply to the Commissions as regards the establishment, powers and tenure of office of members of the Commission. This section of the Decree is deemed to have come into force on 11th August 1967 and the Administration of Justice (Eastern States) Decree 1967 ceased to apply to the two States.[7]

The Administrator for Enugu and the other liberated areas of the Central-Eastern State had with effect from 15th October 1969 powers to legislate by means of Edicts signed by him for the peace, order and good government of the Central-Eastern State.[8] He is not to legislate, however, on any matter included in the Concurrent Legislative List except with the prior consent of the Federal Military Government. The question whether such consent was obtained shall not be enquired into in any court of law.

The Administrator is also vested with all executive functions which immediately before 16th January 1966 was vested in or exercisable by the Governor or any officer or authority of the Eastern Region of Nigeria by virtue of Section 86 or 99 of the Constitution of the Federation.

Immigration

The Immigration (Special Provisions) Decree 1969[9] provides that any person (other than a citizen of Nigeria) shall require an entry certificate, a permit to remain or, as the case may be, a permit to accept or change employment which may be obtained free of charge upon application in writing to the Federal Ministry of Internal Affairs, Lagos or to the appropriate diplomatic Nigerian Mission. In this respect, the provisions of the Immigration Act 1963[10] as to entry, residence and employment are suspended. The Decree does not apply to persons employed by the Federal or any State Government or a corporation or company owned or controlled by any such government or their spouses and children.

The Decree came into force on 4th August 1969 and shall continue in force for a period of 18 months unless sooner extended or repealed.

The Professions

The Architects (Registration etc.) Decree 1969[11] establishes the Architect Registration Council for determining the standards of knowledge and skill to be attained by persons seeking to become members of the architectural profession. No person shall practise or carry on business in Nigeria as an architect unless he is a Nigerian citizen and registered under the provisions of this Decree. A non-citizen may be registered to practise as an architect if reciprocal arrangements exist between his country and Nigeria for Nigerian citizens to practise in that country as architects on the same or nearly similar terms and conditions. There is also established a Disciplinary Tribunal and an Investigating Panel.

The Medical and Dental Practitioners Decree 1969[12] and the Pharmacists (Amendment) Decree 1969[13] enlarge the composition of the Medical Council and the Pharmacist Board respectively. The former further gives the Council powers to conduct postgraduate examinations and confer the appropriate diplomas or licences.

The Veterinary Surgeons Decree 1969[14] provides for an enlarged Veterinary Council of Nigeria and makes new and better provisions for registration and professional discipline.

Judicial Decisions

Civil Servant

In *Wilson* v. *Public Service Commission*,[15] Lambo, J., ruled that where a civil servant intends to file a suit against the State, he can only do so by a Petition of Right under the Petitions of Right Act, Cap. 149.

Chieftaincy Matters

In the several suits relating to the selection and appointment of the Alafin of Oyo, the Courts of the Western State have consistently held that they have no jurisdiction to adjudicate on such matters relating to a chieftaincy question as they are precluded from entertaining such a question by Section 161(3) of the Constitution of the Federal Republic of Nigeria.[16]

Exchange Control

In *Adewuyi* v. *The Board of Customs and Excise*,[17] Taylor, C.J., held that Nigerian currency notes illegally imported into Nigeria contrary to the Exchange Control Act were goods within the definition of the Customs and Excise Management Act and were liable to forfeiture.

Fundamental Rights and Civil Liberties

Despite the continuance of the state of emergency resulting from the civil war, the basic fundamental rights in Chapter 111 of the Republican Constitution were still operative. However, these rights were excluded in the operation of certain decrees.

The investigation and forfeiture of the assets of public officers continued during the year.[18] The Curfew Edict[19] of the Western State which came into force on 16th September 1969 authorised the Governor of that State to impose curfew on any area for the maintenance of and securing public order and another edict directed that the Ex-Olowo of Owo be excluded from entering or residing in any part of the Owo Division of the Western State until such time as the Military Governor may otherwise decide.[20]

A number of detention orders were challenged in the Courts during the period under review.

In *Agbaje* v. *Commissioner of Police, Western State*,[21] the applicant applied for a writ of *habeas corpus* in the High Court of Western Nigeria after being detained by the Respondent on the orders of the Inspector-General of Police under and by virtue of powers conferred by Section 3 of the Armed Forces and Police (Special Powers) Decree 1967.[22] Aguda, J., held that the detention of the applicant was unlawful and he should be released. An appeal lodged by the Respondent was dismissed by the Western State Court of Appeal.[23] In another suit brought by the same applicant in the High Court of Lagos State challenging his continued detention by the Inspector-General of Police, Sowemimo, J., held that it was *ultra vires* the powers of the Inspector-General of Police to detain the applicant and ordered his release immediately.[24]

On 3rd September 1969 the Federal Military Government promulgated a decree entitled Detention Orders (Bar to Certain Civil Proceedings) Decree.[25] It provides that no civil proceedings shall lie or be instituted in any court for or on account of or in respect of any act done or purporting to be done in or in connection with the making of an order made or purported to be made under Section 3 of the Armed Forces and Police (Special Powers) Decree 1967 or in execution of or reliance on or obedience to any such order. The Decree applies to the Inspector-General of Police, The Chief of Staff of the Armed Forces or any person acting under their direction or orders.

In *Ex parte Nwaji*,[26] Ireikefe, J., sitting in the High Court of the Mid-Western State, declared invalid the order signed by the Chief of Staff Supreme Headquarters, Nigerian Army for the detention of the applicant's brother. In *ex parte Mordi*,[27] the applicant was tried by a court martial and sentenced to ten years' imprisonment. Ighodaro, Ag. J., granted the application for a writ of *habeas corpus* as the applicant was not a person subject to military law and could therefore not be tried by a court martial. In re *Olayori & Others*,[28] the Chief Justice of Lagos State ordered the immediate release of the applicants who had been detained for failing to refund money paid to them for services not rendered to the Nigerian Army. However, in *Rabbe & Koki* v. *Inspector-General of Police & Director of Federal Prisons*,[29] Adedipe, J. sitting in the High Court of Lagos State held detention orders issued under Section 3 of Decree 24 of 1967 to be good and valid.

JUDICIAL SYSTEM

There were no significant changes in the judicial systems of the Federation.

Northern States

A constitutional amendment provides that the High Court of any of the Northern States is to be composed of the Chief Justice of the State and such number of judges (not being less than two) as may be prescribed by the Legislature of the State.[30]

Mid-Western State

Any judge in the State may be appointed by the Chief Justice to serve on the Advisory Judicial Committee instead of the Judge next in seniority to the Chief Justice.[31]

No significant legislative development has taken place in these branches of the law.

Judicial Decisions

The interesting point raised in *Sambo & Others* v. *Bashire*[32] is the principle for assessment of damages under Section 7 of the Fatal Accidents Law of Northern Nigeria. The section provides different standards for three classes of persons. The measure of damages for the death of a person not subject to any native law and custom is governed by English law. If the deceased is a Moslem, then Moslem law would apply and in other cases, the particular native law and custom would apply. In this case, the deceased was a Moslem and Moslem law fixed the standard *diya*, i.e. the compensation payable to the heirs irrespective of other benefits, to be 100 camels or 100 *dinars* for involuntary homicide. Bello, S.P.J., fixed the price of a camel at £35 and therefore awarded the plaintiffs £3,500. The learned judge, however, pointed out the anomaly that could arise by treating the three classes of persons mentioned in Section 7 differently. While the dependants of a deceased subject to English law are adequately provided for monetarily, it may well be that there are certain native laws and customs which do not demand monetary compensation for involuntary homicide.

In *Coker* v. *Daily Times of Nigeria Limited*,[33] Sowemimo, J., held that the Report of a Tribunal of Enquiry was not a privileged document under Part 3 of the Schedule to the Defamation Act 1961 and comments thereon are therefore not privileged.

In *Attorney-General, Western State* v. *Oyewole & Others*,[34] Aguda, J., held that the Government of the Western State can take action to enforce a contract entered into by the defendants with the Government of the former Western Region of Nigeria.

Two points arose for a decision in *Fowora* v. *Nigerian Broadcasting Corporation*.[35] The first was whether the plaintiff's case was maintainable in view of the provision of Section 61(1) and (2) of the Nigerian Broadcasting Corporation Act, Cap. 133 namely that the action was not taken within 12 months of the act complained of and that notice of intention to sue was not given to the defendant. Secondly whether there was a breach of the principle of natural justice as the Director-General, who appointed the Tribunal of Enquiry, took part in the deliberations of the Board which considered the findings of the Tribunal. On the first point, Dosumu, J., held that in the circumstances of this case the N.B.C. could not avail itself of the protection given by Section 61(1). On the second point, the learned judge held that it would be an intolerable situation if the Director-General who was the Chief Executive Officer of the Corporation could not take part in the deliberations of the Board when staff matters appertaining to discipline are being discussed.

In the previous case[36] against the Nigerian Broadcasting Corporation, George, J., in an *obiter dictum* said that Section 61(1) contemplates the position where the Corporation on the authority of an Act causes injury or trespass to a person or property. It does not apply to a case where the Corporation is exercising its right based on common law or on a contract e.g. an action for wrongful dismissal.

The reasonableness of a notice of termination of employment arose in two cases. In *Ilaka* v. *National Bank of Nigeria* Limited,[37] Sowemimo, J., held that three months' notice was not reasonable to terminate the contract of employment of the plaintiff, who was secretary to the defendant bank. But in *Shonekan* v. *Royal Exchange Assurance*,[38] Taylor, C.J., thought three months' notice should be considered reasonable to terminate the contract of the Assistant Accountant and Secretary to the defendant company.

COMMERCIAL LAW

Several significant decrees were promulgated by the Federal Military Government during the period under review.

The Banking Decree 1969[39] provides that no banking business is to be transacted in Nigeria except by a company duly incorporated in Nigeria and which is in possession of a valid licence granted by the Commissioner authorising it to do so. Licences issued to banks prior to the commencement of the Decree remain valid. However, a bank which was not, prior to the commencement of the Companies Decree 1968, incorporated in Nigeria is required to incorporate its Nigerian branch or branches in Nigeria on or before 18th February 1969.

A licence for the purpose of carrying on banking business in Nigeria is obtainable on application to the Federal Commissioner for Finance through the Governor of the Central Bank. Any person transacting banking business without a valid licence is guilty of an offence and liable to a fine of £50 for each day during which the offence continues.

No bank is to hold or be granted a licence unless its paid-up share capital is not less than £300,000 in the case of a bank which is not directly or indirectly controlled from abroad and not less than £750,000 in the case of one which is directly or indirectly controlled from abroad. No licensed bank should permit its paid-up capital and statutory reserves to fall below 10 per cent of its total deposits at any given time. The Commissioner may, upon recommendation of the Central Bank, direct any licensed bank to increase the level of its paid-up capital and statutory reserves to an amount consistent with the volume and nature of its business but not exceeding 30 per cent of its total deposits.

The most important legislation relating to the petroleum industry are the Petroleum Decree 1969[40] and the Petroleum (Drilling and Production) Regulations 1969[41] made thereunder. Both came into force on 27th November 1969. The Decree vests the entire ownership and control of all petroleum in, under or upon any lands in Nigeria or under the territorial waters of Nigeria or forming part of the continental shelf in the state. It further empowers the Commissioner for Mines and Powers to grant oil exploration licences, oil prospecting licences and oil mining leases for the purpose of exploring, prospecting or searching for petroleum respectively. Such licences or leases may be granted only to citizens of Nigeria or a company incorporated in Nigeria under the Companies Decree 1968. The Commissioner may also grant a marketer's licence for importing, storing, selling or distributing any petroleum or petroleum products in Nigeria.

The Oil Terminal Dues Decree 1969[42] which is deemed to have come into operation on 1st January 1965 provides for the levy of terminal dues on any ship evacuating oil at any oil terminal and in respect of any services or facilities provided by the Nigerian Ports Authority. It is the duty of the Authority to provide such navigational services or extend such facilities as may be necessary or expedient to serve the public interest in accordance with the requirements of the Convention on the Continental Shelf signed at Geneva on 29th April 1958 and to which Nigeria is a party.

A National Insurance Corporation of Nigeria was established by Federal Military Government[43] with powers to carry on within or outside Nigeria any class of insurance business and in particular to insure any property of any government in the Federation or of any statutory corporation or any property in which such government or corporation has an interest. The Corporation is deemed to be a registered insurer under the Insurance Companies Act 1961 and every other registered insurer must compulsorily reinsure with the Corporation an amount equal to 10 per cent of the sum insured in every policy issued or renewed by it and pay forthwith to the Corporation an amount equal to 10 per cent of the premium received by the registered insurer on the issue or renewal thereof. The Corporation may in its discretion refuse to accept any reinsurance accommodation relating to any particular risk. The share capital of the Corporation is to be held by the Federal Military Government which will grant a loan of £100,000 to the Corporation for its initial expenses and working capital.

Judicial Decisions

Insurance

In *Ogundero* v. *Timothy Kuti and Others*[44] Aguda, J., refused an application to join an insurance company as a defendant in a suit instituted against one of its assured for injuries sustained by the plaintiff in a road accident. The learned judge held that from the provisions of Section 10(1) of the Motor Vehicles (Third Party Insurance) Act, Cap. 126, the only duty of an insurance company is to satisfy judgments which have been obtained against persons injured in respect of Third Party Risks. Wheeler, J., was of the same view in *Cole* v. *Abed Brothers Limited & Another*.[45]

In *Martins* v. *National Employers Mutual General Insurance Association Limited*,[46] the defendants refused to indemnify the plaintiff in respect of damages which had been awarded against him. The defendants, who had insured the plaintiff against third-party risks, contended that they had no notice of the previous proceedings in which the damages were awarded against the plaintiff as required by Section 10(2)(*a*) of Cap. 126. The defendants had been joined in but were later struck out from the previous proceedings. Lambo, J. held that in the circumstances the defendants had notice of the previous proceedings and were liable to indemnify the plaintiff.

INDUSTRIAL LAW

The Trade Dispute (Emergency Provisions) (Amendment) (No. 2) Decree 1969[47] makes provision for the settlement of trade disputes by a standing Industrial Arbitration Tribunal where the machinery for normal negotiations and conciliation fails.

The Tribunal consists of a Chairman, Vice-Chairman and five other members, all of whom are appointed by the Federal Commissioner of Labour. All members of the Tribunal should be persons of good standing and integrity with special knowledge of employment conditions in Nigeria and at least one of them should be a person having a special knowledge of economics, industry or trade.

The functions of the Tribunal are to make awards for the purpose of settling disputes referred to it by the Commissioner and to determine questions referred to it by the Commissioner as to the interpretation of any collective agreement, any award made by it or the terms of settlement of any trade dispute. The Commissioner makes rules for the exercise of the Tribunals functions.

An award or determination of the Tribunal confirmed by the Commissioner is final and binding on the employers and workers to whom it relates as from the date of the award or determination.

REVENUE LAW

The Income Tax (Miscellaneous Provisions) Decree 1969[48] empowers the Federal Commissioner for Finance to acquire the property of any tax defaulter in satisfaction of outstanding tax by executing a certificate setting out the nature and amount of the outstanding tax and annexing thereto a list of the properties to be acquired. The properties then vest in the Federal Board of Inland Revenue. The validity of any certificate issued by the Commissioner is not to be inquired into nor the reason for its issue be open to question in any court.

FAMILY LAW

The development in this branch of the law has, as with previous years, been through Court decisions. The judgment of Thompson, J., in *Akinwande and Others* v. *Dogbo and Others*[49] is perhaps the most significant of all the decisions in the field of family law given in 1969. The plaintiff in this case brought a representative action under the Torts Law of the Western State on behalf of himself as the husband of the deceased and also on behalf of the children of the deceased who died in a car accident. The plaintiff alleged that the deceased was married to him under customary law and one of the issues to be determined by the court was how to prove the existence of such a marriage, in the absence of a marriage certificate. The only evidence of the marriage was the testimony of the plaintiff himself, and counsel for the defendants, relying on the Supreme Court decision in *Lawal* v. *Younan*,[50] submitted that the plaintiff's evidence of itself was insufficient to prove that marriage. Rejecting this submission, Thompson, J., commented as follows:

> "It is my view however, that the above cases refer to proof by *wife* of her marriage under native law and custom, and that they should not be regarded as valid authorities for proof by a man of marriage to a woman under native law and custom. There is a wide gap of difference between proof by husband of marriage under native law and custom. This difference stems out of the status of either spouse under native law and custom. In the case of the wife, she is regarded as part of the chattels of the husband for the purposes of inheritance whereas the husband is regarded as the dominant factor in the home whilst the husband is permitted under Yoruba customary law to marry more than one. In fact there is no limit to the number he could marry, the wife cannot have more than one husband. Furthermore customary law recognises concubinage in favour of the man and disallows it for the woman. It becomes a matter of strict proof therefore for a woman associated with a man to conclude that that association amounts to marriage under native law and custom and not mere concubinage. But if a man declared on oath that a particular woman is his wife, that he has paid dowry and customary presents, that the woman was betrothed to him and that she was handed over to him by her family and there is no evidence to the contrary, then the evidence of the man should be for all practical purposes, a cogent proof of marriage to the woman under native law and custom."

Although the decision in *Lawal* v. *Younan* has been further explained by the Supreme Court in *Agongo* v. *Asekele*,[51] it would seem that the courts are still in doubt as to how a marriage under customary law has to be proved. Thompson, J., had distinguished the case before him on the basis of whether it was the woman or the man testifying, but this distinction on a reading of Lawal's case would seem to be immaterial. In *Abia-Okon* v. *Elias*,[52] also a 1969 decision, George, J., rejected the evidence of the widow as insufficient to prove a customary marriage, while in *Daniel* v. *L.C.G.*,[53] Adebiyi, J., relying on *Angongo's* case held that even when the only evidence available is that of a party to the marriage, so long as that evidence is uncontradicted, the marriage would be deemed proved.

The second issue arising out of *Akinwande* v. *Dogbo* is as to who is an adopted child in the Western State for the purposes of Section 5 of the Torts Law. One of the children claiming as plaintiffs was not a natural child of the deceased, but a child of a deceased's sister who had been staying with the deceased and for whom she was responsible for the maintenance and upbringing. Counsel for the child argued that the child should be regarded as a child adopted under customary law and so coming within the ambit of Section 5 especially as there are now laws for statutory adoption in Nigeria with the exception of Lagos State and the then Eastern Nigeria. Upholding this submission, the learned Judge remarked that under customary law, children of relatives in need of care and protection are regarded as adopted children and made to enjoy the privileges of parenthood without discrimination.

The views of Aguda J., in *Teriba* v. *Teriba & Rickett*[54] will be of interest to students of internal conflict problems, on the legal consequences of "double-decker" marriages. The parties in this case were first married under customary law in 1954 and subsequently in the Marriage Registry in 1962. After reviewing the authorities on the effect of the 1962 Act marriage on the earlier customary marriage, the learned Judge remarked that "the true position is that the customary marriage is converted by the Act marriage which in effect, supersedes it. Therefore, if the Act marriage is subsequently dissolved, the customary marriage cannot revive".

Legitimisation by acknowledgment of paternity is a well-known concept under Yoruba customary law, and the public policy argument has featured prominently in the development of this branch of the law in Nigeria. The decision of Odunlami, J., in *Mopelola* v. *Alamu*[55] is yet another instance of the application of the public policy argument to restrict the concept of acknowledgment. The plaintiff was seeking a declaration of title in respect of farmland situated in the Western State while the defendant claimed to be jointly entitled since he was a son of the deceased — plaintiff's father. The defendant claimed that his mother was married to X, a relation of his deceased father, but that when X was incapable of sexual acts, his mother was given to his deceased father who was responsible for his birth.

In rejecting the defendant's claim, the learned Judge held that there was no evidence that his paternity was acknowledged by the deceased, and it would seem that the learned Judge would still have refused to confer a legitimate status on the defendant even if there was proof of acknowledgment for he held that "the custom whereby a living man would hand over his wife to his brother because of sexual incapacity is foreign to Yoruba customary law and contrary to public policy, equity and good conscience".

CRIMINAL PROCEDURE AND EVIDENCE

The Constitution continues to play a vital role in the reshaping of rules of procedure and evidence. Already, its influence has been felt in the rules governing the claim of State privilege and the admissibility of illegally obtained evidence. In *Yerima* v. *Bornu N.A.*,[56] resort was made to Section 22(2) of the Constitution as a means of invalidating Section 52(1) of the Native Courts Law (Cap. 78 of the Law of Northern Nigeria, 1963). Section 52(1) gave the Inspector of Native Courts the right to appeal against any decision of a Native Court, if in his opinion there has been a miscarriage of justice. No time-limit was placed on this right of appeal and counsel for the accused argued that because of this, the section is invalid in that it infringed the constitutional right to a fair hearing within a reasonable time of a person charged with a criminal offence. This argument was rejected by the Supreme Court which held that Section 22(2) of the Constitution applies only to trials but not to appellate proceedings ". . . a person is charged only until he is convicted and it is the conviction that is to be appealed against and the appeal court has either to suspend or to allow the appeal against conviction. In any case, however, it seems clear to us that the wording of Section 22(2) is dealing only with trials at first instance."

Reliance was also placed on Section 22(2) of the Constitution in *Mohammed* v. *Kano N.A.*,[57] where the Supreme Court held that the accused did not receive a fair hearing when the star witness for the prosecution also assumed the role of the prosecutor. That court also held that a fair hearing means the same thing as a fair trial, and that the true test of a fair hearing is the impression of a reasonable person who was present at the trial as to whether justice has been done in the case.

So far, no attempt has been made to use the constitutional guarantee as a means of controlling the discretion of the prosecution as to whether or not a particular witness must be called or not, and Nigerian Courts have invariably followed the practice of the English Courts in this regard. In *State* v. *Lawson*,[58] Ogunkeye, J., held that the discretion of the prosecution in this regard is unfettered, except that where the name of a witness appears at the back of the information, even though the prosecution has a discretion not to call him, such a witness should be made available to the defence. However, in a very recent decision of Aguda, J., in *State* v. *Oladele*,[59] the impression is created that the prosecution could refuse to call a witness if the evidence of that witness, though relevant, is likely to be against the prosecution. It has often been argued that in situations where the prosecution fails to call a particular witness, the defence can subpoena such a witness or that the trial Judge could call such a witness as a witness of the Court. Although the first suggestion looks attractive, it has its own limitations in that the defence cannot cross-examine such a witness — being its own witness — without first having him been declared a hostile witness. As to the second suggestion, one only needs to refer to the observations of Aguda, J., in *Oladele*, that although Section 200 of the Criminal Procedure Act gives a wide discretion to the Court in the matter of calling, recalling or re-examining a witness of itself, the occasion must be very rare where a Judge of the High Court would take advantage of the provision and call a witness on his own especially where the prosecution is conducted by experienced and well-seasoned advocates.

The Supreme Court decision in *Adegboyega & Others* v. *Igbinosun & Others*[60] is a reminder on the limits to the application of the doctrine of judicial notice as a mode of customary law. Counsel in this case (a Benin case) contended that for a grant to be valid under customary law, there must be witnesses and also putting the grantee into possession. He relied on *Erinosho* v. *Owokoniran*[61] (a Yoruba case) for this proposition, and cited *Awgu* v. *Nezianya*[62] as establishing that unless evidence is established to the contrary, rules of customary law are of general application. This submission was rejected by the Supreme Court, and explaining the dictum in *Awgu* v. *Nezianya* commented thus:

"... Counsel's submission overlooks the significance of the dictum on which he relied and to accept his submission will occasion an outrage on the principles stated in the citation. It is manifest that the passage refers only to general principles of the type to which references had earlier on in the judgment been made and which are not what are in issue herein and obviously not to individual rules of native law and custom on the transfer of land."

One other signicant point in the *Adegboyega Case* is the reference to Section 73(1) of the Evidence Act which provides that the court could take judicial notice of all general customs if certain conditions are fulfilled. The connection between this section and Section 14(2) of the Evidence Act is not clear although in the case under review the Supreme Court doubted whether Section 73 could ever apply to customary law. Whether one comes via Section 73(1) or Section 14(2), the general principle is that a fact must be notorious before it could be judicially noticed. In another recent decision[63] of the Lagos High Court, it has been held that a custom could be judicially noticed under Section 14(2) even if there is only a single decision establishing that custom. Reliance for this proposition was placed on the observations of Brett, F.J., in *Cole* v. *Akinyele*.[64] Although the Supreme Court in *Adegboyega* did not directly avert its mind to this issue, that court approved its earlier ruling in *Giwa* v. *Erinmilokun*,[65] which would seem to run counter to the observation of Brett, F.J.

"It is a well established principle of law that native law and custom is a matter of evidence to be decided on the facts presented before the court in each particular case, unless it is of such notoriety and has been so frequently followed by the Courts that judicial notice would be taken of it without evidence required in proof."

Finally, in the field of evidence, the decision of the Supreme Court in *Esso West Africa Inc.* v. *Oyegbola*[66] shows an awareness by that court of the need to interpret the Nigerian Evidence Act, first enacted in 1943, in a way that is reflective of present-day developments. The interpretation of Section 37 of the Evidence Act was in dispute. The section provides that "entries in books of account regularly kept in the course of business, are relevant whenever they refer to a matter into which the court has to inquire, but such statements shall not alone be sufficient evidence to charge any person with liability". The appellant in this case at the trial stage tendered ledger copies of the statements of accounts of the defendant but the trial judge rejected these documents on the ground that they "do not constitute the type of books of account contemplated by the law (Section 37), as those are usually bound and the pages are not easily replaced". The Supreme Court reversed the trial judge on this issue holding that "the law cannot be, and is not ignorant of modern business methods and must not shut its eyes to the mysteries of the computer. In modern times, reproduction of inscriptions on ledgers or other documents by mechanical process are common place and Section 37 cannot therefore only apply to books of account so bound and the pages not easily replaced."

CRIMINAL LAW

In *Effanga* v. *The State*,[67] the Supreme Court had to consider the principle in *R.* v. *Jordan*[68] dealing with the problem of causation in criminal cases, in the light of Section 312 of the Criminal Code which provides that "when a person causes a bodily injury to another from which death results, it is immaterial that ... his death from that injury might have been prevented by proper care or treatment". The accused in this case attacked the deceased with a matchet and inflicted a wound on his right hand. The deceased died twelve days after this attack and the medical evidence was that "there was haemorrhage from the injured blood vessels. In the circumstances of the time with no medical treatment, the wound was secondarily infected. Probably, if the deceased had had medical treatment in time, his life could have been saved." Counsel for the accused submitted that in the light of the medical evidence, it had not been established that the deceased died as a result of the matchet wound but because of lack of medical care. This submission was rejected by the Supreme Court and, in emphasising the importance of Section 312 remarked that "in this country, where medical facilities are not within easy reach of people, one cannot fail to recognise the need for such provisions in our law. What has to be decided is whether from the legal point of view the death of the deceased was caused by the injuries he sustained and not whether from the medical point of view his death was caused by such injuries." The distinction drawn between legal causation and medical causation is a very fine one, and although one might support the Court's conclusion in the instant case especially as there was evidence that medical attention was not available at the time in question, it is submitted that such a literal interpretation of Section 312 of the Criminal Code will give rise to many harsh and unreasonable decisions.

The end of the Nigerian Civil War has ushered in a wave of armed robberies, and the Supreme Court decision in *Babalolo & Slaboh* v. *State*[69] should be of interest on the interpretation of the offence or robbery in Nigeria. Section 401 of the Criminal Code provides that "any person who steals anything, and, at or immediately before or immediately after the crime of stealing it, uses or threatens to use actual violence to any person or property in order to obtain or retain the thing stolen or prevent or overcome resistance to its being stolen or retained, is said to be guilty of robbery". The accused persons in this case had obtained money from their victim after threatening him with a gun. No evidence was given by the prosecution as to whether the gun was loaded or not. Their Counsel submitted that the robbery charge must fail in that "threatens to use actual violence" means that the prosecution must show that the accused could use *actual* violence, and that they had not shown this in as much as there was no evidence to show that the gun was loaded. The court rejected this submission and held that the test is:

> ". . . whether looking at the circumstances a reasonable man would have been put in fear of actual violence by the threat he received. If a person threatens another with a gun, we think the natural inference is that the threatened person would expect to receive actual violence if he did not accede to the order to hand over his money. He could not be expected to ask the person threatening him to show him whether the gun was loaded or not so as to determine whether he was put in fear of actual violence".

The Court concluded that the test is not whether the person threatening was actually capable of carrying out the threat that he was making, but whether the threatened person reasonably believes in the apparent circumstances that the threat is likely to be carried out.

In *State* v. *Onokoko*,[70] the Supreme Court spelt out in what circumstances a plea of provocation will be allowed if the accused kills Y but not X who offered the provocation. The accused here found his wife having sexual intercourse with X, and in a fight which ensued between him and X, he killed Y who was then asleep in the room where the fighting took place. In sustaining the plea of provocation, the Supreme Court held that the rule that provocation must stem from the deceased is not an absolute rule and that in addition to cases of group provocation, where as in this case, the deceased was killed incidentally, while the accused was acting under provocation, a plea of provocation would succeed.

Another important decision in the field of criminal law is *Akpobasa* v. *State*[71] where the Supreme Court explained its earlier decisions on the use of force to arrest or prevent the escape of a thief. The accused as found by the trial Judge shot an unarmed man because he heard a cry of thief and the man was running away from the spot where the cry came from. Arguing against his conviction for murder, his counsel urged the Supreme Court either to acquit the accused or convict him for manslaughter. He relied on an earlier decision of the West African Court of Appeal in *Obot* v. *Queen*[72] to support his contention for an acquittal. In *Obot*, it was held that "a person who in the night finds another in the act of committing a felony is entitled to use such force as may be necessary to apprehend the felon even to the extent of killing him in order to prevent his escape. . . ." The Supreme Court held that the decision in Obot must be properly limited to the use of force in defence of property such as defending a dwelling house from a breaking and entering with intent to commit a felony and must not be extended or taken out of its context to a situation where the felony has been committed and the person is killed when escaping. The Supreme Court also rejected an argument based on *R*. v. *Aniogo*[73] that the conviction should be for manslaughter on the ground that there was evidence in that case (Aniogo) that the deceased was "possibly armed" when he was shot.

Nigerian law, like the law of other common law jurisdictions, requires that on a charge for receiving under false pretences, it must be established that the representation made by the accused relates to either a past or present fact, and that a representation as to future conduct will not be enough. In *Iyinbor* v. *Commissioner of Police*,[74] the Supreme Court confirmed this long established principle but observed that in determining whether or not a representation is good or bad as laid, recourse must be had to the actual words of the representation alleged in the charge and the evidence in support of the charge. The charge against Iyinbor was that he received money from the complainant "falsely pretending that you had a job of Sanitary Labourer to offer". It was established in evidence that no such job existed and that even if there was, the accused had no authority to give out such a job. The Supreme Court held that although the assigning of a job to the complainant was one to be performed *in future*, a conviction for false pretences was in order in that the substance of the charge was that he made a false representation as to existing facts — the existence of the job and his own personal authority to give out the job whenever it pleases him to do so.

LAND LAW

The only significant decision in this field is the decision of the Supreme Court in *Ayodele* v. *Olumide*,[75] and this has gone a long way to clarify the nature of the title conferred by an allocatee of family land who disposes of his interest to a third party without the consent of the family. Coker[76] takes the view that the disposition "remains only voidable until the family takes steps to set aside any such purported alienation". If this is the true legal position, then the title is in the purchaser from the allocatee until the transaction is voided by the family, and the right of avoidance presumably will be lost if the first purchaser disposes it to a second purchaser. However, in *Ayodele* v. *Olumide* where an allocatee member of the Oloto family disposed of his interest to a purchaser, the Supreme Court held that the legal estate is still with the Oloto family and that what the allocatee had transferred was his right to use and occupation of the land.

One other significant point in *Ayodele* v. *Olumide*[77] is the comment of the Supreme Court on reliance on long possession as a means of proving title. It was argued on behalf of the plaintiff/respondent that even though he had failed to establish title, the fact that he had been in long possession of the disputed property should be enough to get a title declaration against the defendant/appellant. In rejecting this submission, the Court commented as follows:

> "This submission quite overlooks that here the plaintiff was not seeking to rely on undisturbed possession to resist a claim by the Oloto family but was, in counsel's submission, relying on long possession to establish a claim for declaration of title. Not only is long possession and acquiescence really a weapon more of defence than of offence, but it must also be specifically pleaded and this was not done here. In our view the plaintiff's claim stood or fell on etablishing a good title derived from the Oloto family and this she failed to prove while to the contrary the defendant had established that he had a good title from the Oloto family. The plaintiff's long possession, was therefore, only that of a trespasser or a squatter and would not enable her to succeed against the true owner who was in fact proved to be the defendant."

---

1. National Commission for Rehabilitation Decree 1969, No. 41.
2. Administration of Abandoned Properties Edict 1969, No. 8 (Lagos State).
3. Local Government Staff and Other Public Officers (Appointment of Assets Tribunals) Instrument, 1969. W.S.L.N. 123 of 1969.
4. Constitution (Suspension and Modification) Decree 1969, No. 42; see also L.N. 62 of 1969.
5. Statutory Corporations Service Commission (Amendment) Decree 1969, No. 30.
6. The Public Service, etc. (Rivers and South-Eastern States) Decree 1969, No. 5.
7. *Ibid.* Section 1(3), 2.
8. Central-Eastern State (Administration) Decree 1969 No. 46.
9. No. 33.
10. No. 6.
11. No. 10.
12. No. 44.
13. No. 45.
14. No. 37.
15. LD/222/68. Judgment delivered 24th March 1969.
16. See e.g. *Akano* v. *Military Governor, Western State & Others*. I/149/69. Judgment delivered by Somolu, C.J., on 3rd November 1969.
17. LD/598/1968. Judgment delivered 3rd March 1969.
18. The Public Officers & Other Persons (Forfeiture of Assets) (No. 2) Order 1969, W.S.L.N. 99 of 1969. See also L.S.L.Ns. 13 and 14 of 1969.
19. 1969 No. 14.
20. The Ex-Olowo of Owo (Exclusion from Owo Division) Edict 1969, No. 4.
21. M/22/69. Judgment delivered on 18th June 1969.
22. No. 24.
23. *Commissioner of Police* v. *Agbaje*, CAW/81/89. Judgment delivered on 27th August 1969.
24. *Agbaje* v. *Inspector General of Police and the Director of Nigeria Prison Service*. M/84/69. Judgment delivered on 25th August 1969.
25. 1969 No. 3.
26. B/11M/69. Judgment delivered on 13th June 1969.
27. M/35/68. Judgment delivered on 10th January 1969.
28. M/196/69. Judgment delivered on 17th November 1969.
29. M/197/69. Judgment delivered on 21st November 1969.
30. Constitution (Northern States) (Amendment) Decree 1969.

31. Advisory Judicial Committee Edict 1969 No. 2 (Mid-Western State).
32. Z/35/68. Judgment delivered on 12th December 1969.
33. LD/89/1969. Judgment delivered on 5th December 1969.
34. I/188/69. Judgment delivered on 3rd December 1969.
35. LD/553/1969. Judgment delivered on 28th July 1969.
36. *Bankole* v. *Nigerian Broadcasting Corporation*, LD/8/1968. Judgment delivered on 20th December 1968.
37. LD/161/1969. Judgment delivered on 19th December 1969.
38. LD/434/67. Judgment delivered on 24th November 1969.
39. No. 1.
40. No. 51.
41. L.N. 69 of 1969.
42. No. 9.
43. National Insurance Corporation of Nigeria Decree 1969 No. 2.
44. I/50/1968. Judgment delivered on 11th June 1969.
45. K/87/68. Judgment delivered on 1st April 1969.
46. LD/337/68. Judgment delivered on 10th March 1969.
47. No. 53.
48. No. 7.
49. AB/26/68 of 14th July 1969.
50. (1961) 1 All N.L.R. 245.
51. 1967 N.M.L.R. 21.
52. LD/236/67 of 4th August 1969.
53. LD/248/67 of 12th July 1969.
54. I/211/67 of 2nd July 1969.
55. HOY/15A/69 of 18th December 1969.
56. SC.132/68.
57. SC.417/67.
58. AK/6C/69 of 4th July 1969; contrast *State* v. *David & Anor*. AK/15C/68.
59. I/15C/69.
60. SC.207/68 of 10th January 1969.
61. (1965) N.M.L.R. 479.
62. (1949) 12 W.A.C.A. 450.
63. *Oshoko & Others* v. *Macaulay*, LD/117A/68 of 9th July 1969.
64. (1960) 5 F.S.C. 84.
65. (1961 1 All N.L.R. 294.
66. SC.180/68 of 21st November 1969.
67. SC. 117/69 of 31st October 1969.
68. (1956) 40 Cr. A. R. 152.
69. SC.177/69.
70. SC.72/69 of 27th June 1969.
71. SC.253/68 of 7th March 1969.
72. 14 W.A.C.A. 352.
73. 9 W.A.C.A. 62; contrast *R.* v. *Aliechem*, 1. F.S.C. 64.
74. SC.205/69 of 21st November 1969.
75. SC.260/67 of 23rd May 1969.
76. Coker, *Family Property among the Yorubas*, 2nd ed., p. 121.
77. The same observations have been made in *Da Costa* v. *Ikomi* SC.736/66; *Agboola* v. *Abimbola* SC.366/67.

CHAPTER 3

SIERRA LEONE

H. M. Joko Smart

The political storm which broke out in November 1968 resulting in massive arrests and detentions following alleged acts of violence preceding by-elections[1] in certain parts of the Provinces continued to rage in full blast at the dawn of 1969. Events of the past year had shown that though there had been a return to civilian rule, with the formation of a coalition government consisting of members of the All People's Congress and the Sierra Leone People's Party, with Mr. Siaka Stevens as Prime Minister, all was not well with the fusion. Extremist A.P.C. supporters, on the one hand, maintained that as their party had won the General Elections of March 1967, justice would be meted out to them only if their party was in power devoid of all S.L.P.P. elements. Strong S.L.P.P. supporters, on the other hand, while raising a hue and cry over the detention of their party members since November 1968, complained of victimisation from all quarters: Added to this, the treason trial of ex-Brigadier David Lansana and sixteen others,[2] most, if not all, of the accused having been staunch supporters of the S.L.P.P. while that party was in power, left no room in their minds for doubt that the Government was one-sided and that the marriage between the two parties should be dissolved. As a result, on 9th June 1969, the leader of the S.L.P.P., Mr. Salia Jusu-Sheriff, announced in Parliament that his party was henceforth officially in opposition. This announcement had been preceded by the resignation of those S.L.P.P. members who had held Ministerial positions in the coalition government.

Early in the year, the Judicial Committee of the Privy Council reversed the decision of the Sierra Leone Court of Appeal in the celebrated case of *John Akar* v. *Attorney-General of Sierra Leone.*[3] And in June, a Republican Constitution Committee was set up by Government, but as will be shown later, its life was short-lived.

A number of other changes took place in Criminal Law, Contract, Property, Commercial law, and Procedure. These will be considered in their appropriate places as we go on.

CONSTITUTIONAL LAW

There was no major constitutional change. Though there was much talk of a change from a monarchical to a republican system of government, the 1961 Constitution remained in full force.

The Republican Issue

Before the close of 1968 it had been widely rumoured that Government was bent on implementing the Republican Constitution Bill passed for the first time by the last Parliament in 1966. To many who had rallied behind the A.P.C. while in opposition during the election campaign of 1967, such an action was tantamount to a breach of faith since one of the major issues on which the election was contested was that of the Republican Constitution Bill to which the A.P.C. was then vehemently opposed. In order to clear doubts in the minds of many people, Government issued a press release[4] on 2nd January 1969 in which it was strongly denied that any decision had been taken on the matter. But it was admitted that discussions in connection with a republican form of government had taken place and that various points of view had been put forward. Apparently, the discussions occurred only at governmental level since the release promised that the general public would be given the opportunity of expressing their views on the matter.

Shortly after the press release, the Prime Minister, in an address to the British Press on 6th January at the Sierra Leone High Commission in London, announced to the international community that Sierra Leone would be moving over to a republican status "probably before the middle of the year".[5] At home, there was wide speculation that the date of the Republic might coincide with 27th April when the country would have been independent for eight years. On 16th June, the Republican Constitution Committee was set up with the Speaker of the House of Representatives as Chairman.

The Committee consisted of 31 members drawn from various institutions and organisations — political, religious, educational, professional, and mercantile — purporting to represent every shade of opinion in the country. All but the S.L.P.P. and the Sierra Leone Chamber of Commerce agreed to participate in its deliberations. The Chamber of Commerce expressed inability to serve while the S.L.P.P. decided to boycott it on the ground, as stated by the leader of the Opposition, that the setting up of the Committee was unnecessary because:

(*a*) a committee should have been set up as a first step in the process of consulting the people as to whether or not they wanted a change to republican status instead of assuming their acceptance of such status;

(*b*) at least 17 of the members of the Committee were "so obviously members of the A.P.C.".[6]

The terms of reference of the Committee were as follows:

(*a*) "To study the present constitutional position in Sierra Leone and recommend ways and means by which this country can move on to a republican form of government.

(*b*) To spell out the type of Republican Constitution which should be adopted.

(*c*) To advise on any other relevant matter".[7]

In a speech delivered at the inaugural meeting of the Committee,[8] the Prime Minister stressed that it was not within the Committee's terms of reference that recommendations should be made on a monarchical form of constitution which, he said, had "outlived its usefulness and ought to be changed". The reasons advanced for the required change were that:

(*a*) Her Majesty the Queen in Great Britain and Northern Ireland was Head of State and Head of Parliament of Sierra Leone;

(*b*) Her Majesty had formerly to approve all Ambassadorial and other important external diplomatic appointments;

(*c*) The Governor-General was obliged every month to report all important events in the country to Her Majesty the Queen;

(*d*) The Prime Minister, Ministers, Members of Parliament, Judges and senior public officers had to swear an Oath of Allegiance to Her Majesty the Queen residing in England.

With the issue of a one-party state, which died naturally in 1966, still fresh in the minds of many people, there were those who expressed fears that the whole republican issue augured the introduction of a one-party state in disguise; and that the Government intended to have an Executive-President in conformity with the practice of many other African States — a practice to which traditionalists gave no place in Sierra Leone. To test the genuineness of Government, one school of thought held that the rather complicated constitutional position of the country as alleged by Government could be forced on to a procrustean bed of simplification by substituting the word "President" for the word "Queen" wherever the latter appears in the Constitution.[9]

The Government faced its first embarrassment at the national level when at the first and only meeting of the Committee which took place on 23rd June a preliminary objection was raised by some members that Government had not published the terms of reference in the government official Gazette before convening the Committee. The meeting was adjourned in order that the publication might be made as required by law. But the Committee never met again. Government neither stated reasons for not re-convening it nor informed the public of the Committee's dissolution until the 18th of August when the Prime Minister announced that the Committee was to be reconstituted into a Republican Review Commission.[10]

It is premature to deal with the terms of reference of this Commission in this survey. A discussion of it can be appropriately postponed to the survey for 1970. Suffice it, however, to mention that from the constitution of the Commission and its terms of reference, Government appeared to have conceded to the objections of the S.L.P.P. when the Committee was set up.

As in 1967 a very interesting constitutional change occurred again in connection with the office of the Attorney-General. Section 59(1) of the

Constitution had provided that for a person to qualify for appointment as Attorney-General he must be qualified for appointment as a judge of the Supreme Court. According to Section 76(3) of the Constitution "A person shall not be qualified for appointment as a judge of the Supreme Court unless:

(i) he is or has been, a judge of a court having unlimited jurisdiction in civil and criminal matters in some parts of the Commonwealth or a court having jurisdiction in appeals from any such court, or

(ii) he is entitled to practise as an advocate in such a court and has been entitled for not less than ten years to practise as an advocate or solicitor in such court. . . ."

In other words, under the two provisions, in order to become Attorney-General, a person must have been a judge somewhere in the Commonwealth or must have been entitled to practise as an advocate in a court of limited civil and criminal jurisdiction somewhere in the Commonwealth and must have been so entitled for a minimum period of ten years.

Under the National Reformation Council, Section 59 of the Constitution was amended by reducing the minimum number of years for entitlement to practise to seven years.[11]

In the survey for 1967,[12] Dr. Uche could find no very obvious necessity for the change except that the N.R.C. might have had certain individuals in mind who but for the new measure would not have qualified for the post. In actual fact, when the N.R.C. took over, the Bar Association of Sierra Leone was so vehemently opposed to the new régime which the Association termed as illegal that no practising advocate at the local bar was willing to take up the appointment of Attorney-General on the resignation of its incumbent. In the past, when the post of Attorney-General had fallen vacant it was the practice for the most senior official of the Attorney-General's Office, probably the Solicitor General, if he fulfilled the qualifications set out in Section 59 of the Constitution, to be appointed to the post. But by a fortuituous combination of circumstances, none of the senior officials of the Attorney-General's Office was qualified under Section 59 when Mr. Berthan Macaulay resigned in 1967.

The alternatives left to the N.R.C. therefore were either to transfer one of the Judges from the Supreme Court to the post of Attorney-General[13] or appoint someone qualified from outside the country or reduce the minimum qualification so as to accommodate the existing senior officials of the Attorney-General's Office, some of whom had been called to the bar for seven years. The last alternative was adopted and one of the officials was appointed to the post.

The Constitution (Amendment) Act 1969[14] repealed the Attorney-General (Qualification) Decree 1967, and substantially restored the provisions of Section 59(1) of the Constitution with a proviso that a person shall be qualified to act as Attorney-General if he is entitled to practise as an advocate in a court having unlimited jurisdiction in civil and criminal matters in some part of the Commonwealth or a court having jurisdiction in appeals from such court and has been entitled for not less than seven years to practise as an advocate or solicitor in such a court.[15]

Obviously, the object of the Act was to return to the *status quo ante* the N.R.C. régime. But because of the insecurity of person and tenure that had surrounded the office of Attorney-General over the past few months, qualified Sierra Leone nationals were still reluctant to hold the office.[16] In the final analysis an expatriate officer had to be appointed. It is significant to note that the Act had a retroactive effect dating back to 1st June 1968 which date was probably intended to coincide with the appointment of the expatriate officer. As events turned out afterwards, this officer vacated the office.[17] In the event, the proviso to the Act became a saving grace.

Fundamental Rights and Freedom of the Individual

It may be recalled that on 21st November 1968 a State of Emergency was declared in the country.[18] Two days afterwards, the Public Emergency Regulations 1968,[19] were made empowering the Minister of Defence to censor postal communications, suppress newspapers, prohibit the holding of processions and public meetings and to detain any person "with a view to preventing him acting in any manner prejudicial to public safety". These Regulations were revoked on 26th February 1969 with a public notice to that effect[20] and the Public Order (Amendment) Act 1969[21] passed on the same day having a retrospective effect from the 22nd November 1968. The Amendment Act stipulated that without prejudice to the validity of anything lawfully done thereunder, every Regulation made under Section 38 of the Public Order Act 1965 shall cease to have effect at the expiration of a period of four months from the date upon which it came into operation unless, before the expiration of that period, it had been approved by resolution passed by the House of Representatives.[22] Everybody detained under the Regulations was released forthwith. The revocation, nevertheless, did not affect some of the Officers detained by the N.I.C. in 1968 some of whom were later charged with treason in connection with events of the 1967 General Election. Two army officers, the spearheads of the 1968 coup were released from detention on 15th May 1969.[23]

The case of *John Akar* v. *the Attorney General of Sierra Leone*,[24] which was decided by the Court of Appeal in 1968 reversing the Supreme Court decision, took yet another dramatic turn in 1969. The Judicial Committee of the Privy Council, by a majority decision (Lord Guest dissenting), upheld the decision of the Supreme Court though the Board did not adopt all the reasons advanced by the learned Chief Justice for arriving at his decision. Because of the Privy Council's decision it is necessary to repeat here some salient points even though the case has been dealt with exhaustively in a previous survey.[25]

At independence in April 1961, any person born in Sierra Leone who was either a British subject or British protected person automatically became a citizen of Sierra Leone. Thus John Akar born in Sierra Leone whose mother was a native of the country but whose father was of

Lebanese origin became a citizen of Sierra Leone automatically. By Act No. 12 of 1962 the Sierra Leone Constitution was purportedly amended to limit full Sierra Leone citizenship to a person whose father or father's father was a negro of African descent. Any person either of whose parents was a negro of African descent but who did not fulfil the condition laid down in Section 2(*a*) of Act No. 12 of 1962 could, nevertheless, on making the appropriate application, become a citizen of Sierra Leone but he would not be qualified to become a member of the House of Representatives or of any District Council or other local authority until he had continuously resided in Sierra Leone for 25 years after such registration or had served in the Civil Service or regular Armed Forces of Sierra Leone for a continuous period of 25 years.[26]

Another Amendment Act of the same year i.e. Act. No. 39 of 1962 sought to amend Section 23(4) of the Constitution in order to allow discriminatory laws "for the limitation of Sierra Leone citizenship to persons of negro African descent". The overall effect of this Act was to remove Act. No. 12 of 1962 from the category of discriminatory legislation.

Section 23 of the Constitution substantially prohibited discriminatory laws — "discriminatory" being defined by Section 23(3) as "affording different treatment to different persons attributable wholly or mainly to their respective descriptions by race, tribe, place of origin, political opinions, colour or creed whereby persons of one such description are subjected to disabilities or restrictions to which persons of another such description are not made subject or are accorded privileges or advantages which are not accorded to persons of another such description".

But Section 23(4)(*f*) of the Constitution allowed in discriminatory law which "having regard to its nature and to special circumstances pertaining to those persons (against whom the law is passed) or to persons of any other such description is reasonably justifiable in a democratic society".

In the Supreme Court, Akar applied for three declarations and all of them were granted; namely:

(i) that the amendment to Section 1 of the Constitution by Act No. 12 of 1962 was *ultra vires* the Constitution and therefore null and void;

(ii) that the purported amendment by Act No. 39 of 1962 of Section 23 of the Constitution was *ultra vires* the Constitution and therefore null and void;

(iii) that all consequential amendments to other sections of the Constitution were *ultra vires* and void.

The main issues on which the case was contested in the Supreme Court were:

(i) Whether the Sierra Leone Parliament was competent to pass retrospective legislation and its effect.

(ii) Whether Sir Edward Coke's dictum in *Bonham's case*[27] was law in Sierra Leone.

(iii) Whether the Amendment Acts were discriminatory and if so, whether they were justifiable in a democratic society.

With regard to the first issue, the learned Chief Justice had no doubt that the Sierra Leone legislature was competent to pass retrospective legislation but such legislation, he warned, should be passed very sparingly and only when fully justified. The Amendment Acts, he continued, were unnecessary pieces of legislation and their passage was completely unjustified. Holding a contrary view, the Court of Appeal[28] maintained that there was nothing in the Constitution to prevent the legislature from passing a retrospective legislation of whatever nature so long as the legislation specifically states that it is to have a retrospective effect; it was immaterial whether or not such a statute was an immoral piece of legislation.

With respect to the second issue, the learned Chief Justice fully endorsed Coke's reasoning in Bonham's case. The Court of Appeal took a negative view of this. The learned President said:

> "Whether it was a right thing or a just thing for Parliament to have amended the Constitution in the way it did, is, in my opinion, not the concern of this court. This court does not sit in judgment of this kind over parliament."

As the Privy Council did not address itself to this legal aspect of the case it is necessary at this stage to comment on it. Coke's dictum in Bonham's case obviously occupies no place in the laws of Sierra Leone. By its nature, the Constitution is supreme and any Act that is passed which is not in contravention of any of its provisions is valid law which no court can question. Presumably, the learned Chief Justice was advocating law reform and, in so doing, with respect, made *lex lata* and *lex ferenda* undistinguishable when he said: "In my view, the time is ripe for Nations with written Constitutions and I refer particularly to New Independent Nations within the Commonwealth to bring to life as an active legal force the dictum of Coke in Bonham's case."

Another factor that might have influenced the learned Chief Justice is the United States Constitution which empowers the United States Supreme Court to declare Congressional Acts and Acts of the President unconstitutional.[29] So far as the third question was concerned the learned Chief Justice emphatically held that the Amendment Acts were discriminatory and could not be reasonably justifiable in a democratic society. The reasons he advanced were as follows:

(*a*) that the Amendment Acts were not purely legislation on citizenship but were primarily intended to exclude certain persons particularly of Lebanese origin from being elected to the House of Representatives.

(*b*) that it was contrary to the spirit of a democratic society for electors to be debarred from choosing for their representative one who was otherwise unexceptionable or had to wait until he was too old to serve them usefully.

Holding a diametrically opposite view, the Court of Appeal maintained that the Amendment Acts were purely legislation on citizenship; that the only consideration taken by Parliament was descent and not race and this consideration was recognised in the nationality or citizenship laws of many other countries. The court added that even if the Acts were discriminatory, there was no legal proof as to what race Akar belonged.

In the Privy Council,[30] the Board set itself only one main task, i.e. to decide whether or not the Amendment Acts were discriminatory; if so, whether they were reasonably justifiable in a democratic society.

The Board unanimously decided that the Acts were discriminatory, on grounds of race; it had this to say:

"Under the designed amended Section 1(i) a person would become a citizen if (*a*) his father and his father's father are or were negroes of African origin: and (*b*) he was born in the former colony or protectorate; and (*c*) he was on 26th April 1961 a citizen of the United Kingdom and colonies or a British protected person; and (*d*) one of his parents or grand parents was born in the former colony or protectorate. No change would be made in the provision of Section 1(2). It will be seen therefore that the designed change was not one that added anything in regard to having links with Sierra Leone or long family associations with Sierra Leone. The essential change did not involve that a person's father or father's father should have lived in Sierra Leone: what the change involved was that a person's father and father's father had to be negroes, and also negroes of African origin. The new added qualification in Section 1(i) was essentially a racial one."[31]

The majority of the Board (Lord Guest dissenting) also maintained that the Amendment Acts were not reasonably justifiable in a democratic society in order to bring them within the exception in Section 23(3)(*f*) of the Constitution. Their Lordships expressed grave doubts whether an Act that imposed a disability on someone on the ground that someone's father and paternal grandfather were not "negroes of African descent" was something which having regard to its nature was reasonably justifiable in a democratic society.

With regard to the requirement of special circumstances pertaining to the persons subjected to the disability which might make a discriminatory law reasonably justifiable in a democratic society, their Lordships also found that there were no special circumstances pertaining to Akar. "As Section 23 is explicitly against discriminatory laws on grounds of race, race would not be regarded as special circumstances; something more had to be added in order to constitute special circumstances," they suggested.[32]

Indeed, counsel for the Attorney-General of Sierra Leone tried to show a special circumstance which made the laws justifiable in a democratic society, i.e. that Akar and people of his type belonged to an immigrant community whose links with the country were formed more recently than those of others. But their Lordships rejected this argument on the basis that there was nothing in the Acts to show that they were intended to limit citizenship to persons having links or long family associations with Sierra Leone, which perhaps might have provided the special circumstances.

Lord Guest differed from the rest of the Board on this point. In his opinion, the Acts, though discriminatory, were reasonably justifiable in a democratic society: The Attorney-General of Sierra Leone, he said, need not show any special circumstances nor should any motive be imputed to Parliament for passing the Amendment Acts. He added that the courts must interpret the Acts for what they were. As he saw it, there were sufficient special circumstances appearing on the face of the Acts to show that they were reasonably justifiable in a democratic society, i.e. the requirement of negro African descent for citizenship. The learned Lord put the matter quite eloquently in the following words:

"It is said that the exemption does not apply because there is no averment or no statement by the respondent that there are 'special circumstances' within the meaning of that section which made Act No. 12 reasonably justifiable in a democratic society. Although the courts are the guardians of the Constitution I believe that in interpreting the Constitution the ground has to be trod warily and with great circumspection. My answer to the argument that no special circumstances were alleged is that it would not be to the point if they were. The respondent cannot speak for the Parliament of Sierra Leone. Parliament speaks only through the provisions on the statute book. The courts cannot go behind the scenes and enquire what were the motives or policy behind a particular piece of legislation. They can only as a matter of construction decide whether the Act is or is not within the powers of the Constitution. This question must be decided on the terms of the Act in conjunction with the provisions of the Constitution."[33]

In my submission, the reasoning of Lord Guest is to be preferred. On this issue, the majority of the Board, with respect, seemed to have lost sight of a very important canon of statutory interpretation which Lord Guest ably states and is quoted in the preceding paragraph. Sometimes, of course, Homer himself even nodded, but when the repercussion is far-reaching then it is virtuous to be wide awake all the time. Presumably, their Lordships might have unconsciously been guided by the political situation existing in Sierra Leone then and thought it unwise to upset it; for, Akar, the appellant, was appointed Ambassador to the United States of America at the time that the appeal was before the Board for hearing.

THE JUDICIAL SYSTEM

The judicial system remained the same as in the previous year. It is significant to note, however, that though the Courts Act (Amendment) Decree 1967[34] extended the jurisdiction of the Magistrate's Courts in the Western Area to matters affecting customary law, no enthusiasm has been shown by these courts to apply customary law whenever cases dealing with such law come before them. In fact since the passing of the Decree, diligent research has not revealed any instance when a Magistrates' Court in the Western Area took cognizance of the provisions of the Decree. A number of reasons may be advanced for this: First, no list of experts in customary law has yet been drawn up by the Chief Justice as required by the Decree. Secondly, the idea of establishing in the Western Area a Magistrate's Court which is virtually a local court similar to those in the Provinces would appear to be bizarre to courts which had hitherto been

6—AL * *

accustomed to "English" law since the establishment of the Colony in 1808. This is of course conservatism at its peak.

It should, however, be emphasised that the Amendment Decree was the brainchild of the N.R.C. in its effort to grant easy access to a local-court-type court to the many tribal people resident in the Western Area whose personal law is customary law and who but for the Decree would have to return to their home towns if they are to obtain redress for grievances to which customary law is the only applicable law.

As the Decree is still on the Statute Book, its practical utility depends on the Chief Justice. When he has drawn up a list of experts on customary law it is to be hoped that the Magistrates' Courts in the Western Area will show a more compromising attitude at least with the threat of appeals to the Local Division of the Supreme Court hanging over them.

CRIMINAL LAW

In accordance with the Government's declared policy to remove N.R.C. decrees from the Statute Book, as if to regard the period of military rule as an interregnum, while retaining in substance certain provisions of the decrees which are considered good for the country, a number of penal decrees were repealed and re-enacted verbatim. For example, the Corrosive Substance Decree 1967[35] was repealed and re-enacted as the Corrosive Substance Act 1969[36] Similarly, the Statutory Nuisances (Summary Punishment) Decree 1968[37] became the Statutory Nuisances (Summary Punishment) Act 1969.[38]

As illicit diamond mining increased by leaps and bounds, the Alluvial Diamond Mining Act[39] was amended by the Alluvial Diamond Mining (Amendment) Act 1969.[40] Section 4 of the Amendment Act replacing Section 18 of the Principal Act contains a number of penal provisions for illicit diamond prospecting, mining, dealing and exporting with punishment by fine ranging from two hundred leones to five thousand leones and/or imprisonment for terms from six months to two years.[41] An important innovation in the Amendment Act is the addition of a new sub section to Section 24 of the Principal Act providing for the expulsion from any or all diamond areas either for a period of time or for ever any person convicted of an offence or offences under the Act.

The purpose of the Amendment Act was to arrest illicit diamond mining and smuggling which were conducted on a very high scale particularly by persons of non-Sierra Leone origin who had flocked to the areas thus causing a heavy fall in revenue. Tremendous vigilance has been shown by the Police and the Army who have been posted in those areas in search for the culprits and hundreds of persons have been expelled. However, it is too early yet to assess the full impact of the new operation since the more the number of expulsions the more the population of non-licensed diamond mining holders increases in the prohibited areas.

In the wake of rumours in governmental quarters that disgruntled citizens, particularly political opponents, were steadfastly in readiness to disrupt the peace and tranquillity of the country, Parliament passed the Arms and Ammunitions (Amendment) Act 1969.[42] The Act, consisting of only one section, authorised any superior police officer probably not below the rank of a superintendent, having reasonable cause to suspect that Arms or Ammunitions were being unlawfully kept, transported and deposited in any place, himself or other person acting under his direction, without warrant, to enter and search any such place at any time and seize and keep such Arms and Ammunitions and to await due process and determination of law in their regard. The section goes further to empower the officer or his agent to demand from the owner of the Arms or Ammunitions or the occupier of the premises on which they are found the production of his licence or authority. Force may be used by the officer concerned, whether or not he is met with resistance, to break open and enter the premises.

In a country like Sierra Leone where some police officers tend to be overzealous in cases in which politics are involved, such consideration does at times belie the performance of their duties.[43] The absolute discretion given to them to determine when there is a reasonable cause for suspicion and to act accordingly has on many occasions been abused. It is submitted that such a discretion ought to be exercised judiciously and a warrant signed by a magistrate upon the sworn information of the officer concerned may not be asking too much. Again, force should only be used when there is actual resistance by the person whose premises are to be searched.

Homicide

The death penalty exists in Sierra Leone for the offence of murder. But the Court of Appeal which almost invariably is the final appellate Court for many a convicted prisoner,[44] has during the period under review perhaps unwittingly demonstrated disapproval of it by showing a certain degree of reluctance to dismiss appeals in murder cases except where the circumstances surrounding the killing are such that sparing the prisoner's life would be a danger to society. A case in point is that of *Sahr Amara* v. *Reginam*.[45] The appellant/accused who was a native of the Eastern Province of Sierra Leone was visited by the deceased who said that he had come to take away for good his sister, the appellant's wife. From the evidence it would appear that the wife herself had formed the intention of leaving the accused and had sent away to her parents three of their five children. The appellant asked the deceased out of his house which he did. Thereupon the appellant went to another house which was some sixty yards away and the deceased followed him insisting on taking away his sister. Both started insulting each other in the course of which the deceased pushed the appellant and he fell to the ground. When the appellant got up he went to his room, took his gun, came out and shot the deceased dead.

In the Supreme Court the appellant's defence was one of provocation. Summing up to the jury, the learned trial Judge quoted *ipssisima verba* para. 2503 of Archbold's Criminal Pleading, Evidence and Practice (36th Edition) 1966, based on certain words of Viscount Simon in his speech in *Holmes* v. *The Director of Public Prosecution*.[46]

In the final analysis, the learned trial Judge told the jury that there was no evidence to support a verdict of manslaughter; that the verdict should be either murder or an acquittal depending on what weight the jury attached to the evidence. The accused appealed against his conviction on the ground of misdirection on the question of provocation.

The Court of Appeal in upholding the appeal referred to two cases namely, *Lee Chun-Cheun* v. *Reginam*[47] and *R.* v. *Martindale*[48] both of which established that the defence of provocation is not necessarily excluded by the existence of an intent to kill or to inflict grievous bodily harm but may apply where such an intention arises from sudden passion, involving loss of self-control by reason of provocation. The court opined that the question of provocation should have been put to the jury who might or might not have found sufficient evidence of it to justify a verdict of manslaughter. The court therefore gave the benefit of the doubt to the appellant by substituting manslaughter for murder.

On the point of misdirection, the reasoning of the Court of Appeal is difficult to support. The court, perhaps inadvertently, established two categories of the reasonable man. One type would appear to be the sophisticated, educated and civilised man, and the other, the primitive man. Delivering the judgment of the court this is what the learned President had to say:

> "I apprehend that to some persons living in a different social setting with the restraining advantages of education and social pressures, a defence of this kind relied upon by the accused, may amount merely to evidence of a provocative incident and nothing more, and that such evidence would neither support nor provide material for inferring a loss of control by the accused either immediately after the provocative incident or subsequently, and therefore it could be said that there was not sufficient material to go to the jury on the issue of provocation."

In other words, if the accused were a person who fitted into the first category of the reasonable man, there might not be a misdirection by the learned trial Judge. On the second category of the reasonable man, the learned President maintained:

> "The accused in this case was however a tribesman in the backwoods of Africa and was being tried by his countrymen who should have been given the opportunity of deciding whether the words and action of the deceased another tribesman were enough to arouse sudden passion leading to loss of self-control by reason of provocation."

It must be pointed out at this juncture that the law of homicide applicable in England before the Homicide Act 1957 is the law still applicable in Sierra Leone. In England it has been held on a number of occasions that the test to apply in order to reduce murder to manslaughter on the ground of provocation is whether the provocation was sufficient to deprive a reasonable man of his self control; not whether it was sufficient to deprive of his self-control the particular person charged.[49] Moreover, the mode of resentment must bear a reasonable proportion to the provocation, nor should there be a cooling off period.[50]

The Sierra Leone Court of Appeal in *Sahr Amara's case* obviously departed from these established legal principles without showing dissatisfaction with the cases in which the principles were enunciated and without even referring to them.

According to the customary laws that obtain in the Eastern Province of Sierra Leone, it will not be idle to speculate that even if the question of provocation had been put to the jury, their verdict would have been the same. For, any member of a woman's family can lawfully with her consent demand her from her husband. This normally happens when the husband's conduct towards the wife or any of her relations is such that he becomes unworthy of the enjoyment of continued cohabitation with the wife. Furthermore, it is common practice for a wife who has developed an association with another man to leave her husband for that other man; the normal remedy open to the aggrieved husband is to ask the wife's parents or the lover, as the case may be, for the refund of the marriage consideration which he had paid for the wife. The cases that have gone before the local courts in this regard are innumerable.[51]

Much as one would welcome the abolition of the death penalty caution must be exercised in throwing to the winds well-established legal principles without either disapproving them or distinguishing the cases in which they applied from the one before the court.

CONTRACT

Very little change took place in the law of contract. The Control of Betting and Lotteries Decree 1967[52] was repealed and all of its provisions were enacted by the Control of Betting and Lotteries Act 1969.[53] The only change of some significance was in connection with the retiring benefits of employees of the Freetown City Council.

Section 2 of the Freetown Municipality Officers' Superannuation (Amendment) (No. 2) Act 1969,[54] slightly modified Section 18 of the Freetown Municipality Officers' Superannuation Act[55] by adding a new sub-section 3(*d*) which empowers the City Council, by resolution, to retire with full gratuity and pension benefits an officer who has attained the age of 50 years. Hitherto, the normal retiring age was 55 years. The object of the amendment, to quote the Prime Minister, was "to inject fresh blood into the establishment and to make the best use of the Council's funds". In other words, the younger the employees, the greater their output.

TORT

Workmen's Compensation again stole the show in the field of Tort. This was the main area of tort in 1967 when the Workmen's Compensation (Amendment) Decree was passed by the N.R.C.[56] Surprisingly enough, Parliament enacted the Workmen's Compensation (Amendment) Act 1969[57] without repealing the N.R.C. Decree. The Amendment Act, on the face of it, purports to amend certain provisions of the Principal Act, i.e. the Workmen's Compensation Act.[58] But apart from Section 4 of the Amendment Act which amended Section 5 of the Principal Act providing that an employer shall not be liable in respect of any injury which does not incapacitate the workman for a period of at least three days (instead of four as in the Decree) the rest of the amendments is a carbon copy of the 1967 Decree.

PROPERTY

Only a few changes took place in the law of property. First, Government utilised the Commissions of Inquiry (Forfeiture of Assets) (No. 2) Decree 1967,[59] to confiscate certain landed properties of some Ministers, one senior civil servant and two heads of Statutory Corporations who had held offices during the S.L.P.P. régime. Secondly, the Town and Country Planning (Amendment) Act 1969[60] amended the Town and Country Planning Act.[61] On the face of it, the Amendment Act enacted all the provisions of the Town and Country Planning Act (Amendment) Decree 1967[62] with slight modifications such as the substitution of "Minister of Housing and Country Planning" for the expression "the N.R.C. Representative".

Section 3 of the Amendment Act replaced Section 3 of the Principal Act by abolishing the Town and Country Planning Board whose powers became vested in the Minister of Housing and Country Planning. Unlike before when the Principal Act was confined to land in the Western Area alone, the Amendment Act extended the Principal Act to the Provinces as well. This extension came under heavy attack from Parliamentarians from the Provinces where a different system of land tenure operates.

Apart from this, the power to acquire land compulsorily being vested in one man — the Minister — instead of in a Board consisting of at least six persons whose decision to acquire land had to be by majority vote,[63] created some amount of uneasiness for land owners everywhere in the country.

One other statute worth mentioning here is the Alluvial Diamond Mining (Amendment) Act 1969.[64] The most relevant section for our present purpose is Section 2. This Section repealed sub section (1) of Section 4 of the Principal Act[65] and replaced it by the following new sub-section:

> "4.(1)(*a*) subject to the provisions of this section, the Director of Mines may grant an alluvial diamond mining licence to any citizen of Sierra Leone or any firm or company of Sierra Leone nationality, to mine alluvial diamond in any area within a licensed alluvial diamond mining area."

Sub-section 4(*b*) provided for the payment of the prescribed fee before the licence is granted. The amendment took away the right of the Tribal Authority of the area, with the consent of the landowner and occupier of the land, to recommend to the Director of Mines the person or persons to whom licence should be granted. The result has been that in some areas applications by landowners to mine on their own lands have been turned down while the landowners watch, in desperation, strangers mining on their lands without their consent.[66]

COMMERCIAL LAW

In recent years the only field of commercial law in which Parliament has shown great interest is in connection with trade and business by non-citizens of Sierra Leone. The Non-Citizens (Trade and Business) Act 1969,[67] restored the ban which was lifted by the Non-Citizens (Trade and Business) Act 1966 (Repeal) Decree[68] on non-citizens of Sierra Leone undertaking certain types of retail trade in the country. One must not hesitate to say that the ban has had an adverse effect on citizens themselves. Government has therefore decided to lift it partially and to allow non-citizens to engage in some business like road and river transport.

PROCEDURE

Two changes of importance took place in procedure. First, the Supreme Court Rules[69] were amended to make applicable in Sierra Leone rules of civil procedure that applied in the High Court of Justice in England as on the 1st day of January 1960 in circumstances where the existing local rules are silent on any matter concerning procedure.[70] Secondly, new rules of procedure governing appeals from Magistrates' Courts were adopted by the Appeals from Magistrates' Courts Rules 1969.[71] A significant innovation is the introduction of legal aid to litigants in indigent circumstances. This is an important improvement on the administration of justice and it is hoped that the privilege will in due course be extended to similar litigants in appeals from the Supreme Court to the Court of Appeal.

In November 1969 the Court of Appeal decided what would appear to be a test case[72] on criminal procedure. With the consent in writing of a judge of the Supreme Court pursuant to Section 136(1) of the Criminal Procedure Act 1965[73] the Acting Attorney-General preferred an indictment charging Mr. Berthan Macaulay and five others with two counts of treason contrary to Section 3(1)(*a*) and 3(1)(*b*) of the Treason and State Offences Act 1963.[74]

Mr. Berthan Macaulay unsuccessfully moved the Supreme Court to have the indictment quashed on the ground that a preliminary investigation should have been held followed by a committal before an indictment could be preferred against him. He appealed to the Court of Appeal.

His main contention was that indictment for treason was not one of those offences which by law could be preferred with the consent of a judge in accordance with the provisions of Section 136(1) of the Criminal Procedure Act without there being first held a preliminary investigation and committal. Section 136(1) of the Criminal Procedure Act reads as follows:[75]

> "No indictment shall be signed or filed in respect of any criminal offence unless there has been a committal for trial upon a previous preliminary investigation in accordance with Part III or an inquiry or inquest held in accordance with the provisions of the Coroners Act, *except in the case of indictments which by law may be preferred by the direction of or with the consent in writing of a judge,*[76] and in the case of informations known as *ex-officio* informations by the Attorney-General."

The Court of Appeal upheld the appeal of Berthan Macaulay, declared the indictment against him and others null and void and ordered a preliminary investigation to be held since, in their opinion, treason is not one of the cases in which the exception in Section 136(1) could be invoked.

The reasons advanced by the Court were quite easy to comprehend. Section 136(1) of the Criminal Procedure Act did not indicate crimes for which an indictment could by law be preferred by the direction of or with the consent in writing of a judge. The only specific reference in the laws of Sierra Leone when such machinery may be adopted is in the Perjury Act 1911,[77] Section 3 of which stipulates that the Supreme Court can direct the prosecution of persons guilty of wilful and corrupt perjury in any proceedings made or taken before it. If one has to look for any other offence in this regard one must refer to English law; for, according to Section 74 of the Courts Act 1965,[78] subject to the provisions of the Constitution or any other enactment, the common law, doctrines of equity and statutes of general application in force in England on the 1st day of January 1880, are in force in Sierra Leone.

The Vexatious Indictment Act 1859[79] has been held to be a statute of general application and is therefore in force in Sierra Leone.

Under that Act an indictment could be preferred with the consent of a judge in the following offences only, namely, perjury, subornation of perjury, conspiracy, obtaining money by false pretences, keeping a gambling house, keeping a disorderly house and any indecent assault. Small wonder therefore that the Appeal Court took the stand that it did as the offence of treason was completely outside the ambit of the recognised offences to which the exception applies. As will be seen in the survey for 1970 Parliament sought to regularise the situation by passing an Act which purported to increase the number of crimes for which the exception in Section 136(1) of the Criminal Procedure Act may be invoked.

---

1. When the country returned to civilian rule in 1968, 24 election petitions were filed by the A.P.C. unsuccessful candidates against the S.L.P.P. successful candidates in the 1967 General Elections. One of them was later withdrawn. The elections of all the 23 S.L.P.P. candidates were declared null and void. This gave rise to by-elections which were to be held on 8th November 1968.

2. Lansana and others were charged with offences of treason, treason felony, and misprision of treason. A *nolle prosequi* was later entered on behalf of Madam Ella Koblo Gullama one of the accused, as she fell ill during the trial and was admitted to hospital. Later, however, she was charged again together with an S.L.P.P. Member of Parliament. This charge was later dropped and she was again charged with this M.P. and four Army Officers for treason and misprision of treason. Of the 15 people tried in Lansana's case three were acquitted and discharged, two convicted of misprision of treason and treason felony and each sentenced to seven years' imprisonment and ten convicted of treason and sentenced to death. The case which lasted for about two years was concluded in the Supreme Court in April 1969. All the convicted persons appealed against their conviction and the appeals are now pending in the Court of Appeal.

3. The case in the Privy Council is reported in [1969] 3 All E.R. 384.

4. See the Sierra Leone *Daily Mail* of 2nd January 1969.

5. *Ibid.* 7th January 1969.

6. *Ibid.* 23rd June 1969.

7. The terms of reference of the Committee were stated in the Prime Minister's speech in the Committee Room, House of Representatives, on 24th June 1969.

8. *Ibid.*

9. The stiffest opposition for a change over to a Republic came from the University.

10. The Prime Minister made this speech at an informal gathering in Kono during his visit to that district.

11. I.e. by the Attorney-General (Qualification) Law 1967 (N.R.C. Law No. 5).

12. See *Annual Survey of African Law 1967*, p. 81.

13. Though the post of Attorney-General carried more salary than that of a puisne Judge it would appear that a judgeship is more prestigious. Moreover, although the post of Attorney-General was in theory a civil service appointment, in practice it had become so political that it became less attractive to any one who did not want to dabble into politics.

14. Act No. 2 of 1969.

15. Section 2 of Act No. 2 of 1969.

16. The last two Attorneys-General were among the accused in the trial of ex-Brigadier David Lansana and others. It was felt in many quarters that had it not been for their office — being chief legal adviser of government — they might not have been charged. One of them, Mr. A. A. Koroma was eventually acquitted and discharged. It is significant to note that up to January 1970, Mr. Koroma, though on leave prior to retirement, is still substantively Attorney-General. The post has changed several hands in an acting capacity.

17. The circumstances surrounding the vacation of the office by Mr. Oliver Shaw are difficult to explain. On the one hand, Government made a statement that Mr. Shaw was invalidated and retired with full benefits. On the other hand, Mr. Shaw said that he was quite well but was forced to resign.

18. Public Notice No. 91 of 1968.

19. Public Notice No. 92 of 1968.

20. Public Notice No. 24 of 1969.

21. Act No. 7 of 1969.

22. Sec. 2 of Act No. 7 of 1969.

23. By Public Notice No. 33 of 1969. The two officers were Patrick Conteh and Emadu Rogers.

24. See [1968] J.A.L. pp. 89–109.

25. *Annual Survey of African Law* 1967, pp 82–7.

26. Sec. 2.

27. (1610) 3 Co. Rep. f. 7*a*, at f. 8*a*. The dictum is as follows:
"And it appears in our books, that in many cases, the common law will control Acts of Parliament, and sometimes adjudge them to be utterly void: for when an Act of Parliament is against common right and reason, or repugnant, or impossible to be performed, the common law will control it, and adjudge such Act to be void."

28. See [1968] J.A.L. pp 100–9.
29. See Act III Section 2, clause 1 of the U.S. Constitution. The learned Chief Justice did not specifically refer to this clause but quoted certain United States cases in which the clause was invoked.
30. [1969] 3 All E.R. 384.
31. *Ibid.*, p. 389.
32. *Ibid.*
33. *Ibid.* pp. 394–5.
34. Decree No. 56 of 1967.
35. Decree No. 68 of 1967.
36. Act No. 22 of 1969.
37. Decree No. 12 of 1968.
38. Act No. 20 of 1969.
39. Cap. 198 of the revised Laws of Sierra Leone, 1960.
40. Act No. 6 of 1969.
41. Section 5 of the Amendment Act also makes an unlawful possession of diamonds punishable on summary conviction with imprisonment for a term not less than 12 months nor more than two years or on conviction on indictment with imprisonment for a term not less than 12 months nor more than five years.
42. Act No. 8 of 1969.
43. On a number of occasions houses of people have been searched on what would appear to be no reasonable ground for suspicion at all.
44. Legal representation paid for by the Crown is afforded to any person tried for murder up to the Court of Appeal.
45. Unreported. Cr. App 41/68, judgment delivered on 1st April 1969.
46. [1946] 2 All E.R. 124 at 127.
47. [1963]1 All E.R. 73.
48. [1966] 3 All E.R. 305.
49. E.g. *R.* v. *Lesbini* [1914] 3 K.B. 1116; *R.* v. *Alexander* 9 Cr. App. R. 139, *Bedder* v. *D.P.P.* 38 Cr. App. R. 133.
50. *Mancini* v, *D.P.P.* (1942) A.C. 1.
51. I.e. According to the Returns made to the Judicial Adviser in the Provinces. The Judicial Adviser permitted the present writer to see the records for which he is very grateful.
52. Decree No. 64 of 1967.
53. Act No. 3 of 1969.
54. Act No. 14 of 1969.
55. Cap. 71 of the revised Laws of Sierra Leone, 1960.
56. Decree No. 37 of 1967.
57. Act No. 18 of 1969.
58. Cap. 219 of the revised Laws of Sierra Leone, 1960.
59. Decree No. 46 of 1967.
60. Act No. 17 of 1969.
61. Cap. 81 of the revised Laws of Sierra Leone, 1960.
62. Decree No. 41 of 1967.
63. Section 3 of the Principal Act provided for a Board of the nature outlined in the text.
64. Act No. 6 of 1969.
65. Cap. 198.
66. The present writer has been consulted on this issue by a number of persons from these areas.
67. Act No. 9 of 1969.
68. Decree No. 53 of 1967.
69. The Supreme Court Rules in Vol. VI of the revised Laws of Sierra Leone, 1960, were amended by the Supreme Court (Amendment) Rules 1969; Public Notice No. 41 of 1969.
70. The relevant amendment is of Order L 11 Rule 3 which made the English Rules on the 1st day of January 1957 as the residuary rules of procedure.

72. Public Notice No. 25 of 1969.
72. I.e. *Berthan Macaulay* v. *The Acting Attorney-General* Cr. App. 23 A/68 unreported.
73. Act No. 32 of 1965.
74. Act No. 10 of 1963.
75. Act No. 32 of 1965.
76. My italics.
77. Cap. 43 of the revised Laws of Sierra Leone, 1960.
78. Act No. 31 of 1965.
79. I.e. the English Statute.

CHAPTER 4

THE GAMBIA

U. U. Uche

CONSTITUTIONAL LAW

On 18th December 1969, the Republic of the Gambia Bill was passed in the House of Representatives. A previous attempt at introducing a Republican Constitution had fallen through in November 1965, nine months after independence, the reason for this being that the Government were unable to secure the requisite majority in favour of the proposal as provided for in the Independence Constitution.[1] This time the Government had better luck. The Bill did not, however, receive Royal Assent till April 1970 (outside the year under review).[2] Since the Royal Assent that followed the referendum did not affect the form or substance of the Bill, we shall here be looking at some of its salient features.

Firstly the Bill retains in Chapter III protection of fundamental rights and freedoms as contained in the 1965 Independence Constitution.

Secondly the executive power of the Republic vests in the President,[3] who in the exercise of his functions is not obliged to follow the advice tendered by any other person or authority. A person shall be qualified for election as President if he satisfies a number of conditions. These range from the obvious one of being a citizen of the Gambia to being nominated by a hundred registered voters where the Presidential election takes place after a dissolution of Parliament.[4] A Head Chief who is standing for election as President is exempt from at least one of these conditions. He need not be qualified as a voter for purposes of elections to the House of Representatives as provided for under Section 33(*b*) of the Republican Constitution. This is of course understandable, in view of the special position accorded traditional elements in the Republican as in previous Gambian Constitutions. The President and his Cabinet constitute the Executive. There is a Vice-President appointed by the President.[5] The Vice-President is the leader of the House of Representatives.[6]

The third feature of the Bill is the composition of Parliament. The President and the House of Representatives comprise the Gambian Parliament. The House of Representatives is made up of thirty-two elected members, four representatives of Head Chiefs, The Attorney-General if he is not one of the thirty-two elected members, and three others nominated by the President.[7] The elected members, the representatives of Head Chiefs and the Attorney-General constitute the voting membership of the House. The nominated members have no vote. It is interesting to note that the number of nominated members which had been increased from two to four in 1968[8] has now been brought down to three in the Republican Constitution. A nominated member need not be a citizen of the Gambia[9] although he must speak English well enough to take an active part in the proceedings of the House.[10] No doubt this requirement of being able to speak English will influence the Head Chiefs in the election of their four representatives in the House.

Fourthly the amendment procedures in the 1965 Constitution are retained in the Bill.[11] Any amendment at all of the Constitution requires the votes of two-thirds of the membership of the House of Representatives. Any alteration of any of the entrenched provisions which are enumerated under Section 72 of the Bill, require both the two-thirds of the membership of the House and a referendum in which at least half of the electorate or two-thirds of all the valid votes cast are in favour of the proposal.

Another interesting feature of the Bill is the abolition under Section 73 of foreign titles of honour, decoration or other dignity except the President consents to a person accepting such titles or decorations. Distinctions conferred by educational, professional and scientific bodies are excepted.

Sixthly the Gambia is one of the very few Republics that retain appeals to the Judicial Committee of the Privy Council.[12]

Finally Chapter X of the Bill deals with a wide range of matters under the heading "Transitional Provisions". Section 119(3) empowers the President to make by order any amendments to the existing law of the Gambia as may appear to him necessary or expedient for bringing that law into conformity with the provisions of the Republican Constitution or otherwise for giving effect or enabling effect to be given to the provisions of the Constitution.[13] The House of Representatives seized the opportunity to give itself another lease of office by providing that the existing House shall be the House of Representatives during the period beginning with the commencement of the Constitution[14] and ending with the first dissolution of Parliament thereafter. All the existing members were deemed to have been re-elected and the nominated members were also deemed to have been re-nominated accordingly. Section 124 provides for Gambianisation of the Public Service. Compulsory retirements to facilitate appointments of local candidates are not only encouraged but positively canvassed.

Elections

Under this head the Elections (Amendment) Act 1969 has made a number of changes in the electoral law, some of which will be mentioned here. Firstly, instead of the Deputy Supervisor of Elections being appointed by the Governor-General (or under the Republican Constitution, the President), he is now appointed by the Public Service Commission after consulting the President.[15] Secondly, Sections 8 and 9 deal with up-dating of the electoral registers. The Supervisor of Elections shall in his discretion cause to be prepared a number of copies of every master register and master supplementary register sufficient for forseeable elections and for sale to members of the public; one copy of all head and supplementary registers for all constituencies in an administrative area shall be made available by every registering officer in his office for inspection by members of the public during official hours, and such copies shall be brought up to date at each supplementary registration. The registering officer shall certify on the cover of each such copies that he has done so.[16] Thirdly Section 10(*b*) of the Act introduces a new sub-section to Section 26 of the Principal Act. This sub-section makes it an offence for any person to alter, deface or destroy any current voter's card; to sell or give away any voter's card whether current or obsolete. It is also an offence to vote with an obsolete voter's card not bearing the name and photograph of the holder, or to vote with a card issued to a person who has since died but whose name has not been removed from the electoral register. The punishment for the above offences are prescribed under Section 41 of the Principal Act.

Fourthly, the Registrar of Births and Deaths has a duty under Section 11 of the Act under review to notify the Supervisor of Elections every three months of any births and deaths in each district in which registration of births and deaths is in operation.

Finally Section 12 amends Section 28 of the Principal Act by empowering anybody who has lived in a different constituency for at least six months, to apply to the Supervisor of Elections to transfer his name to his new constituency. There is howevei, a proviso to the effect that the Supervisor may refuse such transfer if the application was made immediately before a general election. Apparently the Supervisor could have no such discretion in the event of a by-election. It does seem a little odd that a general election which should be an overriding reason for one to want to vote in a constituency where one has resided for six months, should in this case be used as an excuse to deprive one of the right to vote in a constituency of one's choice. No doubt these detailed electoral provisions in the Gambia are understandable against the background of past litigation fought exclusively on the validity of electoral registers.[17]

JUDICIAL SYSTEM

In view of the introduction of a Republican Constitution and in view of the criticisms often levelled against the Gambia's existing structure of courts, one's curiosity is justifiably aroused to know what changes if any occurred in this area of the law during the review year. The answer to this is that the judicial system was left severely alone in the republican set-up. The Judicial Committee of the Privy Council is still the penultimate Court of Appeal and the legislative authority for the setting up and operation of the various courts in the Gambia, is littered over a vast range of different enactments.

CRIMINAL LAW AND EVIDENCE

Under this heading the Territorial Sea and Contiguous Zone (Amendment) Act 1969,[18] has amended Sections 2 and 3 of the Principal Act in respect of offences committed in the Gambia territorial waters. The territorial sea is now extended to twelve miles and the contiguous zone to eighteen miles. Mention has already been made of the offences created under the Elections (Amendment) Act 1969. There were also a number of judicial decisions in criminal cases in the Gambia Court of Appeal. In *Musa Ceesay* v. *Commissioner of Police*,[19] the appellant, a buying agent for Messrs U.A.C. Limited, was convicted and sentenced on two counts of purchasing groundnuts from persons whom he knew to be members of a Co-operative Society and who were under contract to sell their nuts to the Society. It is an offence under Section 58(*b*) of the Co-operative Societies Act,[20] for any person who knowing of the existence of a contract between a Co-operative Society and any member thereof induces or solicits that member to act in breach of that contract or purchases, other than for his own use, from a person known to him to be, or whom he has reason to believe is a member of a Co-operative Society registered under the Act, any agricultural produce or product of a handicrafts man which the member is contractually bound to sell to the Society. This Section of the Act was amended by Section 16 of the Co-operative Societies (Amendment) Act 1969[21] (discussed in our survey of 1968) in respect of onus of proof. The amendment shifts the onus of proof from the prosecution to the accused in prosecutions under the section. In other words it is up to the accused to prove that the vendor was not a member of a Co-operative Society or that if he was such a member, he was not under any contract to sell to the Society.

One of the issues raised in the appeal was that the trial judge by suggesting that once the prosecution had proved that the accused purchased the nuts from persons whom he knew were members of a Co-operative Society, knowledge of the existence of a contract to sell produce to the Society by the vendor would be presumed unless and until the accused could establish the contrary, had implied that *mens rea* was not an essential ingredient of the charge. On this, Marcus-Jones, J.A., who read the judgment of the Court of Appeal, commented that *mens rea* is still an essential ingredient of the offence and continued:

> "The general principle of law places the burden of persuasion on the prosecution but when in the case of guilty knowledge Parliament placed the 'proof' of the stated fact upon the accused, it did this because the accused alone knew what lawful excuse, if any, he possessed. The prosecution is not expected to negative in advance every conceivable excuse."

Concluding his judgment on this ground of appeal the learned judge gave what in his view is the meaning and purpose of the amendment to be that the onus of proving that the person charged did not know that the vendor was a member of a Co-operative Society contractually bound to sell his products to the Society, shall at all times be on the person charged.

In *Kebba Tabarteh* v. *Commissioner of Police*,[22] the appellant had wanted the Court of Appeal to quash his conviction on grounds of natural justice *inter alia*. What actually happened was that the trial magistrate, on the morning of the trial, had on his own admission been in to see the Commissioner of the Area Council for a chat. The said Commissioner was a vital witness and a prosecutor in the action in which the accused was subsequently convicted. On this basis the accused in his appeal argued that there was a clear case of a judicial officer having interest in a case in which he was adjudicating or bias against a particular accused. There is of course considerable judicial authority for the view that the least trace of pecuniary or legal bias is enough to disqualify a judicial officer as having an interest in the case. The court found however, that this could not be a case of "interest" since all the evidence for it was the brief chat which the magistrate had with the Area Commissioner. The appeal was dismissed on this as on other grounds.

Sulayman Jallow v. *Commissioner of Police*[23] was an appeal against conviction and sentence on the grounds of the admission without warning on the record, of the evidence of accomplices and admitting evidence of confession without first trying the issue of admissibility. The argument of counsel however, was based mainly on the issue of admissibility of a confession made to a police officer without the magistrate first ascertaining the voluntariness of the said confession. The relevant facts here were that both the accused and his counsel were present in court when the police tendered the accused's confession. No objection was raised on the ground of threats made against the accused or on any other ground. The issue of threats was however raised by the accused in his evidence-in-chief. The trial magistrate had therefore ruled that this was an afterthought and did not take it into account in convicting the accused. On counsel's argument on this ground of appeal the court agreed that it was for the judge to decide the issue of admissibility of evidence and continued:

> ". . . the question arises whether at the time the confessions were received in evidence, there was any material before the judge negativing the voluntariness of the confession. In my opinion there was none. If indeed counsel for the appellant had material which on a fair view would lend colour to any threat held out to induce the confession, counsel would have objected to the statement and the learned trial magistrate would have been bound, and indeed it would have been his duty to have heard evidence so as to be able to exercise his discretion whether to exclude the statements."[24]

The appeal was therefore dismissed.

Finally *Mamanding Kuyateh* v. *Commissioner of Police*[25] was a case where the appellant had been charged with forgery but convicted and sentenced for stealing. The Court of Appeal saw nothing out of the ordinary in this, under the provisions of the Criminal Procedure Code of the Gambia. In fact the appeal court had to substitute a conviction for uttering.[26]

CONTRACT AND TORT

Apart from the case of *Musa Ceesay* v. *Commissioner of Police*[27] which has already been discussed above and which involved members of a Co-operative Society selling their produce in breach of a contract with their said Society, there was no significant activity in the area of contract in 1969. In the law of tort however, the case of *Curator of Intestate Estates* v. *N'Jie and Betts*[28] raised a number of interesting legal issues. The facts were that one Omar N'Jie, a learner driver using Abu Betts' car and unaccompanied, had negligently killed one Tejan Foon. The deceased, although unmarried, had acknowledged the paternity of a child *en ventre sa mere*, born six months after his death. He was however, survived by his parents. The Curator of Intestate Estates as Personal Representative of the deceased sued the negligent driver joining the owner of the car under both the Fatal Accidents Act 1846, and the Law of England (Application) Act of the Gambia. The latter Gambian enactment adopts both the Fatal Accidents Act 1846 and the Law Reform (Miscellaneous Provisions) Act 1934 as part of the law of the Gambia. On the advice of the court, the action was conducted under the Fatal Accidents Act 1846 in spite of the fact that certain paragraphs of the statement of claim were also based on the Law Reform (Miscellaneous Provisions) Act 1934, as part of the law of the Gambia. On the curious basis that the parents of the deceased were not his dependants within the meaning of the Fatal Accidents Act 1846 and therefore suffered no pecuniary loss, and that a posthumous child was not entitled under the Act, the learned Chief Justice who heard the case at the Supreme Court level, held that the Curator could not recover any damages under the 1846 Act. He did concede however, that there might well be a case for allowing damages under the 1934 provisions.

Seven issues were raised on appeal to the Court of Appeal namely:

(1) That the learned Chief Justice was wrong in law in holding it was not negligent to hand over a vehicle to a learner-driver, unaccompanied, for the purpose of driving a motor vehicle;

(2) That the learned Chief Justice was wrong in law in holding that the first respondent was not driving for the second respondent;

(3) That the learned Chief Justice found that Tejan Foon came to his death by the negligent driving of Omar N'Jie the first respondent but failed to enter judgment against the said first respondent;

(4) The learned Chief Justice erred in law in holding the payment made by the deceased to his mother and father was in return for furnished accommodation and presumably also for electricity and food;

(5) That the learned Chief Justice was wrong in law that the mother and father of the deceased were not his dependants;

(6) That the learned Chief Justice misdirected himself in holding that the mother and father of the deceased suffered no pecuniary loss; and

(7) That the learned Chief Justice misdirected himself as to the status of the child who was born posthumously.

These could of course be reduced to four grounds namely: the application in the Gambia of the Fatal Accidents Acts 1846–1959 and the 1934 Act; the determination of who the dependants of the deceased were; the question of liability and finally the measure of damages.

Under the first ground, there is no doubt that at common law the death of a person gave no cause of action to others either for mental suffering or material loss. Also at common law the wrong done to the deceased himself died with him. Both these common law rules have been modified by statute in favour of the dependants of the deceased and his estate respectively. The Fatal Accidents Act 1846–1959 and the Law Reform (Miscellaneous Provisions) Act 1934, achieved this in English law. These enactments were made part of the law of the Gambia by the Law of England (Application) Act. It follows therefore that a plaintiff could frame his action under any or both enactments (i.e. 1846 or 1934) without being put to his election by the court to choose either of them as the learned Chief Justice did in this case. The Gambian Court of Appeal upheld this right of the plaintiff to frame his statement of claim under both the Fatal Accidents Acts and the Law Reform (Miscellaneous Provisions) Act 1934.

As to the determination of who the dependants of the deceased were under the Acts, there is a clear insertion under Section 10 of the Gambian enactment that the parents of the deceased qualify as dependants. There is also a provision to the effect that a person shall be deemed to be a parent or child of the deceased person notwithstanding the fact that he was only related to him illegitimately or in the consequence of adoption. In other words both the parents of Tejan Foon in this case and his posthumous child were entitled under the Acts. It must be observed with respect that the learned Chief Justice's ruling that the parents of the deceased were not his dependants was a startling proposition indeed, more so in an African setting. Even if these (i.e. parents of deceased) had not been specifically included under the received law of the Gambia, it would have been perfectly proper for the judge to include them having regards to local circumstances. There is no justification in law or common sense for the exclusion. It is not surprising therefore that the Court of Appeal set aside this ruling on appeal.

On the question of liability the Court of Appeal found that Omar N'Jie the learner driver was negligent and that the deceased came to his death as a direct result of this negligence. It was also found that Abu Betts, the owner of the car was negligent in that he allowed a learner driver to drive his car without either accompanying him himself or arranging for some other qualified driver to accompany him. Both of them were therefore jointly liable.

Finally on the measure of damages the court took into account that the deceased had been paying out a large percentage of his earnings to his dependants. The appeal court cited with approval the dictum of Viscount Haldane in the English case of *Taff Railway* v. *Jenkins*[29] that the basis of the award of damages in such cases was not *solatium* but compensation for pecuniary loss. They agreed with the statement of Lord Wright in a later case that the whole consideration is "a hard matter of pounds, shillings and pence". Accordingly the parents got £300; the son £1,250 and the estate, £200.

REVENUE AND OTHER MONETARY MATTERS

There was considerable legislative activity under this head in the Gambia during the review year. The Currency (Amendment) Act[30] made a number of changes in the Principal Act. Section 2 of the Act amended the interpretation section of the Principal Act by including the meaning for purposes of the Act of such words as "Bank", "Banking Business", "convertible external currencies" and "Special Drawing Rights". In view of the increased activities of the Gambia Currency Board and the importance to the Gambia of their rights in the International Monetary Fund, these insertions are very apt indeed.

Section 3 of the 1969 enactment amends a corresponding section of the Principal Act by empowering the Prime Minister (soon to become the President), to determine the appointment of any director of the Gambian Currency Board without assigning any reasons. Before the 1969 amendment, the Gambian pound derived its value from sterling. Under the new provisions the Gambian pound is given a par value of 2.13281 grammes with a proviso giving power to the Governor-General to declare a new parity after consulting with the appropriate minister and the Board.[31] Section 5 empowers the Board to deal in convertible external currencies, while Section 6 repeals Sections 16 to 22 of the Principal Act by making new provisions for external assets,[32] limits of local assets,[33] and powers of the Board.[34] Section 20 gives the Board the power to licence banks:

"Section 20(1) Notwithstanding the provisions of any other Act, no banking business shall, save as hereinafter provided, be conducted in the Gambia except by a company which is in possession of a valid licence authorising it to conduct banking business in the Gambia."

Thus all banks operating in the Gambia would have to obtain their licence from the Board. Section 21 deals with the Reserve Fund while Section 22 lays down that any liabilities of the Board will be deemed to be those of the Government of the Gambia.

There is also the International Financial Organisations (Amendment) Act 1969[35] which authorised the minister responsible for such matters to communicate the Gambia's acceptance of the Fund's Amendment, and to deposit with the International Monetary Fund an Instrument of Participation in the Special Drawing Account pursuant to Section 1 of Article XXIII of the said Amendment. Section 4(*c*) of the new provisions amends Section 4 of the Principal Act by adding a new sub-section the effect of which is to treat the Gambia's special drawing rights under the fund as part of the external reserves of the country.

The Pool Betting (licensing) (Amendment) Act 1969[36] amends Section 6 of the Principal Act by increasing the tax on bets from 10 per cent to 15 per cent. Section 2 of the Income Tax (Amendment) Act 1969[37] amends Section 9(1)(*t*) of the Principal Act by raising tax-free income from £150 to £200. A new rate of income tax is prescribed under Section 5 (Fourth Schedule) of the new provisions. Other enactments in the year under review that affected revenue and other monetary matters included the Motor Traffic (Amendment) Act 1969,[38] the Permanent Increase of Pensions (Public Officers) Act 1969,[39] the Finance and Audit (Amendment) Act 1969,[40] and the Exchange Control (Specified Foreign Currency) (Amendment) Order 1969.[41] The last mentioned Order made under Section 3 of the Principal Act, includes Ethiopian dollars, Moroccan dirhams and Algerian dinars in the list of exchangeable currencies under the Schedule. This measure was of course, intended to give the necessary boost to the tourist industry which is fast becoming an important aspect of the economic life of the Gambia.

LAND LAW

A number of appeals in this area of the law were heard at the Gambia Court of Appeal. In *Alhaji Tunkara* v. *Isatou M'Benger & anor*,[42] the Court of Appeal was to decide whether long possession could defeat the title of a bona fide purchaser who had obtained a valid title from an administrator.

The facts were that the first defendant and the second defendant were the sister and son-in-law respectively of one Jabel M'Benga (deceased). In 1965 the first defendant had started an action. In 1968 letters of administration of the estate of the late Jabel M. Benga were granted to his son, who later sold the premises in issue as administrator of the estate of his deceased father. In an action for possession by the purchaser against the sister and the son-in-law of the deceased, the Supreme Court took into account the fact that the defendants had been on the premises for about 60 years and decided in their favour. On appeal the Court of Appeal reversed the judgment holding that the plaintiff appellant must succeed. It was further held that any rights which the defendants possessed in the estate of the deceased could be pursued in respect of the proceeds of the sale of the premises.

The issue in *Kamal Milky* v. *Mohamed Makwar*[43] was whether in an action for possession, receipt of rent alone was conclusive evidence of a tenancy agreement. The appellant who was landlord of certain premises in Russel Street, Bathurst had notified the defendant/respondent of an increase in annual rent from £450 to £1,200. The increase was to take effect from the end of December 1965. The appellant later gave respondent notice to quit since he was unwilling to pay the increased rent. In fact the respondent continued staying on the premises and paying the old annual rent of £450 but without a new lease to that effect. In August 1968 the appellant took out an action for possession. The court at first instance found as a fact that although the notice of the increase in rent had been served on the respondent he nevertheless paid the old and lower rent, and that the appellant did not return the sums so paid. On this basis he ruled that a yearly tenancy had revived and that a fresh notice to quit had to be served on the respondent. Against this decision the plaintiff appealed.

At the Court of Appeal Dove-Edwin, P., cited with approval the following statement of the legal position by Sir John Verity in the case of *Hajah Fatmatta Katah* v. *K. Chellaram & Sons*:[44]

"It is not to be assumed that from a mere holding over and acceptance of rent a tenancy from year to year is to be implied. It is in each case a question of fact as to whether in the particular circumstances it is shown to have been the intention of the parties to create such a tenancy or whether the facts go to show that there was no such intention. It is of course upon the party setting up the tenancy to prove its creation . . . if it is to be inferred from the conduct of the landlord that there was no intention to create such a tenancy then no such tenancy is to be implied"

and concluded that there was no new tenancy and that the fact of the holding over of rent was not enough to create one in this case. The appeal was allowed and an immediate order of ejectment was made against the respondent.

Alhaji Momodu N'Jie v. *Abdoulie Barrow*[45] was a case on the priority of two competing judgment debtors; one was secured with an equitable mortgage while the other was not. The Court of Appeal ruled that where one of the judgment creditors was already in possession of an equitable mortgage by deposit of the title deeds and he has done nothing to affect his priority (e.g. by returning the deeds to the mortgagor) his right as a secured creditor to a first charge on the property is not lost and he will be preferred to the other judgment creditor who is not so placed.

MISCELLANEOUS

In February 1969 an agreement was reached in principle for the establishment of a Customs union between the Gambia and Senegal. In April there was a meeting in Dakar of the Senegal-Gambian Inter-State Ministerial Committee to consider interim measures against smuggling until such time that a Customs union will eventually be realised.

Finally a number of notices were made under the Christian Marriage Act.[46] The Roman Catholic Church of the Holy Spirit at Campama (Bathurst)[47] and the Methodist Church at Mansankonko[48] are licensed under Section 4 of the Act to solemnise marriages.

---

1. I.e. half the votes of the whole electorate or two-thirds of all those who actually voted at the referendum. In this case the votes fell short of both electoral stipulations.
2. The delay is explained by the intervening referendum at which the Government obtained about 70 per cent of the votes and therefore satisfied the provisions of Section 48 of the Independence Constitution.
3. Section 42.
4. Section 33(*c*).
5. Section 43.
6. Section 43(1).
7. Section 57.
8. Section 2 of the Constitution (Miscellaneous Provisions) Act 1968. See our Survey of the Gambia for 1968.

9. Sections 58 and 59.
10. Section 58(*b*).
11. Section 72.
12. Section 95.
13. This power is only valid till 24th April 1972.
14. I.e. 24th April 1970.
15. Section 3 of the Elections (Amendment) Act 1969, amending Section 3 of the Principal Act, Cap. 48, Laws of the Gambia.
16. Section 9(*b*).
17. *Sabally & N'jie* v. *Her Majesty's Attorney-General* (1965), 1 Q.B. 273.
18. No. 9 of 1969.
19. Criminal Appeal No. 14/69. Unreported.
20. Cap. 33 Laws of the Gambia (1966 Revision).
21. No. 16 of 1968.
22. Criminal Appeal No. 6/69. Unreported.
23. Criminal Appeal No. 1/69. Unreported.
24. At p. 2 of the judgment.
25. Criminal Appeal No. 9/69.
26. For enactments passed in the Gambia in 1969 that had some marginal connection with criminal law, see Essential Commodities (Regulation of Prices) Act, 1969; Finger-prints (Amendment) Act 1969, the Immigration (Amendment) Act 1969, and Motor Traffic (Amendment) Act 1969.
27. Criminal Appeal No. 14/69. Unreported.
28. Court of Appeal (Civil Appeals) 1969. Unreported.
29. (1913) A.C. 4.
30. No. 17 of 1969.
31. Section 4.
32. Section 16 on value of External assets. These shall be equivalent to not less than 50 per cent of the amount of the Board's Currency Notes and Coins in circulation and its other demand liabilities. The minister can vary the percentage in consultation with the Board. Section 17 makes provision for external assets generally.
33. Section 18 of the Act as amended.
34. Section 19 of the Act as amended.
35. No. 5 of 1969.
36. No. 13 of 1969.
37. No. 21 of 1969. Came into force on 1st January 1970.
38. No. 8 of 1969.
39. No. 24 of 1969.
40. No. 11 of 1969.
41. L. N. 8 of 1969.
42. Civil Appeal No. App/16/69.
43. Civil Appeal No. 19/69.
44. 1955/60 W.A.C.A. Selected Judgments.
45. Civil Appeal; Judgment delivered on 15/12/69. Unreported.
46. Cap. 23 Laws of the Gambia (1966).
47. L.N. No. 1 of 1969.
48. L.N. No. 4 of 1969.

CHAPTER 5

EAST AFRICAN COMMUNITY

Y. P. Ghai

CONSTITUTION

The Treaty for East African Co-operation 1967, which is the basis of the Community was amended once in 1969 by the Treaty for East African Co-operation (Modification) Agreement between the Partner States, Kenya, Uganda and Tanzania (Legal Notice 30). The modification provided for two amendments. Firstly, a new para. 9, was added to Article 66, which deals with the expenditure from the General Fund. The amendment enables the Authority, on the recommendation of the Finance Council, to authorise the payment of any money out of the General Fund as a loan to the East African Development Bank or to any institution of the Community. The Authority may also determine the terms and conditions of such loans. The authorisation by the Authority is sufficient warrant for the disbursement of the money. This provision constitutes an exception to the general rule for the disbursement of money from the General Fund, for para. 4 of Article 66 stipulates that no money shall be paid out of the General Fund except in the manner prescribed by an Act of the Community.

The other amendment relates to the Common Market Tribunal. Its effect is to enable the Tribunal to meet as and when business requires rather than be in permanent session, and to provide for part time rather than full time members of the Tribunal. The specific amendments are to Article 8, para. 1, and Article 10 of Annex VIII. The need for this amendment is alleged to arise both from the difficulties of getting a full time chairman of sufficient competence and prestige and from the small amount of business that has been referred to it. The Tribunal has in fact not met yet.

On 1st June, the East African Railways and Harbour Administration was broken up into the East African Railways Corporation (Legal Notice 16) and the East African Harbours Corporation (Legal Notice 15), and the assets and employees of the Administration divided between the new Corporations (Legal Notices 19–22).

CONFLICT OF COMMUNITY LAW
AND THE LAW OF A PARTNER STATE

The Community has no judicial organs of its own, but as the Community law has the force of law in the partner states, the Community law can be enforced in the courts of the partner state. In case there is a clash between the Community law and the law of the state, the attitude of the national court becomes a matter of crucial interest. The partner states are obliged by Article 95 of the Treaty to take all steps within their power to secure the enactment and the continuation of such legislation as is necessary to give effect to the Treaty, and in particular to confer upon the Acts of the Community the force of law within their territories. The partner states have carried out this obligation through their legislation implementing the Treaty, and the general rule is that the Community law has the force of law in each of the states; in case of a conflict between the Community and the national law, the former prevails, except in instances when the national law states explicitly that it is to have effect notwithstanding a contrary provision in the Community law.[1]

In 1969 the Kenya High Court delivered two judgments in cases where there was a conflict between Community law and the Kenya law. In both cases the conflict was not with the ordinary Kenya law, but with its Constitution. Neither the Treaty nor the implementing Acts deal directly with such a situation, unless the reference to law in both instances is held to include the Constitution as well. In both instances the conflict did not involve the actual provisions of the Treaty, but rather the law enacted by the East African Legislative Assembly.

The first case to be decided, which may shortly and conveniently be referred to as the *Evan Maina* case,[2] concerned certain sections of the East African Customs and Transfer Management Act, which was originally passed in 1952, and which was retained in force by the implementing Act as "existing laws". Maina was employed by the Nairobi Airport services as Deputy Director of Operations. While on duty at the airport, he was involved in an incident with an official of the Customs Department. Two days later the Chief Preventive Officer (another Customs official) wrote to the Director of Airport Services alleging that Maina had assaulted the Customs Officer, and had thus committed an offence under Section 142 of the Act. The Preventive Officer was willing to give Maina three days in which to produce a written explanation. Maina wrote to his Director denying the assault and giving his own version of the incident. A few weeks later, Maina was charged by the Preventive Officer with obstruction of a Customs Officer while in the execution of his duty contrary to Section 142(4)(*d*). He was asked to appear before the Collector of Customs to answer the charges. Maina went to his lawyer, who, being busy on the day fixed for hearing, wrote to the Officer for an adjournment. No further communication was received from the Officer until the date for hearing, when the Principal Collector informed Maina and his lawyer that the matter had been dealt with in his absence in accordance with Section 174 of the Act. The Principal Collector was satisfied that an offence under Section 142 had been committed, and imposed a penalty of 150 s. Maina then moved the court for an order of certiorari to quash the order of the Principal Collector, and to issue a mandamus to him to consider the case in accordance with the law.

Various issues arose during the hearing: whether the Customs Officers, the Preventive Officer and the Principal Collector, were the proper officers, i.e. whether there had been a delegation of the powers of the Commissioner of Customs, in whom was vested the power to impose fines; whether, if such a delegation had been made, it could validly be made, being a power to impose a fine; whether there was a requirement to follow the rules of natural justice, and if so, whether they had been observed. In this chapter we only discuss the additional point considered by the court, namely, whether Section 174 was consistent with the Kenya Constitution. It could be argued that it was unnecessary for the court to deal with the constitutional issue: it was satisfied that the Commissioner was acting in a quasi-judicial capacity and had failed to observe the rules of natural justice that were therefore incumbent on him. On the other hand, there was also an application for mandamus, to determine which the court had to be satisfied as to the validity of the procedures and powers under Section 174.

Before we proceed to examine the court's determination on whether the section was incompatible with the Constitution, it is useful to set out the relevant provisions. Section 142 makes it an offence to obstruct a Customs Officer in the execution of his office. Section 164 provides for the hearing of the offences in subordinate courts of the partner states, but Section 175 enables the Commissioner to settle cases, on the admission by the accused of his guilt. Section 174, however, gives the Commissioner compulsory powers. Where he is satisfied that any person has committed any offence against the Act in respect of which a fine is provided, he may compound such offence and summarily order such person to pay such sum of money, not exceeding two hundred shillings, as he may think fit.

The court held that Section 174 was inconsistent with Section 77(1) of the Constitution. Section 77(1) says: "If any person is charged with a criminal offence, then, unless the charge is withdrawn the case shall be afforded a fair hearing within a reasonable time by an independent and impartial court established by law." The court rejected the contention for the Customs that the offence under consideration was a "customs" rather than a "criminal" offence, and therefore Section 77 of the Constitution had no bearing on the case. Other sub-sections of 77 require the trial to proceed only in the presence of the accused, unless he himself agrees otherwise, or his conduct makes it difficult; he has to be provided an opportunity to defend himself in person or by a legal representative of his choice. Both these provisions were contravened; nor was the Commissioner a "court" within the meaning of the Section. There was therefore a clear clash between Section 174 and the Constitution.

The court then turned to the significance of the clash. Could the Community law be upheld despite the clash? The Kenya law implementing the Treaty, the Treaty for East African Co-operation Act (No. 31 of 1967), provides in Section 10(3) that an Act of Parliament, even if subsequent to the Community law, if inconsistent with that law, is deemed repealed unless a contrary intention is expressed in the Act. At the time the 1967 Act was passed, the Kenya Constitution was not contained in an Act of Parliament, but in Order in Council. The court found it unnecessary to determine whether it was intended to be within the scope of Section 10(3), for the new Constitution, embodied in an Act of Parliament in 1969, contains Section 3 which establishes the supremacy of the Constitution and provides that "if any other law is inconsistent with this Constitution this Constitution shall prevail and the other law shall, to the extent of the inconsistency, be void". This was held to be enough of a "contrary intention" to exclude the application of Section 10(3), and so the Community law had to give way to Section 77.

The court therefore held Section 174 of the Customs legislation void, and granted the certiorari, quashing the proceedings before the Commissioner. It felt unable to issue the mandamus, as the law in question was void.

The other case in which similar issues were posed, arose from constitutional references under Section 67(1) of the Constitution, whereby a subordinate court may if the question of interpretation, is involved, refer it to the High Court for a ruling.[3] The two accused where charged with certain offences against the Official Secrets Act (No. 4 of 1968) of the Community. Since Section 8(1) of that Act lays down that such a prosecution shall not be instituted without the consent of the Counsel to the Community, the point arose as to whether the prosecutions could proceed without such consent. It was argued on behalf of the Kenya Attorney-General that such consent was not necessary, indeed Section 8(1) was invalid in Kenya as it clashed with Section 26(3) of the Constitution, which reads, "The Attorney-General shall have power in any case in which he considers it desirable so to do: (*a*) to institute and undertake criminal proceedings against any person before any court (other than a court-martial) in respect of any offence alleged to have been committed by that person." It was agreed that its terms covered offences under the Community law. Sub-section 8 of Section 26 further provides that in the exercise of his functions under sub section (3), the Attorney-General shall not be subject to the direction or control of any other person or authority. Therefore Section 8(1) of the Community Act is inconsistent with the Constitution, and consequently void.

The court dismissed the contention of the Counsel to the Community (whose appearance as a party to the case was odd, but appears to have been accepted without question by the court and the prosecution), that the requirement of his own consent was a procedural step and in no way could be regarded as limiting the A-G's discretion. If the law was valid, the withholding of his consent would prevent the latter from prosecuting, and was therefore a clog on his power. The Counsel's second point was that even if there was a clash, the Community law ought to prevail, since the partner states had undertaken to give the force of law to Community legislation, and since treaties prevailed over domestic law in cases of conflict, as shown by two decisions of the old Permanent Court of International Justice: The *Greco-Bulgarian Communities*, P.C.I.J., Ser.B, No. 17, 32, and *German Interests in Polish Upper Silesia* (Merits) (1926) Ser.A, No. 7 (I W.C.R., p. 510).

The court found that in the instant case, the conflict was not between the Treaty and Kenya law, but between an Act of the Community and the Kenya Constitution. If the court had to decide a question involving a conflict between Kenya law on the one hand and the principles and usages of international law on the other, and the court found it impossible to reconcile the two, it would be bound, as a municipal court, to say that Kenya law prevailed. Further, the court reiterated its arguments as to the supremacy of the Constitution (as in the previous case) based on Section 3. In further elaboration, the court argued that to hold Section 8(1) of the Community Act to be valid would be to accept that what the Kenya Parliament could not do itself — i.e. amend the Constitution without following the prescribed procedure for its amendment — it could authorise another body to do, particularly a body whose powers of law-making were subsidiary. The court accordingly held Section 8(1) void.

The High Court saw itself primarily as a Kenya municipal court. The result of the decisions is to weaken the Community and to emphasise its dependence on the good will of the partner states. The court gave no consideration to the nature of the institution or organisation set up by the Treaty, but was content to dismiss its law-making power as subsidiary. Another consequence of the decisions is that certain laws of the Community have different status in the different partner states. The offending section of the Official Secret's Act would not be offensive in Tanzania, where the Constitution contains no provision comparable to the Kenya one; similarly, the Customs case would have gone differently in Tanzania. It is clearly unfortunate that the Community law should operate in these diverse ways in the different states. A way out of the problem would be for the Community to formally repeal laws which have been judicially found to offend against the law or Constitution of partner states.

In concluding this section, it is worthwhile to look at another decision of the Kenya High Court in which the standing of the Legal Counsel to enter an appearance was in issue.[4] An employee of the East African Posts and Telecommunications Administration (now Corporation) had been sued for damages arising from an accident when he was driving an official car. The Community or the Administration itself was not sued, nor asked to be made a party to the proceedings, but the Counsel filed the defence. The magistrate held that the Counsel was not entitled, as Counsel, to enter appearance. The Kenya Advocates Act (Cap. 16) allows lawyers in the employ of the Community to appear as advocates in "connexion with the duties of his office". The magistrate held that as the Administration was not a party to the proceedings, the Counsel could not represent the defendant. On appeal, the High Court held that the Community had an interest in the case, as it would be vicariously responsible in case of the defendant's liability. The Counsel was therefore acting in connection with his duties, and was entitled to represent the defendant.

ASSOCIATION AGREEMENT BETWEEN THE E.E.C. AND THE EAST AFRICAN PARTNER STATES

The agreement for the Association was signed on 24th September 1969.[5] It was to come into force on the first day of the month following the date on which the instruments of ratification and the act of notification have been exchanged. It is to last for five years from the entry into force, but in any case to expire by 31st January 1975. Either party can withdraw from the association upon giving six months' notice. Eighteen months before its expiry, the parties have agreed to start negotiations on the terms of a further association. On the East African side, the parties are the individual partner states, so that the Community itself is not a member. On the European side, the E.E.C. as well as the individual member states are parties. The E.E.C. normally has power to conclude agreements on behalf of the member states, but if the content of the agreements goes beyond merely trade matters, then it is felt necessary for the member states to join as parties as well.

Essentially, the agreement seeks to provide a free trade area between the E.E.C. and the Community countries. The actual provisions in fact fall short of a free trade area, although an attempt is made to cast it in that form, primarily to get round the rules of G.A.T.T. and in particular to benefit from the exemption given under its Article 24 against the extension of the concessions of the agreements to all G.A.T.T. members. Products originating in East Africa are guaranteed duty free into the E.E.C. although such goods are entitled to treatment no more favourable than the E.E.C. members accord to goods of one another. The general principle of duty free entry for East African goods is qualified by two provisions. One of these relates to the products covered by the common agricultural policy of the E.E.C. within Article 40 of the E.E.C. Treaty. Here the E.E.C. undertakes to grant East Africa some advantages over third countries, but not necessarily as favourable as that granted *inter se*. Second, the duty free entry for three other products is limited. The duty free quantity for coffee is 56,000 metric tons, for cloves 120 tons, and for tinned pineapple 860. If the export exceeds these quantities in any year, the E.E.C. is free to take, subject to consultation with the Community states, "the necessary measures to avoid serious disturbances in traditional trade flows".

On the part of East Africa, there is even more limited right of duty free entry for the E.E.C. products. Duty free entry has been granted to 59 products which are of special interest to the E.E.C. countries. Even here, it is only technically true to say that the entry is completely duty free. For what the East African states have done is to divide their single tariff duty into two columns, one of which is called fiscal entry and the other Customs duty. It is only the Customs duty which has been eliminated in relation to the E.E.C., while it is the fiscal entry which carries a heavier tariff. The relative lack of duty free entry for the E.E.C. goods is in recognition of the special problems of the developing economies of the East African states. They can retain or introduce duties which are necessary to meet their development needs or which are intended to contribute to their budgets. They can even vary the concessions on the 59 items, so long as the total balance of concessions is maintained, presumably by granting concessions on other items. East Africa is not to discriminate as between the members of the E.E.C.

The position as regards quantitative restrictions is similar: the E.E.C. shall not apply any such restrictions to East African goods that they do not apply *inter se*, except in matters of common agricultural policy, while East Africa, although under a general obligation to abolish such restrictions, may retain or reintroduce them in order to meet their balance of payments or development needs, or in the implementation of a common agricultural policy which is envisaged in the East African Treaty. East Africa is not to discriminate between the E.E.C. states in its policy of quantitative restrictions, and is not to impose an absolute ban, so that the trade channels are kept open. An absolute ban, however, is possible, if this is essential to protect local products, but in this case the E.E.C. members have to be satisfied of the necessity. East African states have further undertaken to provide the most favoured nation treatment to the E.E.C. both in its import and export policies. Both parties have also agreed to refrain from any measure or practice of an internal fiscal nature that directly or indirectly leads to discrimination between its own products and like products originating in the territories of the other.

There are provisions guaranteeing rights to establishments and services, although it seems that in this area the burden on East Africa is considerably heavier than on the E.E.C., both as a matter of law and practice. There is provision for the transfer of capital in so far as payments become due for the goods and services which have been liberalised as a result of the agreement, to the member state in which the creditor or beneficiary is resident.

The freedom of each side to enter into integration or association agreements with its neighbours or other states is recognised. On the part of East Africa, the states are free to form or maintain Customs union or free trade areas; with one or more third African countries, they have similar freedom, except that the rules of origin of goods, which enable East Africa to export to the E.E.C. on favourable terms, are not affected thereby. If there is any incompatibility between the obligations of the East African states under the Association Agreement with the E.E.C. and their obligations under the agreement with other African countries, "measures for the smooth functioning of the Association" shall be taken. If East Africa enters into economic co-operation agreements with third (other, non-African) countries, then such agreement should not be incompatible with the principles or provisions of the Association Agreement. There is thus a very clear restriction on the competence of East African states to pursue independent foreign commercial policies. On the part of the

E.E.C., the obligations are much less onerous. In fact, there is no express provision enabling the E.E.C. to enter into other agreements, it being implied that it has that right. The only obligation it has is to inform the East African states of any request for membership or of association. In some instances there is the obligation to consult with East African states, but only if the potential agreement is with a state whose economic structure and production are comparable with those of the East African states, "and which after examination by the E.E.C.", is referred for consultations. In other words, it is up to the E.E.C. to decide on what negotiations they will consult East Africa. This contrasts with the obligations of the East African states, who have to or can be asked to consult with the E.E.C. on all cases.

The Association Agreement sets up two institutions. The more important is the Association Council which is composed, on the one hand, of the members of the Council and of the members of the Commission of the E.E.C., and, on the other hand, of members of each of the East African states and representatives of the E.A. Community. The Council can meet either at the ministerial level or at the level of their representatives. The precise composition and numbers are unimportant, since each side, i.e. E.A. and E.E.C. have each one vote. The function of the Council is to promote and supervise the implementation of the agreement. It has certain powers of taking decisions, and can make recommendations on most matters pertaining to the matters arising from the agreement.

The other institution is the Parliamentary Committee which meets once a year to discuss matters concerning the Association. It has no specific powers or functions. Its purpose is to enable the parliamentarians of both sides to meet to exchange ideas, and hopefully to put pressures on their governments in favour of strengthening of the Association. It consists on a basis of parity, of members of the European Parliament and of the Parliament's of the East African states. It is significant that on the East African side there is no representation from the East African Legislative Assembly.

In cases of dispute, the Council attempts to resolve it, but if it fails, then either party can demand an arbitration. Each party nominates an arbitrator, while the Council nominates the third. Decisions of the arbitrators are taken by majority vote. Each party to the dispute must take the measures required for the implementation of the decision.

LEGISLATION OF THE COMMUNITY

The East African Legislative Assembly passed 14 Acts. Half of these were appropriations. Four were for the Railways and Harbours Administration (before it was split into separate corporations, and no longer needed to come to the Assembly for appropriations). The remaining three were for the General Fund Services; one was a supplementary appropriation for year ending June 1969, of 12,462,225 Tanzania shillings. The other two were in respect of the year ending June 1970 and together amounted to 310,424,702 Tanzania shillings (original appropriation of 294,254,515 and supplementary appropriation of 16,170,187).

The Assembly passed the Laws of the Community (Interpretation) Act (No. 6), replacing earlier legislation on the subject. On the subject of delegation of powers and functions, it is provided that where by or under any Act the exercise of any power or the performance of any duty is conferred upon the Authority or the Community or the President or any Minister of a partner state or an officer in the service of the Community, they or he may, unless expressly forbidden from doing so, delegate by notice in the Gazette to any person by name, or to the public officer for the time being holding any designated office, the exercise of such power or the performance of such duty subject to such conditions, exceptions or qualifications as they or he may direct. However, no officer in the service of the Community can delegate his powers unless such delegation has been approved by the Authority either generally or in any particular case. Nor can such an officer ever delegate the power to make subsidiary legislation.

Subsidiary legislation, like the parent legislation, has to be published in the Community Gazette, whereupon judicial notice can be taken of it. Subsidiary legislation may operate retrospectively, up to the time of the parent Act, "but no person shall be made or become liable to any penalty whatsoever in respect of any act committed or of the failure to do anything before the date on which such subsidiary legislation is published in the Gazette". Unless otherwise provided, subsidiary legislation may provide for penalties up to a maximum fine of 2,000 Tanzania shillings or imprisonment of two months, or both.

Where any act constitutes an offence under two or more written laws, the offender shall, unless the contrary intention appears, be liable to be prosecuted or punished under either or any such laws, but shall not be liable to be punished twice for the same offence. If a law is amended to change the penalty, the offender, in the absence of express provision to the contrary, is liable to penalty prescribed at the time of the commission of such offence. Subject to the express provisions of any Act, any act which constitutes an offence under any written law [i.e. Act or Community or subsidiary legislation], shall be triable in the partner state in which the offence is alleged to have been committed and the jurisdiction of the appropriate court in that state in relation to the trial and punishment of the person alleged to have committed the offence shall be determined by the Penal Code, the Criminal Procedure Code and any other Act of that state. Forfeits shall, unless the contrary is otherwise provided or unless it is expressed by law to be forfeited to any person, be forfeited to the government of the partner state in which the order for forfeiture was made, and the net proceeds thereof, if it is ordered by a competent authority to be sold, shall be paid into and shall form part of the public revenue of that state. This, however, is not to affect any provision in any written law whereby any portion of any fine or forfeit or of the proceeds of any forfeit is expressed to be recoverable by any person or may be granted by authority to any person. Fines, etc, become payable to the public revenue of the state in which they are levied, but the President of that state may direct the payment to any person of such proportion of such fine or penalty as he may think fit. It is likewise open to the President of the state in which a conviction was recorded, to remit in whole or in part any sum of money which under any written law may be imposed as a penalty, fine or foreiture, on a convicted offender, although such money may be in whole or in part payable to some other person than the government of that state.

The laws of the Community do not affect the rights of the governments of the partner states unless expressly provided otherwise therein, or unless it appears by necessary implication that such government is bound thereby. The words of enactment of Community laws are in terms set out in Article 59 of the Treaty, i.e. "Enacted by the President of the United Republic of Tanzania, the President of the Sovereign State of Uganda and the President of the Republic of Kenya on behalf of the East African Community, with the advice and consent of the East African Legislative Assembly."

Act No. 10, the University College Dar es Salaam (Amend.) Act, provided for two student members on the Council of the College, duly elected by the students themselves to represent the students. Control of Pesticides Act, No. 11, regulates the manufacture, importation, sale and distribution of pesticides in East Africa. It sets up the East African Pesticides Central Organisation, as a body corporate, which has been charged with the implementation and supervision of the purposes of the Act. It has, *inter alia*, the power to license dealers in pesticides. The competence of the Assembly to legislate on pesticides arises from item 9 of Annex X of the Treaty.

Acts of the Community (Miscellaneous Amendments) Act 1969, No. 12, amends the Pensions Cap. 3 Act (by providing a new definition of pensionable emoluments, so as to exclude the non-pensionable part of overseas addition and inducement allowance from being taken into account); the Provident Fund Act (Cap. 10) (by providing a new definition of financial year, 1st January to 31st December, for the Postal Fund, to come into line with the financial year of the Postal Corporation, and 1st July to 30th June for General Fund); the East African Customs and Transfer Tax Management Act (No. 12/1952) and the East African Excise Management Act (No. 13/1952), the object of both cases being to facilitate the change to the metric system of measurements.

East African Income Tax Management (Amend.) Act, No. 5, amends the parent Act in several instances. It extends liability for tax on income received in East Africa by an employee in respect of services performed by him outside East Africa; increases the taxable value of accommodation provided by the employer; restricts the exemption from liability on passage expenditure borne by an employer to expenditure on leave passage for expatriate staff only; extends exemption on employers' contribution to pension funds, etc. to funds providing benefit for employees' dependents; restores a provision defining income of persons in respect of individuals received from resident companies; allows a deduction for revenue expenditure on scientific research and allied subjects; enables personal allowances to be apportioned in the year on which a taxpayer's qualifications for the same ceases; removes allowance for life assurance premiums where a benefit thereunder may be withdrawn at the option of the assured at any time during the continuance of the policy.

East African Customs and Transfer Tax Management (Amend.) Act, No. 13, provides for certain declarations in regard to goods liable to transfer tax and makes provision for the refund of transfer tax on goods which are pillaged or damaged while subject to Customs custody, or when it has been paid in error. Finally, the East African Excise Management (Amend.) Act, No. 14, restricts the movement of beer without the payment of excise — when beer is to be removed from one brewery to another or other licensed premises for the purpose of bottling, or for sampling purposes, the permission of the Commissioner-General is necessary, who may require the deposit of security before giving his permission.

---

1. See *Annual Survey of African Law*, 1968.
2. *In the Matter of an Application by Evan Maina For Leave to Apply For Orders of Certiorari & Mandamus*, Miscellaneous (Case No. 7/1969).
3. *Republic* v. *Mushiyi* — Constitutional Reference No. 2/1969.
   Republic v. *Ombisi* — Constitutional Reference No. 3/1969.
4. *Chite* v. *East African Community*, Civil Case No. 1320/1968.
5. Legal Notice 43/1969.

CHAPTER 6

KENYA

Eugene Cotran

CONSTITUTIONAL LAW

At long last Kenya has a revised Constitution. Since it achieved independence in 1963, the country's Constitution has been mutilated beyond recognition by no less than ten amendments, which include some very major ones, such as the abolition of the Upper House, the Senate, and the abolition of "regionalism". The long title of The Constitution of Kenya Act 1969 (No. 5 of 1969) is "An Act of Parliament to amend the Constitution of the Republic of Kenya and to reproduce the said Constitution in a revised form, and for purposes incidental thereto". The revised Constitution is contained in a Schedule to the Act, which apart from incorporating the amendments, revises the Order of the Chapters, and in a few cases alters the language and content of the provisions. It will not be possible to deal in this short review with the new revised Constitution as a whole, but for the convenience of the reader, I reproduce in an annex to this chapter, the Act itself, and also the Arrangements of Sections of the new Constitution to give the reader some idea of its new structure.

The National Assembly and Presidential Elections Act (No. 13 of 1969) re-enacts the present National Assembly Elections Act (Cap. 7) with amendments and expansion. The Act, together with the Regulations[1] made under it, comprehensively deals with the law and procedure relating to the registration of electors and the holding of elections to the office of President and to the National Assembly. Section 12 makes provision for Presidential elections as required by Section 5(1) of the Constitution. Section 17 contains the provision dealing with preliminary elections for the nomination of party candidates to the National Assembly, as required by Section 34(d) of the Constitution.

The Local Government (Transfer of Functions) Act (No. 20 of 1969) permits the President, by regulations, to make such amendment to any Act of Parliament as may be necessary to transfer to the Government the functions at present exercised by local authorities, other than municipal councils, in relation to education, public health, roads and graduated personal tax. It also empowers him to make such amendments to the Exchequer and Audit Act (Cap. 412) and the Local Government Regulations 1963 (L.N. 256/1963) as may be necessary to transfer to the Controller and Auditor-General the audit of the accounts of local authorities.

The case of *Republic* v. *El Mann*[2] raised the interesting question of the interpretation to be given to Section 21(7) of the Constitution (now Section 77(7) in the revised Constitution) which provides that "No person who is tried for a criminal offence shall be compelled to give evidence at his trial". The proceedings arose out of a reference made to the High Court under Section 28(3) of the Constitution (now Section 84(3)) by the Senior Resident Magistrate, Nairobi. The point for decision was whether the Republic might put in evidence against an accused charged with a contravention of the Exchange Control Act answers given by the accused to an investigation officer pursuant to a mandatory questionnaire under powers conferred by para. 1(1) of the General Provisions as to Evidence and Enforcement set out in Part I of the Fifth Schedule to the Act. By a recent amendment to the said Schedule, it was expressly enacted that "any information obtained under this paragraph shall be admissible in evidence in any prosecution for an offence under this Act of any person from whom it was obtained". When the prosecution sought to put in the answers of the accused at the trial, his counsel objected to their admission in evidence on the ground that the new amendment was unconstitutional as being in contravention of Section 21(7). The short point, as Mwendwa, C.J., put it was "whether Section 21(7) is to be given a liberal and extended construction . . . or to be construed literally and narrowly in accordance with the the exact meaning of the words used". After citing a passage from Craies on Statute Law, and passages from English cases, Mwendwa, C.J., continued:[3]

We have quoted this passage *in extenso*, because both sides agree that it sets out the principles of construction which we have to apply. But, of course, each side lays different emphasis on different aspects of those principles. Counsel for the accused invites us to pay more attention to those passages which stress that regard must be had to the object of the legislation, counsel for the Republic on those which lay the principal emphasis on the language used. There is one point, however, in which, if we have correctly followed the submissions, we detect some difference of approach. It appears to us that counsel for the accused is inviting us to apply a more liberal construction to a constitution than we should adopt in relation to an ordinary enactment of the legislature, and he has cited some passages from *Basu on the Constitution of India* (5th Edn.,) at p. 54 which appear to lend some support to this view. Counsel for the Republic, on the other hand, contends that the same canons of construction apply to a constitution as to any other enactment of the legislature. There are, we consider, dicta which appear to support either viewpoint. But we think that the issue is put into true perspective in the citation which appears on p. 55 of *Basu*, in which Das, J., in *Keshava Menon* v. *State of Bombay*, [1951] S.C.R. 228, a Bombay case, said:

"An argument founded on what is claimed to be the spirit of the Constitution is always attractive for it has a powerful appeal to sentiment and emotion: but a court of law has to gather the spirit of the Constitution from the language of the Constitution. What one may believe or think to be the spirit of the Constitution cannot prevail if the language of the Constitution does not support that view."

We respectfully adopt this dictum as setting out the correct approach to the interpretation of a constitution. We do not deny that in certain contexts a liberal interpretation may be called for, but in one cardinal respect we are satisfied that a constitution is to be construed in the same way as any other legislative enactment, and that is, where the words used are precise and unambiguous they are to be construed in their ordinary and natural sense. It is only where there is some inprecision or ambiguity in the language that any question arises whether a liberal or restricted interpretation should be put upon the words.

In the light of these considerations we now proceed to examine the sub section which we are called upon to construe. It is very short and we repeat it for ease of reference:

"No person who is tried for a criminal offence shall be compelled to give evidence at his trial."

The person who is sought to be protected is a "person who is tried for a criminal offence": the protection afforded is that he shall not be compelled to give evidence: the time at which the protection is to operate is "at his trial". We ask ourselves where is any ambiguity to be found in this short and concise provision?

Nevertheless counsel for the accused has strenuously argued that the intention of the sub section is quite different from what may be gathered from its plain words. He contends that if the provision is narrowly and literally construed, the protection it affords is nugatory, and the guarantee is robbed of all meaning. The words, so he submits, enact a guarantee against self-incrimination. We pause to comment that, in making this submission at the outset of his argument, he appears to us, with respect, to have fallen into the error of first assuming the intention of the legislature and then seeking to spell out the language, by a strained interpretation, the meaning of which has been assumed. He has ranged widely over the constitutions of many countries in the world and has referred in particular to analogous provisions in the constitutions of America and India. In America it is well established that the Fifth Amendment provides protection against self-incrimination which comes into effect long before the trial and extends not merely to evidence in court but to compulsory statements of a self-incriminating character. In India by Article 20(3) of the Constitution protection of a similar kind is afforded although there has been some difference of opinion on the question at what stage the protection begins to operate. As we understood his argument counsel for the accused submits that the framers of the Kenya Constitution, having in mind, as they must have done, such far-reaching guarantees afforded by other constitutions, must have intended to provide some comparable protection in our Constitution. We have no hesitation in rejecting such a submission. We note that the language used in the provisions prayed in aid is quite different from the language of the sub section under consideration, and we base ourselves firmly on the cardinal principle to which we have referred that the intention of the enactment is to be gathered in the first place from the words used. Even if some intention were to be assumed from extrinsic considerations, we should, we think, have no more right to assume that the intention of the legislators was to incorporate guarantees as wide as or wider than those found in other constitutions than to assume that, being aware of practical difficulties which may have arisen from guarantees too widely framed, they intended to substitute some guarantee less far-reaching in its effects. We make neither assumption: we seek to construe what appear to us to be the plain words of the sub section and to give effect to them according to their tenor.

In support of his main submission counsel for the accused is driven to contend that the section, although it appears to refer to evidence given by an accused person at his trial, is intended to be construed as referring to statements made by the accused person before his trial, of which evidence is sought to be given by prosecution witnesses at his trial. We are satisfied that no such construction can be supported and that the words are incapable of the meaning for which counsel for the accused contends. We stress two points. First of all, the words "against himself" are conspicuously absent from the sub section, and in their absence the assumption that the provision is intended to be a general guarantee against self-incrimination can scarcely be supported. Secondly, the protection extends to evidence given at the trial. Even if it were open to argument that "to give evidence" means to provide evidence, the prohibition is limited to evidence provided at the trial, and cannot without doing violence to the plain language of the sub section be extended as counsel for the accused seeks to extend it, to evidence provided by the accused person before the trial began. If, on the other hand, the expression "to give evidence" is to be construed in its natural and obvious sense the prohibition expressly relates not to evidence by prosecution witnesses but to evidence given by the accused. To suggest that when an investigation officer puts in evidence an extrajudicial statement allegedly made by the accused, it is the accused who is giving evidence, is a proposition which we are wholly unable to accept.

Our task is to decide what on its proper construction the Constitution provides, and it is no concern of ours to consider whether wider guarantees ought to be provided or to evaluate the protection which, properly construed, the Constitution affords. But as the submission that the protection afforded by the sub section is of little or no value has been put forward as an argument against construing the sub section according to the natural and obvious meaning of the words, we think it right to add that we do not accept the view that the protection is of minimal importance. Counsel for the Republic has very appositely referred us to sub section (2) of Section 127 of the Evidence Act which provides that in criminal proceedings every person charged with an offence shall be a competent witness for the defence, but includes the proviso that

> "the person charged shall not be called as a witness except upon his own application".

This, we think, is exactly what Section 21(7) of the Constitution in other language provides. Reference has been made by counsel on either side to the passages in Broom's *Legal Maxims* in which the Latin maxim *nemo tenetur seipsum accusare* is considered. At p. 630 of the 9th edition this is referred to as, in the words of Lord Coleridge, "a maxim of our law as settled, as important and as wise as almost any other in it", but the author goes on to note that in many instances, in particular in the laws of bankruptcy and in legislation designed to protect the revenue, it has been entrenched upon. But the passage concludes (at p. 632) with the comment, "the maxim *nemo tenetur seipsum accusare* still holds good to this extent, that the person charged cannot be compelled to enter the witness-box against his will". It is clear that neither the author nor the legislators who enacted the English Criminal Evidence Act of 1898 from which Section 127 of our Evidence Act is ultimately derived, regarded the protection afforded by the proviso as something of little account.

We have said enough to show that in our opinion sub section (7) of Section 21 of the Constitution means no more and no less than is to be gathered from the plain words of the provision, and is not to be given an extended meaning which cannot be spelt out of the words used without doing violence to the language of the sub section. The question which has been referred to us for our decision is whether sub para. (5) of para. 1 of Part I of the Exchange Control Act is *ultra vires* the Constitution of Kenya. For the reasons we have given our answer is in the negative. It follows that in accordance with sub section (4) of Section 28 and sub section (2) of Section 175 of the Constitution, the case will be remitted to the subordinate court to be disposed of in accordance with our decision.

JUDICIAL AND LEGAL SYSTEM

The Statute Law (Miscellaneous Amendments) Act (No. 10 of 1969), although intended only to make minor amendments to various Acts, in fact introduces some important new provisions relating to second appeals from subordinate courts and the High Court. The amendments are to the Civil Procedure Act (Cap. 5 (1948) edition) as follows:

Written Law	*Provision*	*Amendment*
The Civil Procedure Act (Cap. 5 (1948))	Section 71*a*.	Insert a new section as follows— APPEALS FROM APPELLATE DECREES OF A SUBORDINATE COURT Second appeal from subordinate court. 71*a*. Except where otherwise expressly provided by this Act, and subject to such provision as to the furnishing of security as may be prescribed, an appeal shall lie to the High Court from a decree passed by a subordinate court of the first class on an appeal from a subordinate court of the third class, on a question of law only.
	Section 72.	(*a*) Replace the heading with— APPEALS FROM APPELLATE DECREES OF THE HIGH COURT. (*b*) Replace the marginal note with— Second appeal from the High Court.

Written Law	*Provision*	*Amendment*
The Civil Procedure Act (Cap. 5 (1948))—(*Contd.*).	Sections 73, 74.	Delete.
	Section 79*c*.	Insert immediately following Section 79*c* four new sections as follows—

Second appeal from High Court on no other grounds.

79*d*. No second appeal from a decree passed in appeal by the High Court shall lie except on the grounds mentioned in Section 72 of this Act.

No second appeal from High Court in certain cases.

79*c*. No second appeal from a decree passed in appeal by the High Court shall lie in any suit when the amount of value of the subject-matter of the original suit does not exceed one thousand shillings unless special leave has been first obtained from the court before whom the appeal is to be heard.

Section 79*c*.   Appeals by paupers

79*f*. A person who has been allowed to take, defend or be a party to any legal proceedings in a subordinate court as a pauper may not appeal to the High Court, or from the High Court to the Court of Appeal, except with the leave of the court before whom the proceedings appealed against were heard or (if such leave is refused) unless special leave has been first obtained from the court before whom the appeal is to be heard.

CRIMINAL LAW

Kenya has caught up with its neighbours, Tanzania and Uganda, in introducing minimum and generally harsher punishments for criminal offences, especially those involving violence. The Criminal Law Amendment Act (No. 3 of 1969) seeks "to assist in the combating of violent crime" (the words used in the Memorandum of Objects and Reasons to the Bill) by enacting the following provisions:

Section 2 repeals Section 26 of the Penal Code and substitutes therefor the following:

Imprisonment

26. (1) A sentence of imprisonment for any offence shall be to imprisonment or to imprisonment with hard labour as may be required or permitted by the law under which such offence is punishable.

(2) Save as may be expressly provided by the law under which the offence concerned is punishable, a person liable to imprisonment for life or any other period may be sentenced to any shorter term.

(3) A person liable to imprisonment for an offence may be sentenced to pay a fine in addition to or in substitution for imprisonment:

Provided that—

 (i) where the law concerned provides for a minimum sentence of imprisonment, a fine shall not be substituted for imprisonment;

 (ii) where the law concerned provides for imprisonment together with corporal punishment such person shall be sentenced to imprisonment and to corporal punishment.

Section 3 replaces Section 27 of the Penal Code dealing with corporal punishment with the following:

Corporal punishment.

27. (1) A sentence of corporal punishment shall be to receive such number of strokes with a cane as may be specified by such sentence.

(2) No sentence of corporal punishment shall be passed upon any female or upon any male sentenced to death.

(3) Whenever a male person under the age of eighteen years is convicted of an offence for which he is liable to imprisonment the court may, in its discretion, sentence him to corporal punishment in addition to or in substitution for any other punishment to which he is liable:

Provided that no sentence of corporal punishment shall be imposed in default of payment of a fine.

(4) No sentence of corporal punishment shall be carried into effect until after the expiration of the time limited by law for the entry of an appeal in connexion with the proceedings concerned or, if such an appeal has been entered, until after the final disposal thereof.

(5) No corporal punishment shall be inflicted on a prisoner unless, immediately before such infliction, a medical officer has examined the prisoner and has certified that in his opinion such prisoner is physically fit to undergo such punishment.

(6) Corporal punishment shall only be inflicted on a prisoner in the presence of a medical officer, who may at any time during the carrying out of such punishment intervene and postpone the carrying out of the remainder of the punishment if, in his opinion, such postponement is necessary to obviate the risk of grave or permanent injury.

(7) If any person has been sentenced to corporal punishment in substitution for any other punishment to which he might have been liable, and such sentence cannot, either in whole or in part, be carried into effect, such person shall be kept in custody and shall, as soon as possible, be taken before the court which imposed such sentence and such court may, in its discretion, either remit such sentence or the remainder

thereof, or pass upon such person any sentence to which he might have originally been liable.

(8) A person sentenced to corporal punishment without imprisonment may be detained in a prison or some other convenient place for such time as may be necessary for carrying the sentence into effect or for ascertaining that the same should not be carried into effect:

Provided that no person under the age of eighteen years shall be detained under this sub section in a prison.

(9) Corporal punishment shall be inflicted with a rod, cane or other instrument or a type approved for the purpose by the Minister, and the Minister may approve different types of rod, cane or other instrument for different ages of persons.

(10) Where no medical officer is readily available for the purposes of sub section (5) or (6) of this section, the duties and powers imposed and conferred by those sub sections may be carried out and exercised by any medical practitioner.

Section 4 replaces Section 308 of the Penal Code with the following:

Preparations to commit felony.

308. (1) Any person found armed with any dangerous or offensive weapon in circumstances that indicate that he was so armed with the intent to commit any felony is guilty of a felony and is liable to imprisonment with hard labour for a term of not less than ten or more than fourteen years together with corporal punishment.

(2) Any person who, when not at his place of abode, has with him any article for use in the course of or in connexion with any burglary, theft or cheating is guilty of a felony, and where any person is charged with an offence under this sub section proof that he had with him any article made or adapted for use in committing a burglary, theft or cheating shall be evidence that he had it with him for such use.

(3) Any person who is found—

(*a*) having his face masked or blackened, or being otherwise disguised, with intent to commit a felony; or

(*b*) in any building whatever by night with intent to commit a felony therein; or

(*c*) in any building whatever by day with intent to commit a felony therein, having taken precautions to conceal his presence,

is guilty of a felony.

(4) Any person guilty of a felony under sub section (2) or (3) of this section is liable to imprisonment with hard labour for five years or, if he has previously been convicted of a felony relating to property, to such imprisonment for ten years.

Section 5 deals with the offence of "Handling stolen goods", and replaces Section 322 of the Penal Code, which dealt with receiving and retaining stolen property, with the following new section (the definition of "handling" being closely modelled on the English definition contained in the recent Theft Act):

Handling
stolen goods

322. (1) A person handles stolen goods if (otherwise than in the course of the stealing) knowing or having reason to believe them to be stolen goods he dishonestly receives the goods, or dishonestly undertakes, or assists in, their retention, removal, disposal or realisation by or for the benefit of another person, or if he arranges to do so.

(2) A person who handles stolen goods is guilty of a felony and is liable to imprisonment with hard labour for a term of not less than seven or more than fourteen years.

(3) For the purposes of this section—

(*a*) goods shall be deemed to be stolen goods if they have been obtained in any way whatever under circumstances which amount to felony or misdemeanour, and "steal" means so to obtain;

(*b*) no goods shall be regarded as having continued to be stolen goods after they have been restored to the person from whom they were stolen or to other lawful possession or custody, or after that person and any other person claiming through him have otherwise ceased as regards those goods to have any right to restitution in respect of the stealing.

(4) Where a person is charged with an offence under this section—

(*a*) it shall not be necessary to allege or prove that the person charged knew or ought to have known of the particular offence by reason of which any goods are deemed to be stolen goods;

(*b*) at any stage of the proceedings, if evidence has been given of the person charged having or arranging to have in his possession the goods the subject of the charge, or of his undertaking or assisting in, or arranging to undertake or assist in, their retention, removal, disposal or realisation, the following evidence shall, notwithstanding the provisions of any other written law, be admissible for the purpose of proving that he knew or had reason to believe that the goods were stolen goods—

 (i) evidence that he has had in his possession, or has undertaken or assisted in the retention, removal, disposal or realisation of, stolen goods from any offence taking place not earlier than twelve months before the offence charged;

 (ii) (provided that seven days' notice in writing has been given to him of the intention to prove the conviction) evidence that he has within the five years preceding the date of the offence charged been convicted of stealing or of receiving or handling stolen goods.

Section 6 amends Section 7 of the Criminal Procedure Code (Cap. 75) so as to allow a Senior Resident Magistrate or a Resident Magistrate to award the full penalty provided for robbery with violence and attempted robbery with violence (Sections 296 and 297 of the Penal Code) and for preparations to commit felony and handling stolen goods (see Sections 4 and 5 of this Act above).

Section 7 provides for automatic police supervision, and restriction of residence for a period of five years after the release of a person sentenced for any offence mentioned in Section 6 above.

Section 8 makes an amendment to the Prisons Act (Cap. 90) consequential upon the reintroduction of hard labour.

Section 9 together with the Schedules:

(*a*) introduces hard labour imprisonment of varying duration for grave sexual offences;

(*b*) provides for a minimum sentence of 14 years, with a maximum of 20 years, at hard labour together with corporal punishment, for persons convicted of robbery with violence and attempts so to do.

(*c*) makes certain consequential amendments to the Criminal Procedure Code.

The Statute Law (Miscellaneous Amendments) Act (No. 10 of 1969) amends the punishments for attempts by repealing Sections 389 and 390 of the Penal Code, and substituting the following section:

389. "Any person who attempts to commit a felony or a misdemeanour is guilty of an offence and is liable, if no other punishment is provided, to one-half of such punishment as may be provided for the offence attempted, but so that if that offence is one punishable by death or life imprisonment he shall not be liable to imprisonment for a term exceeding seven years and may suffer corporal punishment if such is provided for as a mandatory or discretionary punishment for the offence attempted."

The East Africa Law Reports contain a great number of Kenya cases on criminal law and practice and procedure for the year under review. The following are worth noting:

Njoroge v. *Republic*,[4] where the High Court decided that a person cannot be held guilty of aiding and abetting under Section 20(1) of the Penal Code where the offence is complete before the aid or abetment is given to the offender.

Musisi v. *Republic*[5] involved consideration of the interesting problem of whether a Kenya Court has jurisdiction to convict a person on charges of uttering two forged invoices and of obtaining money by false pretences where the invoices were forged in Uganda, but posted to Kenya. Mwendwa, C.J., held, following English cases, that since the accused's object was to defraud his employer, the Kenya Government, in Kenya, and attempted to induce his employer to act upon the forged invoices in Kenya and to obtain the money by false pretences there, the Kenya Courts had jurisdiction.

In *Karuria* v. *Republic*[6] Rudd, J., considered Section 154 of the Penal Code which provides that "Every woman who knowingly lives wholly or in part on the earnings of prostitution, or who is proved to have, for the purpose of gain, exercised control, direction or influence over the movements of a prostitute in such a manner as to show that she is aiding, abetting or compelling her prostitution with any person or generally, is guilty of a misdemeanour." In this case the appellant was a prostitute living on her own earnings. The Court held:

  (i) the latter part of the section clearly refers to a woman who is not herself a prostitute and the first part of the section must be read *ejusdem generis* with the latter;

  (ii) the section does not intend to make every prostitute living in whole or in part on her own earnings guilty of an offence within the section.

Kaggia and Another v. *Republic*[7] aroused great public interest, involving, as it did, the Vice-President and the Chairman, Homa Bay Branch, of the opposition party, the Kenya People's Union. The appellants were convicted of holding a public meeting which took place without a licence contrary to Section 5(11)(*a*)(ii) of the Public Order Act, and were sentenced by the Kisii Resident Magistrate to one year's imprisonment. The principal grounds of appeal were that there was no public meeting and the appellants did not hold it. There was also an appeal against sentence which the appeal court reduced to six months' imprisonment. It is instructive to quote *in extenso* from the judgment of Farrell, Ag. C.J., on the two main points in the appeal since this is the first case in Kenya which deals with the difficult definitions of a "public meeting" and what is "holding" such a meeting. He said:[8]

> We turn now from the facts to the law. In Section 2 "meeting" is defined as meaning "any gathering or assembly of persons convened or held for any purposes which include any political purpose". There follow certain exclusions which are not altogether easy to understand but which we do not take to be relied on by the appellants. Subject to the determination of the question whether there was a political purpose, we do not understand that it is denied that there was a "meeting" within the meaning of the definition. There is, it is true a suggestion by Mr. Georgiadis that the occasion was a social gathering, but it was not strongly pressed, and we are in any case unable to accept it.
>
> "Public gathering" is defined as "a public meeting, a public procession, and any other meeting, gathering or concourse of ten or more persons".
>
> We next come to the two definitions which are of paramount importance for the purposes of this appeal:
>
> " 'public meeting' means any meeting held or to be held in a public place, and any meeting which the public or any section of the public or more than fifty persons are or are to be permitted to attend whether on payment or otherwise."
>
> " 'public place' means any place to which for the time being the public or any section of the public are entitled or permitted to have access whether on payment or otherwise, and, in relation to any meeting to be held in the future, includes any place which will, on the occasion and for the purposes of such meeting, be a public place."
>
> Before analysing these definitions it will be convenient first to set out the provision under which the charges were laid. Section 5 is in Part III of the Act which is headed "Public Gatherings" and has as marginal note the words "Control of public gatherings". It is a long section with eleven sub sections and the charges are laid under the last sub section which, so far as material reads:

"(11) Any—
  (*a*) public meeting . . . which takes place without a licence under this
    section . . .
    shall be deemed to be an unlawful assembly, and—
      (i) every person who takes or continues to take part in any such
        unlawful assembly shall be guilty of an offence; and
      (ii) every person who holds, convenes, organizes, forms or collects,
        or assists or is concerned in the holding, convening, organiz-
        ing, forming or collecting of, any public gathering such as is
        referred to in para. (*a*) of this sub section . . . shall be
        guilty of an offence and liable to imprisonment for a term not
        exceeding three years."

The charge on which the appellants were convicted alleged that they "held"
a public meeting which took place without a licence contrary to para. (ii)
of the sub section, and the alternative charge on which in his Petition of
Appeal Mr. Georgiadis submits they should have been convicted alleges that
they took part in an unlawful assembly, contrary to para. (i). The
alternative charge was, of course, the less serious of the two and under
Section 17 is subject to a general penalty of a fine not exceeding Shs. 5,000/-
or imprisonment for a term not exceeding six months.

Before the appellants could be found guilty on either charge, it was
necessary first to establish that there was a public meeting, and we must now
look at the definition of "public meeting". It seems to us clear as crystal that
the definition is a double one, and contains two descriptions, each of which
by itself is sufficient to constitute a public meeting. The first is "any meeting
held or to be held in a public place"; the second is "any meeting which the
public or a section of the public or more than fifty persons are or are to be
permitted to attend whether on payment or otherwise". It is true that one
would have expected the word "or" instead of "and" between the two limbs
of the definition, but we note that in the previous definition of "public
gathering" the draftsman also uses "and" where "or" would be more
appropriate. We concede, too, that there appears to be a considerable amount
of duplication and overlapping in this group of definitions. For example, in
the definition of "public gathering", it is difficult to give any meaning to the
expression "any other meeting . . . in any public place", seeing that (if we are
right) any meeting held in a public place is a public meeting. Similarly, it
would appear that in the definition of "public meeting" the words "any
meeting which the public or any section of the public . . . are or are to be
permitted to attend whether on payment or otherwise" are surplusage, since
the place of such a meeting would under the ensuing definition be a public
place and the meeting would accordingly be a public meeting. We do not
think that any construction of the definition is capable of removing all these
superfluities. But whether this is so or not, we still do not consider that there
is any other possible construction of the definition of "public meeting" than
the one that we have propounded. If it had been intended, as a single
definition not only would there have been no comma after the words "public
place", but the words "any meeting" which occur in the second line must, in
our considered view, have been omitted, and the definition would have read:
  " 'public meeting' means any meeting held or to be held in a public place
  and which the public", etc.

There is, if we are right, no requirement that in order to constitute a public
meeting there must be more than fifty persons present. It is this misunder-

standing (if such it is) which seems to us to have distorted the proceedings by causing lengthy evidence to be adduced as to the number of people present, evidence in turn subjected to lengthy cross-examination, lengthy argument as to the trustworthiness of the estimates put forward, and lengthy consideration in the judgment of the question whether it had been established that more than fifty people were present.

In our view all that was necessary in order to establish that the meeting was a public meeting was to show that the place where it was held was a public place, and this was clearly established beyond argument by showing that it was held in a shop, that the doors of the shop were wide open, and that there were no guards of any kind controlling access. We have already discussed the political purpose of the meeting and we are satisfied that it was a public meeting within the definition.

We come now to the most substantial ground of appeal which is set out as follows in para. 3 of the Petition:

> "The Learned Magistrate erred in Law when he omitted to direct his mind at all to the aspect of 'holding' a public meeting in relation to each Appellant under Section 5(11)(ii) of the Public Order Act, which was a necessary ingredient of the charge before he could find either Appellant guilty on the first count, and further had he done so, he would have inevitably concluded that there was insufficient evidence to support that either Appellant 'held' such a meeting."

The only reference to this point in the judgment is where the magistrate says:

> "I have to determine if the accused persons held a public meeting which took place without a licence issued by the District Commissioner under Section 5 of the material Act."

He nowhere considered the meaning of the word "held" although argument was addressed to him on the point from both sides.

It may be observed that para. (i) and (ii) in sub section (11) of Section 5 define what has been described as the passive and the active aspects of attendance at a public meeting. Under para. (i) mere presence is probably sufficient to constitute an offence. Under para. (ii) the primary offence is committed by a person who "holds, convenes, organises, forms or collects" (*inter alia*) a public meeting. It is submitted that the last four words suggest forethought and planning, and that on the principle *noscitur a sociis* (which means that words, like people, are known by the company they keep), a similar connotation should be implied in the word "hold". Mr. Hobbs for the Republic does not concede that the words "form" and "collect" have any such significance, but the words are used transitively and we are inclined to side on that point with Mr. Georgiadis. Mr. Hobbs further points out that "hold" is a word of very general significance and is not a term of art, and that it should not be construed narrowly in this context.

We have not found this an easy question to decide. Many instances have been canvassed. At the one extreme, the speaker who mounts on a soap-box at Hyde Park Corner undoubtedly holds a meeting — if, that is, he is fortunate enough to gain an audience. At the other extreme, the principal speaker at a political meeting, however distinguished a figure he may be, probably does not "hold" a meeting when he rises to speak on the invitation of the chairman flanked by committee members on the platform. In the first case there is no one other than the speaker responsible for collecting the audience; in the other the meeting has ordinarily been convened and advertised by persons other than the speaker. We have to ask ourselves on which side of the line the occasion under consideration lies, and we must consider all the surrounding circumstances. Here we have the sub branch of a party set up in what we take to be a comparatively small trading centre. An office is to be opened, and it is learned that the Vice-President of the party is staying on a visit about ten miles away. We note at the outset a marked disparity between the humble stature of the committee members and the distinction within the party of the principal guest. The chairman of the sub branch asked Mr. Ochok to invite Mr. Kaggia to pay a courtesy call on the proposed sub branch. Mr. Kaggia agreed. All this, according to the evidence of the appellants took place on the morning of February 17th, the day of the meeting. The officials and committee members of the sub branch no doubt had been informed of what was proposed, and were waiting to receive Mr. Kaggia. In fact it is in evidence that Mr. Kaggia told Mr. Ochok to tell the officials to be there between 11 a.m. and noon. Although the proposal for the meeting may have come from the sub branch in the first place, there was at any rate some small degree of preparation on the part of Mr. Kaggia and Mr. Ochok, and probably there would have been no meeting if Mr. Kaggia had not agreed to be present. Whether that is so or not, what clearly emerges from the evidence is that when Mr. Kaggia and his party arrived it was he and Mr. Ochok who took charge of the proceedings, and it was they who decided when the meeting should end and the audience should disperse.

It would in our opinion be wholly unrealistic to decide that in these circumstances the appellants did not "hold" the meeting. "Hold" is in its nature one of the most general words in the English language, and it would require strong argument to show that in this context it is not wide enough to cover the activities of the appellants. The *ejusdem generis* principle is not of universal application, and moreover there is an indication in the immediate context of what is intended by the word "hold". In the sixth line of para. (ii) in relation to public gatherings referred to in para. (*b*), the words "hold or conduct" appear in juxtaposition, and the maxim *noscitur a sociis* may just as readily be applied in the one place as in the other. If there is no significant difference in the meaning of the terms "hold" and "conduct" in this context, and "hold" is to be given the same meaning in both places, it is scarcely any longer open to argument that "hold" in relation to a meeting such as is referred to in para. (*a*) necessarily presupposes some degree of previous planning.

CONTRACT

No legislation on this subject was passed in 1969. Three cases on contract are reported: *Karia & Co. Ltd.* v. *Dhanani*[9] (frustration), *Muhuri* v. *Kiriu*[10] (illegality) and *Mankuleiyo* v. *Otis Elevator Co. Ltd.*[11] (implied terms as to length of service or payment during sickness in a contract of employment).

TORT

No legislation on tort was passed for the year under review, but a few cases deserve special mention.

In *Kimani* v. *Attorney General*,[12] the plaintiff had his name lawfully inserted as owner of certain land in the Record of Existing Rights under the Native Land Tenure Rules. Later an Adjudication Register took the place of the Record of Existing Rights. No legal machinery ever existed for the removal of a proprietor's name from these registers, but the plaintiff's name was removed by Government officials and that of one Bari substituted. After various protests which had no satisfactory result, the plaintiff applied for an order of mandamus, which was refused as being the wrong remedy. He then brought this suit against the Attorney-General for damages. The Attorney-General put forward two defences, namely that the plaintiff had no cause of action, and if he had, he has, by his conduct, debarred himself from succeeding thereon. On the first defence, Trevelyan, J. started by asserting "that the plaintiff had a cause of action is not, to me, in doubt." It is not clear from the judgment, however, on what principle liability rested. The learned judge continued:[13]

> The argument to the contrary was based on the well-known theory of Sir John Salmond that there is a law of torts but not a law of tort so that there is liability only for certain torts, but this theory is now generally rejected, and I take leave to suggest that it is at least to be doubted if it ever represented the true position. The law is a living thing and I believe that a court would be shirking its responsibility were it to say, assuming that there be no existing recognised tort covering the facts of a particular case, "Why then, this must be an end to it". It would undoubtedly be shirking its reponsibilities, for instance, in this case were it to take that stand. With respect, I entirely agree with Danckwerts, J., who, in *Bollinger* v. *Costa Brava Wine Co. Ltd.*, [1960] 1 Ch. 262, said (at p. 283):
>> ". . . the law may be thought to have failed if it can offer no remedy for the deliberate act of one person which causes damage to the property of another."
> The law must, of necessity, adapt itself; it cannot stay still. In *Rookes* v. *Barnard*, [1964] A.C. 1129, the House of Lords particularly asserted its right to adapt the common law to changing social conditions. The plaintiff's name was removed from the register without the slightest legal justification or excuse for this being done and he has lost a valuable right of property as a result. Is the court in the modern society in which we live to deny him a remedy? I believe not.
> In any case the courts have recognised that unlawful interferences with pre-existing rights give a right to damages. One may readily point to the case of *Ashby* v. *White* (1703), 2 Ld. Raym. 938; 92 E.R. 126. In the case now before the court we have a plaintiff who was given, and had, an absolute and unchallengeable right which was flouted and invaded; no justification nor yet excuse has been proffered, even suggested. As Sir John Holt said in *Ashby* v. *White:*
>> "If the plaintiff has a right he must of necessity have the means to vindicate it and a remedy if he is injured in the enjoyment or exercise of it: and indeed, it is a vain thing to imagine a right without a remedy; for want of right and want of remedy are reciprocal."
> And that is as applicable to the facts of the instant case is it was to facts of the other case. His judgment begins:
>> "The single question in this case is whether, if a free burgess of a

corporation, who has an undoubted right to give his vote in the election of a burgess to serve in Parliament, be refused and hindered to give it by the officer, if an action on the case will lie against such officer."

In the final result the plaintiff was awarded £200 by way of damages. Again, quoting the learned Chief Justice:

"If a man gives another a cuff on the ear though it cost him nothing, no not so much as little diachylon, yet he shall have his action . . ."

What happened was that the returning officer maliciously refused to accept the plaintiff's vote, the latter being a duly qualified elector, and it being recognised that he had a pre-existing right, i.e. the right to vote, he was awarded damages for its invasion. Proof of damage was not required nor did the court look to see whether there was a falling within any existing category or tort. The facts of the case now before this court show that the plaintiff had an undoubted and absolute right to have his name on a register, i.e. the register. That right was invaded and I do not see how it can be said that he had no remedy for such invasion.

I am not unaware that the decision in *Ashby* v. *White* has been criticised, but it has been cited with approval by Lord Wright who in *Nicholls* v. *Ely Beet Sugar Factory, Ltd.*, [1936] Ch. 343, a claim for the infringement of fishing rights said, at p. 350:

"the ability to maintain such an action without proof of actual loss depends on a much wider principle, that is the principle that where you have an interference with a legal right the law presumes damage."

In the instant case, of course, the plaintiff has suffered economic loss but that is only for later consideration.

As the Government servants concerned with the operation of the Land Consolidation scheme were surely supposed to know the rules which they were administering they may have acted deliberately and maliciously with the intention unlawfully to injure the plaintiff or they were merely negligent in the way they carried their duties out (particularly so the keeper of the register, for he, above all others, should have known that the removal of the plaintiff's name from the register was not possible in the manner in which it was sought). As I understood the way the case came to me, negligence was one of the bases of the claim put forward, and if not denied, was not challenged. Certainly a "duty situation" existed between the plaintiff and the Government officers concerned. They were, as Lord Atkin would have described their relationship, "neighbours": *Donoghue* v. *Stevenson*, [1932] A.C. 562. That there has, in a case, been no prior recognition of a precise situation by the courts does not matter in the least. As Lord Pearce put it in *Hedley, Byren & Co. Ltd.* v. *Heller & Partners Ltd.*, [1964] A.C. 465 at p. 536:

"How wide the sphere of the duty of care in negligence is to be laid depends ultimately upon the court's assessment of the demands of society for protection from the carelessness of others . . ."

Once the dispute had been decided, as it was, in favour of the plaintiff, he was entitled to be and to remain, so long as it pleased him, the registered proprietor of the land, and to him, and to him alone, did Government owe a duty of care in respect thereof, and the various officers in breach of that duty thereby caused the plaintiff to suffer loss.

Look at it how you will, the plaintiff had a cause of action sounding in damages for the undoubted wrongs done to him.

With regard to the second defence involving the principle *volenti non fit injuria*, the learned judge held:[14]

9—AL * *

He cannot be said to have consented to having his name removed from the register, he undertook to suffer no injury and he sought to adopt no risk. There was, as I think, no risk for him to adopt. His constant endeavour was to try to stop people injuring him. I need not say much about the doctrine itself. It is enough, I think, to mention that whether or not the plaintiff was *volens* is a question of fact, and that for the defence to succeed it must show not only that the plaintiff should have known that there was some degree of risk, but that he appreciated the full extent of it: *Dann* v. *Hamilton*, [1939] 1 All E.R. 59. I do not think that the facts before the court reveal any express or implied consent on the plaintiff's part to suffer any injury in respect of his land or its registration. He has not disentitled himself from receiving damages.

The case went on appeal[15] on the question of damages only, the Court of Appeal holding that Trevelyan, J., was wrong in awarding the plaintiff, in addition to the value of the land, damages for loss of annual profits subsequent to the date of dispossession. The Court also held that interest should run from the date of dispossession until judgment.

The law relating to the torts of malicious prosecution and wrongful arrest was extensively reviewed in two cases in the year under review, namely, *Fernandez* v. *Commercial Bank of Africa Ltd. and Another*,[16] and in *Kagane* v. *Attorney-General*.[17]

The following cases dealing with motor negligence are reported: *Khambi* v. *Mahithi*[18] (apportionment of liability), *Fernandez* v. *Noronha*[19] (duty owed to vehicle on main road and contributory negligence), *Karisa* v. *Solanki*[20] (degree of responsibility and vicarious liability), *Dewshi* v. *Kuldip's Touring Co.*,[21] (*res ipsa loquitur* and inevitable accident).

FAMILY LAW

The Affiliation (Repeal) Act (No. 11 of 1969) repeals the Affiliation Act (Cap. 142) and provides that any affiliation orders in force immediately before the Act shall lapse. The case of *C.T.* v. *M.W.*[22] dealing with corroborative evidence required in affiliation proceedings, was decided before the Act came into force.

In *R.S.* v. *S.S.*,[23] Harris, J., considered the interesting question whether a marriage under the Marriage Act following a potentially polygamous Hindu marriage constituted adultery. The petitioner and the respondent, who were both Sikhs, married by Sikh ceremony in 1957, and this was a valid marriage under the Hindu Marriage, Divorce and Succession Ordinance (Cap. 149). At that time, the marriage was potentially polygamous. In 1958, the respondent went through a civil ceremony of marriage under the Marriage Act (Cap. 150). The wife petitioned for divorce on the ground that the husband committed adultery with the second "wife". Harris, J., accepted the argument of petitioner's Counsel that since marriage under the Marriage Act can only be monogamous, a person already married under the Hindu Marriage, Divorce and succession Ordinance could not validly contract a marriage under the

Marriage Act to a third person; "with the result that what I have referred to as the second marriage did not create a valid matrimonial union so as to prevent the physical relationship which followed it from being, on the part of the respondent, adulterous".[24]

PROPERTY AND SUCCESSION

No legislation on these subjects was passed in 1969. Two cases on the Registration of Titles Act (Cap. 281) are reported, viz. *Boyes* v. *Gathure*,[25] and *Shah Karamashi Panachand & Co. Ltd.* v. *Velji*;[26] and one case on when citation to a person equally entitled to administer the estate with the applicant will be dispensed with under the Indian Succession Act (*Re Mauchauffee*).[27]

COMMERCIAL LAW

The Trade Licensing (Amendment) Act (No. 17 of 1969) introduces amendments to the main Act designed to avoid evasions. The definition of "business" is enlarged to include insurance agents, estate agents and other similar occupations. A new Section 6A deals with the granting of licences to partnerships, which is defined thus: "a partnership is a citizen of Kenya if all the partners therein are citizens of Kenya." Section 6*B* deals with the granting of conditional licences for twelve months. The existing Sections 9 and 10 are replaced; Section 9 now prohibits the transfer of licences except in limited circumstances, and Section 10 provides that a licence shall be displayed in a prominent position on the premises in respect of which it was issued.

EVIDENCE

The Statute Law (Miscellaneous Amendments) Act (No. 10 of 1969) introduces a new Section 47*A* in the Evidence Act (Cap. 80) reading as follows:

> "47*A*. A final judgment of a competent court in any criminal proceedings which declares any person to be guilty of a criminal offence shall, after the expiry of the time limited for an appeal against such judgment or after the date of the decision of any appeal therein, whichever is the latest, be taken as conclusive evidence that the person so convicted was guilty of that offence as charged."

A few cases on evidence are of interest. In *Oduol* v. *Republic*,[28] the High Court held that there was a duty upon a magistrate to consider at the close of the prosecution case whether there was a prima facie case, even if his Counsel made no submission of no case to answer; consequently it was an error of law to call on an accused for his defence if in fact there was no case to answer. In *Odindo* v. *Republic*,[29] Ainley, C.J., considered that it was unwise and improper to receive expert evidence from a policeman as to drunken driving, whilst in *Onyango* v. *Republic*,[30] Mwendwa, C.J. thought that a magistrate was at liberty to accept or reject the opinion of a handwriting expert. In *Nduto* v. *Republic*,[31] it was held that a trial magistrate was entitled to comment adversely on the fact that the accused made an unsworn statement.

Three reported cases on this subject decided by the Court of Appeal are worth mentioning. *Zola* v. *Ralli Brothers Ltd.*[32] concerned affidavit evidence. The Court held that the fact that an affidavit contained irregularities does not render it a nullity. In *Fernandez* v. *Noronha*,[33] the Court took the view that the discretion to recall a witness for further examination and cross-examination should be exercised only in the most exceptional circumstances where the evidence has been completed, and then only if the judge is satisfied that the further evidence is likely to have a material effect on the case and that there is good reason why such further evidence was not given in the normal way. Finally, *Oriental Fire and General Assurance Ltd.* v. *Govinder*,[34] involved several evidential matters, as appears from the head note, viz.

THE ORIENTAL FIRE AND GENERAL ASSURANCE LTD.
v. GOVINDER AND OTHERS

[COURT OF APPEAL AT MOMBASA (Sir Clement de Lestang, Ag. P., Duffus, Ag. V.-P., Spry, J.A.), October 31 and November 29, 1968.]
(186/68)   CIVIL APPEAL No. 39 OF 1968.
    (Appeal from the High Court of Kenya at Mombasa—Mosdell, J.)

Evidence—Of fact clearly implied in pleading.

Evidence—Res gestae—Whether statement after motor accident part of res gestae.

Evidence—Statement—Joint interest of parties not in existence at time of statement.

Insurance—Motor Insurance—Statutory third party liability—Materiality of misrepresentation—Insurance (Motor Vehicles Third Party Risks) Act (Cap. 405), Section 10.

The appellants sued the respondents for a declaration under Section 10(4) of the Insurance (Motor Vehicles Third Party risks) Act (Cap. 405) claiming to be entitled to avoid a motor vehicle policy given to the respondent covering statutory third party liability on the ground that the first respondent had made a representation of fact false in a material particular in that he denied having been involved in an accident in a motor vehicle owned and driven by him. The second and third respondents had been injured in an accident involving the insured vehicle. The Judge held that it was proved that the first respondent had been involved in an accident in a vehicle owned and driven by him, but held that the misrepresentation was not material. The appellant appealed, challenging the finding on materiality. The respondents cross-appealed, alleging that the Judge should not have received evidence of ownership of the vehicle when the fact was not alleged in the pleadings. The second and third appellants also cross-appealed, alleging that the Judge had wrongly admitted as against them the evidence of a statement made by the first respondent to a police officer that he was driving the car involved in the first accident.

Held:

(i) the materiality of the misrepresentation is a question of fact and as there was evidence on which the Judge could find that the misrepresentation was not material, his finding would not be interfered with;

(ii) the judge properly admitted evidence that the first respondent owned the motor car since his ownership of it was clearly implied in the plaint (*Sullivan* v. *Alimohamed Osman*, [1959] E.A. 239, followed);

(iii) as the respondents had no joint interest to maintain at the time it was made, the first respondent's statement to a police officer that he was driving the car was wrongly admitted against the other respondents (*Merchants & Manufacturers Insurance Co. Ltd.* v. *Hunt*, [1941] 1 All E.R. 123 followed);

(iv) the statement of the *res gestae* in that it was not spontaneous or said at or immediately after the time of the accident (*Tustin* v. *Arnold & Sons* (1915), 84 L.J.K.B. 2214 followed).

---

1. Legal Notice No. 221 of 1969.
2. [1969] E.A. 357. For an article on this case, see S. A. Adesanya "The Constitutional Privilege of an Accused to refuse to give Evidence: Republic v. El Mann Examined" in 6 E.A.L.J. pp. 264–78.
3. *Ibid.*, p. 359.
4. [1969] E.A. p. 17.
5. [1969] E.A. p. 493.
6. [1969] E.A. p. 16.
7. [1969] E.A. p. 451.
8. *Ibid.*, p. 455.
9. [1969] E.A. p. 392.
10. [1969] E.A. p. 232.
11. [1969] E.A. p. 568.
12. [1969] E.A. p. 29. For an article on this case, see Peter J. Bayne "Government Liability for Torts by Public Officials" in 6 E.A.L.J. pp. 243–63.
13. *Ibid.*, p. 31.
14. *Ibid.*, p. 33.
15. [1969] E.A. p. 502.
16. [1969] E.A. p. 482.
17. [1969] E.A. p. 643.
18. [1969] E.A. p. 70.
19. [1969] E.A. p. 506.
20. [1969] E.A. p. 318.
21. [1969] E.A. p. 189.
22. [1969] E.A. p. 375.
23. [1969] E.A. p. 229.
24. *Ibid.*, p. 231.
25. [1969] E.A. p. 385.
26. [1969] E.A. p. 194.
27. [1969] E.A. p. 424.

28. [1969] E.A. p. 369.
29. [1969] E.A. p. 12.
30. [1969] E.A. p. 362.
31. [1969] E.A. p. 575.
32. [1969] E.A. p. 691.
33. [1969] E.A. p. 506.
34. [1969] E.A. p. 116.

ANNEXURE

THE CONSTITUTION OF KENYA ACT

No. 5 of 1969

Date of Assent: 10th April 1969

Date of commencement: 18th April 1969

An Act for Parliament to amend the Constitution of the Republic of Kenya and to reproduce the said Constitution in a revised form, and for purposes incidental thereto.

ENACTED by the Parliament of Kenya, as follows:

1. This Act may be cited as the Constitution of Kenya Act 1969.

Short title.

2. In this Act, except where the context otherwise requires—

Interpretation.

"the Constitution" means the Constitution of the Republic of Kenya Contained in Schedule 2 of the Kenya Independence Order in Council 1963, as amended by the Constitution of Kenya (Amendment) Act 1964, the Constitution of Kenya (Amendment) (No. 2) Act 1964, the Constitution of Kenya (Amendment) Act 1965, the Constitution of Kenya (Amendment) Act 1966, the Constitution of Kenya (Amendment) (No. 2) Act 1966, the Constitution of Kenya (Amendment) (No. 3) Act 1966, the Constitution of Kenya (Amendment) (No. 4) Act 1966, the Constitution of Kenya (Amendment) Act 1967, the Constitution of Kenya (Amendment) Act 1968 and the Constitution of Kenya (Amendment) (No. 2) Act 1968;

L.N. 718/1963.
28 of 1964.
38 of 1964.
14 of 1965.
16 of 1966.
17 of 1966.
18 of 1966.
40 of 1966.
4 of 1967.
16 of 1968.
45 of 1968.

"the revised Constitution" means the Constitution of the Republic of Kenya as set out in the Second Schedule to this Act.

3. (1) The provisions of the Constitution specified in the first column of the First Schedule to this Act are amended in such manner as to make them read according to the wording of the provision of the revised Constitution specified in relation thereto in the second column of that Schedule

Amendment of Constitution.

(2) For the avoidance of doubt, it is hereby declared that the amendments effected by sub section (1) of this section do not affect the continued existence or validity of any thing or matter having existence or validity under the Constitution immediately before the commencement of this Act.

Insertion of new sections in Constitution.

4. There shall be inserted in the Constitution new sections identical with those numbered 3, 124, 125, 126, 127 and 128 in the revised Constitution.

Repeal.

5. (1) Sections 10, 66, 85, 157, 162, 166, 177, 212 and 223 and Schedules 9 and 10 of the Constitution are repealed.

L.N. 718/1963.

(2) Sections 13, 14 and 19 of the Kenya Independence Order in Council 1963 are repealed:

Provided that any regulations made under the said Section 19 and in force immediately before the commencement of this Act shall continue in force after such commencement and shall be deemed to have been made under Section 127 of the revised Constitution.

Revised Constitution.

6. The revised Constitution set out in the Second Schedule to this Act (which is a revised version of the Constitution as amended by this Act incorporating revisions as to form only and effecting no changes of substance) is hereby declared to be the Constitution of the Republic of Kenya and to be the authentic version thereof.

Printing and publication of revised Constitution.

7. The revised Constitution may be printed and published by the Government Printer apart from this Act, and the production of a copy of the revised Constitution purporting to be so printed shall be prima facie evidence in all courts and for all purposes whatsoever of the revised Constitution and of its provisions.

Amendment of written laws. Cap. 2.

8. (1) Section 3 of the Interpretation and General Provisions Act is amended by the deletion of the definition of "the Constitution" and the substitution therefor of the following—

"the Constitution" means the Constitution of Kenya set out in the Second Schedule to the Constitution of Kenya Act 1968;"

(2) Any reference in a written law in operation immediately before the commencement of this Act to any of the provisions of the Constitution (as defined for the purposes of that law immediately before the commencement of this Act), being a provision that is specified in the first column of the First Schedule to this Act, shall be construed as a reference to the provision of the revised Constitution specified in relation thereto in the second column of that Schedule.

1969   *Constitution of Kenya*   **No. 5**

FIRST SCHEDULE   (Section 3)

First Column Provision of Constitution	Second Column Provision of revised Constitution	First Column Provision of Constitution	Second Column Provision of revised Constitution
Section 1	Section 87	Section 46	Section 38
Section 2	Section 88	Section 47	Section 45
Section 3	Section 89	Section 48	Section 41
Section 4	Section 90	Section 49	Section 42
Section 5	Section 91	Section 50	Section 44
Section 6	Section 92	Section 51	Section 49
Section 7	Section 93	Section 53	Section 50
Section 8	Section 94	Section 54	Section 51
Section 9	Section 95	Section 55	Section 53
Section 11	Section 96	Section 56	Section 54
Section 12	Section 97	Section 57	Section 36
Section 13	Section 98	Section 58	Section 55
Section 14	Section 70	Section 59	Section 46
Section 15	Section 71	Section 60	Section 48
Section 16	Section 72	Section 62	Sections 56 and 57
Section 17	Section 73		
Section 18	Section 74	Section 64	Section 58
Section 19	Section 75	Section 65	Section 59
Section 20	Section 76	Section 71	Section 47
Section 21	Section 77	Section 72	Section 23
Section 22	Section 78	Section 74	Section 15
Section 23	Section 79	Section 75	Section 16
Section 24	Section 80	Section 76	Section 17
Section 25	Section 81	Section 77	Section 18
Section 26	Section 82	Section 81	Section 19
Section 27	Section 83	Section 82	Section 20
Section 28	Section 84	Section 83	Section 21
Section 29	Section 85	Section 83A	Section 22(2)
Section 30	Section 86	Section 84	Section 22(1)
Section 31	Section 1	Section 86	Section 26
Section 32	Section 2	Section 87	Section 24
Section 33	Section 4	Section 87A	Section 25
Section 33A	Section 5	Section 88	Section 27
Section 33AB	Section 6	Section 89	Section 28
Section 33AC	Section 7	Section 90	Section 29
Section 33AD	Section 8	Section 121	Section 99
Section 33AE	Section 9	Section 122	Section 100
Section 33B	Section 10	Section 124	Section 101
Section 33C	Section 52	Section 125	Section 102
Section 33D	Section 11	Section 126	Section 104
Section 33E	Section 12	Section 127	Section 103
Section 33F	Section 13	Section 128	Section 105
Section 33G	Section 14	Section 163	Section 108
Section 34	Section 30	Section 167	Section 26(4)
Section 37	Section 31	Section 171	Section 60

No. 5   *Constitution of Kenya*   **1969**

FIRST SCHEDULE (—*Contd.*)   (Section 3)

First Column	Second column	First Column	Second Column
	Provision of		*Provision of*
Provision of	*revised*	*Provision of*	*revised*
Constitution	*Constitution*	*Constitution*	*Constitution*
Section 38	Section 32	Section 172	Section 61
Section 39	Section 33	Section 173	Section 62
Section 40	Section 34	Section 174	Section 63
Section 41	Section 35	Sections 176	Section 64
Section 42	Section 39	and 177	
Section 42A	Section 40	Section 178	Section 65
Section 45	Section 37	Section 179	Section 66
Sections 175	Section 67	Section 202	Section 114
and 82		Section 208	Sections 115,
Section 184	Section 68		116
Section 185	Section 69		and 117
Section 186	Section 106	Section 209	Section 118
Section 188	Section 107	Section 210	Section 119
Section 189	Section 109	Section 211	Section 120
Section 190	Section 110	Section 244	Section 121
Sections 191	Section 111	Section 245	Section 122
and 192		Section 247	Section 123
Section 195	Section 112	Sch. 5 Pt. II	Section 43
Section 196	Section 113		

SECOND SCHEDULE   (Section 6)

THE CONSTITUTION OF KENYA
ARRANGEMENT OF SECTIONS

Chapter I—The Republic of Kenya

Section

1—Declaration of Republic.
2—Public Seal.
3—Constitution of Republic of Kenya.

Chapter II—The Executive

Part 1—The President and the Vice-President

4—The office of President.
5—Election of President.
6—Vacancy in office of President.
7—Assumption of office of President.
8—Oath of President.
9—Tenure of office of President.
10—Determination of questions as to validity of Presidential elections, etc.
11—Exercise of President's functions during absence, illness, etc.
12—Removal of President on grounds of incapacity.
13—Salary and allowances of President.
14—Protection of President in respect of legal proceedings during office.
15—The Vice-President of Kenya.

Part 2—Ministers and the Cabinet

Part 3—Executive Powers

Chapter III—Parliament

Part 1—Composition of Parliament

1969   *Constitution of Kenya*   **No. 5**

CHAPTER VIII—THE PUBLIC SERVICE

CHAPTER IX—TRUST LAND

CHAPTER X—GENERAL

CHAPTER XI—TRANSITORY

CHAPTER 7

UGANDA

H. F. Morris

CONSTITUTIONAL AND ADMINISTRATIVE LAW

An interesting question which came before the Court of Appeal for East Africa for decision during 1969 was that of the construction which should be placed on Article 89 of the Constitution.[1] Section 1 of the Article states that appeal from certain decisions of the High Court lies to the "Court of Appeal"; Section 5 states that "Parliament may provide that the Chief Justice may be a member of the Court of Appeal established under this Article"; and Section 6 states that "the Court of Appeal" means "such court of appeal as may be established by Parliament and until such court of appeal is established it means the Court of Appeal for Eastern Africa". An application for leave to file a record of appeal out of time had been brought before a judge of the High Court in his *ex officio* capacity as a judge of the Court of Appeal for East Africa, for the Court of Appeal for Eastern Africa Act, 1962 provides that the Chief Justice and the other judges of the High Courts of the Partner States are *ex officio* members of the Court of Appeal. The judge, however, dismissed the application for want of jurisdiction, holding that Article 89(5) was "indicative of the fact that the puisne judges of the High Court of Uganda are no longer *ex officio* members of the Court of Appeal for East Africa". Reference was accordingly made to the full court and here it was held that Article 89(5) applied only to a Court of Appeal to be established by Parliament and not to the existing Court of Appeal for East Africa and was not indicative of the fact that the High Court judges were no longer *ex officio* judges of the Court of Appeal for East Africa and that these judges remained *ex officio* judges of the higher court. It was, however, added that it was "greatly to be regretted that the provisions of the Constitution and legislation of Uganda in relation to the jurisdiction and membership of the highest and final Court of Appeal for Uganda should be couched in such ambiguous and in some respects contradictory language" and it was suggested "that these provisions be urgently re-examined with a view to their clarification".

The Immigration Act of 1969[2] replaces the Immigration (Control) Act of 1948.[3] An Immigration Control Board is established[4] whose duty it is to determine whether or not an entry permit is to be granted to any person; to determine any question under the Act referred to it by the Minister; and to perform such other functions as may be imposed upon it by law. Any person aggrieved by a decision of the Board in carrying out this duty may appeal to the Minister whose decision is final. The Principal Immigration Officer, who is the Secretary, but not a member, of the Board, performs such duties as the Board may assign to him. Various categories of persons are stated to be prohibited immigrants: these categories are virtually identical to those listed in the previous Act. No person who is not a citizen of Uganda may enter the country unless he possesses a valid entry permit, certificate of residence or pass issued under the Act. Entry permits are of various classes depending on the nature of the employment which the applicant is taking up in Uganda. If a person, other than a prohibited immigrant, applies for the appropriate entry permit, the Board may, in its discretion, issue the permit, provided that it is satisfied that the applicant's engagement in the employment concerned or the purposes for which the entry permit is to be granted will be of benefit to Uganda, or a part thereof, and will not be to the prejudice of the inhabitants generally of Uganda. An entry permit remains valid for a period not exceeding five years and is renewable only once for a period of three years. The Board may also, with the approval of the Minister, grant certificates of residence entitling a person to remain in Uganda for such period as the Minister may determine. The Minister may at any time cancel an entry permit or a certificate of residence without assigning any reason. Furthermore, the Minister may make regulations providing for classes of passes entitling persons to enter and remain temporarily in Uganda and the terms and conditions of issue. An entry permit, certificate or pass issued under the 1948 Act and valid at the time of the enactment of the present legislation continues to have effect according to its terms for a period of twelve months from the commencement of the 1969 Act,[5] during which time application may be made for the appropriate permit, certificate or pass under the new law. Persons born in Uganda who are not citizens of the country and who are not in possession of any permit, certificate or pass entitling them to remain in Uganda must, within twelve months of the commencement of the Act, apply for the appropriate document.

The Constitution provides[6] that there is to be a Public Service Commission and a Teaching Service Commission to advise the President in respect of his powers[7] to appoint persons to hold or act in any offices in the public service of the Uganda Government or of a District Administration or Urban Authority, to exercise disciplinary control over them and to remove them from office. Each of these Commissions is to consist of a chairman and such other members as Parliament may prescribe, all of whom are appointed by the President. Parliament is also empowered, subject to the relevant provisions of the Constitution, to make provisions for the regulating of each of these Commissions in the performance of their functions, including, in respect of the Teaching Service Commission, the establishment of Teaching Service Committees and the prescribing of their functions. This Parliament has done in the Public Service Act and the Public Service (Teachers) Act of 1969.[8] The former Act, which replaces the Public Service Act of 1963,[9] provides that the Public Service Commission is to consist of not less than three, and not more than seven, members in addition to the chairman. The Commission may require any person to attend and give evidence before it. Members of the Commission are to have the same protection and privilege in respect of acts done in the bona fide execution of their duty as a judge has. A Service Committee, the establishment of which in respect of each District and Urban Authority is provided for in the Constitution,[10] has to make recommendations to the Commission in respect of appointments in the service of the District or Urban Authority concerned. Similarly the Public Service (Teachers) Act provides that the membership of the Teaching Service Commission is to consist of not less than three, and not more than seven, members. It has the same power to require persons to attend and its members have the same protection and privilege as in the case of the Public Service Commission. A Teaching Service Committee is established for each District and Urban Authority, consisting of a chairman and not less than three, and not more than seven, other members all of whom are appointed by the Minister. The Committees are required to make recommendations to the Commission in respect of the appointment of, disciplinary control over, and removal of, teachers in primary schools.

TORT

The appeal case of *Onama* v. *Uganda Argus Ltd.*[11] concerns a claim for damages for defamation. A Member of Parliament had made certain allegations against the appellant in the National Assembly, a report of the debate in which this occurred (hereinafter referred to as the "first report") being published by the respondent newspaper. The appellant had challenged the Member to repeat these allegations in a place where parliamentary privilege did not apply, and shortly afterwards the latter had held a press conference at which he had stated that he was holding the conference in reply to the challenge and had then proceeded to make allegations (which were not, in fact, identical to those made in the Assembly) against persons unnamed. A report of this conference (hereinafter referred to as the "second report") also appeared in the *Uganda Argus*. The appellant then sued the newspaper for defamation in respect of the second report. The main issue before the trial court was whether the first report could be relied upon in order to identify the appellant as a person referred to in the second report. The court held that the first report was privileged and could only be relied on if the allegations in it were "expressly or impliedly repeated, approved or adopted in the second report", which had not been the case, and the court found for the respondent. The Court of Appeal was, however, agreed that, since the action was taken in respect of the content of the second report alone, it did not matter whether the first report was privileged or not and that the first report might be referred to to establish the identity of the individuals referred to in the second report.

10—AL　*　*

Furthermore, the Court held (Spry, J.A., dissenting) that on reading the two reports reasonable persons would understand that the appellant was referred to in the second report.

PROPERTY

The Public Lands Act[12] replaces that of 1962[13] and, though much of its content is broadly similar to that of its predecessor, it makes a number of changes many of which reflect the constitutional changes which have since taken place. All rights, titles, estates and interests in land previously vested in the Land Commission[14] continue to be so vested and the powers of the Commission are similar to those conferred by the 1962 Act. In each district there is to be a Land Committee consisting of not more than eight, and not less than four, members appointed by the Minister. The functions of such a committee is to assist the Commission in an advisory capacity on all matters relating to land which may be referred to it and to perform such functions as the Minister may delegate to it. A controlling authority[15] may grant estates and create rights and interests in, manage, dispose of or otherwise deal with, the estate or interest in public land vested in it. The prior consent of the Minister is, however, necessary if the controlling authority wishes to sell land, demolish buildings on it, make a grant in freehold, grant a lease of land outside an urban area to a person who is not an African citizen, grant a lease of land outside an urban area if it is occupied by a person holding by customary tenure, grant more than five hundred acres in leasehold to any one person, or dispose of land declared to be a National Park. The purposes for which public land in rural areas may be alienated include the construction of residential houses, the carrying on of subsistence farming, provided the land required does not exceed fifteen acres, the carrying on of small scale commercial farming or other small scale commercial undertakings, provided the land required is more than fifteen acres and not more than one hundred acres, and the carrying on of large scale farming or other large scale undertakings, provided the land required exceeds one hundred acres. When the Commission makes a grant of public land in freehold, it may impose conditions restricting the subsequent user and subsequent dispositions of the land. A lease of public land in an urban area (other than a lease granted to an urban authority in an urban area listed in Schedule 3 of the Act) may not be for a term exceeding ninety-nine years. It is lawful for any person holding by customary tenure to occupy without grant, lease or licence any unalienated public land vested in the Commission, provided the land is not in an urban area and no tenancy or other right of occupancy has been created in respect of it, and a grant in freehold or leasehold of public land which is occupied by persons holding by customary tenure may not be made without the consent of such persons, who, in the event of such a grant being made, are entitled to such compensation as the Minister may approve. The Minister may, by statutory order, specify any area to be one in which public land not at the time occupied by customary tenure may not thereafter be so occupied. Any person holding by customary tenure may at any time apply for the conversion of the customary tenure into leasehold. If the Commission considers that alienated public land has not, in the case of rural land, been occupied for more than three years, or, in the case of land in an urban area, has not been properly developed in accordance with modern building standards, or is not being used in accordance with town planning zoning for the area, it may give notice of forfeiture of the land.[16] If, within six months of notice being given, the proprietor satisfies the Commission that he intends to use and develop the land to a reasonable extent, the Commission may extend the period within which the land is to be occupied by two, or with the Minister's consent three, years, or, in the case of land in an urban area, specify a period within which the land is to be properly developed. Any person whose estate or interest in land is extinguished by a declaration of forfeiture published in the Gazette may within three months apply to the High Court for relief, which the Court may grant upon such terms as it sees fit.

The Access to Roads Act[17] provides that where the owner of any land [18] is unable through negotiation to obtain leave from owners of adjoining land to construct a road of access to a public highway he may apply to a magistrate for leave to construct such a road of access over land lying between his land and the highway. Notice is then served on the owner of the adjoining land to show cause why leave should not be granted and, after the expiry of one month, a date of hearing is fixed. The magistrate, after hearing such evidence as may be adduced, may then make an order granting the applicant leave to enter upon the adjoining land and to construct the road, subject to such conditions and to the payment of such compensation as the magistrate may decide upon. The road may not exceed twenty feet in width and must be kept in proper repair by the applicant, though if the owner of the adjoining land uses the road he must pay a proportionate share towards the cost of upkeep.

COMMERCIAL AND INDUSTRIAL LAW

The Banking Act of 1969[19] repeals that of 1955[20]. Among the new provisions in the Act are those designed "to safeguard the interests of depositors and to ensure that the commercial banks and credit institutions' operations are in keeping with the new monetary system introduced by Government in the setting up of the Bank of Uganda[21] and can be regulated within the economic and monetary policies of the Government of the day".[22] No one may transact banking or credit institution business without a licence from the Minister for which an annual fee of 5,000 shillings is payable. No licence may be given to a company proposing to transact banking or credit institution business unless it is incorporated in Uganda and its capital, paid up in cash, amounts to at least 20,000 shillings invested in such assets as the Minister may approve in the case of banking businesses, and 2,000,000 shillings invested in such assets as the Minister may approve in the case of credit institution businesses.[23] Every bank or credit institution is required to maintain a minimum holding of liquid assets as may be determined by the Bank of Uganda and also to maintain a reserve fund into which 20 per cent of the annual profits are to be transferred until the fund is equal to the paid up capital. The Minister or the Bank of Uganda may at any time cause an inspection to be made of any bank or credit institution and if it is found that the affairs of the bank or institution are being conducted in a manner detrimental to the interests of the depositors, or prejudicial to the interests of the bank or institution or in contravention of the law, the Minister, or the Bank of Uganda, may order the bank or institution, after it has been given an opportunity to present its views, to take the necessary corrective action or to discontinue the harmful practices or procedures discovered. Moreover, if at any time the Minister is satisfied that a bank or credit institution is carrying on business in a manner detrimental to the interests of its depositors, or has insufficient assets to cover its liabilities to its depositors, or is contravening the Banking Act or Exchange Control Act or if it or any of its officers have been convicted of an offence of dishonesty or fraud, the Minister is to notify the bank or institution of his intention to revoke its licence. The bank or credit institution may then make representations against revocation to the Minister whose decision on the matter is final.

The Trade (Licensing) Act[24] has the following objects: "(*a*) to amend and replace the present Trading Act[25] in order to keep abreast with the prevailing trading and constitutional requirements; (*b*) to bring up to date Uganda's trade licensing procedures; (*c*) to give more trading opportunities to citizens of Uganda by imposing restrictions on trade in certain areas or on certain goods by non-citizens or firms composed predominantly of non-citizens".[26] The Minister may declare areas to be trading centres; he may declare any area of a city, municipality or town to be a general business area; he may declare any trading centre to be an area in which a person who is not a citizen of Uganda is prohibited from trading; and he may declare goods to be specified goods for the purposes of the Act. No one may erect a shop, or trade in any shop, within a radius of two miles outside the boundary of a trading centre.[27] No person who is not a citizen of Uganda may trade outside a city, municipality or town, or in a trading centre in which trade by non-citizens has been prohibited by the Minister; nor may he trade in any area within a city, municipality or town which has not been declared to be a general business area or in any specified goods which are not endorsed on his licence. No person may trade in any goods[28] or carry on any business specified in the Schedule to the Act[29] without a trading licence. A licensing authority[30] may refuse to grant a trading licence without giving any reason, appeal from such refusal lying to the Minister whose decision is final.

The Industrial Licensing Act[31] establishes an Industrial Licensing Board[32] to which applications must be made or a licence by any person wishing to manufacture for sale any article contained in the Schedule to the Act or to erect or operate any factory for the manufacture or sale of any scheduled article. In deciding whether to grant such a licence, the Board is to have regard to the capital and technical skill available to the applicant, the siting of any factory in relation to the availability of power, fuel, labour, transport, raw materials, land and water; the potential production of, and demand for, the articles, the interests and conditions of service of the labour employed and the interests of potential consumers; and the general promotion and orderly development of industries and the prevention of uneconomic competition. A licence may be revoked if the Board is satisfied that the holder has failed to manufacture the articles specified in his licence or to operate the factory, or has failed to maintain a minimum level of production or has failed to comply with any conditions attached to his licence. Appeals from the decisions of the Board lie to the Minister whose decision is final.

A Management Training and Advisory Centre has been established[33] with the following objects:

"(*a*) to assist Government departments [and] public and private institutions with advisory and training services to be given to their personnel concerned with the promotion and development of industry and indigenous entrepreneurship with a view to enabling such personnel to advise, assist and train Ugandan entrepreneurs throughout the country;

(*b*) to assist industry and other economic sectors (including public services and utilities) in introducing or improving management practices, techniques and methods, with a view to raising their productivity;

(*c*) to assist existing and new enterprises in studying designs of new products, models and devices;

(*d*) to prepare citizens of Uganda for managerial, functional and supervisory posts in existing and new industries and business enterprises;

(*e*) to help citizens of Uganda to become entrepreneurs, by providing them with advisory services and instruction in simple management practices, particularly management, accounting and marketing, technological guidance and practical demonstrations;

(*f*) to raise the standard of skill of workers employed in industry through accelerated training, upgrading and in-plant training;

(*g*) to organise and conduct training courses for semi-skilled and skilled workers, foremen, supervisors and technicians, including maintenance workers, on methods and techniques of tool operation as suitable for the equipment and work conditions in the country".[34]

The Centre is generally empowered to do whatever may be calculated to facilitate the carrying out of its functions and, in particular, it may acquire and dispose of property; aid the promotion of any Uganda citizen in trade or business; enter into agreements with Uganda citizens for the establishment, promotion or financing of any business or undertaking; build or purchase business premises; collect and disseminate technical information of interest to entrepreneurs; with the prior approval of the Minister responsible for finance, borrow money; found scholarships, make research grants or otherwise give assistance to Uganda citizens engaged in study or research relating to the productivity of industry; hold classes and lectures and charge fees for them; and published material for sale or otherwise. The Council of the Centre, which is responsible for seeing that the administration and management policy of the Centre is carried out, consists of three *ex officio* members[35] and not more than eight, and not less than four, members appointed by the Minister, all of whom must be persons "of experience in financial affairs, business, administration or professional occupation". Of these members, two are appointed as representatives of employers after consultation with the Employers' Federation, two as representatives of employees after consultation with the Trade Unions and not more than three are appointed after consultation with institutions connected with industry. The Centre may, with the approval of the Minister, make bye-laws respecting the management and conduct of the Centre or any matter connected with its functions. The funds of the Centre consist of grants from the Government and earnings of the Centre such as fees for courses, charges for services provided and proceeds from the sale of goods from its workshops. The Council of the Centre sends an annual report to the Minister on its activities and this, together with the audited accounts, are laid before the National Assembly.

A council known as the Uganda Export Promotion Council has been set up[36] with the functions of promoting, assisting and developing Uganda's exports and of making recommendations to the Government in relation to measures which the Council considers would achieve an increase in Uganda's exports. The Council, which consists of a chairman appointed by the Minister and thirteen members,[37] is empowered to do all such things as are calculated to facilitate, or are incidental or conducive to, the better carrying out of its functions and may, for example, acquire land, establish offices in Uganda and overseas, enter into contracts, organise international trade fairs and exhibitions, publish periodicals and borrow money on such security as may be necessary. The funds of the Council consist of grants from the Government, loans to the Council from the Government or any other person with the prior approval of the Minister, and money accruing to the Council in the course of the discharge of its functions. The annual statement of accounts of the Council must be laid before the National Assembly and published in the Gazette.

The scope of the Workmen's Compensation Act[38] has been widened and the scale of benefits payable to injured workmen under the Act increased.[39] Previously, persons employed, otherwise than by manual labour, whose earnings exceeded 16,000 shillings a year were excluded from the definition of "workman": the figure has now been raised to 24,000 shillings. Provision is made for either an employer or workman who is dissatisfied with the assessment of disability by a medical practitioner, instead of referring the matter to a court of law, to apply to the Labour Commissioner to refer the dispute to the Medical Arbitration Board, which is to be appointed by the Minister in consultation with the Chief Medical Officer and is to consist of a chairman and two medical practitioners. The decisions of this Board are final. Whereas under the previous law the Minister might require any employer or class of employers to insure and keep himself or themselves insured with such insurers as might be approved by the Minister, there is now a statutory obligation on all employers to keep themselves insured with approved insurers.

The Weights and Measures (Amendment) Act,[40] in addition to making certain alterations to the body of the parent Act,[41] adds a new Part to the

Act providing for the conversion of weights and measures to the metric system. The Minister may, by statutory order, specify any area, industry, trade or transaction as being one in which any system, other than the metric system, is prohibited. When such a statutory order has been made, the Superintendent of Weights and Measures may require the surrender of weights and measures and equipment for conversion or disposal. The Minister may also, by statutory order, prohibit the import, manufacture or sale of weights and measures not conforming to the metric system. When the use of any system other than the metric system has been prohibited, metric price conversion tables must be displayed at all places of trade.

The Coffee Marketing Act[42] replaces the Coffee Act of 1963[43] and the Bugisu Coffee Act of the previous year[44] and applies to coffee grown throughout Uganda. The new Act closely resembles the old legislation. A Coffee Marketing Board[45] is established with powers and functions almost identical to those possessed by the Board established under the 1963 Act and so is a Board of Trustees,[46] known as the Trustees of the Bagisu Trust Fund, with duties virtually identical to those of the Board of Trustees set up under the Bugisu Coffee Act of 1962. The Coffee Price Assistance Fund established by the Coffee Ordinance of 1959 remains in existence. The Minister may, by statutory instrument, establish in any district markets for the buying and selling of coffee or any type or grade of coffee and none may be bought or sold except in the appropriate market: nor may any unprocessed coffee be moved from one district to another without the Minister's permission. The owner of a licensed processing factory or a registered co-operative union may apply to the Board to be registered as a buyer or processor of coffee. Registration may be refused if the applicant has been convicted of an offence involving dishonesty or if, in the opinion of the Board, the applicant will be unable to comply with the provisions of the Act relating to the keeping of books and records, or has insufficient funds to conduct business in an orderly and efficient manner. Buyer's licences and processing licences are issued by the Minister to registered buyers and processors of coffee respectively. The Minister may, however, restrict the number of licences granted and impose such conditions as he may think fit. No one, except the Board and its authorised agents, may buy coffee without a buyer's licence and no one may process coffee without a processing licence. The Minister may declare buying seasons and no one, other than the Board or its agents, may buy coffee at other times. The Minister may also fix the price or minimum price at which coffee may be bought from the growers or processors. The processor of coffee pays a coffee cess at such rate as the Minister may, by statutory instrument, impose. The Minister may, in his discretion, permit the erection of a processing factory, if he is satisfied that this will be to the material advantage of the coffee growers in the area. Such a factory must then be licensed before any one may process coffee in it. A licence is also required for a hand pulper. Any one who owns leases or controls a store which is to be used for the storage of coffee must apply to the Board to have the store registered.[47] The Board may cause coffee to be graded prior to, or after, sale or prior to export. The Board may, subject to the approval of the Minister and to the provisions of any international coffee agreement to which Uganda is a party, sell coffee within or outside Uganda by such methods as it thinks the circumstances justify and no person, other than the Board, may sell coffee to a quota market. Any person wishing to export coffee to a non-quota market must apply to the Minister for an export licence, which the Minister may, in his discretion, issue, subject to such terms and conditions as he thinks fit. Rough-hulled and unprocessed coffee may not be exported and no coffee may be exported without a grading certificate.

PROCEDURE

The Criminal Procedure Code (Amendment) Act[48] makes a number of amendments to the parent Act[49] with the main object of ensuring "(*a*) the smoother and quicker administration of justice; (*b*) the lessening of the prison population; and (*c*) the reduction of expense, both to the individual and the State, of criminal proceedings".[50] A sentence imposed by a Magistrate's Court only requires confirmation by the High Court if it is one of imprisonment for two years or more or of preventive detention under the Habitual Criminals (Preventive Detention) Act.[51] The provisions of the Criminal Procedure Code[52] providing for a proclamation in respect of a person who has absconded and for the attachment of his property are repealed. A magistrate's powers in respect of the granting of bail are amplified and, in particular, it is stated that, in deciding whether it is probable that the applicant would appear at his trial, he is to have regard to the following: the nature of the accusation; the gravity of the offence; the antecedents of the applicant; whether he has a fixed abode in the area of the court's jurisdiction; and whether he is likely to interfere with the prosecution witnesses or evidence. Since the old sub section 149(3) of the Criminal Procedure Code was consequentially repealed by Section 11 of the Oaths Act,[53] the position regarding the reception of the evidence of young children in criminal cases has been somewhat obscure in respect of whether the court, before receiving such evidence, must be satisfied that the child is of sufficient intelligence and understands the duty of speaking the truth.[54] The insertion of a new sub section 149(3) now makes it clear that the court must be so satisfied.[55] If a case against the accused is withdrawn, then, if there were no reasonable grounds for his prosecution, the court may, as in the case of a person acquitted under such circumstances, order payment to him of costs. Section 300*A*, dealing with the detention of young offenders, has been reframed and eighteen, instead of sixteen, is now the age below which the term "young offender" applies. A more realistic scale for imprisonment in default of payment of a fine is introduced, ranging from seven days for 20 shillings or less to twelve months for 1,000 shillings or more, and the powers of the court to allow time for the payment of a fine are amplified. Modifications are made to appeal procedure and it is provided that appeals from magistrates' courts are to be heard by not less than two judges as the Chief Justice may direct.[56]

The Criminal Procedure Code (Amendment) Act also introduced provisions dealing with suspended sentences and first offenders. A new Section 298*A* provided that a court[57] might, after taking into account the offence and the age and character of the offender, order that a sentence not exceeding three years be suspended. The sentence would then only be put into effect if the offender committed another offence punishable by a substantive sentence of imprisonment within the following two years. A new Section 299*A* provided that a court might not pass a sentence of imprisonment on a first offender, unless it was of the opinion, having regard to all the circumstances including the character of the offender and the gravity of the offence, that no other method of dealing with him was appropriate. New sub sections 333(3) and (4) provided that an appellate court might on hearing an appeal order a sentence of imprisonment to be suspended or order a sentence which had been suspended by the lower court to be put into effect. The application of the sections dealing with suspended sentences apparently ran into difficulties,[58] whilst it was decided that, in fact, it was unnecessary "for there to be express provision restricting magistrates' powers to imprison first offenders. The fact that a convicted person is a first offender is a matter which will always affect the sentence a court imposes".[59] Five months after the application of the Act amending the Code, a further amending Act was, accordingly, passed[60] which repeals Sections 298*A* and 299*A* and substitutes new sub sections in place of sub sections (3) and (4) of Section 331. Suspended sentences may now only be ordered by an appellate court.

The Civil Procedure and Limitation (Miscellaneous Provisions) Act[61] provides that no suit is to lie or be instituted against the Government, a Local Authority or a Scheduled Corporation[62] until sixty days after written notice has been given. Furthermore, no action founded upon tort or contract may be brought against the Government, a Local Authority or a Scheduled Corporation after the expiration of one year in the case of tort and three years in the case of contract from the date on which the cause of action arose. If any action, prosecution or other proceeding is brought against a person for an act done in pursuance, execution or intended execution of any written law or public duty or authority, or in respect of any alleged neglect or default in the execution of such law, duty or authority, it must be instituted within six months of the act, neglect or default complained of, or, in the case of the continuance of injury or damage, within three months of the ceasing of the injury or damage.

The Witness Summons (Reciprocal Enforcement) Act[63] provides for the enforcement of witness summonses issued in criminal cases by the courts of countries in respect of which the Act is to apply. The Act may be applied by the Minister in respect of any country which the Minister is satisfied has made, or will make, reciprocal provision for the enforcement of a summons issued by a court in Uganda. A summons issued by a court in a country to which the Act applies is served upon the person to whom it is addressed after endorsement by the magistrate within whose area of jurisdiction the person is at the time. A person upon whom such a summons is served may apply to the magistrate who has endorsed the summons for an order excusing him from compliance, which the magistrate may grant if he is satisfied that no adequate provision has been made for the payment of travelling expenses, or that the applicant is too ill to travel, or has been given insufficient time, or that, having regard to all the circumstances, it would be unreasonable to require compliance with the summons. Any person who fails to comply with such a summons and who has not been excused from so doing commits an offence and is liable on conviction to a fine not exceeding 500 shillings.

MISCELLANEOUS

The Engineers Registration Act[64] establishes an Engineers Registration Board[65] for the purpose of regulating and controlling engineers and their activities within Uganda and of advising the Government in relation thereto. Subject to the provisions of the Act, any person is entitled, on making application to the Board and on payment of the prescribed fee, to be registered under the Act, provided he has the following qualifications. He must be either a member of an institution of engineers recognised by the Board as furnishing a sufficient guarantee of academic knowledge of, and practical experience in, engineering, or be over twenty-five and be the holder of a degree, diploma or licence of a university or school of engineering recognised by the Board as furnishing the same guarantee, and, furthermore, have had not less than three years practical experience of such a nature as to satisfy the Board as to his competence.[66] Moreover, the Board may require an applicant for registration to satisfy it that his professional and general conduct has been such as, in the opinion of the Board, would make him a fit person to be registered. The name of every person accepted by the Board for registration is entered in a register maintained by the Registrar and is also published in the Gazette. There is special provision for the temporary registration of persons not ordinarily resident in Uganda. If any registered engineer is convicted of an offence under the Act or is, after an inquiry held by the Board, found to have been guilty of improper or disgraceful conduct in a professional respect, the Board may caution or censure him, or direct that for a period the registration of his name is to have no effect, or direct that his name be deleted from the register. When the Board holds an inquiry into an engineer's conduct, he is entitled to appear in person or to be represented by an advocate. The Board may administer oaths, summon persons to attend and give evidence, and order the production of documents. Any person aggrieved by a decision of the Board to refuse to register his name or to delete his name from the register or to refuse to restore his name or to suspend the effect of the registration of his name, may appeal to the High Court and any ensuing Order of the High Court is final. A person whose name has been entered in the register is entitled to use the style and title of

"Registered Engineer" and any person who, not being a registered engineer, uses this style and title or holds himself out to be a professionally qualified engineer commits an offence, the maximum punishment for which is a fine of 10,000 shillings.

In October 1968 an Agreement was entered between the International College of Tropical Medicine, a body incorporated by Act of Parliament of the Islands of Bermuda and the Uganda Government providing for the establishment in Uganda of an International Centre for Research and Education in Tropical Medicine which would be a Branch of the College and would be administered at the College's expense. The International College of Tropical Medicine (Uganda) Act[67] provides for the implementation of this Agreement.[68]

The Deposit Library and Documentation Centre Act[69] establishes a Centre, which is to be administered by the Institute of Public Administration. In this Centre are to be deposited and kept all books which the Act requires to be delivered to the Centre, together with such other books, publications and material as the Minister may, at his discretion, decide to deposit and keep. The publisher of every book[70] published in Uganda, and any resident of Uganda who is the author of a book published outside the country, must, within one month of publication, deliver a copy of the book to the Librarian of the Centre. Furthermore, if required to do so, the publisher or author must deliver another copy to the Minister. The penalty for failure to comply with these requirements is a fine of one hundred shillings. The Minister may, by statutory order, exempt from the provisions of the Act any specified class of book.

ACTS PASSED DURING 1969

1. Local Administrations (Amendment) Act.
2. Access to Roads Act.
3. International College of Tropical Medicine (Uganda) Act.
4. Shop Hours (Amendment) Act.
5. Workmen's Compensation (Amendment) Act.
6. Witness Summons (Reciprocal Enforcement) Act.
7. Local Government (Rating) (Amendment) Act.
8. Urban Authorities (Amendment) Act.
9. Weights and Measures (Amendment) Act.
10. Hotels (Amendment) Act.
11. Water Boards (Amendment) Act.
12. National Training Corporation (Amendment) Act.
13. Public Lands Act.
14. Trade (Licensing) Act.
15. Industrial Licensing Act.
16. Banking Act.
17. Uganda Export Promotion Council Act.
18. Public Service Act.
19. Immigration Act.

20. Civil Procedure and Limitation (Miscellaneous Provisions) Act.
21. Social Security (Amendment) Act.
22. Pensions (Amendment) Act.
23. Criminal Procedure Code (Amendment) Act.
24. Statistics (Amendment) Act.
25. Bretton Woods Agreements (Amendment) Act.
26. Supplementary Appropriation Act.
27. Stamps (Amendment) Act.
28. Appropriation Act.
29. Management Training and Advisory Centre Act.
30. Liquor (Amendment) Act.
31. Local Administrations (Amendment) (No. 2) Act.
32. Finance Act.
33. Treasury Bills Act.
34. Banking (Amendment) Act.
35. Criminal Procedure Code (Amendment) (No. 2) Act.
36. Public Seal (Amendment) Act.
37. Public Service (Teachers) Act.
38. Deposit Library and Documentation Centre Act.
39. Engineers Registration Act.
40. Coffee Marketing Act.

---

1. *Opoloto* v. *Attorney-General of Uganda* [1969] E.A. 496, [1969] J.A.L. 117–23.
2. Act 19 of 1969.
3. Cap. 60.
4. Consisting of a chairman and not less than six, and not more than eight, members appointed by the Minister.
5. Or for a period of six months if issued under a law in force prior to the 1948 Act.
6. Articles 101 and 102.
7. Under Article 104.
8. Acts 18 and 37 of 1969. Act 37 did not come into force until 17th July 1970.
9. Cap. 227.
10. Article 103.
11. [1969] E.A. 92.
12. Act 13 of 1969.
13. Cap. 201.
14. Article 108 of the Constitution provides that there is to be a Land Commission consisting of not more than five members appointed by the President which is to hold and manage any land vested in it and which is to have such other powers and duties as may be prescribed by Parliament. Under this Article, land which had previously been vested in the Land Boards of the kingdoms and districts is vested in the Land Commission.
15. "Controlling authority" means the Land Commission except in respect of land held on a statutory lease (i.e. a lease granted to an urban authority under Section 15 of the 1962 Act), in which case it means the urban authority concerned.
16. This provision does not apply in the case of statutory freehold (i.e. public land vested in a public body in freehold under the provisions of the 1962 Act). In the case of statutory freehold notice of forfeiture may be given if the public body ceases to occupy the land or to use it for the purposes of the public body.
17. Act 2 of 1969.

18. "Owner of land" includes any person for the time being in actual occupation of the land.
19. Act 16 of 1969.
20. Cap. 88.
21. Established by the Bank of Uganda Act, Act 5 of 1966.
22. Memorandum to the Bill.
23. Banking (Amendment) Act, Act 34 of 1969.
24. Act 14 of 1969.
25. Of 1939, Cap. 100.
26. Memorandum to the Bill.
27. This prohibition does not apply to a shop or store already existing within the radius, nor does it apply to the following trades: (*a*) that of a planter, farmer, gardener, dairyman or agriculturalist in respect of the sale of his own dairy or agricultural produce; (*b*) that of a person in respect of goods made by him on his own premises or by his family or by persons normally residing with him; (*c*) that carried on in a market established under the Markets Act; (*d*) the sale of certain articles by the management of a club to its members within the club premises; (*e*) a trade in respect of which a separate licence is required by law or one for which the Minister has declared that no trading licence is required.
28. Trades listed in note 27 above are excepted.
29. The Schedule lists the trades and businesses of the following: retailer, wholesaler, commission agent, indenting agent, manufacturer's representative, management consultant, insurance broker, estate agent, motor vehicle repairer, hawker and travelling wholesaler.
30. The licensing authority in respect of trading licences is the Town Clerk in cities, municipalities and towns and elsewhere it is a person appointed by the appropriate administration of a district.
31. Act 15 of 1969.
32. Composed of a chairman, a public officer nominated by the Minister responsible for Foreign Affairs and not less than two, and not more than four, other members appointed by the Minister.
33. By the Management Training and Advisory Centre Act, Act 29 of 1969. The Act did not come into force until 1st July 1970.
34. Section 2 of the Act.
35. The Permanent Secretary of the Ministry responsible for Commerce and Industry or his representative, the Permanent Secretary of the Ministry responsible for Education or his representative, and the Permanent Secretary/Labour Commissioner of the Ministry responsible for labour matters or his representative.
36. By the Uganda Export Promotion Council Act, Act 17 of 1969.
37. The Permanent Secretaries of the Ministries of Commerce and Industry and Foreign Affairs or their representatives, the Chairmen of the Uganda Development Corporation, the National Trading Corporation, the Produce Marketing Board and the Uganda Tourist Board or their representatives, the Secretary for Planning or a representative, the Secretary to the Treasury or a representative and five members of the general public appointed by the Minister.
38. Cap. 197.
39. By the Workmen's Compensation (Amendment) Act, Act 5 of 1969.
40. Act 9 of 1969.
41. Cap. 101.
42. Act 40 of 1969.
43. Cap. 230.
44. Cap. 232.
45. Composed of a chairman, a deputy chairman, six members representing registered co-operative unions, the Principal Co-operative Officer in charge of Marketing and a secretary to the Board, all appointed by the Minister.
46. Composed of the Commissioner for Co-operative Development (Chairman), the Commissioner for Agriculture, the Commissioner/Treasury Officer of Accounts

(Secretary), two members from the Bugisu Co-operative Union Ltd. and two members from the Sebei-Elgon Co-operative Union Ltd.
47. And any person "other than a grower storing coffee in his store who stores any coffee otherwise than in a store registered for that purpose" commits an offence (Section 39(4)).
48. Act 23 of 1969.
49. Cap. 107.
50. Memorandum to the Bill.
51. Cap. 112.
52. Sections 110–12.
53. Cap. 52.
54. See H. F. Morris, *Evidence in East Africa*, London, 1968, pp. 179–80.
55. The new sub section also amplifies Section 13 of the Oaths Act in that it requires that the evidence needed to corroborate a child's unsworn evidence must implicate the accused, thus placing on a statutory basis a requirement which case law has earlier held to be necessary: see Morris, *op. cit.*, pp. 177–8.
56. Unlike the provisions of the rest of the Act which came into force on 2nd May 1969, this provision is to come into force on such day as the Minister may, by statutory instrument, appoint: it had not come into force by the end of 1969.
57. The High Court or a court presided over by a Chief Magistrate or a Magistrate Grade 1.
58. See Memorandum to the Criminal Procedure Code (Amendment) (No. 2) Bill. An anomaly to which Section 331(4) gave rise is clearly brought out in *Uganda* v. *Baguma* [1970] E. A. 169. The Director of Public Prosecutions has a right of appeal to the High Court only in the event of an acquittal (see *Hitila* v. *Uganda* [1969] E.A. 219). Hence, although Section 331(4) stated that an appellate court "may, on appeal," order a suspended sentence to be put into effect, in fact, no right of appeal by the prosecution would have lain to the High Court on the ground that the trial court's order that a sentence should be suspended should not have been made, and Section 331(4) could only have been brought into effect in such circumstances by means of a petition for revision.
59. Memorandum to the Criminal Procedure Code (Amendment) (No. 2) Bill.
60. Criminal Procedure Code (Amendment) (No. 2) Act, Act 35 of 1969.
61. Act 20 of 1969.
62. Schedule 3 of the Act lists the following bodies: Uganda Electricity Board, Coffee Marketing Board, Lint Marketing Board, Uganda Development Corporation Ltd., National Housing Corporation, National Insurance Corporation, Uganda Commercial Bank, Uganda Tea Growers Corporation, Bank of Uganda, National Trading Corporation, Dairy Corporation, Apolo Hotel Corporation.
63. Act 6 of 1969.
64. Act 39 of 1969.
65. Consisting of a chairman who must be a registered engineer in the service of the Government and who is appointed by the Minister, three registered engineers in the service of the Government, also appointed by the Minister, and three registered engineers not in Government service appointed by the East African Institute of Engineers.
66. Two of these three years must be after the obtaining of the degree, diploma or licence.
67. Act 3 of 1969. The Act had not yet been brought into force by the end of 1969.
68. Which forms a schedule to the Act.
69. Act 38 of 1969.
70. "Book" includes every part or division of a book, newspaper, periodical, magazine, review, gazette, pamphlet, sheet of letterpress, sheet of music, map, plan, chart or table separately published, but does not include any second or subsequent edition unless this contains additions or alterations.

CHAPTER 8

TANZANIA

James S. Read

Although more than fifty new measures reached the statute book in Tanzania in 1969 — and many of these merit fuller examination than will be possible here — they reflect in the main further consolidation and revision of courses charted in previous years;[1] and consideration of the law must take account also of important events which are not immediately reflected in written law, such as the unanimous adoption by the National Assembly in June 1969 of the Second Five-Year Development Plan,[2] the publication near the end of the year of the Government's proposals for major legislation to integrate the laws of marriage and divorce[3] and the withdrawal of a significant Government Bill for the amendment of the criminal law in the face of Parliamentary resistance to its provisions for the amelioration of the severe penalties prescribed by the Minimum Sentences Act 1963 by the abolition of the mandatory corporal punishment element therein.[4] The latter event, coming towards the end of the life of the First National Assembly established under the single party constitutional system, indicated that the vitality of Parliamentary life was not extinguished. Bills passed by the Assembly include measures which amend the electoral law in anticipation of the elections of 1970, amend the system of criminal justice in various respects, make new provision for the establishment of public corporations and the dissolution of private companies, provide for the conversion of Government leaseholds to rights of occupancy and establish a new statutory framework for the changing educational system.

CONSTITUTIONAL DEVELOPMENTS

1969 saw little change in the basically federal relationship between the two parts of the United Republic, and most of the laws discussed in this chapter apply in the mainland only (Tanganyika) and do not extend to the islands of Zanzibar. In 1968, however, the list of "Union matters" (in respect of which the Parliament of Tanzania has jurisdiction over the entire Republic) had been extended to include "Mineral oil resources"[5] and a Presidential Decree of 1969[6] gives effect to that change by applying to Zanzibar the relevant comprehensive Ordinance of Tanganyika,[7] repealing the shorter Zanzibar Decree[8] which formerly applied. As well as extending to Zanzibar the mainland system of licensing for exploration, prospecting and removal (in place of the former Zanzibar system), this development also vests in the President of Tanzania "the entire property in and control of all natural mineral oil" in Zanzibar (rights which, of course, he already holds in the mainland). The National Assembly, with its substantial minority of (non-elected) members from Zanzibar has never met in Zanzibar, and when a member enquired when it would do so the reply was that the Government was considering Zanzibar, and certain mainland towns as possible future meeting places.[9]

A major revision of the ministerial structure of the central Government occurred in March 1969, less than two years after the previous major changes;[10] although the total number of ministers remains the same as before (16, in addition to the two Vice-Presidents), a Minister for Foreign Affairs was appointed (this portfolio having been formerly retained by the President himself). The President's responsibility for "Co-ordination of Government" is now spelt out, and the Minister for Finance is now responsible for "Co-ordination of East African Community Affairs". A new division of responsibility for the key areas of lands, urban and rural developments and agriculture is introduced: the Minister for Lands adds housing and urban development to his portfolio; state farms, village settlements and farmers' education go to the Minister for Agriculture, Food and Co-operatives, who relinquishes National Parks to the Minister for Information and Tourism, while rural settlement policy and the promotion of ujamaa villages (which by 1969 were regarded as key instruments for development) are allotted to the Minister for Regional Administration and Rural Development. "The formulation and implementation of national transport policy" appears as a new item, the responsibility of the Minister for Communications, Transport and Labour. The maximum grant for the salaries and allowances of the Presidential household and the upkeep of State House has been increased by 50 per cent, to Shs. 3,000,000.[11]

The legislative implementation of the "leadership code", adopted by the Arusha Declaration 1967, has been examined in previous volumes.[12] In 1969 the provisions for enforcing the requirements imposed on Members of the National Assembly were amended,[13] enabling the Attorney General to petition the High Court for a declaration that a member has vacated his seat where he has ceased to be a citizen, or has an interest in a Government contract as prescribed or where he, or his spouse, has infringed the new requirements by any act, or acquisition of property, which attracts disqualification. The amendment also enables a Member who is required to vacate his seat otherwise than by a declaration of the High Court to petition the Court for a declaration that he is not legally obliged to vacate. This amendment conforms to the constitutional stipulation that the High Court has exclusive jurisdiction to determine questions of vacation of Parliamentary seats.[14] In December 1969 the High Court did in fact declare a vacancy, on the petition of the Attorney-General, in the case of a member who had failed to submit statements of his income and assets.[15] The leadership code was also extended to civil servants: the Principal Secretary (Establishments) is authorised to require an officer to lodge a declaration indicating whether he, or his wife, owns shares in a company or holds office as a director, receives two salaries, owns a house which is rented, or employs any workman in a trade, business or profession.[16] Similar requirements were extended also to police and prison officers.[17]

A large number of minor alterations in the law governing the conduct and machinery of Parliamentary, Presidential and local government elections were effected by a comprehensive amending measure.[18] Among the changes was the institution of a new office, that of Director of Elections. (That improvements in the law were required before the elections due in 1970 was hardly surprising; not only was there the experience of the 1965 Presidential and General Election to indicate practical difficulties which arose under the old law, but the latter had been amended in haste on the introduction of the single party system (1965).) A new system was introduced for the registration of voters, and a separate measure reduced the age at which a citizen qualifies to vote from 21 years to 18 years.[19]

In view of the importance attached to the development of Swahili as the national language, it is somewhat surprising that there is still no official version of the Constitution (adopted in 1965) in that language; a Parliamentary question elicited only that the Government is considering this matter.[20]

No doubt the most important single development at the national level in 1969 was adoption of the Second Five-Year Plan 1969–74.[21] As President Nyerere indicated when introducing the Plan,[22] the basic decisions underlying it were taken in effect when the Arusha Declaration was adopted in 1967:[23] development policies will be based upon socialism and self-reliance to bring benefit to all. This reflects a shift in strategy from the First Five-Year Plan, which concentrated public investment in infrastructure and rural economy (including transport, education, irrigation and resettlement) with a major reliance upon private investment for industrial development. The First Plan aimed at an annual growth rate of 6·7 per cent; actual growth is estimated to have been 4·3 per cent per annum to 1967 (it may well have been about 5 per cent in fact). The failure to reach the target is attributed to a number of unforeseen factors including, for example, the drastic fall in world sisal prices, the scarcity of external finance, and the unexpectedly high rate of population growth. Implementation of the First Plan was also affected by policy developments which occurred after its adoption — apart from the Arusha Declaration these included the elaboration of the role of public enterprise and the creation of the National Development Corporation and the adoption of the policy for integrated rural development concentrated in "Ujamaa villages". In consequence,

11—AL * *

"... the Second Plan document is very different from the First. It is much more a statement of strategy and its projections into the future are not always as precise ... the general targets and forecasts are given as a basis for a continual process of progress assessment. ..."[24]

The new plan gives priority to rural development and even sets a modest limit to expenditure on urban infrastructure; it provides for some decentralisation of financial and administrative responsibilities in planning, to encourage local initiative and control. An innovation is the proposal to prepare annual economic plans to achieve flexibility within the general strategy: this should enable account to be taken of both external factors or circumstances beyond Tanzanian control and internal developments such as social pressures and shifts of opinion. Annual reassessments should also serve to redress imbalances which may develop in different parts of the economy due to uneven implementation of a five-year plan. The Second Plan aims at a target growth rate of 6·5 per cent, which is felt to be realistic partly in view of the foundations laid by the First Plan.

Parastatal bodies are clearly the major instruments for the practical implementation of most aspects of development policy, and it is vital that there should be a clear and effective law concerning their establishment, control and operation. The rapid growth of public participation in industry and commerce, culminating in the extensive nationalisations of 1967, had resulted in the creation of a relatively large number of parastatals, often established ad hoc with little overall rationalisation of their general structure and responsibilities. A Presidential Circular of 1969 foreshadowed structural changes and rationalisation, and the Public Corporations Act[25] later provided the means to effect changes. Previously the pattern was that a specific Act was required for the creation of each corporation and any changes in its structure, powers or responsibilities later found necessary required amending legislation, while subsidiary legislation provided the detailed regulations for the operation of the corporation and its staff. The object of the new Act is to provide a basic provision enabling the President to establish any corporation by order, and to prescribe its functions, structure and management and other essential matters in the same way. Moreover, the President may now reorganise any existing public corporation even to the extent of abolishing it — thus having power to repeal by order any Act establishing a parastatal — or transferring any function, assets, liabilities or employees of an existing corporation to another. It may well appear in practice to be the source of the law which has changed in essentials, rather than its content, but the new system undoubtedly gives greater flexibility — for example, for shuffling spheres of activity between parastatals. Thus in 1969 the Act was invoked to rationalise the distribution of functions formerly exercised by the National Development Corporation: its agricultural and tourist activities were transferred to the National Agricultural and Food Corporation and the Tanzania Tourist Corporation respectively, leaving the reconstituted N.D.C. with its industrial and mining interests.[26] The Act preserves the normal present rule that the President may give "directions of a general or specific character" concerning the exercise of functions by the Board or manager of a corporation. The President can delegate any of his powers under the Act, except the power to establish a corporation, to any other Minister. During 1969 orders were made under the Act in respect of the N.D.C., the National Transport Corporation, the Tanzanian Petroleum Development Corporation, the Tanzania Tourist Corporation and the National Agricultural and Food Corporation.[27] Where a parastatal holds all the shares in a subsidiary company (incorporated under the Companies Ordinance), the latter may be dissolved by Ministerial order, its assets vesting in the parastatal or other subsidiary as specified in the order; and the requirement that a registered company must have a minimum number of members no longer applies where a parastatal or its subsidiary has acquired all the shares.[28]

In the field of regulatory and advisory bodies a new creation is the Tanzania Sisal Board, set up by Act to promote the development and improvement of the sisal industry by, *inter alia*, controlling the marketing and export of the crop with power to fix the price to be paid, to require the compulsory registration of all producers, to allocate production quotas and (with the Minister's approval) to impose a levy.[29] This measure repealed the Sisal Industry Act 1965 and revoked the licences granted under that Act to sisal agents. Tourist agents were brought within the requirements of a licensing system in 1969; licensing authorities are appointed by the Minister, to whom appeal lies against refusal, or unreasonable conditions, of a licence, and whose decision is final and not subject to judicial review.[30] Legislation has also provided for the establishment (by Ministerial order) of a Central Road Board, and Regional Road Boards, to advise the Minister regarding the construction, improvement and maintenance of all highways, ferries and aerodromes.[31]

Two significant changes occurred in the field of local government. Chiefs had been the mainstay of the colonial system of administration in Tanganyika which had, indeed, been the prototype of "indirect rule" in East Africa. However, the Government of independent Tanganyika had adopted a new policy in this respect, swiftly revoking all statutory powers granted to chiefs[32] who were replaced by officers of its own and of local elected councils. However, chiefs had exercised authority not merely derived from statute but to some extent based also in the traditional customary law and in some parts of the country at least it has been common for chiefs to continue exercising such powers, no doubt with local assent, even to the extent of punishing those who disobeyed them. Parliament in 1969 specifically deprived chiefs of any function or power which they claimed to exercise in accordance with tradition or customary law; it was made an offence, punishable with a fine of Shs.1,000 (or, for a second offence, Shs.2,000 and up to three months' imprisonment) to exercise or perform any such power or function, or to attempt to do so.[33]

In the wave of "self-help projects", which represented realistic local contributions to development in recent years, difficulties have sometimes arisen from the reluctance of a few persons in an area to participate in such local initiatives. The provision added to the Penal Code in 1962, creating the offence of dissuading persons from assisting with self help schemes,[34] did not satisfactorily meet the problem. This is the background to the provision by statute in 1969 for Ward Development Committees which, the Minister assured Parliament, are intended not to introduce forced labour but to protect the majority against the few.[35] The Minister may direct a local authority to establish such a Committee within any specified ward; the Committee can initiate local development schemes with the Minister's approval (including schemes for agricultural development, roads, social welfare, public utility or industry) and it has power to order all citizens aged between fifteen and fifty resident in the ward to participate in implementing a scheme (with exemptions for teachers, preachers, mothers of children under 3 years or women who expect to deliver a child within 6 months). The Committee can demand contributions in money or kind from citizens who, without lawful excuse, fail to participate. The mode of enforcing such a demand is curious, and reflects a tendency to bypass the ordinary courts: the Committee may report a defaulter to the Area Commissioner who will himself conduct an enquiry, giving the person concerned an opportunity to make submissions. The Area Commissioner may then confirm, vary or reverse the order (not so as to demand a greater contribution) and thirty days after his order has been served on the person concerned, a copy may be lodged in the primary court when it becomes enforceable in the same way as a decision of that court; the citizen has the right to appeal, within twenty-one days, although not to a court but to the Minister, whose decision is stated to be final and not subject to judicial review. It is provided that no court has jurisdiction to enquire into "the validity of any order" by the Area Commissioner or to consider any question as to a person's liability to participate in a development scheme. Thus, even if a person ordered to contribute raises a query as to the jurisdiction of the Committee or Area Commissioner — for example, a doubt as to whether he is in fact a citizen — even this apparently could not be referred to a court, so wide is the exclusion clause.

However, in Tanzania when judicial remedy is excluded the citizen may not be without means of redress: Tanzania's "Ombudsman", the Permanent Commission of Enquiry, reporting in 1969 on its work during the previous year,[36] shows again the range and variety of its work and does not shrink from depicting the incompetence — or worse — which it uncovers in public administration. Complaints received indicate that Tanzanians are very conscious of their rights (cynics might say, of intrusions upon their rights): although there was a sharp drop in the total number of complaints received from 1,627 in the first year of the work to 783 in 1967–8, the proportion of complaints accepted for consideration rose from under a third (567) to over a half (419) indicating better public understanding of the Commission's terms of reference. Of the 585 cases investigated to a conclusion during 1967–8, 114 were found to be "justified cases", twenty-three for "malicious misuse of powers", an equal number for "unreasonable, oppressive, unjust or discriminatory" acts, twenty-one for unjustifiable delays and thirty-one for failure to carry out a duty. District Councils remain top of the list as subjects for complaint, the

Judiciary, Ministry of Home Affairs and Ministry of Regional Administration now following in order. Judicial decisions as such cannot, of course, be investigated but the Commission found difficulty in distinguishing these where, for example, there was unjustified detention in custody not only pending trial but after it too. "Cases of unjustifiable detention by Area and Regional Commissioners have not been uncommon" including, in one case, repeated renewals of detention after the statutory maximum of 48 hours. And again the Commission records regretfully cases of further victimisation of people who have complained to it by officials against whom they have complained. On the other hand, some complaints result merely from impatience or are based upon fabrications. The Commission notes that cases of unjustifiable delay have increased, but cases of "malicious misuse of power" have declined: "it is early to say whether the Commission is deterrent or not, but certainly its effectiveness is beginning to leave its mark in the Public Service". The Commission has enjoyed an auspicious inauguration during its first years, under the chairmanship of Chief E. A. M. Mang'enya who, under the rotational system instituted for Commissioners, retired in 1969 and was succeeded by Mr. Justice Kimicha. Experience (and visits to study comparable institutions in Scandinavia, U.S.S.R., West Germany, etc.) led the Commission to propose certain amendments to the law — particularly, to extend its jurisdiction to embrace the nationalised industries and to give it power to make regulations regarding procedure.

THE JUDICIAL SYSTEM

1969 saw two measures which represent minor incursions into the judicial function: magistrates now share their decision-making powers in two ways. The Magistrates Courts Act 1963,[37] which established a new system of courts to replace the former local courts and old magistrates courts, provided that any magistrates court could sit with assessors in any proceeding where a rule of customary or Islamic law was relevant; the assessors gave their opinions on such a matter before judgment but the magistrate was not bound thereby. However, as amended in 1964, the Act required the primary court, in every proceeding (a term not free from ambiguity), to sit with two assessors whose opinions, although not binding, would be given on the case generally.[38] This arrangement gave rise to difficulty and misunderstanding and has now been replaced.[39] Primary courts are now restructured to consist, for all proceedings, of a magistrate and at least two assessors; all matters are now decided by the majority vote of the magistrate and assessors together, the former having also a casting vote. A trial can continue in the absence of an assessor through illness, but a primary court magistrate can not hear and determine any proceeding alone — at least one assessor must participate. As previously, a district (or resident magistrate's) court may sit with assessors (and may be directed to do so by the appropriate judicial authority) whenever customary or Islamic law is relevant: the magistrate must record their opinions and, while he is not bound to conform to them, if he does not do so he must record his reasons for differing.

As well as revising the position and role of assessors in primary courts, the 1969 amendment has systematised procedures for extra judicial arbitration by the statutory creation of "Arbitration Tribunals".[40] These are established by the Minister who can prescribe their composition, jurisdiction, practice and procedure. He has ordered the establishment of a Tribunal for every ward throughout the country.[41] Each Tribunal consists of five members nominated by the local Branch Committee of the ruling party, TANU; members must be citizens aged at least thirty years and hold office for one year (they may be reappointed); Members of the National Assembly or of local authorities, civil servants, magistrates and judges are disqualified. No member may participate in any proceedings in which he has a pecuniary or other interest. The work is voluntary, there being no provision for pay or allowances. The Regional Commissioner can veto a nomination, or remove a member, if he is "satisfied that it is undesirable" for that person to serve. The jurisdiction of the Tribunals is based upon submission: it extends to disputes of a civil nature referred by primary courts with the concurrence of all the parties to them, and to any disputes referred by any party where the other parties consent to its being determined by the Tribunal. Disputes submitted by the parties may apparently be civil or otherwise in character, but no Tribunal may impose any fine or other punishment whatsoever. Otherwise the Tribunals have jurisdiction over all types of subject matter, with no limitation of value and irrespective of the types of law applicable. The intention to preserve informality in procedure is shown by the provision that the Tribunal "shall investigate and determine any dispute . . . without regard to any law of evidence or procedure applicable to any court and shall . . . be entitled to regulate its own procedure". The machinery is available free of charge: a party may not be required to pay a fee or any payment to the Tribunal or any member. And the ultimate purpose of the scheme is indicated by the requirement that in every proceeding "the Tribunal shall endeavour to bring the parties to the dispute to an amicable settlement". However, when a dispute has been "investigated and settled with consent of all the parties concerned and with consent of all the members of the Tribunal" a certificate may be issued (either by the Tribunal itself or by a primary court magistrate upon the advice of the Tribunal) recording the terms of the settlement: when filed in a primary court, such certificate is "deemed to be an order of the primary court" and is enforceable as such. A party to the dispute can challenge such certificate, but he must satisfy the primary court concerned either that he did not consent to the terms recorded or that he was coerced into accepting them; if the primary court for either reason sets aside the certificate it can proceed to determine the dispute *de novo*, or advise the party to commence proceedings in the court which has jurisdiction to entertain them (for of course primary courts, unlike Arbitration Tribunals, have only limited jurisdiction in terms of subject matter, value and law applicable; thus an order may be deemed to be that of a primary court which would itself have no jurisdiction to make it in an original case). Apparently other defects — such as fraud or corruption — will not serve to invalidate a certificate of settlement.

Each Tribunal will elect its own chairman from among its members; he has the responsibility of convening the Tribunal when a dispute is referred to him or any other member. The Tribunal sits in public (except when it decides to exclude the public in the public interest). A Tribunal which is unable satisfactorily to promote an amicable settlement must report accordingly to the primary court which referred the dispute, or in other cases to the parties (advising them to institute court proceedings). Evidently there was some redrafting of the Regulations, for although a Tribunal is stated to consist of five members, it is later stated that three members out of the seven [*sic*] constitute a quorum and that where the chairman is absent but the *other* two members are present one of these, with the other's consent, may act as chairman; but, again, a Tribunal cannot hear or determine any proceeding with less than three members.

The precise effect of this system can hardly be judged without details, which are not available and unlikely to be so, as to the number and nature of disputes dealt with by Tribunals. Was the intention to relieve the primary courts of cases which are suitable for arbitration? Or was this law designed rather to bring some measure of formal control and political authority to arbitration proceedings which have clearly always continued to be followed in many parts of East Africa, sometimes in preference to official courts? Political leaders, at local levels, have expressed impatience with some of the processes of the courts; there have been some confrontations between political officers and local magistrates; TANU members have sometimes set up their own "courts" to settle local disputes, and this has brought conflict with the proper courts; meanwhile informal dispute settlement within family, clan, village, trade or other social group has continued, adapted to the changing pressures and opportunities of changing conditions. The role of the Arbitration Tribunals will be an interesting new factor in this situation.

An interesting procedural innovation enables a magistrate trying a criminal case under the Employment Ordinance to convert the matter into a civil suit if he considers it can be more conveniently or properly dealt with in that way; if the issues are satisfactorily defined he can then proceed to determine them as if in a suit, without requiring written pleadings.[42]

The niceties of definition in the structure of the Tanzanian judicial system is indicated by the decision of Biron, J., that a District Court presided over by a Senior Resident Magistrate is not a "Court of a Resident Magistrate" which alone has jurisdiction under the Rent Restriction Act.[43] When a magistrate who is hearing a case is transferred, the case may be concluded by another magistrate but under the Criminal Procedure Code the accused may demand the recall of witnesses already heard: if he is not specifically informed of this right, that is a fatal defect and the trial is a nullity.[44]

PROCEDURE AND EVIDENCE

Three measures have introduced significant changes in the machinery of criminal justice. The old Poor Prisoners Defence Ordinance[45] has been repealed and replaced by the Legal Aid (Criminal Proceedings) Act;[46] this now provides for legal aid in criminal trials (or criminal appeals), in any court except a primary court (where advocates may not appear), where the "certifying authority" (who is the Judge in a High Court trial or the Chief Justice in respect of a magistrate's court) certifies that it is desirable in the interests of justice that the accused should have legal aid which his means are insufficient to enable him to obtain. Where it is practicable, the Registrar of the High Court will assign an advocate to the accused. The certifying authority will determine what remuneration the advocate should be paid from the general revenue, but the Act prescribes a minimum of Shs. 120 and a maximum of Shs. 300 (or, "for special reasons" such as complexity or duration of the case, Shs. 500).

A number of amendments were effected in the law of criminal procedure by a single measure:[47] the most interesting is the replacement of the rules governing the conduct of preliminary inquiries by magistrates. Now, instead of an oral hearing of prosecution witnesses and the recording of their evidence in the form of depositions, the prosecution will produce to the court statements by the witnesses it proposes to call at the trial, or written summaries of the substance of such evidence: these will be read over to the accused in a language he can understand. The curious feature is that the rules appear to deprive the court of its discretion: at the outset of the hearing the court now informs the accused that he will be tried later in the High Court, and at the end of the inquiry the court "shall commit the accused for trial". If the magistrate no longer has to determine whether or not there is a prima facie case against the accused, then it may be questioned whether the preliminary inquiry is necessary. The amendments include a rule that no witness can be called at the trial whose statement was not produced at the preliminary inquiry unless reasonable notice in writing has been given to the accused or his advocate. Similarly, the accused is not entitled as of right to have any witness summoned for the trial unless he gave the name and address at the preliminary inquiry.

The Criminal Procedure Code states that all male persons aged between twenty-one and sixty years are liable to serve as assessors. In *Kiwelesi* v. *Republic*[48] the Court of Appeal had inconveniently quashed a conviction for murder where the Chief Justice had tried the accused with the aid of two assessors, one of whom was a woman; taking the point of its own motion, the Court of Appeal held that under the Code women are not eligible to serve as assessors (this not being a case where the masculine embraces the feminine) and therefore, as there was only one eligible assessor present the court was not properly constituted and the trial was a nullity. Thus ended the first trial in East Africa in which a woman had sat as an assessor. The appeal judgment was delivered on 29th November 1968; by a swift legislative reprisal, on 2nd February 1969, Parliament amended the Code to provide that no subsequent proceeding should be invalid by reason of an exempt person serving as an assessor.[49] Nevertheless, the amendment anomalously added "women" to the list of exempt persons; it is difficult to understand why they should not in fact have been specifically made eligible to serve.

The old provision for an appeal, by either party to a criminal case in a subordinate court, by way of "case stated" on a point of law, has been replaced by a right for the Director of Public Prosecutions to appeal to the High Court from a subordinate court's decision on a matter of fact or law, even against an acquittal.[50] (The accused person may appeal on fact or law to the High Court under earlier provisions of the code.[51])

A change in the law relating to insanity in criminal trials now permits a trial court, where it appears that the accused may have been insane so as not to be responsible for his actions, to adjourn the proceedings for a medical examination of the accused and, if the evidence justifies it, to reach the special finding ("not guilty by reason of insanity") — even if no evidence has been directly adduced to prove insanity.[52] Formerly the court could only reach that finding where evidence was given to show that the accused was insane, and the court itself could not take the initiative in the matter.

At a different stage of the criminal procedure, a new Act[53] provides that where a Ministerial order makes provision (contingent upon reciprocal facility being available), the police of a contiguous country may enter a defined area of Tanzania in pursuit of a person reasonably suspected of an extradition crime in that country, and arrest him there; he must then be delivered to a Tanzanian police officer who will bring him before a magistrate who can order his return to the contiguous country if satisfied that he is required there for trial for an extradition offence. The Minister has wide power ("if of the opinion that the circumstances of the case so require") to order the suspect to be discharged. By the end of 1969 the Act had been brought into operation with regard to Kenya, the defined area of Tanzania being that extending from the border to the Tanga-Arusha railway and to a line continuing to Musoma.[54]

Another instance of international co-operation in the field of criminal justice is the new provision regarding witness summonses: where a Minister has ordered application of the Act in respect of another country, contingent upon reciprocity, a summons from a court in that country requiring a witness to attend in a criminal case may be forwarded via the Attorney-General and Registrar of the High Court for endorsement by a Tanzanian magistrate and service in Tanzania. The magistrate, or the Minister, may excuse compliance with the summons. The Act has been applied in respect of Kenya and Uganda.[55]

THE LEGAL PROFESSION

Important amendments to the Advocates Ordinance have revised the disciplinary system of the profession, giving the Advocates Committee, reconstituted to deprive practitioners of their majority, wider powers.[56] The Committee now consists of a High Court judge as chairman, nominated by the Chief Justice, the Attorney-General and one advocate nominated by the Council of the Law Society (previously three practising advocates elected by the Law Society itself formed the majority, sitting with the Attorney-General and an advocate from his chambers whom he chose). The Attorney-General retains his right to convene the Committee (although now he may be requested to convene it by the new chairman) and in doing so "may act upon information brought to his notice in any manner whatsoever". The Committee may consider any allegation of misconduct made by any person against an advocate (previously such allegation had to be by affidavit), and any application by the advocate himself or any other person to remove his name from the roll. After the hearing the Committee itself can disbar, admonish or suspend the advocate; previously these decisions could only be made by two judges of the High Court after considering the Committee's report. Now an aggrieved advocate can appeal to a full bench of the High Court (at least three judges) and there is a right to a further appeal by any party to the Court of Appeal.

A recurrent problem which has faced Tanzanian courts is the awkward question: in what circumstances may an advocate be called as a witness in a case in which he is appearing; may he continue to act as advocate after giving evidence? Is the question affected by the fact that — as in a 1969 case — the advocate has acted for both parties during the negotiations preceding the case? Platt, J., observed that "the practice of giving evidence and conducting cases is to be discouraged"; he noted the argument that this approach "would lead to a convenient method of putting counsel out of the case" but held that if an advocate is called as a witness he should not then act as counsel for the other side.[57]

PENAL LAW

An important new measure in the field of security law is the Prohibited Places and Areas Act.[58] This enables the Minister to declare any premises to be a protected place if he "is of the opinion that it is necessary or expedient that special precautions should be taken to prevent the entry of unauthorised persons": then a permit from the authority specified in the order (or the permission of the authorised officer on duty) is necessary for entry to such premises, although the order may specifically exempt certain persons or classes of persons from these requirements. A protected area is one declared by order where the Minister "is satisfied that it is necessary or expedient that special measures be taken to control the movement and conduct of persons"; such an order may close the area to all except permit holders and may require any person in the area to comply with directions as to movement and conduct given by an authorised officer. The maximum penalty for an offence under the Act is a fine up to Shs. 20,000, imprisonment up to three years, or both, and in any trial the accused has the burden of proving that he was exempted, held a valid permit or had permission to enter from an authorised officer; the latter has wide powers, including unrestricted rights to search persons on the premises or in the area: it is relevant therefore to note who are authorised officers. The Act defines the term to include a police officer of the rank of Assistant Inspector or above, a Regional Commissioner, the local Area Commissioner, any person or class authorised by Ministerial order and any guard or watchman authorised by a Regional or Area Commissioner or an Assistant Superintendent of Police. The powers are somewhat sweeping especially as the term "area" is not defined and appears to be subject to no limit of size (could a whole Region be declared a protected area?) The Act goes even further, providing that the Minister may require an occupier of a protected place or area "at his own expense to take such measures for the better protection of the place or area as the Minister may consider reasonably necessary" and "to take such steps as the Minister may deem necessary in the public interest for the safeguarding of any interest" with regard to such place or area, "or for the security of any classified information or document which may be furnished to such occupier in his capacity as such, by any public officer". The problem in framing such legislation, of course, is that the generality of the provision grows out of the desire to embrace a diversity of particular instances.

In the field of penal policy a remarkable innovation is the introduction of a system for the compulsory resettlement of ex-prisoners.[59] The Minister can establish Resettlement Centres and order certain offenders to remain indefinitely therein. This is therefore a serious form of indeterminate penal restriction operated entirely through administrative discretion: for no court can review a resettlement order. The "offender" will normally have been convicted before a court of law, but this is not invariable for, of the five alternative conditions precedent for the making of an order, two are the existence of a deportation order under the Deportation Ordinance or of a residence order under the Witchcraft Ordinance,[60] both such orders being made by executive authorities. Other circumstances where a resettlement order can be made are where the offender has been convicted of a scheduled offence (being an offence scheduled under the Minimum Sentences Act 1963 or under the Witchcraft Ordinance) or has been convicted of any offence punishable with two years' imprisonment or more (when resettlement is possible only if the Commissioner for Social Welfare recommends it) or has been ordered by a court to give security for good behaviour.[61] The Minister can apply to a Resident Magistrate for a warrant of arrest if he considers that the offender may not comply with the resettlement order. The offender's rights are very circumscribed: the resettlement order must state the reason for which it is required; free transport must be provided to the resettlement centre, and the regulations may provide for a settler to have his dependants (i.e. his wife and children aged under 14 years) with him although of course they cannot be required to remain there; the Minister must review every order annually and at any time on the request of the Commissioner for Social Welfare, and he may review it on the application of the settler or of the officer in charge of the centre. No resettlement order can be made if thirty days have passed since the sentence of imprisonment terminated (or since the conviction, if no sentence of imprisonment was imposed, or the order to give security, as the case may be). A settler commits an offence if he absents himself from his centre without written authority. Obvious criticisms may be offered of this system on grounds of penal policy. The purpose can hardly be to provide a half way stage between imprisonment and normal life for the resettlement, outside the term of imprisonment imposed, actually delays any return to normal life. Isolating offenders in such centres contradicts the aim of re-integrating them in society. If the main purpose is to use persons who have earlier forfeited their freedom to develop under-populated areas — an embryonic direction of labour — it must be noted that the first four centres established were all in the vicinity of existing prisons.[62] In presenting the Bill, the Minister emphasised its preventive nature — it was designed to protect innocent members of society and their property. Difficult questions are raised by the Act: how will ex-prisoners be selected for resettlement — by whom, and upon what criteria? Will courts in future take account of the possibility of resettlement after imprisonment in fixing sentence?

Another interesting event in the field of penal policy was the withdrawal of a Government Bill to effect various amendments when Parliamentary resistance was encountered to proposed changes in the Minimum Sentences Act. When the latter (notorious in Commonwealth Africa for its combination of minimum prison sentences with mandatory corporal punishment for certain offences) was enacted, it was enthusiastically welcomed by Members of Parliament. Despite widespread public opinion to the contrary, the Government had concluded that the corporal punishment provisions had achieved nothing; however, the Bill, which would have removed the mandatory corporal punishment although balancing this improvement with increases in the minimum sentences of imprisonment to three years (from two years) and, for a second offender, or where the property involved exceeded Shs. 10,000 in value, to five years, was withdrawn.[63] This was a significant event in a single party state. (The Bill would also have enlarged the very limited discretion now enjoyed by a court in the case of a first offender under the Minimum Sentences Act.)

The most unusual point of law raised in a criminal appeal during 1969 was probably the ingenious argument presented in *Westcott* v. *Republic*[64] where the appeal was against convictions of being a member of an unlawful society and of assisting in its management. The societies concerned were the Jehovah's Witnesses and the Watchtower Bible and Tract Society, declared unlawful in 1965 under Section 6 of the Societies Ordinance. Before the Court of Appeal it was submitted that Section 6 was invalid as having been *ultra vires* the United Nations Trusteeship Agreement 1946 which was in force when the Ordinance was enacted in 1954 and which required the Administering Authority to ensure in Tanganyika "complete freedom of conscience, and, so far as consistent with the requirements of public order and morality, freedom of religious teaching and the free exercise of all forms of worship" and to guarantee freedom of speech, of the press and of assembly, subject only to the requirements of public order. The argument failed because, the Court of Appeal held, Section 6 was not void *in toto*, for it could have been invoked against societies other than those concerned with religion, in the interests of public order or morality; an order under Section 6 might have been *ultra vires* the Trusteeship Agreement if made before independence to ban religious activity otherwise legitimate, but after independence of course, the Government of Tanzania was not fettered by the Agreement.

Water from a furrow on a neighbouring farm, which has therefore been sufficiently appropriated by the user, is capable of being stolen and it may be theft, even though the accused has permission to take water between 6 a.m. and 9 a.m., if he takes it at other times; but he cannot be convicted on evidence which merely indicates that people connected with him or his wife took water when he may himself have been away.[65]. Is an ostrich egg shell a "Government trophy" possession of which is an offence unless a certificate of ownership is held? This apparently simple question posed a difficult semantic problem for Platt, J., for the statutory definition is that " 'trophy' means any animal, live or dead, and any horn, ivory . . . egg, or other durable portion whatsoever of any animal . . ." and " 'animal' means any kind of vertebrate animal and the eggs and young thereof". So that an ostrich egg is an "animal", and the shell is a portion of that animal and, it was held, is sufficiently durable to rank as a trophy.[66]

An interesting point arose on revision in *Republic* v. *Modest*.[67] Two young men, A and B, were convicted of the abduction of a girl of 12 years, the sister of A, who had in fact been married to B with her father's consent (in place of her older sister for whom B had originally paid bride price but who had then married another). By the time of B's marriage, however, the father was regarded as mentally defective and A had assumed responsibility for the family. The conviction was under Section 133 of the Penal Code, which defines the offence of abducting a "woman of any age" and looking at the scheme of the Code Seaton, J., held that this section refers to adult females only; Section 134 creates an offence in respect of girls under sixteen years which, however, requires that the abduction be against the will of the father, mother or other person in charge of the girl. The convictions were therefore quashed, indicating a curious lacuna in the Code, for it affords no protection to a girl under sixteen years who is forcibly married off by her father (unless he intends that she should have sexual relations with her husband while she is under 12 years, when Section 138 would apply).

TAX LAW

An innovation in local tax law was the adoption of a Sales Tax, at varying rates (10 per cent, 15 per cent, 20 per cent) on a wide variety of goods, whether imported or manufactured in Tanganyika (unless manufactured for export). The Act[68] empowered the Minister to establish an Appeals Tribunal, chaired by a judge or Senior Resident Magistrate nominated by the Chief Justice, to determine disputes by making decisions which are binding and conclusive and not subject to review by any court. The time factor in the introduction of the measure was interesting: the Act was enacted on 9th July 1969 and deemed to have come into operation on 20th June 1969, having been preceded by the Provisional Collection of Taxes (Sales Tax) Order and by the Sales Tax Regulations[69] under the new Act (19th June 1969). Meanwhile, fearing unjustified price increases using the new tax as an excuse (e.g. regarding scheduled goods not actually taxable, for example, because they were held in current retail stock), Parliament had passed the Sales Tax (Prevention of Price Increases) Act[70] making it an offence to offer goods for sale at a price increased by reason of sales tax when the goods are not actually taxable.

Home is where the heart is — thus at least might be paraphrased the humane and philosophical response of Newbold, P., in the Court of Appeal to the call to define "home" in the context of tax legislation. Emphasising that he was not offering an exhaustive definition, he said:

> "The home of a person is a dwelling place, whether the whole or part of a house or a flat, and whether owned or rented, in which, in the absence of special circumstances, one would expect to find that person's family, if he has a family, and the personal belongings which he would gather around him to satisfy his tastes and interests. The special circumstances in which one would not find his family or his personal belongings would include temporary separation, even for a relatively long period, for educational, medical or business reasons, and by business reasons I include the necessity of earning a livelihood."[71]

PROPERTY LAW

The most far-reaching change of 1969 in the field of property law was the extinction of all Government leases and the substitution for them of rights of occupancy.[72] This was the culmination of a process which started with the conversion of all freeholds to Government leaseholds in 1963.[73] All former leaseholders will now hold their land under rights of occupancy under the Land Ordinance[74] for terms equal to the unexpired portions of their leases. Subsidiary interests (derivative leases, mortgages, charges, liens, encumbrances, etc.) subsist with the same effect as if they had originated in respect of rights of occupancy. The incidental provisions of the new Act authorise the Commissioner of Lands to fix the rental payable for the deemed right of occupancy, with a right of appeal to the Minister whose decision is final and not subject to review in any court. But the complexities anticipated in the whole operation are indicated by the provision that the President may by order make such provision as, in his opinion, is necessary or expedient to remove any difficulty which arises in administering the Act.

Government powers over the mining industry have been strengthened by amendments to the Mining Ordinance, re-enacting the provision which vests the entire property in and control of all minerals in Tanganyika in the President and giving the Minister power to refuse to grant or renew any mining lease and the President power to cancel or revoke any mining right, in the national interest, while it is still in force — the exercise of these powers being stated to be final and subject to no questioning in any court.[75]

Another amendment provides for specified dispositions to be exempted by Ministerial order from the operation of the rule against perpetuities.[76] The Customary Leaseholds (Enfranchisement) Act 1968 has been amended *inter alia* to permit an appeal to the Minister from a decision of a Customary Land Tribunal (which determines the landlord's compensation).[77]

In the High Court Duff, J., has held that an "irrevocable authority to sell" granted to an auctioneer in consideration of Shs. 1 is not an "option to purchase" which entitles the auctioneer to enter a caveat on the register.[78] The Court of Appeal has accepted that where Africans are resident on Government land the rights which they enjoy as between themselves are to be decided according to local customary law.[79]

COMPANY LAW

The Minister can now order the winding-up of any company "where, in his opinion, it is in the public interest"; although the order must be filed in the High Court, which then proceeds to make a winding-up order, exercising all its other powers under the Companies Ordinance, the effect of the Ministerial order cannot be questioned. What of companies operating within Tanganyika but incorporated outside? These too are provided for: the Minister is now authorised to order any such company to cease to carry on business in Tanganyika "where, in his opinion, it is in the public interest so to do". The offence of carrying on business after the date specified by the Minister carries a maximum penalty of a fine of Shs. 20,000 plus a further penalty of Shs. 1,000 *per diem* for further offences; every officer, agent or participant in management is deemed to have committed the offence.[80]

SOCIAL DEVELOPMENT

The major legislation in the field of social policy was the new Education Act,[81] which extended and reorganised Government control of schools. The Act gives an enhanced meaning to "education", to embrace "physical, religious and cultural training" as well as "training in general learning" (a curious phrase) and defines the Minister's responsibility to ensure that education policy in Tanganyika is formulated with regard to national, rather than sectional or communal, interests. The formerly mandatory Advisory Council is replaced by an Advisory Committee which may be established, in the discretion of the Minister. The Minister now has power to give directions to the local education authorities (in consultation with the Minister for Local Government); every local authority throughout the country is a local education authority in respect of primary schools. Major changes were introduced in the management and control of schools: "assisted schools" (including mission schools) are now under Government control. There is a Director of National Education who is responsible for assisted and Government schools. The former Boards of Governors were replaced by School Advisory Boards whose functions the Minister in his discretion may restrict to advisory ones. Teachers in assisted schools are deemed to be members of the Unified Teaching Service employed by the state. No school (other than a religious school)[82] may refuse admission to a pupil on grounds of religion or race although preference may be given to citizens. The Minister can censor school literature by prohibiting the use in any school of any book or other material for any reason he may think fit. With regard to religious education, the Act requires Government to provide facilities — that is, opportunities — for it but without incurring any financial expenditure upon it. (The responsibility for providing the religious education in state schools rests with the religious organisations themselves). A parent can request that his child be excused attendance at religious instruction or worship.

Amendments to the Employment Ordinance *inter alia* enabled the Minister to vary progressively the minimum age of employment between the ages of twelve and fifteen. Private recruitment for employment in manual labour is forbidden except regarding domestic service and local work on daily rates of pay.[83]

FAMILY LAW

The most significant contribution to family law in 1969 has produced no specific change in the law itself but merely postulated the principles upon which far-reaching reform of the law of marriage and divorce would be framed in the future: Government Paper No. 1 of 1969, Government's Proposals on Uniform Law of Marriage, summarised the proposals upon the basis of which, after public discussion, legislation will be prepared providing for "the uniformity of laws". Amongst the principles stated are that Christian, Muslim, customary and other marriages should be given equal legal treatment; that certain basic rules should be common to all forms of marriage — e.g. a minimum age of fifteen years for girls, eighteen for men, uniform rules relating to prohibited degrees of relationship, a single marriage register — while preserving the different religious or other ceremonies for the solemnisation of marriage. Upon the vexed question of polygamy, the proposal is that a marriage monogamous in its legal character should be capable of conversion into a polygamous union if both husband and wife agree to this. Validity of customary marriages would not depend upon payment of bride-price which, however, should not be controlled or prevented. The rights of each spouse to his or her separate property would be assured. Cohabitation for two years or more will give rise to a presumption of marriage. Divorce would be possible by judicial decree only, following attempts at reconciliation by Marriage Conciliation Boards, and would be granted only where the marriage has completely broken down save that in a Muslim marriage the court must decree dissolution if the husband has exercised his religious right to dissolve the marriage by pronouncing three *talakas*. The proposals to a large extent follow those made in a lengthy report by a Presidential Commission in Kenya in 1968.[84] They inevitably gave rise to widespread and energetic debate throughout the country; religious and women's organisations were particularly concerned. The Attorney-General assured the bi-annual conference of the Umoja wa Wanawake wa Tanganyika that the White Paper was not intended to interfere with religious faith; yet the heated debate which followed showed that there were misgivings on this, and other points.[85]

Until the new enactment foreshadowed by this Government Paper comes into effect, several different systems of law apply in Tanzania in family matters. Some cases of 1969 recall to mind that although there is a unified judicial system, choice of law questions are still closely related to the choice of forum and vice versa. Thus, a claim for the refund of "bride-price" is a claim under customary law which must be brought in a primary court, in accordance with the Magistrates Courts Act 1963, Section 57[86]: district court proceedings in such a case were therefore a nullity.[87] However, Section 57 applies only to "civil proceedings in respect of marriage, guardianship or inheritance under customary law, or the incidents thereof"; where the claim is by an unmarried woman for the maintenance of her child she has a choice of forum by the exercise of which, a judgment of the late Mr. Justice Hamlyn affirms, she also selects the law to be applied.[88] The applicable law will be the Affiliation Ordinance,[89] under which corroboration of her evidence is required, if the claim is brought in a district court; but if the claim is brought in a primary court, customary law (defined by the Declaration of Local Customary Law[90]) applies under which the onus of proof favours the woman (for the burden of proving that he is not the father rests upon the respondent whom she has named). On the other hand, it should be added that there may also be a great difference between the value of the maintenance which the respective courts may order. Furthermore, Section 57 refers only to marriage and other proceedings under customary law and does not extend to Islamic law claims which, therefore, may be brought in a district court, for the primary court's jurisdiction is then not exclusive.[91]

In an interesting appeal involving Islamic law[92] Seaton, J., held that the validity of a dissolution of a Muslim marriage by a *khula* divorce was not contingent upon the payment of the full consideration agreed, preferring to accept the greater weight of accepted authority to an implication in an earlier East African case.[93] This issue has long been considered in East Africa; the leading study indicates that the answer "really depends on the exact import of the words used: but this seems to be little understood in

Tanganyika . . ."[94] and quotes a Muslim jurist's opinion in a Lindi case which would support the 1969 judgment. Seaton, J., also held that in deciding custody of a child of the marriage, the welfare of the child was the paramount consideration.

CONCLUSION

A survey of Tanzanian law from the published sources alone might serve to inculcate an impression of an over-arching bureaucracy centralised under Ministerial authority rapacious to add new functions to the wide authority already granted by a generally compliant Parliament, with a correlative diminution of the scope of the courts of law to adjudicate upon disputes affecting the individual citizen. The latter can, of course, turn to the Permanent Commission of Enquiry for the redress of his grievances. Certainly there is little reported civil litigation of note, and much of what there is stems from one enactment — the Rent Restriction Act, and often takes the form of appeal against the exercise of the administrative jurisdiction established thereby. This impression of Tanzanian law, inevitably discouraging to the admirer of the common law and no doubt to the practising lawyers of Tanzania, has to be balanced against the fact that the statute book and law reports are not fully representative of the quality or content of national life as a whole. The Reports of the Permanent Commission certainly catch the flavour and style of Tanzania, in both its good and ill aspects, much more richly. The laws as such make little reference to the ruling party with its widespread organisation, or to the actual problems of the relatively small and hard-pressed official bureaucracy in a large and often sparsely inhabited country with poor though improving communications. The effective claims and sanctions upon a citizen's loyalty and industry may still be primarily familial and local in character, despite Tanzania's undoubted success in "nation-building". Yet, even in the context of a determined and realistic socialism, and in face of the problems of poverty and ignorance, the totality of administrative powers grows apace, often to the exclusion of the ordinary courts; it may not always be an adequate defence to state that conditions are such that these powers, though wide, cannot always be effectively exercised.

---

1. See previous volumes in this series.
2. See below, pp. 133–34.
3. See below, pp. 148–49.
4. Criminal Law (Miscellaneous Amendments) Bill 1969. See below p. 144.
5. Act No. 48 of 1968.
6. Extension and Amendment of Laws Decree 1969, Government Notice No. 141.
7. Cap. 399.
8. Cap. 108.
9. *The Parliamentarian*, October 1969, L,4, 317.

10. For which see Government Notice No. 251 of 1967. For the new provision, see Government Notices Nos. 58 and 120 of 1969.
11. Presidential Affairs (Amendment) Act 1969, No. 31.
12. See especially the Annual Survey of African Law, 1967.
13. National Assembly (Qualifications of Members) (Forms and Procedures) (Amendment) Act 1969, No. 24.
14. Interim Constitution of Tanzania, 1965, No. 43, Section 36.
15. *The Standard, Tanzania*, 15th December 1969, cited by A. Mohiddin and A. Mazrui, "Political leadership and the control of temptation: Tanzania's measures against corruption", *The Parliamentarian*, July 1970, LI,3, 180–85.
16. Civil Service (Amendment) Regulations 1969, Government Notice No. 180.
17. Police Service Regulations 1969, Government Notice No. 178; Civil Service (Prisons Service) Regulations 1969, Government Notice No. 179.
18. Electoral Laws (Amendment) Act 1969, No. 51.
19. Elections (Age of Voting) Act 1969, No. 34.
20. *The Parliamentarian*, October 1969, L,4, 317.
21. *Tanzania Second Five-Year Plan for Economic and Social Development, 1st July 1969–30th June 1974*, Government Printer, Dar es Salaam, 4 volumes.
22. In a speech to the TANU Conference, 28th May 1969, reprinted with Volume I ("General Analysis") of the *Plan*, vii-xxiii.
23. ". . . the N.D.C. was then given its very heavy new responsibilities, and other parastatal organizations were created. A similar change affected agriculture . . . The policy of Ujamaa Vijijini, which was adopted by the Party in October 1967, meant the beginning of a change . . ." *Ibid.*, ix.
24. *Ibid.*, ix.
25. No. 17 of 1969. For a precedent see the Statutory Corporations Act 1961 of Ghana, Act 41.
26. This will particularly advance the Government's stated policy of making each parastatal responsible to one sectoral Ministry only, to ease decision-making and ensure co-ordination in each sector.
27. See Government Notices Nos. 90, 248, 140, 91 and 89 respectively. See also Government Notices Nos. 130–2, 184–6 and 250.
28. Written Laws (Miscellaneous Amendments) Act 1969, No. 41.
29. Sisal Industry Act 1969, No. 48.
30. Tourist Agents (Licensing) Act 1969, No. 2.
31. Highways Ordinance (Amendment) Act 1969, No. 40.
32. African Chiefs Ordinance (Repeal) Act 1963, No. 13.
33. African Chiefs Act 1969, No. 53.
34. Section 89C, added by No. 61 of 1962. See, for example, *Ngocho* v. *Republic* [1969] E.A. 82, where the conviction was quashed because the prosecution had not established that the self-help scheme was properly approved.
35. Ward Development Committees Act 1969, No. 6.
36. *Annual Report of the Permanent Commission of Enquiry, July 1967–June 1968*, Government Printer, Dar es Salaam, 1969.
37. No. 55, Cap. 537.
38. No. 67 of 1964.
39. Magistrates Courts (Amendment) Act 1969, No. 18.
40. *Ibid.*, adding Section 15*A* to the parent Act, and the Arbitration Tribunal Regulations 1969, Government Notice No. 219, made thereunder.
41. Two or more may be established in a ward if the Regional Commissioner considers it to be necessary.
42. Employment Ordinance (Amendment) Act 1969, No. 5, amending Cap. 366 *inter alia* by adding a new Section 134*A*.
43. *Allarakhia* v. *Aga Khan* [1969] E.A. 613.
44. *Raphael* v. *Republic* [1969]E.A. 544.
45. Cap 21.
46. No. 21.
47. Criminal Procedure Code (Amendment) Act 1969, No. 10.

48. [1969] E.A. 227.
49. No. 10 of 1969, Sections 25, 26.
50. *Ibid.*, replacing Sections 333–43 of the Criminal Procedure Code, Cap. 20, with a new Section 334.
51. Section 312 etc.
52. No. 10 of 1969, Section 11.
53. Fugitive Offenders (Pursuit) Act 1969, No. 1.
54. Government Notice No. 271 of 1969.
55. Government Notices Nos. 56 and 181 of 1969.
56. Advocates Ordinance (Amendment) Act 1969, No. 39, amending Cap. 341.
57. *Gandesha* v. *Killingi Coffee Estate Ltd. and Another* [1969] E.A. 299.
58. No. 38 of 1969.
59. Resettlement of Offenders Act 1969, No. 8. For Regulations see Government Notices Nos. 133 and 145 of 1969.
60. Cap. 18.
61. Under the Criminal Procedure Code, Cap. 20, Sections 45 and 52.
62. See Government Notice No. 135 of 1969.
63. *The Standard, Tanzania*, 23rd October 1969.
64. *Westcott* v. *Republic* [1969] E.A. 624.
65. *Republic* v. *Ndesario* [1969] E.A. 267.
66. *Mohamed* v. *Republic* [1969] E.A. 287.
67. [1969] E.A. 275.
68. Sales Tax Act 1969, No. 30.
69. Government Notice No. 152.
70. No. 27, enacted on 21st June 1969, and deemed to have come into operation on 19th June 1969.
71. *Commissioner-General of Income Tax* v. *Noorani* [1969] E.A. 685, 689.
72. Government Leaseholds (Conversion to Rights of Occupancy) Act 1969, No. 44.
73. No. 24.
74. Cap. 113.
75. Mining Ordinance (Amendment) Act 1969, No. 22.
76. Rule against Perpetuities (Limitation of Application) Act 1969, No. 23.
77. No. 43 of 1969.
78. *Ramji* v. *Rattansi* [1969] E.A. 309.
79. *Abdalla* v. *Mohamedi and others* [1969] E.A. 444.
80. Written Laws (Miscellaneous Amendments) Act 1969, No. 41, amending Cap. 212.
81. No. 50. Two Bills were published for this measure, the second containing a number of important changes.
82. I.e., any school in which the instruction imparted is wholly or mainly of a religious character.
83. Employment Ordinance (Amendment) Act 1969, No. 5.
84. *Report of the Commission on the law of marriage and divorce*, Government Printer, Nairobi, 1968; for a discussion of the proposals there made see *East African Law Journal, Special issue*, March–June 1969, Vol. V, Nos. 1 and 2.
85. *East African Standard*, 6th September 1969.
86. Unless the Republic or the President is a party or the High Court gives leave.
87. *Francis* v. *Boniface* [1969] E.A. 146.
88. *John* v. *Mnzava* [1969] E.A. 51.
89. Cap 278.
90. Especially Government Notice No. 279 of 1963.
91. *Kara* v. *Osman* [1969] E.A. 34.
92. *Salum* v. *Asumini* [1969] E.A. 255.
93. *Lalli* v. *Asha* (1914) 5 E.A.L.R. 165.
94. J. N. D. Anderson, *Islamic law in Africa*, London 1955. 141.

CHAPTER 9

MALAWI

Vern G. Davidson

CONSTITUTIONAL LAW

Both the Constitution and the Republic of Malawi (Constitution) Act[1] were amended in 1969, the latter by the Republic of Malawi (Constitution) (Amendment) Act 1969,[2] and the former by the Constitution (Amendment) Act 1969.[3]

The Amendment to the Republic Act was relatively unimportant, and probably necessitated by the fact that someone forgot to do his job which was only discovered when drafting the Amendment to the Constitution. The Constitution requires that the Electoral Commission review the boundaries of all constituencies at intervals of not less than three, nor more than five years.[4] The Republic of Malawi Act stated that the Commission is deemed to have done so on 1st April 1964.[5] By the time this was recalled to mind, the time was passed, and on 18th November 1969, Parliament amended the Republic Act so that the constituencies are now deemed to have last been reviewed on 1st April 1966, a date which may indicate the joker in the pack.

This particular action is unimportant, especially when in the near future the number of constituencies would change in any case, but while there is no question of lack of good faith, the system of legislation is dubious at best, and it would appear to be unconstitutional.

When the Republic of Malawi Act was passed, it was passed under a Constitution which required only a simple majority for amendment; and the Act itself established the Republic Constitution as a schedule thereto. Thus, there could be no argument about the Act's validity or anything that by its terms was deemed to have been done. But after it was enacted, the Republic of Malawi Constitution came into effect. That Constitution can only by a two-thirds vote. If we overlook the retroactive aspect of the boundaries legislation, the far more important point remains that the effect was to circumvent the mandate of the Constitution by a simple parliamentary act.

It should be noted that the members of the National Assembly that existed on the appointed day[6] were deemed to have been elected on the appointed day.[7] Can it be supposed that the sections of the Constitution limiting the term of Parliament could be circumvented by an incumbent National Assembly passing an Act which would amend Section 7 of the Republic Act so that "appointed day" would read "July 6th 1984" and thus avoid elections?

The situation is obvious. Clearly neither Constitutional mandates nor vested civil or property rights can be avoided by such circumvention.

The Amendment to the Constitution was indeed significant, although it lumped together the relatively unimportant change in the size of the National Assembly with a major change in the right of appeal to the High and Supreme Courts.

By the Constitution (Amendment) Act, the Constitution is amended in all appropriate sections[8] so as to raise the number of elected members of Parliament to sixty from fifty.

By this same Act, Section 69 of the Constitution is amended as as to make an appeal "subject to the provisions of the Traditional Courts Act relating to appeals". The name "Local Court" is changed to "Traditional Court"[10] and the definition of "Local Court" is deleted and replaced by the definition: " 'Traditional Court' means a court established by or under the Traditional Courts Act".[11]

These changes were of fundamental importance to the judicial and legal system of Malawi and are thus best discussed in that section along with the Local Courts (Amendment) Act 1969,[12] which necessitated their passage.

JUDICIAL AND LEGAL SYSTEM

As was stated above, the Local Courts (Amendments) Act brought about fundamental changes in the judicial and legal system in Malawi as pertains to criminal justice, and necessitated changes in the Constitution.

It has been claimed that the history of this Act, which led to the resignation, or "retirement" of all four British High Court Judges, began with the Limbe murder trials. After a series of unusual and gruesome murders in the Blantyre urban area, five persons were charged with murder before the High Court. At the conclusion of the prosecution case, the Court ruled that there was no case to answer,[13] and acquitted all five defendants.[14]

Whether this claim is true or not, it should be said that this acquittal placed the Government in a very difficult position. There is no question that many people believed beyond doubt that the accused were guilty and feared for their lives if the accused were set loose. This applied especially to the prosecution witnesses, and the effect on future administration of justice can be easily imagined.

In any case, the Government brought forth a series of legislative acts, the major one of which was the Local Courts (Amendment) Act. A short statement of the effect is that the Act gives jurisdiction to the Traditional Courts to hear crimes up to and including homicide, and removes the right of appeal to the High Court. A closer examination is, of course, needed.

Opening the debate on the second reading of the Act, Mr. A. K. Banda, Minister of Finance, Information and Tourism, stated:

> ... as long as a number of the magistrates and judges of the High Court are expatriate lawyers, cases are likely to come before the higher courts of the country raising important issues of African tradition and custom with which the courts themselves, are not readily familiar. ... This being the case, the Government had in mind that there may well be many ... occasions when cases involving complicated problems of customary or traditional behaviour or belief may be more properly and efficiently tried by a Local Court comprised of Malawians who are familiar with the tradition and customary factors involved.[15]

He continued,

> Similarly, as far as appeals are concerned, the Government considers that there would be little purpose as far as cases involving complicated issues of African tradition and customs are concerned, in allowing such cases to be tried by the Local Courts with the right of appeal to expatriate judges who have no familiarity with the customary aspects of the issues involved. In respect of such cases, therefore, it is proposed that the Minister should be able to set up a high-level Traditional Appeal Court. ... .[16]

The Act made the following changes. It repealed Section 11(*a*) of the Principal Act[17] which had excluded from the jurisdiction of the Local Courts all capital offences and ones punishable by life imprisonment. It amended Section 14 of the Act to permit Traditional Courts to impose the death penalty along with all other recognised forms of punishment.

Appeals were handled by leaving the right of appeal from the Traditional Appeal Court to the High Court in Section 33(3), but in adding sub section (4):

> Sub section (3) shall not apply to ... any proceedings declared by the Minister by order published in the Gazette, to be proceedings for the purpose of this Section.

And finally, Section 8 of the Criminal Procedure and Evidence Code [18] which allowed the Chief Justice to declare any case or class of cases to be triable only by the High Court was repealed. This was a last minute amendment in Committee to the original Bill which would have permitted the Minister to direct that any proceedings or class of proceedings would be triable only by the High Court, subordinate courts, or Traditional Courts.[19] It was evidently realised that this would necessitate yet another Constitutional Amendment as the High Court is declared to be a Court of unlimited original jurisdiction by the Constitution.[20]

The Constitutional changes described above were necessitated by the law as it was passed. The Amendment to Section 69 of the Constitution making appeals subject to the provisions of the Traditional Courts Act was necessitated because Section 69 allowed an appeal of right to the High Court from a subordinate court in any case where if the appeal were from the High Court to the Supreme Court of Appeal, it would be right. The question of whether the term "subordinate court" included the Local Courts (now Traditional Courts) was itself answered by the interpretation section of the Constitution.[21] "Subordinate court" means any court established for the Republic other than the Supreme Court of Appeal, the High Court or a court-martial. Is a Local Court a court? "Local Court means a court established by or under the Local Courts Act."

The result of these changes was that the jurisdictional limit on cases or classes of cases that the Minister could designate as triable by a Traditional Court were removed, but that parallel jurisdiction remains with the High Court. Thus, for instance, a murder case can be brought either before the Traditional Court or the High Court, that decision resting, presumably, with the Director of Public Prosecution.

If a case is brought before the Traditional Court, a right to appeal to the High Court does not exist if the Minister designates it as a proceeding for the purposes of Section 33.

It is difficult to argue with the logic of the Minister's remarks to Parliament as quoted above, but it is equally difficult to see their application to what the Act in fact does. It must be remembered that there are no "traditional crimes" recognised as such in Malawi. The cases tried before the courts, Traditional or any other, will be brought under the Penal Code. The law is, presumably, the same regardless of the race of the defendant, or the court before which he is tried. The question of, for instance, whether there is a case to answer is not one that rests on African tradition or custom.

It may be argued that questions of tradition and custom do arise in applying the law. What is provocation in Malawi may well rest on an understanding of Malawi custom, and there is no doubt that an expatriate judge who applies the standard of the man on the Clapham omnibus to determine who is a reasonable man in Blantyre would be out of line. But even granting this, there seems to be little need to take away the right of appeal to the High Court. Custom can be proved like any other law or, if this was a serious concern, findings of fact based on custom could have been made conclusive for the purpose of appeal.

One must feel some apprehension in leaving the intricate questions of law involved in the Penal Code to be decided by a court presided over by men without legal qualifications, where the defendant will not be represented by counsel, and where he will have no appeal to a qualified judge.

EVIDENCE AND PROCEDURE

The Criminal Procedure and Evidence Act,[22] was amended again this year in several important ways.

The amendment to Section 8 of the Act has been mentioned above.

In addition, three other 1969 Acts brought about changes in this area.[23]

Perhaps the most interesting change is the amendment which may have also arisen from the murder case discussed above. In that case acquittals followed a defence motion that there was no case to answer. The Government introduced the Criminal Law (Amendment) Act 1969,[24] by which Section 313 of the Criminal Procedure and Evidence Code which dealt with the presentation of the defence was repealed and replaced by a new section which states:

> 313 — When the case for the prosecution is closed . . . the High Court shall forthwith call on the accused to enter upon his defence.

This should be contrasted with Section 254(1) which deals with procedure before a subordinate (but not Traditional) court and which remained unchanged:

> 254 (1) If, upon taking all the evidence (for the prosecution) . . . , the court is of the opinion that no case is made out against the accused sufficiently to require him to make a defence, the court shall deliver a judgment . . . acquitting the defendant.

What effect does the new Section 313 have? If it was intended to eliminate the right to ask for an acquittal at the end of the prosecution's evidence, it appears to have failed. By the terms of the amendment, the court must call for the defence to be put in after the "case" for the prosecution is closed. Surely it is still open for the court to rule that no "case" has been made to close. If the amendment meant to say that the defence must be made at the end of the evidence supporting the prosecution's case, it could have said so.

This is more than an academic question, since the law in Malawi appears to be that, at least in the case of Section 254(1), if the court rules incorrectly on whether a case has been made out and requires the defence to be made out, the court may not, for the purpose of finding the defendant guilty, look at any evidence that came in from the defence.[25]

Since *Regina* v. *George* rests on the reasoning that the statute is mandatory, the situation as to cases before the High Court would seem to be that Section 313 does not eliminate the right and duty of the court to acquit where no case to answer has been made out, but that the question of whether a conviction based on defence evidence can be upheld on appeal where the court wrongfully ruled that there was such a case made out is not controlled by Malawian precedent. Since Section 313 is anything but mandatory as to acquitting where there is no case to answer, the decision on appeal would have to be decided on policy or non-Malawian precedent.

The final change brought about in procedure by the Criminal Law (Amendment) Act is to change the right of reply by the prosecution. Section 316 of the Criminal Procedure and Evidence Code stated that after the accused or his counsel had summed up his case and commented in reply, counsel for the prosecution was entitled to reply upon the whole case.

The Act now limits the right of the prosecution to making a final reply on the whole case to those cases in which the defendant has called witnesses other than himself. In those cases where no witness other than the defendant is called, the prosecution is limited to the right to reply before the accused or his counsel sums up his case.

The Criminal Procedure and Evidence Code (Amendment) Act, 1969,[26] has completely reversed the law as it had been concerning criminal appeals by the Director of Public Prosecution against acquittals. Under the Act as it stood, there might have been an appeal on a matter of law, but "nothing in this section shall authorise the High Court to convert a finding of acquittal into one of conviction. . . ."[27]

Section 346 of the parent Act was amended to spell out the right of the D.P.P. to appeal, Section 353 (2) was amended so as to eliminate the quoted words above, and the new sub section 353(2)(*c*) was added to dictate the procedure on successful appeals from an acquittal. If the acquittal was arrived at before the defence had been called, the case is remitted with direction to proceed with the trial; in any other case the acquittal is converted into a conviction. The High Court may then pass sentence itself or remit to the subordinate court for sentence.

This raises the question of what is the situation as to an appeal from an acquittal by the High Court of Appeal?

According to the Courts Act[28] the appellate criminal jurisdiction of the High Court is exercised in accordance with the law in force relating to criminal procedure. That law is certainly clear.

The appellate criminal jurisdiction of the Supreme Court of Appeal is stated quite differently. An appeal may be brought by the Director of Public Prosecution against any judgment of the High Court if he is dissatisfied with the judgment on a point of law.[29] In such a case, the Act states:

> On an appeal under Section 11(3) the court shall hear and determine the question or questions of law arising on such appeal and may remit the case to the High Court with the opinion of the court thereon with such directions as it may deem necessary, or may make such other order in relation to the appeal as to the court may seem fit, or may dismiss the appeal.[30]

The obvious question is, has the enlarged powers of the High Court to subordinate court changed the powers of the Supreme Court of Appeal in the case of an acquittal by the High Court?

It is pertinent that the Supreme Court of Appeal Act states that where the Act does not make provision for any particular point of practice or procedure, the court shall follow the practice and procedure of the Court of Criminal Appeal in England.[31]

CIVIL LAW

There was again no case law in Malawi of importance in this area, but it is worth noting that Malawi did enact a Partnership Act,[32] which removes the previous application of the United Kingdom Partnership Act of 1890. The new Partnership Act is, however, substantially the same as the United Kingdom Partnership Act of 1890 in its present-day form.

1. The Constitution of Malawi is the Second Schedule to the Republic of Malawi (Constitution) Act of 1966 which established the Republic.
2. Act. No. 27 of 1969.
3. Act No. 25 of 1969.
4. Malawi Constitution Section 31(4).
5. Republic of Malawi (Constitution) Act, Section 8(2).
6. 6th July 1966.
7. Republic of Malawi (Constitution) Act, Section 7(2).
8. The sections of the Constitution so amended are 19(1), 21(1) and 31.
9. Act No. 25, 1969, Section 5.
10. *Ibid.*, Section 6, amending Section 70(3) of the Constitution.
11. *Ibid.*, Section 7, amending Section 98(1) of the Constitution.
12. Act 31 of 1969. The apparent inconsistency of Section 70(3) of the Constitution in referring to the "Traditional Courts Act" is explained by the fact that Section 2 of the Local Courts (Amendment) Act changes the name of the Principal Act from Local Courts Act to Traditional Courts Act.
13. This ruling itself was the cause of further legislation discussed below.
14. See Malawi — Criminal Jurisdiction, *The Review*, I.C.J., No. 5, March 1970.
15. Hansard, Seventh Session, First Meeting, 1969, Revised Edition, pp. 56, 57.
16. *Ibid.*, p. 57.
17. Local Courts (now Traditional Courts) Act, Cap. 3:03.
18. Cap. 8:01.
19. Local Courts (Amendment) Bill 1969, Section 10, *The Malawi Gazette Supplement*, 12th November 1969.
20. Malawi Constitution, Section 62(1).
21. Malawi Constitution, Section 98(1).
22. Cap. 8:01.
23. Acts 5, 30, 32 of 1969.
24. Act 32 of 1969.
25. See *Regina* v. *George*, 1961–3 ALR Mal., 423.
26. Act No. 5, 1969.
27. Cap. 8:01 Section 353(2).
28. Cap 3:02, Section 18.
29. Supreme Court of Appeal Act, Cap. 301, Section 11(3). It should be noted that the D.P.P. may appeal to the High Court if he is dissatisfied on either a point of fact or a point of law. See Cap. 8:01, Section 346(2).
30. *Ibid.*, Section 12(4).
31. *Ibid.*, Section 7(*a*).
32. Act No. 4 of 1969.

CHAPTER 10

ZAMBIA

G. Care

1969 in Zambia saw legislation on all fronts designed to carry further into effect President Kaunda's Statement of the Blueprint for Economic Development of the Republic on 19th April 1968.[1] There were constitutional hurdles to be overcome before the Government could proceed to acquire full control of the natural resources of the country, and probably at the same time lay to rest some doubts upon the question whether the loss of trading rights of non-citizens was compensable or not. The main hurdle was the existence of one of the entrenched provisions of the Constitution inserted at Independence — Section 18. Section 18 protected persons from deprivation of their property except upon the payment of full adequate and prompt compensation.

None of the Fundamental Rights could be altered except with the approval of a two-thirds' majority of the National Assembly and also the approval of a majority of those of the electorate entitled to vote on a referendum.[2]

A Referendum was held on 17th June 1969 to remove Section 72(3) of the Constitution which required a Referendum to be held prior to the amendment of the fundamental freedoms and certain other sections. An overall majority was duly obtained approving this course.[2] This approval was not obtained without some pockets of resistance based not so much upon any opposition to the economic reforms but upon suspicion of the Government's motives behind the far-reaching nature of the disentrenchment of the fundamental rights which the Government had clearly indicated its intentions upon.

The programme of legislation which is required to implement fully both the Economic Reforms and the President's Policy on Humanism[3] will not be completed overnight and it is anticipated that the process of building the nation anew on sound economic foundations on the socialist lines predicated by the President on so many occasions in his speeches and writings will be spread over several years.

160

PUBLIC AND CONSTITUTIONAL LAW

The Referendum which has been referred to was the first in the history of Zambia (some may remember the suggestion that one be held in 1952 to test reaction to Federation). Before it was held detailed administrative machinery had to be set up and the country had to be prepared for this novel event both practically and politically. The Referendum Act was therefore suitably amended[4] and a Referendum Commission was set up under the chairmanship of a very experienced and able judge.[5] The Commission organised and supervised the referendum from announcement to result — in the course of so doing the Chairman probably became the Best-Known TV Personality of the Year.

Having removed the need for a referendum to amend the Constitution, amendments were then made to Chapters III and VII of the Constitution (dealing with fundamental freedoms) and Sections 71(2), 72 and 73 of the Constitution (dealing with legislative procedures, the alteration to the Constitution and the laying before Parliament of Statutory Instruments (Constitution (Amendment) (No. 5) Act No. 33 of 1969). The Act is too long to set it out in full here, but a fairly detailed summary is necessary in order to indicate not only what was changed but also directions of future detailed legislation.

Firstly, those sections dealing with property.

The Barotseland Agreement of 18th May 1964 between the Government of Northern Rhodesia (as Zambia was then called) and the Litunga (or paramount chief) of Barotseland, whereby it had been agreed that the Litunga should retain his earlier treaty rights to property within Barotseland.[6]

Section 18[7] of the Constitution was repealed and replaced by a new section changing the conditions under which a person was protected from deprivation of his property.

Under the new section[8] compensation for property compulsorily acquired is no longer required to be prompt and adequate and neither is the adequacy, apparently, judiciable: the purposes for which the property may be taken are no longer limited as before. However property now may be acquired only under the authority of an Act of Parliament which provides for the payment of compensation which in default of agreement shall be determined by resolution of the National Assembly.[9] The Act, under which the property is so taken shall prescribe the principles upon which the compensation shall be calculated and also that it shall be paid in money.

The circumstances in which it shall be deemed that any taking shall not be inconsistent with this section contain many of the usual exceptions, but in addition some new ones are worthy of special note. Section 18(4)(*a*)(ii) refers to property taken pursuant to ". . . conviction of an offence . . ." instead of "conviction of a criminal offence under the law in force in Zambia . . .".

The precise significance of this change is not clear, unless it be in service of economy of words. If it is intended to cover a person convicted of an offence and subjected to a penalty by the courts of another country (which becomes in some way enforceable in Zambia) then it is submitted that to tuck away such an important departure from present practice is unsound. Perhaps the words "law in force in Zambia" could raise a doubt on construction as to when any such law is in force; but why remove the word "criminal"?

Section 18(4)(*a*) provides that the section shall not be deemed to apply to property the removal out of or into Zambia has been attempted in contravention of any law which renders it liable to seizure.

Section 18(4)(*a*) provides that property which is abandoned, unoccupied, unutilised or undeveloped may be acquired without compensation.[9]

Also under Section 18(4)(*a*) the property of absent or non-resident owners may be taken without compensation.[9]

Under Section 18(4)(*a*) property taken in pursuance of any law relating to trusts or settlements does not fall within the section.[10]

Under Section 18(4)(*a*) property taken in pursuance of the exploitation of minerals for the marketing of property[12] is not compensable.

Under Section 18(4)(*a*) the acquisition of shares on terms agreed to by nine-tenths of the class of shareholders whose shares are acquired falls outside the protection of the section, as does property which consists of a licence or a permit.[13]

Fundamental rights

Section 10 of the Constitution, which allowed reciprocal rights of non-discrimination against Commonwealth citizens, and which was the subject of argument in *Thixton* v. *A.G.* in 1967[14] was repealed. Section 26[15] (dealing with non-derogation from fundamental rights) was amended so that its operation extended over all the fundamental rights[16]; it also changed the "reasonably justifiable in a democratic society" formula which had received judicial interpretation by Magnus, J., in *Kachasu* v. *A.G.* The new section is unusual and for this reason it is set out in full — however whether the new formula replacing the "reasonably justifiable" one will make the court's task any easier remains to be seen, but one may venture to suggest that since a court is in no position to pronounce upon policy matters it will be in no better position to decide whether putting itself (in point of time at the date of the Act upon which it is called upon to adjudicate) in the shoes of the legislature it can be expected to judge whether the circumstances could reasonably have been thought to have been necessary. The circumstances would to have been so outrageously out of proportion that only something akin to bad faith or a mental blackout could be an explanation of why the legislature acted in such a manner. One wonders whether, if this is the best that can be devised, it would not be preferable to abandon altogether any attempt at such illusory guarantees of freedom in an Act of the legislature which is supposed to be superior to other Acts.

Section 26 in full reads as follows:

"Nothing contained in or done under the authority of any law shall be held to be inconsistent with or in contravention of Sections 15, 18, 19, 21, 22, 23, 24, or 25 of this Constitution to the extent that the law in question authorises the taking, during any period when the Republic is at war or when a declaration under Section 29 of this Constitution is in force, of measures for the purpose of dealing with any situation existing or arising during that period; and nothing done by any person under the authority of any such law shall be held to be in contravention of any of the said provisions unless it is shewn that the measures taken exceeded anything which, having due regard to the circumstances prevailing at the time, could reasonably have been thought to be required for the purpose of dealing with the situation in question."

Section 24(4) and (5) and Section 26(2) to (4) are repealed and replaced by Section 26*A*. The new section provides one common method of dealing with persons who are restricted and persons who are detained. The detainee or restrictee must be informed of the reasons for his detention or restriction as the case may be within fourteen days, the fact of his detention or restriction must be advertised in the *Gazette* within one month and his entitlement to a review of his case by an independent Tribunal is after twelve months (as opposed to one month in the case of detentions and six months in the case of restrictees as was the case before).

Hitherto any declaration of emergency had to be renewed by Resolution of the National Assembly every six months. There has been in force in Zambia a Declaration of Emergency under Section 29 of the Constitution ever since UDI in Southern Rhodesia. Under the new section once a declaration has been made by the President and approved by the National Assembly, it remains in force until revoked by the President or by the National Assembly, or until there is a change, by election in the holder of the office of President.

There is added to Section 65(2) of the Constitution a new sub section (*f*) under which a person is disqualified from standing for election as a member of the National Assembly who is either restricted or detained under the Constitution for over six months. This amendment was made following upon the election of a member of the Opposition Party, A.N.C., to the National Assembly whilst he was in restriction.

The changes in the qualifications for judges will be dealt with under the next heading.

General

The post of Secretary-General to the Government was created. It would seem that the appellation "Grand Co-ordinator" would briefly describe the main duties attaching to this post (significantly the first incumbent of the post is a lawyer Mr. Mwanakatwe). Provision was also made for the payment of remuneration to the person recognised by the Speaker as Leader of the Opposition.[17]

Some changes were made in the requirements for nomination of a candidate for the National Assembly[18]. Apart from the proposer and seconder, seven nominators are required who must be registered as voters in the Constituency in which the Candidate is standing and the nomination paper must be signed in the presence of the Returning Officer for that Constituency.[19]

Two items of note on the domestic side of the political scene are of interest; first the Mumbwa District of A.N.C. was declared an "unlawful society".[19] For this district Edward Mungoni Liso, who figures in the case noted below, holds a seat in the National Assembly — one of the few Opposition members. Regulations under the Preservation of Public Security Ordinance Cap. 265 provided that a District Governor (who is the President's personal representative in a district) may compel the attendance at any meeting of any Chief or Headman. In *Liso* v. *A.G.* [20] the Court of Appeal for Zambia pronounced upon the meaning of Section 65(2)(*c*) of the Constitution. This section reads thus:

> "An elected member of the National Assembly shall vacate his seat in the Assembly . . . if he is sentenced by a court in Zambia to . . . imprisonment . . . for a term exceeding 6 months."

Liso had been sentenced to eighteen months' imprisonment by a Magistrate in 1968.[21] This sentence was later reduced on appeal to six months. The question which fell to be considered by the Court of Appeal was "had Liso forfeited his seat in the National Assembly?" The court, in allowing the appeal from the Chief Justice holding that he had, held that "sentenced" meant, in the section, "finally sentenced". As has been noticed in two Articles in the *Zambia Law Journal*[22] this raised an interesting side issue, which was whether Liso was entitled to receive the emoluments of his office for the period during which he had been suspended by the Speaker? Perhaps one aspect of the issue has been dealt with in the new Section 8*A* of the Ministerial and Parliamentary Offices (Emoluments) (Amendment No. 2) Act No. 35 of 1969, which denies the right to receive any pay whilst any member is serving a sentence of imprisonment imposed by the court (perhaps not?).

In *Kachasu* v. *A.G.* the fundamental freedom of religion was raised (Section 21 of the Constitution).

The facts of the case were that Paul Kachasu, a minor, was suspended from his school in 1966. Paul and his father were members of the Watchtower sect (Jehovah's Witnesses). Paul had apparently refused to salute the national flag or sing the national anthem because, he said through his father who brought the application on his behalf, it was contrary to his religious beliefs so to do. As a result Paul was suspended from school and remains so.

By Regulations made under Section 12(1)(*b*) of the Education Act of 1966 students at primary and secondary schools may, under certain circumstances, be required, in pursuit of national unity, to sing the national anthem and to salute the national flag — provided that it is not as part of a religious ceremony.[23] the first question was whether the regulations were *ultra vires* Sections 24 and 25 of the Principal Act: it was decided that they were not.

The second question was whether Paul's right to exercise freedom of religion under Section 21 of the Constitution was hindered by his having been required to sing the anthem and salute the flag and upon his refusal to do so his being suspended from school.

The court held that the onus of proving hindrance was upon the applicant; it also held that the onus of proving that the restrictions were not reasonably justifiable in a democratic society was likewise upon the applicant. The court further held that the applicant had discharged the onus of showing that Paul had been hindered in the exercise of his freedom of religion but that such hindrance (inherent in the regulations compelling students to sing and to salute on pain of suspension from school) was "reasonably justifiable in a democratic society, which Zambia was". Magnus, J., in the course of his judgment remarked that whether an Act was or was not reasonably justifiable was hardly a decision which a court of law was in a position to pronounce upon.[24]

Perhaps the words of Blagden, C.J., ". . . the State is not under any mandate to provide education" point to the need for constitutions to lay more emphasis upon reminders to the state as to what its duties are towards its people rather than attempt to set out somewhat unrealistic rights which these people are supposed to enjoy. The third case was not concerned with the Constitution, but with the duties of local authorities when sitting as licensing authorities under the Trades Licensing Acts. Gardner, J., held in *Chendaeka* v. *Luanshya Municipal Council*[25]:

(i) that, when sitting to decide whether to grant or refuse a licence the Council was acting in a quasi-judicial capacity
(ii) that the applicant for a licence was entitled to be informed of the reasons for the refusal of the licence
(iii) that where the refusal was on the ground of it being contrary to public interest, "public interest" in this context as used in the Act meant the local public interest.

JUDICIAL AND LEGAL SYSTEM

Under the Constitution (Amendment) (No. 5) Act No. 33 of 1969, Section 99(3) of the Constitution was amended so that in addition to the existing qualifications a person may be appointed to the Bench of the High Court or the Court of Appeal if he has for five years held any of the specified qualifications required by the Legal Practitioners Ordinance Cap. 144 for a person to be admitted in Zambia as a barrister and solicitor. The requisite period of five years' standing may be reduced and a person appointed by the President with less than five years' standing if in special circumstances the Judicial Service Commission so advises. Circumstances were envisaged when suitable black Zambian lawyers could not be appointed to the Bench because they had not held the specified qualifications for long enough. The Legal Practitioners Ordinance was amended yet again in the Legal Practitioners (Amendment) Act No. 17 of 1969 which enabled students who were citizens or residents of Zambia on 1st March 1968 and pursuing courses of study leading to their qualification as lawyers in

Commonwealth countries with common law jurisdictions to enjoy similar exemptions from the local Qualifying Examination and practical experience, to their counterparts engaged on courses of study in England or Ireland. The Act also empowered the Council of Legal Education to recognise accounts examinations which had been taken and passed in countries outside Zambia. Hitherto it had seemed that solicitors were unable to place Clients' Money on deposit with a Building Society. This was expressly permitted by an amendment to Section 37 of the Legal Practitioners Ordinance.

The Local Courts (Administration of Estates) Rules[26] made under the Local Courts Act 1966 laid down the procedure to be followed by the local courts when making orders for the appointment of administrators of estates under the Act.

CRIMINAL LAW

The position of spouses to customary marriages, when called as witnesses in criminal trials — as to competence and compellability — was put on the same footing as spouses to a marriage of Christian type. This required an amendment to Section 141 of the Criminal Procedure Code Cap. 7 and the repeal of Section 142.[27]

The continued and alarming increase in cases of armed robbery and violent assaults led to the imposition of minimum sentences for persons convicted of aggravated robbery or aggravated assault.[28] A comprehensive statute was passed to deal, mainly, with espionage. Zambia's political and geographical position render it specially vulnerable to subversive activities from inside and out, it called for a legislative answer to a situation very much akin to that which gave rise to the war-time rubric "Carelessness costs Lives". Section 4 does in fact make carelessness in particular circumstances punishable most severely.[29]

A number of cases decided during the year call attention to some procedural and criminological points.

In *Kalebwa* v. *D.P.P.*[30] the Court of Appeal held that what the accused said when he was called upon to plead to the charges could not be relied upon by the prosecution to fill the gaps in its case. The case of *Mulundika* v. *D.P.P.*[31] also decided in the Court of Appeal held that Section 14(3)[32] of the Court of Appeal Act did not give to that court the power to suspend any part of the sentence which had been imposed upon the appellant by the court below.

The Court of Appeal in *Vunika* v. *The People*[33] made a small contribution to the principles of punishment when it held that it was undesirable to combine corporal punishment with a long term of imprisonment especially where the accused was an adult. The accused had, in this case, been convicted of rape but, apart from the questionable (to put it mildly, for is it not an undignified and savage punishment?) usefulness or desirability of whipping there would seem to be no good reason for limiting this decision to cases of rape and even better reasons for applying it *a fortiori* in cases where the accused is under 21.

In the course of its judgment the court declined to apply the principle enunciated in *Reg.* v. *Green 1968*, All E.R. P77, saying that the principle that legal aid should be granted where there was a risk of a long sentence being imposed had little application in Zambia. In fact it is hoped that the Director of Legal Aid would always try to make sure that an accused in such circumstances was represented.

LAW OF PROPERTY

The Economic Reforms were pursued in two Acts during the year which are of considerable importance. In addition the Lands Acquisition Bill NAB 45 of 1969 was also tabled which would deal with the compulsory acquisition of undeveloped land and property owned by absentee owners. This Bill will be dealt with fully in next year's volume.

The Mines and Minerals Act No. 46 of 1969 vested all rights of ownership in mineral deposits in the President and provided that the acquisition of mineral rights shall henceforth be limited to Zambian citizens and companies incorporated under the laws of Zambia.

Wholesale trading was put on the same footing with regard to the issue of licences as retail trading.[34] In essence only Zambians will be granted licences to carry on wholesale trade except in the central areas of some of the larger towns and cities where existing licences, whether held by Zambians or not, may be renewed. The same Act gave to the President the power to revoke any trading licence by statutory order.

The Rent Control (Temporary Provisions) Act 1968[35] was extended yet again for another year without any major change being made to it.[36]

INDUSTRIAL AND COMMERCIAL LAW

The method of computing the tax upon the major export commodity of the country, copper, is based upon the price quoted upon the London Metal Exchange (the L.M.E.). The Copper (Export Tax) Act No. 12 of 1969 laid down the method of calculating that price. First one must calculate the mean price during the month of each of the four types of copper sales on the market (wirebars, wirebars three months and cathodes and cathodes three months) and take the mean price of those four means thus obtained and multiply the result by 0·99. Perhaps one may be forgiven for dragging in at this point the observation that protestations of desire to aid developing nations made by the capital-exporting countries have a hollow ring in the ears of the former as they see little evidence of a serious and urgent attempt to help them to help themselves by effective steps to stabilise the often violently fluctuating price of primary commodities. Zambia confirmed its participation in the Special Drawing Rights (S.D.R.'s) of the International Monetary Fund[37] although by the end of the year it had made no drawing against its allocation. Although not obviously a part of the programme for economic reform, the minimum age for persons to be eligible as directors of companies was set at 21 years.[38] This, when coupled with the definition of a Zambian Company, which requires the directors to be citizens of Zambia, effectively precludes business owned by companies from being handed over to the infant children of the non-Zambian effective owners; if this could be done the policy behind the Trades Licensing Act could be defeated.

The Agreement between Tanzania and Zambia of October 1968 concerning the building of the railway between Zambia and Tanzania (incidentally expected to be completed in about 1976) was placed under a statutory Corporation for the purposes of its implementation and operation. The Corporation is subject to the normal laws of the land.[39] The Loans and Guarantee (Authorisation) Act No. 28 of 1969 provides (*inter alia*) that in the case of any loans raised by the Government from non-residents the repayment or performance of the contract may be guaranteed by any Body Corporate, Local Authority in Zambia, Public Utility or company in which the Government holds shares. The Act does not apply to certain international multilateral financing such as the World Bank.[40]

Agricultural marketing was controlled by the National Agricultural Marketing Act No. 30 of 1969. The Board established thereunder may declare any agricultural products to be controlled products, whereupon when they are grown they vest in the Board (Section 30) and must be delivered to it. The Board will fix prices which will be paid to the producer by the Board (Section 17).

The Hire-Purchase (Amendment) Act No. 16 of 1969 gives to the Minister the power to reclassify categories of goods, add thereto or delete therefrom, vary the percentages of interest and deposits and he may also discriminate between Zambians and non-Zambians in the application of the Act (Section 26(8)(*a*)) by regulation.

In the case of *The Stamp Duty Commissioners* v. *The African Farming Equipment Co. Ltd.*[41] the Defendants attempted to mitigate the burden of stamp duty under head 8(1) of the Schedule to the Stamp Duty Ordinance Cap. 78 by drawing an agreement for the repayment of money lent in the form of a receipt. The sole security for a loan attracts *ad valorem* duty whereas a receipt only attracts a small fixed sum. The court held that the document was chargeable to *ad valorem* duty notwithstanding that "it masqueraded as a receipt".

Zambia acceded to the Conventions on Protection of Industrial Property (patents and the like), Paris Convention 1883 as supplemented up to 1958, in April 1965. It is not known whether it considers itself to be bound by the International Copyright Conventions 1908–28.

---

1. *Annual Survey of African Law*, Vol. I, 1967, p. 175.
2. Act No. 10 of 1969, Constitution (Amendment) (No. 3) Act was the Act which was put to the electorate in the Referendum on 17th June 1969. There was a gross poll

of 69·63 per cent. Of the total registered electors of 1,584,574, 904,337 voted "Yes" — Zambia Information Services *Background*, No. 41, 69.

3. *Humanism in Zambia* by K. D. Kaunda, published by Zambia Information Services.
4. Referendum (Amendment) Act No. 5 of 1969.
5. Mr. Justice Thomas Picket. He has been on the Bench in Zambia for over fifteen years and is now Judge of Appeal.
6. Barotseland Agreement, 18th May 1964. See Zambia Independence Order Section I. No. 1652 of 1964. S 20 which together with Section 18 of the Constitution were amended annulling this Agreement.
7. See *Annual Survey of African Law*, Vol. II, 1968 p. 178, No. 4.
8. Section 18(4) of the Constitution as amended.
9. See The Lands Acquisition Bill, NAB 45, of 1969.
10. Trusts Restrictions Act 1970 will be dealt with in the next volume.
11. See, *infra*, State Direction of Trade.
12. *Ibid.*
13. See *Annual Survey of African Law*, Vol I, 1967, p. 228.
14. *Selected Judgments of Zambia*, 10, 1969.
15. The Constitution of Zambia.
16. Section 11 of Act No. 33 of 1969.
17. Ministerial and Parliamentary Offices (Emoluments) (Amendment) Act No. 23 of 1969.
18. Electoral (Amendment) Act No. 18 of 1969.
19. Section I. No. 307 of 1969 made under the Societies Ordinance Cap. 262.
20 *Selected Judgments of Zambia*, No. 1, 1969.
21. *Annual Survey of African Law*, Vol. II, 1968. p. 166.
22. Vol. I, *Zambia Law Journal*, Part 1, 1969.
23. Education (Primary and Secondary Schools) Regulations 1966, Regs. 25 and 31(1)(*d*).
24. See, *supra*, p. 162.
25. *Selected Judgments of Zambia*, No, 14, 1969.
26. Section I. No. 297 of 1969.
27. Criminal Procedure Code (Amendment) Act No. 20 of 1969.
28. Penal Code (Amendment) (No. 2) Act No. 40 of 1969.
29. State Security Act No. 36 of 1969.
30. *Selected Judgments of Zambia*, No. 17, 1969.
31. *Selected Judgements of Zambia*, No. 18, 1869.
32. Section 14(3) of the Court of Appeal Act, Cap. 12, which reads:
    "On appeal against sentence the court shall, if it thinks that a different sentence should have been passed, quash the sentence passed at the trial and pass such other sentence warranted in law (whether more or less severe) in substitution therefor as it thinks ought to have been passed, and in any other case shall dismiss the appeal."
33. *Selected Judgments of Zambia*, No. 16, 1969.
34. Trades Licensing (Amendment) Act No. 41 of 1969.
35. Act No. 42 of 1969.
36. *Annual Survey of African Law*, Vol. II, 1968, p. 192.
37. Bretton Woods Agreement (Amendment) Act No. 7 of 1969.
38. Companies Ordinance (Amendment) Act No. 31 of 1969.
39. Tanzania Zambia Railway Authority Agreement (Implementation) Act No. 6 of 1969.
40. Loans and Guarantee (Authorisation) (Amendment) Act No. 39 of 1969.
41. *Selected Judgments of Zambia*, No. 15, 1969.

CHAPTER 11

RHODESIA

H. Silberberg

CONSTITUTIONAL LAW, PUBLIC and ADMINISTRATIVE LAW

In September 1968 the Appellate Division of the High Court of Rhodesia had acknowledged the Rhodesian Front Government as the *de jure* Government and the 1965 Constitution as the only valid Constitution of Rhodesia.[1] It is not surprising, therefore, that the gravamen of constitutional law in 1969 shifted from the courts to the legislature. Since the Government had planned for some time to introduce an entirely new constitutional framework, it made no attempt to amend the 1965 Constitution, except that Section 81(2) was amended so as to enable Parliament to declare a state of public emergency for a period of twelve months instead of only for three months at a time.[2] Instead the Referendum Act 1969 (34/69) was passed instructing the Officer Administering the Government to appoint a day for the holding of a referendum "for the purpose of determining the opinion of the voters" whether they were in favour of or against (*a*) the adoption of a republican form of government and (*b*) certain draft proposals for a new Constitution which were to be published in due course.[3] These proposals were published as a White Paper in a Government Gazette Extraordinary on 21st May 1969,[4] and shortly afterwards the Constitution Amendment (No. 2) Act (42/69) provided for the referendum to be held on 20th June 1969, the repeal of the 1965 Constitution, the introduction of a new Constitution and fundamental changes in the legal system of Rhodesia.[5] At the referendum an overwhelming majority of registered voters signified their approval of a declaration of a republic and of the constitutional proposals which were then embodied in three Acts of Parliament, viz. the new Constitution for Rhodesia (54/69), the Land Tenure Act 1969 (55/69) and the Electoral Act 1969 (56/69).[5a]

The 1969 Constitution

The constitution is preceded by a "Dedication" in which "(t)he peoples of Rhodesia humbly acclaim the supremacy and omnipotence of Almighty God and acknowledge the ultimate direction by Him of the affairs of men". A "Preamble" refers to the referendum of 20th June 1969 according to which "the voters of Rhodesia are in favour of the adoption of a republican form of government and . . . of the . . . constitutional proposals" (*supra*) and to the Constitution Amendment (No. 2) Act 1969 which had empowered the legislature "to enact such laws as may be deemed necessary or desirable to give effect to the wishes of the voters". It concludes with the traditional statement (as amended after UDI) according to which the new Constitution was "enacted by His Excellency the Officer Administering the Government, as the representative of the Queen's Most Excellent Majesty, by and with the advice and consent of the Parliament of Rhodesia".[6]

The Constitution itself is divided into eight chapters. Chapter I provides that the *Head of State* shall be "a President in and over Rhodesia" who shall also be Commander-in-Chief of the Armed Forces (Section 1). He will be appointed by the "Executive Council" (i.e. the Cabinet) for a period not exceeding five years and a President who has held office for two terms shall not be eligible for reappointment. He may be removed from office on a resolution passed by two-thirds of the total membership of the House of Assembly on the grounds of misconduct or inability to discharge efficiently the functions of his office.[7]

The legislative power is vested in *the Legislature* consisting of the President and Parliament, which has two chambers: the Senate and the House of Assembly.[8]

The *Senate* has twenty-three members:[9] ten Europeans, ten African Chiefs[10] and three senators nominated by the President. A European senator must be a registered voter, at least forty years old and have lived in Rhodesia for at least ten years during the fifteen years preceding his nomination. An African senator must hold the office of Chief. European senators are elected by the European members of the House of Assembly, who for this purpose constitute an "electoral college". African senators are elected by an electoral college consisting of at least fifteen members of the Council of Chiefs.[11] The Senate shall have a President and a Deputy President.[12]

The President of the Senate appoints the *Senate Legal Committee*. It consists of at least three members who must be either a retired judge of the High Court, or an attorney or advocate qualified to practise for not less than ten years, or a magistrate who has held office as such for at least ten years. The function of the Senate Legal Committee is to report on proposed legislation in advance and on subsidiary legislation (statutory instruments) in retrospect whether or not any provision therein contained would be, or is, inconsistent with the Declaration of Rights.[13]

The *House of Assembly*[14] consists, for time been, of sixty-six members of whom fifty are Europeans and sixteen are Africans.

Provision for an *increase in the number of African members* is made on the following basis:[15] When the aggregate of the income tax assessed on the income of Africans exceeds sixteen sixty-sixths of the aggregate of the income tax assessed on the income of Europeans and of Africans, the number of African members shall, with effect from the next dissolution of

Parliament, be increased so that it bears the same proportion to the total number of members in the House of Assembly as the aggregate of the income tax assessed on the income of Africans bears to the aggregate of the income tax assessed on the income of Europeans and of Africans. In the calculation of the income tax contributions from Africans and Europeans respectively, all tax chargeable in terms of the income tax law shall be taken into account, provided however that any income tax assessed on the income of a person other than an individual shall be disregarded.

When the number of African members in the House of Assembly equals the number of European members there shall be no further increase of African members. The Constitution thus envisages ultimate parity of the races in Parliament and excludes proportionate representation.

African and European members must be qualified and actually registered as voters and have been "ordinarily resident" in Rhodesia for at least five years during the period of seven years immediately prior to their nomination. An African is disqualified if he is a chief or headman and every person is disqualified irrespective of race if he is holding public office other than that of minister or deputy minister or as an officer or member of the armed forces or in the police reserve.[16]

Any Bill may originate in the House of Assembly and any Bill, other than a Money Bill or a private Bill, may originate in the Senate.[17] A Bill which originated and has received its final reading in the House of Assembly shall be transmitted to the Senate for consideration. The Senate may reject or amend any Bill submitted in this manner other than a Bill which the Speaker of the House of Assembly has certified to be a Money Bill; in respect of such a Bill the Senate may only recommend amendments. If the Senate and the House of Assembly cannot reach agreement upon a Bill originating in the House of Assembly within 180 days such Bill may none the less be presented to the President for assent.[18]

Special provision is made for the Prime Minister to certify a Bill originating in the House of Assembly which has been given a final reading as being so urgent that it is not in the national interest to delay its enactment. If a Bill which has been so certified is not agreed upon by the Senate within eight sitting days after its introduction into the Senate, the House of Assembly may resolve that it shall not be held up and be presented to the President for assent. These special provisions, however, shall not apply to a constitutional Bill or a Bill amending any entrenched provision of the Electoral Law or of the law relating to tenure of land, including Tribal Trust Land.[19]

No Bill shall become law unless the President has assented thereto and has signed it and whenever a Bill is presented to him for assent he shall declare, subject to the law and constitutional convention, that he assents or refuses to assent thereto, provided that no law shall come into operation until it has been published in the Gazette or the date of its commencement been specified in some other law which has been duly gazetted.

Parliament shall be summoned by the President in every calendar year so that there shall be never more than twelve months intervening between the last sitting of either House in any one session and the first sitting in the next session. The President *may* at any time prorogue or dissolve Parliament and he *shall* dissolve Parliament before the expiration of five years reckoned from the first day of the first sitting after a General Election, or at any other time when so advised by the Prime Minister. If the President considers that Parliament should be dissolved according to constitutional conventions and the Prime Minister does not advise the dissolution of Parliament, then the President may in his discretion dissolve Parliament.[20]

The executive government is vested in the President acting on the advice of the Executive Council consisting of the Prime Minister and Cabinet Ministers appointed by the President on the Prime Minister's advice.[21] The Prime Minister himself is appointed by the President in his discretion, provided that the President shall appoint as Prime Minister the person who in his opinion is best able to command the support of a majority in the House of Assembly. Generally speaking, the President shall act only with the advice of the Executive Council or the appropriate Minister or the Prime Minister, unless he is required under the Constitution or any other law to act in accordance with the advice of any other person. In any legal proceedings a court shall not, however, enquire on whose advice the President has acted, the nature of any advice tendered, or whether any advice was either tendered or acted upon; nor shall the court enquire into the manner in which the President may have exercised his discretion.[22]

The President shall in particular exercise the prerogative of mercy and he may at any time declare a state of public emergency.[23] In certain circumstances, the President *shall* declare or revoke a state of emergency if the House of Assembly so resolves.

The *judicial authority* is vested in the High Court. The Chief Justice and all other judges are appointed by the President on the advice of the Prime Minister who shall consult with the Chief Justice before he advises the President on the appointment of any judge other than the Chief Justice. The qualifications of a judge of the High Court shall be a prior appointment as judge of a superior court in a country in which the common law is Roman-Dutch and English an official language or admission to practise as an advocate in Rhodesia or in a country from which a judge might be appointed. A judge may be removed from office by the President for inability to discharge the functions of his office, but only after an independent Tribunal appointed by the President has recommended his dismissal.[24]

There is a general power vested in the legislature to amend, add to or repeal the Constitution,[25] provided that any such amendment is duly passed by a two-thirds majority of the total membership of the House of Assembly and of the Senate. If a proposed amendment — i.e. a constitutional Bill — does not receive the approval of the two-thirds majority of the total membership of the Senate, the House of Assembly may, after the expiration of 180 days reckoned from the day on which the amendment was first introduced into the Senate, resolve that the constitutional Bill containing that amendment should be again transmitted to the Senate for further consideration; and if the amendment is then accepted by the Senate by a simple majority of its total membership, then it shall be deemed to have been duly passed by Parliament.[26]

A *Declaration of Rights* is contained in the Second Schedule to the Constitution. This Declaration is not enforceable in court and in particular: "No court shall inquire into or pronounce upon the validity of any law on the ground that it is inconsistent with the Declaration of Rights."[27] Its legal effect will therefore require further clarification which may be forthcoming if and when the Senate Legal Committee should report that the provisions of any Bill or statutory instrument are, in its opinion, inconsistent with the Declaration of Rights. All that can be said at this stage is that the Declaration of Rights has the same significance as is usually attached to the preamble in written constitutions elsewhere. The following summary gives an outline of the main provisions of the Declaration.

The right to life is protected in so far as no person shall be deprived of his life intentionally, except in execution of the sentence of a court in respect of a criminal offence or as the result of a lawful act of war. But no law shall be construed as inconsistent with the protection of the right to life to the extent that it provides for the use of force in circumstances in which such force is necessary to prevent the commission of an offence. No person shall be deprived of his personal liberty unless it is reasonably justifiable for the purposes of national defence, public safety or public order or public health. Detention and restriction without trial fall into the first three categories and provision is made for the review of the cases of persons so detained or restricted by an independent Tribunal. The Declaration postulates further protection from slavery and forced labour as well as from inhuman treatment. It protects property and prohibits the search of persons or the entry and search of a dwelling house, except for certain clearly lawful purposes and generally "in the interests of defence, public safety, public order, public morality, public health or town and country planning". Every person is entitled to a fair hearing within a reasonable time by an independent and impartial court in all civil and criminal matters. Any person charged with a criminal offence is presumed to be innocent until he is proved or has pleaded guilty and must be afforded adequate time and facilities for his defence. The Declaration establishes the maxims *nullum crimen et nulla poena sine lege* and prohibits in particular the imposition of a heavier penalty than the one that was applicable at the time the criminal offence was committed.[28] Freedom of conscience, expression, assembly and association is likewise embodied in the Declaration, provided that no law shall be construed as being inconsistent with these freedoms in so far as it restricts them in the interests of defence, public safety, public order, public morality, public health or the economic interests of the State or to protect rights and freedoms of other persons.

As regards the functions of the Senate Legal Committee it seems clear that it can only report on whether a Bill is compatible with the Declaration of Rights and that it cannot prevent the passing of such a Bill. The Constitution envisages that the Senate will normally accept the recommendations of its Legal Committee, but it may nevertheless agree to pass a Bill which is, or appears, to be inconsistent with the Declaration of Rights if it resolves that the enactment of the provision or provisions which are not consistent with that Declaration are necessary in the national interest. The House of Assembly can, furthermore, pass any Bill which has been rejected by the Senate, if such a Bill is reintroduced into the House after a period of 180 days and this power would seem to cover Bills which the Senate has not agreed to after the Legal Committee has reported upon it as being in conflict with the Declaration of Rights. If this is correct then it would *a fortiori* apply to a Bill originating in the House of Assembly which, after it has been given its final reading, is certified by the Prime Minister as being so urgent that it is not in the national interest to delay its enactment. It would, therefore, appear that the effect of an adverse report by the Senate Legal Committee will be determined in the long run by developing a constitutional convention, although the effect of any report of the Senate Legal Committee may well depend on the authority which its members can command, just as the authority of judgment often depends on the authority of the judge who has delivered it.

The Electoral Act 1969

This Act constitutes a fundamental departure from the previous system of parliamentary representation on non-racial lines based on common voters rolls which made it possible for an African to represent a pre-dominantly European constituency and for a European to be elected by a majority of African voters. Now provision is made for separate African and European voters rolls and the Act states categorically that "A European shall not be enrolled as a voter on an African Roll" whilst, conversely, "An African shall not be enrolled as a voter on a European Roll".[29] The Act defines an "African" as "any member of the aboriginal tribes or races of Africa and the islands adjacent thereto, including Madagascar and Zanzibar; and any person who has the blood of such tribes or races and who lives as a member of an aboriginal native community", whilst a "European" is defined simply as "a person who is not an African".[30] An Asian or Coloured thus counts as a European for the purposes of the Electoral Act. To give effect to these innovations a Delimitation Commission shall be appointed as may be required from time to time. The functions of the first Commission so appointed are de-fined by the Act which provides for the division of the whole of Rhodesia into fifty European Roll constituencies (with at least eighteen rural constituencies) and eight African Roll constituencies (of which four each are allocated to Mashonaland and Matabeleland respectively).[31] In addition, the Act establishes eight tribal electoral college areas — again four each in Mashonaland and Matabeleland. Each tribal electoral college consists of all the chiefs, headmen and elected councillors of the African councils in the area. Thus the fifty European members of the House of Assembly are elected by the European voters registered in the fifty European constituencies. Eight of the sixteen African members are elected by the Africans registered as voters in the eight African constituencies, whilst the eight tribal electoral colleges elect the other eight African members.[32]

Every Rhodesian citizen who has attained the age of twenty-one years with an adequate knowledge of the English language (which is the only official language of Rhodesia)[33] and who is not otherwise disqualified[34] shall be entitled to be registered as a voter on the appropriate voters roll, provided that he possesses certain residential and means qualifications or a combination of means and educational qualifications. The educational and means qualifications for registration on the European Roll are as follows:

1. Either a bona fide income of at least £900 during each of the two years immediately preceding his claim for registration — or ownership of immovable property in Rhodesia valued at not less than £1,800.
2. Alternatively: a bona fide income of at least £600 during each of the two years immediately preceding his claim for registration — or ownership of immovable property in Rhodesia valued at not less than £1,200 *and* completion of a course of not less than four years' secondary education "of a prescribed standard".[35]

The corresponding qualifications for registration on the African Roll are:

1. Either a bona fide income of at least £300 during each of the two years immediately preceding his claim for registration — or ownership of immovable property in Rhodesia valued at not less than £600.
2. Alternatively: a bona fide income of not less than £200 during each of the two years immediately preceding his claim for registration — or ownership of immovable property in Rhodesia valued at not less than £400 *and* completion of a course of not less than two years' secondary education "of a prescribed standard".[36]

A married woman is deemed to have the same means qualifications as her husband. If a man is married under a polygamous system and in fact has more than one wife, then only that wife to whom he has been married for the longest period shall be deemed to have the same means qualification as her husband. A minister of religion and members of religious orders under vows of poverty shall, irrespective of their race, be deemed to have the required means qualifications.[37]

Provision is made for the means qualifications to be varied from time to time so as to adapt them to changes in the cost of living.[38] In addition to these variations which depend entirely on economic factors the Act provides for further and independent increases in the means *and* educational qualifications for the registration of African voters. Such increases shall be made "as the number of African members of the House of Assembly is increased"[39] so that when the numbers of African and

European members in the House of Assembly are equal, the means and educational qualifications for registration as a voter on the African Roll and on the European Roll will also be the same.[40]

Most of the provisions of the Electoral Act which have so far been discussed are entrenched in the Constitution. The remainder of the Act deals mostly with procedural and administrative matters, the prevention of corrupt and illegal practices and other offences relating to elections. Of these only the following require consideration. A person claiming to have had a right to be elected at an election of members of the Senate or the House of Assembly, and person alleging himself to have been a candidate at such election, a constituency member, or in the case of a senator or tribally elected member, any member of the electoral college concerned, may present a petition to the High Court, complaining of an undue return or election of a member of the Senate or the House of Assembly. The grounds on which such a petition may be based are lack of qualification, corrupt practice, irregularity "or any other cause whatsoever".[41] The other provision which ought to be mentioned in this context is that no person shall in any legal proceedings, whether taken to question the election or return or otherwise, be required to state for whom he has voted.[42]

Judicial control of Administrative Tribunals

In *Lapham* v. *Liquor Licensing Board, Rhodesia, et al.*, 1969 (4) S.A. 337, the High Court pointed out that an application for permission to inspect the record of the Liquor Board's proceedings held in private will not be granted as a matter of course, but only if the applicant can show that the information he seeks relates to matters which he clearly requires to enable him to substantiate the grounds on which he wishes to base an appeal against the decision. It is clear, therefore, that "fishing expeditions" will be disallowed. But if the applicant has good reason to believe that such information as has been supplied to him is not a true or bona fide reflection of the Board's reasons or findings, or that irregularities have occurred at the private proceedings, his application will be granted.

In two decisions the factors which the Board may take into account when exercising its discretion whether the grant of a liquor licence is "necessary in the public interest, having regard to the number of existing licences" (Section 52 Liquor Act) were considered. In *Kashangura* v. *Liquor Licensing Board, Rhodesia*, 1969 (1) S.A. 338 (A.D.), the court pointed out that these words must not be interpreted as meaning "necessary" or "essential in the interests of the public". They must be construed on the basis that it is the policy of the Legislature to impose certain restrictions and controls on the sale of intoxicating liquor to the public designed to reduce the risk of harm which the consumption of liquor involves, bearing in mind that draconic measures to control the consumption of alcohol have generally been shown to be ineffective and harmful. No hard and fast rules can be laid down. In short, the public is entitled to "reasonable facilities". Africans are in this regard no longer to be treated on a different basis from Europeans. Although the poverty of an area may, the race of an area cannot, be legitimately be taken into account. In *Savania* v. *Liquor Licensing Board*, 1969 (2) S.A. 598 (A.D.), it was held that the effect of the grant of an additional liquor licence on other licences in a particular area does not *per se* affect the public interest.

The Land Tenure Act 1969

The Act divides all land in Rhodesia into three categories: a "European Area", an "African Area" and a "National Area". The total extent of all the land in the European Area shall not differ by more than 2 per cent from one half of the combined extent of both the European and the African Area, and the same applies conversely to the African Area. A similar provision is made to prevent encroachment on, or an extension of, the National Area.[43] Each area is geographically defined in several schedules which form part of the Act. The National Area, parks and wild life land in the European and African areas are vested in the President.[44]

It is specifically laid down that "The European Area shall be an area in which the interests of Europeans are paramount" and that "The African Area shall be an area in which the interests of Africans are paramount".[45] Subject to certain exceptions an African shall not own, lease or occupy land in the European Area, and the owner, occupier or other person who is in control of land in the European Area shall not dispose or attempt to dispose of such land to an African; or lease it to an African, or permit or suffer an African to occupy such land. The same restrictions are imposed upon Europeans as far as land in the African Area is concerned.[46] The Minister responsible for the administration of the Act may from time to time prescribe that attendance for specified purposes at specified places or premises shall constitute "occupation" for the purposes of the Act. In particular, a person who attends a school or other educational institution as a teacher or pupil, or a hospital or other medical institution as a doctor or other employee or as a patient, or who stays at a hotel or boarding house, is regarded, for the purposes of the Act, as occupying the land on which such institution or hotel is situated.[47]

Land in the European Area which is zoned for residential, commercial or industrial purposes may be declared "a non-racial residential area" and special provision is made for African townships in the European Area, in which Africans may own, lease and occupy land, whilst a European is generally not permitted to occupy land in such townships without a special permit.[48] Corresponding provisions are made for the establishment of European townships and the declaration of non-racial areas in the African Area.[49]

An African employee working in the European Area may occupy land for the purpose and in connection with his employment in that area, provided that he is in possession of an appropriate permit. Again the same applies *mutatis mutandis* to Europeans working in the African Area.[50]

The occupation of Tribal Trust Land is governed by specific regulations.[51] It forms a geographically defined area which no person other than a tribesman shall occupy, except persons who acquired a right to such occupation before the Act came into force. In addition, persons who are not tribesmen may occupy Tribal Trust Land for administrative, religious or educational or medical purposes in the interests of tribesmen; or for the exercise of rights granted in respect of forest produce and other natural resources or the conduct of hotels established for the convenience of travellers. A tribesman is defined as a person who under African customary law is recognised as a member of a community under the control of a chief. The importance attached to the administration and use of Tribal Trust Land is emphasised by the fact that the President shall be responsible for ensuring that such land is used and occupied solely and exclusively by tribesmen subject only to the above-mentioned exceptions, although otherwise the Minister shall be responsible for its administration together with a Board of Trustees for the African Area. The President may add other land in the African Area to Tribal Trust Land and convert any Tribal Trust Land into freehold tenancy after consulting the general wishes of the tribesmen living in any area of Tribal Trust Land. Conversely, the President may certify that any Tribal Trust Land is required for any of the following purposes; mineral development, defence, improvement of communications or any other public purpose, and after consultation with the Board of Trustees,[51a] he may then declare that such areas as are so required shall cease to be part of the Tribal Trust Land. Whenever a tribesman or a tribe is dispossessed of the right to occupy land because it has been specified as being required for any of the aforegoing purposes, such tribesman or tribe shall be given a right to occupy alternative land so far as is reasonable and practicable. If alternative land is not available the tribesman or tribe shall be entitled to monetary compensation.

Whenever an individual or a class of persons occupy land in contravention of the Act the Minister may require such individual or class of persons to move from the land which he or they so occupy. If such person or persons (who must be given at least three months' notice) fail to vacate the land occupied by them, he or they may be evicted together with all their property. No compensation shall be payable to persons required to move from land which they have occupied in contravention of the Act.[52]

As far as the racial classification of statutory authorities and voluntary associations is concerned, the Minister may declare that a statutory authority or a voluntary association shall be regarded as "a European" or as "an African" for the purposes of this Act. In the case of a voluntary association or company the Minister shall establish whether the controlling interest therein is held by Europeans or Africans and the classification shall be made accordingly. In the case of a statutory authority, however, it is possible that a statutory authority may be declared as European or African, although a controlling interest therein is held by persons of another race.[53] As these particular provisions affect a number of multi-racial organisations, including churches and mission schools and hospitals, it is envisaged by the Act that such organisations may apply to the Minister for authority to own or lease land in the European Area or the African Area, irrespective of the race of their members, and that the Minister may then grant such authority subject to such terms and conditions as he thinks fit.[54]

The Act provides for the establishment of a Board of Trustees for the European Area and of a Board of Trustees for the African Area.[55] The chairman for both Boards of Trustees shall be the Chief Justice or any other judge or a retired judge of the High Court, subject to the approval of the Chief Justice. The functions of these Boards shall be, in particular, to determine whether a proposed transfer of land from the European, African or National Area to any other Area is desirable and to make recommendations on such transfers to the President. Their other functions are laid down throughout the Act. Finally, it should be noted that the basic provisions of the Act are entrenched in the Constitution.[56]

Tax law

The Finance Act 1969 (39/69) introduces a number of important amendments. Sections 20 and 21 repeal Parts III and IV of the Income Tax Act 1967 relating to the levy of supertax and undistributed profits tax. The Act also introduces new and reduced rates of tax for individuals (Section 37 RA) and special abatements for immigrants to Rhodesia after the 1st April 1968.

The Personal Tax (Repeal) Act 1969 (36/69) abolishes the levy of personal tax in Rhodesia.

Honours and Awards Act 1969

This Act (50/69) authorises the Officer Administering the Government to create honours and awards for long and meritorious service to Rhodesia, bravery, outstanding achievement, or any other purpose which he may deem fit.

JUDICIAL AND LEGAL SYSTEM

A significant change in the legal system of Rhodesia was made by the introduction of the African Law and Tribal Courts Act 1969 (24/69). It confers a far greater autonomy on African courts than they ever had before in the history of Rhodesia. The first part determines the range of cases in which African customary law shall be applied. Customary law is defined as "the legal principles and judicial practices" of a particular African tribe "except in so far as such principles or practices are repugnant to natural justice or morality; or to the provisions of any enactment: Provided that nothing in any enactment relating to the age of majority, the status of women, the effect of marriage on the property of the spouses, the guardianship of children or the admonistration of deceased estates, shall affect the application of customary law, except in so far as such enactment has been specifically applied to Africans". Customary law shall be applicable in any case between Africans which relates to seduction or adultery; the custody or guardianship of children; the devolution otherwise than by will of movable property on the death of an African (except as otherwise provided by Section 17 of the Administration of Estates Act). Customary law shall also determine, as between Africans, rights in land not held under individual registered title, matters affecting marriage consideration and generally the consequences of a marriage between Africans contracted under customary law, irrespective of whether or not such a marriage has been solemnised under the African Marriages Act. The general law of Rhodesia shall be applicable in any other case and the court may depart from customary law if the justice of the case requires and where no express rule is applicable to any matter in issue, the court shall apply the principles of justice, equity and good conduct. Where the custody of children is in issue, the paramount consideration shall be the best interests of the children. The legal capacity of Africans shall be governed by the general law of Rhodesia, but if the existence of any right or obligation depends upon customary law, the capacity of an African in relation to such right or obligation shall be determined according to customary law. A conflict between different systems of customary law may be resolved by agreement. Otherwise the customary law of the place where the cause of action arose shall be applied as a general rule. Magistrates' Courts have jurisdiction in civil cases between Africans, but where a case between Africans or between an African and a non-African is governed by customary law, it shall be transferred to a District Commissioner's Court.

In addition, disputes between Africans may now also be decided by tribal courts. A tribal court shall consist of a chief or headman who will preside over the proceedings and at least two assessors chosen by the President according to customary practice. The limitations previously imposed on the jurisdiction of African courts have been removed, except that a tribal court shall have jurisdiction only over civil cases which are to be decided according to customary law and that no tribal court can dissolve a marriage contracted under the Marriage Act 1964 — i.e. a marriage concluded according to Christian rites or by civil ceremony before a marriage officer. A tribal court also has jurisdiction in a civil case between an African and a non-African in which the aforegoing requirements are satisfied and if the non-African consents to the jurisdiction.

A tribal court is entitled to try a criminal case in which the accused is an African and the complainant is either also an African or, if he is a non-African, he has consented to the jurisdiction of the tribal court, or where there is no complainant other than the Government. A tribal court has no criminal jurisdiction over an accused who is a member of the police force, a prison officer, or a district messenger, unless a senior officer of the accused consents to the jurisdiction.

A tribal court's jurisdiction is limited to the common law offences of theft (excluding the theft of certain types of property) and malicious injury to property (excluding damage to structures used or designed for the accommodation of persons). A tribal court has no jurisdiction, even in regard to these common law offences, if the value of the property stolen or damaged exceeds £20 ($40.00).

A tribal court may impose a fine not exceeding £20 ($40.00), or in the case of a male under the age of nineteen years, a moderate whipping, or such other penalty recognised by customary law as may be prescribed.

In civil cases the only appeal from a tribal court lies to the Tribal Appeal Court. In criminal cases the accused may appeal first to the Tribal Appeal Court and from there to a Provincial Magistrates' Court and finally to the Appellate Division of the High Court. A District Commissioner may set aside the proceedings if the tribal court had no jurisdiction. Any such annulment and certain other remedial actions by a District Commissioner are limited as he is merely given powers of supervision (as has been seen); there is no appeal to his court and normal powers of review are exercised by the General Division of the High Court. There is no right of legal representation before a tribal court, except as required or permitted by customary law.

Matters of procedure and evidence in tribal courts and in Tribal Appeal Courts (in civil and criminal cases) are governed by customary law. A Tribal Appeal Court is constituted for each province and has three members who are chiefs and presidents of tribal courts.

The Advocates Act 1969 (15/69) lays down revised conditions for the *admission of advocates* of the High Court of Rhodesia. An applicant must satisfy a Board of Examiners that he has passed an examination in Latin and that he is proficient in written and spoken English, unless he was previously appointed as one of Her Majesty's Counsel in the United Kingdom or a Senior Counsel in the Republic of South Africa, in which case he shall *ipso facto* be admitted. The qualifications required of any other applicant are that he has obtained a South African law degree and passed the local examinations; or that he has obtained the post-graduate Diploma in Law of the University College of Rhodesia; or that he has obtained a recognised overseas law degree and been admitted as a barrister in the United Kingdom or as an advocate in the Republic of South Africa and is entitled to practise in the country in which he was admitted, and further, that he has either passed the local examinations or obtained the aforementioned Diploma in Law. There are certain alternative qualifications and provisions for exemptions. An applicant must either have practised as an advocate or barrister or, at any rate, read in chambers for at least three months and he must not within the six months immediately preceding his application have practised or otherwise been connected with the practice of an attorney, solicitor, conveyancer or notary public, either in Rhodesia or elsewhere. The Act also provides for the removal of an advocate from the Roll of Advocates on his own application or on that of the Attorney-General or on the application of the majority of advocates practising in Rhodesia. The sole right of audience in the High Court is preserved.

Attention is also drawn to the High Court Amendment Act 1969 (57/69), the Witnesses Compulsory Attendance Act 1969 (13/69) and the Legal Assistance and Representation Act 1969 (20/69).

In *R.* v. *Schaube-Kuer*, 1969 (2) S.A. 40 (A.D.)[57] the Appellate

Division considered the question whether it had the right to *overrule a decison of the Federal Supreme Court of Rhodesia and Nyasaland* "which was a court of comparable jurisdiction to this court". Beadle, C.J., thought that the Appellate Division should regard a decision of the Federal Supreme Court in much the same way as the court regarded its own decisions and as the Appellate Division would regard its own decisions. The Federal Supreme Court had accepted that it had jurisdiction to overrule its own decisions: see *Attorney-General of Northern Rhodesia* v. *Dimakopoulos*, 1961 R. & N. 833. The Privy Council and the South African Appellate Division both consider that they have the right to overrule their own decisions and as they were also previously (the Privy Council until 1968 and the South African Appellate Division until the establishment of the Federal Supreme Court) the final Court of Appeal for Rhodesia there was thus "strong precedent for the proposition that this court can overrule one of its own decisions", particularly since the Appellate Division had "in effect stepped into the shoes of the Federal Supreme Court". However, in exercising the right to overrule the decision of the Federal Supreme Court, the Appellate Division would apply the same degree of caution as it would apply in overruling one of its own decisions and after paying due regard to the principle of *stare decisis*.

CRIMINAL LAW

During the year under review the High Court decided a number of interesting cases which raised *inter alia* problems of causation and foreseeability, the defence of automatism and of "impossible attempts".

In *R.* v. *Dick*, 1969 (3) S.A. 267, the accused was charged with inciting another man to murder a woman by the administration of D.D.T. The accused had originally given the other man certain herbs and asked him to administer them to the woman in the hope that she would consent to live with him. In addition, the accused gave the other man a quantity of D.D.T. powder which he asked him to administer to the woman if the herbs failed to fulfil their purpose. The herbs were quite useless for the accused's object and the D.D.T. was equally harmless as the quantity supplied was too small. It was held that neither this fact nor that the incitement to murder was conditional upon the failure of the herbs, precluded the court from convicting the accused of incitement to murder as he clearly had the intention of bringing about the woman's death if the herbal treatment failed.

In *R.* v. *Kantor*, 1969 (1) S.A. 457 (A.D.), the question arose whether a person can be convicted of an offence which he intended to commit, but finds out afterwards that he did not, in fact, commit it. The appellant, a dealer in stamps and coins, had been convicted of contravening the Rhodesian Exchange Control Regulations which prevent the export of goods in excess of £25 in value without a valid export permit. He had bona fide acquired several sheets of stamps from a private individual which appeared to be misprints and therefore valuable from a collector's point of view. At the time, the Rhodesian Post Office had issued stamps with an official overprint and it was this type of stamp which the appellant had acquired because he thought that the fault which made them valuable was contained in the overprint. He received an offer for them from a private collector in Johannesburg and took the stamps personally to South Africa where he sold them for £2,250. Subsequently, it was discovered that the person from whom the appellant had acquired the stamps had forged the overprints. The appellant informed the buyer and agreed to refund the purchase price as the stamps were either valueless or, at the most, worth their face value which was less than £25. It was not, therefore, possible for him to achieve his criminal purpose. It was conceded that "on principle the fact that an accused's criminal purpose cannot be achieved, because the means are, in the existing or in all conceivable circumstances, inadequate, or because the object is, in the existing, or in all conceivable circumstances, unattainable, does not prevent his endeavour from amounting to an attempt". (Per Schreiner, J.A., in *R.* v. *Davies and Another*, 1956 (3) S.A. 52.) But it was argued that the contravention of the Exchange Control Regulations was one of those exceptions where an attempt to contravene a statute is not an offence if the object which the accused seeks to achieve is absolutely impossible of attainment. The contention was that the relevant regulations are not concerned with the export of valueless goods as there is no reason to prohibit the export of such goods. Therefore, it could be inferred from the purpose of the Act that it was never intended to make what the appellant did an offence. These arguments were rejected. Firstly, it has been finally decided that an attempt may be criminal, though the attainment of the accused's object is absolutely impossible. Secondly, the argument based on the purpose of the regulations would apply to almost any attempt to contravene a statute where it was absolutely impossible for the accused to achieve his criminal object. For example (Beadle, C.J., pointed out) if it were a statutory offence to administer poison unlawfully to a person and the accused, genuinely intending to administer arsenic, by mistake put sugar in his victim's food: there can be no doubt that such an act would constitute an attempt. As regards the general purpose of the Exchange Control Regulations, it seemed that it was to prohibit and discourage the export of goods over £25 in value and that for this reason the accused's conduct constituted an attempt.

Two cases raised problems of *causation and foreseeability*. In *R.* v. *John*, 1969 (2) S.A. 560 (A.D.), it was held that on a charge of culpable homicide (manslaughter) "foreseeability is an essential element to be considered in deciding whether a causal connection exists between the unlawful act or omission and the death of the victim". The somewhat complicated facts may be summarised, as follows: The accused and his wife were involved in a prolonged fight. Eventually the wife, who was six months' pregnant, broke away and ran some 200 yards when she either fell into or took refuge in a fairly large deep pool of water where she drowned. The accused had chased his wife carrying a hoe. He had threatened to kill her, but there was no acceptable evidence that he had prevented her from leaving the pool when she made efforts to do so. It was argued that there was no causal connection sufficient in law to say that the accused had caused his wife's death. Macdonald, J.A., examined the relationship between causation and foreseeability; after an exhaustive survey of Roman-Dutch authorities and of the views expressed by Hart and Honoré in their work on Causation in the Law and of various other writers he came to the conclusion that foreseeability must be regarded as a separate element in the form of *mens rea* and that the degree of foreseeability which has been described as the "guilt nexus is not something different from the degree of foreseeability required to establish the causal nexus for the purpose of legal liability". In the result, it was held that the accused ought to have foreseen that the deceased fleeing terror-stricken might "in her headlong flight collide violently with some obstacle, fall . . . into a hole or other pitfall, or fearing death or serious injury at the hands of the appellant, take an avenue of escape which . . . was scarcely less dangerous than the threatened assault". The accused had, therefore been rightly convicted of culpable homicide.

The question of causation and foreseeability was again considered in *R. v. Douglas and Another*, 1969 (4) 239 (A.D.), where the two accused had assaulted their victim who had died as a result of the assaults. At the trial it had been argued in mitigation of sentence that the court should not take too serious a view of the crime because the accused could hardly have foreseen that death would result from their actions. The trial judge remarked that he did not find it necessary to go into the question of the extent to which the accused could have foreseen death resulting from their actions. On appeal Beadle, C.J., pointed out that the case had been decided before the judgment in *R. v. John* (*supra*) had been delivered and that until then "it was not customary for the courts of this country to go into the question of 'foreseeability' in charges of culpable homicide". He thought that on the facts of the case there was no doubt whatsoever that the accused ought to have foreseen the likelihood of death resulting from their actions. But he went on to consider the "procedural point" whether in all cases of culpable homicide a court should expressly mention that it had applied its mind to the question of "foreseeability". The learned Chief Justice thought that in the overwhelming majority of cases it will be found that the accused ought to have foreseen that death might result from his actions "even though death may not often result from the particular type of assault with which the case is concerned". In these cases the court will not be criticised if it fails to draw attention to what is quite obvious and does not state that it has considered the question of foreseeability, though in exceptional cases where there may be some doubt trial courts should draw attention to the fact that they had not overlooked that question. It would seem, therefore, that the attitude of the Rhodesian courts was correctly expressed by Macdonald, J.A., in *R. v. John* (*supra*) when he said that "the determination of legal cause whether in civil or criminal cases necessarily involves at some point the application of common sense and human experience to arrive at what is essentially a value judgment".

The problems involved in the defence of "*sane automatism* were" considered in *R*. v. *Senekal*, 1969 (4) 478 (A.D.). The accused had been charged with murder in the following circumstances. He had been fighting with another man at a workmen's club. Others tried to restrain him, but he broke away and went to his room to fetch a knife and returned to the club with the object of renewing his attack. Again other workmen intervened and in the course of the struggle which ensued the accused stabbed a man who tried to wrest the knife from him. That man subsequently died. The accused raised the defence that as a result of alcohol which he had consumed and of injuries which he had received to his head during the fight, he did not know what he was doing when he stabbed the deceased. In the trial court the accused was acquitted. On appeal the Attorney-General submitted that the accused was at the most entitled to a special verdict in terms of Section 231 of the Criminal Procedure and Evidence Act (Chap. 31) read in conjunction with Section 31(1) of the Mental Disorders Act (Chap. 164). The latter section provides that if it is found that an accused committed an offence, but that he was at the time when he committed it "mentally disordered or defective so as not to be responsible according to law for his action", a special verdict shall be returned "to the effect that the accused is guilty of the act . . . charged against him but was mentally disordered or defective as aforesaid when he did the act . . .". The problem was, therefore, to determine the type or types of mental disorders which the law recognises as relieving a person from responsibility for his actions. The Mental Disorders Act defines a "mentally disordered or defective person" as a person "who is suffering from mental illness, arrested or incomplete development of mind, psychopathic disorder or any other disorder or disability of mind". This definition which was introduced by an amendment in 1967 has no counterpart in the South African Mental Disorders Act on which the Rhodesian statute was originally modelled. The South African cases dealing with this problem and according to which a special verdict can be brought only in the case of persons who are permanently mentally disordered (*R*. v, *F*., 1960 (4) S.A. 27; *S*. v. *Mahlinza*, 1967 (1) S.A. 408) are, therefore, only of limited assistance. None the less, Beadle, C.J., considered the principles enunciated in them and concluded that their effect was to extend, and not to limit, the meaning of the Rhodesian definition (*supra*). In the result, the learned Chief Justice came to the following conclusions. Firstly, "for an accused to be mentally disordered or defective so as not to be responsible according to law for his action, it is not necessary that the disorder or defect of the mind be of a permanent nature or of a nature that is likely to recur. It is sufficient if it is of a purely temporary character". Secondly, "the cause of the mental disorder or disability is irrelevant". An accused who, because of an injury to his head, does not know what he is doing thus suffers from a "disability of mind" and is not responsible in law for his action because he acted in a state of automatism due to the injury which he received. But such persons are not entitled to a verdict of not guilty and only a special verdict can be returned against them. Beadle, C.J., stressed, however, that he was dealing only with the case of automatism caused by injury — where the mind is so seriously disabled from an injury that the accused is quite unconscious of his actions. He expressly left open the question whether "there is such a thing as 'sane automatism' under Rhodesian statutory law" and he refused to "express any view on the place such automatism now occupies in our criminal law".

It now seems clear that a woman can be convicted of *rape* in Rhodesian law. In *R. v. D.*, 1969 (2) S.A. 591 (A.D.), it was held that where an accused has induced fear in his mind of his victim which disables her from exercising a free choice, then, whether he himself commits rape upon her or causes her to submit to a third party who may well believe on reasonable grounds that she is a consenting party, *the accused himself* is guilty of rape. Nor does it seem to be necessary that a person who has induced such fear in a woman that she will submit to a third party must be present when the sexual intercourse takes place. The all-important question, so far as the person inducing such fear in a woman's mind as will cause her to submit to sexual intercourse is concerned, seems to be only whether he in fact succeeded in inducing the necessary degree of fear in her and if such is the case, then the maxim *qui facit per alium facit per se* will apply. In the above case two men were involved, but the principle enunciated in the case should logically also apply to a woman. The only question which remains is whether a court will, when a woman will one day actually be charged with rape, bridle at the suggestion that she is a "principal" and refer to Lord Wright's statement that the logic of the law is not always exact. (Cf. *R. v. Bourne*, (1952) 36 Cr. App. R. 125.)

It is, of course, clear that in the above case the court was influenced by the fact that the moral turpitude of a person (be it a man or a woman) who coerces a girl or a woman to submit to sexual intercourse against her will should not go unpunished. It is interesting, therefore, to compare *R. v. D.* with the attitude of the court in *R. v. M.*, 1969 (1) S.A. 328. In that case the accused was charged with committing an unnatural offence on a girl under the age of twelve years with whom he had sexual intercourse *per anum*. Some of the older Roman-Dutch law authorities regarded unnatural intercourse of a man with a woman as a crime, but it is no longer referred to as such by later writers including Huber and van der Linden. But since none of these writers dealt with the question at all it is doubtful whether or not in Voet's day such conduct constituted a crime. However, the court accepted that even if it was a crime in those days, it has since been abrogated by disuse and, therefore, considered whether the accused could be convicted of any other offence, although no alternative charge had been preferred against him. Beadle, C.J., would probably have adopted this course if the matter had been *res nova*, but as the Appellate Division of the Supreme Court of South Africa had expressed a different view in *R*. v. *M*., 1959 (3) S.A. 332, he categorically declined to adopt an approach which would be in conflict with the South African view.

There was no major legislation affecting criminal law in 1969, though mention should be made of the Criminal Law Amendment Act 1969 (12/69) which amended a number of sections of the Criminal Procedure and Evidence Act (Chap. 31) and also introduced a new section (403A) dealing with the power of the courts to hold criminal proceedings *in camera*. This Act also repealed the Libel Act (Chap. 41), but revived specifically the common law relating to the offence of criminal *injuria* to the extent to which it had been substituted by the Libel Act.

CONTRACT

In *Springvale Ltd.* v. *Edwards*, 1969 (1) S.A. 464 (A.D.), the question of the extent to which a term should be implied into a contract was considered in a context in which other civil law systems would probably have approached the comparatively simple problem of this case through the doctrine of *culpa in contrahendo*. The facts which were not in dispute may be summarised as follows: In 1962 the defendant entered his son on the waiting list of the private school conducted by the plaintiff. He then received a prospectus which contained a reservation which gave the plaintiff the right to alter and increase its fees — then ammounting to £270 *per annum* — by giving one term's notice. Conversely, parents of pupils at the school had the right to remove their children from the school by giving one term's notice on the first day of each term. During the first term in 1965 the plaintiff offered the defendant a place at the school as from the first term in 1966. This offer was accepted in March 1965 and the defendant acknowledged in writing that the fees for the first term 1966 would be payable, unless a term's notice in writing was given. Meanwhile the plaintiff increased the amount of its annual fees from £270 to £300. It is not quite clear whether that increase was announced before or after the defendant had accepted the place offered to his son, but it was not disputed that when he accepted that place, he bona fide believed that the fees were still £270 per year. In October 1965 the defendant "cancelled" his acceptance. By then, the third term of 1965 had begun and it was, therefore, impossible for the defendant to give one term's notice for the first term in 1966. He justified his cancellation on the ground that the plaintiff had failed to advise him of the increase in fees and that a notification to this effect should have been given either when he accepted the place or as soon thereafter as the increase had been decided upon. The plaintiff refused to accept this explanation and sued the defendant for payment of the fees for the first term of 1966. It must be assumed that the defendant cancelled the contract as soon as he learnt of the increase in fees. The court refused to imply a term imposing on the plaintiff the obligation to advise the defendant of the increase in fees because it would involve an alteration of the express provision requiring only "one term's notice" of an increase in fees. In the circumstances, the court thought that clearly there was no basis for implying such an alteration. One cannot help wondering to what extent the fact that the increase in fees was comparatively small influenced the decision. It was pointed out that the defendant knew when he accepted the offer of a place that he was contracting to pay the current fees and he also knew that these were subject to alteration. If the exact (!) amount of the fees was important to him he should, the court thought, have enquired whether they had been or were about to be altered.

In *Florencio* v. *Kreuter*, 1969 (2) S.A. 673, the question arose in what circumstances a building contractor was entitled to a *quantum meruit* payment. The defendant had entered into a contract for the construction of a dwelling house by the plaintiff for £6,400. He alleged that the contract had not been properly completed and retained almost £800 to cover the costs of remedying certain defects and omissions, alternatively as damages. Although not every complaint was held to be justified, the plaintiff was unable to establish that he had complied with some of the contract requirements and the court acknowledged that the defendant was within his strict rights in insisting on compliance with the terms of the contract. But the question was whether the complaints which the defendant justifiably made about defects supported a finding of failure to complete the contract as a whole which depended on whether "an important attribute to the house has not been completed". The costs of remedying the defects came to just over £200 and the plaintiff had already agreed, albeit without prejudice, to rectify £170 worth of these defects. In the circumstances, judgment was given for the plaintiff on his claim less an amount of some £40 in respect of a defect which could not be remedied and subject to the proviso that £170 should be paid only after the plaintiff had carried out the repairs which he had promised. The court approached the case on the basis that an owner may not withhold substantial sums under a building contract simply because the contractor has failed to comply with all his obligations, if the owner would be unjustly enriched in the result. In such a case the contractor would qualify for payment on a *quantum meruit* basis and in order to establish such a claim, the contractor "must show that the owner has been unjustly enriched by the contract works to the extent of the unpaid portion of the contract price less the cost of remedying any defects and that he did not wilfully abandon the contract before completion, but bona fide believed he had completed the contract at the time when the owner took occupation".

DELICT

There is no case law or legislation affecting or concerning the principles of the Roman-Dutch law of delict in Rhodesia to report for the year under review. It should be noted, however, that at long last a draft Apportionment of Damages Bill, which will *inter alia* abolish the common law doctrine of contributory negligence, appears to have reached the stage at which it may confidently be expected to become law in the course of the year 1970.

FAMILY LAW

In *Hill* v. *Hill*, 1969 (3) S.A. 544 (A.D.), the Appellate Division reversed the decision of Goldin, J. reported in 1968 (4) S.A. 179. A comparison between the two judgments shows how difficult it really is to draw the line between the guilt and the breakdown principle in the law of divorce. In this case the husband had instituted divorce proceedings against his wife in terms of Section 3(c) of the Matrimonial Causes Act (Chap. 179) on the ground that she had treated him with such cruelty as made the continuance of married life insupportable. He had also asked for the custody of the minor children (aged twelve, eleven and seven years respectively). His complaint was that his wife's conduct after she had adopted the Jehovah's Witness faith had made life unbearable for him. The wife spent a great deal of her time attending religious meetings and going from house to house preaching her faith. This practice made social life difficult and caused embarrassment to the husband. At home the wife insisted on making her views known not only to her husband but also to the children who thus learnt that in their mother's view the Roman Catholic Church was fathered by the devil and that the Anglican Church (to which the husband still belonged and of which the wife had also been a member before she embraced her new faith) is an off-shoot of the Roman Catholic Church; that the world was bound to come to an end in about ten years' time and that this period should be used to preach the Gospel and not be wasted on making long-term educational and vocational or professional plans; that it was wrong to submit to medical treatment (such as blood transfusions) and to acknowledge any other authority than that of God (and that it was inconsistent with her belief to recognise for instance the National Anthem or to undergo military training). At one time, the wife had insisted on taking the children to her religious meetings and she had tried actively to influence them beyond making her views known to them. At the trial, however, the wife genuinely acknowledged that the father's rights in the exercise of the parental power are greater than those of the mother and the children's upbringing in the faith of the Anglican Church was accepted by her. Moreover, the trial judge appeared to be satisfied that the mother would not prevent a blood transfusion or similar medical treatment, if it should become necessary for the children — this was a point about which the father had expressed concern — and that she had generally accepted that "in any such matter applying to the children" her husband's decision would be binding on her. As regards the children who had given evidence, the learned judge had formed the "clear impression that they (were) perfectly normal, well-adjusted and happy children (who were) extremely fond of both parents and the only cause of unhappiness mentioned related to their fear that their parents (might) decide to break up what they consider(ed) to be a happy home". In the result, he refused to grant the divorce. He thought that no individual act of cruelty alleged by the plaintiff was sufficiently serious to make the continuance of married life insupportable, but accepted that "an accumulation of minor acts of ill-treatment could amount to cruelty as required by law for the granting of a . . . divorce" and that there is always "the last straw which breaks the camel's back". Nevertheless, not everything which a spouse resents or finds difficult to tolerate amounts to cruelty in law: "married couples have often to deal with differences of opinion, honestly and sincerely held and with conviction that the other is in grave error". Not every act or conduct which might be described as "cruel" justifies the granting of a divorce on the grounds of cruelty, for "otherwise one goes from one case on the edge, to a case a little more on the edge, as this is, and in the end the whole thing becomes absurd".

The Appellate Division took an entirely different view. To begin with, it placed far greater emphasis on certain facts than the trial judge had done — namely that the husband's health had suffered and that the companionship and cohabitation essential to the marriage had come to an end. As far as the wife's change of religion was concerned, the court said that no hard and fast rule can be laid down, whether a departure from the beliefs upon which the marriage was founded amounts to mental cruelty and that in each case the degree of a change and its effect upon the lives of the parties must be examined. In this case, there was no doubt that the wife never intended to be cruel to her husband and that she honestly believed she was doing the best for him and the children, but a subjective intention to be cruel is not essential, and whilst allowance must be made for changes in the intellectual and spiritual development of the spouses, there was here "a fundamental departure from the basis on which the marriage was concluded" and the wife had adopted "a way of life different from that of most religions founded upon the Bible". In addition, her whole way of life was different from the husband's in every other respect. He believed in loyalty to his country, whilst she would prefer the children to be imprisoned rather than undertake military service. He wanted to give his children a secure future — she told them that Armageddon was at hand. Nor did the Appellate Division regard the offer to acknowledge the husband's superior parental power as sufficient. On all these grounds the court held that the husband was entitled to a divorce and to the sole guardianship and the custody (if necessary the sole custody) of the minor children despite the declared preference of the two elder boys, because the husband's influence was more likely to make them into useful members of society.

In two cases, *Jagoe* v. *Jagoe*, 1969 (4) S.A. 59, and *Ex parte Walton*, 1969 (3) S.A. 340, the court emphasised again that in all cases concerning the *custody of minor children* the interests of such children are paramount, irrespective of the rights and wrongs of the dispute between the parents. See also the discussion of *Jagoe*'s case *infra*: Conflict of Laws.

The question whether intercourse between a husband and wife a few days before the trial of a divorce action pending between them amounts to *condonation* was considered in *B.* v. *B.*, 1969 (2) S.A. 584. The wife who claimed a divorce on the grounds of cruelty alleging excessive drinking, profligate behaviour and perpetual dishonesty, had when the husband came to see her "succumbed to the temptation to have intercourse with her husband, prompted by her natural physical desire". But in such circumstances it cannot be assumed that a true reconciliation takes place, and in this particular case the cruelty was in any event immediately revived when the husband showed shortly afterwards that he had in no way changed his mode of life and conduct.

Mountford v. *Mukukumidzi*, 1969 (2) 56 (A.D.), decided that in *affiliation proceedings* the court may take into consideration the resemblance between the child (even when it is only a few months old) and the alleged father, although too much weight should normally not be given to resemblance and colour. Furthermore, whilst the evidence of the unmarried mother must be assessed critically and with caution, the degree of proof required is no higher than that in any other civil dispute.

PROPERTY

Section 75 of the Town and Country Planning Act (Chap. 135) seems to be a perennial source of litigation. It provides that no person shall sub-divide or enter into any agreement for the sub-division of any property, unless the permission of the Minister responsible for the administration of the Act has first been obtained. Since any agreement for the sale or alienation of a property and any agreement whereunder a person is given a right, whether vested or contingent or conditional, to acquire any portion of a property or a right to erect a building on any portion of a property belonging to another person, is regarded as an agreement for the sub-division of that property, the number of disputes over the effect of this section is not very surprising. In *Rensford* v. *Rainsford*, 1969 (1) S.A. 13, the defendant claimed the right to enter upon a portion of the plaintiff's land in reliance on a document in terms of which the plaintiff had agreed "to an appropriation . . . of one thousand acres of land (by the defendant) to be transferred when (certain) instalments had been paid". At the time of the agreement the rights to the land of which the 1,000 acres were a portion were held jointly by the plaintiff and the defendant, but the land was subsequently registered in the name of the plaintiff only and it seemed clear that the "appropriation agreement" in favour of the defendant was made in anticipation of the termination of the joint venture. When the defendant sought to exercise his rights the plaintiff objected on the grounds that the agreement was void because it was an agreement for the sub-division of the land for which the consent of the Minister had not been obtained. This contention was upheld, but the court was clearly not satisfied that the plaintiff should succeed upon what seemed to be a technicality and indicated that it might grant the defendant some other remedy in regard to the recovery of what was obviously "his share of the land". The result was, as the report shows, a request for a postponement *sine die* — obviously for the purpose of arriving at a settlement between the parties.

In *Savvas* v. *Liquor Licensing Board, Rhodesia, et al.*, 1969 (4) S.A. 333 (A.D.), the appellant had applied for the issue of a new bottle liquor licence in respect of two shops which he had leased for a period of ten years. The Board refused the application on the ground that such a lease was "an agreement for the sub-division of (the) property" and that ministerial permission therefore had not been obtained so that the lease was void and the appellant had no legal right of occupation to the premises. It is clear that Section 75 (*supra*) does not apply to short leases, i.e. leases of less than ten years, but a long lease, i.e. one of ten years or more which is capable of registration in the Deeds Office, has for certain purposes been regarded as an alienation, and it was treated as such for the purposes of Section 75 of the Town and Country Planning Act in *Brymoira (Pvt.) Ltd.* v. *Lalla*, 1968 (3) S.A. 150; however, the court distinguished that case on the facts and relied on the juxtaposition of the words "alienation" and "sale" in Section 75 to give the former its ordinary grammatical meaning, viz. "to transfer ownership". Accordingly, a long lease does not amount to a sub-division of property and the Board was ordered to consider the application on its merits.

The most important legislation affecting the law of property in 1969 was, no doubt, the Land Tenure Act. Indeed, its effect is so fundamental that it was thought appropriate to deal with it in the section: Constitutional, Public and Administrative Law.

An Act which reflects the importance attached to agricultural development is the Agricultural Land Settlement Act 1969 (59/69). It authorises the Minister to establish schemes for the settlement of persons on and the alienation to such persons of agricultural land; the training of persons in farming and the development of a farming industry. It envisages applications for the allocation, in particular, of Government land to individuals who will develop such land for agricultural purposes. Any such allocations will, in the first instance, be made on the basis of a lease and it is interesting that in this Act the word "alienate" includes lease.

Attention is also drawn to the following statutes: Mines and Minerals Amendment Act 1969 (17/69), Mines and Minerals Amendment (No. 2) Act 1969 (61/69), Town and Country Planning Amendment Act 1969 (21/69).

Industrial property

The Registered Designs Amendment Act 1969 (31/69) amends various sections of the Registered Designs Act 1958. In particular, it introduces a new definition of the circumstances in which a design shall be deemed to be "a new and original design" capable of registration under the Act. It amends the provisions relating to the display of designs at industrial or international exhibitions and the section of the Principal Act relating to the copyright in registered designs (which subsists for a period of fifteen years from the date of registration).

The Copyright Act 1966 is amended by the Copyright Amendment Act 1969 (29/69) which brings the Principal Act into line with the new provisions of the Registered Designs Act.

Lonrho Ltd. v. *Salisbury Municipality*, 1969 (2) S.A. 678, was concerned with the question whether the nominee of the actual *first and true inventor* could acquire the rights of a patentee under the (now repealed) Patents Act (Chap. 222) of the 1939 Edition of the Rhodesian Statutes and then, by assignment, confer upon the actual inventor the protection of the Patents Act. It was held that Chapter 222 was modelled on the Canadian, and not the English, legislation and that only the actual first and true inventor could acquire the rights of a patentee on registration of the invention. Chapter 222 was replaced by the Federal Patents Act, 13 of 1957 which is still in force in Rhodesia and which introduced considerable alterations into the Rhodesian Patent Law. *Inter alia* it expressly excludes the "communicatee" of a patent from the definition of "inventor" (Section 2) and does "not contain the restrictive limitation as to prior knowledge or user of the invention anywhere else in the world" which was a feature of the previous law.

SUCCESSION

The limits beyond which the court may not go in the construction of a statute which it regards as outdated are well illustrated in *Perlmutter et al.* v. *The Master*, 1969 (1) S.A. 8, which was reversed by the Appellate division *sub nom. Braude N.O.* v. *Perlmutter et al.*, 1969 (4) S.A. 101 (A.D.). The case turned on the meaning of Section 2 of the Deceased Estates Succession Act (Chap. 52), which provides that a last will "executed by any person prior to marriage, shall become null and void unless such person endorses on such will that it is declared that the same shall remain of full force and effect" after that person's marriage and, further, that such endorsement "shall be duly signed and witnessed in the manner required in the case of a will". Here the testator had executed a valid will in 1937 shortly before his marriage. It was clearly made in contemplation of that marriage and the intended wife was unequivocally identified and referred to as "my future wife" in a number of provisions of that will. Reference was also made to "any children born of my marriage with (my said future wife)". The marriage was duly celebrated, and lasted until the testator's death in 1964. It was then discovered that the will had never been endorsed so that it was prima facie null and void. The judge at first instance was obviously loath to accept this result in the case of a perfectly reasonable and fair will. He, therefore, thought it permissible to extend the *ratio decidendi* of *Sanua* v. *The Master*, 1956 (1) S.A. 158 (A.D.), where it had been held that Section 2 (*supra*) does not require a formal endorsement in the strict sense of that word, but that it is sufficient if the testator includes a clause *in* his will in which he directs *expressis verbis* that the will shall remain in force after his marriage to the woman named therein. The learned judge, therefore, declared the will as valid, having regard to its unequivocal meaning.

The Appellate Division felt that the decision in the court below placed too much emphasis upon the intention of the testator and disregarded the intention of the Legislature with which the court must be concerned when it construes a statute. *Sanua*'s case was clearly distinguishable. To uphold the decision of the court *a quo* would result in a process of judicial interpretation which would erode the statute to a point where it ceases to have any practical significance. Only the legislator could remedy the unsatisfactory consequences of a decision which compelled the court to hold that the will in this case was null and void.

The Administration of Estates Amendment Act 1969 (30/69) introduces certain minor amendments into the Principal Act.

COMMERCIAL LAW

Kortessis v. *Prudential Assurance Co. Ltd.*, 1969 (3) S.A. 335, concerns the construction of apparently well settled and familiar clauses in two insurance policies — one against risk of fire and the other against loss of business profits. The plaintiff's claim for about £12,800 arose from a fire in his business premises on 28th February 1968. It was duly submitted to the defendant who rejected it on 11th April 1968 in bald terms alleging an unspecified breach of warranty which was amplified on 23rd April 1968 when the defendant relied on a breach of the safe and books clause in the fire policy. On 14th June 1968 the defendant called upon the plaintiff to proceed to arbitration to determine the amount due as a condition precedent to the institution of proceedings by the plaintiff under the policies. The defendant intimated that it preferred to have the issue of liability (which was disputed altogether) to be determined before the *quantum* was submitted to arbitration. The parties thereupon agreed on 18th June 1968 that the defendant's liability should first be determined by the High Court. The plaintiff issued summons against the defendant on 17th August 1968. The defendant now took the point that all benefits under the policies had been forfeited because the plaintiff had failed, as required by the policies, to commence his action within three months after the rejection of his claim. The plaintiff contended that the period of three months had begun to run only on 18th June 1968 when the parties had agreed that arbitration proceedings should be deferred until after the defendant's liability had been established in principle. Since the policies provided not only that action must be commenced within three months after the rejection of a claim, but that in the event of arbitration taking place, that action need only be instituted within three months after the arbitrator's award, and since the plaintiff had justifiably believed that the claims would first be submitted to arbitration, the defendant could not now be heard to say that the period of three months had already started to run when the claim was rejected. In further support of this contention — and also independently — the plaintiff relied on the fact that the defendant had continued to investigate the claim after it had been rejected. The court did not accept these conditions. The wording of the policies was clear: action had to be commenced within three months of the repudiation of the claim and only in the event of arbitration taking place was that period extended until three months after the arbitrator's award. There was sufficient time between 18th June and 22nd July (when the three months from the rejection of the claim expired) to commence action. As for the continued investigation of the claim after repudiation the defendant had reserved all its rights and it would seem that even without such reservation it could not be said to have reprobated and approbated merely because it continued its investigations. But can it not be said that there was at least some substance in the first point raised by the plaintiff? Until 18th June he had no reason to prepare for the commencement of an action. Why should he now be compelled to do so within just over a month merely because he had fallen in with the defendant's suggestion to have the issue of liability determined before the *quantum* of the claim?

EVIDENCE AND PROCEDURE

Summary judgment and declaration of rights in civil proceedings

In *Windsor Diesels (Pvt.) Ltd.* v. *Shangani Saw Mills (Pvt.) Ltd.*, 1969 (3) S.A. 145, the plaintiff applied for summary judgment against the defendant for payment of £2,000 odd being the cost of transportation of 31,195 cubic feet of timber @ $\frac{1}{4}$d. per cubic foot between 1st April and 30th November 1966. The plaintiff alleged that the amount claimed represented a "reasonable remuneration" which the defendant had expressly or impliedly agreed to pay. No details of the distance over, or the manner in, which the timber had been carried were given. The defendant filed no replying affidavits. The question arose whether the claim was one for a "debt or liquidated demand only". If it was not, summary judgment would not be granted. After a review of English, South African and Rhodesian authorities the court held that the claim was capable of speedy ascertainment and therefore was a debt or liquidated demand.

Gelcon Investments (Pvt.) Ltd. v. *Adair Properties*, 1969 (3) S.A. 142 raised the question in what circumstances an applicant may ask the court for a "declaration of rights". Here the applicant asked the court to determine the meaning and effect of certain clauses in a contract between the parties. The court has a discretion whether or not it will grant such a declaration and it may exercise its discretion in the applicant's favour, notwithstanding that he "cannot claim any relief consequential upon such determination". Does this mean that the court should make no declaration when the applicant *can* claim consequential relief — i.e. should he be required to proceed by action and ask for judgment against the defendant? The South African courts have not yet reached a conclusion on this point.

The Rhodesian High Court held that an applicant may ask for a declaration of rights even though he could proceed by way of action.

Criminal procedure and evidence

The vexed question as to the admissibility of an accused's statements was considered by Beadle, C.J., in *R.* v. *Moyo*, 1969 (3) S.A. 720. The accused was charged with murder and the Crown had at the close of a preparatory examination produced a certified copy of a statement alleged to have been made by the accused (Section 80 Criminal Procedure and Evidence Act, Chap. 31). At his trial in the High Court the accused denied that he had ever made that statement. It was suggested that the statement was inadmissible because it had never been proved that it had actually been made by the accused. The court rejected this contention. The statement had been correctly introduced at the preparatory examination and could be received in evidence without further proof "unless it was shown that (it) was not in fact duly made . . ." The court must of course examine all the evidence critically and be satisfied that the statement was in fact that of the accused and whether it was true or not. But if the accused challenges a statement, the onus to substantiate his challenge is upon him. Whether he discharges that onus by raising a reasonable doubt or whether he must refute the statement on a balance of probabilities remains an open question because in this case the accused's evidence was regarded as so unsatisfactory that he did not even raise a reasonable doubt in the court's mind.

In *R.* v. *Wood*, 1969 (4) S.A. 188 (A.D.), the accused was charged with driving under the influence of liquor. During the trial a police officer had given evidence of a conversation he had with the accused in which the latter had admitted that he had been drinking and also that he was unaccustomed to drink. It was argued on appeal that the statement was inadmissible as it had not been proved that the accused was in his sound and sober senses when he made it. The Appellate Division disposed of this submission that the police officer had related this conversation in response to questions put to him in cross-examination by accused's attorney. It was admissible, therefore, because it had been introduced by the defence, presumably, *in favorem innocientiae*. But as a general rule, a witness must not be allowed to give evidence of statements made by himself when the accused was not present — except in very special circumstances, e.g. to prove that other statements which he did make in the presence of the accused were not fabricated by him: *R.* v. *Mack*, 1969 (4) S.A. 55.

Sentences

In *R.* v. *Nyati*, 1969 (4) S.A. 389, the accused had been convicted of stock theft and sentenced to one year's imprisonment with hard labour and a fine of £60 and in default of payment, to one (further) year's imprisonment with hard labour. It was obvious that the accused was unable to pay the fine. A magistrate rejected his plea of poverty on the ground that his father had sufficient assets to assist him and that in any event the accused, "even if he has to do a bit of begging", would be able to pay the fine. On review, Beadle, C.J., pointed out that it was quite wrong to impose a fine on an

15—AL * *

accused which is much greater than would normally be imposed on the average person in the accused's station of life, simply because the latter happens to have wealthy parents or friends.

CONFLICT OF LAW

In *Coluflandres Ltd.* v. *Scandia Industrial Products Ltd.*, 1969 (3) S.A. 551, the plaintiff, a Belgian company which had obtained judgment in Belgium against the defendant, a Rhodesian company, issued a provisional sentence summons (founded on the Belgian judgment) against the defendant in Rhodesia. The defendant opposed the application for provisional sentence on various grounds. Firstly: that it had not been proved that the Belgian judgment was a final judgment; secondly: that it had not received notice of the trial in Belgium; and thirdly: that the Belgian court had no jurisdiction in the action in which it had given judgment. The Rhodesian court held: although it would, clearly, enforce only a final judgment, this fact need not necessarily be formally proved in the case of a foreign judgment which was final on the face of it, unless the defendant was able to rebut at least prima facie the presumption that it was a final judgment. The onus was on the defendant to show that the foreign judgment was vitiated by a failure of natural justice, as far as its allegation that it did not receive notice of the foreign trial was concerned. Finally, where the jurisdictional facts relied on by the plaintiff for the foreign court's jurisdiction are matters very much in controversy, the plaintiff must prove that the foreign court had jurisdiction.

The question of how far a Rhodesian court was bound by an order awarding the custody of a minor child to one of the parents after their marriage had been dissolved in America was considered in *Jagoe* v. *Jagoe*, 1969 (4) S.A. 59. In that case an Alabama court had granted the husband (the respondent in these proceedings) a decree of divorce on the grounds of his wife's (now the applicant) cruelty. The custody of the only child of the parties, a girl less than one year old, had been awarded to the mother by consent. But the father had access to the child and early in 1967 he removed the child from the mother's custody and took her with him on a trip through Europe, the West Indies and South America. Finally, in March 1968, he settled in Rhodesia. He did not inform the mother of his or the child's whereabouts. When the mother had at long last traced the father and child, she came to Rhodesia and made application to the High Court for the return of the child on the strength of the Alabama order. She intended to take the child with her back to America. The Rhodesian court did not regard itself bound by the foreign order, but thought that it had to make a decision as to what was now in the best interests of the child according to the principles of Rhodesian law. It took into consideration that the father had not lightly consented to the custody of the child being given to the mother in the first instance and that he was unusually concerned in the child's welfare. In the result, the court came to the conclusion that the interests of the child would be best served if her custody was given to the mother, but only on the condition that she would not remove the child from Rhodesia. Therefore, the mother had to settle in this country if she wanted to keep the custody of the child. The father was to have reasonable access to the child at all times, but was likewise forbidden to remove her from the jurisdiction of the Rhodesian court.

MISCELLANEOUS

AFRICAN CUSTOMARY LAW

Matambo v. *Matambo*, 1969 (3) 717 (A.D.), illustrates the approach of the courts to African customary law. In this case an African had died intestate leaving considerable property which included two farms in an African Purchase Area. He was survived by seven wives (whom he had married according to African custom) and 35 children. Clearly, the estate devolved according to customary law. But the difficulty was to reconcile that law with Section 6 of the African Wills Act (Chap. 108) which provides that "(t)he heir at African law of any deceased African shall succeed in his individual capacity to any immovable property (of the deceased) not devised by will". According to the tribal law of the deceased, his eldest sister, the *vatete* (advised by a brother) distributes his property among his children, though *semble* it is given in trust to the eldest son of the deceased's senior wife to deal with to the best advantage for the other members of the family. In this case that particular son was unpopular with, and distrusted by, the family. Therefore, the *vatete* gave him one of the farms outright and the remainder of the estate to the second son of the senior wife. The eldest son objected to this decision of the *vatete* and took the matter to court. A magistrate held that the eldest son was the *only* "heir at African law" and, therefore, in terms of Section 6 (*supra*) entitled to succeed in his *personal* capacity to *all* the *immovable* property in the estate. The younger son maintained that, although the eldest son was the only spiritual heir of his father and succeeded to his name, the *vatete* was entitled to appoint other heirs, too, and distribute among them portions of the estate and adduced substantial evidence supporting this contention. The eldest son took his stand on the wording of the Act and claimed, at any rate, all the deceased's immovable property. Beadle, C.J., thought the word "heir" in Section 6 (*supra*) must be given its ordinary meaning — i.e. it referred to such persons as, in regard to intestate succession, are entitled to succeed to the property of the deceased. The crisp question, therefore, was whether according to the tribal law of the deceased some person or persons in addition to the eldest son of the senior wife might be *entitled* to succeed to the property of the deceased. On this basis the learned Chief Justice paraphrased Section 6 so that "(t)he person at African law who is entitled to succeed to the property (of the deceased) shall succeed in his individual capacity to any immovable property". At the same time, he emphasised that the word "property" embraced movable and immovable property. In this particular case the question who, according to the deceased's tribal law, was entitled to succeed to the property, had not been sufficiently investigated and Beadle, C.J., therefore, ordered further evidence to be taken on this point. It would seem that the decision will ultimately depend on the extent to which the *vatete* is given a discretion by customary law to distribute the deceased's property — or whether she is bound by certain customary rules. In either case customary law would, at least prima facie, prevail.

Drugs Control Act 1969 (14/69)

This Act reflects the growing concern in Rhodesia about the world-wide problem of the use of drugs. A drug is defined as *inter alia* any substance which is used or represented as suitable for the diagnosis and treatment of any mental or physical illness or, generally, for "restoring, correcting or modifying any organic function in man". It provides for the establishment of a Drugs Control Council and the registration of drugs (which shall be approved if the availability of a particular drug is in the public interest and its safety and therapeutic efficacy regarded as satisfactory), their advertisement and distribution. Contraventions of the Act are subject to certain penalties: A fine of £500 and/or imprisonment up to six months in the case of a first offender, and a fine of £1,000 and/or imprisonment not exceeding one year in the case of a second or subsequent offence.

---

1. *R. v. Ndhlovu and Others* 1968 (4) S.A. 515 (A.D.). For further details on the internal constitutional conflict between the courts and the Government see *Annual Survey of African Law* Vol. I at pp. 236 ff. and Vol. II 1968 at pp. 180 ff.; Allott's *Judicial and Legal Systems in Africa* (2nd ed.) 218 ff. and 289 ff.
2. Constitution Amendment Act 1969 (1/69). Emergency Powers Amendment Act 1969 (25/69).
3. It has been pointed out (University of South Africa Constitutional Law II RS 2/2/70 at p. 34) that the so-called referendum was no referendum in the legal sense because the result had no legal force. Cf. the pre-republican plebiscite in South Africa and see also Section 105 of the 1965 Constitution.
4. The White Paper was in the form of a broad outline and a statement of policy rather than a detailed commentary such as the *Whaley* Report (Report of the Constitutional Commission 1968).
5. See Sections 3, 4, 5. The Act (42/69) also provided for the adaptation of the Electoral Act then in force to the requirements of a referendum having regard *inter alia* to the cross-voting system of A and B Rolls. See Referendum Regulations 1969 G.N. 368*A* of 1969.
5a. Approximately 80 per cent of the registered voters cast their votes at the referendum. In favour of the Constitution: 50,724 — against 20,776. In favour of a republic: 61,130 and 14,327 against it. The discrepancy between the votes cast for and against the declaration of a republic and the new Constitution can be explained by the fact that the voters to the "right" *and* to the "left" of the Government Rhodesian Front party voted against the Constitution, but only those to the "right" of the Government voted in favour of a declaration of a republic whilst those to the "left" rejected it along with the Constitution.

6. The legal significance of a "preamble" to a written constitution is of course problematic. But eminent jurists in all countries with written constitutions acknowledge that it may be referred to in the construction of constitutional provisions.

7. Sections 3 and 4. A resolution removing the President can be passed only "after a report prepared by a committee of (the House of Assembly) appointed at the request of the Prime Minister has recommended (the President's) removal". Semble: only the Prime Minister can initiate steps for the President's removal; Section 4(3). Cp. *infra* n. 20 Section 52(1) and Section 52(4) on the President's position in regard to the prorogation and dissolution of Parliament. For the protection of the President's dignity cp. Section 8 (Any act calculated to violate the President's dignity is an offence punishable by a fine up to $1,000 or imprisonment up to five years).

8. Chap. II Pt. I, Sections 10–12.

9. *Ibid.*, Pt. II, Sections 13–17.

10. Five each from Matabeleland and Mashonaland (the main tribal divisions in Rhodesia).

11. Sections 56 and 65 Electoral Act. Senators may be members of the Cabinet or serving army or police officers, but hold no other public office. For further details on electoral colleges see *infra* the section on the Electoral Act.

12. For their qualifications, tenure and procedural matters relating to their election see Sections 15, 16.

13. Sections 14, 43–6, 71–5. The functions of the Senate Legal Committee are discussed further in their relevant context.

14. Chap. II, Pt. III, Sections 18–21.

15. Section 18. The number of African members must always be increased by two or in multiples of two to preserve the equilibrium between Matabeleland and Mashonaland representation.

16. For the expulsion and suspension of members of the House of Assembly and of the Senate in the event of a member being convicted of certain offences see Sections 26, 27.

17. For the procedure regarding the introduction and passing of bills generally see Chap. II, Part VI, Sections 40–50, and for the restrictions placed upon the debate and passing of a Money Bill Section 40(4). Definition of a Money Bill: Section 92.

18. Section 42.

19. Sections, 45, 80.

20. Chap. II, Pt. VII, Sections 51, 52, 54. In the case of a disagreement between the President and the Prime Minister it would seem that the President's view must prevail. *Quaere* whether the President may dissolve Parliament after the Prime Minister has asked the House of Assembly to appoint a commission to enquire into the President's conduct.

21. Chap. III, Sections 53, 56. For the general powers of the President (e.g. to appoint and recognise diplomatic representatives, proclaim martial law, declare war) see Section 54.

22. Section 57.

23. Section 61.

24. The members of such a Tribunal must be either the speaker, or a former judge from Rhodesia or a country from which he could be appointed as a judge in Rhodesia; or an advocate or attorney of not less than ten years' standing nominated by the Bar Council or the Law Society respectively.

25. A Bill which, when enacted, would have the effect of amending, adding to or repealing any of the provisions of the Constitution is referred to as a "Constitutional Bill" — Section 92 ("Interpretation").

26. Chap. VI, Sections 76–9. It should be noted that not every proposed amendment of the Constitution (i.e. not every Constitutional Bill) requires the special two-thirds majority referred to in the text. On the other hand, a Bill which would

have the effect of amending the entrenched clauses of the Electoral and Land Tenure Acts ranks as a Constitutional Bill.

27. Section 84. See also *infra* in the text where the role of the Senate Legal Committee as a "watchdog" in relation to the Declaration of Rights is discussed.

28. On the effect of an increase in the punishment for an offence between the commission of such an offence and the time by which the offender is brought to trial see *R*. v. *Sillas* 1959 (4) S.A. 305 (App. Div. of South Africa) which is likely to be followed in Rhodesia.

29. Section 17(3) and (4).

30. Section 2.

31. Cp. *supra* Nos. 10 and 14. Additional African constituencies will be created as the number of African members of the House of Assembly is increased: *supra* text following No. 15. But whenever this happens, the number of constituencies must be increased equally in Mashonaland and Matabeleland, Section 5(3).

32. Electoral Act Sections 3 to 6. Constitution Section 18. Provision is also made for an increase in the number of tribal electoral college areas, Section 7 Electoral Act.

33. Section 81 of the Constitution.

34. Section 28 provides for the disqualification of persons on the ground of certain criminal convictions, mental disorders and also disqualifies "any person who for a continuous period of one year has been in receipt of Government rations or a maintenance allowance . . .".

35. Section 19.

36. Section 20.

37. Sections 22, 23.

38. Section 24. A commission shall investigate the price structure affecting the cost of living at least every three years and if prices have either increased or decreased by not less than 10 per cent the means qualifications shall be adjusted accordingly.

39. In terms of Section 18(4) of the Constitution — *supra* text ad No. 15.

40. Section 26.

41. Chap. IX, Sections 164 to 177.

42. Section 179.

43. Sections 4, 5.

44. Part V, Sections 56 ff. Land in the National Area shall not be disposed of to any person. But this provision is not entrenched in the Constitution, and land int his area may be leased for a period which does not exceed ninety-nine years.

45. Sections 11, 24.

46. *Ibid.*

47. Section 3. *Quaere* the significance of the inclusion of "other employee" in medical institutions only. "The Minister responsible for the Administration of the Act" is hereafter referred to as "the Minister". The term "occupy" seemingly includes throughout the Act the regular attendance at a certain place for a certain length of time so that a person working at such a place apparently occupies it for the purposes of the Act. See No. 48 *infra*.

48. Sections 14, 15, 18. An African may own, lease or occupy land in a non-racial area for residential purposes. A permit for a European to occupy land in an African township will normally be issued only in connection with the Administration of such a township.

49. Sections 28–31.

50. Sections 16, 17, 30, 31, 32.

51. Part IV Sections 37–55. Second Schedule Part IV.

51a. See text *infra*.

52. For further details see Section 67. It seems that this section applies also to persons who have occupied land before the Land Tenure Act 1969 came into force and who only now occupy such land in contravention of the provisions of this Act.

53. Sections 68, 72.
54. Section 72(2).
55. Sections 6, 7. Each Board consists of the chairman and two other members who shall be Europeans in the one case and Africans in the other case and who shall be selected for their suitability to represent the interests of the race to which they belong.
56. For details see the 4th Schedule to the Act.
57. Most Rhodesian decisions are reported first in the South African Law Reports and subsequently a separate series of Rhodesian Law Reports is published. In the text references to the South African Law Reports are given.

CHAPTER 12

BOTSWANA

S. Roberts

The National Assembly again completed a heavy legislative programme, but much of what came before it was of no greater importance than the business dealt with in the previous year. Developments in only two areas stand out. The first of these was the enactment of a Customary Law (Application and Ascertainment) Act, designed to clarify the hitherto uncertain relationship between customary law and the common law. The second was the passage of a comprehensive body of labour legislation, a reminder of coming industrial growth rather than a response to urgent contemporary need.

PUBLIC LAW

The Constitution

Two statutes passed during the year contained amendments to the Independence Constitution of 1966. The first, the Constitution (Amendment and Supplementary Provisions) Act,[1] contained two unrelated amendments to the Constitution. The first of these concerned citizenship, and is considered separately below.[2] The second was a drafting amendment to the chapter of the Constitution dealing with the protection of fundamental rights and freedoms of the individual. Section 15 of this chapter prohibits the enactment of discriminatory legislation, but contains an exemption making provision for the differential operation of customary laws. This exemption is now extended to small "communities" of Africans living outside the tribal territories, unattached to any of the principal tribes, and arguably excluded from the existing range of persons to whom the exemption applied.[3]

The Constitution of 1966 made provision for the discharge of the functions of the President by the Vice-President during the former's absence from the country or illness, but made no provision for the discharge of these functions where both were ill or out of the country at the same time. The Constitution (Second Amendment) Act[4] now provides for this eventuality by enabling any other Minister to be authorised to carry them out.[5]

A further statute, the Presidential Elections (Supplementary Provisions) Act,[6] makes provision, in pursuance of the Constitution, for the administration of a Presidential Election. It makes detailed rules for such matters as the appointment of authenticating officers, the preparation of nomination forms and the choice of colours and symbols by a candidate for the purposes of the election.

Citizenship

The Constitution of 1966 contained a provision under which Commonwealth citizens and citizens of specified African countries were entitled, as of right, to registration as citizens of Botswana once they had been lawfully resident in Botswana for a period of five years immediately preceding the application.[7] This right is now qualified so that registration may be refused in the case of a person who:[8] is a prohibited immigrant; in the opinion of the Minister responsible for the administration of matters of citizenship, "is not of good character by reason of drunkenness, prostitution, perversion or other objectionable practices or is a member of a group whose beliefs or practices are not generally acceptable in Botswana"; or, is a citizen of a Commonwealth country whose law does not make equally favourable provision for the acquisition of citizenship of such country by citizens of Botswana.

Public order

Two measures were introduced during the year aimed at the prevention of various forms of racial discrimination. The first of these was the creation of a new offence of "discrimination" for inclusion in the Penal Code. For the purposes of this offence a person discriminates against another "if on the grounds of colour, race, nationality or creed he treats such person less favourably or in a manner different to that in which he treats or would treat any other person".[9] A person found guilty of this offence is liable to a fine not exceeding R500 and to a term of imprisonment not exceeding six months. The other was directed specifically towards instances of discrimination on licensed premises, and enabled the Minister responsible for the administration of the Liquor Proclamation to cancel a licence where he "is of the opinion that discrimination is practised on any licensed premises".[10] Such an act of cancellation disqualifies the licensee from holding another licence for a period of five years, and is "final and shall not be questioned in any court".[11]

COMMERCE AND INDUSTRY

Recent prospecting discoveries, notably of diamonds at Orapa, necessitated the enactment of a Precious Stones (Protection) Act,[12] providing *inter alia* for the notification of all discoveries by registered prospectors, and for the prohibition of all dealing in rough and uncut precious stones except by licensed dealers.[13] Accelerating economic development in another sphere was evidenced by the passage of an Insurance Act,[14] designed to regulate the transaction of all insurance business in Botswana.

LABOUR LAW

The immediate prospect of rapid industrial growth led also to the enactment of a comprehensive body of labour law. This legislation consists of a Regulation of Wages and Conditions of Employment Act,[15] a Trade Disputes Act[16] and a Trade Unions Act.[17] The first of these statutes gives the Minister charged with its administration power to establish a Wages Council in connexion with any sector of employment in respect of which existing machinery for the regulation of wages appears inadequate.[18] Such Councils are to be composed of even numbers of representatives of management and labour and an odd number of independent members.[19] The Trade Disputes Act follows up this provision with some sophisticated machinery for dealing with industrial disputes where the normal negotiating procedures break down. Part II of the Act requires unsettled disputes to be referred to the Commissioner of Labour and, where necessary, on to the Minister responsible, who may attempt what further efforts at reconciliation that he considers appropriate. Part IV of the Act prohibits certain forms of industrial action. Section 19 provides:

> Where it appears to the Minister that there is an actual or threatened strike or lockout in any trade or industry and the Minister is of the opinion —
> (*a*) that the strike or lockout has any object other than or in addition to the furtherance of a trade dispute within that trade or industry; and
> (*b*) that the strike or lockout is designed or calculated to coerce any employer or employee in any other trade or industry in respect of his conduct in or in connexion with that trade or industry, either directly or by inflicting hardship on the community —
> the Minister may by order in the *Gazette* declare any strike or lockout in that trade or industry to be unlawful.

Any strike may also be prohibited pending the holding of a secret ballot, where the Minister considers this desirable. The Minister further has power to declare strikes in breach of a negotiated agreement unlawful. And any strike directed towards the maintenance of a closed shop is automatically unlawful.

The Trade Unions Act consolidates and extends the existing law relating to trade unions. A Register of trade unions is to be kept in pursuance of this Act, and the Registrar may refuse registration if "he is satisfied that", *inter alia*, the trade union is to be used for unlawful purposes, or if "any other trade union or employees' association registered under the Act is sufficiently representative of the interests in respect of which the application for registration is made", or if it appears that the purpose of the combination is not primarily to regulate relations between employers and employees or between employees and other employees. The Act also protects a registered trade union from action in tort in the traditional terms of Section 3 of the 1906 Act.

THE LAW OF PROPERTY

A Tribal Land (Amendment) Act[20] made several small amendments to the principal statute. Among these, two are particularly important. The first deletes a provision of the Act which could have been interpreted as authorising the Land Boards to make individual grants of grazing land.[21] The second removes the absolute prohibition against non-tribesmen holding land in the tribal territories under customary forms of tenure; such persons may now do so with the written permission of the Minister responsible for the administration of the Act.[22]

THE ASCERTAINMENT AND APPLICATION
OF CUSTOMARY LAW

As is the case in many of the former British African territories, the relationship between customary law and the common law in Botswana has always been rather vague. References to it in early constitutional provisions tended to assume rather than expressly confirm its continued application,[23] and the jurisdictional limitations placed upon the various courts avoided the necessity for choice of law rules. The traditional authorities retained their judicial powers over Africans, and in doing so naturally applied customary law, while the jurisdiction of the first common law courts established in the Bechuanaland Protectorate did "not extend to any matter in which natives only are concerned, unless in the opinion of such court the exercise of such jurisdiction is necessary in the interests of peace, or for the prevention or punishment of acts of violence to person or property".[24] The simplicity of this dual system had obvious attractions, but it could only be maintained as long as Africans refrained from involving themselves in transactions foreign to customary law and the administration resisted the temptation to legislate in areas hitherto the sole concern of the traditional authorities. Under the changing social and economic conditions prevailing in the years following the declaration of the Protectorate neither could long be the case, but despite the enactment of legislation in areas previously governed by customary law and the increasing subjection of Africans to the common law in certain fields, choice of law problems continued to be hidden by the jurisdictional limitations inherent in the dual system of courts, and they remained so even after independence.

The Customary Law (Application and Ascertainment) Act[25] attempts for the first time to clarify the relationship between customary law and the common law by the provision of choice of law rules. The Act begins by conferring upon the courts of Botswana generally power, within the limits

of their jurisdiction, to "apply customary law in all cases and proceedings
in which, by virtue of the provisions of this Act, or any other law,
customary law is properly applied and where it is not properly applied
such courts shall apply the common law".[26] The rules governing the
making of this choice are then set out in two general sections, the first
relating to disputes between "tribesmen"[27] and the second to disputes
between "tribesmen and non-tribesmen". A further three sections
making special provision for disputes involving custody of children,
intestate succession and personal injuries. A final section tackles the
problem of legal capacity.

The section laying down general choice of law rules to be applicable in
disputes between tribesmen provides:[28]

> Save as is otherwise provided under this Act or any other law, customary
> law shall be applicable in all civil cases and proceedings where the parties
> thereto are tribesmen unless:
> (*a*) it shall appear either from express agreement, or from all relevant
>   circumstances, that each intended or may reasonably be deemed to
>   have intended the matter to be regulated according to the common law;
>   or
> (*b*) the transaction out of which the case or proceedings arose is one
>   unknown to customary law; or
> (*c*) the parties express to the court their consent to the Common Law being
>   applicable and any consent referred to in this paragraph shall be
>   recorded in writing and attached to the court record of the case and
>   shall be irrevocable.

This formulation provides a general guide, but it can be seen that much is
left to the court applying it, and no doubt a considerable case law will
develop around it. It is interesting to speculate how the courts will
interpret the provision relating to transactions "unknown to customary
law"; contracts of insurance and hire purchase agreements seem obvious
examples of what the draftsman is getting at, but the categories are by no
means clear cut. The circumstances under which a dispute involving a
non-tribesman may be disposed of according to customary law are much
narrower. The Act provides:[29]

> Subject to any written law, where in any cases or proceedings between
> tribesmen and non-tribesmen:
> (*a*) it shall appear either from express agreement, or from all relevant
>   circumstances, that each intended or may reasonably be deemed to
>   have intended the matter to be regulated according to customary law;
>   or
> (*b*) the parties express to the court their consent to any customary law
>   being applicable;
> that law shall be applied accordingly, and any consent referred to in para-
> graph (*b*) shall be recorded in writing and attached to the court record of the
> case and shall be irrevocable.

Here again, much is left to the courts. One curious feature of the
provisions is that the choice of law rules provided by Section 4 are limited

to "civil cases and proceedings" whereas no such limitation appears in Section 5. The whole Act is silent on the question of the customary criminal law, and no other statute deals with the matter, but it appears from reading Sections 3 and 4 together that, in the case of tribesmen at least, the courts have no jurisdiction to apply customary criminal law. This is unsatisfactory, as although in dealing with criminal matters the customary courts are now required to be "guided by" the Penal Code,[30] the majority of customary courts in fact settle the multitudinous cases of assault and wrongful taking which come before them according to customary law.

Turning to the three topics excluded from the general choice of law rules, it is provided in respect of the first that "in any case relating to the custody of children the welfare of the children concerned shall be the paramount consideration irrespective of which law or principle is applied".[31] This formulation avoids, without directly tackling, the problem which has sometimes arisen when the custody of African children whose parents are married under the Marriage Proclamation comes in issue. It is nowhere provided whether the custody of such children should be resolved under customary law or the common law, and the courts have from time to time been left in doubt as to the proper approach; now the difficulty is avoided. The provision should give rise to no difficulty in the customary courts, as, although the child of a married couple is according to the law of all the Tswana tribes a member of the descent group to which the father belongs,[32] questions of physical custody seem invariably decided according to the welfare principle.

The special provision relating to intestate succession requires that "customary law shall be applicable in determining the intestate heirs of a tribesman and the nature and extent of their inheritance".[33] While the intention of this section is reasonably clear, it is unhappily drafted in view of the fact that customary wills are widely made by Tswana tribesmen and recognised in the customary courts.[34] Had the section referred expressly to wills made in conformity with the Wills Proclamation, the difficulty would have been avoided.

The necessity for making special provision for claims arising out of personal injuries and death is due to the inadequate rates of compensation sometimes ordered in respect of these wrongs in the customary courts. In these days when motor vehicles and modern agricultural machinery are widely found in the tribal territories, and questions of insurance arise where an accident occurs, legal issues may also be present with which the customary courts are unfamiliar, and to deal with which the common law is better equipped. For these reasons, it is provided that the general choice of law rules contained in Section 4 shall not "prevent the application of the common law where the claim arises out of personal injury to, or the death of, any person". It is also provided that the fact that a claim has already been determined under customary law shall not preclude the institution of proceedings under the common law, although in assessing damages any such previous determination may be taken into account.

A novel feature of the Act is that it endeavours to resolve the difficult conflictual problems associated with questions of legal capacity. It provides:

> (1) Where the existence or extent of any right held or alleged to be held by a tribesman or of any obligation vesting or alleged to be vesting in any tribesman depends upon or is governed by the customary law, the capacity of the tribesman concerned in relation to any matter affecting the right or obligation shall be governed by customary law.
>
> (2) In any case other than such a case as is referred to in sub section (1) the capacity of any tribesman to enter in any transaction or to enforce or defend any rights in a court of law shall, subject to any written law affecting any such capacity, be determined in accordance with the common law.

Through this formulation it is hoped to avoid, for example, the inappropriate importation of common law notions of majority into disputes otherwise wholly subject to customary law.

The Act also makes provision for resolving internal conflicts between the different bodies of customary law. Again the relevant section is best quoted in full:[35]

> 10. (1) In any case where customary law is applicable and the question arises as to which system of customary law is applicable —
>
> (*a*) in land matters the applicable customary law shall be the customary law of the place where the land is situate;
>
> (*b*) in cases and proceedings arising from inheritance the appropriate customary law shall, subject to the provisions of paragraph (*a*), be the customary law applying to the deceased;
>
> (*c*) subject to the provisions of paragraphs (*a*) and (*b*) the court shall apply the customary law which the parties intended or may reasonably be deemed to have intended should regulate their obligations in the matter or, in the absence of such actual or deemed intention, the customary law of the place where the action arose.
>
> (2) If the system of customary law cannot be ascertained in accordance with sub section (1) or if the customary law is not ascertainable, the court shall determine the matter in accordance with the principles of justice, equity and good conscience.

Curiously, the notion of a personal customary law is nowhere invoked in the Act except in sub section (*b*); are we to assume that "the customary law applying to the deceased" is the law of the tribe to which he belongs?

In ascertaining what the customary law on a particular point is, the Act authorises a court to refer to reported cases, textbooks "and other sources", and to receive written or oral opinions,[36] provided that in doing so all such sources shall be made available to both parties and any oral opinion given shall be given in the same manner as oral evidence. The decision as to what sources are to be consulted is one for the court, to be reached after hearing any submissions the parties to the case may wish to make.

Two other enactments passed during 1969 touch upon the question of the application of customary law. The Court of Appeal (Amendment) Act[37] adds a further section to the principal Act requiring that:

In the hearing and determination of any appeal or question of law reserved the law to be applied shall be the law properly applicable to the case in the court from which the appeal is brought or by which the question of law was reserved.

This provision ensures that, in the exercise of its appellate jurisdiction, the Court of Appeal shall apply customary law under all circumstances in which such law was properly applied, or should properly have been applied, in the court from which the appeal lies. Such an occasion may frequently arise, as the Court of Appeal lies at the apex of the appelate system leading through the magistrates' courts and the High Court from the customary courts. Similarly, customary law may be relevant in appeals upon matters heard in the first instance in the magistrates' courts and the High Court, where these courts properly apply customary law in accordance with the Customary Law (Application and Ascertainment) Act.

Notwithstanding the general authority to apply customary law conferred upon all courts by the Customary Law (Application and Ascertainment) Act, subject to the choice of law rules which that Act contains, it is still desirable in the majority of cases that matters involving customary law should continue to be dealt with in the customary courts. These courts have (or ought to have) a natural familiarity with customary law, whereas the High Court and many of the magistrates' courts continue to be staffed by persons who often have no direct experience of customary law or the dispute settlement procedures traditionally employed among tribesmen. Such reasoning has led to the introduction of the following provision designed to restrict the circumstances under which disputes involving customary law are dealt with in the magistrates' courts:[38]

> Where, at any time after the commencement of any proceedings, a subordinate court is of the opinion —
> (*a*) that, by virtue of the provisions of Section 4 of the Customary Law (Application and Ascertainment) Act, 1969, or any other law, customary law is applicable to the principal matter in issue; and
> (*b*) that it is not contrary to the interests of justice to do so;
> it shall order that the case be transferred to a customary court of competent jurisdiction.

Such a provision leaves much to the discretion of the magistrate concerned, and the legislature was perhaps right not to spell out too clearly the circumstances under which transfer would be inappropriate. Obviously, such a case would arise where there was doubt whether a fair trial could be had in the customary court concerned (as, for example, where the dispute involved the traditional authority presiding over the court, or a member of his immediate family). It is clear, although the Act does not say so, that this power of transfer is for use only in cases coming before a magistrate in the exercise of his original, as opposed to his appellate, jurisdiction.

THE RECORDING OF CUSTOMARY LAW

During 1969 the Botswana Government's programme for recording Tswana customary law continued. This survey, commenced under the direction of the Attorney-General in association with the Minister of Local Government and Lands in the previous year,[39] was designed to provide Government with accurate information as to the contemporary state of selected areas of customary law. The areas chosen for initial investigation were family relations, land and succession to property; and the survey was to be confined in the first instance to the eight Tswana tribes occupying defined tribal territories. It was hoped that the information thus gathered might provide a basis for the preparation of restatements of these areas of customary law for use in the courts, and for any necessary remedial legislation if it was found that the law had failed to accommodate itself to changing social conditions.

Previous investigations of Tswana customary law had been largely carried out through rule-centred interviews with informants. This method formed the basis of the research on which Schapera's classic, *A handbook of Tswana law and custom*, was written;[40] it was also used in later investigations carried out on behalf of the Botswana Government by A. C. Campbell and J. M. Walker.[41] While this research revealed the existence of a rich mass of stated legal norms, it could not in its very nature indicate with any certainty the part which these norms played in the dispute settlement process. For this reason it was decided that the new survey should be directed towards ascertaining how disputes were actually settled in the customary courts. This line of investigation was greatly facilitated by the fact that the chiefs' courts of the eight tribes concerned had all kept quite full written records of cases tried before them; in every case these records went back to the 1950's, and in some much earlier records survived.[42] The procedure decided upon was for the records kept by the chief's court of each tribe under investigation during the previous ten years to be indexed and classified. Records of disputes falling within the areas of law under consideration were then to be abstracted and analysed. Once this had been done, the information obtained was to be checked and expanded in discussion with selected informants drawn from the tribe concerned. At this stage the direction of the investigation was to remain focused upon actual disputes, rather than the extraction from informants of stated legal norms.

In the early months of 1969 the classification and analysis of the records of the Kgatla chief's court at Mochudi, covering the years 1954–68, was completed, and a series of meetings held with Kgatla informants to supplement the information so gathered. On the basis of this investigation three draft Restatements of Kgatla law, covering Domestic Relations, Succession to Property, and Land and Natural Resources, were prepared and submitted to the Attorney-General. These Restatements were subsequently published to enable the public to comment upon them.[43] The remainder of the year was devoted to the classification and analysis of the case records of the chiefs' courts of the Malete, Tlokwa, Kwena and Ngwaketse tribes.[44]

It is hard to generalise about the findings which have come out of this survey, particularly in the limited space available here. But some important developments are noticeable over a wide area. Considering first the field of family law, earlier studies had shown that the traditional Tswana law and its dispute settlement mechanisms were embedded in, and dependent for their effectiveness upon, the system of kinship organisation prevailing among the Tswana tribes. Marriages were formed, family disputes were settled and matrimonial relief was obtainable only within the context of the kinship groups to which the parties belonged, and the range of a man's obligations to provide material support for needy kinsmen was wide, although well defined. Today, changing social and economic conditions have everywhere in Botswana placed great strains upon the traditional kinship organisation, and in some areas it has largely broken down. In the majority of the tribal territories the customary courts are trying to accommodate the law to these new conditions. To take a few examples: the kinds of orders as to property typically made in the customary courts where a divorce is granted take into account the fact that the woman will not now necessarily be able to fall back on members of her own descent group for her subsequent maintenance as she was able to do in the past; the kinds of association recognised as giving rise to a valid marriage are being extended, enabling more parties to qualify for matrimonial relief; in some areas a degree of recognition for the purposes of material relief is being granted to wholly informal unions; unmarried women who have been impregnated are now themselves being allowed to bring actions and to recover compensation against the man responsible, the orders made in such cases being directed towards the maintenance of the child. Behind all these developments, but central to them, have been changes in the traditional dispute settlement procedures. The first level dispute settlement procedures, located within the descent groups to which the parties belong, have naturally shown signs of decay as the organisation of these groups has crumbled. The higher level agencies, ward courts and the chiefs' courts, have met this situation by allowing parties to appear before them without insisting upon prior attempts at settlement at descent group level and without insisting upon the presence in court of senior supporting relations. Thus these higher level courts have enabled disputes to be settled and relief to be obtained by the parties themselves, unimpeded by the absence or non-co-operation of their kin.[45]

Changes of a similar character are noticeable in the law of succession to property. Where the head of a household died, the bulk of the cattle held by him traditionally passed to a single male heir, who himself became head of the household and took over the responsibilities for the members which had previously been borne by his father, using the herd that he had inherited to carry them out. These responsibilities ranged at least as far as his widowed mother, any of his unmarried sisters, and his younger brothers (and their households, as such brothers married and set up their own homesteads). Today, it is widely complained that the beneficiaries who looked in the past for support to the principal heir can no longer do so with any confidence. The courts are responding to this situation by developing rules of inheritance to provide for the *division and distribution* of a dead man's estate instead of the *transfer of its management* from one family head to another. Obviously, the speed of development, and the devices used to secure distribution, differ a great deal from place to place, but the general movement noted can be seen in all the tribal territories in Botswana.[46]

The same can be seen in relation to arable lands. Their administration and division was traditionally carried out exclusively by the tribal authorities, ranging from the chief at the top to the head of a local descent group at the bottom. Recently, even prior to the passing of the Tribal Land Act,[47] control over land distribution has been slipping out of the hands of the tribal authorities (particularly at a lower level), and land transfers between individuals, often unannounced to the authorities, have become a normal way of acquiring and disposing of arable holdings. In many areas it is clear that these transfers are now made for consideration, particularly where the plot in question is favourably situated in relation to water and not too remote from the urban areas.

The survey has also revealed information as to the way in which the traditional courts themselves have developed following their incorporation into the court system of the Protectorate under the Native Tribunals Proclamation, 1934, and subsequent enactments. Here, the records kept by the chiefs' courts of the various tribes tell how far these courts have remained the agencies to which tribesmen take their disputes for settlement. Much seems to have depended upon the calibre of the individual traditional authorities, and how they have reacted towards the restrictions progressively placed upon their authority outside the judicial sphere. In those areas where the chieftaincy remains strong, the recognised customary courts continue to constitute the real as well as the official forum for the settlement of family, land, succession and other disputes between tribesmen traditionally disposed of under customary law. Into this category fall the Chief's Courts, Chief's Representative's Courts and many of the larger ward courts of the Ngwaketse, Ngwato, Tawana, Kgatla and Malete tribes. However, the records show that the chiefs' courts of the Kwena and Tlokwa tribes, while retaining jurisdiction officially, have effectively ceased to be used by tribesmen for the settlement of disputes subject to customary law. The manner in which such disputes are disposed of in those tribes would constitute an interesting topic for research.

---

1. No. 30 of 1969.
2. See Section 2, *infra*.
3. Section 15 as amended by the Constitution (Amendment and Supplementary Provisions) Act 1969.
4. No. 43 of 1969.
5. Section 37.
6. No. 41 of 1969.

7. Botswana Independence Order 1966, No. 1171, Art. 9; Constitution of Botswana, Section 25; Citizenship of Botswana (Supplementary Provisions) Law 1966.

8. Citizenship of Botswana (Supplementary Provisions) (Amendment) Act, No. 56 of 1969.

9. Section 89*D* of the Penal Code, inserted by Penal Code (Amendment) Act 1900.

10. Section 62*A*, inserted in the principal Proclamation by the Liquor Proclamation (Amendment) Act, No. 61 of 1969.

11. Sub sections (2) and (3).

12. No. 3 of 1969.

13. Sections 3 and 6.

14. No. 21 of 1969.

15. No. 22 of 1969.

16. No. 28 of 1969.

17. No. 24 of 1969.

18. Section 4(1).

19. Schedule to the Act.

20. No. 48 of 1969.

21. Section 20 as amended.

22. *Ibid.*

23. For example, under the Order in Council of 9th May 1891, the High Commissioner, in issuing Proclamations, was required to:[2]
    ". . . respect any native laws or customs by which the civil relations of any native chiefs, tribes or populations under Her Majesty's protection are now regulated, except so far as such may be incompatible with the due exercise of Her Majesty's power and jurisdiction".

24. Proclamation of 10th June 1891, Section 8.

25. No. 51 of 1969. This statute is reproduced in full, together with a comment by A. N. Allott, in 13 *J.A.L.* 98.

26. Section 3.

27. For the purposes of the Act, "tribesman" means a "member of a tribe or similar group of any other county in Africa prescribed by the Minister by notice in the *Gazette* for the purposes of the Customary Courts Proclamation 1961, and includes the legal personal representative of such member".

28. Section 4.

29. Section 5.

30. Customary Courts Proclamation 1961, Section 9, as amended by the African Courts (Amendment and Supplementary Provisions) Act, No. 57 of 1968.

31. Section 6.

32. An exception to this rule, under which an adulterine child may be repudiated by the husband (thereafter becoming a member of the wife descent group), is recognised in some tribes.

33. Section 7.

34. See Schapera, *A handbook of Tswana law and custom*, (2nd ed.), 1955, at page 230; Roberts,"Kgatla Law and Social Change", *Botswana Notes and Records*, Vol. 2, 1970, at p. 56.

35. Section 10.

36. Section 11.

37. No. 15 of 1969.

38. Section 31*A*, inserted in the principal Proclamation by Subordinate Courts (Amendment) Act, No. 44 of 1969.

39. The survey was carried out by the author of this chapter, who was given Special Leave of Absence from the London School of Economics and Political Science to act as Customary Law Adviser to the Botswana Government; the appointment being arranged under the Special Commonwealth African Assistance Plan.

40. At the time Schapera did his research for this work, the recording of disputes in the Tswana customary courts was only just beginning, and few records were therefore available to him. In his Preface to the Second Edition (1955), he acknowledges the

great importance of the case materials, and in work completed after the *Handbook* he used the records extensively. See, for example, "The Work of the Tribal Courts in the Bechuanaland Protectorate", *African Studies*, Vol. 2, 1943, 27; and "Contract in Tswana Case Law", 9 *J.A.L.*, 142. Schapera must be regarded as the first scholar working in Africa to perceive the crucial importance of this material.

41. Campbell prepared an account of Ngwaketse Family Law for the Botswana Government during 1965, and he and Walker surveyed the whole field of Malete law during 1967. Of this work the only part so far published is an article by Walker, "The Bamalete Law of Contracts", *Botswana Notes and Records*, Vol. 1, 1969. However, their unpublished manuscripts proved invaluable in the subsequent programme initiated in 1968.

42. A detailed account of the surviving customary court records found in Botswana in the course of the survey, together with a brief explanation of the research methods used, can be found in an article by the author of this chapter entitled, "The Recording of Customary Law: Some Problems of Method", *Botswana Notes and Records*, Vol. 3, 1971.

43. Simon Roberts, *A Restatement of the Kgatla Law of Domestic Relations*, Government Printer Gaborone, 1970; *A Restatement of the Kgatla Law of Succession to Property*, Government Printer Gaborone, 1970; *A Restatement of the Kgatla Law Relating to Land and Natural Resources*, Government Printer Gaborone, 1969.

44. See the article referred to in note 42, *supra*.

45. Some of these developments, so far as they are visible in the case of one Tswana tribe, the Kgatla, are reported in an article (by the author of this chapter) entitled "The Settlement of Family Disputes in the Kgatla Customary Courts: Some New Approaches", 15 *J.A.L.*, 60.

46. The nature of these developments in the Kgatla tribe is considered in an article "Kgatla Law and Social Change", *Botswana Notes and Records*, Vol. 2, 1970, p. 56.

47. No. 54 of 1968, referred to in the Botswana chapter of the 1968 volume of the *Annual Survey of African Law*.

CHAPTER 13

LESOTHO

S. M. Poulter

PROPERTY

According to the 1966 census figures around 87 per cent of the population of Lesotho is dependent upon agriculture and in 1966–7 agriculture accounted for over 70 per cent of the Gross Domestic Product. However since the Basotho are almost exclusively subsistence farmers and there is an acute land shortage the average annual *per capita* income was recently estimated to be a mere R57.7, one of the lowest in Africa.[1]

There are many factors which are responsible for the present under-developed state of agriculture — one of which may be the land tenure system itself which permits an individual the right of occupation and enjoyment of land, though not ownership[2] — but even within the existing system there is room for much reform in the use to which the land is put. An important legislative step in this direction was taken by the enactment of the Land Husbandry Act, No. 22 of 1969.

The Act empowers the Minister of Agriculture to make regulations in respect of agricultural land which in his judgment will ensure that land is employed in the most beneficial uses. In particular these regulations may prescribe the uses to which designated land may be put, control the growing of various crops, prevent soil erosion, provide for the maintenance of contour furrows, protect water resources, restrict the number of persons permitted to graze livestock on desig-nated land and provide for the proper management of trees (Section 4). The Act declares that the position of chiefs and headmen *vis-à-vis* the allocation and deprivation of land in terms of Section 7 of the Laws of Lerotholi is now to be subject to regulations made under the Act (Section 4). These regulations may make it an offence, punishable in the first instance by a fine not exceeding R50 (or in default, imprison-ment for up to three months), to contravene or fail to comply with the regulations Section 7).

These sanctions for bad husbandry will supplement the existing nalty of forfeiture in terms of Section 7(3) of the Laws of Lerotholi which provides that a chief or headman may at his discretion take land away from any of his subjects who through continued absence or for insufficient reason fails for two successive years to cultivate it properly.

SUCCESSION

The vexed question of the inheritance rights of widows which was the subject of much controversy in the cases of *Lekhaota* v. *Lekhaota*[3] in 1963 and *Khatala* v. *Khatala*[4] in 1964 arose again in the case of *Tsosane* v. *Tsosane* (Civ./A/6/68) which was decided by Jacobs, C.J., in 1969. The case concerned a dispute over the estate of the deceased between his two widows. The appellant was the deceased's first wife by a customary marriage, while the respondent was his second wife by a civil marriage contracted in South Africa. The only child of the deceased was a daughter of the first marriage. The disputed property consisted of a mill bought jointly by the deceased and the respondent on hire-purchase and a post-office savings bank book. During the last two years of the deceased's life he and the respondent had jointly operated the milling business and the profits had been deposited in the savings account.

In the court of first instance the appellant was successful in her claim to be the heir of the whole estate under customary law as the senior widow. On appeal to the Judicial Commissioner's Court this decision was reversed.

In the High Court, Jacobs, C.J., mentioned at the outset that:

> "Both the courts below and counsel appearing for the parties in this court . . . dealt with the matter on the basis that Basuto law recognises the existence side by side of a civil marriage and a customary union and that a 'second house' was created by the civil marriage."

The view that such an arrangement can be countenanced by the law of Lesotho[5] and that it does not amount to the offence of bigamy coincides with that of the present writer[6], but conflicts with that of Harlow.[7]

The court proceeded to follow the decision of the Court of Appeal in *Khatala* v. *Khatala*[8] in holding that despite the fact that the deceased's marriage to the respondent was a civil one the intestate succession rights were to be governed by the customary law. In terms of Section 11(2) of the Laws of Lerotholi if there is no male issue in any house the senior widow is the heir, but this rule only applies in respect of unallocated property. The case therefore turned upon the applicability of Section 14(1) of the Laws of Lerotholi which regulates the position of allocated property as follows:

> "If a man during his lifetime allots his property amongst his various houses but does not distribute such property . . . his wishes must be carried out, provided the heir according to Basuto custom has not been deprived of the greater part of his father's estate."

The question was whether the mill and the savings bank book could be said to have been allocated to the respondent during the deceased's lifetime. The court held that the evidence did lead to this conclusion, especially in view of her assistance in the business and the joint hire-purchase agreement. Therefore the respondent while not the heir, was protected by Section 14(2) of the Laws of Lerotholi which allows a widow with no male issue to have the use of property allocated to her house for the rest of her life.

It was submitted on behalf of the appellant that the allocation of the mill and the savings bank book to the respondent deprived her, as the heir, of the greater part of the deceased's estate and therefore it was invalid. However the court found that this submission had not been established on the evidence.

The only doubt arising from the decision relates to the omission of any discussion as to whether the allocation could have been regarded as invalid for lack of family publicity. The existing decisions cited in Duncan's *Sotho Laws and Customs*[9] show that there is uncertainty as to whether this requirement is necessary. The only High Court decision seemingly in point, *Mantsebo Seeiso* v. *Bereng Griffith*[10] held that the validity of an allocation did not depend on the presence of the heir and publicity within the family, but Duncan considered that the decisions to the contrary reflected the true legal position.[11] The question therefore still seems to be an open one.

CONFLICTS (Succession.)

One of the areas in which the conflict between the two branches of Lesotho's dual legal system is most marked in the law of succession. Whereas by statute (amending the common law position) there is complete freedom of testation, the customary law as reflected in the Laws of Lerotholi gives a man only a restricted right to regulate the disposition of his property after his death by putting his wishes in writing.

On the one hand, the Law of Inheritance Act of 1874 provides:[12]

"Every person competent to make a will shall have full power by any will . . . to disinherit or omit to mention any child, parent, relative or descendant without assigning any reason for such disinheritance or omission, any law, usage or custom now or heretofore in force in Basutoland notwithstanding, and no such will as aforesaid shall be liable to be set aside as invalid, either wholly or in part, by reason of such disinheritance or omission as aforesaid."

On the other, the Laws of Lerotholi in Section 14(1) declare:

"If a man . . . dies leaving written instructions regarding the allotment (of property) on his death his wishes must be carried out, provided the heir according to Basuto custom has not been deprived of the greater part of his father's estate."

Whereas most choice of law questions are left to the common law, and the courts must therefore establish suitable tests for exercising their discretion in favour of one system or the other, the choice in the law of inheritance is partially regulated by statute. The Administration of Estates Proclamation[13] contains the following provision:

> "This Proclamation shall not apply . . .
> (*b*) to the estates of Africans which shall continue to be administered in accordance with the prevailing African law and custom of the territory; provided that such law and custom shall not apply to the estates of Africans who have been shown to the satisfaction of the Master to have abandoned tribal custom and adopted a European mode of life and who, if married, have married under European law."

The uncertainty of an African testator who had married "under European law" as to whether he would be deemed by the Master under the archaic wording of the section to be fit to have his estate regulated by the Proclamation, furnished the background to the dispute in *Hoohlo* v. *Hoohlo* (Civ./A/4/69).

The testator left a widow and five sons and in his will, which had been drawn up by his attorneys, he bequeathed his house to his youngest son. The preamble to the will recited that the testator had borne in mind the provisions of Section 14(1) of the Laws of Lerotholi, but had taken account of the fact that he had already spent a considerable sum of money on the education of his eldest son (the heir according to customary law) and that this sum represented considerably more than half of what the estate would have been worth if it had not been spent. Provision for the testator's widow was also made in the will and by a codicil she was appointed sole executrix. The eldest son challenged the bequest of the house to the youngest son alleging that the estate should be administered under customary law and that he was entitled as heir to inherit the property.

Since the Master had already accepted the estate for administration under the Proclamation the simple issue was whether he had erred in doing so on the basis that the deceased had not been shown to have "abandoned tribal custom and adopted a European mode of life".

Although the Master's certificate merely stated baldly that he had accepted the estate because he found the conditions for doing so had been satisfied, both the High Court and the Court of Appeal held that there was ample evidence in the will itself on which he was entitled to reach this conclusion. In the words of the Court of Appeal:

> "This revealed that the deceased had lived in the Maseru Reserve and not in a tribal area under a chief; that he had been married by civil rites as well as by customary union; that he had possessed motor vehicles; that he had a saving account with a Bank, that he had had his will drawn up by a firm of attorneys in the form appropriate to the requirements of the civil, that is the Roman-Dutch, law as practised in South Africa and Lesotho. It also showed that the deceased had spent a substantial sum of money on the education of his eldest son, the appellant, in order to fit him to earn a living in a non-tribal environment; for the appellant is described in the papers as an electrical engineer in the employ of the Lesotho Government and residing in Maseru; a fact of which it is not impossible that the Master may have had personal knowledge.

In my view there is no substance in the appellant's contention as to the deduction to be drawn from the references to customary law in the preamble of the will. According to the respondent and the attorney who drew the will those references were inserted because of uncertainty during the lifetime of the testator as to whether the will would eventually be accepted by the Master for administration in terms of the civil law, and uncertainty as to the outcome of a conflict between the civil law and the customary law in the administration of the estate. And so far from indicating that the deceased adhered to tribal law and custom the references seem to indicate the reverse. The testator was endeavouring to escape from the customary law and to exercise that freedom of testation, denied by customary law but available to him under the civil law, which enabled him in disposing of his estate to take into account the various amounts which he had spent during his lifetime on the education of his children, and also to make bequests to his widow which he might not have been able to make under the customary law."

Counsel for the eldest son had further submitted that the Master had merely "rubber-stamped" the will without any inquiry into the requirements of the relevant section. The Court of Appeal while agreeing that the Master's functions were quasi-judicial and therefore he was bound to have regard to the effect of his decision on the rights of possible heirs and beneficiaries, nevertheless held that the eldest son had had sufficient opportunity of adducing evidence that the deceased had not abandoned tribal custom and yet had not availed himself of it.

Aside from the decision itself which, it is submitted with respect, was correct, Roper, P., expressed his views on the direct conflict between the rules of customary law and the Law of Inheritance Act of 1874 which permits disinheritance of the heir "any . . . usage or custom now or heretofore in force in Basutoland notwithstanding". The Law of Inheritance Act was imported from the Cape Colony and the word "Basutoland" was only inserted in place of "this colony" (i.e. the Cape) in 1960.[14] Roper, P., discussed its history and application as follows:

"The object of this Act as of the earlier Cape Act No. 26 of 1873, was to abolish or modify certain provisions of the Roman-Dutch law, which of course was, as it still is, the common law of the Cape Colony, and it is not concerned with the customary law under which the native tribes of the Cape Colony were living. The 'usage or custom' referred to is not the customary law of the African tribes but usage and custom such as was recognised by the Roman-Dutch law as having legal force among people living under that system.

In those days the Legislature of the Cape simply shut its eyes to the existence of native customary law. British Kaffraria had been annexed to the Colony by Act No. 3 of 1865 and though native law and custom had been recognised in that territory before the annexation the statute made no provision whatever for its recognition after that event. Yet it was not replaced by the common law of the Cape as between natives living in the tribal way. Notwithstanding the absence of any express provision as to the customary law among natives living under tribal conditions, that law, as modified from time to time, has throughout been recognised between natives who have not been married by Christian rites or become detribalised. A reference to Whitfield's chapter on 'Succession and Inheritance' will show that restriction upon freedom of testation still holds good among tribes living in what was Cape Colonial territory, notwithstanding the provisions of the statutes of 1874 and 1876. The customary laws of the Basotho and the Laws of Lerotholi are not affected by that legislation."

Maisels, J.A., concurred with Roper, P., while Schreiner, J.A., stated that he preferred to express no opinion on this question. However it is respectfully submitted that the majority viewpoint is the correct one in restricting the operation of the statute to wills that are in the form prescribed by the common law or statute and not extending it to encompass "written instructions" in terms of Section 14(1) of the Laws of Lerotholi. They are indeed two completely different concepts.

CONFLICTS (Family law.)

In *Rakhoabe* v. *Rakhoabe* (Civ./T/11/68) the issue was whether the law governing a division of the joint estate upon judicial separation was the common law, the customary law or the statute law of the Republic of South Africa.

The parties were married by civil rites in South Africa at a time when the husband was domiciled in Lesotho. The wife petitioned for a decree of judicial separation on the ground of adultery and for a division of the joint estate. The first question to be determined was the law applicable since according to the statute law of South Africa marriages *between Africans* are not in community of property unless the parties have declared in prescribed form prior to the marriage their intention that community of property shall take place.[15] On the other hand the reverse position applies under the law of Lesotho, all civil marriages (regardless of the parties' race) being in community of property unless otherwise agreed.

In the High Court Evans, J., held that the *lex domicilii* prevailed, but that the parties could not approbate and reprobate and have it both ways and therefore the law applicable to the particular circumstances of the case was the customary law. He therefore granted a decree of judicial separation *a mensa et thoro*, but refused to order a separation of the joint estate. The wife appealed against this refusal.

The Court of Appeal followed the South African decision in *Frankel's Estate* v. *The Master*[16] and upheld the decision of Evans, J., to the effect that the *lex domicilii* governed the property rights of the parties and further held that the South African statute was no part of the law of Lesotho and therefore the marriage was in community of property. However the court found it difficult to follow the reasoning of Evans, J., where he stated:

"they cannot approbate or reprobate in that the community excluded by statute in South Africa can still apply in Lesotho at common law"

nor did it agree that the law applicable was the customary law.

"The marriage was a civil one and I am unable to see why the ordinary proprietary consequences of such a marriage should not apply. It follows therefore in my view that the marriage between the parties was in community of property."

The Court of Appeal was accordingly prepared to order a division of the joint estate.

It is submitted with respect that while the reasoning of Evans, J., was totally unconvincing, his decision as to the law applicable may nevertheless have been the correct one. At any rate the reasons given by the Court of Appeal were too succinctly stated to be really satisfying.

The question whether the marital property régime of a civil marriage is governed by the common law or customary law is not regulated by statute in Lesotho. As a result of missionary influence extending now for well over a century a large percentage of the population are Christians. For many years now it has been common practice for parties to go through two ceremonies of marriage, one in church and the other according to customary rites. Whether the intention that the property consequences should be governed by the common law can justifiably be attributed to the parties simply because they decide to follow the conventional practice of a church wedding seems highly questionable. This seems especially so if they continue to regulate their affairs according to a customary mode of life after marriage.

These considerations seemed to gain recognition by the Court of Appeal in 1964 in *Khatala* v. *Khatala*[17] where it was stated:

"In the absence of express provision to that effect there is no good reason for holding that all marriages under the provisions of the Marriage Proclamation carry the consequences of a marriage governed by Roman-Dutch law. It is unnecessary to express a view on whether all marriages by Basuto in Basutoland have identical proprietary consequences; it is enough to say that where, as here, Basutos living 'according to the Basuto custom' marry according to Basuto rights as well as according to Christian rites, their proprietary relations during their joint lives and their intestate succession rights after the death of one of them are governed by Basuto law."[18]

Khatala's *case* was admittedly a stronger one for the application of customary law because in *Rakhoabe* v. *Rakhoabe* not only was there no evidence of a concurrent customary marriage but the civil marriage itself was contracted before a magistrate and not in church. For these reasons it might be considered that the parties could only have intended the common law to regulate their property régime. However there was evidence that the wife at the time of the marriage had not properly understood the significance of the concept of community of property and so far as her subsequent mode of life was concerned she had pursued all the usual customary procedures within the family for settling the dispute before coming to court.

The facts of *Mosakeng* v. *Mosakeng* (Civ./T/15/68) which was also decided in 1969 by Evans, J., were closer to *Khatala* v. *Khatala* in that the parties were married both in church and according to customary rites.

The wife petitioned for a decree of judicial separation and division of the joint estate. The court made both orders as prayed in terms of the common law without any discussion of the law applicable and without any evidence as to the mode of life of the parties.

It seems clear therefore that the time is ripe for a detailed analysis by the courts of the exact legal consequences of a marriage contracted by civil rites in terms of the marriage Proclamation[19] and the factors involved in making the choice of law.

ECONOMIC DEVELOPMENT

Three statutes were enacted in 1969 with the purpose of fostering speedier economic development particularly in the industrial sector.

The Pioneer Industries Encouragement Act, No. 19 of 1969, provides tax incentives for approved manufacturers and related industries as well as for hotel and casino-keepers and building companies if they are establishing their businesses for the first time or if they are expanding their operations. A Pioneer Industries Board is created with the power to grant, subject to the agreement of the Minister responsible for commerce and industry, the necessary approval to an applicant satisfying the following requirements (Sections 7,13,15,17):

(i)   It must be registered as a company or co-operative society in accordance with the laws of Lesotho;

(ii) it must undertake to establish a new factory or plant engaging in manufacturing or a similar process, or a new hotel or casino (or to expand any of these) or, in the case of a building contractor, to construct, own and lease dwellings at a capital cost of not less than R100,000 or one or more industrial buildings to such standards as the Board may approve; and

(iii) it must satisfy the Board that in one of these ways it will contribute to the economic development of Lesotho.

An approved manufacturer is given a choice of two types of tax incentive and has to make its election between them on or before its date of production. One incentive is a six-year tax holiday including the carry forward of any overall losses during the six-year period which may be set off against income arising after the exemption period (Section 8,9). The alternative incentive is in the form of various special deductions in respect of the normal income tax payable, including a write-off allowance for new machinery of 100 per cent on top of a machinery investment allowance of 45 per cent, various building and industrial housing allowances, a utilities and transportation allowance and citizen training and wages allowances (Sections 8,10).

The tax incentives available to existing manufacturers as well as to hotel and casino-keepers and building contractors are similar to the special deductions granted to manufacturers, but the tax holiday is not applicable to them. (Sections 14,16,18).

The Casino Act, No. 26 of 1969, empowers the Gaming-Liquor Control Board to grant to an applicant, subject to the agreement of the Minister responsible for commerce, an exclusive authorisation to establish and operate casinos. The applicant must be incorporated in Lesotho and satisfy the Board that it has adequate financial means to develop the casino industry and that its directors are persons of integrity (Section 9). An exclusive authorisation is valid for a period of ten years in the first instance and may be renewed (Section 9). The Board may grant the holder of an exclusive authorisation a casino licence subject to certain conditions, one of which is that the holder may be required to provide such facilities as hotel rooms, restaurants, swimming pools, conference rooms, gaming rooms and bars (Section 10). The casino-keeper is required to pay annual licence fee of R2,000 in respect of each casino, a gaming levy of 20 per cent of the income derived from gaming and the normal rate of income tax, but the licence fee and gaming levy are deducted from gross income in assessing the total taxable income (Section 11). An obligation is imposed upon the casino-keeper to take all reasonable precautions to ensure that no person under the age of eighteen is present in a gaming room open for play (Section 20), and that residents of Lesotho participate in gaming on a cash basis only (Section 21).

The Act itself grants an exclusive authorisation and licence to Amalgamated Hotels (Lesotho) (Pty.) Ltd. together with the necessary approval in terms of the Pioneer Industries Encouragement Act to entitle it to special deductions from income tax. The same group also operates the casino recently established in Swaziland and it is noticeable that the Casino Act is drafted in very similar terms to the Swaziland Casino Proclamation.[20] An interesting omission however, from the Lesotho Act is the Swaziland provision that it is an offence for a public servant to participate in gaming in a casino.

The Industrial Licensing Act, No. 27 of 1969, is designed to establish an orderly system for the licensing of manufacturers. Every person engaged in a manufacturing enterprise and who manufactures for sale any product at any place within Lesotho must be in possession of a licence granted by the Pioneer Industries Board (Section 7). Moreover the Board may, subject to the approval of the Minister responsible for commerce and industry, grant a licence giving exclusive protection to a manufacture in respect of particular products provided it is satisfied that this is in the public interest and in the interest of the efficient development of the industry concerned (Section 16). The protection may be conferred for a period not exceeding five years in the first instance, but may be renewed for a further period not exceeding five years (Section 16).

A further enactment of note in relation to economic development is the Lesotho Constitution (First Amendment) Act, No. 14 of 1969, which abolished the National Planning Board. This Board was established by Section 90 of the 1966 Constitution with *inter alia* the following functions:

(i) to prepare plans for the economic development of Lesotho, including in particular the development, conservation and use of land and other natural resources;
(ii) to co-ordinate and supervise the preparation of such plans by the Government and other public authorities; and
(iii) to advise the Government and other public authorities in relation to the economic development of Lesotho.

It was felt, apparently, that the Board's executive powers conflicted with the responsibility of the Government in this sphere. The Prime Minister has announced that a National Planning Consultative Council will be set up with advisory powers only.

INTERNATIONAL LAW

Molefi v. *The Principal Legal Adviser* was the case which attracted most public interest in Lesotho during 1969. It was virtually a test case on the position of South African refugees in Lesotho and thus touched on controversial political issues. The case was also notable for being the first case from Lesotho to go on appeal to the Judicial Committee of the Privy Council since independence and, at the same time, the last.[21]

Molefi, a journalist, was a South African citizen who fled to Lesotho after being charged in South Africa with being a member of the unlawful Pan Africanist Congress and with furthering its aims. He was charged with contravening certain provisions of the South African Suppression of Communism Act, No. 44 of 1950. The charges against him related to alleged activities during 1960–1. He left South Africa in 1961 while he was released on bail and came to live in Lesotho where he resided up to the time of the present action.

In October 1968 he was informed by the Lesotho Government that, being an "Alien" in terms of the Aliens Control Act,[22] he was required to leave the country within three days. Since Lesotho is completely surrounded by South Africa this would have involved him in a return to South Africa or at any rate transit through that country.

Section 38 of the Aliens Control Act however provides:

"(1) If any international treaty or convention relating to refugees is or has been acceded to by or on behalf of the Government of Lesotho, an alien who is a refugee within the meaning of such a treaty or convention shall not be refused ... sojourn in Lesotho, and shall not be expelled from Lesotho in pursuance of the provisions of this Act except with his consent or except to the extent that is permitted by that treaty or convention ..."

Molefi relied for his protection on the 1951 Geneva Convention Relating to the Status of Refugees and sought an interdict preventing his expulsion from Lesotho. Various interim interdicts were granted during the hearings, but his substantive application was eventually refused by the High Court, and his appeals to the Court of Appeal and to the Judicial Committee of the Privy Council were both dismissed.

Before each court there were two main issues for determination. The first was whether the Convention Relating to the Status of Refugees had in fact been "acceded to by or on behalf of the Government of Lesotho" in terms of Section 38 of the Aliens Control Act. In this connection it was contended that a letter addressed to the Secretary-General of the U.N. by the Prime Minister constituted an accession. The letter ran as follows:

22nd March 1967

"Your Excellency,

The Government of the Kingdom of Lesotho is mindful of the desirability of maintenance, to the fullest extent compatible with the emergence into full independence of the Kingdom of Lesotho, of legal continuity between Lesotho and the several States with which, through the action of the Government of the United Kingdom the country formerly known as Basutoland enjoyed treaty relations. Accordingly, the Government of the Kingdom of Lesotho takes the present opportunity of making the following declaration:

2. As regards bilateral treaties validly concluded by the Government of the United Kingdom on behalf of the country formerly known as Basutoland, or validly applied or extended by the said Government to the country formerly known as Basutoland, the Government of the Kingdom of Lesotho is willing to continue to apply within its territory, on a basis of reciprocity, the terms of all such treaties for a period of twenty-four months from the date of independence (i.e. until October 4, 1968) unless abrogated or modified earlier by mutual consent. At the expiry of that period, the Government of the Kingdom of Lesotho will regard such of these treaties which could not by the application of the rules of customary international law be regarded as otherwise surviving, as having terminated.

3. It is the earnest hope of the Government of the Kingdom of Lesotho that during the aforementioned period of twenty-four months, the normal processes of diplomatic negotiations will enable it to reach satisfactory accord with the States concerned upon the possibility of the continuance or modification of such treaties.

4. The Government of the Kingdom of Lesotho is conscious that the above declaration applicable to bilateral treaties cannot with equal facility be applied to multilateral treaties. As regards these, therefore, the Government of the Kingdom of Lesotho proposes to review each of them individually and to indicate to the depositary in each case what steps it wishes to take in relation to each such instrument — whether by way of confirmation of termination, confirmation of succession or accession. During such interim period of review, any party to a multilateral treaty which has, prior to independence been applied or extended to the country formerly known as Basutoland, may, on a basis of reciprocity, rely as against Lesotho on the terms of such treaty.

5. It would be appreciated if Your Excellency would arrange for the text of this declaration to be circulated to all Members of the United Nations.

Please accept, Sir, the assurance of my highest Consideration.

Leabua Jonathan, *Prime Minister*."

Since the Convention had been extended to Basutoland by the United Kingdom prior to Lesotho's independence the question was whether the last sentence of para. 4 of the letter amounted to an accession.

In the High Court (Civ./Appn./31/68) Jacobs, C.J., held that it did not and that it was nothing more than an undertaking that where reciprocal rights and obligations arose under a particular treaty, the Government of Lesotho would honour its terms if the party with whom it was dealing at any particular time was prepared to do the same.

In the Court of Appeal (Civ./A/3/69) the three learned judges took up differing positions. Roper, P., agreed with the view of Jacobs, C.J., that the letter merely referred to an interim arrangement during a period of review.

> "This Convention . . . is one of those which are based on purely humanitarian grounds and are part of a general agreement to behave in an enlightened way towards a class of persons deserving of sympathy. It embodies no reciprocal obligations between states and in my view the letter has no application to this Convention.
>
> In my opinion the letter cannot be construed as an accession or adherence to the Convention; indeed it seems to me to be the reverse."

Schreiner, J.A., found it unnecessary to decide this point at all since he considered the appeal should be dismissed on other grounds.

Maisels, J.A., on the other hand, treated the question at length and after a most careful analysis concluded that the letter did indeed amount to an accession to the Convention by the Government. His reasoning found favour with the Privy Council and is therefore set out in some detail.

> "It seems to me that the terms of the letter manifest a plain desire on the part of the Government of Lesotho not to denounce but rather to adhere, albeit for a limited time and perhaps subject to certain conditions, to pre-independence treaties made by the Government of the United Kingdom in respect of Basutoland . . . . Professor O'Connell in *State Succession in Municipal Law and International Law*, volume II, page 113, *et seq*, points out (p. 113) that the former colonial and protected territories following independence have acted with respect to treaty continuity in contradictory fashion. There have apparently been three different positions taken. Certain states have adopted a generally negative attitude towards the question, i.e. they have not admitted succession to treaties entered into by the former colonial powers and have started with a clean slate. A number of States (p. 114) have acknowledged succession of the treaties, whereas others have adopted the 'Nyerere Doctrine' which is styled by the learned author as the 'temporising position' (p. 115). The learned author says at page 116:
>
>> 'When it became independent, Tanganyika did not wish to compromise its position in respect of one or two sensitive questions by signing a devolution agreement with the United Kingdom, and chose instead to make a declaration embodying what is known in Africa as "the Nyerere doctrine". Prime Minister Nyerere stated that for a period of two years Tanganyika would continue to apply British treaties. During that period these would be examined, and the other parties would be notified of the treaties which Tanganyika wished to continue. At the expiry of the period all treaties not confirmed would be deemed to have lapsed, save those succeeded to in virtue of customary international law. Largely because Tanganyika was linked with Uganda and Kenya in the East African Common Services Organization, these two States adopted the Tanganyikan

declaration (though in Uganda's case the period of review was eighteen months), so that treaties affecting the work of the Organization would expire in the case of both Tanganyika and Uganda at about the same time. Malawi adopted the Tanganyikan text, but prefaced it by an expression of desire to maintain existing treaty relations to the full extent compatible with independence, and gave itself a period for examination of a little more than one year. Botswana on 6 October 1966 and Lesotho on 22 March 1967 varied the text of this declaration. Following the making of each of these declarations, the United Kingdom wrote to the Secretary-General of the United Nationas stating that the United Kingdom had ceased to have the obligations or rights which derived from the relevant treaties.'

The terms of the Declaration by Mr. Nyerere, the Government of Kenya and by the Prime Minister of Malawi appear in *The Effect of Independence on Treaties*, a publication of the International Law Association, at pp. 370, 387 and 388 respectively. An examination of these declarations shows that the wording of the letter by the Prime Minister of Lesotho now under consideration must have been largely, if not entirely, based on the declarations of the Prime Minister of Malawi. Indeed *mutatis mutandis* and save that the period of the twenty-four months mentioned in para. 2 and 3 in the Lesotho Declaration is eighteen months in that of Malawi, the Malawi and Lesotho Declarations are in identical terms. Professor O'Connell on page 119 *op. cit.* states:

"The Nyerere doctrine, in essence, embodies the claim that the successor State is free to determine which treaties it wishes to continue and which it wishes to reject. This raises serious questions concerning the legal basis for continuity during the period of review. Certainly the doctrine operates as notice to terminate those treaties which are terminable on notice, and to this extent it is merely an unusual device of lawful denunciation. But inasmuch as it purports to achieve the termination of treaties which would not lapse on independence and are interminable, it operates only on the principle of tacit consent. And inasmuch as it depends for its achievement on customary international law, it has no advantage over the devolution agreements or other policy statements on treaty succession, and its main utility lies in the diplomatic value of letting all parties know where they stand . . .'

The letter itself starts with the statement 'The Government of the Kingdom of Lesotho is mindful of the desirability of maintenance . . . (of) legal continuity between Lesotho and the several States which through the action of the Government of the United Kingdom, the country formerly known as Basutoland enjoyed treaty relations'. The word 'accordingly' is the first word in the next sentence and everything that follows in the letter must, I consider, be read bearing in mind the declaration on the part of the Government of Lesotho that it is mindful of the desirability of legal continuity of pre-independence treaties . . . . As was recognised by the Government of Lesotho, it is obvious that multilateral treaties could not be treated in the same way as bilateral treaties, for example, questions of continuation, abrogation or modification of such treaties might well have to be dealt with in quite a different way. Consequently, it seems to me that it wished to have an undefined time to enable it to make up its mind as to what steps it wished to take with regard to each instrument 'whether by way of confirmation of termination, confirmation of succession or accession'. What was to happen during the time it was making up its mind in regard to the multilateral treaties? Were the treaties to be considered as not binding on Lesotho, or were they to be considered as binding? For an answer I turn to the words of the Declaration itself, viz:

> 'During such interim period of the review any party to a multilateral treaty which has prior to independence been applied or extended to . . . Basutoland may on a basis of reciprocity rely as against Lesotho on the terms of such treaty.'

In my opinion the meaning of the Lesotho Government Declaration in question is that the pre-independence multilateral treaties are to continue in existence and will be considered as binding on Lesotho until such time as the Government of Lesotho makes up its mind what it wants to do finally in regard to all or any one of these treaties, whether to terminate them, to succeed to them or to accede to them. Some difficulty is, however, occasioned by the words appearing in para. 4 of the letter 'on the basis of reciprocity'. It may be said that before the convention can be considered binding on Lesotho other States would have to agree that they accept the Lesotho Declaration. In Jowett's *Dictionary of English Law*, the following definition is given of 'reciprocity':

> 'The term is used in international law to denote the relation existing between two States when each of them gives the subjects of the other certain privileges, on condition that its own subjects shall enjoy similar privileges at the hands of the other State.'

Reciprocity in this sense really has no place in a Convention of the nature now under consideration. Indeed this Convention deals with cases where the citizen or national of one State flees from his own State . . . On the question of reciprocity, it is of course possible in the ordinary sort of case such as is dealt with in the definition quoted above, for the other States to refuse to accept the terms of the Lesotho Declaration, but in the Convention under consideration, having regard to its objects to the methods of accession and denunciation provided for therein, I doubt whether this situation can really arise . . . It may be argued that as in the ordinary sense of the word there appears to be no question of reciprocity in this Convention, the Declaration cannot constitute an accession to the Convention in view of the use of the words 'on a basis of reciprocity'; in other words, that the Declaration is limited to those Conventions where there may be said to be reciprocity in the ordinary sense of the word. The Convention now under consideration is not the only one where reciprocity in the ordinary sense of the word is not apparent. Other examples are Conventions on genocide, forced labour and slavery, human rights, the Geneva Convention for the care of the wounded. In my view full meaning is given to the Declaration by reading the words 'on a basis of reciprocity' as limited to those cases where reciprocity is required to make the treaty effective, but in those cases where this is not so, these words are to be treated as surplusage. C. Wilfred Jenks, in an article on 'State Succession in respect of Law-making Treaties' in the *British Year Book of International Law* 1952 p. 105 at p. 108–9 says:

> 'The psychology of newly won independence is a formidable reality, and juristic speculations on state succession which ignored it would be an altogether unprofitable exercise. The obligations of multipartite legislative instruments are not, however, badges of continuing servitude; they are a necessary part of full co-operation in the international community and participation in them must therefore be regarded as one of the hallmarks of

emancipation. Fischer Williams has reduced it to a truism: "The life of human-kind is a process of perpetual change, and legal rights cannot be made an exception to this process." If the contention that law-making treaties survive changes of sovereignty were inconsistent with this principle it would be wholly unrealistic, but it is not more inconsistent with the mutability of human affairs than the principle that a new member of the international community is bound by existing customary international law or the principle that a change of sovereignty does not automatically change the law governing private relationships. It is not a matter of perpetuating the dead hand of the past, but of avoiding a legal vacuum. Subject to any special obligations binding upon it as the result of the circumstances of its creation or recognition, the new state will have the same rights of denunciation under legislative instruments as existing states and, with the exception of the few instruments designed to effect a permanent and basic change in the law, virtually all multipartite legislative instruments now make reasonable provision for denunciation. In these circumstances, the independence of the new state is in no way impaired by the substitution of orderly processes of development and change for the uncertainty, confusion, and practical inconvenience of a legal vacuum which may be gravely prejudicial not only to the interests of other states concerned but equally to the interests of the new state itself and its citizens. The suggestion sometimes made that there is no treaty vacuum because pre-existing treaty obligations will generally continue to be binding on an existing state misconstrues the nature of the problem. There *is* such a vacuum in respect of the territory and citizens of the new state, which may comprise hundreds of thousands of square miles and millions of citizens, and in a wide range of cases the effectiveness of law-making treaties which cease to be applicable to them, even temporarily, will also be impaired elsewhere.'

I think these remarks are apposite in the present case. The Declaration by the Government of Lesotho was an intimation, I consider, of its recognition that multilateral treaties 'are a necessary part of full co-operation in the international community' and of its intention to be bound by those entered into on its behalf by the United Kingdom pending an examination of each one, a matter which in the very nature of things would take time.

It was also contended on behalf of the respondents that the Declaration was merely a notification that the Government of Lesotho would carry out the treaties but would not be obliged to do so — a statement of policy without binding obligations. The use of the words 'may rely' seems to me to negate this interpretation. The Declaration was deposited with the Secretary-General of the United Nations who in terms of the Convention (Article 39) is the depositary, and reading the Declaration as a whole, it does in my opinion constitute an instrument of accession by the Government of Lesotho to the Convention which is an international convention relating to refugees. That being so the Convention has been made part of the municipal law of Lesotho by virtue of the provisions of Section (38(1) of the Aliens Act *supra*."

As stated above the Privy Council (P. C. Appeal No. 27 of 1969) substantially agreed with Maisels, J.A., and held that the Prime Minister's letter was a declaration that pending individual examination of those multilateral treaties which had resulted in treaty relations between Basutoland and other states, Lesotho would adhere to such treaties.

The second main issue in the case was whether or not Molefi was a "refugee" within the meaning of Article 1 of the Convention. This term was defined to refer to any person who:

> "as a result of events occurring before 1st January 1951 and owing to well-founded fear of being persecuted for reasons of race, religion, nationality, membership of a particular social group or political opinion, is outside the country of his nationality and is unable, or, owing to such fear, is unwilling to avail himself of the protection of that country; or who, not having a nationality and being outside the country of his former habitual residence as a result of such events, is unable or, owing to such fear, is unwilling to return to it".

The important part of the definition was the opening phrase, "as a result of events occurring before 1st January 1951", since it was necessary for Molefi to establish that he left South Africa as a result of such events despite the fact that he did not actually leave until 1961. The events he relied upon were the coming to power of the Nationalist Party in 1948, the repressive policy of the South African Government against Africans and the enactment of repressive measures, including the 1950 Suppression of Communism Act.

The difficulty faced by the courts was to determine what test applied in deciding the meaning to be attached to the words "as a result of events . . .".

In the High Court, Jacobs, C.J., declared:

> "Now I am prepared to assume that the words 'as a result of events' in the Convention do not require a direct and immediate causal connection between the events and the result but that they i.e. the words, should be construed to have been used in a somewhat broad, practical sense, connoting causal relationship not necessarily as between the result and the cause nearest to that result, but as between a result and a cause not too remote from it or, to use the words of Sir Samuel Evans in *H.M.S. London* (L.R. 1914 p. 72 at 77), 'Sufficiently near for the courts to give effect to it'. Employing this 'empirical or common sense view of causation' (Lord Wright's words in *Smith, Hogg and Co.* v. *Black Sea and Baltic General Insurance Co.*, 1940 A.C. at p.1003) I consider that the enactment of the [Suppression of Communism Act] by the South African Parliament in 1950 . . . may have been a *causa sine qua non* of the charge against him but that it was the charge itself, based on the applicant's activities long after 1951, which was the *causa* of his flight from South Africa."

In the Court of Appeal Roper, P., applied the same test of causation and reached the same conclusion as Jacobs, C.J. He found that the reasons for Molefi's flight were his membership of the Pan-Africanist Congress (which could not have been before 1959, as it was only founded then), his resulting prosecution in 1961 and his fear of conviction and the direct and indirect penalties which might and probably would result from it.

> "Properly regarded, the pre-1951 South African legislation and the repressive Government policy referred to . . . were merely the background to these events, or, as it was put by Lord Wright (*loc. cit.*), a part of the history or narrative."

Schreiner, J.A., reached the same conclusion. He did not attempt to formulate exactly what the meaning of the expression "as a result of events" was, but simply stated:

"In the absence of explanation the fact that he did not make the change of residence until some ten years after the passing of the 1950/1951 legislation leads me to reject the view that it is more probable than not that he emigrated because of the 1950/1951 legislation or because of any other event or events happening before 1st January 1951".

Maisels, J.A., concurred with Roper, P., and Schreiner, J.A., on this question.

In the Judicial Committee their Lordships considered that the phrase "as a result of events occurring before 1st January 1951" must be applied

"with common sense while remembering that one event may often lead to another which in turn may lead to another or others. The words do not call for legalistic or philosophical examination. A mean can be found between too much stiffness of interpretation and too much easiness of application. When the facts of a situation are ascertained and known then in a fair-minded way those facts must be surveyed and an answer given to the straightforward question which is posed. If after a fair-minded approach an answer is readily and clearly given it may not be one that requires or permits of detailed elaboration."

The Privy Council, after pointing out that the Pan-Africanist Congress only came into existence in 1959 and only became an unlawful organisation in 1960, and that Molefi had remained in South Africa for thirteen years after the 1948 elections and eleven years after the passing of the Suppression of Communism Act, upheld the decisions of the lower courts and dismissed the appeal.

---

1. *Annual Statistical Bulletin*, 1967.
2. See Sheddick, *Land Tenure in Basutoland* (H.M.S.O., 1954).
3. (1963–6) H.C.T.L.R. 38.
4. (1963–6) H.C.T.L.R. 97.
5. Under South African law, which does not generally recognise the validity of marriages by customary rites, the effect of the civil marriage would be to dissolve the prior "customary union", but the property and succession rites of the first "wife" under customary law would be preserved — *Nicambula* v. *Linda*, 1951 (1) S.A. 377.
6. (1969) J. A. L. 127 at 134–5; see also Ramolefe, *Restatement of the Sesotho Customary Law of Marriage* (unpublished).
7. See (1966) J.A.L. 168 at 170.
8. *Supra*
9. (O.U.P., 1960), p. 16.
10. H.C.C. No. 6 of 1946 (unreported).
11. *Op. cit.*, p. 17.
12. Part II, Section 5.
13. Proc. 19 of 1935.
14. By the Law Revision Proclamation, No. 12 of 1960.
15. Act 38 of 1927, Section 22(6).

16. 1950 (1) S.A. 220 (A.D.).
17. *Supra.*
18. At p. 100.
19. Proc. 7 of 1911.
20. No. 56 of 1963.
21. Appeals were finally abolished by the Court of Appeal and High Court Order, No. 17 of 1970, Section 7(1).
22. No. 16 of 1966.

CHAPTER 14

SWAZILAND

N. N. Rubin

This survey covers the first full calendar year of Swaziland's independence. Most of the major structural changes in the constitutional, judicial and legal systems had occurred before or at the time of independence. The year under review was thus mainly one of legislative consolidation, with a number of significant developments in the fiscal and private law fields but no event of overwhelming importance in the area of public law.

CONSTITUTIONAL LAW AND GOVERNMENT

Acting in terms of the Swaziland Independence Order in Council,[1] King Sobhuza II of Swaziland issued a legal notice[2] which modified or adapted a large number of laws already on the statute book to "bring them into conformity with the Constitution". Some 188 measures were amended, and the amendments are given in the schedule to the order. Most of them are textual and are designed to take account of changes which follow from Swaziland's new status, both as an independent state and as a Kingdom.[3] One amendment to the General Interpretation proclamation[4] is of constitutional importance, however. A new Section 23 replaces the old one, and reads:

> "*Saving of the rights of His Majesty and the Government.*
> 23. No law shall in any manner whatsoever affect the rights of His Majesty the King or of the Government unless it is therein expressly stated or unless it appears by necessary implication that His Majesty or the Government, as the case may be, is bound thereby."

In view of the considerable personal and proprietary privileges and rights enjoyed by the King in terms of the Constitution, the protection thus afforded him may be a source of future legal controversy.

Treaty obligations

The contractual and treaty obligations of the Swaziland Government were dealt with prior to independence, by a British Order in Council[5] which inserted the following provisions into the Constitution:

235

"Transfer of rights and obligations
10*A*. (1) All rights, liabilities and obligations of Her Majesty in right of the Government of Swaziland subsisting under the law of Swaziland immediately before the appointed day[6] shall, as from the appointed day, be rights, liabilities and obligations of the Government of the Kingdom of Swaziland and, subject to the provisions of any law, shall be enforceable by or against the Government.

(2) In this section, reference to rights, liabilities and obligations arising under contract [sic] of otherwise but, except in the case of any agreement expressed to be between Swaziland and the International Bank for Reconstruction and Development or between Swaziland and the International Development Association, shall not include rights, liabilities and obligations arising under any treaty, convention or agreement with another country or with any international organisation."

This disavowal of succession to treaty obligations was, however superseded and modified, at least for a period of two years, as a result of a declaration made by the Swaziland Minister of State for Foreign Affairs on 22nd October 1968 at the United Nations. The Minister stated that, for a period of two years from 6th September 1968, Swaziland accepted all treaty rights and obligations entered into prior to independence by the British Government on behalf of the Kingdom of Swaziland. Such treaties would be examined during the two-year period, and at the end thereof it would be determined which rights and obligations would be adopted, which terminated and which adopted with reservations.[7]

The Order in Council also vested all property rights and assets which previously inhered in the Queen of England "for the purposes of the Government of Swaziland" in the Swaziland Government, subject to any subsisting rights or interests which had been granted to or vested in any other person.[8]

Parliament

The procedure relating to Private Bills and their introduction was established by order of the Speaker of the House of Assembly and the President of the Senate in terms of the Constitution.[9] A private Bill is defined as follows:

"Unless it is introduced by a Minister or the presiding officer decides otherwise, every Bill for the particular interest or benefit of any person or persons shall be treated by the House as a private Bill."

The procedure provides for advertisement, examination, opposition and the rights of petitioners in opposition to private bills to be heard.

Local government

The Urban Government Act[10] provides at length for the establishment of municipalities by the Minister for Local Administration, and for the election or appointment of municipal or town councils. The statute also provides detailed rules for the meetings of councils and committees; management committees; staff; duties and powers of councils; land, streets and public places; bye-laws; various matters relating to the financial and accounting procedures; and for central control and inspections. Other statutory provisions relate to towns and town boards, bribery and the limitation of actions in respect of acts or omissions on the part of councils to a period of one year from the date on which the claimant had knowledge or could reasonably have had knowledge of the act or omission alleged.[11] Urban Government Financial Regulations and Elections regulations were also issued during the course of the year.[12]

JUDICIAL AND LEGAL SYSTEM

A number of minor amendments were introduced in respect of the Court of Appeal by the omnibus legal notice issued by the King and already referred to on p. 235, and this was also done in respect of the High Court. New Rules of the High Court were introduced[13] and replace the previous rules.[14]

The Water Act[15] amended the 1967 Act of the same name by the introduction of a new section dealing with the status and composition of the court, as follows:

"*Constitution of Water Court.*
41. (1) A Water Court shall be a superior court of record and shall be presided over by the Chief Justice, or by a person appointed by him who possesses the qualifications which would entitle him to be appointed a Judge of the High Court.
(2) A Water Court shall consist of the Chief Justice or a Judge appointed by him in terms of sub section (1) sitting alone or, if the Judge presiding over the Court so directs, with one engineer assessor and not more than two lay assessors, appointed or selected as hereinafter provided."[16]

It also went on to provide the following new section relating to assessors:

"*Appointment of Assessors.*
44. At any hearing before a Water Court the assessor shall advise the judge presiding over the Court on all matters of fact which the Court is called upon to decide but the decision of the Judge shall be the decision of the Court."

Rules of the Water Court were issued by the Chief Justice during the course of the year.[17]

King Sobhuza's omnibus legal notice also contained amendments relating to the Subordinate Courts Proclamation[18] which provided for appointment, through a notice in the *Gazette*, by the Judicial Commission, of magistrates and assistant magistrates to hold subordinate courts of a class specified in such notice. The Chief Justice is authorised by the amended provision to confer jurisdiction, with the concurrence of the Minister of Local Administration, on a District Officer to hold a subordinate court of the first class, and on a Cadet to hold a subordinate court of the second class. Unless the notice in the *Gazette* containing such appointments specifies otherwise, any conferment of jurisdiction in this way by the Chief Justice or by the Judicial Service Commission, is deemed to confer jurisdiction to hold a court within any District in Swaziland.[19]

The Legal Practitioners (Amendment) Act[20] amended the 1964 Legal Practitioners Proclamation so as to provide that a period of pupillage in the Attorney-General's Chambers shall rank as the equivalent of articles of clerkship.

CRIMINAL LAW

The principal new statute introduced during the year in this field was the Fugitive Offenders (Commonwealth) Act.[21] As the name indicates, it provides in detail for the arrest, detention, commital and return of a person "found in Swaziland who is accused of a relevant offence in any other country" in the Commonwealth, to that country. The relevant offences are specified in a schedule to the Act. They are subject to an overall restriction to the effect that they must be punishable by not less than twelve months' imprisonment (except where the act or omission alleged would constitute an offence against the law of Swaziland if it took place within Swaziland).[22] The Act also specifically excludes the application of any of the procedures which it establishes to offences "of a political character", as well as those which appear to the Prime Minister, the court of commital or the High Court to involve an offence which

> ". . . (though purporting to be made on account of a relevant offence) is in fact made for the purpose of prosecuting or punishing [a person] on account of his race, religion, nationality or political opinions";

or that

> "he might, if returned, be prejudiced at his trial or punished, detained, or restricted in his personal liberty by reason of his race, religion, nationality or political opinions".[23]

Similarly, the provisions do not apply where, if the person were charged with the offence in Swaziland, he would be discharged under any law relating to previous acquittal or conviction.[24] Furthermore, a person may not be returned to a country unless the law of that country (or an arrangement with that country) provides that he will not be tried in respect of any offence other than the offence in respect of which his return is requested, or a lesser offence established by the same facts, or such other relevant offence as the Prime Minister of Swaziland consents to.[25]

It should be noted that, since the Act only applies to Commonwealth countries, it does not apply to the return of offenders to the Republic of South Africa.[25a]

An unusual offence is created in terms of the Road Traffic Law of 1965 by means of regulations issued thereunder,[26] in respect of eight designated urban areas. It is an offence to convene, attend or take part in a meeting or procession of persons or vehicles (other than in connection with funerals, weddings or for Naval, Military or Police purposes) without the prior permission in writing of a District Officer for the relevant area. The penalty for breach is a fine of up to R.100 (one hundred Rands) or imprisonment for three months, or both the fine and imprisonment. The definition of a meeting is very broad. It means:

"an assembly, gathering or concourse of *more than seven* persons held or convened for any purpose, *including a lawful purpose*".[27]

FISCAL AND FINANCIAL LAW

The International Financial Organisations Act[28] provided for Swaziland's membership of the International Monetary Fund, the International Bank for Reconstruction and Development, the International Finance Corporation and the International Development Association. The Articles of Agreement of the various institutions are incorporated as Schedules to the Act.

A major alteration in the basis of Swaziland's Government revenue resulted from the conclusion of a new Customs Agreement between the governments of Botswana, Lesotho, Swaziland and South Africa. This was made in December 1969, and was published in the *Gazette*.[29] In view of its importance, it is appended in full at the end of this chapter. What follows is a summary of its effect, in the context of the *status quo ante*.[30]

The 1969 agreement superseded one made in 1910, in terms of which the three countries received a fixed proportion amounting to 1.31097 per cent of the duty on goods passing through South Africa. This percentage was, in turn, divided among the three former High Commission Territories (Basutoland, now Lesotho; Bechuanaland Protectorate, now Botswana; and Swaziland) as follows:

	1910–64	1964–9
Botswana	0.27622 per cent	0.30971 per cent
Lesotho	0.88575 per cent	0.47093 per cent
Swaziland	0.14900 per cent	0.53033 per cent
	1.31097 per cent	1.31097 per cent

In terms of the new agreement, no fixed percentage of the total Customs revenue is distributable. The amount available to each of the three countries other than South Africa will vary, but will be based on the following formula, which is expected to increase the total sum available: for each of the countries, a calculation will be made of its imports plus the production of goods subject to excise and sales duties. This will be divided by the total imports plus production of excisable and goods subject to sales duty in the entire Customs area, i.e. including South Africa. The quotient is then multiplied by a factor of 1.42 to give the percentage of the common revenue pool from Customs, excise and sales duties that goes to each territory.

The new agreement was due to come into operation from March 1970, but was ante-dated to April 1969. In respect of the fiscal year 1967–8, Swaziland was to receive R.7.1 million, Lesotho R.5 million and Botswana R.4.1 million.

The immediate effect of this re-allocation was that the increased revenue offset nearly all of Swaziland's budgetary deficit (which had, however, been met by a grant-in-aid from the British Government). The longer-term effect would not be noticeable in financial terms, since Britain was expected to withraw its budgetary aid in view of Swaziland's increased revenue. In general, then, the effect can be seen as decreasing Swaziland's dependence on Britain and increasing its dependence on the common Customs area.

One of the complaints against the 1910 agreement was that the absence of tariff barriers within Southern Africa prevented the three smaller countries from offering protection to industries in need thereof. This has been rectified by Article 6 of the new agreement which enables Botswana, Lesotho and Swaziland (but not South Africa) to levy additional duties on imports to meet competition from other manufacturers in the common Customs area. Any such additional duties must, however, be removed within a period of eight years.

In addition, where one of the other three countries specifies an industry as being of importance to its economy, South Africa will undertake not to reduce the common Customs duty in respect of the product concerned, and will give "sympathetic consideration" to any application from one of the other three countries for the imposition of a higher duty where protection is needed.

South Africa has agreed to consult with the three territories concerning general changes in duties, though its right to determine these is unaltered.

CONTRACT AND DELICT

In the field of contract, the main development was the passage of the Hire Purchase Act,[31] which applies to both movable and immovable property.

In respect of immovable property sold after the date of commencement of the Act[32] (other than that sold by the Government) a buyer who has agreed to pay the purchase price in more than two instalments at specified periods, and who has paid at least 50 per cent of the purchase price, is entitled to demand, in writing, that the seller transfer the property to him against registration in favour of the seller of a first mortgage bond over the property to secure the balance of the purchase price (and any interest) payable in terms of the agreement of sale. If the seller fails to transfer the property within three months of receiving such a written demand, the buyer may cancel the agreement. He may also recover from the seller (against the return of the property, if the seller is not in possession thereof) the total amount paid by him in pursuance of the agreement, together with an amount in respect of damages which he has sustained.[33] The wording of the relevant provision indicates that the cancellation of the agreement and the pecuniary remedies afforded apply only where a buyer who is already in possession vacates it in favour of the seller.

The remaining provisions of the Act apply only to movable property, and agreements in respect thereof. The Act distinguishes between a "hire-purchase agreement" and an "instalment agreement". The former is defined as:

"any agreement whereby goods are sold subject to the condition that the ownership in such goods shall not pass merely by the transfer of the possession of such goods, and the purchase price is to be paid in instalments, two or more of which are payable after such transfer; and includes any other agreement which has, or agreements which together have, the same import, whatever form such agreement or agreements may take:
Provided that any agreements which together provide for the letting and hiring of goods—
  (*a*) with the right to purchase such goods only after two or after more than two instalments subsequent to such transfer have been paid in respect thereof; or
  (*b*) with the right, after two or after more than two instalments subsequent to such transfer have been paid in respect thereof, to continue or renew from time to time, the right to be in possession of the goods, without any further payment or against payment of a nominal periodical or other amount
shall, whether or not the agreement may at any time be terminated by either party or one of the parties, for the purposes of this Act, be deemed to be of the said import."

An "instalment agreement" is defined as:

"any agreement of purchase and sale whereby ownership in the goods sold passes upon delivery, and the purchase price is to be paid in instalments, two or more of which are payable after delivery, and under which the buyer is prohibited from alienating or encumbering the goods sold until the purchase price has been paid in full or the full purchase price becomes payable if the buyer alienates or encumbers the goods sold, or the seller would be entitled to the return of the goods if the buyer should fail to comply with any one or more provisions thereof, and includes any other agreement which has or agreements which together have the same import whatever form such agreement or agreements may take."

The Act enables the Minister of Commerce, Industry and Mines to prescribe the portion of the cash price of any movables which must be paid on conclusion of the agreement: if he does not do so, the portion is fixed by Section 9(1)(*a*) at a minimum of 10 per cent thereof; the Minister may also prescribe the maximum period within which the total purchase price must be paid. Other sections of the Act provide that a prospective buyer must be informed of the cash-sale price of goods (Section 5); that agreements must be in writing and that a copy must be supplied to the buyer, failure to comply with the first part of this requirement rendering the agreement void (Section 6). Section 7 prescribes the necessary clauses in an agreement (including details of the cash price, amount and dates of instalments payable, description of the goods, and any terms as to the reservation and passing of ownership in the goods). It is also necessary to include details of all sums included in the purchase price, each separately itemised. No mention is made of any need to state the amount of interest charged, though it is possible that the need to give each item would cover this. Failure to "substantially comply" with this section does not invalidate the agreement; it gives rise to an offence.

An agreement is of no force and effect in respect of a movable if the appropriate prescribed portion of the cash price has not been paid, and if the period prescribed for the payment of the entire purchase price is exceeded.[34] The wording of the provision is far from easy to interpret, especially because of the number of negatives contained in it, but it would seem that both elements — in respect of the cash deposit and the time — must be absent if invalidity is to ensue.

There are a number of provisions which appear to be designed to protect buyers. Section 14 renders a seller disentitled to enforce a provision for the acceleration of payment of any instalment unless an instalment amounting to not less than a tenth of the purchase price is due and unpaid; or where two or more instalments amounting to not less than a twentieth of the purchase price are unpaid. The effect is to make it easier for the seller to enforce such a provision as the number of unpaid instalments increases. By relating the right to accelerate to the ratio of instalments outstanding on the total purchase price rather than the balance due, the protection afforded the purchaser is also considerably diminished. The section also requires a seller to give a buyer at least ten days' notice in writing at his last known address before seeking to enforce a contractual right to a claim for damages, forfeiture, penalty or the acceleration of instalment payments. Section 15 entitles a buyer to be reinstated in possession of goods recovered by the seller for non-payment of instalments if, within twenty-one days of the seller's repossession, he pays all arrears due in terms of the agreement.

If the buyer wishes to terminate the agreement, he may do so at any time. But where he does so, he must give written notice to the seller of his intention to do so; and he must tender to the seller the return of the goods. He must also place the seller in the financial position he (the seller) would have been in if all the obligations of the buyer had been performed thereunder.[35]

The buyer may at any time pay an instalment in advance of the date on which it is due. He may also accelerate payment of the entire balance due in respect of the contract. In the latter case, he must pay all interest due up to the date of payment; and (except where he does so in respect of the last payment due) he is entitled to a reduction of each instalment not yet due at the time of payment at the rate of $7\frac{1}{2}$ per cent per annum.[36] Generally, the buyer is protected from performing any act or obligation, in the event of termination or rescission of the contract, which would have the effect of placing the seller in a better position than he would have been in if the agreement had expired through regular performance of all the buyer's obligations.[37] Other Sections of the Act deal with the valuation of goods, the powers of a court, the creation of an automatic interdict prohibiting the use or removal of goods which are the subject of a summons issued by a seller; and a bar on the issue of a decree of civil imprisonment or a garnishee order as a means of enforcing payments under an agreement, or arising from its termination or rescission, or as damages for any breach thereof.

There was virtually no legislation passed during the year on the law of delict. The omnibus order referred to above repealed the Crown Liabilities Proclamation;[38] an Apportionment of Damages Bill was introduced during the year, but does not appear to have been passed before the year ended.[39]

FAMILY LAW

An Adoption of Children (Amendment) Act[40] was the only legislative development in this field, and it introduced only minor changes, most of which were designed to give control over the adoption procedures, in independent Swaziland, to the Minister for Local Administration. A new Section 15 makes it clear, however, that the statutory rules shall not "be construed as preventing or affecting the adoption of a child in accordance with Swazi law and custom".

PROPERTY

A considerable number of amendments were introduced in this field by the omnibus amending order issued by King Sobhuza II. A large proportion of these are purely textual and are designed either to accord with Swaziland's new status (e.g. by substituting the word "Government" for the word "Crown") or to tidy up legislation. Occasionally, however, textual amendments can produce substantive changes, as where the word "Africans" in the Ancillary Rights Proclamation[41] is replaced by the words "Swazi people" — an alteration which does not, however, deviate from what was probably the intended scope of the previous legislation.

There is a very large number of amendments to the Mining Proclamation and the Mining Regulations,[42] the import of which can only be indicated in general terms. The effect seems to be to put beyond doubt the dominant role of the King (as Nggwenyama)[43] in respect of title to minerals and the right to mine for them, as well as that of the Government acting through the Minister of Commerce, Industry and Mines.

During the course of the year the following sets of regulations were also issued: The Standard Building Regulations[44] (91 pp.); the Buildings Operations Regulations[45] (23 pp.); the Mines and Quarries (Machinery) Regulations[46] (78 pp.); the Mines and Quarries (Safety) Regulations[47] (42 pp.).

PROCEDURE AND EVIDENCE

Among the numerous minor alterations introduced into laws which come under this heading by means of the omnibus order, there are several which establish the role of the Attorney-General as the principal official "vested with the right and entrusted with the duty of prosecuting in the name and on behalf of His Majesty in accordance with the powers conferred on him by Section 91 of the Constitution".[48]

A new offence, with equivalent penalties to those for perjury, was created in connection with conflicting statements made under oath: the effect is that it is unnecessary for the prosecution to show more than a conflict between the statements, without proving which was false, to establish the offence.[49]

A Criminal Procedure and Evidence and Road Traffic (Amendment) Act[50] introduces new sections into the main Proclamation dealing with the taking of fingerprints, palm prints, footprints and specimens of blood,[51] and the use of these in evidence.[52] It also introduces a section dealing with the taking and use of breath tests in connection with persons suspected of driving under the influence of alcohol.[53]

MISCELLANEOUS

It is worth noting that a new Public Health Act[54] was passed during the year, and that a comprehensive set of Aviation Regulations (in 280 pp.) was issued in terms of the Aviation Act.[56]

---

1. I.e., the Constitution, Section 5 (3).
2. No. 8 of 1969, dated 5th March 1969.
3. Some of those which did involve substantive changes will be referred to elsewhere in this chapter.
4. Cap. 2, Laws of Swaziland.
5. Swaziland Constitution (Amendment) Order, Statutory Instrument No. 727 of 1968.
6. I.e. independence, on 6th September 1968.
7. See explanatory note, Legal Notice No. 35 of 1969, dated 30th June 1969.
8. A new Section 10*B* incorporated these provisions but saved the reservation made in Section 89 of the Constitution.
9. Legal Notice No. 17 of 1969, dated 12th March 1969.
10. Act No. 8 of 1969, brought into force from 1st July 1969 by Legal Notice No. 31 of 1969.
11. Section 116.
12. By Legal Notice No. 32 of 1969, and Legal Notice No. 36 of 1969 respectively.
13. By Legal Notice No. 3 of 1969, incorporating an order of the Chief Justice dated 21st November 1968; this was later amended by Legal Notice No. 27 of 1969; incorporating an order by the Chief Justice dated 20th May 1969.
14. Cap. 19 of the Laws of Swaziland.
15. Act No. 1 of 1969.
16. See, on Water Courts, "Swaziland" in *Judicial and Legal Systems in Africa*, edited by A. N. Allott, pp. 238–240.
17. Legal Notice No. 26 of 1969, incorporating an order by the Chief Justice dated 19th May 1969.
18. Cap. 20, Laws of Swaziland.
19. New Section 4, Subordinate Courts Proclamation.

20. No. 23 of 1969.
21. No. 9 of 1969.
22. *Ibid.*, Section 5.
23. *Ibid.*, Section 6(1).
24. *Ibid.*, Section 6(2).
25. *Ibid.*, Section 6(3).
25a. A separate treaty of extradition with S. Africa came into force on October 5th 1968; it also excludes political offences.
26. Road Traffic (Public Meetings) Regulations, Legal Notice No. 12 of 1969, amended by Legal Notice No. 41 of 1969.
27. Emphasis added.
28. No. 27 of 1969.
29. Legal Notice No. 71 of 1969, dated 11th December 1969.
30. For a description of the problems associated with the formation of this agreement see B. Turner, "The Southern African Customs Union" in *African Affairs*, Vol. 70 No. 280, pp. 269–76.
31. No. 11 of 1969.
32. 16th May 1969.
33. Hire-Purchase Act Section 30.
34. Section 9, the first sub-section of which reads:
    "*Invalidity of Certain agreements*
    9(1). No agreement in respect of the sale of a movable shall be of any force or effect:
    (*a*) until at least the appropriate prescribed portion of the cash price of such movable or, if no such portion has been prescribed, at least one-tenth of such price has been paid; and
    (*b*) unless the period within which the full purchase price is payable does not exceed the appropriate prescribed period (if any)."
35. Section 16(1)(*a*) read with Section 17(1)(*b*).
36. Section 16(1)(*b*).
37. Section 17(1)(*a*) and (2).
38. Cap. 23, Laws of Swaziland.
39. For the Bill, see the Supplement to the Swaziland Government Gazette dated 25th July 1969, Part *A*, Section 5.
40. No. 22 of 1969, amending Cap. 34 of the Laws of Swaziland.
41. Cap. 138, Laws of Swaziland.
42. Cap. 145, Laws of Swaziland.
43. This is the traditional title of the Swazi King: the spelling was altered to include a second "g" in various statutes by the omnibus order.
44. Legal Notice No. 22 of 1969.
45. Legal Notice No. 19 of 1969.
46. Legal Notice No. 66 of 1969.
47. Legal Notice No. 67 of 1969.
48. The wording of the new Section 7 of the Criminal Procedure and Evidence Proclamation, Cap. 35 of the Laws of Swaziland.
49. *Ibid.*, new Section 130(3), inserted by the Criminal Procedure and Evidence (Further Amendment) Act, No. 41 of 1968, dated 21st January 1969.
50. Act No. 19 of 1969.
51. Cap. 35, new Section 335.
52. *Ibid.*, new Section 336.
53. *Ibid.*, new Section 337. The Act also amended the provisions relating to the relevant offence by introducing a new Section 121 in the Road Traffic Act No. 6 of 1965.
54. No. 5 of 1969, replacing Cap. 86 of the Laws of Swaziland.
55. Legal Notice No. 70 of 1969.
56. Act No. 31 of 1968 as amended by Act No. 4 of 1969.

LEGAL NOTICE NO. 71 OF 1969

THE CUSTOMS PROCLAMATION
(*Cap.* 200)

CUSTOMS UNION AGREEMENT BETWEEN THE
GOVERNMENTS OF SWAZILAND, BOTSWANA, LESOTHO
AND SOUTH AFRICA
(under Section 74)

In exercise of the powers conferred upon him by the above-mentioned proclamation, the Honourable the Prime Minister has been pleased to enter into the agreements set out in the Schedule.

W. A. RAMSDEN
Attorney-General

Mbabane,
11th December 1969

SCHEDULE

CUSTOMS UNION AGREEMENT BETWEEN THE
GOVERNMENTS OF SWAZILAND, BOTSWANA, LESOTHO
AND SOUTH AFRICA

The Governments of the Kingdom of Swaziland, the Republic of Botswana, the Kingdom of Lesotho and the Republic of South Africa—

Being desirous of maintaining the free interchange of goods between their countries and of applying the same tariffs and trade regulations to goods imported from outside the common customs area as hereinafter defined;

Recognising that the Customs Agreement concluded on 29th June 1910, as amended from time to time, requires modification to provide for the continuance of the customs union arrangements in the changed circumstances on a basis designed to ensure the continued economic development of the customs union area as a whole, and to ensure in particular that these arrangements encourage the development of the less advanced members of the customs union and the diversification of their economies, and afford to all parties equitable benefits arising from trade among themselves and with other countries;

Have agreed as follows:

ARTICLE 1

Definitions.

In this Agreement, unless inconsistent with the context—

"additional duties" means duties imposed in terms of Article 6 of this Agreement;

"Botswana" means the area of the Republic of Botswana;

"common customs area" means the combined areas of Botswana, Lesotho, South Africa and Swaziland;

"customs duties", "excise duties" and "sales duties" mean customs duties, excise duties and sales duties as defined in the customs and excise legislation in force in the countries of the contracting parties;

"financial year" means the period of twelve months commencing on the first of April;

"Lesotho" means the area of the Kingdom of Lesotho;

"South Africa" means the area in respect of which the Government of the Republic of South Africa is a contracting party to the General Agreement on Tariffs and Trade;

"Swaziland" means the area of the Kingdom of Swaziland'

and cognate expressions shall be construed accordingly.

ARTICLE 2

Interchange of Domestic Products.

Except as elsewhere provided herein, a contracting party shall not apply quantitative restrictions or impose any duties on goods grown, produced or manufactured in the common customs area on importation of such goods from the area of any other contracting party.

ARTICLE 3

Interchange of Goods Imported from outside the Common Customs Area.

Except as elsewhere provided herein a contracting party shall not impose any duties on goods which were imported from outside the common customs area on importation of such goods from the area of any other contracting party.

ARTICLE 4

Customs and Sales Duties on Imported Goods.

(1) Except as elsewhere provided herein, the customs tariff and duties and the sales duties as in force in South Africa from time to time shall be applied to goods imported into the common customs area from outside such area.

(2) Any rebates, refunds or drawbacks of customs duty or sales duty on imported goods granted by the Government of Botswana, Lesotho or Swaziland in respect of such goods for use in or used in any industry shall be identical to any such rebates, refunds or drawbacks in force in South Africa in respect of such goods for use in or used in a corresponding industry in South Africa.

(3) Subject to paras. (2) and (4), all other rebates, refunds or drawbacks of customs duty or sales duty on imported goods granted by the Government of Botswana, Lesotho or Swaziland in respect of such goods shall be similar to any such rebates, refunds or drawbacks in force in South Africa.

(4)   (*a*) A contracting party may grant a full rebate of the customs and sales duties in respect of goods imported into its area:
     (i) for the relief of distress of persons in cases of famine and other national disaster;
     (ii) under any technical assistance agreement; and
     (iii) in terms of an obligation under any multilateral international agreement to which such contracting party is or becomes a party.

   (*b*) A contracting party may, with the prior approval of the other contracting parties, grant a full rebate of the customs and sales duties in respect of goods imported into its area for such other purposes as may be agreed upon by the parties to this Agreement from time to time.

ARTICLE 5

Imposition and Amendment of Customs Duties.

(1) Subject to the provisions of para. (2) of this Article, the Government of South Africa shall give the other contracting parties adequate opportunity for consultations before imposing, amending or abrogating any customs duty with respect to goods imported into the common customs area from outside such area.

(2) Para. (1) of this Article shall not apply if the imposition of, or the removal of, or an amendment to any customs duty either forms part of the measures of the Government of South Africa designed primarily for fiscal purposes, or is resorted to as an interim measure designed to assist a local industry in the common customs area pending the completion of an investigation by the appropriate South African authorities.

ARTICLE 6

Imposition of Additional Duties for Protective purposes by Botswana Lesotho or Swaziland.

(1) The Government of Botswana, Lesotho or Swaziland may levy additional duties on goods imported into its area to enable new industries in its area to meet competition from other producers or manufacturers in the common customs area, provided that such duties are levied equally on goods grown, produced or manufactured in other parts of the common customs area and like products imported from outside that area, irrespective of whether the latter

goods are imported directly or from the area of any other party to this Agreement and subject to payment of the customs duties applicable to such goods on importation into the common customs area.

(2) Before any such duties are imposed or amended the Government concerned shall consult the other contracting parties in terms of Article 20, and such parties may make recommendations thereon. If the recommendations of any such parties are not acted upon, the Government concerned shall inform the other contracting parties of the reason for its decision.

(3) Protection which is afforded to a new industry in terms of this Article shall not be given for a period exceeding eight years without the prior consent of the contracting parties.

(4) In this Article, "new industry" in relation to any contracting party means an industry which has been established in the area of that party for not more than eight years.

ARTICLE 7

Specification of Industries of Major Importance to Botswana, Lesotho or Swaziland.

(1) The Government of Botswana, Lesotho or Swaziland may with the concurrence of the other contracting parties—
  (*a*) specify industries which are or are likely to be of major importance to its economy; and
  (*b*) specify periods in relation to such industries for the purposes of para. (2) of this Article.

(2) The customs duties applicable to goods, imported from outside the common customs area and competing with those of any industry specified in terms of this Article, shall not for the period specified in terms of para. (1)(*b*) above in relation to that industry be decreased or abrogated without the consent of the Government specifying the industry; and during such period the Government of South Africa shall with due regard to the interests of the other contracting parties and to the criteria usually applied by it in the consideration of representations for tariff assistance and relief, give sympathetic consideration to proposals by any other contracting party to increase any customs duty applicable to such goods or to afford relief of customs duty applicable to any material, used directly in the production or manufacture thereof and to requirements for such industries, where the Government concerned regards such increase or relief necessary to assist the establishment of such industry or to prevent its contraction.

ARTICLE 8

Excise and Sales Duties on Goods produced in the Common Customs Area.

(1) The excise duties and the sales duties as in force in South Africa from time to time shall be applied to goods grown, produced or manufactured in the common customs area.

(2) Any rebates, refunds or drawbacks of excise duty or sales duty granted by the Government of Botswana, Lesotho or Swaziland in respect of goods grown, produced or manufactured in the common customs area, for use in or used in any industry shall be identical to any such rebates, refunds or drawbacks in force in South Africa in respect of such goods for use in or used in a corresponding industry in South Africa.

(3) All other rebates, refunds or drawbacks of excise duty or sales duty granted by the Government of Botswana, Lesotho or Swaziland in respect of goods grown, produced or manufactured in the common customs area shall be similar to any such rebates, refunds or drawbacks in force in South Africa.

ARTICLE 9

Duties on Goods produced by Specified industries.

(1) If goods grown, produced or manufactured in Botswana, Lesotho or Swaziland, by an industry specified in pursuance of Article 7 of this Agreement, are subject to excise duties, the margin of protection afforded by the customs duty applicable to such goods shall be maintained for period specified under that Article and may be changed only with the agreement of the Government specifying the industry.

(2) During the specified period the Government of South Africa shall with due regard to the interests of the other contracting parties and to the criteria usually applied by it in the consideration of representations for tariff assistance and relief, give sympathetic consideration to proposals by such a Government to reduce or abrogate any excise duty applicable to such goods where such a Government regards such duty as injurious to that industry.

ARTICLE 10

Laws relating to Customs, Excise and Sales Duties

Subject to the provisions of Articles 4 and 8, the Governments of Botswana, Lesotho and Swaziland shall apply laws relating to customs, excise and sales duty similar to such laws in force in South Africa from time to time.

ARTICLE 11

Import and Export Prohibitions and Restrictions.

(1) The contracting parties recognise the right of each party to prohibit or restrict the importation into or exportation from its area of any goods for economic, social, cultural or other reasons.

(2) Except in so far as may be agreed upon between the parties from time to time, the provisions of this Agreement shall not be deemed to suspend or supersede the provisions of any law within any part of the common customs area which prohibits or restricts the importation or exportation of goods.

(3) The provisions of paras. (1) and (2) shall not be so construed as to permit the prohibition or restriction of the importation by any contracting party into its

area of goods grown, produced or manufactured in other areas of the common customs area for the purpose of protecting its own industries producing such goods.

(4) A contracting party shall upon request by any other contracting party take such steps as may be agreed upon between the parties concerned (including action to make such steps legally enforceable within its area) to prevent the exportation or unrestricted exportation from its area to the area of such other contracting party of such prohibited or restricted goods imported from outside the common customs area or grown, produced or manufactured in its area or to prevent the exportation or unrestricted exportation from its area to a country outside the common customs area of such prohibited or restricted goods imported from the area of such other contracting party.

(5) The contracting parties shall co-operate in the application of import restrictions with a view to ensuring that the economic objectives of any import control legislation in any country in the common customs area are attained.

ARTICLE 12

Arrangements for Regulating the Marketing of Agricultural Products.

(1) Whenever an arrangement for regulating the marketing of an agricultural commodity is in operation in any area of the common customs area, such arrangement shall be applied on an equitable basis to similar commodities produced in any other area of the common customs area and marketed in the area where the marketing arrangement is in operation, and the contracting parties concerned, cognisant of the advantages deriving from the effective operation of these arrangements, shall co-operate in such arrangements on a basis to be mutually agreed upon.

(2) The contracting parties agree to consult from time to time on matters affecting production and consumption of agricultural commodites and the improvement and extension of marketing arrangements, for such commodities.

ARTICLE 13

Pool of Customs, Excise, Sales and Additional Duties.

Any customs, excise, sales and additional duties collected in the common customs area shall be paid quarterly into the Consolidated Revenue Fund of South Africa.

ARTICLE 14

The Pool of Customs, Excise, Sales and Additional Duties.

(1) The common revenue pool of the common customs area shall consist of the gross amounts of customs, excise, sales and additional duties leviable and collected on goods imported into or produced in the common customs area, and any other duties collected in terms of Article 19(3), but shall not include any

duties rebated or refunded under the provisions of any law relating to customs, excise and sales duty (including any rebate or refund specifically provided for in any such law but which is paid from voted funds and not deducted from customs, excise and sales duty revenue).

(2) The contracting parties agree that in determining the share of Botswana, Lesotho or Swaziland of the common revenue pool in respect of any financial year the following formula shall be used:

The cost-insurance-freight value at border of goods from all sources imported during the financial year into the area of each party, *plus* the value of excisable and sales duty goods produced and consumed in such area during such year, *plus* the excise and sales duties paid thereon during such year shall be expressed as a percentage of the cost-insurance-freight value of the goods imported during the financial year into the common customs area, *plus* the customs and sales duties paid thereon during such year, *plus* the value of excisable and sales duty goods, produced and consumed during such year in the common customs area, *plus* the excise and sales duties paid thereon during such year. The amount calculated by the application to the common revenue pool of the percentage so obtained, enhanced by a multiplying factor of 1·42, shall represent the share of each of the three countries in respect of that financial year.

(3) There shall be paid from the Consolidated Revenue Fund of South Africa to the Governments of Botswana, Lesotho and Swaziland, in respect of their share of the common revenue pool, amounts calculated on the following basis:

(*a*) in respect of the financial year 1972/73 and each financial year thereafter:

    (i) an amount resulting from the application to the formula referred to in para. (2) above, of the relevant data for the financial year two years before the financial year in question;

plus or *minus*

    (ii) a first adjustment in respect of the financial year two years before the financial year in question equal to the difference between the total amount actually received by each country in respect of that year and the amount due to each country in terms of the formula referred to in para. (2) above, recalculated on the basis of the latest available data for that particular financial year;

plus or *minus*

    (iii) a final adjustment in respect of the financial year three years before the financial year in question equal to the difference between the total amount actually received by each country in respect of that year and the amount due to each country in terms of the formula referred to in para. (2) above, recalculated on the basis of the final data for that particular financial year:

(*b*) in respect of the financial year 1971/72:

    (i) an amount resulting from the application to the formula referred to in para. (2) above of the relevant data for the financial year 1969/70;

plus or *minus*

(ii) an amount in respect of the financial year 1969/70 equal to the difference between the total amount actually received by each country in respect of that year and the amount due to each country in terms of the formula referred to in para. (2) above, recalculated on the basis of the latest available data for the financial year 1969/70;

(*c*) in respect of the financial year 1970/71: an amount resulting from the application to the formula referred to in para. (2) above, of the relevant data for the financial year 1968/69 except that in the case of import values 1968 data shall be used and that agreed estimates of the values of sales duty goods produced and consumed in the financial year 1969/70 and the sales duties collected thereon shall be included;

(*d*) in respect of the financial year 1969/70: an amount equal to the difference between the total amount actually received by each country in respect of that year and the amount due to each country in terms of the formula referred to in para. (2) above, calculated on the basis of the relevant data for the financial year 1968/69, except that in the case of import values 1968 data shall be used, and that no imputed allowances for the values of sales duty goods produced and consumed and the sales duties thereon shall be included.

(4) The amount referred to in sub paras. (*a*) and (*b*) of para. (3) above shall be determined and agreed upon between the contracting parties approximately six months before the beginning of the financial year in question.

(5) The amounts referred to in sub paras. (*a*), (*b*) and (*c*) of para. (3) above shall be remitted in equal quarterly instalments during the financial year in question.

(6) The payment referred to in sub paras. (*d*) of para. (3) above shall be made before the end of the financial year 1969/70.

(7) The Government of South Africa undertakes to consult the Governments of Botswana, Lesotho and Swaziland prior to the introduction of changes in the fiscal structure of South Africa where these are expected to have a substantial effect on the structure of taxation measures relating to the common revenue pool.

(8) This Article shall be deemed to have come into operation on the first day of April 1969, and to have been substituted from that date for the corresponding provisions of the Customs Agreement concluded on the 29th June 1910.

ARTICLE 15

Rail and Road Traffic.

(1) The contracting parties undertake that the transit through their areas of goods imported from outside the common customs area to or exported to a country outside the common customs area from the areas of the other contracting parties shall not be subject to transport rate discrimination.

(2) Each contracting party shall ensure that the tariffs applicable within its area to the conveyance of goods by publicly-owned transport to and from the other areas of the common customs area shall be no less favourable than the tariffs applicable to the carriage of similar goods within its area.

(3) Each contracting party undertakes to extend to the motor transport operators registered in the areas of the other contracting parties treatment no less favourable than that accorded to motor transport operators registered within its own area for the conveyance of goods or passengers for reward or in the course of any trade or business.

ARTICLE 16

Freedom of Transit.

A contracting party shall afford freedom of transit without discrimination to goods consigned to and from the areas of the other contracting parties: Provided, however, that a contracting party may impose such conditions upon such transit as it deems necessary to protect its legitimate interests in respect of goods of a kind of which the importation into its area is prohibited on grounds of public morals, public health or security, or as a precaution against animal or plant diseases, parasites and insects, or in pursuance of the provisions of a multilateral international convention to which it is a party: And provided, further, that a contracting party shall not be precluded from refusing transit, or from taking any measures deemed necessary by it in connection with such transit, for the purpose of protecting its security interest.

ARTICLE 17

Bilateral Consultations.

Notwithstanding the provisions of Article 2, if, as a result of unforeseen developments, any product is being introduced into the area of one of the contracting parties from the area of another contracting party in such increased quantities and under such conditions as to cause or threaten serious injury to producers or manufacturers of like or directly competitive products in the area into which such goods are so introduced, the Government of the latter area shall have the right to require the other party to consult at the earliest possible opportunity and to co-operate with it in finding as soon as possible a mutually acceptable solution.

ARTICLE 18

Consultations on Zoo-Sanitary and Phyto-sanitary matters.

Subject to the provisions of Article 11, the contracting parties recognise the importance of measures prescribing zoo-sanitary and phyto-sanitary requirements aimed at the prevention of the spread of animal and plant diseases, parasites and insects and agree to consult from time to time to achieve such aim in the common customs area with due regard to the need to facilitate the flow of trade in products affected by such measures.

ARTICLE 19

Trade Agreements with Countries outside the Common Customs Area.

(1) A contracting party shall not, without the prior concurrence of the other

contracting parties and subject to such conditions as may be agreed upon by the contracting parties, enter separately into or amend a trade agreement with a country outside the common customs area in terms of which concessions on the duties in force in the common customs area are granted to that country.

(2) A contracting party may enter separately into or amend a trade agreement, other than a trade agreement mentioned in para. (1), with a country outside the common customs area, provided the terms of such an agreement or amendment do not conflict in any way with the provisions of this Agreement. Such contracting party shall, as soon as possible after the conclusion of the agreement or amendment, supply each of the other contracting parties with a copy of the agreement or amendment.

(3)   (*a*) A contracting party, having an agreement with a country outside the common customs area which provides for the importation into its area from such country of goods at lower rates of duty than those applicable to like goods in the common customs area, shall collect the duties payable on importation into its area.

     (*b*) Unless the contracting parties have otherwise agreed in respect of any such agreement, where such goods are to be removed from the area of such contracting party to the area of any of the other contracting parties the duties applicable in the common customs area shall become due and payable and the contracting party from whose area such goods are to be removed shall, prior to such removal, collect the differences between the lower duties paid and the duties applicable. If proof of payment of the differences in duty cannot be furnished in the area to which the goods are subsequently removed, the goods shall be liable to forfeiture.

     (*c*) Any duties and differences in duties thus collected shall be paid into the Consolidated Revenue Fund of South Africa. Any payments due by that contracting party under such agreement with a country outside the common customs area, shall be paid on its behalf from the Consolidated Revenue Fund.

ARTICLE 20

General Consultations

(1) A Customs Union Commission shall be established comprising representatives of all the contracting parties, for the purpose of discussing any matter arising out of this Agreement.

(2) The Commission shall meet once a year. A contracting party may, however, at any time request a meeting of the Commission for the purpose of discussing a matter connected with this Agreement and the Commission shall meet as soon as possible thereafter.

(3) Where contracting parties have consulted on a matter which may affect the rights of the other parties under this Agreement and arising under Article 12, 17 or 18 or on a matter arising under para. (5) of this Article, a report on the results of these consultations shall be furnished to the Commission before its next meeting.

(4) Where a matter has been referred to the Commission for discussion, the Commission shall use its best endeavours to find a mutually agreeable solution to the particular problem or difficulty and the representatives shall report to their respective Governments for consideration of any remedial measures.

(5) Any difficulty or problem arising out of this Agreement which does not directly affect the interests of all the contracting parties may, with the concurrence of all the contracting parties, form the subject of direct consultation between the parties affected with a view to seeking a solution thereof.

ARTICLE 21

Termination of 1910 Agreement.

The Customs Agreement concluded on the 19th June 1910, as amended from time to time, shall terminate on the entry into force of this Agreement.

ARTICLE 22

Entry into Force of, and Withdrawal from, Agreement.

This Agreement shall, subject to the provisions of Article 14(8) enter into force on the 1st March 1970.

If a contracting party wishes to withdraw from this Agreement that party shall give notice thereof to all the other contracting parties.

If after consultation the contracting parties fail to agree on the date and conditions of the withdrawal, this Agreement shall remain in force until twelve months from the date of such notice and shall then cease to apply to the withdrawing party.

In witness whereof the undersigned, being duly authorised thereto by their respective Governments, have signed this Agreement.

Done at Pretoria, in quadruplicate, in Afrikaans and English texts, each of which texts shall be of equal authenticity, this eleventh day of December 1969.

For the Government of the Kingdom of Swaziland:

For the Government of the Republic of Botswana:

For the Government of the Kingdom of Lesotho:

For the Government of the Republic of South Africa:

MEMORANDUM OF UNDERSTANDING

With reference to the Customs Union Agreement dated the 11th December 1969, between the Governments of Swaziland, Botswana, Lesotho and South Africa, it is desired to place on record the following additional understandings on which agreement has been reached among the four Governments and which shall be read with, and shall form part of the Agreement:

AD ARTICLES 3, 4, 8 AND 10

Administration of Customs, Excise and Sales Duty Provisions.

(1) The Governments of Botswana, Lesotho and Swaziland undertake to establish customs and excise administrations capable of administering the terms of the Agreement and any arrangements thereunder, customs and excise storage and manufacturing warehouse provisions, excise provisions and the collection of excise duties and sales duty provisions and the collection of sales duties.

(2) The contracting parties agree that:

(*a*) goods (including goods for warehousing) destined for Botswana, Lesotho or Swaziland and imported through any place of entry in South Africa (including Lourenco Marques and Jan Smuts Airport) shall be entered for customs, excise or sales duty purposes through South African customs and for that purpose the laws relating to customs, excise and sales duty of South Africa will apply to such goods as if such goods were destined for South Africa: Provided that if the laws relating to customs, excise and sales duty of Botswana, Lesotho or Swaziland as the case may be, should, in relation to such goods, differ in respect of any restriction, prohibition, tariff or rebate under the Agreement, the relative law of the country of destination of such goods shall in that respect be deemed to be the law relating to customs, excise or sales duty, as the case may be, of South Africa in relation to such goods;

(*b*) goods destined for South Africa and imported other than by road through any place in Botswana, Lesotho or Swaziland shall be entered for customs, excise or sales duty purposes at the place of entry in South Africa. Goods so destined and imported by road shall be so entered at the place of entry into the common customs area;

(*c*) goods destined for Botswana, Lesotho or Swaziland and imported directly into the country in question shall, subject to the provisions of sub para. (*a*), be entered for customs, excise or sales duty purposes in that country;

(*d*) goods for warehousing in any customs and excise storage warehouse established in the area of Botswana, Lesotho or Swaziland shall be cleared for warehousing at places of entry in South Africa for removal to such warehouse without further entry, but any clearance ex such warehouse of such goods and collection of any customs, excise or sales duty thereon shall be the responsibility of the country in whose area the warehouse is situated;

(*e*) the administration of any customs and excise manufacturing warehouse (including the collection of any customs, excise or sales duty on any goods manufactured in such warehouse) in Botswana, Lesotho and Swaziland shall be the responsibility of the country in whose area the warehouse is situated; and

(*f*) provisions relating to drawbacks of duty on goods used in the manufacture of exported goods shall be administered by the Government in whose area the exporter is situated, but the Government of South Africa shall accept responsibility for the processing of claims for drawback of any duty emanating from exporters in Botswana, Lesotho or Swaziland in respect of goods exported from the common customs area and payment of such claims shall be effected from the Consolidated Revenue Fund of South Africa.

Done at Pretoria, in quadruplicate, in Afrikaans and English texts, each of which texts shall be of equal authenticity, this eleventh day of December 1969

For the Government of the Kingdom of Swaziland:

L. LOVELL

For the Government of the Republic of Botswana:

J. G. HASKINS

For the Government of the Kingdom of Lesotho:

P. N. PEETE

For the Government of the Republic of South Africa:

J. F. W. HAAK

PART II

L'Afrique Francophone
(Francophonic African Countries)

Sous la Direction du
Professeur D. G. Lavroff
par le Centre d'Etude d'Afrique
Noire de Bordeaux

CHAPTER 15

MAURITANIE

L. G. Verdun

DROIT ADMINISTRATIF

Carte d'identité: Le décret n° 69.143 du 7 mars 1969 institue la carte nationale d'identité délivrée par l'autorité administrative la plus proche de son domicile (commissaire de police ou à défaut préfet ou chef d'arrondissement) à tout ressortissant mauritanien âgé de quinze ans au moins qui en fait la demande. Ce document est valable dix ans à compter du jour de sa délivrance (J.O. du 26 mars 1969, p. 159).

Education nationale: La loi 69.269 du 1er août 1969 porte réorganisation de l'enseignement du second degré. Cet enseignement est dispensé en 2 cycles (4 années pour le premier cycle, trois années pour le deuxième cycle) par trois catégories d'établissements d'enseignement du second degré: les lycées dispensant les enseignements du premier et du deuxième cycle, les collèges dispensant uniquement les enseignements du premier cycle, et l'Institut national des hautes études islamiques dispensant les enseignements du premier et du deuxième cycle en langue arabe. Le but de cette réforme est de "maintenir et développer la culture mauritanienne traditionnelle inspirée des valeurs spirituelles de l'Islam — et de faire acquérir aux futurs cadres les connaissances propres à accélérer la promotion technique, économique et sociale de la Mauritanie" (J.O. du 27 août 1969, p. 299).

Etablissements publics: Le décret 69.131 du 28 février 1969 porte organisation de la Caisse Nationale d'Epargne, établissement public à caractère commercial, destiné à faire fructifier les sommes qui lui sont confiées en les immobilisant pour partie à terme, pour partie à vue. Cet établissement est placé sous la tutelle du ministre chargé des Postes et Télécommunications, son directeur est nommé par décret sur proposition de ce dernier, son agent comptable est nommé par arrêté du ministre des Finances, sur proposition du ministre de tutelle (J.O. du 26 mars 1969, p. 148).

Fiscalité: La loi n° 68.352 du 31 décembre 1968 modifie le Code des Impôts directs et indirects concernant l'imposition sur les bénéfices industriels et commerciaux et sur les bénéfices des exploitations agricoles. Les contribuables peuvent bénéficier de l'imposition suivant le régime du forfait ou suivant le régime du bénéfice réel. Un impôt minimum forfaitaire frappe les sociétés et personnes morales. Il est dû au titre d'une année déterminée en fonction du chiffre d'affaires du dernier exercice clos, le tarif de cet impôt variant de 100.000 francs pour un chiffre d'affaires inférieur à 10.000.000 francs, à 1.500.000 francs pour un chiffre d'affaires égal ou supérieur à un milliard. Quant à l'impôt sur les bénéfices non commerciaux, il est assis sur les bénéfices des professions libérales, des charges et offices dont les titulaires n'ont pas la qualité de commerçant, et de toutes les occupations, exploitations lucratives et sources de profits non soumises à un impôt spécial sur le revenu (J.O. du 29 janvier 1969, p. 45).

Fonction publique: La loi 69.266 du 26 juillet 1969 porte réforme du statut des cadis, fonctionnaires nommés par décret du Président de la République, sur proposition du ministre de la Justice pour assurer le service des tribunaux de droit coutumier (J.O. du 27 août 1969, p. 299).

Organisation territoriale: la loi 69.063 du 25 janvier 1969 supprime les communes urbaines et les communes pilotes instituées par les lois du 16 janvier 1960 et du 18 janvier 1964. Elle modifie les dispositions de la loi du 30 juillet 1968 portant organisation générale de l'administration territoriale en ce qui concerne la structure des budgets régionaux qui sont établis selon un plan type qui comprend des recettes ordinaires et des recettes extraordinaires et une énumération des dépenses ordinaires obligatoires (J.O. du 29 janvier 1969, p. 64).

DROIT PRIVÉ

Droit commercial

La loi n° 69.22 du 20 juin 1969 fixe les règles de commercialisation et d'utilisation des produits pétroliers. L'importation des produits pétroliers est soumise à un agrément; une commission paritaire des produits pétroliers est chargée de donner son avis sur les questions techniques de caractère général intéressant l'importation, le stockage, distribution et la vente de ces produits (J.O. du 23 juin 1969, p. 235).

DROIT PÉNAL ET PROCÉDURE PÉNALE

La loi 69.050 du 21 janvier 1969 réprime le délit d'abandon de famille, sanctionné par une amende de 25.000 à 500.000 francs et par une peine d'emprisonnement de 3 mois à 1 an. (J.O. du 29 janvier 1969, p. 55).

La loi n° 69.270 du 1er août 1969 interdit la pratique des jeux de hasard destinés à procurer un gain, à l'exception de ceux pratiqués dans des établissements autorisés dans les conditions fixées par voie réglementaire. La non-observation de cette règle est sanctionnée par une amende de 36.000 à 200.000 francs et par une peine d'emprisonnement de 2 mois à 6 mois (J.O. du 27 août 1969, p. 300).

Chapter 16

SENEGAL

L. G. Verdun

L'examen des textes législatifs et réglementaires de l'année 1969 traduit la volonté des pouvoirs publics de tirer les enseignements de la crise de mai-juin 1968: textes sur l'état d'urgence, l'état de siège, la diffusion de la propagande politique; réformes sur l'enseignement mises en train; sur le plan financier, recours à un emprunt national obligatoire et réformes fiscales.

DROIT PUBLIC

Droit constitutionnel

Incompatibilités: La loi nº 69.75 du 30 décembre 1969, dite loi Joseph Mathiam, fait bénéficier de la non application des règles relatives aux incomptabilités entre l'exercice d'une fonction publique et l'exercice d'un mandat parlementaire, la totalité des personnels enseignants de l'université de Dakar et les médecins des formations hospitalières publiques (auparavant seuls les personnels titulaires de l'enseignement supérieur étaient exemptés de l'application des règles relatives aux incompatibilités) (J.O. du 31 janvier 1970, p. 99).

Indemnités: le décret 69.442 du 14 avril 1969 fixe les indemnités des ministres, secrétaires d'Etat, ainsi que des membres du cabinet du Président de la République et des cabinets ministériels (J.O. du 10 mai 1969, p. 530).

Libertés publiques

La loi 69.29 du 29 avril 1969 fixe les règles relatives à l'état d'urgence et à l'état de siège. L'état d'urgence est déclaré par décret sur tout ou partie du territoire, soit en cas de péril imminent résultant d'atteintes graves à l'ordre public, soit en cas de menées subversives compromettant la sécurité intérieure, soit en cas d'évènements présentant par leur nature et leur gravité un caractère de calamité publique. Durant l'état d'urgence, l'autorité administrative peut interdire toutes manifestations sur la voie publique, instituer des zones de sécurité où le séjour des personnes est réglementé ou interdit, assigner à résidence ou procéder à l'internement administratif des personnes dont l'activité présente un danger pour la sécurité publique, réquisitionner les personnes et les biens. En période d'état de siège, les pouvoirs dévolus à l'autorité civile pour le maintien de l'ordre et de la police sont transférés à l'autorité militaire (J.O. du 10 mai 1969, p. 571).

La loi 69.30 du 29 avril 1969 définit les conditions d'exercice du droit de réquisition des personnes, biens et services dans les cas prévus par les lois sur l'organisation générale de la défense et sur les états d'exception (J.O. du 10 mai 1959, p. 573).

La loi 69.31 du 29 avril 1969 soumet à autorisation administrative préalable l'introduction et la diffusion de brochures, tracts, affiches, insignes, enregistrements sonores ou visuels d'origine ou de provenance étrangère présentant un caractère de propagande politique (J.O. du 10 mai 1969, p. 576).

Relations internationales: le décret 69.438 du 14 avril 1969 ordonne la publication au Journal Officiel du statut de l'Organisation des Etats riverains du Sénégal, signé à Labé le 24 mars 1968 (J.O. du 26 avril 1969, p. 476).

DROIT ADMINISTRATIF

Education nationale

Le décret 69.001 du 9 janvier 1969 crée une commission nationale pour la réforme de l'université et des sous-commissions de facultés (J.O. du 1er février 1969, p. 112).

Le décret 69.131 du 11 février 1969, relatif à la planification de l'emploi, de la formation et des structures scolaires, ainsi qu'à l'attribution des bourses et allocations d'études et de stages crée, sous la présidence du Président de la République, un conseil interministériel chargé de coordonner les activités des différents services ayant à connaître des problèmes d'emploi, de formation et d'enseignement, d'établir des directives sur les structures scolaires et universitaires ainsi que sur celles de tous autres moyens de formation, sur le nombre et la répartition des bourses et allocations scolaires de toute nature (J.O. du 1er mars 1969, p. 264).

Le décret 69.332 du 27 mars 1969 institue une commission nationale pour la réforme des enseignements primaire, moyen et secondaire ainsi que des sous-commissions techniques. La commission nationale est chargée d'étudier et de proposer une réforme portant sur les structures, les programmes et les méthodes, les sous-commissions étant chargées de l'étude des problèmes pédagogiques particuliers à chaque ordre d'enseignement. (J.O. du 12 avril 1969, p. 450).

Le décret 69.402 du 31 mars 1969 crée à l'université de Dakar un Institut des Sciences et Médecine vétérinaires, institut d'université à caractère interétatique ayant double vocation d'enseignement et de recherche. L'Institut est dirigé, sous l'autorité de son conseil d'administration, par un directeur nommé pour trois ans par le recteur, sur présentation successive du conseil d'administration et du conseil de l'université (J.O. du 26 avril 1969, p. 484).

La loi 69.33 du 19 juin 1969 modifie la loi 67.47 du 13 juillet 1969 relative à l'université de Dakar. Les libertés indispensables à l'objectivité de l'enseignement et de la recherche sont garanties aux membres du personnel enseignant, aux chercheurs et aux étudiants, qui jouissent également de la liberté d'exprimer leurs opinions politiques, philosophiques et religieuses, ainsi que de la liberté d'association dans le cadre de la législation en vigueur. L'exercice de ces libertés doit toujours s'inspirer des "principes d'objectivité et de tolérance". Les étudiants ne peuvent à l'aide de violences, menaces ou manoeuvres porter atteinte à l'ordre public et au fonctionnement régulier des institutions universitaires, "même lorsqu'ils s'abstiennent de suivre les enseignements par suite d'une décision concertée". Par ailleurs, la nomination d'un enseignant, ressortissant d'un Etat "africain étranger" devra être approuvée au préalable par le gouvernement de cet Etat lorsque celui-ci aura sur ce point conclu un accord réciproque avec l'Etat sénégalais (J.O. du 28 juin 1969, p. 827).

Finances publiques

Emprunt: la loi n° 69.01 du 15 janvier 1969 autorise l'émission d'un emprunt national et fixe ses modalités de souscription. Cet emprunt obligatoire est destiné à financer le plan quadriennal de développement. Les personnes physiques et morales passibles de l'impôt sur les bénéfices industriels et commerciaux ou de l'impôt sur les bénéfices non commerciaux sont tenues de justifier d'une souscription au moins égale à 50% du montant des impôts dûs par les intéressés au titre de l'année fiscale 1968: les personnes assujetties à l'impôt général sur le revenu sont tenues de justifier d'une souscription au moins égale à 20% du montant de l'I.G.R. dû par les intéressés sur les revenus de l'année 1967, lorsque ce montant est supérieur à 50.000 francs CFA. Les titres émis à 12 ans et remboursables par tirage au sort portent intérêt de 4% (J.O. du 18 janvier 1969, p. 67).

Fiscalité: La loi n° 69.02 du 15 janvier 1969 porte réforme de l'impôt du minimum fiscal: cet impôt perçu au profit de l'Etat est dû par toute personne résidant au Sénégal âgée d'au moins 14 ans. Le taux de l'impôt varie de 500 à 4.000 francs CFA selon les catégories établies en fonction des professions et du niveau des ressources des contribuables (J.O. du 18 janvier 1969, p. 71).

La loi 69.03 du 15 janvier 1969 supprime la contribution mobilière, tandis que la loi 69.05 du même jour crée une taxe complémentaire à l'impôt général sur le revenu et une taxe complémentaire à la contribution des patentes (J.O. du 18 janvier 1969, p. 72 et 77).

Le décret 69.475 du 22 avril 1969 crée un comité de lutte contre la fraude fiscale composé de représentants des divers ministères, qui sera chargé de coordonner les moyens de lutte contre la fraude et la contrebande, et d'étudier les mesures permettant d'accroître l'efficacité de l'intervention des services de répression (J.O. du 17 mai 1969, p. 581).

Fonction publique

Concours administratifs: le décret 69.179 du 18 février 1969 fixe à 50 ans l'âge limite des candidats aux concours professionnels (J.O. du 8 mars 1969, p. 299).

Conseil supérieur de la Fonction publique: sa composition est modifiée par le décret 69.135 du 12 février 1969. Désormais le Conseil supérieur comprend 16 membres titulaires: 8 représentants de l'administration et 8 fonctionnaires choisis sur proposition de l'organisation syndicale nationale la plus représentative (J.O. du 8 mars 1969, p. 297).

Statuts particuliers

Le décret 69.257 du 17 mars 1969 porte statut particulier des fonctionnaires des archives et des bibliothèques. Les fonctionnaires des catégories A et B sont groupés dans un cadre unique composé de 3 corps: corps des conservateurs d'archives et de bibliothèques, corps des archivistes, bibliothécaires et documentalistes, corps des sous-archivistes, sous-bibliothécaires et sous-documentalistes (J.O. du 12 avril 1969, p. 436).

Le décret 69.445 du 14 avril 1969 modifie le statut particulier des fonctionnaires de la Statistique qui désormais sont classés en cinq corps: ingénieurs, ingénieurs des travaux, adjoints techniques, agents techniques, agents de la statistique (J.O. du 10 mai 1969, p. 550).

La loi 69.54 du 16 juillet 1969 fixe le statut général de la Fonction publique communale applicable aux agents qui, nommés dans un emploi permanent des communes, ont été titularisés dans un grade de la hiérarchie des corps communaux. Les fonctionnaires communaux, qui sont nommés par le Président de la République, appartiennent à un cadre unique (J.O. du 2 août 1969, p. 980).

La loi 69.64 du 30 octobre 1969 fixe le statut du personnel des Douanes qui est réparti en 6 corps hiérarchisés: inspecteurs et officiers des douanes, contrôleurs, agents de constatation, sous-officiers, agents brevetés, et préposés. Ces personnels ne peuvent être ni électeurs ni éligibles, ils ne jouissent ni du droit de grève ni du droit syndical, leurs libertés d'expression, d'aller et de venir, de réunion, d'association, sont limitées par décret en fonction des nécessités du service (J.O. du 8 novembre 1969, p. 1820).

Planification

La loi 69.53 du 16 juillet 1969 institue un troisième plan quadriennal de développement économique et social qui entrant en vigueur le 1er juillet 1969 arrivera à son terme le 30 juin 1973.

Police administrative

La loi 69.49 du 16 juillet 1969 définit la notion de débit de boissons. "tous les lieux ouverts au public et offrant à la vente des boissons à consommer sur place". L'ouverture des débits de boissons est subordonnée à autorisation préalable de l'autorité administrative (J.O. du 2 août 1969, p. 978).

DROIT PÉNAL ET PROCÉDURE PÉNALE

La loi 69.72 du 23 décembre 1969 abroge et remplace l'article 392 du Code pénal:

Sera puni d'un emprisonnement de 3 mois à 3 ans et d'une amende de 50.000 à 500.000 francs CFA ou de l'une de ces deux peines seulement, quiconque à l'aide de violences envers les personnes ou envers les choses, voies de fait, menaces, manoeuvres frauduleuses ou propagation de fausses nouvelles, aura porté atteinte ou tenté de porter atteinte au libre exercice du travail.

Sera puni d'un emprisonnement d'un mois à deux ans det d'une amende de 20.000 à 100.000 francs CFA ou de l'une de ces deux peines seulement, quiconque dissuadera ou tentera de dissuader toute personne "d'exercer ses droits et libertés en matière d'éducation et de culture", quiconque aura participé à toute forme d'action collective ayant pour effet ou pour but "de troubler le fonctionnement d'un établissement public ou privé, notamment par l'occupation irrégulière des locaux" (J.O. du 24 janvier 1970, p. 68).

La loi 69.73 du 23 décembre 1969 sanctionne le refus d'exécuter un ordre de réquisition par une peine d'emprisonnement de deux mois à deux ans et par une amende de 20.000 à 500.000 francs, pose des sanctions disciplinaires sans observation de garanties, par le licenciement sans préavis ni indemnités (J.O. du 24 janvier 1970, p. 68).

La loi 69.49 du 16 juillet 1969 réprime l'ivresse publique: toute personne condamnée deux fois pour ivresse publique et manifeste, sera déclarée incapable d'exercer les droits civiques, civils et de famille, et frappée pour une durée d'un an par la suspension du permis de conduire. Quant au débitant de boissons, son établissement sera fermé si des boissons alcoolisées ont été servies ou vendues à des personnes manifestement ivres ou à des mineurs de 18 ans (J.O. du 2 août 1969, p. 978).

CHAPTER 17

MALI

P. Y. Laporte

A la suite du coup d'Etat du 19 novembre 1968, le gouvernement du Lieutenant Moussa Traore éprouve le besoin de diriger le pays de façon moins idéologique et plus pragmatique que l'ex-Président Modibo Keita. Cette orientation politique l'amène à décider d'une série de réformes, notamment dans le domaine économique qui devient en 1969 le principal objet des préoccupations gouvernementales.

DROIT PUBLIC

Droit constitutionnel

Aucun texte n'a été pris en ce domaine en 1969.

Droit administratif

Le nouveau gouvernement poursuit d'abord les réformes purement institutionnelles et politiques qu'il avait commencées à mettre en oeuvre à la fin de 1968.

L'ordonnance n° 1 CMLN du 5 février 1969 modifie le statut des membres de la Cour suprême tel qu'il était fixé par la loi n° 65.2 ANRM du 13 mars 1965 portant réorganisation de la Cour suprême du Mali. L'ordonnance prévoit en effet que les fonctions des membres de la Cour suprême prendront désormais fin à l'expiration de la période pour laquelle ils ont été nommés. Pour sa part, la loi de 1965 stipulait qu'ils étaient inamovibles sauf pour cause d'incapacité, de faute professionnelle ou de condamnation pour crime et délit, éléments que la nouvelle ordonnance ne reprend pas.

L'ordonnance n° 16 PGP/RM du 1er mars 1969 modifie la loi n° 66.9 du 2 mars 1966 portant Code Municipal sur un point qui est important pour le nouveau gouvernement. Elle prévoit en effet la nomination par le gouvernement de délégations spéciales chargées de remplir les fonctions des conseils municipaux, lorsqu'après leur dissolution ou la démission de tous leurs membres, de nouveaux conseils ne peuvent être constitués Quant à la capitale, Bamako, elle se voit octroyer un statut particulier par l'ordonnance n° 20 CMLN du 15 mars 1969.

Mais c'est surtout dans le domaine fiscal et économique qu'interviennent les textes qui vont marquer l'année.

Deux ordonnances du 21 février 1969 réorganisent le régime fiscal malien. La première, l'ordonnance n° 9 CMLN, porte codification de l'impôt sur les Affaires et Services, et modifie la loi n° 62.80 du 31 décembre 1962 créant l'impôt sur les Affaires et Services, en donnant en particulier une nouvelle définition des personnes et affaires imposables, des obligations des redevables de l'impôt et des pénalités qu'ils encourent éventuellement. La seconde ordonnance, n° 10 CMLN, porte codification des taxes locales et concerne notamment les taxes sur les boissons alcoolisées, les carburants et le tabac.

Le souci d'insuffler un dynamisme nouveau à l'économie conduit également le gouvernement à refondre le statut des Entreprises nationales. L'ordonnance n° 23 CMLN du 11 avril 1969 annule donc la loi n° 67.40 AN du 18 juillet 1967 portant statut des Entreprises nationales, ainsi que les textes ultérieurs qui l'ont modifiée, et fixe le nouveau statut général de ces entreprises. Ce statut vise à dépolitiser la gestion des entreprises nationales et à accroître leur rentabilité. A cet égard, il est significatif qu'il mentionne désormais la nécessité pour ces entreprises d'être financièrement rentables, qu'il ne reprenne pas les expressions politiquement valorisées du précédent statut telles que "l'exploitation de l'homme par l'homme ... est abolie une fois pour toutes" ou qu'il les remplace par des expressions plus neutres—"planification" devient "objectifs assignés par le gouvernement". Il est également significatif que le comité de gestion de l'entreprise, que la précédente loi voulait prépondérant pour des raisons politiques, soit ramené à un simple rôle consultatif. C'est le conseil d'administration de l'entreprise, où dominent les experts, qui assume désormais "la haute responsabilité de l'administration de l'entreprise". Quant au Directeur général, il n'est plus qualifié de "militant responsable ... de l'éducation politique des travailleurs" mais il se voit avant tout confier des responsabilités techniques précises.

Trois ordonnances du 23 mai 1969 viennent encore témoigner des efforts du gouvernement pour rompre avec la politique économique du régime précédent. L'ordonnance n° 29 CMLN portant fixation du Code des Investissements accorde divers avantages, dont un régime fiscal et douanier particulièrement favorable, aux entreprises étrangères que l'on voudrait ainsi inciter à investir dans le pays. L'ordonnance n° 31 CMLN modifie la loi n° 63.51 ANRM du 31 mai 1963 portant régime des substances minérales au Mali. Elle favorise en effet désormais l'investissement de capitaux privés dans ce domaine et met à part les hydrocarbures. C'est maintenant l'ordonnance n° 30 CMLN qui organise la recherche, l'exploitation, le transport par canalisation et le raffinage des hydrocarubres, en prévoyant également l'investissement de capitaux privés.

La dernière touche apportée à cette nouvelle politique économique prend la forme de l'ordonnance n° 60 CMLN du 11 novembre 1969 instituant un Code de la chasse. Nul doute que, tout en essayant de sauvegarder la faune du pays, ce Code soit aussi un élément important d'une politique touristique visant à accroître les rentrées de devises étrangères.

DROIT COMMERCIAL

Réorganisant le secteur commercial en accord avec l'esprit des mesures économiques précédémment décrites, trois textes marquent l'année 1969. C'est d'abord l'ordonnance n° 8 du 18 février 1969 autorisant le gouvernement à ratifier la convention relative au commerce de transit des pays sans littoral. C'est ensuite l'ordonnance n° 12 CMLN du 1er mars 1969 portant réglementation de la profession de commerçant. Cette ordonnance complète la loi n° 65.14 AN du 25 mars 1965 portant statut général de la profession de commerçant en rendant plus facile le développement d'un secteur commercial privé parallèle au secteur commercial étatisé. C'est enfin le décret n° 48 CRM du 11 mars 1969 portant organisation du commerce et qui concerne notamment le commerce de gros et de demigros ainsi que le commerce de détail.

DROIT PÉNAL

L'ordonnance n° 32 CMLN du 6 juin 1969 modifiant la loi n° 59.17 ALP du 23 janvier 1959 fixe le régime pénitentiaire des condamnés pour atteinte aux biens publics. Elle précise en effet que les travaux forcés et peines d'emprisonnement seront désormais subis dans des salines ou en tout autre lieu déterminé par le gouvernement.

CHAPTER 18

NIGER

F. Constantin

L'année législative 1969 n'est marquée au Niger par aucune innovation fondamentale. Mises à part quelques réformes dans l'aménagement des structures juridictionnelles et de nouvelles modifications apportées à la législation pénale, l'essentiel des mesures prises reste lié aux circonstances, notamment aux problèmes économiques propres à la République du Niger. L'année politique au Niger, relativement calme, explique l'absence de grand changement dans le domaine du droit public. On remarque seulement le souci du gouvernement nigérien d'améliorer le régime de prévoyance sociale des militaires des Forces Armées du Niger.

DROIT PUBLIC

Droit Constitutionnel

La loi 69.4 du 18 février (J.O.R.N., p. 141) apporte quelques modifications à la loi 61.28 relative à l'organisation et au fonctionnement de la Cour suprême: la plus importante concerne la désignation des membres de la Cour constitutionnelle (a. 25 de la Loi 61.28). Celle-ci comprenait le vice-président, deux conseillers désignés annuellement par décret du Président de la République pris en Conseil des ministres et quatre personnalités nommées par décret pour 5 ans, deux étant désignées par le Président de la République et deux par le Président de l'Assemblée nationale. Désormais, les conseillers passent au nombre de 3, et ils sont désignés par le Président de la Cour suprême (Personnalité nommée par décret du Président de la République). En ce qui les concerne, l'influence de l'exécutif est donc médiatisée.

Droit Administratif

La restructuration des collectivités locales effectuée au cours des années précédentes ne connaît aucune modification en 1969. Seule exception, la création du nouvel arrondissement d'Arlit (Loi n° 69.29 du 10 avril, J.O.R.N., p. 310) dote ainsi le centre de production d'uranium d'une personnalité propre à l'intérieur du département d'Agadez.

Les préoccupations économiques apparaissent encore en matière administrative avec la création d'une Commission d'Etude de la Réglementation des Marchés (Décret n° 69.74/MF du 25 mars, J.O.R.N., p. 215). Cette Commission, formée de hauts fonctionnaires, est chargée de proposer au gouvernement de nouvelles modalités concernant la passation des marchés publics. Cependant, aucun texte nouveau n'est publié dans ce domaine en 1969.

La loi de Finances n° 69.42 du 30 septembre (J.O.R.N., p. 684) contient, outre les dispositions conjoncturelles, quelques modifications concernant la répartition des charges entre les collectivités territoriales et l'Etat (a. 2 et 3), et complète la loi n° 61.32 par un article 14 bis consacrant l'existence de deux catégories de crédits: Les crédits "evaluatifs", servant à acquitter, éventuellement au delà des dotations budgétaires, "les dettes de l'Etat résultant de dispositions législatives spéciales, de conventions permanentes approuvées par la loi, ou de décision de justice", et les crédits "limitatifs".

Notons enfin que le Décret n° 69.35/MAECI du 11 janvier (J.O.R.N., pp. 112) fixe les conditions d'application de la loi 68.24 portant Code des Investissements, et organise à cet effet la Commission d'Investissements prévue par le Code.

DROIT SOCIAL

Les conditions de vie du paysannat nigérien constituent un problème fondamental pour le gouvernement d'un pays où l'urbanisation reste très limitée.

Diverses mesures législatives ont été prises depuis l'Indépendance. Des structures d'assistance économique, technique, sociale avaient été définies, sinon mises en place. Il faut cependant attendre le décret 69.149 MER-CGD du 19 octobre (J.O.R.N., p. 777) pour voir définies les modalités d'application de la Loi n° 60.28 fixant les règles de mise en valeur et de gestion des aménagements agricoles réalisés par la puissance publique, et dont l'objet était de remplacer les structures héritées de la colonisation (Société de Prévoyance, SMDR).

Le nouveau décret pose comme principe que ces aménagements ne peuvent être mis en valeur que par faire valoir direct, et par un paysannat familial (a.1).

L'une des préoccupations du gouvernement est cependant d'accélérer le transfert des charges d'entretien de ces aménagements de l'Etat aux paysans bénéficiaires grâce à l'amélioration de leur revenu net (a. 3 à 6). Une fois pris en charge par les organisations coopératives paysannes, ces aménagements cesseront d'appartenir au domaine public de l'Etat, et entreront dans le domaine public de la collectivité territoriale interessée. Le décret incite donc les paysans à s'organiser sur une base coopérative (a. 2 et 9).

Le problème de l'attribution des terres est particuliérement détaillé dans le chapitre IV du Décret. Si les détenteurs de droits coutumiers bénéficient d'une priorité d'établissement (a. 13) la répartition des terres doit se faire en fonction des capacités de travail de chaque famille paysanne exploitante (a. 14). Autrement dit, le gouvernement cherche à assurer une transition prudente entre les structures traditionnelles et les impératifs d'une meilleure rationalité, sans imposer de cadre général trop précis. La composition des Commissions d'arrondissement prévues par l'a. 16 illustre cette recherche d'équilibre puisque doivent y participer des représentants du pouvoir politique, de l'administration, et des autorités traditionnelles, associés aux représentants des Conseils d'exploitants (a. 27). C'est la Commission d'arrondissement qui procède à la répartition des unités de culture et contrôle l'exploitation faite par les paysans. L'encadrement administratif de ces opérations est précisé par le chapitre V du Décret.

Les liens entre les exploitants et l'organisme de gestion (qui aura passé une convention de gérance avec la puissance publique) sont définis par contrat, dont les éléments fondamentaux (durée, obligations, avenants. . .) sont définis dans les a. 32 à 35 du Décret.

Si ce Décret traduit la volonté de mettre en place un paysannat pilote, il ne signifie pas que le gouvernement nigérien abandonne une politique générale placée sous le signe de la Promotion Humaine. En effet, un décret 69.101 MEN/CGD du 30 mai (J.O.R.N., p. 465) met en place un Comité Permanant des Ressources Humaines composé de hauts fonctionnaires des ministères et administrations centrales s'occupant des questions sociales. Son objet est de coordonner les mesures gouvernementales prises en vue de valoriser les ressources humaines (Définition des objectifs, des moyens, formation, rendement).

L'abondance relative de la législation sociale en faveur des militaires nigériens semble répondre autant à des objectifs de justice sociale qu'à un souci politique. Il s'agit de satisfaire un corps dont le poids n'est pas négligeable dans l'exercice du pouvoir. Ainsi, le Décret 69.25 MDN du 11 janvier (J.O.R.N., p. 101) étend le bénéfice de l'institution d'un capital-décès au profit des ayants-droits des fonctionnaires décédés aux ayants-droit des militaires des FAN. Un autre décret n° 69.52 MDN du 18 février (J.O.R.N., p. 154) aménage le régime des retraites de ces militaires, et le décret 69.81 MDN du 29 mars (J.O.R.N., p. 227) définit avec précision le mode de calcul des rémunérations des enfants de troupe et militaires nigériens en stage à l'étranger.

DROIT PRIVÉ (DROIT CIVIL)

En matière civile, la seule innovation importante pour 1969 consiste dans l'adoption du Décret 69.102 MJ du 30 mai qui fixe les modalités d'application de la Loi 66.14 portant statut de la magistrature. Le Décret organise la carrière des magistrats dans tous ses aspects (recrutement par concours direct et concours professionnel, rémunération, notation et avancement). Le formalisme ne perd pas ses droits, puisque le chapitre V du décret est consacré au "Costume" imposé aux magistrats selon la nature des audiences, costume qui n'est en rien africanisé.

DROIT PÉNAL ET PROCÉDURE PÉNALE

Droit pénal

La loi n° 69.40 du 30 septembre (J.O.R.N., p. 735) institue la contrainte par corps pour le recouvrement de certaines dette civiles et commerciales. Cette procédure est ouverte seulement aux collectivités publiques, aux établissements publics et aux sociétés d'économie mixte (a. 1) lorsque le débiteur a été condamné définitivement pour une créance supérieure à 25.000 F (a. 2). On peut remarquer que le plancher ainsi fixé est relativement bas. Certaines personnes sont toutefois protégées contre cette mesure (a. 3). La demande d'exécution de contrainte par corps ne peut intervenir qu'après un délai de trois mois. C'est le juge du domicile du débiteur condamné qui doit être saisi de la demande. La durée de la contrainte varie selon l'importance de la dette (a. 6). L'article 12 précise que la nouvelle loi peut être appliquée pour des décisions intervenues avant son entrée en vigueur. Toutefois, le décret d'application prévu par la loi n'a pas été publié au terme de l'année législative.

Procédure pénale

La loi 69.5 du 18 février (J.O.R.N., p. 142) apporte de nouvelles modifications au Code de Procédure pénale, la loi 61.33 du 14 août 1961 restant cependant le texte de base.

Certaines de ces modifications sont seulement des ajustements d'ordre matériel. En particulier, les articles 618 à 620 du CPP concernant la procédure de règlement de conflits de compétence (Réglement de juges) sont réécrits, les seules modifications de fond portant sur l'effet suspensif de la requête en réglement de juges. Désormais la juridiction saisie n'est plus libre de prononcer ou non la suspension de la procédure. Celle-ci est automatique si la Cour suprême ordonne la communication de la requête aux parties (a. 619 nouveau). Ce n'est qu'en cas d'opposition à l'arrêt portant réglement de juges que la Cour suprême conserve sa liberté d'appréciation.

D'autre part, la loi complète l'a. 564 par un alinéa 3 qui porte à quinze jours le délai de pourvoi en cassation lorsque les assises siègent hors de Niamey.

CHAPTER 19

GUINÉE

L. G. Verdun

DROIT PUBLIC

Droit administratif

Le décret n° 134 PRG du 10 mars 1969 fixe l'organisation du ministère du domaine social. Ce ministère comprend, outre le cabinet, le secrétariat d'Etat à la Santé publique, le secrétariat d'Etat aux affaires sociales, le secrétariat d'Etat à la jeunesse et à la culture populaire, le secrétariat d'Etat à la fonction publique et au travail, le secrétariat d'Etat à l'education nationale, le service central des organismes internationaux (J.O. du 15 mai 1969, p. 95).

DROIT PRIVÉ

Droit commercial

Le décret 182 PRG du 12 avril 1969 interdit à toute entreprise d'Etat, d'économie mixte ou privée exerçant une activité industrielle en Guinée, d'assurer la distribution commerciale de sa production. Les entreprises doivent céder leur production exclusivement aux entreprises commerciales d'Etat qui en détiennent le monopole d'acquisition et de vente (J.O. du 1er juillet 1969, p. 134).

Procédure civile

Aux termes du décret n° 494 PRG du 27 novembre 1968, toutes les fonctions anciennement dévolues aux notaires, huissiers ou officiers d'exécution, commissaires priseurs — quand elles ne concourent pas directement à l'administration de la justice — ainsi que toutes les prérogatives des divers services contentieux des entreprises publiques ou à caractère agricole, industriel et commercial de l'Etat, sont transférées à un service public national d'Offres ministérielles et de règlement des créances, l'O.R.C., organisme rattaché à la présidence de la République.

Sous la direction d'un administrateur général nommé par décret, les agents de l'O.R.C. sont répartis en 3 sections: section du notariat, section de rédaction, de signification d'actes de procédure et d'exécution des décisions de justice, section de règlement des créances de l'Etat et des particuliers, de la vente aux enchères publiques et du recouvrement des amendes pénales (J.O. du 15 janvier 1969, p. 10).

DROIT PÉNAL ET PROCÉDURE PÉNALE

Le décret 127 PRG du 7 mars 1969 sanctionne certaines violations des dispositions réglementaires de la circulation routière par l'arrestation immédiate et une condamnation obligatoire à des peines d'emprisonnement, même dans l'hypothèse d'accident n'ayant entraîné que des dégâts matériels (J.O. du 15 mai 1969, p. 94).

CÔTE D'IVOIRE

F. Constantin

La stabilité politique en Côte d'Ivoire n'est pas fondamentalement remise en cause au cours de 1969. Certes, Abidjan connaît à son tour l'agitation étudiante, et le Président de la République juge bon de consacrer une grande partie de son temps à un dialogue direct avec les représentants de tous les groupes professionnels, économiques, sociaux existants en Côte d'Ivoire afin de dissiper des malentendus dont la persistance ternirait l'image paisible que veulent offrir au monde extérieur les dirigeants ivoiriens.

Ces contacts sont trop proches de la fin de l'année pour avoir quelque effet sur l'année législative 1969. Celle-ci, plus encore que l'année politique, est particulièrement calme, même si elle est marquée par une réforme d'importance, le découpage administratif de la République.

DROIT PUBLIC

Droit administratif

La loi n° 69.241 du 9 juin (J.O.R.C.I. n° 27, p. 819) pose le principe du remplacement des 6 départements existants depuis 1963 par 24 départements. Les décrets 69.504 du 4 décembre (J.O.R.C.I. n° 54, p. 1768), 69.538 et 539 du 22 décembre (J.O.R.C.I. 1970 n° 1, p. 3 et 5) fixent les conditions d'application de la loi et précisent le ressort territorial d'un certain nombre de sous-préfectures.

Ce nouveau cadre administratif est l'aboutissement d'un morcellement progressif qui va dans le sens d'un rapprochement entre l'Administration et les administrés. Officiellement, il s'agit d'une décision élaborée rationnellement, rendue nécessaire par le développement économique du pays, et devenue possible grâce à la formation du personnel d'autorité compétent. En fait, on peut lier cette mesure au développement de tensions locales plus ou moins sérieuses. Ainsi, la réforme peut présenter un double aspect: d'un côté, c'est un moyen pour le pouvoir central de renforcer l'encadrement des populations ivoiriennes; en sens inverse, elle doit permettre une meilleure circulation de l'information et éviter que certaines circonscriptions territoriales se sentent oubliées du pouvoir central, sauf lorsqu'il s'agit de payer l'impôt.

Quoiqu'il en soit, la réforme reste uniquement territoriale, la structure centralisée n'étant en aucune façon remise en cause.

Dans le même domaine administratif, diverses réformes techniques interviennent dans l'organisation des ministères, poursuivant un mouvement que l'on avait pu noter dans les années antérieures. Elles concernent cette année les administrations dont la fonction est essentiellement sociale: Ministère de l'Education nationale (décret n° 69.04 du 4 janvier, J.O.R.C.I. n° 3, p. 69) de la Santé publique et de la Population (décret 69.48 du 20 février; J.O.R.C.I. n° 12, p. 324), de la Jeunesse, de l'Education populaire et des Sports (décret 69.174 du 25 avril, J.O.R.C.I. n° 21, p. 639). D'autre part l'Ecole Nationale d'Administration, régie par une loi de 1960, fait l'objet d'un nouveau décret redéfinissant sa structure, ses fonctions, et l'organisation des programmes (décret n° 69.403 du 2 septembre, J.O.R.C.I. n° 43, p. 1375).

L'interventionnisme économique se poursuit malgré les apparences: la création en 1969 des sociétés "Palmivoire" et "Palmindustrie" a pour conséquence de nouvelles mesures d'intervention avec notamment la création d'un Fonds de Développement agricole et d'un Fonds social (décret 69.152 et 153 du 17 avril, J.O.R.C.I. n° 20, p. 596). Ces fonds, alimentés principalement par l'Etat (en tant qu'actionnaire des deux Sociétés) sont destinés à favoriser le financement d'opérations d'intérêt général et la protection du paysannat ivoirien suivant qu'il est concerné (F.S.) ou non (F.D.A.) par le développement du palmier à huile. Ces Fonds n'ont pas de personnalité juridique propre et sont gérés dans le cadre du budget spécial d'investissement.

Du point de vue financier, on peut noter le désir de renforcer le contrôle de l'administration des Finances sur les activités de gestion. A la suite de l'adoption en 1968 du nouveau Code de Prévoyance sociale, le décret 69.59 du 20 février (J.O.R.C.I. n° 12, p. 332) institue un contrôle financier auprès de la Caisse nationale de Prévoyance sociale et de la Caisse de Retraite des Travailleurs salariés. Le contrôleur dispose d'un véritable droit de veto à l'égard de tous les engagements de dépense, sous le contrôle du ministère de tutelle et du ministère des Finances. D'autre part, le décret n° 69.416 du 16 septembre (J.O.R.C.I. n° 44, p. 1409) auquel est annexé une circulaire d'application précisant les modalités de passation des Marchés passés sur le budget de l'Etat et les budgets annexes, rappelle les conditions d'exercice du contrôle financier sur ces marchés, et les liens entre ce contrôle et celui exercé par la Direction Générale des Marchés. La circulaire prévoit dans le détail les procédures à respecter afin d'obtenir des autorités compétentes l'approbation des marchés.

Droit international public

Par décret n° 69.159 du 17 avril (J.O.R.C.I. n° 20, p. 573), le gouvernement ivoirien a ratifié le protocole additionnel facultatif à la Convention internationale des Télécommunications de Montreux (1965) relatif au réglement obligatoire des différends.

D'autre part, le décret 69.445 du 22 octobre (J.O.R.C.I. n° 48, p. 1563) interdit le chalutage de fond aux navires étrangers dans la zone contiguë aux eaux territoriales de la Côte d'Ivoire. Toutefois, des dispositions spéciales sont prévues (mais non encore définies) si des accords de réciprocité ont été passés avec d'autres Etats en la matière.

DROIT SOCIAL

Prévoyance sociale

Après l'adoption du Code de Prévoyance sociale, l'activité législative et réglementaire est limitée. Des mesures de circonstance interviennent, comme le relèvement du taux des prestations familiales (décret 69.457).

Deux mesures importantes pour deux catégories particulières de travailleurs sont prises:

Pour les militaires, le décret 69.77 du 8 mars (J.O.R.C.I. n° 14, p. 382) institue une allocation temporaired' invalidité lorsque celle-ci résulte d'un accident de service entraînant une incapacité permanente ou d'une maladie imputable au service. Le bénéfice de ces dispositions s'étend aux soldats du contingent. La procédure et le calcul du montant de l'indemnité sont fixés par le décret.

Pour les marins, le décret 69.444 du 22 octobre (J.O.R.C.I. n° 48, p. 1562) met en place la Commission sociale de la Marine marchande et des Pêches maritimes. C'est une commission d'étude des problèmes professionnels (recrutement, formation, condition de travail) qui — le fait est assez rare pour être noté — est composée essentiellement de représentants des syndicats d'armateurs et de marins (8 au total), les représentants de l'Administration étant en minorité (4). Cependant, c'est le ministre des Travaux publics qui est seul habilité à convoquer la Commission et qui fixe son ordre du jour.

DROIT PRIVÉ

Deux auxiliaires de la justice voient au cours de l'année publier leur statut professionnel.

Il s'agit des huissiers de justice [loi n° 69.242 et décret d'application n° 69.243 du 9 juin: J.O.R.C.I. n° 27, p. 820 et 823] et des notaires [loi n° 69.372 et décret d'application 69.373 du 12 août: J.O.R.C.I. n° 38, p. 1224].

En matière commerciale, le gouvernement ivoirien a ratifié la Convention de Bruxelles de 1924 sur l'unification de certaines règles concernant la responsabilité du transporteur en matière de transport maritime (connaissement).

DROIT PÉNAL ET PROCÉDURE PÉNALE

Droit pénal

Le décret 69.356 du 28 juillet (J.O.R.C.I. n° 35, p. 1104) définit les contraventions de simple police et les peines qui leur sont applicables.

Trois catégories de contraventions sont ainsi établies en fonction de la gravité du fait sanctionné.

Les contraventions de lère classe sont punies d'une amende de 200 à 2 000 F CFA; une liste de treize faits se rapporte à la police de la voirie, des immeubles ou à des menus vols. Les contraventions de 2e classe sont sanctionnées par une amende de 1 000 à 10 000 F CFA ou 10 jours d'emprisonnement, les deux peines pouvant se cumuler. Ceci concerne vingt trois types d'activités répréhensibles allant de l'entrave au fonctionnement des services publics au refus de recevoir la monnaie ayant cours légal; on trouve encore dans la liste les dégradations commises sur les édifices publics, certains cas de coups et blessures involontaires, les mauvais traitements infligés à des animaux, les incitations publiques à la débauche, etc... Enfin, les contraventions de 3e classe sont punies de 2 000 à 72 000 F CFA d'amende ou d'un emprisonnement de dix jours à deux mois, les deux peines pouvant être cumulées. Les quinze faits énumérés dans cette catégorie sont notamment l'opposition caractérisée à l'exercice de l'autorité légitime, uniforme, la dégradation des chemins publics, le vol des récoltes (sous réserve de l'a. 388 du Code pénal), les violences légères, les lettres anonymes, l'organisation de jeux de hasard, l'exercice du métier de devin ou "d'interprète des songes", le défaut de tenue des registres exigés des hôteliers, aubergistes, etc...

Ce décret, qui dans son souci de précision, ne manquera pas cependant de poser des problèmes d'interprétation au juge, abolit la vieille législation héritée de la colonisation.

Signalons d'autre part le décret 69.189 du 14 mai (J.O.R.C.I. n° 24, p. 712) qui fixe la réglementation des établissements pénitentiaires, c'est-à-dire essentiellement les conditions dans lesquelles les peines privatives de liberté sont exécutées. Les prévenus, contraints et condamnés à un emprisonnement de simple police, sont soumis au même régime de détention.

Pour les autres condamnés, divers régimes sont prévus, en fonction de leur personnalité telle qu'elle s'est révélée au cours des procès, en fonction de la nature de la peine, et en fonction de leur conduite au cours de la détention. En principe, les mineurs doivent bénéficier d'un régime spécial. Le régime disciplinaire, les conditions de travail des détenus, leur rémunération, l'assistance sociale et médicale sont organisés dans les chapitres suivants du décret.

Procédure pénale

La loi 69.371 du 12 août (J.O.R.C.I. n° 38, p. 1217) apporte diverses modifications au Code de Procédure pénale adopté le 14 novembre 1960.

L'économie générale du texte n'est guère modifiée; les réformes portent sur des points très particuliers comme les conditions de notification, certains délais de recours ou de prise de connaissance des dossiers, l'expertise; les modification se bornent parfois à mettre à jour le Code en tenant compte des réformes législatives intervenues depuis sa publication (comme le décret du 28 juillet 1969 cité ci-dessus.).

CHAPTER 21

HAUTE-VOLTA

L. G. Verdun

DROIT PUBLIC

Droit administratif

Etablissements publics industriels et commerciaux: l'ordonnance n°
69.64 du 20 novembre 1969 crée un centre de Formation féminine et
artisanale, établissement public industriel et commercial doté de la
personnalité civile et de l'autonomie financière, dont l'objet est
"d'assurer aux jeunes filles une éducation féminine complète, leur formation à un travail d'artisanat, et contribuer à la valorisation de l'artisanat
voltaïque". L'établissement est placé sous la tutelle technique du
ministère de l'Education nationale et sous la tutelle financière du
ministère des Finances (J.O. du 27 novembre 1969, p. 616).

Finances publiques

Budget de l'Etat (exercice 1969): l'ordonnance n° 69.67 du 2
décembre 1969 constitue loi de finances pour l'exécution du budget
1970. Les produits et revenus applicables au budget de l'Etat sont
évalués à 9.761.861.000 francs CFA dont 2.213.000.000 au titre des
impôts directs et 6.506.500.000 au titre des impôts indirects. Les
crédits ouverts sont répartis de la façon suivante: Dette publique
(Titre 1): 710.231.000; Dépenses de fonctionnement (Titre 2):
6.947.704.000; Interventions publiques (Titre 3): 1.064.510.000;
Equipement et investissements (Titre 4): 904.416.000 (J.O. du 15 janvier 1970, p. 31).

Fiscalité: quatre ordonnances, 69.9 du 10 mars 1969 (J.O. du 20
mars 1969, p. 167), 69.54 du 17 octobre 1969 (J.O. du 30 octobre
1969, p. 533), 69.61 du 15 novembre 1969 (J.O. du 27 novembre,
p. 608), 69.72 du 31 décembre 1969 (J.O. du 8 janvier 1970, p. 18)
apportent des modifications et des compléments au Code des Impôts
directs et indirects et du monopole des Tabacs. L'ordonnance du 10
mars modifie la liste des redevables de l'impôt forfaitaire sur le
revenu, celle du 17 octobre institue une taxe anuelle d'un montant de
5.000 francs CFA sur les postes récepteurs de télévision, celle du 15

novembre traite des taxes frappant les biens de mainmorte, des taxes sur le bétail, des taxes sur le chiffre d'affaires, celle du 31 décembre fixe le tableau des exemptions de la taxe sur le chiffre d'affaires ainsi que la liste des marchandises soumises à un taux réduit.

Fonction publique

L'ordonnance 69.56 du 21 octobre 1969 modifie la loi 37.61 du 24 juillet 1961 instituant le régime général de retraite des fonctionnaires de la République de Haute-Volta. La limite d'âge de 55 ans est ramenée à 53 ans: les fonctionnaires qui atteindront l'âge de 53 ans seront admis d'office à la retraite et feront valoir leurs droits à pensions d'ancienneté ou proportionnelle. Toutefois, pour des nécessités impérieuses de service, le Conseil des ministres pourra, à titre exceptionnel, maintenir le fonctionnaire en service au-delà de cette limite d'âge et pour une période ne pouvant en aucun cas excéder deux ans (**J.O.** du 6 novembre 1969, p. 574).

Le décret 69.247 du 18 novembre 1969 abroge les dispositions du décret du 31 decembre 1960 et fixe les barêmes des traitements des agents temporaires de l'administration et des établissements publics. Ces personnes sont classés en 5 catégories subdivisées en 2 échelles comportant 13 échelons (**J.O.** du 27 novembre 1969, p. 612).

Terres domaniales

L'ordonnance 69.14 du 4 avril 1969 fixe les prix d'aliénation qui varient de 1 à 1.500 francs CFA le mètre carré selon les régions et selon l'implantation du terrain en zone commerciale, résidentielle, industrielle, suburbaine et hors lotissement. Le montant des redevances est fixé à 1/20 du prix du terrain, avec minimum de 1.000 francs (**J.O.** du 17 avril 1969, p. 212).

DROIT PRIVÉ

Droit commercial

Banques: l'arrêté n° 556 du ministre des Finances en date du 16 octobre 1969 porte fixation du capital minimum des Banques et établissements financiers. A compter de l'exercice 1969–1970, toute banque commerciale devra justifier d'un capital dont le montant, sans pouvoir être inférieur à 50 millions de francs CFA devra être égal ou supérieur à 8% des risques figurant à son bilan ou hors bilan à la date de clôture.du plus récent exercice (**J.O.** du 30 octobre 1969, p. 554).

DROIT AÉRIEN

L'ordonnance n° 69.25 du 12 mai 1969 porte Code de l'Aéronautique civile. La première partie de ce Code, intitulée "Navigation aérienne" est divisée en 6 titres traitant successivement des aéronefs, du personnel aéronautique, des aérodromes, des services auxiliaires, des conditions et règles de la circulation aérienne, et des enquêtes sur les accidents d'aviation: la deuxième partie intitulée "Services aériens" divisée également en 6 titres, traite successivement des définitions et règles générales, des services aériens de transport public, du travail aérien, des services aériens privés, des aéroclubs et écoles d'aviation, et de la responsabilité; la troisième partie traite des infractions et pénalités. Le Code de l'Aéronautique civile se réfère à la Convention relative à l'Aviation civile internationale signée à Chicago le 7 décembre 1944 et à la convention relative aux infractions et à certains actes survenant à bord des aéronefs, signée à Tokyo le 14 septembre 1963 (J.O. du 8 septembre 1969, numéro spécial).

CHAPTER 22

TOGO

F. Constantin

A l'image de bien des militaires au pouvoir, le Général Eyadema, Président de la République togolaise considère superflu de s'imposer la présence d'une Assemblée législative. Les source écrites du Droit restent donc les Ordonnances présidentielles et les décrets gouvernementaux. La facilité d'action qui en découle n'est cependant pas utilisée en 1969 pour effectuer des modifications fondamentales dans l'ordre juridique pas plus que dans le domaine politique. L'année est finalement relativement calme, si l'on considère qu'il y a eu un seul remaniement ministériel, même s'il touche les principaux ministères : le ministre de la Justice (Colonel Dadjo), le ministre du Travail et de l'Economie rurale (M. Adossama), le ministre des Finances (B. Djobo), le ministre de l'Education national (S. Babelème) sont remplacés et disparaissent de la formation gouvernementale le 4 août.

Exerçant seul le pouvoir, le Général Eyadema doit conserver le contrôle sur ses collaborateurs pour qui la fidélité est, autant que la compétence, un gage de longévité ministérielle.

DROIT PUBLIC

Droit Constitutionnel

Le retour à un régime civil annoncé pour 1969 n'a pas lieu : des manifestations populaires ont été organisées au début de l'année pour réclamer le maintien de l'armée au pouvoir.

Droit Administratif

Les mesures les plus marquantes concernent la poursuite des opérations de restructuration de l'Administration centrale déjà amorcée en 1968.

Le décret 69.139 du 9 juillet (J.O.R.T. n° 421, p. 453) crée, sous l'autorité du ministre des Finances, la Direction et les services extérieurs des Douanes. Il organise la structure générale de cette administration, les circonscriptions territoriales et précise les fonctions des différents agents, de la Direction centrale aux agents locaux.

Le décret 69.174 du 5 septembre (J.O.R.T. n° 425, p. 602) procède à la restructuration du ministère de l'Economie rurale. Il crée un "collège" chargé de la définition des objectifs et de la coordination des programmes, une Direction générale de l'Economie rurale, composée de directions techniques et reliée "de manière fonctionnelle" aux Services para-administratifs agissant dans le même secteur.

De même, les Directions techniques du ministère de l'Education nationale sont réaménagées par le décret 69.178 du 1er octobre (J.O.R.T. n°4 27, p. 630).

A ce même niveau structurel, on trouve le souci du gouvernement de définir, au début de l'année, les cadres administratifs chargés d'appliquer la législation sociale qui sera précisée dans les mois suivants.

Un décret n° 69.25 du 14 janvier (J.O.R.T. n° 406, p. 62) fixe la composition et les fonctions de la Direction générale du Travail, de la Main d'Oeuvre et de la Sécurité sociale, et des services de contrôle et d'application (Inspection du Travail et Service de la Main d'Oeuvre).

Le décret n° 69.121 du 10 juin (J.O.R.T. n° 419, p. 365) crée, sous l'autorité du ministre de la Santé publique, trois organes consultatifs: le Conseil national de la Santé publique, qui associe le ministre et les représentants des professions et des oeuvres privées intéressées; le "Collége du ministère", composé de hauts fonctionnaires de cette Administration; le Comité permanent de planification qui fait intervenir, outre les hauts fonctionnaires, le représentant de l'O.M.S. à Lomé. D'autre part, les diverses attributions des Directions du Ministère et les structures locales d'encadrement sont précisées par le Décret.

DROIT SOCIAL

Prévoyance sociale

Le gouvernement togolais intervient à tous les niveaux de l'action sociale. Au niveau de la conception, le décret 69.137 du 30 juin (J.O.R.T. n° 420, p. 432) consacre l'existence du Conseil interministériel de l'Action sociale, assisté d'un Comité technique, chargé de définir les objectifs de la protection sociale et d'harmoniser la législation.

Au niveau local d'exécution, le décret 69.53 du 10 mars (J.O.R.T. n° 412, p. 221) institue des "Centres sociaux", établissements publics autogérés constituant les "bases opérationnelles du service social polyvalent".

En ce qui conserne la législation sociale proprement dite, le décret 69.205 du 27 octobre (J.O.R.T. n° 429, p. 672) précise les obligations incombatant aux employeurs en tant qu'ils sont débiteurs de la Caisse Nationale de Sécurité Sociale pour les cotisations dûes au titre des régimes de prestation familiale, des accidents du travail, des pensions. Les modalités du prélèvement et du versement sont précisées par les articles 2 à 5 du décret; un système allégé est prévu en faveur des entreprises employant moins de 20 salariés. Les sanctions (majorations, procédure de contrainte) sont aménagées pour les retardataires par les a. 6 à 11 du décret.

L'Arrêté n° 244 MTAS.FP du 6 juin (J.O.R.T. n° 416 (Spécial), p. 12) fixe le règlement général du régime des pensions annoncé par une Ordonnance présidentielle de 1968: Ce régime s'applique à tous les travailleurs soumis au Code du Travail, y compris les salariés de l'Etat et des collectivités publiques ne bénéficiant pas d'un régime dérogatoire, ainsi que les adhérents volontaires, admis dans les conditions fixées par les a. 5 à 10 de l'arrêté. Chaque travailleur ainsi assujetti a un livret d'assurance signé par ses employeurs successifs. Les conditions d'attribution des pensions de vieillesse, d'invalidité à l'intéressé ou à ses ayants droits sont fixées par le chapitre III de l'Arrêté: l'âge minimum est en règle générale de 55 ans. La procédure du versement et de liquidation sont précisées dans l'arrêté (Chapitre IV, V, VI).

Signalons enfin un bref arrêté n° 87 MTAS.FP.MSP du 20 février (J.O.R.T. n° 409, p. 169) qui fixe les conditions du congé de maternité des femmes non fonctionnaires des Services administratifs de l'Etat et des collectivités secondaires (Durée totale: 14 semaines, salaire versé pour moitié par l'Administration, pour moitié par la Caisse nationale de Sécurité sociale).

Droit du Travail

Complétant cette série de mesures se rapportant à la prévoyance sociale, le gouvernement togolais met au point au cours de l'année les statuts de diverses catégories de travailleurs de l'Etat et des collectivités publiques.

Tout d'abord, signalons la publication du Décret 69.113 du 28 mai (J.O.R.T. n° 416 (Spécial), p. 3) fixant les diverses mesures d'ordre statutaire nécessaires pour la mise en application du Statut général du Fonctionnaire (publié en 1968). Le décret précise l'organisation des Cadres et Corps de la Fonction publique, le recrutement et la formation des fonctionnaires, et de façon plus générale, le déroulement de leur carrière et la procédure disciplinaire. L'ensemble de cette réglementation s'inspire directement de la tradition de la fonction publique des démocraties libérales.

Dans le même temps, divers statuts particuliers sont adoptés pour la Police (Ordonnance n° 11 du 10 juin — J.O.R.T. n° 418, p. 332; décret n° 69.122 du même jour — J.O.R.T. n° 419, p. 368), le personnel du Port Autonome de Lomé (décret 69.136 du 23 juin, J.O.R.T. n° 420, p. 422) et de la Régie nationale des Eaux (décret 69.125 du 30 octobre, J.O.R.T. n° 429, p. 675). Pour le personnel de Police, l'obligation générale de discrétion en matière d'expression des opinions est renforcé (a. 9 et 11) et la liberté syndicale ne leur est pas reconnue (a. 10). La nature des fautes susceptibles d'entraîner des sanctions disciplinaires est précisée en termes généraux par l'a. 92 de l'Ordonnance. Les diverses règles concernant les conditions de travail, de recrutement, d'avancement, de cessation des fonctions ainsi que les garanties sociales sont précisées par l'ordonnance et le décret d'application pris le même jour.

On retrouve les mêmes éléments mais très allégés dans les statuts du Personnel du Port Autonome de Lomé et de la Régie nationale des Eaux.

Enfin, un bref décret n° 69.112 du 28 mai (J.O.R.T. n° 416 (Spécial), p. 3) fixe le mode de calcul des congés payés pour tous les travailleurs soumis au Code du Travail. La règle est que pour 12 mois de travail, le travailleur a droit au maximum à 30 jours de congés payés. Cette mesure particulièrement favorable est entrée en vigueur le 1er juillet 1969.

Ainsi, on ne peut qu'être frappé par l'importance de l'effort effectué par le gouvernement togolais pour régler avec précision la situation sociale des travailleurs salariés qui constituent une population dont l'importance politique n'est pas négligeable, surtout dans le Sud du Togo.

DROIT PRIVÉ

Il n'y a pas à proprement parler d'innovation importante en cette matiére au cours de l'année.

Toutefois, le secteur des Assurances, qui avait été l'objet d'une réglementation générale en 1968 voit publier le décret d'application attendu: c'est le décret 69.119 du 2 juin (J.O.R.T. n° 418, p. 352). Il fixe les conditions d'agrément des Sociétés d'Assurance (en distinguant selon que les sociétés sont togolaises ou étrangères), et les conditions d'exercice des fonctions de courtiers et représentants légaux des sociétés. Le titre II du décret précise les modalités de la liquidation.

Signalons d'autre part que l'Ordonnance n° 15 du 3 juillet (J.O.R.T. n° 420, p. 416) ratifie l'accord commercial signé le 4 mai 1966 entre le Togo et le Nigeria.

DROIT PÉNAL

Deux ordonnances importantes interviennet dans ce domaine. L'ordonnance n° 5 du 17 février (J.O.R.T. n° 410 (Spécial), p. 3) institue les juridictions pour enfants, destinées à juger les mineurs de dix huit ans lorsque leur cas peut être disjoint de celui de co-inculpés plus âgés (a. 3). Le juge compétent est choisi parmi les juges en place en raison de l'intérêt qu'il porte aux problèmes de l'enfance (a. 6).

L'ordonnance n° 16 du 9 juillet (J.O.R.T. n° 421, p. 451) modifie certaines dispositions du Code Pénal relatives à la répression des fraudes sur les billets de banque (a. 132 à 138) et des contrefaçons ou falsifications de sceaux officiels.

CHAPTER 23

DAHOMEY

F. Constantin

Commencée avec un régime militaire, l'année 1968 s'était achevée avec un régime civil. Au terme de 1969, les militaires sont à nouveau au pouvoir. Autant dire que le jeu des rivalités politiques est loin d'être achevé et que les préoccupations circonstancielles (Maintien au pouvoir) l'emportent largement sur le souci de mettre au point des réformes d'envergure dont on craint d'ailleurs qu'elles ne créent de nouvelles catégories de mécontents. Dans ces conditions, les activités essentielles ne concernent que le perpétuel réaménagement des structures administratives centrales, la définition du statut des agents publics les plus importants (forces de l'ordre, comptables publics, douanes) et la répression des atteintes à la sûreté de l'Etat, mesures pourtant bien insuffisantes pour atteindre leur objectif, c'est-à-dire la sûreté du gouvernement en place.

DROIT PUBLIC

Droit constitutionnel

Doit-on accorder une place importante à la publication d'un nouveau texte constitutionnel sous la forme de "Charte du Directoire" (Ord. n° 69.53 du 26 décembre, J.O.R.D. n° 31, p. 885) sinon pour signaler qu'il confirme la chute du gouvernement civil du Président E.D. Zinsou ? On peut à la rigueur attirer l'attention sur le caractère unilatéral du texte publié par le triumvirat militaire, dont le chef est "le Lieutenant-Colonel du FAD... le plus ancien dans le grade le plus élevé". On retrouve au passage des dispositions inspirées de la Constitution française à ceci près que ce qui est là du domaine de la loi devient ici du domaine de l'Ordonnance, ce qui rend la distinction bien formelle entre le pouvoir législatif et le pouvoir réglementaire; il n'est en effet nulle part envisagé la mise en place d'un Corps législatif.

La Cour suprême se voit reconnaître une autorité suprême en matière constitutionnelle, administrative, judiciaire et fiscale et veille à

289

la régularité d' "opérations électorales" nulle part prévues dans la Charte, sinon pour un avenir incertain, dans l'a. 42.

Seule assemblée délibérante, le Conseil économique et social reste en fonction à titre consultatif. Son règlement intérieur avait été approuvé par un décret 69.56 PR/SGG du 17 février (J.O.R.D. n° 6, p. 293).

Droit administratif

Le souci de renforcer et d'améliorer les structures administratives peut être symbolisé par la création d'une Commission nationale de la Réforme administrative (décret n° 69.55 PR/MFPRAT/SG du 17 février, J.O.R.D. n° 7, p. 239), chargée de la "rationalisation, de la diminution des coûts, et l'élévation de la conscience professionnelle des fonctionnaires et agents de l'Etat". La Commission est placée sous la responsabilité du Ministre de la Fonction publique.

Dans le même temps, l'organisation de certains ministères dahoméens est révisée — révision que l'on rencontre dans d'autres Etats africains voisins — Ceci concerne en particulier le ministère de la Fonction publique (décret 69.54 PR/MFPRAT/SG du 17 février, J.O.R.D. n° 7, p. 237), de la Santé (décret 69.45 PR/MSPAS/ du 17 février, J.O.R.D. n° 7, p. 260), de l'Education nationale (décret 69.146 PR/MEN du 19 juin, J.O.R.D. n° 16, p. 450), de l'Intérieur (décret 69.325 D/SGG du 17 décembre, J.O.R.D. 1970 n° 7, p. 186). L'objectif essentiel est de renforcer la position des Secrétaires généraux des ministères afin d'assurer un meilleur contrôle sur les agents des services intéressés.

La tentative de reprise en main porte aussi sur l'Armée. Aux mesures déjà prises en 1968 par le gouvernement civil s'ajoute une refonte des Conseils de discipline (décret 69.6 PR/SGDN, J.O.R.D. n° 3, p. 110), dont la fonction est seulement consultative. La composition du Conseil, la procédure suivie sont aussi l'objet de nouvelles dispositions qui laissent malgré tout à "Haute Autorité chargée de la Défense nationale" le pouvoir de décision.

L'une des dernières ordonnances du Président Zinsou concerne justement l'organisation générale de la Défense nationale. L'ordonnance 69.48 PR/DN du 9 décembre (J.O.R.D. 1970 n° 7, p. 186) souligne là encore le rôle fondamental du Secrétaire général à la Défense, "cerveau" de la Défense nationale (a. 14).

Enfin, les diverses mesures concernant la Gendarmerie nationale déjà prises en 1968 font l'objet de nouvelles précisions: le décret 69.270 PR/DN du 21 octobre (J.O.R.D. n° 27, p. 769) définit les missions de la Gendarmerie nationale et les modalités d'exercice, en axant l'exposé des dispositions sur les relations avec les autorités civiles nationales et locales, les rapports avec l'Armée devant faire l'objet d'une instruction spéciale (a. 200).

C'est encore la pression des évènements qui amène l'adoption de l'ordonnance 69.15 du 19 juin (J.O.R.D. n° 15, p. 437) puisqu'elle porte sur le recouvrement de l'impôt. Il est vrai que c'est un problème chronique pour les autorités dahoméennes qui se succèdent au pouvoir. Parallèlement à la retenue mensuelle à la source de l'impôt sur le revenu,[1] un versement trimestriel est prévu pour les non salariés.

DROIT SOCIAL

Prévoyance sociale

Aucune mesure fondamentale n'intervient en 1969. Signalons simplement que par décret 69.315 PR/MAE du 9 décembre (J.O.R.D. 1970 n° 7, p. 191) le gouvernement dahoméen annonce son adhésion au Protocole du Statut International des Réfugiés complétant la Convention de Genève de 1951.

Travail

Le décret 69.117 PR/MFPRAT/DTLS du 8 mai 1969 (J.O.R.D. n° 14, p. 428) organise le Conseil national du Travail prévu par le Code du Travail de 1967. Il est composé d'Administrateurs spécialisés qui se réunissent au moins deux fois par an.

Dans le domaine du droit du travail, une autre législation fondamentale fait l'objet d'une refonte étroitement liée aux circonstances politiques: il s'agit du droit de grève que réglemente l'ordonnance n° 69.14 PR/MFPRAT du 19 juin (J.O.R.D. n° 15, p. 438). Sa portée est générale, puisqu'elle vise non seulement les salariés du secteur public, mais aussi ceux des entreprises privées "chargées de la gestion d'un service public ou (dont le) fonctionnement est nécessaire à la vie de la Nation" (a. 1). La grève ne peut intervenir qu'après un préavis de 5 jours, et après l'échec dûment constaté par les parties intéressées des tentatives d'accord négocié (a. 2 à 5). Les grèves tournantes ou perlées sont interdites (a. 5). Chaque ministre reste libre de déterminer par des mesures ad hoc les personnels qui ne pourraient participer à la grève (a. 6). Les réquisitions individuelles ou collectives sont largement autorisées (a. 8–9). Le non respect des dispositions de l'ordonnance peut entraîner pour les contrevenants des sanctions prises selon une procédure expéditive (a. 7, 11).

Par ailleurs, une nouvelle série de statuts particuliers est publiée, touchant des travailleurs dont la place dans la Nation est fondamentale: il s'agit des comptables publics (ordonnance 69.5 PR/MEF du 13 février, complétée par le décret 69.48 PR/MEF du 17 février[2] — J.O.R.D. n° 6, p. 204 et 207), du personnel des douanes et droits indirects (décret 69.16 PR/MFPRAT du 8 mai — J.O.R.D. n° 22, p. 618) et du personnel militaire de l'Armée dahoméenne (ordonnance 69.34 PR du 17 octobre — J.O.R.D. n° 27, p. 759, abrogeant le statut antérieur adopté en 1968 par le gouvernement militaire du Lieutenant Colonel Alley).

DROIT PRIVÉ

Là encore, on est seulement en présence de mesures de circonstance dont les plus importantes concernent encore une fois les problèmes monétaires et financiers.

Une circulaire n° 5 MEF/CAB du 14 janvier (J.O.R.D. n° 4, p. 140) définit les conditions et la procédure de la domiciliation bancaire des opérations d'importation et du paiement des marchandises étrangères importées au Dahomey. En sens inverse, la circulaire n° 6 MEF/DGAE du même jour (J.O.R.D. n° 4, p. 144) organisé la domiciliation des exportations sur l'étranger et le contrôle du rapatriement de leurs produits (une annexe A indique toutefois pour ces deux circulaires la liste des produits dispensés de ces formalités).

En application de la législation mise en place en 1968, une autre circulaire n° 15 MEF/CAB du 20 janvier (J.O.R.D. n° 4, p. 148) fixe les conditions d'ouverture et de gestion des comptes étrangers en francs et devises de valeurs mobilières ouverts à des non-résidents.

D'autre part, le contrôle des changes pour tous les déplacements à l'étranger (c'est-à-dire hors de la zone franc) est précisé par l'Arrêté 173 MEF/AE/DG du 21 février (J.O.R.D. n° 10, p. 324) qui fixe la forme et le contenu des carnets de change.

Dans le même sens, une série de circulaires n° 142 à 149 MEF/AE/DG du 17 septembre (J.O.R.D. n° 23, 634 et suivantes) précise pour toute une série de cas particuliers (Secours, transferts de salaire, délivrance de devises, paiements courants) les modalités des réglements monétaires hors des frontières du Dahomey.

DROIT PÉNAL ET PROCÉDURE PÉNALE

Droit pénal

L'année 1969 voit une aggravation progressive de la législation pénale. Les actes délictueux sont définis avec une précision accrue et surtout recouvrent un domaine d'activité de plus en plus étendu.

L'ordonnance 69.10 PR du 14 mai (J.O.R.D. n° 14, p. 413) complète la Loi de 1961 sur la Sécurité publique en précisant que si le délinquant est un fonctionnaire, il pourra faire l'objet de santions supplémentaires en vertu du Statut général de la Fonction publique, sans bénéficier des garanties de la procédure statutairement prévues.

L'ordonnance 69.22 PR/MJL du 4 juillet (J.O.R.D. n° 17, p. 485) organise la répression de la propagation des fausses nouvelles par tous moyens portant atteinte à la paix publique, au moral de la nation, à l'intérêt du pays (a. 1). Les infractions seront poursuivies d'office par le Ministère public, suivant la procédure de flagrant délit

De façon plus générale, l'ordonnance 69.33 PR du 15 octobre (J.O.R.D. n° 25, p. 723) définit les "attentats, complots et autres infractions contre l'autorité de l'Etat et l'intégrité du territoire national" et les "crimes tendant à troubler l'Etat par le massacre ou la dévastation" et les" crimes commis par la participation à un mouvement insurrectionnel". Elle fixe le régime des peines encourues par les responsables et abroge toutes les dispositions antérieures, notamment les a. 87 à 108 du Code Pénal.

Ces réformes marquées par une aggravation des sanctions n'ont pas arrêté les comploteurs. Mais si le gouvernement civil du Président Zinsou n'a pas pu empêcher la prise du pouvoir par les militaires, ceux-ci entretiennent la tradition, l'un de leurs premiers actes étant la publication du Décret 69.324 D/DAI/A du 16 décembre (J.O.R.D. n° 31, p. 890) qui interdit toutes manifestations de rue, sans préciser les sanctions encourues par les contrevenants. Il est vrai que même les manifestations favorables au Directoire sont interdites.

Procédure pénale

Parallèlement à ce mouvement général, l'Ordonnance 69.9 PR du 7 mai (J.O.R.D. n°11, p. 361) créait une Cour de Sûreté de l'Etat compétente pour connaître de tous crimes et délits se rapportant à la sûreté de l'Etat et des autorités légitimes. La Cour est composée exclusivement de magistrats civils (sauf lorsqu'est en cause la discipline des armées). Les arrêts rendus par la Cour sont susceptibles d'un recours en cassation. L'ordonnance précise en outre le déroulement de la procédure.

Autrement fondamentale, parce que moins liée aux évènements politiques, paraît être l'Ordonnance 69.33 PR/MJL du 10 juillet (J.O.R.D. n° 17, p. 485) concernant le jugement des infractions commises par des mineurs de 18 ans. La compétence des tribunaux pour enfants est ainsi précisée (a. 2 et 3). La procédure de l'instruction fait l'objet des a. 7 à 16 de l'ordonnance. Le chapitre III (a. 17 à 28) concerne la procédure à suivre en matière correctionnelle et le chapitre IV (a. 29 à 33) la procédure à suivre en matière criminelle. Le régime des peines est précisé par l'a. 32. Enfin, le chapitre V (a. 34 à 67) organise les modalités d'exécution des mesures de garde provisoire ou définitive en vue de la protection, de la surveillance ou de la rééducation du mineur. L'ensemble de ces dispositions confère au juge pour enfant une responsabilité très lourde, notamment dans le cas de la liberté surveillée.

Publiée en 1969, cette organisation nouvelle doit fonctionner à partir de 1970.

---

1. Qui, d'ailleurs, au lieu d'être égale au 1/12 de l'impôt de l'année précédente, est fixée pour l'année en cours à 1/6. . .
2. Qui prévoit la prestation de serment et le dépôt d'un cautionnement.

CHAPTER 24

REPUBLIQUE FEDERALE DU CAMEROUN

J. L. Balans

Dix ans après son accession à l'indépendance, la République fédérale du Cameroun connaît encore des troubles politiques sporadiques qui se traduisent dans le domaine juridique par la mise en oeuvre de mesures d'exception. Cependant, on notera la volonté de l'Etat de mieux assurer son emprise sur les collectivités et d'améliorer le contrôle exercé sur ses différents organes. Les conflits juridiques issus de la structure fédérale de la République du Cameroun trouveront une meilleure solution avec la mise en place de la Cour fédérale de Justice que l'on peut considérer comme l'innovation législative la plus importante de l'année.

DROIT PUBLIC

Droit constitutionnel

Il n'y a pas de réforme constitutionnele en 1969.

Droit administratif

La mesure la plus importante en Droit public est la loi 69.LF.1 du 14 juin (J.O.R.F.C. supplémentaire du 1er juillet, p. 2) fixant la composition, les conditions de saisine et la procédure devant la Cour fédérale de Justice. Cette Cour peut tranchen les conflits de compétence en matière civile qui pourraient résulter en déni de justice, dans les cas notamment où les cours suprêmes du Cameroun oriental et du Cameroun occidental confirmeraient un arrêt de refus de compétence. Mais surtout c'est elle qui décide des interprétations du Droit fédéral. Deux types d'action sont alors possibles: action dans l'intérêt des parties, à la suite d'une décision d'une cour suprême at action dans l'intérêt de la Loi par l'avocat général ou le procureur général auprès de la Cour fédérale. Enfin, c'est à la Cour fédérale de Justice qu'est attribué le contentieux en matière administrative (contentieux à l'encontre de la République fédérale, des Etats fédérés, des collectivités et établissements publics). Ce contentieux inclut les recours en annulation pour excès de pouvoir, en indemnisation des préjudices et aux concessions de services publics. Dans ces cas l'Assemblée plénière de la Cour fédérale siégeant à Yaoundé juge seulement en appel des décisions rendues en première instance par les chambres administratives de la même cour qui siègent à Yaoundé et à Buéa. Les régles de procédure sont alors analogues à celles du Droit administratif français.

Un certain souci d'améliorer le contrôle administratif des organes de l'Etat se manifeste par le décret 69.DF.15 du 17 janvier (J.O.R.F. C. du 1er février, p. 140) transformant la direction générale du contrôle d'Etat en inspection générale de l'Etat placée sous l'autorité d'un ministre délégué, et le décret 69.DF.151 du 26 avril (J.O.R.F.C. du 1er mai, p. 697) supprimant les cabinets ministériels et créant dans chaque ministère un secrétariat particulier plus étroitement lié à la fonction publique. Le décret 69.DF.160 du 3 mai (J.O.R.F.C. du 15 mai, p. 841) organise la Sûreté nationale. Force civile dirigée par un délégué général mais sous l'autorité du Président de la République, elle est mise à la disposition des autorités fédérales et fédérées.

En matière de Droit administratif général, notons le décret 69.DF.201 du 2 juin (J.O.R.F.C. du 15 juin, p. 1028) qui, faisant application de la loi 67.LF.21 du 12 juin 1967, étend l'application du système métrique à six unités de mesure de base à l'ensemble de la République fédérale.

Le Droit public économique est bien entendu marqué par la loi de Finances pour l'exercice 1969–1970. La loi 69.LF.7 du 14 juin (J.O.R.F.C. supplémentaire du 1er juillet, p. 5) établit le niveau des produits et revenus applicables ainsi que les charges publiques à 32.667.398.000 CFA. Le décret 69.DF.316 du 14 août (J.O.R.F.C. du 15 août, p. 1336) institue un blocage des prix. Cette mesure a pour objet de permettre un réajustement général des frais généraux et des marges bénéficiaires admissibles. Les taux révisés sont inscrits en annexe du décret 69.DF.408 du 2 octobre (J.O.R.F.C. du 15 octobre, p. 1931) qui lève le blocage des prix.

Enfin les décrets 69.DF.101 du 27 mars (J.O.R.F.C. du 1er avril, p. 483) et 69.DF.412 et 413 du 3 octobre (J.O.R.F.C. du 15 octobre, p. 1935) prorogent l'état d'urgence dans les régions où il est en vigueur depuis 1961.

DROIT SOCIAL

Prévoyance sociale

Il n'y a pas de mesures nouvelles en matière de prévoyance sociale.

Droit du Travail

En 1969, deux textes importants interviennent dans le domaine du Droit du Travail.

Le décret 69.DF.15 du 17 janvier (J.O.R.F.C. du 1er février, p. 140) établit une commission nationale paritaire des conventions collectives et des salaires. Cette commission est composée de représentants des centrales syndicales d'employeurs et de travailleurs les plus représentatives nommés pour cinq ans. Ses attributions sont essentiellement consultatives puisqu'elle a pour mission de soumettre des suggestions au gouvernement dans le domaine de la législation et de l'extension des conventions du travail et d'émettre des recommandations aux employeurs concernant l'application des conventions collectives. Elle peut aussi prendre des décisions exécutoires concernant les classifications professionnelles, les taux de salaire minimum par catégories d'emplois.

La décret 69.DF.287 du 30 juillet (J.O.R.F.C. du 1er août, p. 1395) établit les règles concernant les contrats d'apprentissage. Ces règles reprennent l'essentiel des dispositions existant en droit français.

DROIT PRIVÉ

Droit civil

Nous nous trouvons en présence d'un seul texte à portée générale, la loi 69.LF.3 du 14 juin (J.O.R.F.C. supplémentaire du 1er juillet, p. 8) qui réglemente l'usage des noms, prénoms et pseudonymes. Les règles générales sont analogues à celles existantes en Droit français. On peut cependant noter que le souci de faciliter une meilleure intégration d'une société aussi composite que la société camerounaise a fait autoriser le changement de nom pour "... toute personne en instance de naturalisation dont le nom patronymique présente une consonnance spécifiquement étrangère de nature à gêner son intégration dans la communauté nationale" ou si "... la consonnance du nom est de nature à gêner l'assimilation dans une communauté religieuse dont le demandeur partage la foi". Cette loi est complétée par le décret 69.DF.419 du 20 octobre (J.O.R.F.C. du 1er novembre, p. 1978) qui précise les règles de procédure à suivre concernant le changement de nom.

Droit commercial

Aucun texte important n'est à signaler.

Procédure civile

Aucun texte important n'est à signaler.

Droit international privé

Aucun texte important n'est à signaler.

DROIT PÉNAL ET PROCÉDURE PÉNALE

Droit pénal

Aucun texte important n'est à signaler.

Procédure pénale

Dans le domaine de la justice pénale, on peut noter le décret 69.DF.50 du 13 février (J.O.R.F.C. du 15 février, p. 224) qu supprime le tribunal militaire temporaire de Douala créé en 1960 et transfère ses compétences au tribunal militaire permanent de Yaoundé et au tribunal militaire provisoire de Bafoussam.

CHAPTER 25

REPUBLIQUE CENTRAFRICAINE

P. Y. Laporte

Comme les années précédentes, on peut difficilement parler d'activité législative au sens propre du terme en R.C.A. puisque le pays ne comporte pas de Parlement et que le Général Bokassa gouverne par ordonnances.

Les trois remaniements ministériels de l'année n'ont pas affecté la stabilité des institutions et les textes pris par le gouvernement concernent principalement des problèmes de portée restreinte. Toutefois, certains textes concernant la création ou la réorganisation de Services publics et l'intervention économique de l'Etat ont une portée évidemment beaucoup plus grande.

DROIT PUBLIC

Droit constitutionnel

Aucun texte n'a été pris en ce domaine en 1969.

Droit administratif

Sans remettre en cause les grandes lignes de l'ordonnance n° 58.09 du 30 décembre 1958 portant création d'un Code Générale des Impôts, l'ordonnance n° 69.01 du 25 janvier 1969 en modifie cependant 73 articles, notamment ceux portant sur le barême des impôts, sur les pénalités éventuelles encourues par les contribuables ainsi que sur les obligations des tiers et les privilèges du Trésor.

L'ordonnance n° 69.04 du 13 janvier 1969 modifie la loi n° 63.367 du 1er février 1963 portant statut de la magistrature, en matière de poursuites disciplinaires contre les magistrats.

L'ordonnance n° 69.50 du 1er août 1969 confie le Service public des Postes et Télécommunications à un Office des Postes et Télécommunications, établissement public à caractère industriel et commercial doté de la personnalité civile et de l'autonomie financière. L'Office centrafricain des Postes et Télécommunications exerce un monopole postal, télégraphique et téléphonique, et se trouve placé sous la tutelle du ministre des Postes et Télécommunications.

Mais l'année va également être marquée par les mesures prises par le gouvernement en matière économique. C'est d'abord l'ordonnance n° 69.16 du 22 avril 1969 créant une Société Nationale d'Economie Mixte Centrafricaine de Diamant Industriel, et l'ordonnance n° 69.20 du 25 avril 1969 modifiant le Code minier et réprimant les fraudes sur l'or et les pierres précieuses. C'est ensuite l'ordonnance n° 69.47 du 2 septembre 1969 modifiant la loi n° 62. 355 relative au Code des Investissements, et le décret n° 69.322 du 22 octobre 1969 portant rétablissement de l'activité de l'Office National du Diamant. C'est enfin l'ordonnance n° 69.48 du 19 septembre créant un Office National d'Affrêtements et l'ordonnance n° 69.68 du 18 novembre 1969 abrogeant la Convention de Gestion par l'ATEC de la flotte marchande centrafricaine et créant une Agence centrafricaine des communications fluviales.

DROIT SOCIAL

Prévoyance sociale

L'ordonnance n° 69.40 du 4.7.1969 stipule que le comité de gestion de l'Office centrafricain de Sécurité sociale, prévu par la loi n° 60.04 du 6 mai 1964 instituant l'O.C.S.S., fait place à un Conseil Supérieur de la Sécurité Sociale institué auprès du ministre de la Fonction publique, du Travail et des Affaires sociales. Ce Conseil est chargé de l'étude des questions concernant l'application de la législation sociale dont il est saisi par le ministre.

Droit du Travail

Aucun texte n'a été pris en ce domaine en 1969.

DROIT PRIVÉ

Droit civil

L'ordonnance n° 69.33 du 1er juillet 1969 réglemente l'état civil en R.C.A.

DROIT PÉNAL ET PROCÉDURE PÉNALE

L'ordonnance n° 69.06 du 14.2.1969 portant répression des infractions à la législation sur le contrôle des changes prévoit que les contraventions aux mesures visées dans l'ordonnance n° 68.063 du 27 novembre 1968, portant réglementation des relations financières avec l'étranger, sont passibles d'un mois et un jour à trois mois d'emprisonnement, de la confiscation du corps du délit, et d'une amende de la somme sur laquelle a porté l'infraction ou la tentative d'infraction. Les infractions ainsi réprimées sont constatées, poursuivies et jugées, et les peines infligées sont exécutées selon les grandes lignes des règles applicables aux infractions à la réglementation douaniére définies par l'acte n° 8.65 du 14.12.1965 du Conseil des Chefs d'Etat de l'Union Douanière et Economique de l'Afrique Centrale.

CHAPTER 26

GABON

J. L. Balans

L'année 1969 est une année assez calme pour la République gabonaise. Le Président BONGO poursuit l'affermissement de son autorité personnelle en inspirant de légères retouches constitutionnelles. Un certain souci se manifeste aussi dans le domaine de la protection sanitaire et sociale.

DROIT PUBLIC

Droit constitutionnel

Une première loi constitutionnelle (loi 1/69 du 1er juin — J.O.R.G. du 1er juillet, p. 525) apporte des retouches à l'article 20 en affirmant la prééminence du Président de la République ("chef des armées et des forces de sécurité, et des administrations civiles et militaires). Les attributions de la Cour suprême sont également précisées par l'article 23 nouveau (les projets de lois et d'ordonnances lui sont soumis avant les conseils des ministres) et 61/10 (la Cour suprême donne son avis sur toutes les questions juridiques ou administratives que le Gouvernement lui soumet).

Une deuxième loi constitutionnelle (loi 15/69 du 31 décembre — J.O.R.G. du 1er mars 1970, p. 141) allonge la liste des actes du Président de la République dispensés du contreseing ministériel (article 13), précise l'origine des ministres qui peuvent être membres de l'Assemblée nationale ou non, leurs indemnités ainsi que les incomptabilités fixées par la loi (article 21), élargit les cas d'irrecevabilité opposables aux projets de lois ou d'amendements émanant des parlementaires (article 46 1°), prévoit l'assistance ou la représentation des membres du gouvernement auprès de l'Assemblée nationale par des commissaires du gouvernement.

L'ordonnance 13/69 du 26 février (J.O.R.G. du 1er avril, p. 279) établit le texte du serment que devront prêter les membres du gouvernement, le Président de la Cour suprême et le Président du Conseil économique et social: "Je jure de remplir consciencieusement et scrupuleusement les devoirs de ma fonction vis-à-vis du peuple gabonais, de me comporter en toutes circonstances avec dignité, de conserver religieusement le secret des délibérations auxquelles j'aurai participé et d'agir toujours fidèlement et loyalement envers le chef de l'Etat".

L'ordonnance 63/69 du 30 septembre (J.O.R.G. du 1er novembre, p. 810) précise la composition du Conseil économique et social prévu par l'article 64 de la Constitution: sept représentants des salariés, sept représentants des entreprises industrielles et sept personnalités qualifiées nommées pour cinq ans. Leur fonction est incompatible avec une fonction gouvernementale ou un mandat de député. Le Conseil économique et social tient une session annuelle dont la durée ne peut excéder quinze jours.

Enfin, comme à l'accoutumée, le Président de la République est autorisé à légiférer par ordonnances pendant la période d'intersession parlementaire (loi 6/69 du 1er juin au J.O.R.G. du 15 juillet, p. 574).

Droit administratif

L'année 1969 n'apporte guère d'éléments nouveaux en matière d'organisation administrative. On peut relever cependant l'ordonnance 5/69 du 20 janvier (J.O.R.G. du 15 février, p. 138) qui crée un emploi de secrétaire dans chaque collectivité rurale.

Des mesures plus importantes sont prises dans le domaine des Finances publiques et du droit public économique.

L'ordonnance 68/69 du 6 octobre (J.O.R.G. du 15 novembre, p. 834) porte refonte et modification du code général et du code local des impôts directs. Plusieurs lois des années précédentes sont ainsi codifiées:

La loi 47/62 du 31 décembre 1962 qui prévoit un impôt minimum forfaitaire à la charge des sociétés devient les articles 277 à 286.

La loi 7/63 du 11 janvier 1963, et la loi 3/64 du 2 janvier 1964 qui instituent des taxes sur les terrains inexploités ou insuffisamment exploités deviennent les articles 287 à 291.

La loi 26/65 du 27 décembre 1965 instituant un versement forfaitaire à charge des employeurs devient les articles 312 à 318.

Le Code général et le Code local des impôts directs sont regroupés en un seul code intitulé "code général des impôts directs de la République gabonaise".

La loi 14/69 du 31 décembre (J.O.R.G. du 1er mars 1970, p. 142) suspend en matière fiscale l'application de la régle de prescription quadriennale.

Dans le domaine du Droit public économique, le gouvernement veut se donner les moyens de mieux contrôler l'intervention économique de l'Etat. Tout d'abord l'ordonnance 64/69 du 7 juillet (J.O.R.G. du 15 août, p. 651) crée la Caisse autonome d'amortissement de la République gabonaise. Cette caisse, érigée en établissement public a pour mission d'assurer le service de la dette de l'Etat, d'émettre les emprunts publics et d'en gérer les fonds, d'assurer l'émission et la gestion des obligations jusqu'alors assurés par la Banque gabonaise d'Investissement. Elle est contrôlée par un Conseil de gérance composé des ministres intéressés et des représentants des administrations financières intéressées. En plus des resources budgétaires affectées au service de la dette publique, elle peut bénéficier des subventions du Trésor et des prêts de toutes sortes consentis à la République du Gabon. Les textes antérieurs qui fixaient les attributions de la Banque gabonaise d'investissement (ordonnance 3/63 du 24 janvier 1963) et du fond gabonais d'investissement (ordonnance 36/67 du 1er août 1967) sont modifiés en conséquence.

Le décret 159/PR du 17 février (J.O.R.G. du 15 mars, p. 247) crée un comité national exécutif du Plan chargé de suivre la mise en oeuvre du Plan national de développement en cours et la préparation du Plan qui doit en prendre le Relais. Le Comité est composé des ministres des Finances et du Budget, des Affaires économiques, Commerce Industrie et Economie rurale, du Secrétaire d'Etat au Plan et au Développement, du Secrétaire général adjoint au Président de la République, du conseiller économique et financier du Président de la République.

Enfin, l'on peut mentionner l'ordonnance 16/69 du 26 février (J.O.R.G. du 1er avril, p. 280) relative à l'utilisation des moyens d'information, qui rappelle que l'information, la radiodiffusion et la télévision sont à la disposition du Président de la République qui seul a pouvoir de les requérir.

DROIT SOCIAL

Prévoyance sociale

L'essentiel du travail législatif de l'Assemblée nationale gabonaise lors de sa session de mai-juin aura été consacré à la protection sanitaire et sociale. La loi 21/69 du 1er juin (J.O.R.G. du 15 juillet, p. 573) modifie la Loi 13/63 du 8 mai 1963 en matière de protection contre les maladies endemo-épidémiques. Désormais l'ensemble des populations est soumis à des prospections périodiques et il est délivré une carte sanitaire provisoi re jusqu'à la mise en circulation de la carte nationale.

Les vaccinations contre la variole et la fièvre jaune sont obligatoires, ainsi que la vaccination contre la rougeole pour les moins de six ans et le vaccin BCG pour les moins de 20 ans et certaines catégories de personnel exposées plus particulièrement à la contagion, telles que le personnel médical ou le personnel des industries alimentaires.

La loi 3/69 du 1er juin (J.O.R.G. du 15 juillet, p. 574) a trait à la protection des filles mineures: "Toutes personne ayant séduit et mis enceinte une élève de moins de vingt ans devra l'épouser." Les plaignantes, ou leurs parents, disposent d'une action devant le tribunal de grande instance dans l'année qui suit l'accouchement. Toute manoeuvre dolosive en vue d'échapper à l'obligation créée par cette loi peut être punie de peines de prison allant de 1 à 5 ans de prison, ou d'amendes allant de 24.000 à 500.000 F CFA.

Le gouvernement a cependant jugé préférable de statuer par ordonnance sur le problème controversé de la contraception. L'ordonnance

64/69 du 4 octobre (J.O.R.G. du 15 novembre, p. 831) porte une interdiction de principe de l'utilisation des moyens contraceptifs. Certaines exceptions sont cependant prévues: en cas de nécessité absolue, mais seulement pour les personnes âgées de plus de 25 ans; par mesure préventive décidée par un conseil de trois médecins nommés par le ministre de la Santé. Dans tous les cas une ordonnance médicale est requise et la pharmacien doit tenir à jour un carnet à souches.

A côté de ces trois mesures importantes, il est possible de mentionner la loi 4/69 du 1er juin (J.O.R.G. du 15 juillet, p. 574) modifiant la loi 61/69 sur l'assurance vieillesse et permettant à un travailleur étranger qui quitte le Gabon avant l'admission à la retraite de demander le remboursement de ses cotisations, ainsi que la loi 5/69 du 1er juin (J.O.R.C. du 15 juillet, p. 574 également) plaçant au rang de créances privilégiées les cotisations de sécurité sociale dûes à la Caisse gabonaise de prévoyance sociale.

Droit du Travail

Aucun texte important n'est à signaler.

DROIT PRIVÉ

Droit civil

Une seule mesure est à inscrire au chapitre du Droit civil en 1969: la loi 11/69 du 31 décembre (J.O.R.G. du 1er mars 1970, p. 141) qui crée une obligation alimentaire au père d'un enfant né hors mariage. La mère dispose d'une action en justice pendant les trois ans qui suivent l'accouchement ou la fin du concubinage.

Droit commercial

Une seule loi intervient dans le domaine commercial: la loi 13/69 du 31 décembre (J.O.R.G. du 1er mars 1970, p. 141) modifiant la loi du 14 juillet 1867 sur les sociétés et ayant trait aux fonctions et statuts des commissaires aux apports.

Procédure civile

Aucun texte important n'est à signaler.

Droit International Privé

Aucun texte important n'est à signaler.

DROIT PÉNAL ET PROCÉDURE PÉNALE

Droit pénal

Une seule mesure est susceptible de se rattacher, en 1969, à la réglementation pénale.

Il s'agit de l'ordonnance 30.69 du 11 avril (J.O.R.G. du 20 décembre,

p. 899) relative à la police de la route fixant les sanctions correspondant aux infractions de conduite en état d'ivresse, délit de fuite, obstruction à la circulation et falsification au mauvais usage de plaques d'immatriculation, sont également précisées les règles relatives à la suspension ou au retrait du permis de conduire.

Les mesures sont intégrées au décret 837/RR/MTPT du même jour (J.O.R.G., p. 901) portant Code de la route.

Procédure pénale

Aucun texte important n'est à signaler.

CHAPTER 27

CONGO—(KINSHASA)

Johan M. Pauwels

INTRODUCTION

There is considerable delay in the publication of legislation in the Congo. The *Moniteur Congolais*,[1] the official gazette of the Democratic Republic of the Congo, ought to be issued twice a month, but several issues of 1968, 1969 and 1970 have not appeared up to now.[2]

Congolese lawyers use less frequently the official publications than the private (but state-backed) compilation of legal texts: P. Piron and J. Devos, *codes et Lois du Congo belge*, Brussels, F. Larcier, 8th edition, 3 volumes, 1959–1960. Supplements to these Codes, covering the last ten years, are now being published: P. Piron, with the collaboration of L. de Wilde and Ph. Piron, *Supplément aux Codes congolais — Législation de la République Démocratique du Congo, 1960–1970*, Brussels — Kinshasa, F. Larcier — Office National de la Recherche et du Développement, 1970; fasc. I, *Matières civiles, commerciales et pénales*; fasc. II, *Matières judiciaires et administratives*. The third volume and general tables will follow very soon. This important publication makes it possible to evaluate the scope of legislative movement in the Congo since independence. As some legal texts, which have not been published officially yet, figure in this publication, we shall indicate the place of examined texts in the Codes, preceded by the abbreviation: *Suppl. Codes*.

From the viewpoint of legislation, 1967 was an important year, because of the promulgation of the new Constitution. 1968 too was important: the Judicial Code was promulgated that year and a profound reform of local urban administration took place. Important enactments were few in 1969: the main innovations were the law on procedure in the Supreme Court of Justice and the (new) Investment Code.

CONSTITUTIONAL LAW
AND ADMINISTRATIVE LAW

Structure of the Government

The *ordonnance* n° 69/147 of 1st August 1969 (*Suppl. Codes*, II, p. 61) develops Articles 20, 24, 27, 29, 31 and 47 of the Constitution of 1967.

Article 1 reaffirms the basic principles of the presidential régime (the president exercises the executive power, he determines and leads the policy of the Republic; he has reglementary power with respect to matters which do not fall within the field of legislation) and declares that the President is assisted by the Government and the *Bureau* of the Presidency. The latter is governed by a separate statute (cf. *infra*).

Article 2 provides that the Government is composed of *ministres d'Etat*, ministers and vice-ministers. The latter assist a minister placed at the head of a department.

Article 3 enumerates the special tasks entrusted with the *ministre délégué à la présidence* (cf. also Article 6).

Articles 5 to 9 specify certain duties of the members of the Government.

The following articles deal with the mechanisms of the Government: the inter-ministerial committees (Articles 10 to 16) and the cabinets (*conseil des ministres*) (Articles 17 to 21).

The number, designation and competence of the ministries are determined by the *ordonnance* n° 69/146 of 1st August 1969 (*Suppl. Codes*, II, p. 65).

Bureau of the Presidence

This very important body is governed by the *ordonnance* n° 69/905 of 8th May 1969, replacing the *ordonnance* n° 67/452 of 7th October 1967 (*Moniteur*, 1969, n° 10, p. 396; modified by *ordonnance* n° 69/149 of 18th August 1969, *Moniteur*, 1969, n° 16, p. 661; *Suppl. Codes*, II, p. 63).

The *Bureau* is in charge of multiple tasks, defined by Article 2: the study of various questions, the keeping of the originals of legislative documents, the protocol and the secretariat of the Presidency, the preparation of presidential decisions about the administration of the portfolio of the state and about planning. The *Bureau* is directed by the *ministre délégué à la présidence* (Article 3) and by a *directeur* (Article 4); it is composed of a group of counsellors (Articles 4 and 8).

Security of the state

A *Conseil National de Sécurité* (National Security Council) was created by the *ordonnance-loi* n° 69/033 of 25th July 1969 (*Moniteur*, 1969, n° 15 p. 615; *Suppl. Codes*, II, p. 64). It is composed of the President, several ministers, the commander-in-chief of the army and the chief of the *Sûreté Nationale*. It deliberates upon all matters regarding the external and the internal security of the state.

Other legislative measures affect the *Sûreté Nationale*, which becomes the *Centre National de Documentation* (National Centre of Documentation) (*ordonnance-loi* n° 69/037 of 9th August 1969, *Moniteur*, 1969, n° 16, p. 660; *ordonnance-loi* n° 69/038 of 9th August 1969, *Moniteur*, 1969, n° 16, p. 660 *ordonnance* n° 69/159 of 9th August 1969, *Moniteur*, 1969, n° 16, p. 667).

Public finances

The finance Act (*loi financière*), resulting from the *ordonnance-loi* n° 69/061 of 5th December 1969 (*Suppl. Codes*, II, p. 103)[3] specifies the rules applying to the preparation, the presentation and the execution of the annual budget law, and to the annual Act approving Government accounts.

Tax law

Two statutes rerfoming tax law were promulgated: the *ordonnance-loi* n° 69/009 of 10th February 1969 on income tax (*contributions cédulaires sur les revenus*) (*Moniteur*, 1969, n° 13, p. 515); the *ordonnance-loi* n° 69/006 of 10th February 1969 on land rates (*contribution réelle* on land and vehicles) (*Moniteur*, 1969, n° 12, p. 475).

No fundamental reform of the tax system results from these enactments.

Rights and duties (*statut*) of civil servants

Two *ordonnances-lois*[4] permit the recruitment or the advancement of some categories of civil servants in derogation of the statutory rules (*décret-loi* of 20th March 1965, *Moniteur*, 1965, special issue of 30th April 1965, p. 287; *Suppl. Codes*, II, p. 231).

The *ordonnance-loi* n° 69/035 of 1st August 1969 (*Suppl. Codes*, II, p. 264) determines certain rules applicable to the academic, scientific and higher executive personnel of the universities. It applies not only to the personnel of the State University of Lubumbashi (*Université Officielle du Congo*), but also to the personnel of the two private universities, the Lovanium University of Kinshasa and the *Université Libre du Congo* in Kisangani.

Public contracts: works and supplies

The *ordonnance-loi* n° 69/054 of 5th December 1969 (*Suppl. Codes*, II, p. 110)[5] provides that public deals (i.e. deals concluded by the Republic, the cities, the local entities and, as a rule, by public corporations) have to be concluded by public allocation. Numerous exceptions to the rules of public allocation are admitted (limited allocation or transaction by mutual agreement.

Public corporations — Nature Conservation

The *ordonnance-loi* n° 69/041 of 22nd August 1969 (*Moniteur*, 1969, n° 18, p. 739) creates the *Institut de la conservation de la nature du Congo* (I.C.N.C.), which is entrusted with the task of protecting nature and encouraging scientific research and, to a certain extent, tourism in the "réserves naturelles intégrales" (i.e. among others, the *Parcs nationaux* of the Congo).

Local government

Ever since the colonial period, local administration has been based in the Congo on two types of local administrative entities: (*a*) the *circonscriptions indigènes* (i.e. *secteurs* and *chefferies*, more or less traditional communities, and *centres*, small agglomerations of recent origin); (*b*) *communes* grouped in cities (*villes*), in the urban areas.

The legislation on *villes* and *communes* was profoundly modified in 1968 (*ordonnances-lois* of 20th February 1968). The *décret* of 10th May 1957 on the *circonscriptions indigènes* (*Bulletin Officiel*, 1957, p. 1254; Piron and Devos, *Codes et Lois*, 8th ed., Brussels, 1960, II, p. 210) was repealed and replaced by the *ordonnance-loi* n° 69/012 of 12th March 1969 (*Moniteur*, 1969, n° 7, p. 257; *Suppl. Codes*, II, p. 85).[6]

It is stressed that the reform of local rural administration performed by this Act is not a very profound one. In addition to purely formal changes (the main one being that the former *circonscriptions indigènes* are called *collectivités locales* from now on), two major innovations were introduced. The first measure, the abolition of the *collège permanent*, which formerly was a body of assistants to the local chief, strengthens the power of the chiefs of the *collectivités*. The second measure, that chiefs will in future be appointed by the Interior Minister (*ministre de l'Intérieur*), no longer by a subordinate local executive, strengthens the power of the Government. Both modifications illustrate the trend towards centralisation which is very distinct in the Congo at present.[7]

JUDICIAL AND LEGAL SYSTEM[8]

The Constitution of 1967 created the Supreme Court of Justice (*Cour Suprême de Justice*), which combines the functions of the *Cour de cassation* and of the *Conseil d'Etat*, of Continental European countries.

The organisation and jurisdiction of the Supreme Court were fixed by the *Code de l'organisation et de la compétence judiciaires* (*ordonnance-loi* of 10th July 1968, *Moniteur*, 1968, n° 14, p. 1340; *Suppl. Codes*, II, p. 1). Minor modifications of this Code result from the *ordonnance-loi* n° 69/010 of 11th February 1969 (*Moniteur*, 1969. n° 5, p. 154; *Suppl. Codes*, *loco citato*).

As to the procedure in the Supreme Court, (cf. *infra*).

TORT

State liability

The *ordonnance-loi* n° 69/044 of 1st October 1969 on damage caused by disturbances (*Moniteur*, 1969, n° 19, p. 787; *Suppl. Codes*. I, p. 102), abolishes the liability of the state for damage caused either by rioters or rebels, or by military or police force acting against the former. Reparation of damage caused by the armed forces will be obtained, however, if evidence is given that the tort was committed outside the operations against the rioters or rebels and that the armed force committed a fault (*faute*).

Article 2 of the *ordonnance-loi* specifies that judicial decisions which had condemned the state to such damages before this Act became effective, will not be executed.

Up to now, the liability of the state and other public authorities was based on Article 258 of the Congolese Civil Code, Book III, Obligations (the equivalent of Article 1382 of the Napoleonic Code) and on the *ordonnance-loi* n° 11/215 of 21st May 1960, which is now repealed.

COMMERCIAL LAW

Investment Code

The *ordonnance-loi* n° 69/032 of 26th June 1969[9] repeals and replaces the first Congolese Investment Code (*décret-loi* of 30th August 1965), which had to be adapted to the situation resulting from the economic and monetary reform of 1967.

Two régimes are provided for: the so-called general régime, allowed by way of assent of the Government, and the conventional régime for especially important investments. Peculiar advantages are offered in case of reinvestment of benefits, and to non-resident investors. Special regulations will be issued for small investments (i.e. less than 50.000 Zaïres or 100.000 U.S. $).

A *commission des investissements* is created. Disputes will be settled by arbitration.

EVIDENCE AND PROCEDURE

The *ordonnance-loi* n° 69/2 of 8th January 1969 (*Moniteur*, 1969, n° 2, p. 58; *Suppl. Codes*, II, p. 23) regulates the procedure in the Supreme Court of Justice.[10]

The Act is influenced by Belgian and French legislation on procedure in the *Cour de cassation* and the *Conseil d'Etat*; but quite original is the attempt to unify as far as possible judicial and administrative procedures.

---

1. Services du Moniteur Congolais, Palais de Justice, Kinshasa-Kalina.
2. At the moment of drafting this contribution (December 1970), the only issues at my disposal were n°s 1 to 20 of 1969, none of 1970.
3. Cf. also *ordonnance-loi* n° 69/008 of 10th February 1969, on the financial engagements of the state (*Moniteur*, 1969, n° 6, p. 217; *Suppl. Codes*, II, p. 105).
4. *Ordonnance-loi* n° 69/028 of 16th June 1969, *Moniteur*, 1969, n° 13, p. 540; *Suppl. Codes*, II, p. 249; *ordonnance-loi* n° 69/043 of 25th September 1969, *Suppl. Codes*, II, p. 250.
5. See also *ordonnance* n° 69/279 of 5th December 1969, executory provisions (*Suppl. codes*, II, p. 111).

6. See also *ordonnance* n° 69/157 of 9th August 1969, executory provisions (*Moniteur*, 1969, n° 18, p. 744; *Suppl. Codes*, II, p. 92).
7. On Congolese administrative law, see de Burlet, Jacques, *Précis de droit administratif congolais*, I, Brussels , Larcier, 1969.
8. See Rubbens, Antoine, *Le droit judiciaire congolais*, I, *Le pouvoir, l'organisation et la compétence judiciaires*, Brussels, Larcier and Kinshasa, Université Lovanium, 1970.
9. This *ordonnance-loi* was not yet published either in the *Moniteur* or in the Supplement to the Codes Piron. We consulted a private edition made available by the Centre d'Etude et de Documentation pour les Investissements Outre-Mer (C.E.D.I.O.M., 34, rue de Stassart, Brussels), *Le Code congolais des investissements*, 1970, mimeographed. The *Centre* published also Congolese legislation on labour law and on tax law.
10. The Supreme Court was installed on 21st November 1968, and gave its first decision on 9th July 1969. The first decisions of the court were published in the *Revue Congolaise de Droit*, I(1970), n° 1 (Kinshasa, Office National de la Recherche et du Développement) and in the *Revue Juridique du Congo*, XLVI (1970), n° 1 (Lubumbashi, Société d'Etudes Juridiques du Katanga).

CHAPTER 28

BURUNDI

Louis De Clerck

DROIT CONSTITUTIONNEL

La constitution du Burundi a été suspendue par arrêté royal du 8 juillet 1966. Le 28 novembre de la même année la République fut proclamée. Le décret-loi du 19 décembre 1966 décide que le pouvoir législatif s'exerce provisoirement par voie de décrets-loi pris par le Président de la République sur rapport des Ministres intéressés, et après avis consultatif de la *Commission de législation*. Cette commission de législation fut créée par décret-loi du même jour.

Par décret-loi du 24 avril 1969 la commission de législation est supprimée. Un décret présidentiel du même jour crée la *Commission technique chargée des problèmes de la législation*. Cette commission est chargée d'élaborer des textes législatifs et réglementaires dans les matières qui lui sont soumises par le Président de la République. Le Président de la République peut également, s'il l'estime opportun, demander l'avis de la commission sur les projets de textes législatifs et réglementaires qui lui ont été communiqués par un Ministre. La commission peut adresser au Président de la République toutes suggestions relatives à des problèmes de législation. La commission est présidée par le Ministre de la justice. Les membres sont nommés et révequés par le Président de la République; leur nombre n'est pas déterminé. Par décret présidentiel du 22 mai 1969 les membres de la commission ont été désignés. Ce sont trois ministres, quatre hauts magistrats et le Président de la Banque de la République.

DROIT INTERNATIONAL

Le Président de la République a approuvé et ratifié plusieurs accords internationaux, notamment:

l'accord commercial avec la République de Zambie.
les actes de l'Union postale universelle.
le statut des réfugiés (protocole de 1967).
la convention relative au commerce de transit des pays sans litteral adoptée par la conférence des Nations Unies le 8 juillet 1965.

la convention du 17 février 1967 pour le règlement des différends relatifs aux investissements entre Etats et ressortissants d'autres Etats.
la convention d'association entre la Communauté économique européenne et les Etats africains et malgache associés (convention de Yaoundé du 29 juillet 1969).

DROIT ADMINISTRATIF

Afin d'améliorer le fonctionnement de l'administration publique, le décret présidentiel du 14 juillet 1969 crée le *Comité national de réforme et modernisation du secteur public.* Il a pour tâche de collecter les rapports des différents départements et d'élaborer un plan de réforme et de modernisation du secteur public en vue de son adaptation au développement économique et social du pays. Le Comité est assisté d'un "suppor-administratif" qui est le *Service central d'organisation et de gestion.*

Le décret-loi du 6 août 1969 fixe *les principes généraux de la Fonction publique,* et un décret présidentiel du même jour porte *statut des fonctionnaires de la République.* Ces textes remplacent respectivement la loi du 9 mars 1965 et l'ordonnance législative du 8 mars 1961, ainsi que les textes portant statut du personnel des écoles officielles et des agents du Ministères des affaires étrangères.

Dans ses premiers articles le décret-loi du 6 août 1969 définit la qualité de fonctionnaire. Il prévoit trois catégories de fonctionnaires: la catégorie de direction, la catégorie de collaboration et la catégorie d'exécution. Le législateur détermine ensuite les principes qui régissent le recrutement et l'avancement en grade. Les Articles II et 12 définissent les devoirs et incompatibilités qui découlent de la qualité de fonctionnaire. Il est prévu notamment que le fonctionnaire ni son épouse ne peuvent avoir une occupation quelconque qui serait de nature à nuire à l'accomplissement des devoirs du fonctionnaire ou ne se concilierait pas avec sa fonction. Est toujours considéré incompatible avec une fonction publique tout mandat ou service, même non rétribué, dans les affaires privées à but lucratif, sauf si ce mandat est exercé au nom de l'administration. La fonction politique est incompatible avec la fonction publique: l'article 13 dispose que le fonctionnaire chargé d'un mandat politique est placé en suspension d'activité pour la durée du mandat.

Les Articles 14 et 15 fixent les principes généraux en matière de traîtement. Le traîtement est indentique pour tous les fonctionnaires revêtus du même grade. Les fonctionnaires bénéficient d'augmentations annuelles de traîtement.

Pour être promu (Article 16) le fonctionnaire doit avoir un minimum d'ancienneté et avoir les connaissances et aptitudes nécessaires. Le passage à une catégorie supérieure est subordonné à la réussite d'une épreuve et ne peut se faire qu'au cas ou une fonction est vacante.

Un signalement annuel est destiné à établir le mérite et les aptitudes du fonctionnaire (Article 19). L'article 20 édicte les principes en matière de sanctions disciplinaires. Aucune sanction ne peut être appliquée que si elle est prévue par le statut. Le fonctionnaire doit toujours étre averti des griefs formulés contre lui et doit pouvoir présenter sa défense.

L'article 21 prévoit comment prend fin la carrière du fonctionnaire, et l'article 22 établit le droit à la pension en cas ou il est mis fin à la carrière pour limite d'âge ou inaptitude physique. En cas de décès du fonctionnaire la veuve et les orphelins ont droit à une rente.

Le décret présidentiel du 6 août 1969 constitue le statut des fonctionnaires, rédigé en application des principes posés ci-dessus.

Entr'autres conditions nécessaires pour être nommé fonctionnaire, il faut posséder les diplômes ou certificats pris en considération pour l'accès au grade auquel le recrutement doit s'effectuer (Article 3). Des étrangers peuvent être engagés dans la fonction publiaue en cas d'absence ou de pénurie candidats Barundi (Article 5).

Le chapitre II (Article 6 à 10) traite du recrutement. Pour être recruté au grade inférieur de la catégorie d'exécution il faut avoir un diplôme d'études primaires. Pour être recruté au grade inférieur de la catégorie de collaboration il faut avoir un diplôme de fin d'études secondaires (six années) ou un certificat ou diplôme assimilé. Pour accéder au grade inférieur de la catégorie de direction il faut un diplôme universitaire de licence, ou d'études assimilées.

Les fonctionnaires de la catégorie de direction sont nommés par le Président de la République, les autres par le Ministre ayant la fonction publique dans ses attributions. Les nominations ne peuvent avoir lieu que dans les limites prévues par le cadre organique et par la loi budgétaire annuelle.

Les fonctionnaires ne peuvent être nommés à titre définitif qu'après un stage de un ou deux ans à l'issue duquel un rapport de stage propose soit leur admission à titre définitif, soit leur licenciement.

La chapitre VI (Article 21 à 25) traite successivement des congés (vingt jours ouvrables par an), de la suspension d'activité, de la disponibilité et du détachement.

Au chapitre VII (Articles 26 à 34) il est question de la rémunération. Les traîtements vont de 20.000 fr. burundi (230 dollars) par an pour le grade le plus bas (auxiliaire) à 195.000 fr. burundi (2.241 dollars) par un pour le grade de directeur général. Outre le traîtement, la rémunération comprend les indemnités familiales pour l'épouse (si celle-ci n'exerce pas d'activité lucrative), et pour les enfants, ainsi que l'indemnité de logement. D'autres frais de service, indemnités compensatoires et indemnités pour services particuliers sont prévues.

Les fonctionnaires bénéficient des soins médicaux et pharmaceutiques dans les hopitaux du gouvernement. Une retenue forfaitaire pour soins de santé est effectuée mensuellement sur leurs traîtements.

Le chapitre VIII traîte des modalités du signalement, et le chapitre IX de l'avancement. Pour être promu il faut, sauf exception, trois ans d'ancienneté dans le grade, avoir obtenu la mention "très bon" les deux dernières années, et la mention "apte" lors du dernier signalement.

Le régime disciplinaire fait l'objet du chapitre X (Articles 43 et 44) Il y a cinq peines disciplinaires: le blâme, la retenue du traîtement pendant cinq jours minimum et quinze jours maximum, la suspension de fonction pour une durée d'un mois (avec retenue de la moitié du traîtement) et la révocation. Le fonctionnaire contre lequel une action disciplinaire est introduite a un droit de recours.

L'article 49 énumère limitativement les cas et conditions dans lesquels il peut être mis fin à la carrière des fonctionnaires.

La limite d'âge est de 55 ans. Elle peut être portée au maximum â 60 ans (Article 52). Il peut être mis fin à la carrière avant l'âge limite de 55 ans quand le fonctionnaire a atteint 30 ans de services (Article 53).

Il peut être mis fin à la carrière pour inaptitude physique constatée par une commission médicale (Article 55) et pour inaptitude professionnelle constatée par la chambre de recours (Article 56).

Les Articles 60 à 74 constituent des dispositions particulières aux fonctionnaires des cadres du Ministère des affaires étrangères. Les fonctionnaires recrutés dans le cadre de ce Ministère ne sont admis au stage qu'après la réussite d'un concours (Article 64). Les fonctionnaires des autres Ministères, même nommés à titre définitif, qui sont trasférés dans les cadres du Ministère des affaires étrangères, sont soumis au stage dans ce Ministère, mais l'admission à ce stage n'est pas nécessairement subordonnée à la réussite d'une épreuve (Article 65).

Les promotions, au Ministère des affaires étrangères, sont toujours subordonnées à la réussite d'une épreuve (Article 72).

Les Articles 77 à 84 sont des dispositions qui adaptent le statut à la situation particulière des fonctionnaires des cadres de l'enseignement.

Des dispositions transitoires (Articles 85 et 86) prévoient la régularisation des situations acquises par les fonctionnaires déjà en service.

POLICE ET SURETE

Le décret-loi du 22 mai 1969 sur le droit de résidence permet au Ministre de l'intérieur, par ordonnance motivée, de contraindre toute personne qui, par sa présence ou sa conduite, compromet ou menace de compromettre gravement l'ordre public, de s'éloigner de certains lieux ou d'une certains région du pays, ou d'habiter dans un lieu déterminé du Burundi. La mesure de résidence ne peut dépassar deux ans mais peut être renouvelée.

La personne contre qui une mesure de résidence est prise peut interjeter appel de l'ordonnance auprès d'une commission présidée par le Ministre de la justice. En outre tous les trois mois la personne contrainte à résidence peut demander au Ministre de l'Intérieur le réexamen de sa situation. Le Ministre doit statuer sur cette demande de révision dans les trente jours, est sa décision est également susceptible d'appel. Des sanctions pénales sont prévues pour ceux qui ne respectent pas les mesures de résidence. Ce décret-loi complète et modifie la législation sur le droit de résidence qui existait antérieurement.

ACTIVITÉS ECONOMIQUES

Le décret-loi du 4 juin 1969 approuve le plan quiquennal (1968–1972) de développement économique et social du Burundi. Le Ministère du plan est chargé de la supervision et de la coordination de ce plan; il est assisté à cet effet d'une *Commission nationale du plan*, créée par décret présidentiel du 4 juin 1969. La Commission est consultative. Elle est composée des ministres du plan, des affaires étrangères, des finances, de l'économie, de l'agriculture, de l'intérieur, ainsi que des Présidents de la Banque de la République et de la Banque Nationale de Développement économique.

PUBLICATIONS JURIDIQUES

La *revue administrative et juridique du Burundi*, qui parait quatre fois par an à Bujumbura, a continué à publier des articles de doctrine sur le droit du Burundi et de la jurisprudence des juridictions nationales. Parmi les articles de doctrine juridique: ceux de J. de Boe sur le contrat de travail à l'essai, et sur la protection de la maternité dans la législation du travail du Burundi. Egalement un article du professeur Verbrugghe sur la tutelle en droit coutumier rundi. *La Revue Juridique et Politique — Indépendance et Coopération* (Octobre — Décembre 1969 pp. 535 à 542) a publié une étude de M. L. Nzeyimana, intitulée "L'organisation judiciaire du Burundi en matière civile et la réforme du 26 juillet 1962".

CHAPTER 29

RWANDA

J. Vanderlinden

Si on excepte un texte intéressant le droit social et portant mesures d'exécution du Code du Travail en ce qui concerne les formes et modalités d'établissement et de visa du contrat de travail à durée déterminée (ou nécessitant le déplacement du travailleur hors de sa résidence habituelle) et la durée du préavis (J.O.R.R., 1969, n° 5, pp. 21–4), les seuls textes méritant d'être remarqués dans la législation rwandaise de l'année 1969 ressortissent tous au droit public, qu'il soit constitutionnel ou administratif. A cet égard, il importe d'ailleurs de noter que l'année fut une année d'élections législatives et présidentielles dont le seul effet fut de confirmer la position du Président G. Kayibanda et de son parti (le parmehutu) au pouvoir par une écrasante majorité de l'électorat.

Aussi, n'est-il guère étonnant qu'une partie importante de la législation soit consacrée aux modalités techniques des élections (J.O.R.R., 1969, n° 11–15 et 16, pp. 117–23, 196–206 et 225–54). Si les deux derniers de ces textes sont des arrêtés ministériels au caractère purement technique, le premier, la loi du 19 mai 1969, présente davantage d'intérêt puisqu'elle redéfinit certains principes en matière électorale tels que les définissait la loi du 5 juillet 1967. C'est ainsi notamment que:

il faut désormais savoir lire et écrire pour être éligibles aux Conseils communaux (Article 26);
le nombre des cadidats présentés sur les listes des partis politiques ne peut excéder le double des mandats à pourvoir (Articles 33 et 110);
le vote se fait désormais à domicile, tandis que le Ministre de l'Intérieur reçoit pouvoir de prendre les mesures propres à garantir le secret et la liberté de vote (Article 42 ancien, 63 nouveau);
pour être bourgmestre, il faut avoir été élu Conseiller communal, tandis que l'on peut désormais justifier d'une formation équivalente à celle obtenue après quatre années d'études primaires (Article 94);
le bourgmestre n'est plus élu directement par les électeurs, mais bien nommé par le Président de la République au sein et sur la proposition des conseillers élus (Article 21);
les candidats à l'Assemblée nationale peuvent avoir une formation équivalente à celle obtenue après six années d'études primaires (Article 103);

les listes de candidats des partis à l'élection à la Présidence ne peuvent comprendre qu'un nom (Article 153).

Toutes les autres modifications introduites par la loi sont d'ordre technique.

Sur le plan administratif, mais aussi économique, il faut signaler deux textes législatifs, l'un créant les Régies agricoles, des Eaux & Forêts et d'Elevage et l'autre réglementant la pratique de l'aviation civile au Rwanda. La première ordonnance-loi datée du 19 mai 1969 (J.O.R.R., n° 11, pp. 123–5) confère au Président de la République de créer et d'organiser en régie des exploitations, établissements et services agricoles à caractère commercial ou industriel. Il s'agit d'administrations personnalisées jouissant d'une certaine autonomie administrative et financière sous la tutelle du Ministre de l'Agriculture et de l'Elavage et les modalités essentielles de leur fonctionnement sont fixées par l'ordonnance-loi. Quant à l'ordonnance-loi du 30 mai 1969 (J.O.R.R., n° 12, pp. 133–40), elle pose les principes d'organisation de l'aviation civile dans la République en accord avec la Convention de l'aviation civile internationale dont elle est signataire. Il s'agit essentiellement de la définition de la souveraineté nationale sur l'espace aérien du pays, du droit de survol, des autorités en matière aéronautique, de l'immatriculation des aéronefs, des aérodromes, des servitudes aéronautiques, des enqêtes, des autorisations de transport et de travail aérien, etc.

Enfin, l'année 1969 a vu promulguer diverses dispositions relatives à l'armée et à la police. C'est ainsi que deux arrêtés du 23 avril 1969 (J.O.R.R., n° 10, pp. 73–107) portent respectivement statut des officiers et adjudants de la Garde nationale, c'est-à-dire de l'armée rwandaise, et des officiers de la Police nationale; une annexe à ce dernier texte définit en outre l'organisation et les fonctions de la Police nationale. Quant aux arrêtés ministériels des 9 et 14 juillet 1969 (J.O.R.R., 1969, n° 14, pp. 169 à 192), ils concernent la discipline des mêmes corps.

PART III
Other African Countries

CHAPTER 30

LIBERIA

Steven L. Werner

During 1969 several important portions of the Liberian Code of Laws Revised, supplanting the Liberian Code of Laws of 1956, became law and are summarised under appropriate headings *infra*. Also important in the development of Liberian law are three volumes published during 1969 under the sponsorship of the Liberian Codification Project: (1) *Reports and Opinions of the Attorney-General of the Republic of Liberia, 15th December 1922–31st July 1930, Louis A. Grimes, Attorney-General* (Ithaca, N.Y.: Cornell University Press, 1969); (2) *Opinions of the Attorney General of the Republic of Liberia, 10th September 1964 – 13th August 1968, James A. A. Pierre, Attorney-General* (Ithaca, N.Y.: Cornell University Press, 1969); and (3) *Liberian Law Reports, Cumulative Index and Table of Cases, Volumes 1–16* (Ithaca, N.Y.: Cornell University Press, 1969).

The first of the two volumes of opinions of the Attorney-General (1922–30) is a reprint (with new index) of a volume originally published nearly 40 years ago and long out of print. The second volume of opinions of the Attorney-General (1964–9) contains a foreword in which Attorney-General, James A. A. Pierre, sets forth the view that "it is the duty of the Attorney-General to publish his opinions in the performance of the duties of his office". Presumably, therefore, publication of the Attorney-General's opinions may be expected to be continued on a regular basis, adding a valuable new dimension to the interpretation of Liberian law, particularly in the constitutional and administrative areas.

The newly published cumulative index and table of cases to Volumes 1–16 of the *Liberian Law Reports* amounts to a comprehensive synopsis of more than a century of Liberian case law — from the first cases in Volume 1 (January Term 1861) through Volume 16 (March through October Terms 1964). The series of *Liberian Law Reports* (which is to be supplemented by a new series of Chambers Opinions) will, of course, be continued to be published as the official reports of cases adjudged in the Supreme Court of Liberia. However, no new Liberian case law was published during 1969.

CONSTITUTIONAL, PUBLIC AND ADMINISTRATIVE LAW

Executive Law. Title 12 of the Revised Code became effective in 1969 supplanting Title 13 of the 1956 Code as the Executive Law of Liberia and incorporating considerable legislation enacted since 1956. The new law delineates the organisation of the Executive Branch of the Liberian Government with the aim of clearly defining the jurisdiction of each department, bureau and agency. Legal authority and responsibility for each department is expressly vested in the chief officer of that department. The head of each department or independent agency in the Executive Branch is now authorised (Rev. Code 10.4) "subject to the approval of the President, to prescribe regulations not inconsistent with law for the operation of the department or agency, the accomplishment of its lawful functions, the conduct of its officers and employees, and the distribution and performance of its business".

The powers of the President, some of which were previously defined only in temporary or emergency legislation or derived by implication from the Constitution of Liberia with analogical reference to the United States Constitution, are codified and explicitly stated in the new Executive Law. Section 3.3, headed "Power during internal emergency", spells out the extent of the President's powers "Whenever there occurs any insurrection, riot, rebellion, lawless violence, or natural disaster sufficient to create an internal emergency . . .". This section confers on the President a full panoply of powers to deal with any emergency situations — or, rather, recognises powers which the President was already in a position to exercise as Chief Executive and Commander-in-Chief of the armed forces. Some of these provisions are taken from the previous Emergency Powers Act, others have been added.

Chapter 4 of the new Executive Law provides for filling any vacancy in the office of President or Vice-President; for conduct of the office of President in the event of temporary Presidential disability; for conduct of that office when the President is absent from the country; and for death, refusal to serve, disqualification or disability of a President-elect. The new provisions for filling any vacancy in the offices of President or Vice-President (Rev. Code 12:4.1, 4.2) are the same as in Article III, Section 2 of the Liberian Constitution (in case of the removal of the President from office or his death or resignation, the Vice-President becomes President; when a vacancy occurs in the office of the Vice-President, the President must immediately call a special election to fill the vacancy) except that the constitutional provision also refers to disability of the President — a subject treated in full in Section 4.4 of the new law.

The 1956 Code provided that the Secretary of State should "discharge the duties of President" in case of removal, death, resignation or disability of both President and Vice-President (1956 Code 13:5). The new law provides that if such a vacancy occurs in both offices, "then the Speaker of the House of Representatives and the President *pro tempore* of the Senate, in this order, and who is not under a constitutional disability shall act as President and shall within 90 days call a special election to fill the vacancy in the office of the President" (Rev. Code 12:4.3).

Section 4.4 of the new Executive Law provides for the disability of a President by prescribing that: "Whenever it becomes apparent that the President is unable to discharge the powers and duties of his office, the Legislature shall by two-thirds vote declare that the President is unfit to hold office and shall instruct the Secretary of State to publish such declaration in a special edition of the Liberian Official Gazette whereupon the Vice-President shall immediately assume the powers and duties of the President." Section 4.5 provides that when the President is out of the country, "The Government of the Republic shall be conducted by the Cabinet under the direction of any member thereof or of any Under or Assistant Secretary of any of the departments of the Executive Branch of the Government who may be at the time acting in the capacity of Secretary, whom the President shall designate by letters patent, and the person so designated shall exercise such further and other authority as the President may direct". Section 4.6 provides that in case of the death, refusal to serve or disqualification of a President-elect, the President shall issue a proclamation for an election to fill the vacancy; and in the case "the President-elect suffers a disability which prevents him from being inaugurated as President, the President shall serve as President until the disability is removed and the President-elect takes the oath of office".

Chapter 20 of the new Executive Law (Rev. Code 12:20.1 *et seq.*) strengthens and clarifies provisions for archives and record-keeping. The responsibility of the Director of National Archives and Record Service for records management, somewhat vaguely indicated under the 1956 Code, is now defined. Methods for management of Government records — a subject heretofore unprovided for in Liberian Law — are detailed in Chapter 81 (Rev. Code 12:81.1 *et seq.*).

Chapter 21 of the new Executive Law (Rev. Code 12:21.1 *et seq.*) which deals with the organisation of the Department of the Treasury, follows closely the provisions of L. 1961–2, ch. XXXIV which effected the reorganisation of that Department. However, in accordance with subsequent developments, the new law divests the Secretary of the Treasury of authority to formulate the budget plan and to administer the central procurement and general supply services. The Bureau of the Budget has been placed in the office of the President and the supply services are to be taken care of by a new General Services Agency (Rev. Code 12:52.1 *et seq.*).

The 1956 Code failed to designate responsibility in a Government agency for construction (as distinguished from maintenance) of public buildings or works other than highways, streets, roads and bridges. (See 1956 Code [1958 Supp.] 13:400.) This omission is remedied in the Revised Code which authorises (Rev. Code 12:27.2(b)) the Secretary of Public Works "to be in charge of" such construction "either directly or by contract".

Chapter 54 of the new Executive Law authorises the President to "create in the Executive Branch of the Government an agency to be known as the Public Welfare Agency" (Rev. Code 12:54.1), responsible for all public welfare and relief to the poor and underprivileged (Rev. Code 12:54.2). This agency, when established, will take over, on a modern, centralised administrative basis, the functions formerly distributed among various local authorities under the old Public Welfare Law which constituted Title 33 of the 1956 Code.

The provisions of Chapter 80 (Management and Disposal of Government Property), Chapter 81 (Management of Government Records) and Chapter 82 (Administrative Procedure), comprising Part V of the new Executive Law are almost entirely new. Chapter 80 (Rev. Code 12:80.1 *et seq.*) is designed to end loose practices with regard to the management of Government property and contains a blueprint for the conduct of heads of agencies in regard to the handling and disposal of property under their control. Chapter 81 (Rev. Code 12:81.1 *et seq.*) places the Director of National Archives and Records Services in charge of a complete programme of records management. Chapter 82 (Rev. Code 12:82.1 *et seq.*) constitutes an administrative procedures law which will prescribe the fundamentals of procedure for determination and review of cases under the jurisdiction of administrative agencies where no other statutes are expressly applicable. These provisions are adapted, for the most part, from the Federal Administrative Procedure Act of the United States (5 U.S.C. Sections 1004–11) and the Model State Administrative Procedure Act of the American Law Institute (9C Un. L. Ann. 110).

Local Government Law. Title 21 of the Revised Code, became effective in 1969 supplanting the same-numbered title of the 1956 Code as the Local Government Law of Liberia and taking account of the conversion of provinces and hinterland districts into four new counties under President Tubman's National Unification Program. The four new counties (Loffa, Bong, Nimba and Grand Geddah) are divided into districts in conformity with the system in the older counties of Montserrado, Grand Bassa, Sinoe, Maryland and Grand Cape Mount. Although the National Unification Program envisions the ultimate homogenisation of Liberia's political, economic and juridical systems, the realities of the existing situation in which a large segment of local government must necessarily be conducted on the tribal level are recognised in Chapter 5 of the new law (Rev. Code 20:5.1 *et seq.*) which prescribes procedure for the conduct of tribal government through chiefs. A system of tribal courts is continued (Rev. Code 20:6.1 *et seq.*) under the general supervision of the Secretary of Internal Affairs. The former Aborigines Law which constituted Title 1 of the 1956 Code has been repealed.

Public Contracts Law. Title 31 of the Revised Code, became effective in 1969, supplanting the former Public Works Law (Title 34 of the 1956 Code). The new law governs procurement of contracts by all agencies of the Liberian Government whether within or without the country and codifies procedures for competitive bidding and awards. All purchases and contracts by Government agencies are now required "to be made on a competitive basis to the maximum practicable extent; that is competitive proposals ('bids' in the case of procurement by formal advertising, 'proposals' in the case of procurement by negotiation) shall be solicited from all such qualified sources as are deemed necessary by the contracting officer to assure such full and free competition as is consistent with the procurement of types of supplies and services necessary to meet the requirements of the agency concerned" (Rev. Code 31:1.3(1)). Procurement by "bids" is generally required on contracts involving payments of $5,000 or more (Rev. Code 31:1.3(2)).

The Government is given the right to recover the amount of "any fees or kickbacks by sub contractors on negotiated contracts" from the "sub contractor or the recipient thereof by setoff of moneys otherwise owing to the sub contractor, either directly by the Government, or by a prime contractor under any contract or by an action in an appropriate court of Liberia" (Rev. Code 31:1.7(3)). Detailed procedures are established for negotiation and evaluation of bids and for award of contracts on either the basis of negotiation or formal advertising (Rev. Code 31:1.8 *et. seq.*). Procedures are also laid down for posting of "performance bonds" (Rev. Code 31:41. *et seq.*); for inspection of supplies and services to determine whether they conform to contract requirements (Rev. Code 31:5.1 *et seq.*); and for advance, progress or partial payments under procurement contracts (Rev. Code 31:6.1 *et seq.*).

CRIMINAL LAW

The penalty for conviction of the offence of gambling (1956 Code 27:365) was increased by an Act approved 18th April 1969 from a fine of not more than $100.00 to "a fine of not more than $1,000.00 or imprisonment for one calendar year, nor less than $500.00 or imprisonment for six calendar months".

The Penal Law was also amended by addition of new Section 304-A and 304-B making a crime of "criminal trespass" chargeable against any person "who shall (*a*) enter upon, occupy and improve real property not having fee simple title thereto, or permission of the owner, or (*b*) dispose of real property by sale, mortgage or otherwise without having proper and valid ownership to the same, or (*c*) lease, rent, mortgage or otherwise convey real property to another without a deed or other instrument of conveyance establishing ownership thereof in himself". The penalty is one to three years' imprisonment. The rightful owner of the property (except where the owner is the Government) may collect damages for trespass.

EVIDENCE AND PROCEDURE

The new Civil Procedure Law which became effective in 1968 as the first title of the Revised Code was amended in 1969 by the addition of sub chapter F of Chapter 16, governing special proceedings concerning mentally disabled and incompetent persons. The new sub chapter is designed primarily to provide more humane procedures for hospitalisation, commitment and release of persons suffering from mental or emotional illness or deficiency and who require hospitalisation or commitment to custody for their own welfare or the protection of others. Jurisdiction over such persons (when not charged with crime) as well as over the property of adjudicated incompetents is vested in the country probate courts.

Emergency hospitalisation for not more than five days may be instituted on a showing of reasonable cause in a written application to the superintendent of a government or government-approved institution by any sheriff, police officer or health officer. In all other cases, the only method of instituting proceedings for hospitalisation or commitment to custody of mentally disabled persons is by petition for an order of the probate court. Provisions are made for a hearing in which the respondent may demand a jury trial in the circuit court. If a jury trial is not demanded, the probate court has jurisdiction to hear the matter without a jury. In any case, the probate court has the responsibility of determining and ordering either (*a*) that the petition be dismissed; or (*b*) that the respondent be hospitalised in such manner and under such conditions as the court finds necessary for his welfare or the protection of others; or (*c*) that the respondent be committed to the custody of a person or persons willing and able properly to care for him at a place other than a mental institution.

Any hospitalised person may be provisionally released by the superintendent of the institution where he has been a patient. This form of administrative release may be conditional and is subject to revocation without a court order. Judicial discharge of persons hospitalised or committed to custody may be procured but procedures similar to those required for hospitalisation or commitment.

An adjudication as to hospitalisation or commitment to custody, or discharge from hospitalisation or from commitment to custody, is statutorily distinguished from an order or adjudication as to incompetency or restoration to legal capacity — separate proceedings being authorised for each type of order. However, in hearing and determining a petition respecting hospitalisation or commitment to custody, the court may in the same proceeding hear and determine a petition as to incompetency or restoration to legal capacity. In all proceedings under this sub chapter, provision is made for adequate legal representation of any alleged mentally disabled or incompetent person, the court being given the responsibility of appointing counsel where required.

TAXATION

A new Revenue and Finance Law which became effective in 1969 as Title 36 of the Revised Code supplants Title 35 of the 1956 Code. The new law standardises administrative procedures for the collection of all taxes and prescribes penalties and methods of appeal not merely with respect to income taxes but applicable to taxes of every other kind. The Secretary of the Treasury is authorised to collect unpaid taxes (except for real property taxes and certain Customs imposts) by summary warrant "under his official seal directed to the Judge of the Tax Court in Montserrado County, requesting that he command the clerk of his court to file the warrant and to record the entries thereon with respect to the unpaid tax in the judgment books kept by him in accordance with the Civil Procedure Law" (Rev. Code 36:2.15(1)). This form of collection by summary warrant cannot be utilised without prior notice of 30 days, during which the delinquent taxpayer may appeal to the tax court. Such an appeal will stay the entry of the judgment which, if issued under warrant without previous notice, would, in any case, be subject to review under the provisions of the Civil Procedure Law generally applicable to judgments by default.

If the Secretary of the Treasury "believes that the collection of any tax imposed by this title will be jeopardised by delay" (Rev. Code 36:2.16(1)), he is authorised to demand immediate payment "whether or not the time otherwise prescribed by law for making return or paying such tax has expired".

The somewhat complicated system of income tax review formerly provided in Section 180 *et seq.* of the 1956 Code is superseded by procedures for administrative review under rules to be promulgated by the Secretary of the Treasury (Rev. Code 36:3.1, 3.2) whose determinations may be appealed to the tax court (Rev. Code 36:3.3).

Tax rates have not been generally revised, but a newly provided method of computing taxes on the income of partnerships will increase the amount of those taxes in many instances. Liberian law has always tended to regard business partnerships or joint ventures as legal entities rather than mere associations of individuals. The new Revenue and Finance Law modifies the entity theory, at least for tax purposes (Rev. Code 36:11.21 *et seq.*) to the extent of treating any income in excess of $20,000 derived by an individual from a partnership as taxable first at the rate applicable to partnerships and secondly in the individual's tax return with credit for the amount of tax paid by the individual on the partnership return. A joint venture in which any member is a corporation is now taxable (Rev. Code 36:11.21) at the rates levied against corporations (Rev. Code 36:11.41) instead of (as under the 1956 Code) at the rates levied against partnerships. Tax rates on corporations (Rev. Code 36:11.41) remain unchanged.

Although the rates of real property taxes remain basically the same (Rev. Code 36:13.1), the standard of assessment is clarified by a new provision that "all buildings and other improvements on real property . . . shall be assessed according to the same standard of true value which shall be the actual cost of construction" (Rev. Code 36:13.2). The tax list is enlarged to include "buildings and other improvements . . . situated on public land owned by the Government of the Republic of Liberia which is leased to private persons" (Rev. Code 36:13.1(3)(f)). Enforcement of the realty lease tax (Rev. Code 36.19.1 *et seq.*) of 10 per cent on rent collected from leases of real property is strengthened by extension of the tax to "other consideration paid in lieu of rent or in consideration of rent" (Rev. Code 36:19.2(2)).

MISCELLANEOUS

Petroleum Act. In anticipation of the development of petroleum resources, the Legislature enacted and the President approved on April 18, 1969, "An Act to Regulate the Operation of the Petroleum Industry in Liberia". The regulation of petroleum production under the 1956 Code would presumably have been subject to general provisions controlling the development of mineral resources (1956 Code 25:140 *et seq.*). The new law declares that "property in petroleum existing in its natural condition in strata in the territory of Liberia, including its submarine area, is vested in the State". A system of licensing for production is established.

Vehicle and Traffic Law. Title 38 of the Revised Code was enacted and approved in 1969, superseding the former Vehicle Traffic Law (1956 Code Title 37). The new law prescribes, for the first time in Liberia, a complete set of provisions controlling issuance, suspension and revocation of automobile operators' licences. The issuance of licences will depend on examinations which "shall include a test of the applicant's eyesight, his ability to read and understand signs regulating, warning and directing traffic, and his knowledge of the Republic; and shall include an actual demonstration of his ability to exercise ordinary and reasonable control in the operation of a motor vehicle" (Rev. Code 38:2.26(1)). A system of compulsory liability insurance is authorised (Rev. Code 38:4.1 *et seq.*) subject to (*a*) the enactment and effectiveness of a new Insurance law as part of the Revised Code; and (*b*) a declaration by the Attorney-General "that automobile liability insurance is available to the Liberian public at a reasonable premium". Chapter 5 of the new law (Rev. Code 38:5.1 *et seq.*) provides civil liability for negligence in the operation or use of a motor vehicle when such negligence is attributable to the owner, who is made liable for the negligence of any person operating the vehicle with the owner's permission, express or implied.

Chapter 12 of the new Vehicle and Traffic Law (Rev. Code 38:12.1 *et seq.*) sets up a system of numbered summonses or "tickets" for traffic violations similar to that in use in many parts of the United States.

CHAPTER 31

SUDAN

Natale Olwak Akolawin

INTRODUCTION

The year 1969 witnessed an epoch which opened a new chapter in the history of the Sudan; the establishment of a Socialist system of government instead of the liberal Parliamentary system of government based on the Westminster model.

On 25th May 1969, a leftist group of young Army Officers led by Colonel Gaafar Mohamed El Nimeiry took over the reins of power in the country after carrying out a successful bloodless *coup d'état* and established a Socialist Revolution — the 25th of May Socialist Revolution. This radical change in the political, social and economic system of the Sudan brought with it inevitable changes in the law. This year is therefore particularly rich in legislation covering many aspects of the law.

CONSTITUTIONAL AND ADMINISTRATIVE LAW

Technical committee on the constitution

The forty-man constitutional committee set up by the Constituent Assembly on 22nd July 1968, continued with its task of revising the provisions of the Draft Constitution of the Sudan 1967. It appointed on 11th February 1969, a three-man Technical Committee on the Constitution which was charged with supplying the committee with background studies on various aspects of the Constitution and with its final drafting.[1]

The new constitutional order

The Coalition Government of the Democratic Unionist Party Umma (Imam) and the Southern Front as well as the Parliamentary system of government was overthrown on the 25th May 1969.

The leaders of the Revolution on their first day in power, issued three Orders, called Republican Orders, dealing with the new constitutional set-up, the defence of the Revolution and the appointment of the members of the Council of Ministers.[2]

The Republican Order No. I declared the Sudan a Democratic Republic in which the sovereignty rests in the people and is exercised on their behalf by the Council of the Revolution.[3] It suspended the Sudan Transitional Constitution as amended in 1964 and dissolved the following constitutional bodies:

(*a*) The Supreme Commission,
(*b*) The Council of Ministers,
(*c*) The Constituent Assembly,
(*d*) The Public Service Commission,
(*e*) The Election Commission.[4]

It also dissolved all political parties and prohibited the establishment of any political party, institution or organisation except with the permission of the Council of the Revolution.[5]

All laws in force before the suspension of the Constitution were to continue in force until repealed or amended by a competent authority except that every reference in such laws to the Supreme Commission was to be construed as referring to the Council of the Revolution.[6]

Except as provided in the Republican Order No. I all persons holding offices in the Republic of the Sudan were to continue in the exercise of their functions unless an order to dismiss or suspend them had been made by a competent authority.[7]

Instead of the dissolved legislative and executive bodies, the Republican Order No. I established two constitutional organs; the Council of the Revolution, which is the supreme constitutional authority in the country and the Council of Ministers.

The two organs exercise both legislative and executive powers. There is no clear demarcation of powers between them except that the Council of the Revolution can set aside any legislation or executive Act made by the Council of Ministers. The Council of the Revolution issues Decrees or Orders, which have the force of Law.

The Council of Ministers, is appointed by the Council of the Revolution and is collectively responsible to it for the discharge of its functions.[8]

The Council of the Revolution appoints, dismisses or accepts the resignation of Ministers on the recommendation of the Prime Minister, who is himself appointed by the Council of the Revolution.[9]

The Ministers before exercising their ministerial functions have to take an oath before the Council of the Revolution. They are individually responsible to the Prime Minister for the conduct of their ministries.[10]

The quorum of the Council of the Revolution or the Council of Ministers is half the number of its members. The decision in each council is made by absolute majority.[11]

The Republican Order No. II dealt with the defence of the newly established order. It gave the Council of the Revolution and the Council of Ministers wide administrative powers to protect the Revolution. Any measure taken by the Council of the Revolution for the protection of the Revolution is deemed an Act of State and is not contestable before any court of law.[12]

The Council of the Revolution has under this Order "full power without having recourse to any disciplinary measures, to dismiss any person holding an official post in any organ of the State if the Council is of the opinion that such person is not competent to perform his duties or there is suspicion as to his honesty, integrity or good reputation or if his continuance in such a post constitutes a hindrance to the aims of the Revolution".[13]

The Council of Ministers is also given the same power of dismissal as the Council of the Revolution in respect of any official in the Civil Service.[14] The Council of Ministers on the recommendation of the Minister of Interior and in the interest of public security may order any person to be detained in any place it deems fit, within the boundaries of the Sudan whether that place is the ordinary place of residence of such person or not. Any order made by the Council of Ministers for the detention of any person in any place under this Republican Order, is deemed to be made under Section 92D (4) of the Code of Criminal Procedure and is not questionable before any court.[15]

Any offensive act against the Revolution contravenes the provisions of the Republican Order No. II and is punishable under it.[16] Offensive acts against the Revolution are defined by Article 3 of this Order to include "every act the object of which is to arouse opposition to or contempt against the régime in the Sudan or to defame the same".

Defamation of the Council of Revolution or any of its members or of the Council of Ministers or any of its members or insult to any of them, is deemed to constitute opposition to the Revolution.

The following acts constitute acts against the Revolution if performed with intent to cause opposition to or contempt against the régime in the Sudan or to defame the same:

(*a*) word of mouth, sign or writing,
(*b*) organising processions or meetings,
(*c*) printing, publishing, distributing or possessing books, posters, leaflets or newspaper,
(*d*) broadcast by radio or television.[17]

According to Article 5 of this Order, whoever commits the following acts namely:

(*a*) does any act the object of which is to form political institutions, parties or organisations without the permission of the Council of the Revolution,
(*b*) Possesses, receives, assigns or disposes of any property whether immovable or movable for political purposes,
(*c*) disposes of the possession or ownership of any property whether immovable or movable deposited or registered in the name of any political party or political organisation or in the name of the President of such party or political organisation or in the name of any other person on behalf of such party or organisation,
(*d*) goes on strike or does any act with intent to cause damage or sabotage to the economic system of the state, or

(*e*) does any act which is likely to arouse hatred between classes of persons because of difference in religions, creed or social status intending hereby to damage or harm the social system in the Sudan.

contravenes the Republican Order No. II and is punishable under it.

Anyone who commits an offensive act against the Revolution or any act in contravention of the provisions of Article 5 of this Order, is punishable with death or with imprisonment for a term which may extend to ten years.[18]

All the offences committed under Republican Order No. II and all offences under Chapters IX, XI, XI*A* and XII of the Penal Code of the Sudan, namely; offences against the State, offences against the Military Forces, Offences relating to Police Forces, and offences against Public Tranquillity as well as any other offence under any law which the Council of the Revolution so decides are exclusively triable by court martial.[19]

The Council of the Revolution is empowered by the Order to make regulations providing for the constitution and procedure of courts-martial to try offences specified in the Orders but until such regulations are made, the Constitution and procedure of such courts should be in accordance with the provisions of the Armed Forces Act 1957 and the rules and regulations made thereunder.[20]

The Republican Order No. III dealt exclusively with the Constitution and appointment of the Council of Ministers of the Government of the Revolution.

The Council of the Revolution appointed a Council of Ministers consisting of twenty-three Ministers, twenty-one civilians and two military officers under the premiership of Sayed Babiker Awadalla, a former Chief Justice of the Sudan, with three vacant Ministries left to be filled later.

Though the Council of Ministers, was predominantly civilian, the Council of the Revolution consisted of ten members, nine military and one civilian, the Prime Minister, who is also the Deputy President of that Council.

The Council of the Revolution and the Council of Ministers acting in accordance with provisions of Articles 10 and 11 of the Republican Order No. II carried out purges in the Army, the Judiciary, the Civil Service and in other organs of the State.

The former members of the Supreme Commission and of Council of Ministers as well as any persons whose arrest was necessary in the interest of public security were placed under detention.

Political corruption

The Council of Ministers in July 1969, passed a special retroactive enactment, the Punishment of Corruption Act 1969[21] to punish corruption in politics, in the Administration and in the press. This Act is deemed to have come into force as from 10th June 1965 and its provisions apply to "any person who during the period from 10/6/1965 to 25/5/1969, was President of the Supreme Commission or a member thereof or a Minister, or a Speaker of the Constituent Assembly or a member thereof or a member of an Executive Council or of any Local Government Council established under the Local Government Ordinance 1951, or a public servant in the central or local government or in any corporation or organisation or committee established by law or a chairman or a member of any Board of Directors of such corporation or organisation or an owner of a newspaper, magazine or a press agency or an editor in such newspaper, magazine or press agency, and generally to any person who was entrusted with or holding an office of public nature or had a representative public capacity".[22]

The Act defines in detail the offences of corruption in politics, the administration and the press. The provisions of Chapters V, VI, VII and VIII of the Sudan Penal Code relating to joint acts, abetment, attempts to commit offences and criminal conspiracy apply in relation to offences committed under this Act.[23] The offences punishable under the Punishment of Corruption Act, which are at the same time punishable under the Penal Code or any other law are to be dealt with in accordance with the provisions of this Act.[24]

Persons accused of committing offences under this Act or the Prevention of Unlawful Enrichment Act 1966, are to be tried exclusively by courts martial in accordance with the procedure provided for in Article 8 of the Republican Order No. II.

The offences under these Acts are to be investigated and prosecuted by a Prosecution Council specially appointed by the Minister of Justice for that purpose, consisting of a chairman and members.[25]

The Prosecution Council has the power to conduct an investigation against any person where there is reasonable suspicion that such person had committed an offence under this Act or the Prevention of the Unlawful Enrichment Act 1966.[26] The Prosecution Council is given wide powers for discharging its functions of investigation or inquiry, including all the powers of a Magistrate of the First Class under the Code of Criminal Procedure relating to issue of summons to witnesses or accused persons, the issue of warrants of arrest of any accused person, the production of material evidence necessary for investigation, and issue of search warrants.[27]

The investigation under this Act is conducted under complete secrecy. Even the advocate for the accused is not allowed to be present during the course of investigation and neither the accused nor his advocate is permitted to have access to the records of investigation.[28]

Any person found guilty of an offence under this Act, is punishable with imprisonment for life or for any shorter period and is deprived of his political rights of life. The court may in addition to the above punishments impose forfeiture of private property, movable or immovable, fine or prohibition from holding any public office for such period as the court may deem suitable.[29]

The Minister of Justice acting in accordance with the provisions of Chapter 111 of the Act, set up Prosecution Councils which carried out investigations with persons suspected of having committed offences under this Act.

Elections

The Registration for the General Elections Act 1967 and all the Rules and Orders made under it and the Constituent Assembly Elections Act 1968 and all the Rules and Orders made under it were repealed by the Elections Enactments (Repeal) Act 1969.[30]

Amnesty Law

The Council of Ministers in execution of the declared Government Policy towards the Southern Provinces of the country announced on 9th June 1969 which recognised the right of the people of the Southern Sudan to regional autonomy and the right to develop their culture within a united Socialist Sudan, and which promised the continuation and extension of the Amnesty Law, amended the Indemnity Act 1966,[31] in order to grant amnesty or immunity against any action or other legal proceedings whether civil or criminal against any person in any court of law "for or on account of any act or matter done as from the 18th day of August 1955, and such act or matter was done in connection with mutiny or sedition in the Southern Provinces", provided that that person surrenders himself and the arms (if any) in his possession to the authorities concerned and accepts to stay in the Peace Villages or in any other suitable place not inconsistent with security requirements as determined by the said authorities.[32]

The Indemnity Amendment Act 1969, is deemed to have come into force as from 19th October 1969 and is to continue in force for one year.

Prohibited political activities

In addition to the provisions of the Republican Order No. II on hostile political activities against the new political order, the Council of Ministers enacted a law, the Prohibited Political Activities Act 1969[33] the primary purpose of which was to prohibit the activities of the sectarian youth organisations and any other para-military organisations. The Act defines "prohibited political activity" as "any act against the Revolution and includes any speech or writing or any other activity whether by signs or visible representation or otherwise".

"Prohibited Organisation" under the Act includes any sectarian Youth organisation, or any other organisation which is declared by the Council of the Revolution as a sectarian organisation engaged in political activities or any organisation which is engaged in prohibited political activity or which is likely to be exploited for carrying out such activities, whether such organisation is registered or not.

It also prohibits any "training or manoeuvre or parade of a military nature" except that which is carried out by the Armed forces of the Sudan or the Police or Prison forces or any training authorised by the Council of the Revolution.[34]

Any act which contravenes the provisions of the Prohibited Political Activities Act, are exclusively triable by courts martial.

Any person found guilty of an offence under the Act, is punishable with imprisonment for a period not exceeding three years or with a fine or with both, provided, that if the act constitutes also an offence under the Republican Order No. II and the court is satisfied that the circumstances of the offence are of such a grievous nature as to necessitate awarding punishment prescribed under the said Order, the court may award that punishment.

In all cases, whether an offence is committed under this Act or the Republican Order No. II, the court on conviction must order the closure of all premises used for committing the offences and confiscation of all the money and property found therein.[35] The Minister of Interior by Order, may close down any premises or club or any other place owned or possessed or used as a meeting place by any prohibited organisation.[36]

Ministry of Justice

The Attorney-General's Powers Distribution Act 1968 (1968 P.O. No. 19) was repealed by the Ministry of Justice (Re-organisation) Act 1969.[37] The Act provides for the creation of a post of and appointment of an Under-Secretary, Ministry of Justice, who shall be responsible to the Minister of Justice for the efficient functioning of the Ministry.

Any reference in any other law to the Attorney-General, Solicitor-General, the Advocate-General or Prosecutor-General is to be read and construed as a reference to the Under-Secretary, Ministry of Justice. The Act authorises the Under-Secretary by Order published in the Gazette, to delegate all or any of the powers vested in him by virtue of this Act to any of his deputies, namely, the Advocate-General, the Prosecutor-General or the Solicitor-General or any person officiating as such deputy.

The Minister of Justice may make regulations for carrying out the provisions of this Act and without prejudice to the generality of the powers of delegation by the Under-Secretary, such regulations may provide for all or any of the following matters, namely:

(*a*) organisation of the Ministry of Justice,
(*b*) formation of sections and distribution of work among them,
(*c*) responsibilities of officers in charge of sections so formed.

Martial law

The Armed Forces Act 1957, was amended twice during the year. The first Amendment[38] affected Section 54 of the Act, which empowers the Kaid El-Amm to confer upon any officer of the rank of Liwa, commanding a command or corps, the power to deal summarily with charges against any officer below the rank of Mukaddam and of other rank commanding a command or corps, the power to deal summarily with charges against any officer below the rank of Rayed, provided in both cases, the officers upon whom such powers are conferred may inflict only the punishments of reprimand, severe reprimand or forfeiture of technical allowances or special allowances.

The second Amendment[39] affected Sections 54, 102 and 104. In Section 54(1) "Chief of Staff" was substituted for Assistant Kaid".

The amended Section 54(2) empowers the Kaid-El-Amm to confer upon any Deputy Chief of Staff or any officer commanding a command or corps, the power to deal summarily with charges; in cases of any Deputy Chief of Staff, against any officer below the rank of Mukaddam and in case of any other officer, against any officer below the rank of Rayed.

Any Deputy Chief of Staff or officer upon whom such power is conferred may award any one or more of the following punishments, namely:

  (i) Reprimand or severe reprimand,
  (ii) Forfeiture of technical allowances or special allowance.

Under the amended Section 102, the confirming officer, when confirming the finding and sentence of a court martial, may:

  (*a*) mitigate the punishment awarded or commute such punishment for any less punishment to which the officer could have been sentenced by the court martial; or
  (*b*) remit the whole or any part of the punishment awarded, or
  (*c*) suspend the execution of the whole or any part of such punishment, or
  (*d*) refuse to confirm the finding and the sentence of the court martial and may for reasons to be recorded in writing order a fresh trial by another court martial.

The amended Section 104 deals with the powers of the confirming officer in cases of fresh trial ordered under Section 102. Where the finding of the court martial on any charge is one of not guilty, such finding is to be confirmed by the confirming officer. If the finding of the court martial on any charge is one of guilty, the confirming officer may exercise any of the powers conferred on him under Section 102.

The Civil Service

The Civil Service Pensions Act 1962, was amended[40] and this amendment was deemed to have come into effect on 25th May 1969.

This Amendment deals with two closely related topics, compensation payable in addition to pension or gratuity on termination of the service of a Government Official either by retirement or discharge and the notice he is entitled to receive.

It fixes the compensation payable under Section 30 of the Act, either on retirement or upon discharge as three months' salary of the retired or discharged official. Notice is fixed as three months' notice in case of discharge under Section 28.

The vacuum created by the dissolution of the Civil Service Commission by the Republican Order No. 1 with regard to the Civil Service and officials of other organs of state, was eliminated by two legislations on this matter, namely the Public Corporations (Transfer of Powers) Act 1969[41] and the Officials Discipline (Amendment) Act 1969.[42]

The Public Corporations Act 1969 transferred to the Council of Ministers or any person specified by the Council all powers conferred by any law on any authority relating to determination of terms and conditions of service of officials and other employees of any Public Corporation established by law and any reference in such law to such authority in relation to its powers of determining such terms and conditions of service are to be construed as a reference to the Council of Ministers or the person specified by the Council.

The Officials Discipline (Amendment) Act 1969, is deemed to have come into force on 25th May 1969. This Amendment makes the Officials Discipline Ordinance on and from its commencement "have the effect as it stood immediately before the commencement of the Sudan Transitional Constitution (amended 1964)".

Aliens

Section 25 of the Passports and Immigration Act 1960[43] was amended[44] in order to include in the residence permit granted to an alien not only his wife or wives living with him and his dependent children but "also his parents and sisters and brothers who reside with him and are dependent on him".

THE JUDICIARY AND LEGAL SYSTEM

The Judiciary

The Council of the Revolution acting in accordance with Section 10 of the Republican Order No. II, retired on 19th June 1969, all the members of the Civil Supreme Court, two High Court Judges and the Chief Registrar of the Civil Division as well as the Grand Kadi, the Mufti and two members of the Sharia Supreme Court.

The Supreme Civil Court Act 1967 and the Supreme Sharia Court Act 1967 were repealed by the Judiciary Act 1969.[45] The Judiciary Act 1969 restored the organisation of the Judiciary, more or less as it was prior to the 1966 Amendment[46] of the Sudan Transitional Constitution which created two separate and independent Divisions of the Judiciary, the Civil and the Sharia Divisions.

Under this Act, the administration of Justice in the Democratic Republic of the Sudan is performed by an independent body called "The Judiciary", which is directly responsible to the Council of the Revolution for the performance of its functions and is represented by the Minister of Justice in the Council of Ministers.[47]

It consists of two Divisions, the Civil Division, and the Sharia Division, of which the Chief Justice and the Grand Kadi are the respective presidents and judicial heads.[48]

The Civil Division comprises the Courts and exercises the jurisdiction specified in the Civil Justice Ordinance, the Penal Code, the Code of Criminal Procedure, the Chiefs' Courts Ordinance 1931 and the Native Courts Ordinance 1932 or any amendments of the same, and such other courts and jurisdiction as may from time to time be conferred upon it by law.[49]

The Sharia Division on the other hand comprises the Courts and exercises the jurisdiction specified in the Sharia Courts Act 1967 or any law amending or substituting it.[50]

Any conflict of jurisdiction arising between the Civil and Sharia Divisions, is settled by a Court of Jurisdiction consisting of the Chief Justice as the President, the Grand Kadi, two judges of the Civil High Court and one judge of the Sharia High Court.[51]

The Chief Justice, the Grand Kadi and members of the High Courts are appointed by the Council of Revolution on the advice of the Prime Minister, who consults the appropriate president with the consent of the Council of Ministers, in accordance with the provisions of the Judiciary Regulations.

The members of the Judiciary holding office immediately before the commencement of this Act are to continue in office and are deemed to have been appointed under this Act.

No appointment may be made which would effect an increase in the number of the members of the Judiciary unless such increase is authorised by law.[52]

The Chief Justice and the members of the Civil High Court on appointment take an oath or make a declaration before the Council of the Revolution in the form set out in the Schedule to the Act. Members of the subsidiary Civil Courts on appointment take the said oath or make the said declaration before the Chief Justice.[53]

The Chief Justice, the Grand Kadi, the Mufti and members of the High Courts may be retired by the Council of the Revolution and the members of the subsidiary courts may be retired by the appropriate president, at any time after they attain the age of 55 years in accordance with the provisions of the Judiciary Regulations, and must be so retired on attaining the age of 60 years.

However, notwithstanding the foregoing provision on compulsory retirement on attaining the age of 60 years, the Council of the Revolution, if it is of the opinion that the Chief Justice, the Grand Kadi, the Mufti or member of a High Court or subsidiary court is engaged in service of an exceptional nature which should in the interest of public service be completed by him before retirement, may on the advice of the Council of Ministers extend the age of compulsory retirement for a period of one year at a time with a maximum not exceeding five years for the completion of the said service.

Subject to the provisions of the Government Pension Ordinance 1919 or the Civil Service Pensions Act 1962 as the case may be, the Chief Justice, the Grand Kadi, the Mufti and members of the High Courts may at any time resign office by notice in writing addressed to the Council of the Revolution.[54]

Subject to the provisions of retirement on grounds of old age under Section 11(1) and (2), the Chief Justice, the Grand Kadi, the Mufti and the members of the High Courts shall not be removed from office except by the Council of the Revolution, in pursuance either of a formal resolution by the said Council or of a recommendation to that effect made by the appropriate president and a majority of the members of that High Court other than the member in question.[55]

Members of subsidiary courts may be removed from office by the appropriate president with the consent of the Council of Ministers and may also be removed under Section 32(*b*) of the Government Pension Ordinance 1919 or Section 30(*b*) of the Civil Service Pensions Act 1962 as the case may be.[56]

The Chief Justice and the Grand Kadi are authorised by the Act to delegate to any member or members or the Chief Registrar of their respective Divisions, such powers vested in them as the administrative or judicial heads of their Divisions except their powers under Section 8.[57]

The salaries and pension rights of the members of the Judiciary are to be laid down by law and in the meantime they shall be those in force immediately before the commencement of this Act, provided that neither salary nor pension rights of a member of the Judiciary shall be varied to his disadvantage after his appointment.

Subject to the provisions of this Act, the conditions of service of the members of the Judiciary including provisions as to recruitment, appointment, promotion, transfer, retirement, discipline and pension shall be laid down by the Chief Justice in case of the Civil Division or the Grand Kadi in case of the Sharia Division, and with the consent of the Council of the Revolution on the advice of the Council of Ministers and in the meantime all the existing regulations are to continue in force as if made under this Act.

The said regulations are to provide for the creation of two Judicial Service Boards of which the Chief Justice shall be President as far as the Civil Division is concerned and the Grand Kadi as far as the Sharia Division is concerned.

The Judicial Staff, which is defined by the Act as persons other than the members of the Judiciary who hold classified or unclassified posts in the Judiciary Budget or are paid against that Budget, are deemed to be officials or employees in the service of the Central Government, and their terms and conditions of service are to be in all respects the same as those applicable to such officials or employees, and the appellate powers under the Officials Discipline Ordinance and the powers of the Head of Department are to be vested in and exercisable by the Chief Justice in respect of the Civil Division and the Grand Kadi in respect of the Sharia Division.[58]

All petitions relating to appeals, revisions, reviews, confirmations or any other petition raised to the Supreme Civil Court or the Supreme Sharia Court immediately before the commencement of this Act and still pending, are to be heard and determined in accordance with the provisions of this Act.

Any amendment introduced by the repealed Supreme Civil Court Act in the Code of Criminal Procedure or the Civil Justice Ordinance or any other enactment is repealed by the Act and the said enactment is revised as if it had not been amended.[59]

The proviso to Section 14(1) of the Judiciary Act 1969, which states that "neither salary nor pension rights of a member of the Judiciary shall be varied to his disadvantage after his appointment" was deleted by the Judiciary (Amendment) Act 1969.[60]

Section 2(6) of the Number of Judges Ordinance 1950, was amended by the Number of Judges (Amendment) Act 1969[61] as follows:

> In sub section 6(ii) the words "Kadis of the Sharia High Court" are substituted for "Sharia Inspectors". For (iii) the following are substituted: "Province Kadis, twelve".

In sub section 6(iv) the words "Thirty-Four" are to be substituted the words "Twenty-Six".

The Law Commissions

The Provisional Order No. 20 of 1968, which provided for the constitution of commissions for the reform of law together with all orders made under it were repealed by the Law Commissions Provisional Order (Repeal) Act 1969.[62]

CRIMINAL LAW, PROCEDURE AND EVIDENCE

There has not been major amendments of the Sudan Penal Code and the Code of Criminal Procedure as would have been expected. This is so, because all possible or expected offences of a political nature against the new Régime were made punishable under either, the Republican Order No. II or the Prohibited Political Activities Act 1969.

CRIMINAL LAW

There was only one amendment of the Penal Code during the year, the Penal Code (Amendment) Act 1969.[63] The sections of the Code on Cheating were amended in order to prohibit expressly the giving of an uncovered cheque or the endorsement, delivery or acceptance of a cheque known to be uncovered as well as misrepresentation by the drawee that funds to cover an issued cheque are non-available.

After Section 362*A* the following new sections were added:

Giving an Uncovered Cheque

"362*B*. Whoever gives to any person a cheque which is dishonoured by the drawee because:
   (*a*) he has no account with the drawee at the time the cheque is presented for payment; or
   (*b*) he has insufficient funds with the drawee, or
   (*c*) he has countermanded the payment of the cheque; and without a reasonable cause; or
   (*d*) his credit, to his knowledge, is not available for payment; or
   (*e*) he intentionally draws the cheque in such an irregular manner that the drawee refuses to honour it

shall be punished with imprisonment for a term which may extend to seven years or with fine or with both."

Explanation

The term "drawee" includes a banker or any other person who carries wholly or in part the business of banking.

The Endorsement, Delivery or Acceptance of a Cheque Knowing That it is Uncovered . . . etc.

"362*C*. Whoever indorses, delivers or accepts a cheque knowing that there is no credit to meet it, that the credit is insufficient or that it has been countermanded,
shall be punished with imprisonment for a term which may extend to seven years or with fine or with both."

Misrepresentation by the Drawee that Funds are Non-available

"362*D*. Whoever being a servant or an agent of a drawee, intentionally misrepresents that the drawee has no credit, that the credit is insufficient to meet the cheque, or that the credit is not available for payment,
shall be punished with imprisonment for a term which may extend to two years or with fine or with both."

The Residual Control Act 1966, was amended twice during the year. The first Amendment[64] introduced enhanced punishments for the hoarding or the concealment of any article of commerce or selling of such article at a price above the maximum fixed by an order made under Section 4 of the Act.

Under the amended Act, hoarding or concealment of any article of commerce is made punishable with death or imprisonment for life and selling above the maximum price fixed under Section 4, is punishable with imprisonment for a term which shall not be less than one year nor more than seven years. The Court shall also impose a fine but in both cases an order for forfeiture of property and the forfeiture of the Trader's licence is made mandatory.[65]

Besides the enhanced punishment, this Amendment re-introduced the doctrine of minimum and maximum punishments. Normally, the Sudan Penal Code, while fixing the maximum punishment a court may impose on the offender, it leaves to the discretion of the court, the punishment to be imposed in a particular case. Under the Amendment, the court on convicting any person of selling any article of commerce above the maximum fixed price or for contravening the provisions of any regulations made under Section 6, is bound to impose a minimum sentence of one year's imprisonment, if it does not impose a longer term.[66]

The punishments imposed under this Act are in addition to and not in derogation of any other punishment, penalty or procedure to which such person may be liable or subject under any other law.[67]

The offences committed under this Act are triable by a special court constituted by the Chief Justice in consultation with the Council of the Revolution.[68]

In addition to any person on whom the Minister of Supply may confer the powers provided for in Section 4 of the Act, any policeman and any member of the Armed Forces is authorised to enter and search any place in which any article of commerce is reasonable suspected of being hoarded or concealed and to seize such article. They are also authorised to arrest anyone reasonably suspected of contravening the provisions of the Act, Orders and regulations made under it.[69]

The Second Amendment[70] which dealt only with Section 8(1), confined death sentence or life imprisonment to cases of hoarding or concealment of any article or articles of commerce the value or aggregate value of which exceeds five thousand Sudanese pounds. The other provisions of this section remain as they were under the First Amendment.

There were some important judicial decisions made during the year in the field of Criminal Law on Abetment, Consent, Joint act, Provocation, Right of Private Defence and Vicarious Criminal Responsibility.

Parties — Abetment and Joint Act

There was a very important decision by the Chief Justice on the complex subject of parties to an offence and their respective individual responsibility.

He had to decide in *Sudan Government* v. *El Sheikh Agab El Dor and others*,[71] a case involving robbery, tribal affray and homicide, whether persons who agreed to commit robbery jointly, and committed robbery, are also jointly liable for any murder or culpable homicide not amounting to murder, committed by one of them.

The Chief Justice had to tackle the complex but inter-related issues of abetment, joint act, intention and knowledge of the consequence of one's act.

He held that in order to convict several or more persons of joint act, it must be proved that they had a common intention to commit that act. Osman El Tayeb, C.J., states:

> "In my opinion the common intention cannot exist, unless there is the element of agreement between the offenders, that they thought of the crime, had it in their minds at one time and made their pre-arranged plan for it or for the mode through which to carry it out. This is to be proved by the conduct of the accused and the circumstances in which the offence was committed. The fact that the accused had a common intention to steal the camels does not prove the common intention to kill the owners of the camels who came up in pursuit.
>
> It is important to emphasise that common intention to commit a crime is different from knowledge of each one of accused that the commission of that crime would be a likely consequence of their acts. Intention and knowledge are two distinct elements of any offence . . . Where the law makes intention alone an ingredient of the offence, the proof of knowledge would not, by itself incriminate him. In the case of joint acts under the Sudan Penal Code, Section 78, where the existence and proof of a common intention is essential, the proof of knowledge that death would be the probable or a likely consequence of a common or same or similar acts of the accused, would not bring them within the ambit of that section."

He went on to point out that the appropriate law to be applied to this type of case is the law of Abetment, particularly Section 88 of the Sudan Penal Code, in that those who took part in the fight in either side, abetted the members of their group, by encouraging or aiding them to assault the members of the other group and are liable for the act abetted and the abettor would be liable for the consequence of the act abetted, but which the abettor had not intended, provided he had the knowledge that those consequences were likely to happen.

Consent

It was held in *S.G.* v. *Abdel Wahab Musa Margan*[72] that consent which was given by a girl about 16 years of age under fear of death to have sexual intercourse with the accused, was not free consent within the meaning of Section 39 of the Sudan Penal Code and that the accused was guilty of rape under Section 317 of that Code.

Provocation

It was held in *S.G.* v. *Suleiman Mahmoud Hassab El Rasoul*[73] that a slap on the face coupled with abusive words from a woman to a man constitutes a provocative act under the Sudan Penal Code, Section 249(1).
Osman El Tayeb, C.J., states in his judgment:

> "I think that the abusive words uttered by deceased coupled with the slap on the face, and moreover pushing accused until he fell down on the sarif, all taken together are too much and especially when emanating from a woman. In the society of the accused, the woman is looked upon as a person of lower grade than that of a man, and any insult by words or other acts to a man is considered as a condemnation of that man. The slap on the face is universally taken as a serious provocative act, and it was not alone; it was preceded by abusive words and succeeded by a push on a sarif; and all that done by a weak woman. Accused was subjected to great humiliation and contempt. In these circumstances, I am of opinion that there was grave and sudden provocation in this case."

The right of private defence

The Chief Justice in *S.G.* v. *El Sheikh Agab El Dor and Others*[74] dealt with a very important aspect of the right of private defence on which the Sudan Penal Code is silent and which is dealt with in Section 105 of the Indian Penal Code, namely the beginning and the continuation of the right of private defence.
He held that the right of private defence of property, which extends to causing of death under Section 62 of the Sudan Penal Code, continues up to the point of recovery of property stolen by the thieves and robbers.

> "Under the Sudan Penal Code, Section 62, the right of private defence of property extends to the causing of death. It does not exist only for the protection of the property by preventing the robbers or the thieves from taking it, but it continues up to the point of recovery of the property. This is the rule applicable to the hue and cry or the faza'a (as it is locally known). When robbers or thieves get in possession of stolen animals, and run away with them, the owners collect their people with their arms and pursue them, with intention of recovering their animals."

S.G. v. *Mohamed Yousif Mohamed*[75] gives an interesting novel application of Section 61(*a*) of the Sudan Penal Code, as to the meaning of *reasonable apprehension of death or grievous hurt*. It was held that for the right of private defence of body to extend to causing of death, it is essential that the accused must have believed in the existence of danger to his body which causes reasonable apprehension of death or grievous hurt. The accused in this case, since he believed that the knife would not penetrate his skin because of the amulet he wore on his body, could not have reasonable grounds of fear of death or grievous hurt and therefore could not benefit from the provision of Section 61(*a*).

S.M.A. Attig, J., states in his judgment:

"The question whether in the circumstances of a given case, the accused could have had reasonable grounds for apprehending death or grievous bodily injury is a question of fact to be decided upon the facts of each case. In this case, accused firmly stated in his confession that being amuletized, the knife did not penetrate his skin. Since the accused had this belief, then it cannot be said that he had reasonable grounds of fear of death or grievous hurt. It is immaterial that that belief was fabulous. It is essential that the accused must have believed in the existence of danger to his body and that he must have had reasonable cause for it. Since the accused had a belief in his amulet, a belief that the knife will not penetrate his skin, then there was no reasonable ground for fear of death or grievous hurt. Hence the accused's mind was not affected by the attack with the unsheathed knife, then there is no room for applying the test of the reasonable man who should be from the accused's society.

At any rate the test comes into play whenever the accused had entertained a bona fide apprehension of fear that death or grievous hurt would otherwise be the consequence if he fails to defend himself. The test is applied for ascertaining the reasonableness of the accused's apprehension of fear then and there.

Consequently, accused cannot avail himself of the plea of self defence."

S.G. v. *Hamouda Kodi*[76] dealt with the standard of proof required in order to establish a plea of the right of private defence. It was held that an accused person raising the plea of right of private defence under the Sudan Penal Code, Section 61, is not required to prove it in the same manner as the prosecutor is required to prove his case. It is enough, if the accused creates in the mind of the court a reasonable doubt as to the existence of such right.

S.M.A. Attig, J. states:

"The question whether in the circumstances of a given case the accused could have had reasonable grounds for apprehending grievous bodily injury is a question of fact to be decided upon the facts of each case. The test in such a case is not whether there was actual danger, but whether there was reasonable apprehension that such danger existed. This apprehension may be mistaken, but if bona fide it gives rise to a right of private defence . . .

An accused person raising the plea of self-defence is not to prove it in the same manner as the prosecution is required to prove its case. The standard of proof required is very low. It is enough if the accused creates in the mind of the court a reasonable doubt as to the existence of such right."

Vicarious criminal responsibility

The decision of Osman El Tayeb, C.J., in *Sudan Government* v. *Mohamed Abdo Rabo Mohamed*[77] is an important contribution to a very complex and controversial field of Criminal Law — Vicarious criminal responsibility.

This decision is made on revision of a conviction made under Rule 9 of the Prices and Charges Order, which was punishable under the Residual Control Act 1966, Section 8(1)(*c*). This offence for which the accused was tried was committed before the First Amendment of the above Act in July 1969. In this case, the accused the owner of a shop, who was not in charge of sales, but had an agent in the shop, was charged of selling a three-inch diesel pump, above the fixed price.

This case provides an excellent exposition of Sudanese and English precedents on the topic.

It was held, that the owner of a shop is presumably vicariously criminally responsible for the act of his servants in contravention of the Prices and Charges Order, Rule 9. Such presumption is rebuttable by pleading and establishing that the servant, at the time the offence was committed, was not acting within the course of his employment.

> "In this case where there is an absolute prohibition not to sell goods above the prescribed maximum prices, the seller to whom the prohibition is directed is the owner of the shop in which the goods are sold, and the owner of the goods that are being sold, in the sense that he was the person who brought or authorised them to be brought in the shop for sale for profit in the ordinary course of business. When the sale is being carried out by a servant or agent, it is being so done on behalf of the shop owner, and it is attributable to him, as if it was done by him personally. Here arises a legal presumption that the offences committed by the sale of goods at a price higher than the maximum prescribed, made by the servant, is the master's offence, and he would be criminally responsible for it. That is so even if the servant had been in charge of the full management of the shop; for fixing the prices and showing them on labels attached to the goods, and even if the shop owner had no knowledge of or intention to fixing prices higher than the maximum prices prescribed by law. This presumption is rebuttable by pleading and establishing that the servant at the time the offence was committed, was not acting within the course of his employment, and therefore the master would not be criminally responsible for the offence committed by his act. The butcher is criminally responsible for his servant's act, when the servant sold meat in excess of the maximum prices, and the baker is also criminally responsible for the act of his servants, when they sold bread in excess of the maximum prices, unless he had proved that the servants acted outside the course of their employment.
>
> In the present case the appellant prisoner is the owner of the shop, and owner of the goods, and the engine in question was imported by him. He is employing Mohamed Alawi to be in charge of the shop, he did not make the defence that Mohamed Alawi was acting outside the course of his employment. The prisoner is therefore the seller within the meaning of Rule 9, and if the price fixed and shown on the engine was above the maximum prices, then he would be committing the offence by demanding more than the maximum price for that engine."

There being a doubt as to whether the price for which the engine was offered for sale, was above the fixed maximum price the conviction of the accused was quashed with a direction that he should be set at liberty.

CRIMINAL PROCEDURE AND EVIDENCE

The Code of Criminal Procedure, was amended[78] by adding Section 134*A* which provides that:

> "No proceedings shall be instituted under Section 362*B*, 362*C*, or 362*D* of the Penal Code, except upon a complaint made by some person aggrieved by such offence."

Schedule 1 to the Code of Criminal Procedure was amended accordingly.

The Commissions of Inquiry Ordinance was amended twice during the year. The first Amendment[79] substituted "any Minister concerned" for "the Minister of Interior" under Section 3, 5, 6(2) and 7. The second Amendment[80] repealed Section 3 of the Ordinance and substituted it with the following:

> "3(1) The Prime Minister may, with the approval of the Council of Ministers, issue an order appointing one or more Commissions for the purpose of inquiring into any occurrence or matter in which an inquiry would in his opinion, be for the public welfare, and the Commission may inquire in any Ministry or any other body.
>
> (2) Any Minister concerned may, in the same manner and for the same reasons provided for in the preceding sub section, appoint a Commission for the purpose of inquiring into what falls within his jurisdiction."

In Section 5, the words "The Prime Minister or the Minister concerned" were substituted for "the Minister concerned".

In Sections 6(2) and 7, the words "The Prime Minister" was to be inserted before the words "the Minister concerned" wherever they occur.

The purpose of the second Amendment, was to empower the Prime Minister, or any Minister with the approval of the Council of Ministers, to appoint a Commission to inquire, in case of the Prime Minister, into any Ministry or any other body and in case of any Minister, in what falls within his jurisdiction.

There were five important judicial decisions on Criminal Procedure dealing with the use of Case Diary in Criminal Trial, Joint Trial, Plea of guilty to a charge of attempted murder under Section 259 of the Penal Code, Powers of Confirming Authority, particularly the procedure to be followed by the Trial Court, when a case is returned by the Confirming Authority for revision of Finding or Sentence and for retrial and Sentences in case of conviction of several offences at one trial.

Case Diary

It was held in the *Sudan Government* v. *Ramadan Adam Gazal & Others*[81] that the statements recorded in the Case Diary are not admissible as evidence against the accused but they may help the court or the appellate authority in trying to come to the truth of the matter and to form an opinion about the credibility of the witness, especially when the witness makes different statements.

The judgment of Osman El Tayeb, C.J., in this case deals exhaustively with the use of Case Diary, either in inquiry, or trial or by the appellate authority.

According to the express and plain words of Section 116 of the Code of Criminal Procedure statements recorded in the Case Diary are not evidence and are not admissible against any accused person in any inquiry or trial.

> "The Case Diary as the record of the Police Investigation, its main purpose, is the collection and piling up of all informations, statements and other material with respect to an offence suspected of being committed, and the detection or pointing out the persons involved in the commission of that offence. It is rather an administrative action to indicate or show whether there is a case for prosecution to be taken before a court of justice that will pronounce the final word about. And the judicial control or interference exercisable by Magistrates, as given to them by law, is necessary only to assist the investigator to carry out their duties; when they want, for the purposes of investigation, to make arrests, searches, etc.

> The statements in the Case Diary are not taken on oath, and they are not taken in a judicial proceedings and for that they are not admissible in evidence in any inquiry or trial. The confession of an accused person, or the dying declaration of a deceased person as to the cause of his death when recorded in the Case Diary are not exceptions to that rule, because they have to be proved by the person who recorded them.

> The statements of persons recorded in the Case Diary may be referred to by a court holding an inquiry or trial to test the credibility of the person who made that statement, when he is giving evidence on oath before the court, and to refresh the memory of the witness to make full disclosure of all the facts within his knowledge. The provisions of the Code of Criminal Procedure, Section 116 are sufficiently clear on these points.

> When, as confirming and appellate authority we refer to the Case Diary, as we usually do, we do it with that same view expressed in the above-mentioned section. We seek that necessary aid in trying to come to the truth of the matter, to form an opinion about the credibility of the witness especially when it is found that he made different statements here and there. We try to place ourselves in the position of the Trial Court and do what it ought to have done, but for lack of experience neglected to do."

Joint trial

It was held in *S.G.* v. *Eisa Isagha Ismail & others*[82] that omission to obtain the sanction of the Province Judge for joint trial in case of tribal fights according to Section 206(*h*) of the Code of Criminal Procedure, is not a mere formality or technical error within the meaning of Section 261 of the said Code. Any joint trial held under Section 206(*h*) without prior sanction of the Province Judge is illegal and therefore null and void.

Though joint trial in case of tribal affrays is stated clearly by para. 3 of the Criminal Court Circular No. 5 to be illegal, this case disposes with the effect of illegality or non-compliance with requirement of Section 206(*h*) on sanction. Non-compliance with this provision of the Code on joint trial, the purpose of which is to avoid embarrassment or prejudice to the accused by bringing evidence relating to them together, vitiates all the proceedings.

Plea

The decision in *S.G.* v. *Abdel Rahman Bakheit Gaidoom*[83] is a further elaboration to the Note to Section 150 of the Code of Criminal Procedure on Plea and the Criminal Court Circular No. 11 which instructs the magistrate that before convicting on a plea of guilty he must satisfy himself that the accused has clearly understood the meaning of the charge in all its details and essentials and also the effect of the plea. That on accepting a plea of guilty it may necessary to examine the record of any proceedings taken before the trial and to call witnesses whose evidence appears in such proceedings.

It was held in the above case that the court should not convict upon a plea of guilty for a charge under Section 259 of the Penal Code, because such a charge cannot be easily understood by the accused, as it involves legal implications, i.e. it may be shown that the accused is entitled to one of the exceptions laid down under Section 249 of the Penal Code. Therefore, in case of such a plea, the court should proceed to examine such legal implications before convicting the accused upon his plea of guilty. Though the court has the discretion to convict on his plea of guilty, this discretion has to be exercised judiciously.

Powers of confirming authority

The Chief Justice, in *Sudan Government* v. *Suleiman Mahmoud Hasab El Rasoul*[84] gave specific directions on the procedure to be followed by the Province Judge and the Magistrates when the proceedings of a case are sent back by the confirming authority in exercise of its powers under Section 256 of the Code of Criminal Procedure for revision of finding or for retrial.

In the case of sending back the proceedings for revision of the finding, the court is not allowed to hear additional evidence unless expressly authorised. The duty of the court is to sit, bring the accused before it, explain to him the opinion of the confirming authority, invite him to put forward any argument relating to that opinion, and then the court makes up its mind on the finding and the reasons thereof and bring the accused and explains to him the revised finding. This is to be made on the same record of the trial, filing at the end of it the Note on confirmation containing the order of the confirming authority, placing after it the record of anything that might have been said by the accused, then the rest of trial form starting by the page for the finding up to the sentence. The revised reasons for the finding must be limited and restricted to that part of them on which the return of the proceedings for revision was based and which was virtually reversed by the confirming authority.

Retrial or fresh trial can only be conducted when the confirming authority has refused to confirm the finding, and directs that there should be retrial or fresh trial by the same court or by another court, on the same charge or a new charge. Subject to that direction the court can hear fresh evidence or the evidence previously heard, and make a new finding, new reasons, and a new sentence.

Sentences in case of conviction of several offences at one trial

S.G. v. *Abdel Moneim Sharif Salih*,[85] is no doubt an important additional contribution[86] to knowledge on a difficult but interesting subject — sentence in cases where the accused is charged of and convicted of several offences at one trial.

The accused in this case was separately charged and convicted in one trial of careless driving under the Road Traffic Act, Section 22, and the Sudan Penal Code, Section 256, of causing death by rash or negligent act. The issue which came on revision to the Chief Justice, was whether the accused should be visited with one sentence for the two offences or with two sentences each one for one offence.

It was held on revision, that the offence of careless driving under the Road Traffic Act, Section 22, and the offence of causing death by rash or negligent act under the Penal Code, Section 256, are not offences of the same nature, even though emerging from one transaction. The accused therefore should be visited with two sentences one for each of the two offences.

> "These are not offences of the same nature. It may be argued that the careless driving was the same negligent act that was an important ingredient for the second offence. This may be true in such a case but it is not generally true that every rash or negligent act within the meaning of the Sudan Penal Code, Section 256, must be due to careless driving. The distinction is clear between these two offences, in one parcel, and the two of theft and housebreaking to commit theft in the other.... Offences under two different enactments having totally different objects, cannot in my opinion be considered as being of the same nature. The Sudan Penal Code and the Road Traffic Act are two different enactments with different underlying principles and objects, and therefore offences created by them are not of the same nature even though emerging from one transaction."

Evidence

There is no legislation on criminal evidence.

There are also no cases dealing directly with evidence in criminal trial except for *Sudan Government* v. *Mohamed Yousif Mohamed* and *Sudan Government* v. *Hamouda Kodi*,[87] which raised issues of proof as to the accused's belief in the existence of danger to his body which causes reasonable apprehension of death or grievous hurt and the standard proof required in order to establish a plea of the right of private defence under the Sudan Penal Code.

These two cases have been examined under the Right of Private Defence.

THE LAW OF CORPORATIONS AND COMMERCIAL LAW

Law of Public Corporations

State direction, control and management of some aspects of the national economy is not a new feature brought about by the May Socialist Revolution.

Public Corporations, state-owned but run by Boards on private commercial basis are well known in the commercial, industrial and agricultural life of the country. The typical example of this type of venture in the field of agriculture is the Gezira Scheme — run by the Gezira Board, a public corporation.

Because of the dominant role played by statutory corporations in the national economy, the Law of Corporations deserves a special recognition. Though it is a bridge between the worlds of private and public law, I shall treat it here as a special component of Commercial Law.

Under the Law of Corporations I include any law regulating any state-owned, partially-owned statutory corporation which operates in the fields of Agriculture, Banking, Industry, Trade and Transport.

The Constituent Assembly passed in April the Banking Regulations Act 1969[88] which virtually imposed complete Government control on all aspects of operations of foreign banks carrying on business in the Sudan. Government control over banking business is exercised by the Bank of Sudan and the Minister "for the time being responsible for matters relating to finance in the Sudan".[89]

The Act dealt *inter alia* with licensing of Banks, their Capital, Reserve Funds, Dividends, Balance Sheets, Prohibited Business, Minimum Liquid Assets, Inspection, Audit, Appointment of Auditors and Penalties for Contraventions of its Provisions.

No banking business shall be carried on in the Sudan except by a company, which must be in possession of a valid licence granted by the Bank of the Sudan with the approval of the Minister.[90]

Any company proposing to carry on banking business in the Sudan must before commencing any such business, apply to the Bank of Sudan for a licence under this Act in the prescribed form. The Bank of the Sudan, would grant the licence, if it is "satisfied on inquiry made in this behalf, having regard to the financial standing and history of the applicant, the character of the management, the adequacy of the capital structure and earning prospects, the structure of the proposed bank including the intended network of its branches, the convenience and the needs of the community to be served", that it is necessary in the public interest to do so. Every person who immediately before the commencement of this Act was carrying on banking business in the Sudan, is to be given a provisional licence by the Bank of Sudan, which will cease to be valid on the expiry of one year or such longer period as the Bank of the Sudan, may specify on the grant of licence.[91] The Bank of Sudan has the power to inspect the books, accounts and records of any person if it has reason to believe that such person is carrying on banking business in contravention of the provisions of the Act.[92]

The Bank of Sudan with the approval of the Minister is authorised to revoke any licence if the holder ceases to carry on banking business in the Sudan, or is declared bankrupt or is wound up or otherwise dissolved.

It may also with the approval of the Minister revoke any licence if in its opinion the bank is carrying on its business in a manner detrimental to the interests of the depositors of the bank or has insufficient assets to cover its liabilities to its depositors and creditors or is contravening the provisions of this Act or if the bank or any of its officers has been convicted of any offence under this Act.[93]

Under the Act every bank in the Sudan is required at all times to have a paid share capital, unimpaired by losses or any other cause, not less than Ls.1,000,000 or such higher amount as the Bank of Sudan may determine.

The Act also ensures Sudanese control over the shareholdings in any bank operating in the Sudan, by requiring that not less than 75 per cent of the share capital of any bank must at all times be owned or controlled by Sudanese nationals.[94]

The banks are prohibited to pay any dividends on shares until all capitalised expenditure, not represented by tangible assets has been completely written off. No bank is allowed to grant any person any advance or credit facility or give any financial guarantees or incur any other liabilities in respect of such person at any time exceeds 30 per cent of the sum of the paid-up capital and the published reserves of the bank nor grant any advance or credit facility against the security of its own shares.

It shall not grant or permit to be outstanding unsecured advances or unsecured credit facilities which in the aggregate exceed the sum of Ls. 2,000 to any one of its directors or to dependent members of their families, whether obtained by its directors of such members jointly or severally nor grant or permit to be outstanding in respect of any one of its officers (other than a director) or employee, unsecured advances of credit facilities which in aggregate exceed one year's emoluments of such officer or employee.[95]

The banks are prohibited under the Act *inter alia* from engaging whether on its own account or on a commission basis and whether alone or with others, in the wholesale or retail trade, including the import or export trade except in the course of the satisfaction of debts due to them.[96] The Act prohibits investment by any bank in any financial, commercial, agricultural, industrial or other undertaking, if its share-holdings in such an undertaking exceed in the aggregate 25 per cent of the sum of the paid-up capital and published reserves of that bank.[97]

The Act also imposes restriction on the rate of interest payable to or by the banks.[98]

Every bank is required under this Act to maintain a minimum holding of liquid assets which shall be equal to such percentage of its sight and time liabilities as the Bank of Sudan may from time to time prescribe. "Sight liabilities" are defined by the Act as "the total liabilities of any bank which must be met on demand" and "time liabilities" as "the total liabilities of a bank to be met otherwise than on demand, including the liabilities arising from savings accounts".[99]

The Bank of Sudan is given wide powers of inspection by the Act and may periodically or at its discretion cause an inspection to be made by one or more of its officers of any bank and its books and accounts in order to ensure compliance with the provisions of the Act.[100]

Every bank has to appoint annually an auditor approved by Bank of Sudan, whose duty shall be to make a report upon its annual balance sheet and accounts. The Bank of Sudan, may appoint such an auditor, if any bank fails within reasonable time to appoint an auditor or to fill up a vacancy of such auditor. The report of the auditor shall be read at the annual meeting of the shareholders of the Bank.[101]

The Bank of Sudan, is made under this Act, the Official Liquidator in any proceedings for the winding up of a bank in the Sudan. It can, if it considers in the interests of the depositors of a bank, by order prohibit the bank from carrying on banking business and impose a moratorium on any action against or continuance of any action, for a period which shall not exceed six months.[102]

In case any bank in the Sudan becomes unable to meet its obligations or suspends payment, its assets in the Sudan, according to the Act, must be used to meet all deposit liabilities of the bank in the Sudan and such deposit liabilities shall have priority over all other liabilities of the bank.[103]

No bank operating in the Sudan can be merged or consolidated with any other bank or banks without application to, and authorisation by the Bank of Sudan approved by the Minister. The Bank of Sudan with the approval of the Council of Ministers may in the public interest cause mergers between banks.[104] The Act provides penalties for contraventions of its provisions and vests the Bank of Sudan, with wide powers of supervision and control.

The Act also amended specifically Section 8(3*A*) of the Companies Ordinance as well as Sections 3, 46, 48 and 51 of the Bank of Sudan Act 1959.

Besides the amendments in the Banking Regulations Act 1969, there were two other amendments of the Bank of Sudan Act 1959 during the year. The first Amendment[104] fixed the reserves of the Bank of Sudan in addition to the special drawing rights and any foreign exchange proceeds from their use held on behalf of the Democratic Republic of the Sudan at no less than the equivalent of seven million Sudanese pounds.

The second Amendment[105] deleted the sentence occurring at the end of that Act.

The Agricultural Bank of the Sudan Act 1957 and the Sudanese Estate Bank Act 1966, were amended[106] in order to fix the authorised capital of each of these Banks at seven million pounds, 40 per cent of which shall be subscribed by the Government and 60 per cent by the

Bank of Sudan, provided that the contribution of the Government to the paid-up capital shall not exceed 40 per cent of the paid-up capital.

The Rural Water and Development Corporation Act 1967, was amended[107] in order to make the Minister of Co-operation and Rural Development responsible for the general supervision of the operations and activities of the Corporation.

The Industrial Planning Corporation Act 1968, was repealed by the Industrial Planning Corporation (Repeal) Act 1969.[108]

Commercial Law

Four important laws were passed during the year in the field of what can be called now traditional commercial law dealing with trade marks, registration of the importers, the monopoly of goods and grant of concessions to public companies.

The Monopoly of Goods Act 1968,[109] was repealed by the Monopoly of Goods Provisional Order (Repeal) Act.[110]

The Trade Marks Ordinance 1931 and the Regulations made under it were repealed and replaced by the Trade Marks Act 1969[111] and the Trade Marks Rules 1969.[112]

Under the Trade Marks Act 1969, trade marks may be registered with the Registrar of Trade Marks at the Offices of Commercial Registry, Ministry of Economics, Commerce and Supply, Khartoum, or at such places as may be appointed by the Minister by an order published in the Democratic Republic of the Sudan Gazette.

Registration is effective only for ten years but it can be renewed at the expiration of every ten years.

Section 12 of the Act, provides that, should the Democratic Republic of the Sudan, become a party to any international convention for mutual protection of trade marks, then any person who has duly filed a first application for registration of a trade mark in another state, party to such convention or his successor in title, shall, on his request, be deemed to have applied for registration in the Democratic Republic of the Sudan, on the day of his first application. However, the registered owner of the trade mark shall not be entitled to recover damages for the infringement prior to the date on which the mark is registered in the Democratic Republic of the Sudan.

Only persons of Sudanese nationality are eligible under this Act to act as Trade Marks Agent.

The Importers Registration Act 1969[113] provides for registration of all persons who carry on the business of import of commodities into the Democratic Republic of the Sudan for the purpose of sale.

No person shall carry on business as an importer of any commodity specified in the Schedule to this Act unless he is in possession of a valid certificate of registration issued under this Act.

The Minister of Economics, Commerce and Supply can reject the application for registration as an importer or approve it subject to such conditions as he deems fit. The decision of the Minister is final and is not questionable in any court of law.[114]

The Registrar of the Importers may with the approval of the Minister cancel the registration of any person, either temporarily or permanently if he is convicted under the Residual Control Act 1966 or the Regulations or Rules or Orders made or deemed to be made under it.[115]

The Public Companies (Grant of Concessions) Act 1969[116] introduced a new feature of public company, which is totally different from concession companies established under the Approved Enterprises Act 1956 which are intended to produce import substitute goods or commodities, but a hybrid between a co-operative society and ordinary public company.

A Public Concession Company is defined by the Act, as a public company that has been granted concessions under this Act and which by its articles of association gives the Minister of Economics, Commerce and Supply the exclusive power to fix from time to time the value of the share and the maximum number of shares held by each member. Such a public company is not by law allowed to distribute dividends out of profits unless 20 per cent of such profits are first allocated to the Development Fund and a further 10 per cent to the Reserve Fund of the company.

The Miscellaneous Amendments Act 1969[117] was passed in August in order to amend the Companies Ordinance, the Registration of Business Names Ordinance, the Trade Marks Act and the Traders' Licence and Taxation of Business Profits Ordinance 1929, so as to catch up with the re-organisation of the economic Ministries.

There were no judical decisions in the field of Law of Corporations and Commercial Law during the year worth noting except one very important decision dealing with excuses for delay in making a protest under Section 45 of the Bills of Exchange Ordinance 1916.

It was held in *Mustafa Amin* v. *Kristo Balandrious*[118] that the Bills of Exchange Ordinance, Section 48(1), is made of two parts. The first part deals with delay that is caused by circumstances beyond control of the holder; this is the excusable delay, that which occurs after the two business days following, the day of payment. The second part deals with delay that is caused by any other circumstances in spite of the fact that the holder has taken all reasonable diligence. In case of the second kind of delay, the section does not fix a certain period within which the protest has to be made. It was held that this is question of fact to be decided by the court.

CONTRACT AND TORT

There was no legislation in this field.

There were no judicial decisions on Contract during the year. There is, however, one case on Tort dealing with the liability of private carrier of goods.

It was held in *Sudan Safari & Company* v. *Baychand Premchand*[119] that a private carrier who carries goods on occasions or under special contract, is a bailee of the goods and is bound to take due and proper care of the goods entrusted to him.

It was further held that a private carrier for hire or reward is liable in tort for his own and for his servant's negligence which is committed in the course of employment.

The Court also adopted the definition of the defence of act of God, as laid down in *Greenock Corporation* v. *Caledonian Railway Co.*[120] as "an act of nature unaccompanied by the agency of man, which no human foresight could anticipate, and of which no reasonable man could be expected to guard against".

EVIDENCE AND CIVIL PROCEDURE

There was no legislation dealing directly with Evidence and Civil Procedure except Section 25 of the Civil Justice Ordinance 1929 which was amended by the Civil Justice (Amendment) Act 1969.[121]

Section 25 as amended empowers the Chief Justice to confer upon any District Judge of the First Grade all or any of the powers of Province Judge or upon any District Judge of the Second Grade all or any of the powers of a District Judge of the First Grade generally or for any particular purpose or purposes.

There was only one case, *Ibrahim Rizig* v. *Millad Fanous*[122] which dealt with some aspects of the law of Evidence. This decision affirms the decision of the Court of Appeal in *Hellenic Community* v. *Petit Bazaar*[123] and *Costis Trizis* v. *Idris El Kanzi*[124] that the appellate court has the power to re-examine the evidence given in the trial court so as to draw an inference from proved facts.

There were three decisions on Civil Procedure dealing with costs, inherent powers and attachment before judgment which are worth noting.

It was held in *Nicolas C. Mavikios* v. *S. A. Mikhielides*[125] that costs should be paid on the sum actually decreed and not on the sum claimed by the plaintiff.

> "The Civil Justice Ordinance, Section 100 ordains that the question of costs is within the discretion of the court to decide upon. Of course the discretion has to exercised judiciously. It seems to me that according to the Civil Justice Ordinance, Section 100(2), that the costs shall not follow the event is the exception rather than the rule. Hence the applicant should pay the fees on the sum actually decreed. It is obviously unfair to make him pay costs at the rate of the sum claimed rather than the sum actually decreed."

Gamal Mustafa Abu Samra v. *Abul Ela Engineering Co.*[126] dealt with the use of inherent powers of the court under Section 226 of the Civil Justice Ordinance. It was held that the inherent powers of the court cannot be exercised in order to extend the period of limitation on any grounds of equity and justice. The court cannot resort to its inherent powers in defiance of the express provisions of the Civil Justice Ordinance. It is only when there is no clear provision in the Ordinance that inherent jurisdiction can be invoked.

Salah Eddin Hassan, J., in a very important decision concurred in by other two members of the Court of Appeal laid down in *Mustafa Abdel Hamid Abul Izz* v. *Gabir Abdel Hamid Abu Izz*[127] fourteen guiding principles which must be considered by the court when deciding on application for attachment before judgment under Section 135 of the Civil Justice Ordinance. This decision laying down conditions for granting an order of attachment of property before judgment provides further contribution to knowledge of the subject as laid down in *Christos Symos* v. *Yousif Naoum Gange*[128] that the object of Section 135 of the Civil Justice Ordinance is to provide for furnishing of security in order to ensure the satisfaction of any decree that may be passed in the case. Furnishing of security is therefore the first process the court must have in mind. It is only when the defendant fails to furnish security that an order for attachment is to be made under Section 135 of the Civil Justice Ordinance.

The Court of Appeal laid down the following fourteen principles which the court must have in mind when deciding to grant or not to grant an order for attachment before judgment:

"1. That an order under the Civil Justice Ordinance, Section 135, can only be issued, if circumstances exist as are stated therein.

2. Whether such circumstances exist is a question of fact which must be proved to the satisfaction of the court.

3. That the court would not be justified in issuing an order for attachment before judgment, or for security, merely because it thinks that no harm would be done thereby or that the defendants would not be prejudiced.

4. That the affidavits in support of the contentions of the applicant, must not be vague, and must be properly verified. Where it is affirmed true to knowledge or information or belief, it must be stated as to which portion is true to knowledge, the source of information should be disclosed, and the grounds for belief should be stated.

5. That a mere allegation that the defendant was selling off his properties is not sufficient. Particulars must be stated.

6. There is no rule that transactions before suit cannot be taken into consideration, but the object of attachment before judgment must be to prevent future transfer or alienation.

7. Where only a small portion of the property belonging to the defendant is being disposed of, no inference can be drawn in the absence of other circumstances that the alienation is necessarily to defraud or delay the plaintiff's claim.

8. That the mere fact of transfer is not enough, since nobody can be prevented from dealing with his properties, simply because a suit has been filed; there must be additional circumstances to show that the transfer is with an intention to delay or defeat the plaintiff's claim. It is open to the court to look to the conduct of the parties immediately before suit, and to examine the surrounding circumstances, and to draw an inference as to whether the defendant is about to dispose of the

property, and if so, with what intention. The court is entitled to consider the nature of the claim and the defence put forward.

9. The fact that the defendant is in insolvent circumstances or in acute financial embarrassment, is a relevant circumstances, but not by itself sufficient.

10. That in the case of running businesses, the strictest caution is necessary and the mere fact that a business has been closed, or that its turnover has diminished, is not enough.

11. Where however, the defendant starts disposing of his properties one by one, immediately upon getting a notice of the plaintiff's claim and/or where he had transferred the major portion of his properties shortly prior to the institution of the suit and was in an embarrassed financial condition, these were grounds from which an inference could be legitimately drawn that the object of the defendant was to delay and defeat the plaintiffs' claim.

12. Mere removal of properties outside jurisdiction is not enough, but where the defendant with notice of the plaintiffs' claim, suddenly begins removal of his properties outside the jurisdiction of the appropriate court, and without any other satisfactory reason, an adverse inference may be drawn against the defendant. Where the removal is to a foreign country, the inference is greatly strengthened.

13. The defendant in a suit is under no liability to take any special care in administering his affairs, simply because there is a claim pending against him. Mere neglect, or suffering execution by other creditors, is not a sufficient reason for an order under the Civil Justice Ordinance, Section 135.

14. The sale of properties at a gross undervalue, or benami transfers, are always good indications of an intention to defeat the plaintiff's claim. The court must however be very cautious about the evidence on these points and not rely on vague allegations."

There is no doubt that the guiding principles embodied in the two cases would be of considerable help to the trial courts when dealing with attachments before judgments.

FINANCIAL AND FISCAL LAWS

A good number of enactments were passed during the year in the field of finance and taxation dealing with fiscal policy, advance appropriations, revenue, royalties and road traffic licences.

Treasury Bills

The Treasury Bills Act 1966[129] was amended by the Treasury Bills Amendment Act 1969.[130] Section 3 as amended authorises the Minister of Treasury to borrow by issue of Bills in the Democratic Republic of the Sudan provided the face value of such Bills outstanding any time shall not exceed Ls. 10,000,000.

Under the amended Section 6(i), the Bank of Sudan, shall issue every Bill for amount of Ls. 10,000 or a multiple thereof for sale to commercial Banks and Financial Institutions and Ls. 1,000 or Multiples thereof for sale to other investors. However the proviso to the sub section authorises the Minister of the Treasury, in case of financial Institutions other than Banks and of other investors, to fix a lower denomination than that stipulated above.

Special Drawing Rights

The Amendments to the Articles of the International Monetary Fund with regard to the Special Drawing Account, approved by its Board of Governors in their Resolutions Nos. 23–5, was ratified by the Special Drawing Rights (Ratification) Act 1969.[131] Section 32(2) of the Bank of Sudan Act 1959 dealing with Special Drawing Rights was amended accordingly.

Advance Appropriations

Two Acts were passed authorising the 1969/70 Advance Appropriations. The first Advance Appropriations Act 1969[142] provided for the Government Services and the second Act[133] provided for Development.

Taxation

The Hut and Poll Tax Ordinance 1925 and the Tribute Ordinance 1925 and all the regulations and orders made under them were repealed by the Hut and Poll Tax Ordinance Repeal Act 1969[134] and the Tribute Ordinance Repeal Act 1969[135] respectively.

Two Finance Acts were passed during the year. The first Act[136] introduced new Customs tariffs on various items of goods and commodities imported into the Democratic Republic of the Sudan as well as Excise and Consumption Duties and increased Additional Tax and the Royalties rates. This Finance Act which came into effect on 1st July 1969 amended the Customs Ordinance, the Excise and Consumption Duties Ordinance 1924, the Additional Tax Act 1966, and the Royalties Order 1939.

The Finance (No. 2) Act 1969[138] also amended the Customs Ordinance and provided that rates levied on new cars shall be applied in the same proportion on such cars if secondhand in accordance with the assessed value of each car.

The Customs Ordinance was also amended by the Customs (Amendment) Act 1969,[138] which added a new sub section to Section 74, which provided that "notwithstanding the provisions of sub section (2), the value of any secondhand Motor Car shall not in any case, be less than half the value of such Motor Car when new".

A special tax, known as the Emergency Tax, collected as if it were personal Income Tax under the Income Tax Act 1967, deductible from wages and salaries, and not exceeding 10 per cent of the monthly salaries of employees in the Public and Private sectors, for a period of one year, was imposed by the Emergency Tax Act 1969.[139] The Emergency Tax Act 1969, was deemed to have come into force as from 1st August 1969 until 31st July 1970.

Any person contravening the provisions of the Emergency Tax Act 1969, is liable to the same penalties specified under the Income Tax Act 1967.

The Petroleum Resources Development Act 1958, was amended by the Petroleum Resources Development (Amendment) Act 1969.[140]

In Section 9, clause (*b*) of sub section (4) the following clauses were substituted:

"(*b*) A royalty on petroleum produced which shall be calculated at the rate of 15 per cent on the well head value of all crude oil and natural gas produced, provided that the Minister of Finance and Economics may elect to take petroleum or petroleum products in kind in satisfaction or part satisfaction of the royalty due in any one year.

(*c*) An income tax on the net profits of the lessee derived by him from petroleum produced which will be calculated at the rate of 50 per cent of such profits for any one year, provided that the income tax so calculated will be reduced by the royalty paid in accordance with clause (*b*) above."

After sub section (6), a new sub section (7) was added, namely:

"(7) Any lessee who is liable to pay income tax under Section 9(4)(*c*) of this Act, shall be exempt from the payment of any tax chargeable under the provisions of any other law relating to tax on income or business profits in respect to the net profits of the lessee derived from petroleum produced."

The Road Traffic Act 1962, was also amended by the Road Traffic (Amendment) Act 1969.[141] This Amendment is deemed to have come into force as from the first day of January 1967. It repealed the second Schedule to 1962 Act and substituted with it a totally new Schedule of licence fees for different kinds of vehicles, provided that any fees paid in excess of any fees specified in the Schedule as it existed before the commencement of this Act in the belief that the fees so paid had been increased to that extent shall be deemed to have been levied and collected in accordance with the law and shall not be liable to be refunded.

The Amendment saved the licensing authorities from refunding fees charged since 1st January 1967, in excess of the fees laid down in the second Schedule of 1962 Act without prior legislative sanction.

Avoidance of double taxation

The Democratic Republic of the Sudan signed and ratified during the year an Agreement for Avoidance of Double Taxation with the Republic of Italy.[142]

LOAN AGREEMENTS

The Democratic Republic of the Sudan ratified also three financial or loan Agreements during the year, two Agreements with the United Kingdom of Great Britain and Northern Ireland and one Agreement with the Republic of Italy.

Under the first Agreement[134] with United Kingdom, the Democratic Republic of the Sudan was granted as an interest-free loan, a sum not exceeding Ls. 459,000, towards the cost of new sluice gates and ancillary equipment at the Sennar Dam.

Under the second Agreement[144] the Democratic Republic of the Sudan received another sum not exceeding Ls. 200,000, as an interest-free loan; as financial assistance to the Sudan Railways Corporation towards the cost of the purchase of ten diesel electric locomotives.

These two loans are to be used exclusively for purchases in United Kingdom.

Under the Financial Agreement with the Republic of Italy[145] the Democratic Republic of the Sudan received a financial credit for an amount of Italian Lire 7,500 million (Seven billions and five hundred million) payable within a period of 12 years. The financial credit is to be used for the purpose of effecting payments relating to imports into the Democratic Republic of the Sudan of Italian goods and services foreseen by the list annexed to the Agreement.

INSURANCE LAW

The Constituent Assembly earlier in the year passed the Social Insurance Act 1969[146] which provided for a comprehensive Social Insurance Scheme based on proportioned contributions of the employer and the insured person. The Social Insurance Scheme under the Act applied to all those employed under written or oral contract with the exception of the Government Officials, members of the Armed and the Police Forces and foreign subjects serving in diplomatic or international missions.

This Act was repealed by the Social Insurance (Repeal) Act 1969.[147]

There is only one judicial decision in the field of insurance law, dealing with compulsory insurance under Section 49 of the Road Traffic Act, 1962. The Court of Appeal in *Babiker Babiker Kazan* v. *Sudan Insurance Co. Ltd.*[148] held that according to Road Traffic Ordinance, Section 49, compulsory insurance covers the use of the motor vehicle as well as the person or persons using it. This decision of the Court of Appeal will be welcomed by everyone who travels in or uses a motor vehicle.

LABOUR AND INDUSTRIAL LAW

Four enactments were passed during the year dealing with employment, trade disputes and Trade Unions.

The Employers and Employed Persons Ordinance 1948 was amended by the Employers and Employed Persons (Amendment) Act 1969.[149] This amendment introduced major changes in the law aimed at improving the terms of employment for the benefit of the employed persons.

Section 10(2) of the Ordinance as amended lays down six conditions under which the employer may dismiss his employed persons immediately and without notice or gratuity and four conditions under which an employed person may cease to work before the expiration of the period of his contract of service and without giving his employer any notice.

In all the cases specified under Section 10(2)(*a*) and (*b*) the employer shall not dismiss the employed person and the employed person shall not cease to work unless the dispute is referred to the Commissioner of Labour and his consent thereto is obtained. The Commissioner of Labour must give his decision within a period of not more than seven days.

If the employed person is dismissed by the employer for reasons other than those specified in Section 10(2)(*a*) or if he is dismissed before the Commissioner of Labour makes his decision upon the dispute referred thereto, the dismissal is deemed prejudicial the consequence of which is that the employed person shall either be reinstated to his work and is paid by his employer a full wage for the period during which he was suspended from work up to the date on which the decision of reinstatement was made or that the employed is forced to pay him in addition to any gratuity and other entitlement a compensation equalling three months' wages.

If the employed person intends to determine the contract of service for reasons other than those specified in Section 10(2)(*b*), or before the Commissioner of Labour makes his decision upon the dispute referred to him, the employed person shall by registered post send to the employer a notice to the effect that he intends within thirty days to leave the service otherwise the employer shall be entitled to receive from him compensation not exceeding thirty days' wage.

Where the employed person is engaged on the basis of a daily wage, each party may terminate the contract of service after three months from the date of the commencement of the contract.

Irrespective of the reasons that led to the dismissal of the employed person or the cessation of his work the employer is required to give the employed person on termination of his service, a certificate specifying his name, the work he was performing, the period he spent at his service and the wage he was receiving.

The amendment also gave the employed persons the right to be given holidays on public holidays as stated by the Government with pay. It laid down new schemes for payment of wages during illness, making the employed person unable to attend at his place of employment and of gratuity on termination of service.[150]

The amendment has considerably improved the working conditions of employed women. An employed woman, after completing one year of service is entitled to leave and for each subsequent year for delivery with full pay, calculated as follows:

Four weeks before delivery and four weeks after delivery provided that the date for the probability of delivery and the actual date in which delivery takes place is certified by a licensed doctor in accordance with Section 14 of the Public Health Ordinance 1939.

Employed persons are entitled to annual leave with full pay after completing eighteen continuous months of service, calculated as follows:

If the period of his service is less than five years, he shall be granted fifteen days. after the completion of five years of service but less than ten years, he shall be granted twenty days.

After the completion of ten years of service but less than twenty years he shall be granted twenty-five days. After the completion of twenty years of service or more, he shall be granted thirty days.

An employed person with the consent of the employer may adjourn his leave in any year to the next subsequent year and in this case he shall be granted leave equal to double his entitlement in one year.[151]

The Trade Dispute Act 1966, was amended by the Regulation of Trade Disputes (Amendment) Act 1969[152] by substituting the following new section for Section 27:

> "No worker shall stop partially or completely or go slow and no employer shall look-out his place of work wholly or partially unless he acquires the approval of the Ministry of Labour."

The Trade Unions Ordinance 1949, was also amended by the Trade Unions Ordinance (Amendment) Act 1969[153] by substituting a new section for Section 17, empowering the Registrar to issue a temporary certificate of any trade Union upon its application for registration to enable it to perform any act in furtherance of the purposes for which it has been formed.

There is only one case of significance in this field of law, dealing with gratuity on termination of service. It was held in *Abul Ela & Ahmed Abdel Karim Co.* v. *Ali El Bayoumi*[154] that an employed person who was in service before 12/2/1949, the date of the coming into force of the Employers and Employed Persons Ordinance, is entitled to gratuity under Section 24 of the said Ordinance from the date the said Ordinance came into force and not before. It was held also that disability to continue in service due to old age, is not a voluntary act of leaving the service and that it frustrates the contract of service.

> ". . . It is a rule of law that a contract for personal services is discharged by supervening incapacity. A contract to perform services which can be rendered only by the promisor personally necessarily contemplates that his state of health which at present is sufficiently good for the fulfilment of his obligations, will continue substantially unchanged, and if this ceases to be so owing to his health or illness, the court decrees that both parties shall be discharged from further liability."[155]

LAND LAW

There were four enactments in the field of Land Law all of which are not of major legal significance.

The Public Premises Eviction Act 1969[156] was passed in order to deal with a problem which had become chronic; public servants refusing to vacate Government houses when asked to do so.

The Act defines "public premises" as "any premises owned or taken on lease by the Government or any provincial, municipal, or other local authority or any public body established by law".

The Act also defines "competent authority" under it, as "the Ministry of Housing or any provincial or municipal or other local authority or a public body established by law, each in relation to its premises".

The Act authorises the competent authority to give at any time notice to any person in occupation of any public premises to vacate such premises within such time as may be specified in the notice.

If on the expiration of such period, the public premises is not vacated; the Minister of Interior may, on application made to him by the competent authority and notwithstanding any provisions to the contrary contained in any other law, order the Police Authorities to effect the vacation of such premises and to use such force as may be necessary for that purpose.

Applications to Minister of Interior are to be made through the Solicitor-General.

Any notice given or action taken before the commencement of the Act, is deemed to have been given or taken in accordance with the provision of this Act.

Any order or action made or taken or deemed to have been made or taken under this Act is not questionable before any court.

The Rent Restriction Ordinance 1953, was amended by the Rent Restriction (Amendment) Act 1969,[157] which repealed Section 10*A* and substituted it with the following:

> "Notwithstanding any thing to the contrary contained in this Ordinance, and from the first day of August 1969, the actual rent payable by the tenant (including the sub tenant) to the landlord for residential premises shall be reduced as hereinafter mentioned, provided that the reduced rent shall, for the purposes of this Ordinance, be the standard rent:
> (*a*) 25 per cent as regards premises whose monthly rent is less than twenty pounds,
> (*b*) 20 per cent as regards premises whose monthly rent is twenty pounds, and does not exceed fifty pounds".

The Town and Village Planning Act, 1961 and the Town Replanning Ordinance 1950, were amended by the Town and Village Planning (Amendment) Act 1969[158] and the Town Replanning (Amendment) Act 1969[159] respectively, in order to make the Minister responsible under these legislations, the Minister of Housing. There were other minor amendments particularly of the Town and Village Planning Act 1961 necessitated by the transfer of responsibility from the Minister of Local Government to the Minister of Housing.

There were six cases of Land Law, dealing with Landlord and Tenant, Prescription, pre-emption and customary rights in land.

It was held in *Abdel Rahman Ahmed Abdel Rahman* v. *Hamza Yassin Hamza*[160] that where rent is lawfully due under Rent Restriction Ordinance, Section 11(*a*) and is not paid at the time of institution of the suit, there must be eviction and that the principle of reasonableness is not applicable, because there is no such provision in the Rent Restriction Ordinance 1953.

This case follows the decisions of the Court of Appeal in *Ahmed Ramadan* v. *Dina Kosta*[161] and *Muhrath Diyab* v. *Khalid Ahmed Suliman*,[162] which rejected the application of the principle of reasonableness in cases of eviction on ground of non-payment of rent lawfully due.

Ibrahim Rizig v. *Millad Fanous*[163] dealt with eviction on grounds of personal use under Section 11(*d*) of the Rent Restriction Ordinance. It was held in this case that the need for personal use is not confined to the person of the landlord but includes his dependants who live with him.

> "The interpretation of the word need in the Rent Restriction Ordinance, Section 11(*d*) is not confined to the person of the landlord, but includes his dependants.
>
> The landlord and his dependants are one single unit and the need of each member of the complete whole is the need of the other or others. The landlord can, therefore, plead his children and other dependants who live with him to prove essential need for possession of his property on grounds of personal use".

This case dealt also with the definition of the word "essential" in Section 11(*e*) of the Rent Restriction Ordinance which was defined in *Helen Dirpiatis Case*[164] to mean "indispensably requisite or absolutely necessary".

It was held by the Court of Appeal, that words or phrases like "indispensable requisite, genuine need, convenience" are questions of facts which may differ from case to case. That the best method of interpreting such words is to subject them to the merit of every case.

That though convenience could be a factor *inter alia* of indispensable need, it cannot by itself alone, provide a footing for a successful claim for personal use.

Fatima Mohamed Nasir v. *El Amin Siddik & others*[165] dealt with the relation between the landlord and tenant after the expiration of a long-term lease and the question whether an owner can acquire by way of prescription an easement over his own property.

In this case, the applicant, a lessee of land registered in the name of Sudan Government claimed a right of light over adjoining land registered also in the name of the Government.

It was held on the first issue, that on termination of a long-term lease, the lease is transformed into an annual tenancy if it is not renewed.

As to the second issue, the Court of Appeal refused to follow English law on this point, which allows a lessee to acquire a right of light over the land of another lessee even though the two lands were owned by one landlord,[166] not because it is undesirable but because it is expressly prohibited by Section 6*A* of the Prescription and Limitation Ordinance. This section prohibits *establishment of* an easement "over any land after it has been registered in the name of the Government", and held that an owner cannot acquire by way of prescription an easement over his own property.

"An easement is a benefit to one person and a restriction on another. It follows that identity of ownership or occupation negatives easements. To say that an owner of land can acquire an easement over the adjourning land which also belongs to him will be contradiction in terms. Ownership is the entirety of rights that can be enjoyed over a thing. Hence there would remain nothing for an owner to acquire by way of an easement over his own property. He has everything that could be had."

The decision of the Court of Appeal in *Mohamed Ahmed Khalifa* v. *Mohamed Hamad Ahmed*[167] follows an important decision of that Court of Appeal in *Aman Omer Hassan* v. *Besharia Hassan El Malik & others*[168] which dealt with rights in land in the so-called Native Lodging Areas in towns in which the Government allots plots to the individual citizens on temporary basis to erect temporary buildings for residence. In addition to the issue of the legal relation of the Government and the allottees of land in such areas, the Court of Appeal had to decide, whether the right or interest in land of the allottee comes within orbit of word "property" as defined in the Pre-emption Ordinance, Section 4(*b*).

It was held by the Court of Appeal, that the legal position between the Government and the allottees of land in the Native Lodging Areas creates tenancy at will, which is determinable by the lessor at any time without notice and by the death of the lessee and which does not by itself create a right in land. And since a tenancy at will is not a right or an interest in land, it was held by the Court of Appeal, that it does not come within the orbit of the word property as defined in Section 4(*b*) of the Pre-emption Ordinance and therefore not subject to pre-emption. The rights of the occupants of the Native Lodging Areas "are limited and restricted right of occupation, that is not capable of being transferred or alienated."

Sudan Government v. *El Amin Bedrawi*[169] dealt with interpretation of Section 6(*a*) of the Prescription and Limitation Ordinance, which prohibits establishment of prescriptive rights or titles over land registered in the name of the Government.

It was held that Section 6(*a*) bars claims by prescription for periods after registration is effected in the name of the Government but does not prohibit establishing prescriptive titles for periods prior to the registration in the name of the Government.

The Court of Appeal in *Suleiman Abdalla Hamza* and *others* v. *Abdalla Noura & others*[170] dealt with customary land right known as *mirin*. In this case there was a dispute over ownership of land between the west-bankers and the east-bankers of a river. Mahdi Mohamed Ahmed, J., on the nature and significance of a mirin states:

"A mirin is an imaginary line drawn along the middle of the river, 'Medium filum aquae'. Usually it is drawn by agreement or settlement. A mirin drawn by a settlement becomes permanent and governs the future distribution of the river-bed between the highlanders on the opposite banks. A mirin thus sited can only be altered by a decree of a higher court. It will not be affected by the fluctuation on the course of the river.

Hence it is the primary duty of a settlement officer in the case of river-bed land to start his work by an inquiry as to the existence and whereabouts of any mirins in the settlement area. I admit it is a difficult job to find out about and locate a mirin. The people, in the hope that they will get more land than they are entitled to, will more often than not, withhold such information. But once a settlement officer discovers and locates a mirin he will find that his troubles are over. All he has to do is to grant land east of the mirin to the Eastern-Bankers and the land to the west of it to the Western-Bankers.

Where a mirin exists a settlement officer is bound to take as the established boundary and divide the land between the two bankers accordingly. To set up a fresh mirin on every settlement or resettlement will annul the whole work of the previous settlements and undermines the existing register."

THE LEGAL PROFESSION

The Legal Profession (Regulations) Act 1966, was amended by the Legal Profession (Regulation) Amendment 1969.[171] Section 7(2) and (4) were amended to provide for holding of Legal Profession Examinations at least twice a year, in four branches of law instead of seven, namely:

(*a*) Criminal Law,
(*b*) Law of Criminal Procedure,
(*c*) Law of Civil Procedure,
(*d*) Law of Evidence.

The Legal Profession Regulations 1967, were amended accordingly by the Legal Profession (Amendment) Regulations 1969.[172]

MEDICAL PROFESSION

The Medical Council Ordinance 1955 was amended by the Medical Council (Amendment) Act 1969.[173] The Amendment provides for the establishment of a council, "the Medical Council" an independent body corporate endowed with a legal entity and having perpetual succession and a common seal, which can sue or be sued on its own. The Council exercises the powers and carries out the duties imposed on it by this Act. The Medical Council is directly responsible to the Council of Ministers through its chairman or the person acting on his behalf. The Act vests the Council with powers to licence those who practise medicine and dental surgery under the Public Health Ordinance as well as power to licence those who practise pharmacy under the Pharmacy and Poisons Act 1963.

It provides for registration of practising members of the Medical Profession. No licence to practise medicine, dental surgery or pharmacy shall be granted by the Medical Council except to those persons whose names are registered under this Act in the General Register.

Once the name of any physician, dentist or pharmacist has been erased by the Medical Council from the Register, his licence shall automatically be revoked and he shall not be allowed to practise medicine, dental surgery or pharmacy until his name is restored on the Register and he is again licensed.

The Medical Council prescribes the conditions in Regulations under which licence to practise medicine, dental surgery or pharmacy may be granted. The licence granted by the Council shall either be provisional, temporary or full. The Act deals also with the finance and accounts of the Medical Council.

FAMILY LAW

There was no legislation in the field of Family Law although an attempt was made by the Government to amend the controversial last clause of Section 5(1)(*a*) of the Sharia Court Act 1967, which extended the jurisdiction of the Sharia Courts in family matters and therefore the application of Sharia (Islamic) Law to Christians and Jews.

The Democratic Republic of the Sudan, like many countries in Africa and Asia has a multiplicity of personal laws, of which Sharia Law is the most dominant, being the personal law of the majority of the population. There has been political agitation for a long time to make Sharia Law the fundamental law of the state. This goal was supposed to have been achieved by the Sharia Courts Act 1967, at least in family matters.

The Act gives Sharia Courts jurisdiction in family matters if (i) the marriage to which the suit relates was celebrated in accordance with the Sharia or (ii) all the parties to the marriage are Muslims or (iii) "one of them believes in any of the Holy Books".

Prior to 1967, the Sharia Courts had no jurisdiction in family matters if any party to the suit was a non-Muslim. The aim behind the clause "one of them believes in any of the Holy Books" was to bring mixed marriages between Muslims and those who believe in the Holy Books under the jurisdiction of the Sharia Courts and therefore ensuring the application of Sharia Law.

The Holy Koran recognises only two Holy Books besides itself, the Torah and the Bible. So unless the Holy Books are interpreted to include the Holy Koran, those who believe in the Holy Books would be only the Jews and Christians.

Besides the intolerant feature of this provision, it did not achieve its purpose, because marriage between a Muslim and a non-Muslim other than a Christian or a Jew does not come within the last clause of Section 5(1)(*a*) and therefore within the jurisdiction of Sharia Courts.

This provision did not only encroach on religious rights of Jews and Christians guaranteed them by the Sudan Transitional Constitution but also introduced for the first time religious intolerance and bigotry.

The Minister of Justice having noticed that the Act did not confer jurisdiction on the Sharia Courts in case where one party is a Muslim while another is a non-believer in any of the Holy Books presented a Bill, the Sharia Courts (Amendment) Act 1969, to the Constituent Assembly on 28th April 1969 amending the Sharia Courts Act 1967, "to endow the

Sharia Courts with jurisdiction over family matters whenever of the parties to the dispute is a Muslim irrespective of the faith of the other party".[174]

The proposed amendment provided that the last words in Section 5(1)(*a*), namely "*or one of them believes in any of the Holy Books*" be deleted and the words "or any one of them is a Muslim" should be substituted instead.

Though the proposed amendment was relatively an improvement over the situation under the Sharia Courts Act 1967, in that it excluded from the jurisdiction of the Sharia Courts and therefore from the application of Sharia Law, marriages between non-Muslims; the Bill met with stiff opposition in and outside the Constituent Assembly and the Government was forced to withdraw it from the Assembly. The non-Muslims in and outside the Assembly demanded the deletion of the last clause of Section 5(1)(*a*) and the return to situation prior to 1967.

The Sudan Council of Churches, in a petition addressed to the President and members of the Supreme Council, Speaker of the Constituent Assembly, the Prime Minister, the Minister of Justice and the Leaders of Ansar and Khatimia Religious Sects rejected the proposed amendment and called for the repeal of the last offending clause of Section 5(1)(*a*) and the return to the status quo prior to 1967.

When the Parliamentary System was overthrown on 25th May 1969, the Sudan Council of Churches on 29th May 1969 petitioned the President of the Council of the Revolution and the Prime Minister on the same subject matter. The Government by letter dated 12th July 1969[175] assured the Sudan Council of Churches that the amendment has not been passed and will not be passed. The letter was however silent about the repeal of the last clause of Section 5(1)(*a*) of the Sharia Courts Act 1967.

There was only one decision in this field of law worth noting.

In *Maria Adwok* v. *Gideon Tokmae*[176] it was held by the High Court that in determining the custody of a child, it is the paramount interest of the child, namely, his physical, financial, educational and spiritual welfare which should the primary concern of the court rather than the rights of the parties. The suit in this case involved the custody of a child $9\frac{1}{2}$ years old born out of wedlock. The applicant, the mother, is a Shilluk and the defendant, a Dinka. Each parent was claiming custody in the light of his tribal law and custom and there was diversity in this respect. The Court in such situation is instructed by Section 9 of the Civil Justice Ordinance to act in accordance with justice, equity and good conscience.

It was stated by the applicant that according to Shilluk law and custom, the custody of the child belongs to the mother's family and should the father claim the child he is obliged to pay compensation. It was claimed by the defendant that according to Dinka law the child's custody goes with the father.

It was decided by the court that since both parties are sophisticated and live in Khartoum, the diversity of custom would be only important in case of payment of compensation for legitimation. As the issue of legitimation was not important and the issue for settlement was the custody of the child, the court ignored the competing tribal laws.

Guided by the paramount interest of the child and for reasons enumerated in the judgment, the High Court awarded the custody of the child to the defendant. The order was not however, unqualified.

"The applicant being the child's mother is still entitled to see the child and she is entitled to come to court at any time and apply for varying the above order, if there are reasons which warrant the application. It is obvious that this is so owing to the fact that it is the child's interest which is of paramount importance.

Furthermore, it is inevitable for the psychological upbringing of the child that it should grow up with the feeling that he has a mother and that he is wanted and he belongs. Thus respondent is bound to allow the applicant to see the child. This may be arranged by the parties who should be maturated by the interest of the infant rather than by their own grudges and selfish motives."

PUBLIC INTERNATIONAL LAW

Agreements and treaties ratified

Besides the financial and loan agreements with the Republic of Italy and United Kingdom already mentioned, the Democratic Republic of the Sudan ratified during the year bilateral Agreements with many countries on trade and other fields of international co-operation as well as multi-lateral Agreements.

Bilateral agreements
Air transport

The Democratic Republic ratified an Agreement with the People's Republic of Bulgaria[177] on Air Transport between their respective territories.

International co-operation

In the field of international co-operation, the Republic ratified Cultural Co-operation Agreements with the Lebanese Republic,[178] The Somali Republic,[179] the Socialist Republic of Romania[180] and the Syrian Arab Republic.[181] It ratified Cultural and Scientific Co-operation Agreements with the Democratic Republic of Germany,[182] the People's Republic of Hungary,[183] the Socialist Republic of Czechoslovakia[184] and the Union of Soviet Socialist Republics,[185] as well as Cultural, Scientific and Technical Co-operation Agreement with the People's Republic of Poland.[186]

It ratified Economic Co-operation Agreement with the United Arab Republic[187] and the Protocol Amending the Sudan-Bulgaria Economic Co-operation Agreement.[188] It ratified Economic and Cultural Co-operation Agreement with Arab Republic of Yemen,[189] Economic and Technical Co-operation Agreement with the German Democratic Republic[190] and the Kingdom of Netherlands,[191] Economic, Scientific,

Technical and Cultural Co-operation Agreement with United Arab Republic[192] as well as an Economic Integration and Technical Agreement.[193] In the field of International Trade, the Democratic Republic of the Sudan ratified Trade Agreements with the Arab Republic of Yemen[194] and the Republic of Kenya,[195] the Trade Protocols with the Polish People's Republic,[196] the Socialist Republic of Romania[197] and the Trade Protocols Amending Trade Agreements with the Syrian Arab Republic[198] and the United Arab Republic.[199]

Multilateral agreements

The Democratic Republic of the Sudan ratified a good number of multilateral Agreements dealing with International and Arab Regional co-operation.

The Republic ratified the Agreement between the Office of the United Nations High Commissioner for Refugees and the Government of the Democratic Republic of the Sudan concerning the establishment of a Branch Office of the High Commissioner in Khartoum,[200] and adhered to the Agreement on the Rescue of the Astronauts, the return of the Astronauts and the Return of the Objects launched into the Outer Space.[201]

It ratified five regional Arab Co-operation Agreements, namely, the Agreement for a Middle Eastern Regional Radio-Isotope Centre for the Arab Countries,[202] the Agreement for Economic Unity among the Arab League Countries,[203] the Agreement for Arab Co-operation in the Use of Nuclear Power for Peace Purposes,[204] Diplomatic Immunities and Privileges Agreement of the Arab Organisation for Standardisation and Meteorology of League of the Arab States[205] and the Agreement establishing the Arab Organisation for the Standardisation and Meteorology of the League of the Arab States.[206]

Of the five Agreements on Arab States Regional Co-operation, the Agreement for Economic Unity among the Arab Countries, signed in 1957 by the Sudan but remained unratified until 1969, has far-reaching effects as it aims creating closest co-operation among the States of the Arab League on equal reciprocal basis and without detriment neither to them nor the interest of their subjects. The Agreement aims at establishing an Arab Common Market, in which there is freedom of movement of persons and capital, of exchange of domestic and foreign goods, or residence, work, employment and the exercise of economic activities, transport, transit and use of means of transport, ports and civil airports as well as freedom of ownership, making legacies and inheritance.

The Agreement though passed earlier in the year by the Constituent Assembly was a subject of bitter controversy and because of the sharp division in the Supreme Commission, it did not receive the assent of that body till the Parliamentary System of Government was overthrown on 25th May 1969.

1. The Technical Committee consisted of (i) Ahmed Mutwali Atabani, former Judge of the High Court and former Attorney-General of the Sudan; Chairman; (ii) Abbas Musa Mustafa, Attorney-General, and Natale Olwak Akolawin, Lecturer, Faculty of Law, University of Khartoum.
2. Special Legislative Supplement to the Democratic Republic of the Sudan Gazette No. 1076, dated 25th May 1969.
3. Article 2.
4. Article 3.
5. Article 8.
6. Article 9.
7. Article 10.
8. Article 4.
9. Article 5.
10. Article 6.
11. Article 7.
12. Republican Order No. 11, Article 9.
13. Article 10.
14. Article 11.
15. Article 12.
16. Article 2.
17. Article 4.
18. Article 6.
19. Article 7.
20. Article 8.
21. 1969 Act No. 31.
22. Section 2(1).
23. Section 2(2).
24. Section 2(3).
25. Section 7(1).
26. Section 8.
27. Section 9.
28. Section 13.
29. Section 6.
30. 1969 Act No. 38.
31. 1969 Act No. 79.
32. Section 3(1)(*a*) and (*b*).
33. 1969 Act No. 94.
34. Section 2.
35. Section 7.
36. Section 4(2).
37. 1969 Act No. 83.
38. 1969 Act No. 19.
39. 1969 Act No. 87.
40. 1969 Act No. 43.
41. 1969 Act No. 69.
42. 1969 Act No. 70.
43. 1960 Act No. 40.
44. 1969 Act No. 78.
45. 1969 Act No. 23.
46. Amendment No. 4.
47. Section 4.
48. Section 5.
49. Section 6.
50. Section 7.
51. Section 8.
52. Section 9.
53. Section 10.
54. Section 11(1), (2) and (3).

55. Section 11(4).
56. Section 11(5).
57. Sections 12 and 13.
58. Section 14.
59. Section 15.
60. 1969 Act No. 68.
61. 1969 Act No. 92.
62. 1969 Act No. 71.
63. 1969 Act No. 33.
64. 1969 Act No. 34.
65. Section 8(1).
66. Section 8(1)(*b*) and (3).
67. Section 8(4).
68. Section 11.
69. Section 12.
70. 1969 Act No. 81.
71. AC-CP-591-1969.
72. AC-CP-608-1969
73. AC-CP-739-1969.
74. See Note 71 *supra*.
75. AC-CP-805-1969.
76. AC-CP-385-1969.
77. AC-CR-REV-211-1969.
78. 1969 Act No. 32.
79. 1969 Act No. 26.
80. 1969 Act No. 41.
81. AC-CP-391-1969.
82. AC-CP-107-1969.
83. AC-CP-474-1969.
84. AC-CP-739-1969.
85. AC-CP-380-1969.
86. See Section 74 Sudan Penal Code, Section 23 Code of Criminal Procedure and Criminal Court Circular No. 26.
87. See notes Nos. 75 and 76 respectively.
88. 1969 Act No. 7.
89. Section 2(*h*).
90. Section 3.
91. Section 5.
92. Section 6.
93. Section 7.
94. Section 8.
95. Section 12.
96. Section 13.
97. Section 14.
98. Section 18.
99. Section 19.
100. Section 20.
101. Section 23.
102. Section 24.
103. Section 25.
104. 1969 Act No. 45.
105. 1969 Act No. 88.
106. 1969 Acts No. 46 and 47 respectively.
107. 1969 Act No. 48.
108. 1969 Act No. 74.
109. 1968 P.O. No. 14.
110. 1969 Act No. 62.
111. 1969 Act No. 8.

112. 1969 L.R.O. No. 19.
113. 1969 Act No. 58.
114. Section 6(4).
115. Section 8.
116. 1969 Act No. 67.
117. 1969 Act No. 65.
118. AC-REV-442-1969.
119. AC-REV-426-1968.
120. (1917) AC 556.
121. (1969) Act No. 75.
122. AC-REV-231-1969.
123. (1956) SLJR 4.
124. (1960) SLJR 222.
125. AC-REV-580-1968.
126. AC-REV-584-1968.
127. AC-REV-669-1969.
128. (1961) SLJR 163.
129. 1966 Act No. 2.
130. 1969 Act No. 15.
131. 1969 Act No. 18.
132. 1969 Act No. 28.
133. 1959 Act No. 29.
134. 1969 Act No. 24.
135. 1969 Act No. 25.
136. 1969 Act No. 30.
137. 1969 Act No. 39.
138. 1969 Act No. 40.
139. 1969 Act No. 42.
140. 1969 Act No. 9.
141. 1969 Act No. 64.
142. 1969 Act No. 98.
143. 1969 Act No. 76.
144. 1969 Act No. 77.
145. 1969 Act No. 84.
146. 1969 Act No. 14.
147. 1969. Act No. 27.
148. AC-REV-394-1968.
149. 1969 Act No. 1.
150. Sections 21, 25 and 26.
151. Section 22.
152. 1969 Act No. 36.
153. 1969 Act No. 35.
154. AC-REV-273-1968.
155. per B.M.A. Baldo, J.
156. 1969 Act No. 37.
157. 1969 Act No. 57.
158. 1969 Act No. 59.
159. 1969 Act No. 60.
160. AC-REV-209-1968.
161. AC-REV-300-1966.
162. AC-REV-431-1967.
163. AC-REV-231-1968.
164. (1960) SLJR 165.
165. AC-REV-95-1967.
166. Section 3, English Prescription Act 1832 and *Morgan* v. *Fear* (1907) A.C. 425.
167. AC-REV-548-1967.
168. AC-REV-511-1964.
169. AC-REV-260-1968.

170. AC-REV-607-1967.
171. 1969 Act No. 61.
172. 1969 L.R.O. No. 22.
173. 1969 Act No. 2.
174. Preamble to the Bill.
175. MW/1/A/5/4/587, Subject: Bill of Sharia Courts, Amendment 1969.
176. HC-CS/182/1969.
177. 1969 Act No. 16.
178. 1969 Act No. 49.
179. 1969 Act No. 41.
180. 1969 Act No. 56.
181. 1969 Act No. 53.
182. 1969 Act No. 54.
183. 1969 Act No. 51.
184. 1969 Act No. 55.
185. 1969 Act No. 52.
186. 1969 Act No. 50.
187. 1969 Act No. 63.
188. 1969 Act No. 100.
189. 1969 Act No. 73.
190. 1969 Act No. 93.
191. 1969 Act No. 10.
192. 1969 Act No. 20.
193. 1969 Act No. 99.
194. 1969 Act No. 53.
195. 1969 Act No. 80.
196. 1969 Act No. 86.
197. 1969 Act No. 85.
198. 1969 Act No. 91.
199. 1969 Act No. 21.
200. 1969 Act No. 11.
201. 1969 Act No. 12.
202. 1969 Act No. 17.
203. 1969 Act No. 72.
204. 1969 Act No. 82.
205. 1969 Act No. 96.
206. 1969 Act No. 97.

CHAPTER 32

SOMALI DEMOCRATIC REPUBLIC

Haji N. A. Noor Mohammed

CONSTITUTIONAL LAW

Introduction

The Somali Democratic Republic is composed of the former Trust Territory of Somalia under Italian Administration and the former British Somaliland Protectorate, which joined together on 1st July 1960 to form the Republic, and the Constitution[1] which was originally drafted for the Trust Territory was applied to the whole Republic.

The Constitution contemplated a parliamentary system of government with a President of the Republic elected by the National Assembly as the Head of the State, a National Assembly elected by the people by adult franchise, a Government consisting of the Prime Minister and Ministers responsible to the National Assembly and a Judiciary with the Supreme Court as the highest judicial organ of the Republic. The Supreme Court: (i) exercised judicial review of administrative action; (ii) constituted as the Constitutional Court, it exercised judicial review of legislative action; and (iii) constituted as the High Court of Justice, it had jurisdiction over proceedings against the President of the Republic, the Prime Minister and the Ministers. In order to guarantee the independence of the Judiciary, a Higher Judicial Council was also contemplated.

Revolution

After nine years of civilian government, the Armed Forces took over power in the Republic at 0300 hours on 21st October 1969, in a bloodless Revolution.

In a press conference held in Mogadiscio on 26th October 1960, the President of the Supreme Revolutionary Council stated that the Armed Forces took over power "after having seen the danger that was threatening our independence and existence". He said that the aim of the Revolution was "to normalise, to restore true democracy which was being threatened, to carry on all possible developments which would lead to progress and the prosperity of our people and to hand over power again to a civilian government at an appropriate time".[2]

Following the Revolution, the Armed Forces issued the First Charter of the Revolution and Law No. 1 of 21st October 1969, under which they dissolved the National Assembly, deposed the Government and abolished the Higher Judicial Council. Furthermore, the said Charter and Law No. 1 vested in the Supreme Revolutionary Council the functions and powers of the President of the Republic, the National Assembly, the Council of Ministers, individual Ministries, the Constitutional Court and the High Court of Justice and provided that the said functions and powers shall be exercised in the manner established by the existing laws until otherwise provided by the Supreme Revolutionary Council. The Charter and the Law also suspended the provisions of the Constitution which were contrary to, or inconsistent with, the spirit of the Revolution.[3]

The Supreme Revolutionary Council has not yet enacted a fundamental law defining the functions and powers of the various organs of the State. However, the significant changes effected after the Revolution in the organisational set-up of the State are mentioned below.

The Supreme Revolutionary Council

The Supreme Revolutionary Council consists of twenty-five Army and Police Officers.

The President of the Supreme Revolutionary Council is elected by the Members of the Council in a secret ballot, by a two-thirds majority in the first ballot and by an absolute majority in the second ballot.[4] He is the Head of the State, Head of the Government and Commander-in-Chief of the Armed Forces.

The Supreme Revolutionary Council exercises legislative and executive functions. The legislative functions include the approval of the Annual Budget, Annual Accounts of the State and legislation. In the exercise of its executive functions, the Council lays down the general policy of the State and approves the appointment of high officials.

The Government

After the Revolution, the Supreme Revolutionary Council has appointed a "Government of Technicians" and has restored to it the functions pertaining to government.

The Government consists of the President and Vice-President of the Supreme Revolutionary Council and the Secretaries of State. Their meeting constitutes the Council of Secretaries, which is presided over by the President of the Supreme Revolutionary Council.

The Secretaries of State are appointed and dismissed by Decree of the President of the Supreme Revolutionary Council subject to the approval of the Supreme Revolutionary Council.

The Council of Secretaries mainly deals with the following matters: major questions of policy and public order; approval of draft laws to be presented to the Supreme Revolutionary Council; proposals concerning international treaties and major questions of international policy; proposals for the appointment of high officials; and approval of the Annual Budget and Annual Accounts of the State.

Central organisation

The Central Administration of the Republic is organised into the Presidency of the Supreme Revolutionary Council and the following fifteen Ministries: Justice, Religion and Labour; Foreign Affairs; Interior; Defence; Information and National Guidance Education; Health; Planning; Finance; Public Works; Rural Development and Livestock; Communications and Transport; Industry and Commerce; Agriculture; Mineral Resources.

Territorial organisation

The territorial organisation of the State consists of eight Regions and fifty-nine Districts. After the Revolution, Regional and District Revolutionary Councils have been appointed throughout the Republic.[5] These Councils consist of Army and Police Officers and are competent to decide on problems of the Region or District concerned. The posts of Regional Governors and District Commissioners are held by Army Officers.

Local administration

By Decree No. 4 of 25th October 1969, all the Local Councils were dissolved and Extraordinary Commissioners have been appointed for all Local Administrations. The Extraordinary Commissioners exercise the functions of the Local Councils and of their chairmen.

ADMINISTRATIVE LAW

During the period under review, the Supreme Court delivered two leading judgments on administrative law in respect of matters relating to the political elections held in 1969.

In the first case, viz., *Popular Movement for Democratic Action* v. *The Minister of Interior*,[6] the Supreme Court dealt with petitions filed in connection with the presentation of lists,[7] some of which were against the orders of the Regional Courts rejecting certain lists, and some against the orders of the Regional Courts validating the lists presented by local committees of political parties. While declaring the petitions inadmissible, the Supreme Court explained at length the law governing the subject.

The Supreme Court observed that, under Article 14 of the Political Elections and Local Councils Election Law,[8] a petition would be admitted only if it fulfilled the following conditions:

(*a*) It should be filed by the representatives of the list.
(*b*) It should state the grounds of law on which it was based.

(*c*) It should be against the order of the Regional Court rejecting a petition filed before it.

(*d*) It should be filed within three days from the date of the said rejection.

The court said that the representatives who filed petitions should be lawful representatives, i.e. they might be members of either the central committee or the local branch of the political party concerned and that all the three representatives contemplated by Article 12, para. 5 of the Law[9] should jointly sign the petitions presented before the Regional Court and the appeals filed before the Supreme Court. Otherwise the petitions would be inadmissible.

As regards the grounds of appeal, the court said that, even though Article 14, para. (4) of the Political Elections and Local Councils Election Law provided that an appeal might be preferred even by telegram without any particular procedural formality, such telegram should specify the questions of law on which the appeal was based or separate grounds of appeal should be filed before the court within the specified time limit. Telegrams of appeal which did not specify any grounds of law would at best be considered as evincing the intention of the party to appeal against an order of rejection, but the court would be misinterpreting the law if appeals were admitted in cases where the questions of law were not specified in the telegrams or separate grounds were not presented within the prescribed time limit.

Furthermore, the Supreme Court also held that appeals might be filed before it only against orders of rejection by Regional Courts of petitions filed before them. In respect of this ruling, the court followed a previous decision of a Full Bench of the Supreme Court in *Somali National Congress* v. *the State*.[10]

Regarding the statutory period of limitation prescribed in Article 14 of the Political Elections and Local Councils Election Law, the Supreme Court noted that there was a conflict between the Italian, English and Arabic texts of the Law. The court said that the English version expressly states that the period begins to run from the date of the order of rejection, i.e. within three days from the date of such rejection. On the other hand, the Italian text reads, *entro tre giorni successivi*, i.e., "within three successive days", not excluding public holidays, while the Arabic text reads: "In the course of three days". Since it was not possible for the court to check within the short time available as to which of the versions was the original, it decided to interpret the provision in question according to the English text and ruled that the word "within" must bear whatever meaning may be attributed to it in the English language. The court, therefore, held that "limitation period must commence to run from the date of the order in question".

In the second case, *Islao Osman Nur Amer* v. *Chairman of the Central Electoral Office*,[11] the Supreme Court dealt with the question as to whether it had jurisdiction to deal with appeals filed against the decision of the Central Electoral Office respecting complaints pertaining to the operations in the political elections pursuant to Article 59 of the Political Elections and Local Councils Election Law[12] and against the proclamation of the final results of those elections by the chairman of the Central Electoral Office.

In order to decide the above question, the court had to examine the nature of the decisions of the chairman of the Central Electoral Office, that is to say, whether the said decisions are judicial decisions or administrative acts.

In a prior decision[13] on petitions filed in connection with the political elections held in 1964, the Supreme Court held that the chairman and other officers in the Central Electoral Office performed functions of an executive nature, that the decisions given by the chairman of the Central Electoral Office were not judicial decisions but administrative acts, and that an appeal against his decision was an administrative action contemplated under Article 39 of the Constitution.[14]

In overruling the previous decision, the Supreme Court held that the Central Electoral Office "is nothing more than an *ad hoc* body that is created to play the role of the midwife in the process of the birth of the new National Assembly", that it need not be classified as legislative or executive. It added that the category of administrative matters in respect of which the Supreme Court had jurisdiction under Article 94 of the Constitution[15] was different from the category of electoral matters and that "it is futile to endeavour to squeeze both categories in a single pigeon hole". In respect of political elections, the Supreme Court had jurisdiction only to entertain petitions challenging the qualifications of deputies under Article 59 of the Constitution; and the Political Elections and Local Councils Elections Law did not confer any jurisdiction on the Supreme Court over appeals against the decisions of the Central Electoral Office and the proclamation of final results by the chairman of the said office by way of administrative action. The soundness of this decision is open to question.

TORT

In the Somali Democratic Republic, torts committed by Somalis are governed by customary law.

In *Ismail Hassan Egeh and another* v. *the Abdi Haji Mohammed Behi and another*,[16] the Supreme Court had to consider the question of guardianship of minors in cases relating to compensation under customary law.

In the above case, the respondents sued the appellants for compensation in respect of injuries inflicted on the second respondent by the first appellant. The first appellant was a minor and, since his father was in Djibuti (French Somaliland), the second appellant, who was the paternal grandfather of the minor and *Akil*[17] of the *dia*-paying group[18] to which the minor belonged, was appointed by the court as guardian. In the course of the proceedings, the second appellant admitted liability for the compensation in question. The trial court gave a decree in favour of the respondents for a sum of Sh.So.3325. An appeal was filed before the Court of Appeal, Hargeisa. The appellate court dismissed the appeal. It, however, reduced the *quantum* of compensation to Sh.So.2430.

In the second appeal filed before the Supreme Court, the appellants challenged the decision of the courts below on the grounds that: (*a*) the second appellant was not the natural guardian of the first appellant; (*b*) there was a conflict of interest between the minor and the second appellant as *Akil* of the *dia*-paying group in respect of the acceptance of liability relating to the compensation in question.

As regards the first contention, the Supreme Court observed that the minor's father was in Djibuti, which was outside the jurisdiction of the court, and that, therefore, the second appellant, who was the paternal grandfather of the minor, was the natural guardian of the minor under both Sharia and customary law.

The Supreme Court also stated that in admitting liability regarding the compensation in question there was no conflict of interest between the two appellants.

EVIDENCE AND PROCEDURE

In *Ismail Yahya Gaileh* v. *Mohamed Ahmed Abobaker*,[19] the Supreme Court gave a leading decision relating to evidence and procedure.

In the above case, the appellant's case was that he rented from the respondent a building, where he stored 600 hides, 300 sacks and 70 ropes and that during his absence the respondent demolished the building, destroying the goods stored therein. The appellant therefore claimed the value of the goods. The District Court of Burao gave a decree in favour of the appellant.

On appeal, the Court of Appeal, Hargeisa, noted that there were procedural irregularities in the proceedings before the trial court. It, however, allowed the appeal on the ground that the evidence in the case was not sufficient to prove the claim.

In the second appeal filed before the Supreme Court, the appellant contended that: (*a*) the judgment of the Court of Appeal was against the weight of evidence; (*b*) if the Court of Appeal had noticed procedural irregularities in the proceedings of the District Court, it should have set aside the said proceedings and remanded the case for retrial. The Supreme Court rejected both the grounds.

As regards the first contention of the appellant, the Supreme Court observed that the appellant did not prove the number of the goods alleged missing or the value thereof. There was not even evidence in the case to prove that the said goods were stored in the building at all. The appellant had thus failed to establish his basic claim that some hides, sacks and ropes were in the building when the respondent demolished it. The Supreme Court, therefore, ruled that the Court of Appeal gave its decision after properly weighing the evidence produced in the case.

Regarding the procedural defects, the Supreme Court noted that the procedure of the trial court was "a complete mess". The Court said that the case was brought under the Civil Law as distinguished from the Somali Customary Law and the trial court nevertheless did not hear either the appellant or the respondent on oath. There was only a vague entry in the trial court proceedings that the appellant gave a sworn statement. The Supreme Court stated that the entry was by no means what the trial court should have done; it should have, on the other hand, heard the actual statement of the appellant as given by him. There was also no indication that the respondent was allowed to cross-examine the appellant.

The Supreme Court, however, observed that, despite the procedural irregularities in the proceedings of the trial court, the decision of the Court of Appeal was in accordance with Section 43 of the Somaliland Order in Council 1960, which provides that in applying the Indian and British Statutes, procedural niceties should be disregarded and judicial decisions should be based on substantial justice.

---

1. For text of the Constitution, see Official Bulletin of the Somali Republic, No. 1 of 1st July 1960; Armos J. Please, *Constitutions of Nations*, Vol. I, "Africa", 773–803, the Hague (1965). Haji, N. A. Noor Muhammad, *The Development of the Constitution in the Somali Republic*, 179–229, Government of the Somali Republic, Ministry of Grace and Justice, Mogadiscio (April 1969).

2. *Somali Democratic Republic, New Era*, 12, Ministry of Information and National Guidance, Mogadiscio (February 1970).

3. The Constitution was later repealed by Decree of the Supreme Revolutionary Council, No. 38 of February 24 1970.

4. First Charter of the Revolution dated 21st October 1969.

5. Law No. 1 of 25th October 1969.

6. See judgment of the Supreme Court dated 23rd February 1969, delivered by Abdul Rahman Sheikh Ali, President.

7. Political Elections and Local Councils Elections Law (Law No. 13 of 6th June 1968) provided for the list system of proportional representation. Under this system, political parties had the right to file lists of candidates for elections in every electoral district.

8. Political Elections and Local Councils Elections Law, Article 14 reads as follows:

"*Article 14*
Presentation of the Lists

1. The lists of candidates shall be presented to the Office of the District Commissioner territorially competent before 6 p.m. of the forty-fifth day prior to the date of voting. Such time limit shall, however, be extended until all the supporters, who are present in front of the District Commissioner's Office at the time fixed for closing, have completed the operations relating to the signature of the lists.

2. The District Commissioner shall immediately verify whether the lists and annexes are regular, allot to each list, which is regular, a progressive number issuing a receipt, and return the lists which are not regular to the representatives of the lists referred to in Article 12(5) stating in writing the reasons for rejecting them.

3. The representatives may file a petition in writing on questions of law before the Regional Court territorially competent against the order rejecting the presentation of the list within three days from the date of such rejection; and the court shall decide within three days from the date of the filing of the petition. An appeal shall lie to the Supreme Court against the decision of the Regional Court rejecting the petition within three days from such decision. The Supreme Court shall decide the appeal at least thirty days prior to the date of voting and its decision shall be final.

4. The petition and appeal provided for in the previous paragraph may be preferred even by telegram, without any particular procedural formality."

9. *Id.*, Article 12(5). The above provision reads as follows:

"5. The list shall indicate the names and addresses of three voters who shall be empowered to: (*a*) present the list in accordance with Article 14; (*b*) prepare all other incidental acts of a procedural and executive nature."

10. Judgment of the Supreme Court dated 5th Nov. 1969 by Dr. Giuseppe Papale, President; see, Somali Republic, Somali Law Reports, Hargeisa and Burao Regions 1961–3, 208–23.

11. See, judgment dated 30th June 1969, delivered by Abdul Rahman Sheikh Ali, President. It dealt with forty-five petitions, out of which forty-four related to political elections and one with local council election.

12. Under Article 59 of the Political Elections and Local Councils Election Law, the Chairman of the Central Electoral Office had the power to decide on complaints regarding voting and counting operations and to proclaim the final results in the political elections.

13. See, judgment of the Supreme Court dated 7th March 1964, delivered by Dr. Haji N. A. Noor Muhammad, Vice-President.

14. The Constitution, Article 39 read as follows:

"Article 39

Protection against Acts of Public Administration

Judicial Protection against acts of the public administration shall be allowed in all cases, in the manner and with the effects prescribed by Law."

15. The Constitution, Article 94 read as follows:

"Article 94

Supreme Court

1. The Supreme Court shall be the highest judicial organ of the Republic. It shall have jurisdiction over the whole territory of the State in civil, criminal, *administrative*, and accounting matters, and on any other matter specified by the Constitution by Law." (Italics added.)

16. Supreme Court Civil Appeal No. 130 of 1968, judgment dated 2nd February 1969 delivered by Mohamoud Sheikh Ahmed, Vice-President.

17. *Akil* means the tribal chief appointed by Government.

18. *Dia* means blood money.

19. Supreme Court Civil Appeal No. 112 of 1968, judgment dated 7th January 1969 delivered by Mohamoud Sheikh Ahmed, Vice-President.

AFRICAN LEGAL BIBLIOGRAPHY

J. Vanderlinden

The African Law Bibliography 1969 includes books and articles dealing with African legal problems and published primarily during the year 1969, but also in 1967 and 1968. Within books and articles are included government reports, but not legislative materials published under one form or another; essays included in collective works are also covered. By African legal problems, one means studies which have a definite legal import. The dividing line between law on the one hand and anthropology, economics, politics and sociology on the other being what it is, the compiler has attempted to be restrictive in his choice in order to keep the bibliography within satisfactory limits; thus studies of which the major import is either anthropological, economic, political or sociological have in most cases been omitted. The whole African continent is considered, as the Centre for African Legal Development has been assigned such geographical limits by its promoters. Only published works (and thus no archives or thesis) are incorporated in the bibliography.

J. Vanderlinden
Director
Centre for African Legal Development
Faculty of Law
Haile Sélassie I University

AFRICA — AFRIQUE

"Acquisition and Use of State Lands in Africa: A Bibliography", *African Law Studies*, 1(3): 23, 1969.

Adegbite, L.O. "African Attitudes to the International Protection of Human Rights", *International Protection of Human Rights*, 69.

The African Law Reports, Commercial — 1964, 2 vol., Dobbs Ferry 1969.

The African Law Reports, Commercial — 1966, Vol. 2, Dobbs Ferry 1969.

The African Law Reports, Commercial — 1967, Vol. 1, Dobbs Ferry 1969.

African Penal Systems, London 1969.

Balandier, G. "Les relations de dépendance personnelle: présentation du thème", *Cahiers d'études africaines*, 9: 345, 1969.

Allott, A.N. "Local Customary Courts in the Former British Territories in Africa", *L'organisation judiciaire en Afrique noire*, 247.

Arowolo, E.A. "The Taxation of Low Incomes in African Countries", *International Monetary Fund Staff Papers*, **15**: 322, 1968.

Bartoli, A.L. "Decolonizzazione africana e successione nei trattati internazionali", *Diritto Internazionale*, **23**(1): 338, 1969; **24**(1): 129, 1970.

Bekombo, M. *Vie familiale et délinquance juvénile en Afrique noire*, Paris 1968.

Bentil, J.K. "Economic and Customs Union of Central Africa and the Convention on Investment", *Journal of World Trade Law*, **3**: 98, 1969.

Bentsi-Enchill, K. "The Colonial Heritage of Legal Pluralism", *Zambia Law Journal*, **1**(2): 1, 1969.

Bentsi-Enchill, K. "Plaidoyer pour une Commission du Droit africain", *Revue sénégalaise de droit*, **(5)**: 64, 1969.

Blanc-Jouvan, X. "Codification du droit du mariage dans les pays d'Afrique noire francophone", *Ius Privatum Gentium*, Vol. 2, 909.

Cano, G.J. "Relationship between Water and Other Natural Resources. Physical and Economical Aspects of the Problem", *International Law Association. Report of Conferences*, **53**: 531, 1968.

Cours international de criminologie — Travaux du 16ème cours, Abidjan 1966, Paris 1968.

David, R. "Derechos de Africa y de Madagascar", *Boletin Mexicano de Derecho Comparado*, **1**: 65, 1968.

De Clerck, L. "Droit de développement", *Revue administrative et juridique du Burundi*, **(4)**: 37, 1969.

Dekkers, R. "Justice bantoue", *Ionasco Collection*, 57.

Farer, T. *Africa's Goals; the Options of International Law*, New York 1968.

Filesi, T. *L'istituto della famiglia nelle costituzioi degli stati africani*, Milano 1969.

Filesi, T. "L'istituto della famiglia africana — Problematica del presente e dell'avvenire". *Africa (Roma)*, **24**: 349, 1969.

Flores, X.A. "Institutional Problems in the Modernization of African Agriculture", *A Review of Rural Cooperation in Developing Areas*, 199.

Gilissen, J. and Vanderlinden, J. "L'organisation judiciaire en Afrique noire — Essai de synthèse", *L'organisation judiciaire en Afrique noire*, 9.

Goody, J. "Inheritance, Property and Marriage in Africa and Eurasia", *Sociology*, **3**(1): 55, 1969.

Grundmann, H.E. "Patent Laws in New African States", *Journal of the Patent Office Society*, **50**: 486, 1968.

Halloy, G. "Quelques considérations sur la justice en Afrique noire", *L'organisation judiciaire en Afrique noire*, 103.

Hazard, J.N. "La familia de sistemas juridicos de inspiracion marxista en Africa", *Libro — Homenaje a la memoria de Roberto Goldschmidt*, 131.

Hazard, J.N. "Modernization and Codification", *Revue roumaine des sciences sociales*, **12**: 63, 1968.

Heidelberg, W. *Grundzüge des Niederlassungsrechts in den afrikanischen Staaten*, Vol. 2, Hamburg 1969.

Huber, S.K. "Legal Education in Anglophonic Africa: With Particular Attention to a Text-Book", *Wisconsin Law Review*: 1188, 1969.

Hunt, H.F. "African Folklore: The Role of Copyright", *African Law Studies*, **(1)**: 87, 1969.

Ideas and Procedures in African Customary Law, London 1969.

Jensen, J. "Verfassung, politische Institutionen und Stammeswirklichkeit in den neuen Staaten Afrikas", *Internationales Afrika Forum*, **5**: 685, 1969.

Kiefe, R. "Water and Air Pollution and the Public Health", *The Review of the International Commission of Jurists*, **(5)**: 28, 1970.

Lampué, P. *Droit d'Outre-Mer et de la coopération*, Paris 1969.

Lavroff, D.G. "Le régime juridique des investissements étrangers en Afrique noire", *Afrika Spectrum*, **4**(3): 64, 1969.

Mair, L. *African Marriage and Social Change*, London 1969.

Mangin, G. "Die Legislative in den frankophonen Staaten Afrikas", *Internationales Afrika Forum*, **4**: 430, 1968.

Mangin, G. "Droits de l'homme dans les pays de l'Afrique francophone", *Les droits de l'homme*, 1: 453, 1968.

Mangin, G. "Le régime disciplinaire des magistrats en France et dans les Etats de l'Afrique francophone", *Revue juridique et politique, Indépendance et coopération*, 23: 1115, 1969.

M'Baye, K. "Réalités du monde noir et les droits de l'homme", *Les droits de l'homme*, 2: 382, 1969.

McNamara, S. "Development Corporation Laws", *African Law Studies*, (1): 23, 1969.

Meek, C.K. *Land Law and Custom in the Colonies*, London 1969.

Melady, T.P. "The Right to Be Educated in the New Africa", *The Right to Be Educated*, 204.

Newman, B.S. "To Further a System of Justice: Legal Aid in Africa", *African Law Studies*, 1(3): 97, 1969.

Obeng, A. "The Inspection and Control of Government Services in Seven African States", *Cahiers africains d'administration publique*, (2B): 12, 1967.

Ochola, J. "Ownership of Land in African Customary Tenure", *Vierteljahresberichte*, 38: 423, 1969.

L'organisation judiciaire en Afrique Noire, Bruxelles 1969.

Palley, C. "Rethinking the Judicial Role — The Judiciary and Good Government", *Zambia Law Journal*, 1(1): 1, 1969.

Payne, R.H. "Divided Tribes: a Discussion of African Boundary Problems", *New York University Journal of International Law and Politics*, 2: 243, 1969.

Perlin, M.L. "The Insanity Defense in English-Speaking African Countries", *African Law Studies*, (2): 73, 1969.

Paul, J.C.N. "The Development of Legal Education in Developing African Countries" *Conference on World Peace through Law, 3rd Conference*, 458.

Quenum-Possy-Berry, M. "Traditionelle Werte und neue Institutionen in den Afrikanischen Staaten", *Internationales Afrika Forum*, 3: 314, 1967.

Read, J.S. "Censored", *Transition*, 7(1): 37, 1967.

Robertson, A.H. "Commission on Human Rights for Africa?", *Les droits de l'homme*, 2: 696, 1969.

Salacuse, J.W. *An Introduction to Law in French-Speaking Africa*, Charlottesville 1969.

Schott, R. "Interdisziplinäre Forschungen auf dem Gebiet der Rechtsethnologie", *Afrika Spectrum*, 4(2): 5, 1969.

Schröder, D. "Das Recht zur interafrikanischen Intervention", *Verfassung und Recht in Uebersee*, 2: 29, 1969.

Seidman, R.B. "The Reception of English Law in Colonial Africa Revisited", *Eastern Africa Law Review*, 2: 47, 1969.

Sedler, R.A. "Law Reform in the Emerging Nations of Sub-Saharan Africa: Social Change and the Development of the Modern Legal System", *St Louis University Law Journal*, 13: 195, 1968.

Stibich, R. "Family Law in Some English-Speaking African States", *African Law Studies*, (2): 49, 1969.

Tabatoni, P. "Fiscalité et développement en Afrique", *Cahiers de droit fiscal international*, 53(1): 249, 1968.

Verhelst, T. *Safeguarding African Customary Law: Judicial and Legislative Processes for its Adaptation and Integration*, Los Angeles 1968.

"Water Resources Law", *International Law Association. Report of Conferences*, 53: 509, 1968.

Yakemtchouk, R. "L'Afrique en droit international", *Cahiers économiques et sociaux*, 7: 383, 1969.

Yakemtchouk, R. "Régime international des voies d'eau africaines", *Revue belge de droit international*, 480, 1969.

AFRICA (CENTRAL) — AFRIQUE (CENTRALE)

Borella, F. "Union des Etats de l'Afrique centrale", *Annuaire français de droit international*, 14: 167, 1968.

Botte, R. Dreyfus, F. Le Pape, M. and Vidal, C. "Les relations personnelles de subordination dans les sociétés interlacustres de l'Afrique centrale", *Cahiers d'études africaines*, 9: 350, 1969.
Lukusa, T. "L'U.E.A.C.", *Congo-Afrique*, (30): 503, 1968.
Ngoie, J. "Le traité de Kampala et l'intégration économique en Afrique orientale et centrale", *Congo-Afrique*, (24): 168, 1968.

AFRICA (EAST) — AFRIQUE (ORIENTALE)

Allott, A.N. "Customary Law in East Africa", *Afrika Spectrum*, 4(3): 12, 1969.
Cotran, E. *Tribal Factors in the Establishment of the East African Legal Systems*, London 1969.
Diamond, P.A. "Effective Protection of the East African Transfer Taxes", *East African Economic Review*, 4(2): 37, 1968.
Durand, P.P. "The Doctrine of Estoppel as Applied in East Africa", *East African Law Journal*, 5: 200, 1969.
Durand, P.P. "Evidence of Business Entries by Persons Unknown", *East African Law Journal*, 5: 291, 1969.
Ghai, Y.P. "Legal Aspects of the Treaty for East African Cooperation", *East African Economic Review*, 3(2): 27, 1967.
Ghai, Y.P. and Whitford, W.C. "Reform of Private Law in East Africa", *Mawazo*, 2(1): 43, 1969.
Hazlewood, A. "The Kampala Treaty and the Accession of New Members to the East African Community", *East African Economic Review*, 4(2): 49, 1968.
Hazlewood, A. "Notes on the Treaty for East African Cooperation", *East African Economic Review*, 3(2): 63, 1967.
Helleiner, G.K. "Transfer Taxes, Tariffs and the East African Common Market", *East African Economic Review*, 3(2): 53, 1967.
Huber, H. "Woman Marriage in Some East African Societies", *Anthropos*, 63–64: 745, 1968–1969.
Huber, S.K. "Co-operative Legislation in East Africa", *Journal of the Denning Law Society*, 2(2): 114, 1969.
Huber, S.K. "Use of Marginal Notes in East Africa", *Eastern Africa Law Review*, 2: 107, 1969.
Katende, J.W. "Company Law in East Africa: Present and Future", *Eastern Africa Law Review*, 2: 135, 1969.
Martin, R. "Sociology and Legal Change", *Eastern Africa Law Review*, 2: 101, 1969.
McAuslan, J.P.W.B. "Succession and Elections in East Africa", *Eastern Africa Law Review*, 2: 269, 1969.
Nadel, B. "Curtailment of the Right to Counsel in the Determination of Income Tax Liabilities", *East African Law Journal*, 4: 203, 1968.
Newbold, C.D. "How an Advocate Should Prepare and Argue an Appeal in the Court of Appeal for East Africa", *Journal of the Denning Law Society*, 2(2): 94, 1969.
Newbold, C.D. "The Value of Precedents Arising from Cases Decided in East Africa as Compared with Those Decided in England", *Eastern Africa Law Review*, 2: 1, 1969.
Ngoie, J. "Le traité de Kampala et l'intégration économique en Afrique orientale et centrale", *Congo-Afrique*, (24): 168, 1968.
Orloff, N. "Economic Integration in East Africa: the Treaty for East-African Co-operation", *Columbia Journal of Transnational Law*, 7: 302, 1968.
Private Enterprise and the East African Company, Dar es Salaam 1969.
Rahim, B. "Legislative Implementation of the Arusha Declaration", *East African Law Journal*, 4: 183, 1968.
Risch, A. "Selected Bibliography of Recent Publications on East African Law", *Afrika Spectrum*, 4(3): 43, 1969.
Rogers, M. *Outline of the Commercial Law of East Africa*, Nairobi 1968.
Singh, C. "Some Notes on the Development of Law in East Africa to the End of the Consular Jurisdiction", *East African Law Journal*, 5: 149, 1969.

Smith, A.H. "Employment, Self-Employment and the Non-Citizen", *East African Law Journal*, **4**: 166, 1968.
Spreen, G. "Elements of East African Law", *Afrika Spectrum*, **4(3)**: 5, 1969.
Spry, J.F. *Civil Procedure in East Africa*, Nairobi 1968.
Svoboda, J.L. "Transfer Tax and Development Bank: A New Look for the East African Community", *African Law Studies*, **(2)**: 93, 1969.
Thanawalla, S. "Commercial Law and Foreign Investment", *Afrika Spectrum*, **4(3)**: 37 1969.
Thomas, P.A. "The Advantages of the Being LTD", *Transition*, **7(5)**: 51, 1968.
Thomas, P.A. "The Doctrine of Ratification in East Africa", *Eastern Africa Law Review*, **2**: 259, 1969.
Whitford, W.C. "The Doctrine of Fundamental Breach in East Africa". *Eastern Africa Law Review*, **2**: 87, 1969.

AFRICA (NORTH) — AFRIQUE (SEPTENTRIONALE)

Von Muralt, J. "Rural Institutions and Planned Change in the Middle East and North Africa", *A Review of Rural Cooperation in Developing Areas*, 277.

AFRICA (WEST) — AFRIQUE (OCCIDENTALE)

Chukura, O. *A Digest of Decisions of Her Majesty's Privy Council in Appeals from West Africa, 1841 to 1964*, Ibadan 1969.
Hazard, J.N. "Marxist Models for West African Law", *Ius Privatum Gentium*, Vol. 1, 285.
Ighodaro, I.E.B. "Changing Patterns of Marriage and Family Life in West African Society", *Ibadan*, **(26)**: 36, 1969.
Oloruntimehin, B.O. "The Treaty of Niagassola, 1886: An Episode in Franco-Samori Relations in the Era of the Scramble", *Journal of the Historical Society of Nigeria*, **4(4)**: 601, 1969.
Rabl, K. "Westafrikanische Verfassungsprobleme", *Internationales Afrika Forum*, **3**: 311, 1967.
Woodman, G.R. "Some Realism about Customary Law — The West African Experience", *Wisconsin Law Review*, —: 128, 1969.

COMMONWEALTH — COMMONWEALTH

Head, I.L. "Alien's Access to Local Remedies: The African Commonwealth Countries Experience", *Vanderbilt Law Review*, **21**: 701, 1968.

ETATS AFRICAINS ET MALGACHES ASSOCIES
AFRICAN AND MALAGASY ASSOCIATED STATES —

Aliboni, R. "Renewal of the Yaounde Convention", *Africa Quarterly*, **9**: 95, 1969.
Aliboni, R. "The Yaounde Convention: A Conflict of Doctrines", *Africa Quarterly*, **9**: 275, 1969.
Bruyas, J. "Yaoundé II", *Annales africaines*, –: 123, 1969.
Clauss, M.W. "Die dritte Phase der europäisch-afrikanischen Assoziierung — Zur Erneuerung des Abkommens von Jaunde", *Verfassung und Recht in Uebersee*, **1**: 453, 1968.
Kovar, R. "Relations extérieures. Le renouvellement de la Convention de Yaoundé", *Revue trimestrielle de droit européen*, **5**: 534, 1969.
Lucron, C. "Les orientations nouvelles de l'association entre la Communauté économique européenne et les états africains et malgaches associés", *Chronique de politique étrangère*, **22**: 651, 1969.
Merkel, C. "Das Abkommen von Jaunde II in Kamerunischer Sicht", *Verfassung und Recht in Uebersee*, **2**: 485, 1969.
O'Malley, C.K.H. "Some Legal Issues Involved in the Association of the European

Economic Community with the African and Malagasy States", *African Law Studies*, (1): 53, 1969.
Le renouvellement de la Convention de Yaoundé, Bruxelles 1969.
Riccardi, F. "Réflexions sur la nouvelle Convention d'association de Yaoundé", *Revue française d'études politiques africaines*, (46): 37, 1969.

ALGERIE — ALGERIA

Baumann, H. "Mechanismus der obersten Staatsorgane Algeriens in der Entwicklung einer nationaldemokratischen Staatsmacht", *Staat und Recht*, **18**: 1903, 1969.
Bedjaoui, M. "La nouvelle organisation judiciaire en Algérie", *Revue juridique et politique Indépendance et coopération*, **23**: 521, 1969.
"La charte de la wilaya", *Revue algérienne des sciences juridiques, économiques et politiques*, **6**: 853, 1969.
"Le code communal algérien", *Cahiers africains d'administration publique*, **(1B)**: 1, 1967.
Collot, C. "Le régime juridique de la presse musulmane algérienne", *Revue algérienne des sciences juridiques, économiques et politiques*, **6**: 343, 1969.
El Hassar, M. "A propos de l'article 7 du Code de Procédure civile", *Revue algérienne des sciences juridiques, économiques et politiques*, **6**: 7, 1969.
Favret, J. "Relations de dépendance et manipulation de la violence en Kabylie", *L'Homme*, **8(4)**: 18, 1968.
Fenaux, H. "L'article 7 du Code de la Procédure civile", *Revue algérienne des sciences juridiques, économiques et politiques*, **6**: 845, 1969.
Fenaux, H. "Eléments de droit judiciaire algérien (3)", *Revue algérienne des sciences juridiques, économiques et politiques*, **6**: 11, 1969.
Ghozali, S.A. and Burger, J.J. "Les hydrocarbures en Algérie — leur régime juridique", *Revue algérienne des sciences juridiques, économiques et politiques*, **6**: 165, 1969.
Lampué, P. "La justice administrative en Algérie", *Revue juridique et politique, Indépendance et Coopération*, **23**: 167, 1969.
Lapassat, E.J. *La Justice en Algérie 1962–1968*, Paris 1969.
Loussouarn, Y. "Du caractère confiscatoire des mesures prises par l'Etat algérien à l'encontre des entreprises françaises", *Recueil Dalloz Sirey*, 241, 1969.
Mahiou, A. and Amadio, M. "La réforme de la wilaya", *Revue algérienne des sciences juridiques, économiques et politiques*, **6**: 1077, 1969.
Salaheddine, A. "De quelques aspects du nouveau droit judiciaire algérien", *Revue algérienne des sciences juridiques, économiques et politiques*, **6**: 435, 1969.
Sauvel, J. "L'accord franco-algérien du 27 décembre 1968 relatif à la circulation, au séjour et à l'emploi en France des ressortissants algériens et de leur famille", *Revue juridique et politique, Indépendance et coopération*, **23**: 275, 1969.
Soulier, G. "Le droit constitutionnel algérien: situation actuelle et perspective", *Revue algérienne des sciences juridiques, économiques et politiques*, **6**: 793, 1969.

ANGOLA — ANGOLA

Carvalhal, J.E. "A legislaçao vigente em Angola em face dos preceitos da Convençao International do Trabalho n. 26", *Trabalho*, **20**: 97, 1967.
Fidalgo, M. "A Evoluçao socio-laboral do Direito de Cabinda apos 1885", *Trabalho*, **20**: 35, 1967.
Mota, M.F. "Demarcaçao de terrenos em Angola. Direitos do requerente", *Scientia Iuridica*, **18**: 228, 1969.

BOTSWANA — BOTSWANA

Crawford, J.R. "The History and Nature of the Judicial System of Botswana, Lesotho and Swaziland — Introduction and the Superior Courts", *South African Law Journal*, **86**: 476, 1969.

Griffiths, J. "A Note on Local Government in Botswana", *Botswana Notes and Records*, **(2)**: 64, 1969.
Roberts, S. "Kgatla Law and Social Change", *Botswana Notes and Records*, **(2)**: 56, 1969.
Roberts, S. "The Malete Law of Contract — A Reply", *Botswana Notes and Records*, **(2)**: 62, 1969.
Schapera, I. "Uniformity and Variation in Chief-made Law: A Tswana Case Study", *Law in Culture and Society*, 230.
Suter, A.C. *Labor Law and Practice in Botswana*, Washington 1968.
Walker, J.M. "Bamalete Contract Law", *Botswana Notes and Records*, **(1)**: 65, 1968.
Werbner, R. "Land and Chiefship in the Tati Concession", *Botswana Notes and Records*, **(2)**: 6, 1969.

BURUNDI — BURUNDI

De Boe, J. "L'engagement à l'essai et le Code du Travail au Burundi", *Revue administrative et juridique du Burundi*, **(3)**: 1, 1969.
De Boe, J. "La protection de la maternité et le Code du Travail au Burundi", *Revue administrative et juridique du Burundi*, **(1)**: 7, 1969.
Helvetius, M. "Fonctionnement de la justice en milieu coutumier au Burundi", *L'organisation judiciaire en Afrique noire*, 227.
Maquet, J. "Institutionalisation féodale des relations de dépendance dans quatre cultures interlacustres", *Cahiers d'études africaines*, **9**: 402, 1969.
Nzeyimana, L. "L'organisation judiciaire du Burundi en matière civile et la réforme du 26 juillet 1962", *Revue juridique et politique, Indépendance et coopération*, **23**: 535, 1969.
Nzeyimana, L. "L'organisation judiciaire du Burundi en matière pénale", *Revue juridique et politique, Indépendance et coopération*, **23**: 729, 1969.
Verbrugghe, A. "La tutelle en droit coutumier rundi", *Revue administrative et juridique du Burundi*, **(2)**: 39, 1969.

CAMEROON — CAMEROUN

Brain, R. "Bangwa (Western Bamileke) Marriage Wards", *Africa*, **39**: 11, 1969.
Crozes, G. "Législation fiscale du Cameroun" *Bulletin for International Fiscal Documentation*, **23**: 204, 1969.
Gonidec, P.F. *La République fédérale du Cameroun*, Paris 1969.
Marticou-Riou, A. "L'organisation judiciaire du Cameroun", *Penant*, **79**: 33, 1969.
Marticou-Riou, A. "Les statuts personnels en République fédérale du Cameroun", *Revue sénégalaise de droit*, **(5)**: 40, 1969.
Mboui, J. "La parenté et la terre dans la stratégie du développement: l'exemple du Sud Cameroun", *Bulletin de l'Association française pour les recherches et études camerounaises*, **4**: 1, 1969.
Ngongang-Ouandji, A. "L'assistance judiciaire et la socialisation de la pratique du droit au Cameroun", *Revue juridique et politique, Indépendance et coopération*, **23**: 1293, 1969.
Ngongang-Ouandji, A. "L'organisation judiciaire du Cameroun en matière pénale", *Revue juridique et politique, Indépendance et coopération*, **23**: 733, 1969.
Ngongang-Ouandi, A. "La juridiction administrative au Cameroun", *Revue juridique et politique, Indépendance et coopération*, **23**: 927, 1969.
Ngongang-Ouandji, A. "Les auxiliaires de la justice au Cameroun", *Revue juridique et politique, Indépendance et coopération*, **23**: 1231, 1969.
Ngongang-Ouandji, A. "Les magistrats au Cameroun", *Revue juridique et politique, Indépendance et coopération*, **23**: 1122, 1969.
Nzouankeu, J.M. "Remarques sur la Constitution camerounaise", *Civilisations* **19**: 216, 1969.

CONGO (BRAZZAVILLE) — CONGO (BRAZZAVILLE)

Gonidec, P.F. "Le Droit et la pratique des conventions collectives de travail au Congo (Brazzaville)", *Penant*, **79**: 279, 1969; **79**: 429, 1969.

Rey, P.P. "Articulation des modes de dépendance et des modes de reproduction dans deux sociétés lignagères", *Cahiers d'études africaines*, **9**: 415, 1969.

CONGO (KINSHASA) — CONGO (KINSHASA)

"A propos du colloque futur sur le droit mortuaire des époux", *Revue juridique du Congo*, **45**: 114, 1969.

Balanda, G. "L'organisation judiciaire chez les Basakata, les Badja et les Baboma", *L'organisation judiciaire en Afrique noire*, 109.

Balanda-Idzumbuir, M.J. "L'établissement de garde et d'éducation de l'Etat de la Kasapa et les mineurs internés", *Problèmes sociaux congolais*, (87): 3, 1969.

Balekomoso, F. "L'organisation judiciaire du Congo-Kinshasa en matière pénale", *Revue juridique et politique, Indépendance et coopération*, **23**: 745, 1969.

Boeck, A. "Auxiliaires de la Justice et représentants de l'Ordre", *Revue juridique du Congo*, **45**: 167, 1969.

Bourland, M. "Les représentants du personnel dans les entreprises congolaises", *Revue du travail*, **70**: 1, 1969.

De Burlet, J. *Précis de droit administratif congolais*, Kinshasa 1969.

De Sousberghe, L. "L'immutabilité de l'alliance dans les sociétés patrilinéaires du Congo", *Anthropos*, **62**: 433, 1967.

Dethier, A. "L'appel en droit judiciaire privé congolais", *Revue juridique du Congo*, **45**: 1, 1969; **45**: 141, 1969; **45**: 234, 1969.

Dupriez, P. "La réforme monétaire du 24 juin 1967 en République démocratique du Congo", *Cahiers économiques et sociaux*, **6**: 72, 1968.

De Wilde, L. "La réforme de la justice au Congo", *L'organisation judiciaire en Afrique noire*, 69.

Herbots, J.H. "La justice de paix dans le nouveau Code de l'organisation et de la compétence judiciaires", *Etudes congolaises*, **12(3)**: 98, 1969.

Joris, A. "Les réglementations congolaises sur les transactions invisibles et leurs effets sur la perception de l'impôt sur le revenu professionnel des entreprises", *Publications de l'Université officielle du Congo*, (19): 215, 1969.

Kalambay, G., Kapeta-Nzovu, H. and Lamy, E. "Analyse statistique de l'activité du Tribunal de Ville de Lubumbashi — 1963 et 1964", *Revue juridique du Congo*, **45**: 80, 1969.

Kanyinda-Lusanga, T. "Les institutions traditionnelles luba — Structures et fonctionnement", *Congo-Afrique*, (34): 187, 1969.

Kikassa, F. and Vundowe, F. "Origines et évolution des institutions communales et urbaines au Congo", *Congo-Afrique*, (29): 449, 1968.

Lejeune, C. "Contentieux financier belgo-congolais", *Revue belge de droit international*, 535, 1969.

Lessedjina, S. "Principes d'organisation des juridictions urbaines au Congo", *L'organisation judiciaire en Afrique noire*, 203.

Mafema, C. "Organisation judiciaire en pays lunda", *L'organisation judiciaire en Afrique noire*, 131.

M'Bela, M.B. "L'évolution et l'organisation du service diplomatique congolais de 1960 à 1968", *Cahiers économiques et sociaux*, **7**: 437, 1969.

Mulumba, C. "Le pouvoir législatif dans la Constitution congolaise du 24 juin 1967", *Cahiers économiques et sociaux*, **7**: 119, 1969.

Pauwels, J. "Les tribunaux coutumiers de Léopoldville: note sur leur histoire et leur activité", *L'organisation judiciaire en Afrique noire*, 215.

Phanzu, V. "Le régime disciplinaire des magistrats en République démocratique du Congo", *Revue juridique et politique, Indépendance et coopération*, **23**: 1132, 1969.

Piron, P. *Introduction au droit congolais*, Louvain 1969–1970.

Promontorio, V. *Les institutions dans la Constitution congolaise*, Kinshasa, s.d.

Rigaux, F. "L'influence des changements de souveraineté territoriale sur les conflits de lois et les conflits de juridiction", *Cahiers économiques et sociaux*, 7: 359, 1969.

Rubbens, A. "La réforme judiciaire du 10 juillet 1968 en République démocratique du Congo", *Cahiers économiques et sociaux*, 7: 411, 1968.

Schmitz, A. "Projet de réforme de la législation forestière en République démocratique du Congo", *Publications de l'Université officielle du Congo*, (19): 151, 1969.

Sibille, P. "Rapports entre les systèmes fiscaux et le développement économique dans les pays en voie de développement. Le cas du Congo-Kinshasa", *Cahiers de droit fiscal international*, 53(1): 97, 1968.

Sibille, P. "Systèmes fiscaux et développement — Le Congo-Kinshasa", *Revue fiscale*, 26: 25, 1969.

Sohier, J. "Remarques sur l'avenir de l'organisation judiciaire en République démocratique du Congo", *L'organisation judiciaire en Afrique noire*, 99.

Vanderlinden, J. "Aspects de la justice indigéne en pays zande en 1956, 1957 et 1958", *L'organisation judiciaire en Afrique noire*, 143.

Vanderlinden, J. *Coutumier, manuel et jurisprudence de droit zande*, Bruxelles 1969.

van Mensel, A. "Arbeidsovereenkomst naar kongolees recht", *Rechtskundig Weekblad*, 32: 1825, 1969.

Verhaegen, J. "Légalité formelle et pays en voie de développement", *Cahiers économiques et sociaux*, 7: 431, 1969.

Vliebergh, H. "Les structures politiques de la République démocratique du Congo", *Revue juridique et politique, Indépendance et coopérations*, 23: 183, 1969.

Vundowe, F. "L'organisation judiciaire du Congo-Kinshasa en matière administrative", *Revue juridique et politique, Indépendance et coopération*, 23: 937, 1969.

Vundowe, F. "L'organisation judiciaire du Congo-Kinshasa en matière civile et la réforme du 10 juillet 1968", *Revue juridique et politique, Indépendance et coopération*, 23: 554, 1969.

Vundowe, F. "L'organisation judiciaire du Congo-Kinshasa en matière pénale", *Revue juridique et politique, Indépendance et coopération*, 23: 757, 1969.

Vundowe, F. "Le rôle de la Cour suprême de justice du Congo-Kinshasa", *Revue juridique et politique, Indépendance et coopération*, 23: 975, 1969.

Yakemtchouk, R. "Le 'bassin conventionnel' du Congo", *Cahiers économiques et sociaux*, 6: 347, 1968.

Zuyderhoff, L. "Note sur l'organisation judiciaire en République du Congo", *L'organisation judiciaire en Afrique noire*, 91.

CÔTE D'IVOIRE — IVORY COAST

Aggrey, A. "L'organisation judiciaire de la Côte d'Ivoire en matière pénale", *Revue juridique et politique, Indépendance et coopération*, 23: 761, 1969.

Aggrey, A. "Les auxiliaires de la justice en Côte d'Ivoire", *Revue juridique et politique, Indépendance et coopération*, 23: 1241, 1969.

Augé, M. "Statut, pouvoir et richesse: relations lignagères, relations de dépendance et rapports de production dans la société alladian", *Cahiers d'études africaines*, 9: 461, 1969.

Basque, E. "L'inspection générale des services administratifs en République de Côte d'Ivoire", *Cahiers africains d'administration publique*, (2B): 32, 1967.

Boni, A. and Goudot, G. "Les nouveaux pouvoirs de la Chambre judiciaire de la Cour suprême en matière pénale d'après l'article 589 bis", *Revue ivoirienne de droit*, 1(4): 13, 1969.

Du Bois, V.D. "Crime and the Treatment of the Criminal in Ivory Coast", *American Universities Field Staff. Reports — West African Series, Vol. 11, 1, Ivory Coast.*

Haeringer, P. "Structures foncières et création urbaine à Abidjan", *Cahiers d'études africaines*, 9: 219, 1969.

Mourgeon, J. *La République de Côte d'Ivoire*, Paris 1969.

Perrot, C.H. "Hommes libres et captifs dans le royaume agni de l'Indiéné", *Cahiers d'études africaines*, 9: 482, 1969.

Snyder, F.G. "L'acculturation juridique du droit forestier au Sénégal et en Côte d'Ivoire", *African Law Studies*, 1(3): 53, 1969.

DAHOMEY — DAHOMEY

Dangou, I. "L'organisation judiciaire dahoméenne en matière pénale", *Revue juridique et politique, Indépendance et coopération*, **23**: 769, 1969.
Glele, M.A. *La République du Dahomey*, Paris 1969.
Houngbedji, A. "La sélection des magistrats au Dahomey", *Revue juridique et politique, Indépendance et coopération*, **23**: 1137, 1969.
Huber, H. "Le principe de la réciprocité dans le mariage nyende", *Africa*, **39**: 260, 1969.

ETHIOPIA — ETHIOPIE

Bilillign Mandefro. "Agricultural Communities and the Civil Code", *Journal of Ethiopian Law*, **6**: 175, 1969.
Bodman, T.P. "Income Tax Exemption as an Incentive to Investment in Ethiopia", *Journal of Ethiopian Law*, **6**: 215, 1969.
Doresse, J. "Les nouveaux accords culturels franco-éthiopiens", *Revue juridique et politique, Indépendance et coopération*, **23**: 383, 1969.
Assafa Dula. "Land Tenure in Chercher Province", *Ethiopia Observer*, **12**(2): 137, 1968.
The Fetha Nagast, Law of Kings, Addis-Ababa 1969.
Fisher, S.Z. *Ethiopian Criminal Procedure: A Source Book*, Addis-Ababa 1969.
Geraghty, T.F. "Field Research in Ethiopian Law", *African Law Studies*, **1**(3): 17, 1969.
Krzeczunowicz, G. "The Present Role of Equity in Ethiopian Civil Law", *Journal of African Law*, **13**: 145, 1969.
Leclercq, C. *L'Empire d'Ethiopie*, Paris 1969.
Pankhurst, R. "Tribute, Taxation and Government Revenues in Nineteenth and Early Twentieth Century Ethiopia", *Journal of Ethiopian Studies*, **5**: 37, 1967; **6**: 21, 1968; **6**: 93, 1968.
Sand, P.H. "Reform des äthiopischen Erbrechts — Problematik einer synthetischen Rezeption", *Rabels Zeitschrift für ausländisches und internationales Privatrecht*, **33**: 413, 1969.
Schiller, A. "Customary Land Tenure among the Highland Peoples of Northern Ethiopia", *African Law Studies*, **(1)**: 1, 1969.
Schwab, P. "The Agricultural Income Tax and the Changing Role of Parliament in Ethiopia", *Genève Afrique*, **8**: 34, 1969.
Ullendorff, E. "The Anglo-Ethiopian Treaty of 1902", *Bulletin of S.O.A.S.*, **30**: 641, 1968.
Vanderlinden, J. *The Law of Physical Persons*, Addis-Ababa 1969.
Yohannes Berhane, *Delict and Torts*, Asmara 1969.

GABON — GABON

Augé, L. "De la formation des magistrats gabonais", *Revue juridique et politique, Indépendance et coopération*, **23**: 1153, 1969.
Mangongo-Nzambi, A. "La délimitation des frontières du Gabon (1885–1911)" *Cahiers d'études africaines*, **9**: 5, 1969.

GAMBIA — GAMBIE

Cissoko, S.M. "La royauté chez les Mandingues occidentaux d'après leurs traditions orales", *Bulletin de l'IFAN*, **21**(B): 325, 1969.

GHANA — GHANA

Acquaye, E. "The Administration and Development of Stool Land in Ghana", *Review of Ghana Law*, **1**: 174, 1969.
Amissah, A.N.E. "The Police and the Courts", *Review of Ghana Law*, **1**: 31, 1969.
Asante, S.K.B. "Interests in Land in the Customary Law of Ghana", *University of Ghana Law Journal*, **6**: 99, 1969.

Audat, P.L. and Obeng, A. "Structure and Resources of Regional and Local Administrations in Ghana and the Role of these Administrations in Regional and Local Development", *Cahiers africains d'administration publique*, **(1B)**: 29, 1967.

Brobbey, S.A. "Actions for Maintenance of Children", *Review of Ghana Law*, **1**: 74, 1969.

Brobbey, S.A. "A Disgression on Proof. Is Majolagbe v. Larbi dead?", *Review of Ghana Law*, **1**: 152, 1969.

Daniels, W.C.E. "Signing a Divorce Petition", *Review of Ghana Law*, **1**: 148, 1969.

Das Gupta, P. "The Ghana Constitution: An Assessment", *Africa Quarterly*, **9**: 220, 1969.

Date-Bah, S.K. "Tsede v. Nubuasa: A Welcome Inroad into the Doctrine of Consideration", *University of Ghana Law Journal*, **6**: 60, 1969.

Dei-Anang, K.K. "The Pre-Incorporation Contract and Section 13 of the Companies Code", *University of Ghana Law Journal*, **6**: 1, 1969.

"Divorce Jurisdiction — What Basis?", *Review of Ghana Law*, **1**: 235, 1969.

Fiadjoe, A. "Juliana Ashong v. Daniel Cobblah Ashong: An Exercise in Excessive Judicial Caution", *University of Ghana Law Journal*, **6**: 53, 1969.

Fiadjoe, A. "The Pre-Incorporation Contract and Section 13 of the Companies Code — A Rejoinder", *University of Ghana Law Journal*, **6**: 140, 1969.

Fiadjoe, A. "Recent Judicial Pronouncements on Matrimonial Property", *Review of Ghana Law*, **1**: 62, 1969.

Goody, J. " 'Normative', 'Recollected' and 'Actual' Marriage Payments Among the Lowili of Northern Ghana", *Africa*, **39**: 54, 1969.

Hellawell, R. "Taxation and Economic Development", *University of Ghana Law Journal*, **6**: 89, 1969.

Heydon, J.D. "Gratuitous Options: Section 8(1) of the Contracts Act, *University of Ghana Law Journal*, **6**: 40, 1969.

Kom, E.D. "Declaration of Title to Land", *University of Ghana Law Journal*, **6**: 18, 1969.

Kyerematen, A. "The Royal Stools of Ashanti", *Africa*, **39**: 1, 1969.

Mensah-Brown, A.K. "Chiefs and the Law in Ghana", *Journal of African Law* **13**: 57, 1969.

Miracle, M.P. and Seidman, A. *State Farms in Ghana*, Madison 1968.

Narayan, K. "Extension of Time within Which to Appeal", *Review of Ghana Law*, **1**: 225, 1969.

Nukunya, G.K. *Kinship and Marriage among the Anlo Ewe*, London 1969.

Ofori-Boateng, J. "Ejectment Orders and Procedure Under the Rent Act 1963 (Act 220)", *Review of Ghana Law*, **1**: 87, 1969.

Ofosu-Amaah, G.K.A. "Law Reform Commission — N.L.C.D 288", *University of Ghana Law Journal*, **6**: 142, 1969.

Osew, E.A. "The Role of a Parliamentary Commissioner", *Review of Ghana Law*, **1**: 45, 1969.

Police and Crime", *Review of Ghana Law*, **1**: 122, 1969.

Quist, C.C. "Professional Conduct and Etiquette", *Review of Ghana Law*, **1**: 71, 1969.

"Registration of Churches and Other Social Organisations", *Review of Ghana Law*, **1**: 115, 1969.

Seidman, R.B. "A Note on the Construction of the Gold Coast Reception Statute", *Journal of African Law*, **13**: 45, 1969.

Tetteh, E.K. "Extorting Property by Threats", *Review of Ghana Law*, **1**: 230, 1969.

Tetteh, E.K. "Quicquid plantatur solo, solo cedit", *Review of Ghana Law*, **1**: 151, 1969.

Tetteh, E.K. "Refusal to Be Sworn", *Review of Ghana Law*, **1**: 214, 1969.

"Titles of Cases: Different Names for the Same Legal Personality", *Review of Ghana Law*, **1**: 183, 1969.

Twumasi, Y. "Ghana's Draft Constitutional Proposals", *Transition*, **7(6)**: 43, 1968.

Woodman, G.R. "Common Customs bf Ghana: Common Law or Customary Law?", *University of Ghana Law Journal*, **5**: 1, 1968.

Woodman, G.R. "Estoppel by Judicial Decision in Ghana", *Journal of African Law*, **13**: 80, 1969.

Woodman, G.R. "Palliatives for Uncertainty of Title: The Land Development (Protection of Purchasers) Act 1960 and The Farm Lands (Protection) Act 1962", *University of Ghana Law Journal*, **6**: 146, 1969.

Woodman, G.R. "Two Problems of Matrilineal Succession", *Review of Ghana Law*, **1**: 1, 1969.

Zabel, S. "The Legislative History of the Gold Coast and Nigerian Marriage Ordinances", *Journal of African Law*, **13**: 64, 1969; **13**: 158, 1969.

GUINÉE — GUINEA

Ernst, J. "Parlament und Verfassung im progressistischen Guinea", *Afrika Spectrum*, **4(1)**: 18, 1969.

Gulphe, P. "Réflexions sur la législation guinéenne en matière de mariage", *Annales africaines*, 89, 1969.

GUINÉ ECUATORIAL — EQUATORIAL GUINEA

Dilg, K.G. "Die Verfassung der Republik Äquatorial — Guinea unter besonderer Berücksichtigung der politischen und verfassungsmässigen Entwicklung bis zur Unabhängigkeit im Jahre 1968", *Verfassung und Recht in Uebersee*, **2**: 291, 1969.

Zaragoza, J. de M. "La république de Guinée Equatoriale", *Revue juridique et politique, Indépendance et coopération*, **23**: 213, 1969.

GUINÉ PORTUGUESA — PORTUGUESE GUINEA

Da Silva, A.A. "Usose Costumes juridicos dos Mandingas", *Boletim Cultural da Guiné Portuguesa*, **24**: 5, 1969.

KENYA — KENYA

Abel R.L. "A Bibliography of the Customary Laws of Kenya", *African Law Studies*, **(2)**: 1, 1969.

Abel, R.L. "Case Method Research in the Customary Laws of Wrongs in Kenya", *East African Law Journal*, **5**: 247, 1969.

Abel, R.L. "Customary Laws of Wrongs in Kenya", *American Journal of Comparative Law*, **17**: 573, 1969.

Anderson, J.N.D. "Comments with Reference to the Muslim Community", *East African Law Journal*, **5**: 5, 1969.

Bayne, P.J. "Administrative Authorities and Government Policy", *Eastern Africa Law Review*, **2**: 343, 1969.

Cotran, E. *Restatement of African Law, Kenya, vol. 2, The Law of Succession*, London 1969.

Derrett, J.D.M. "Comments with Reference to Hindu Law", *East African Law Journal*, **5**: 21, 1969.

Devine, D.J. "International Law Implications of the Commonwealth Immigrants Act, 1968", *Acta juridica*, 101, 1968.

Durand, P.P. *Index of East African Cases Referred to 1868–1968*, Nairobi 1968.

Fliedner, H. "Die Wandlung der Agrarstruktur in Kenia", *Geographische Rundschau*, **20(3)**: 81, 1968.

Ghai, Y.P. "Judicial Protection of the Individual against the Executive in Kenya", *Gerichtsschutz gegen die Executive*, 599.

Hall, P.A. "District Magistrate Training in Kenya", *East African Law Journal*, **5**: 299, 1969.

James, R.W. " 'Benami' and the Equitable Doctrine of Resulting Trust", *Journal of the Denning Law Society*, **2(2)**: 106, 1969.

Kahn-Freund, O. "Law Reform in Kenya", *East African Law Journal*, **5**: 54, 1969.

Kassam, F.M. "Report of the Kenya Commission on Marriage and Divorce: A Critique", *Eastern Africa Law Review*, **2**: 179, 1969.

Kassam, F.M. "Comments on the White Paper", *Eastern Africa Law Review*, **2**: 329, 1969.

Legal and Economic Factors Relating to Mineral Development in Kenya, Nairobi 1967.

Le Pelley, P. "Vagrancy and the Law in Kenya", *East African Law Journal*, **5**: 195, 1969.

Le Pelley, P. "A Practitioner's Comments on the Marriage and Divorce Report", *East African Law Journal*, **5**: 141, 1969.

Okoth-Ogendo, H.W.O. "Land Tenure and Agricultural Development in Kenya and Tanzania", *Journal of the Denning Law Society*, **2**(2): 30, 1969.

Ollennu, N.A. "Comments with Special Reference to Customary Law", *East African Law Journal*, **5**: 97, 1969.

Patel, L.R. "The Interaction of Social and Economic Forces with the Legal Order", *Journal of the Denning Law Society*, **2**(2): 143, 1969.

Patel, L.R. "The Report of the Kenya Commission on the Law of Succession: A Comment", *Eastern Africa Law Review*, **2**: 221, 1969.

Read, J.S. " 'Living on Her Own Immoral Earnings', Karuria v. Republic", *East African Law Journal*, **5**: 214, 1969.

Read, J.S. "Marriage and Divorce: A New Look for the Law in Kenya", *East African Law Journal*, **5**: 107, 1969.

Schiller, A.A. "The Draft Legislation and Customary Law", *East African Law Journal*, **5**: 88, 1969.

Singh, C. "Hindu Law in Kenya", *East African Law Journal*, **5**: 310, 1969.

Wako, S.A. "An Assessment of the Marriage and Divorce Commission Report in Kenya", *Journal of the Denning Law Society*, **2**(2): 73, 1969.

Whetham, E. "Land Reform and Resettlement in Kenya", *East African Journal of Rural Development*, **1**(1): 18, 1968.

LESOTHO — LESOTHO

Crawford, J.R. "The History and Nature of the Judicial System of Botswana, Lesotho and Swaziland — Introduction and the Superior Courts", *South African Law Journal*, **86**: 476, 1969.

Poulter, S. "The Common Law in Lesotho", *Journal of African Law*, **13**: 127, 1969.

Proctor, J.H. "Building a Constitutional Monarchy in Lesotho", *Civilisations*, **19**: 64, 1969.

LIBERIA — LIBERIA

Barndt, R.V. "The Liberian World of Promise", *Liberian Law Journal*, **5**: 1, 1969.

Gibbs, J.L. Jr. "Law and Personality: Signposts for a New Direction", *Law in Culture and Society*, 176.

Grimes, L.A. *Reports and Opinions of the Attorney-General of the Republic of Liberia, 1922–1930*, Ithaca 1969.

Liberian Law Reports — Cumulative Index and Table of Cases (1861–1964), Ithaca 1969.

Pierre, J.A.A. *Opinions of the Attorney-General of the Republic of Liberia, 1964–1968*, Ithaca 1969.

Topor, W. "Stammesgerichtsbarkeit und staatliche Gerichtsbarkeit in Liberia", *Zeitschrift für das gesamte Familienrecht*, **81**: 488, 1969.

MADAGASCAR — MADAGASCAR

Cadoux, C. *La République malgache*, Paris 1969.

Comte, J. *Les communes à Madagascar*, Tananarive 1967.

Decary, R. "Le règlement des affaires en brousse sous l'ancienne administration française", *Cahiers du Centre d'étude des coutumes*, (5–6): 7, 1968–1969.

"Enquête sur le mariage effectuée en pays merina", *Cahiers du Centre d'études des coutumes*, (5–6): 89, 1968–1969.

Faublée, J. "Les bases religieuses du droit malgache", *Annuaire 1967–1968, Ecole pratique des hautes études Vème section, sciences religieuses*, 93, 1967.

Germishuizen, W.A. "A Factual and Legal Survey of the Republic of Malagasy's Role as Trading Partner in Southern Africa", *Comparative and International Law Journal of Southern Africa*, **2**: 188, 1969.

Guichon, A. "La législation et la réglementation de l'exploitation forestière à Madagascar et leur application", *Terre malgache*, (**6**): 137, 1969.

Guichon, A. "Note sur le régime domanial des forêts malgaches", *Terre malgache*, (**4**): 219, 1968.

Cherkaoui, A. *Le contrôle de l'Etat sur la commune*, Rabat 1968.

Guth, J.M. "Le code pénal malgache de 1962 et les problèmes posés par sa réforme", *Revue internationale de criminologie et de police technique*, **23**: 195, 1969.

Hébert, J.C. "Moeurs et coutumes des Sandrangoatsy", *Cahiers du Centre d'étude des coutumes*, (**5–6**): 21, 1968–1969.

Hébert, J.C. "Coutumes de l'Ambongo", *Cahiers du Centre d'étude des coutumes*, (**5–6**): 165, 1968–1969.

Jamet, L. "L'Assemblée nationale malgache", *Annales malgaches — Droit*, (**6**): 177, 1969.

Massiot, M. *Guide formulaire d'actes*, Tananarive 1967.

Massiot M. *Les institutions politiques et administratives de la République malgache*, Tananarive 1967.

"La mort d'un roi Antaisaka: prétexte à documentation", *Cahiers du Centre d'études des coutumes*, (**5–6**): 177, 1968–1969.

Pain, G. "Le procès des francs-maçons contre les jésuites à Madagascar de 1891 à 1892", *Bulletin de l'Académie malgache*, **45(1)**: 57, 1967.

Ramangasoavina, A. "L'assistance judiciaire et la socialisation de la pratique du droit à Madagascar", *Revue juridique et politique, Indépendance et coopération*, **23**: 1296, 1969.

Ramangasoavina, A. "L'emploi de professionnels non-juristes dans l'administration de la justice civile à Madagascar", *Revue juridique et politique, Indépendance et coopération*, **23**: 1219, 1969.

Ramangasoavina, A. "L'organisation judiciaire malgache en matière civile", *Revue juridique et politique, Indépendance et coopération*, **23**: 566, 1969.

Ramangasoavina, A. "L'organisation judiciaire malgache en matière pénale", *Revue juridique et politique, Indépendance et coopération*, **23**: 785, 1969.

Ramangasoavina, A. "Le corps des magistrats malgaches", *Revue juridique et politique, Indépendance et coopération*, **23**: 1155, 1969.

Ramangasoavina, A. "Note sur l'organisation judiciaire malgache", *L'organisation judiciaire en Afrique noire*, 271.

Ramangasoavina, A. "Le rôle de la Cour suprême dans l'évolution du droit privé à Madagascar", *Revue juridique et politique, Indépendance et coopération*, **23**: 995, 1969.

Ramangasoavina, A. "Le rôle de la Cour suprême de Madagascar en matière politique", *Revue juridique et politique, Indépendance et coopération*, **23**: 978, 1969.

Rodiere, R. "Un nouveau code de droit maritime: le Code privé malgache", *Droit maritime français*, **19**: 115, 1967.

Rouhette, A. "Remarques sur les régimes matrimoniaux non-mérina", *Cahiers du Centre d'étude des coutumes*, (**5–6**): 49, 1968–1969.

MALAWI — MALAWI

The African Law Reports — Malawi 1961–1963, Dobbs Ferry 1969.

MALI — MALI

Diarra, T.D. "La juridiction administrative au Mali", *Revue juridique et politique, Indépendance et coopération*, **23**: 939, 1969.

Diarra, T.D. "L'organisation judiciaire du Mali en matière pénale", *Revue juridique et politique, Indépendance et coopération*, **23**: 801, 1969.

MAROC — MOROCCO

Caillé, J. *Le Consulat de Tanger (des origines à 1830)*, Paris 1967.

Decroux, P. "La délégation de pouvoir au Maroc", *Revue juridique et politique, Indépendance et coopération*, **23**: 357, 1969.

Dubois, A. "Association de la Tunisie et du Maroc à la Communauté", *Revue du Marché commun*, 355, 1969.
Khattabi, M. "L'organisation judiciaire marocaine en matière civile", *Revue juridique et politique, Indépendance et coopération*, **23**: 577, 1969.
Khattabi, M. "L'organisation judiciaire marocaine en matière pénale", *Revue juridique et politique, Indépendance et coopération*, **23**: 804, 1969.
Khattabi, M. "Le rôle de la Cour suprême marocaine", *Revue juridique et politique, Indépendance et coopération*, **23**: 999, 1969.
Mennens, E. "Associatieovereenkomsten tussen de E.E.G. en Tunisië en Marokko", *Sociaal-Economische Wetgeving*, **17**: 562, 1969.
Rousset, M. "L'administration marocaine", *Bulletin de l'Institut international d'administration publique*, **12**: 7, 1969.
Rousset, M. "L'exception de recours parallèle dans le contentieux administratif du Maroc", *Revue juridique et politique, Indépendance et coopération*, **23**: 367, 1969.

MAURITANIE — MAURETANIA

Piquemal-Pastre, M. *La République islamique de Mauritanie*, Paris, 1969.
Sy, S.M. "La loi mauritanienne du 11 juillet 1967 portant loi organique relative aux lois de finances", *Revue sénégalaise de droit*, **(6)**: 5, 1969.
Tandia, Y. "Les juridictions pénales en République islamique de Mauritanie", *Revue juridique et politique, Indépendance et coopération*, **23**: 817, 1969.
Tandia, Y. "Les juridictions civiles en République islamique de Mauritanie", *Revue juridique et politique, Indépendance et coopération*, **23**: 597, 1969.

NIGER — NIGER

Dandobi, M. "L'organisation judiciaire du Niger en matière pénale", *Revue juridique et politique, Indépendance et coopération*, **23**: 819, 1969.
Murphy, R.F. "Tuareg Kinship", *American Anthropologist*, **69**: 163, 1967.

NIGERIA — NIGERIA

Adaramaja, A. " 'Character' as a Basis of Criminal Liability in Nigerian Law", *Nigerian Law Journal*, **3**: 116, 1969.
Adegbite, L.O. "Civil Suits by and against Public Corporations", *Nigerian Law Journal*, **3**: 41, 1969.
Adejuyigbe, O. "Local Boundary Disputes in Western Nigeria: The Example of Edunabon Enclave", *ODU*, N.S. **(2)**: 78, 1969.
Adeogun, A.A. "The Legal Framework of Industrial Relations in Nigeria", *Nigerian Law Journal*, **3**: 13, 1969.
Adesanya, S.A. "The Exclusion of the Application of the Nigerian Codified Form of Common Law of Evidence from the Customary Courts and the Machinery for Filling the Gaps", *Northern Ireland Legal Quarterly*, **20**: 349, 1969.
Adesanya, S.A. "Marriage According to the Local Islamic Rites of Southern Nigeria", *Journal of Islamic and Comparative Law*, **2**: 26, 1968.
Adeyemi, A.A. "The Age of Criminal Responsibility — A Research Design", *Lagos Notes and Records*, **2(1)**: 13, 1968.
Akande, J.O. "The Rights of Women in Property in Nigeria", *Lagos Notes and Records*, **2(1)**: 15, 1968.
Akanki, O. "Reflections on Some Recent Constitutional Issues in Nigeria", *Nigerian Law Journal*, **3**: 102, 1969.
Commission of Inquiry into the Selection of an Alafin of Oyo, Ibadan 1969.
Elias, T.O. *The Prison System in Nigeria*, Lagos 1968.
Heidelberg, W. "Einige Bemerkungen zur Reform der Gesellschaftsrechts in Nigeria", *Afrika Spectrum*, **4(1)**: 44, 1969.
Hill, D.J. and Abbas, A.S. "Comparative Survey of the Islamic Law and the Common Law Relating to the Sale of Goods", *Journal of Islamic and Comparative Law*, **2**: 88, 1968.

Ijaodola, J.O. "The Proper Place of Islamic Law in Nigeria", *Nigerian Law Journal*, 3: 129, 1969.

Jegede, M.I. " 'Equity' and Nigerian Law", *Nigerian Law Journal*, 3: 57, 1969.

Kanam, Y.M. "The Effect of Custom on Certain Aspects of Maliki Law in the Northern States of Nigeria", *Journal of Islamic and Comparative Law*, 2: 79, 1968.

Kasunmu, A.B. "Admissibility of Illegally Obtained Evidence in Nigeria", *Nigerian Law Journal*, 3: 83, 1969.

Kasunmu, A.B. "Proof of a Polygamous Marriage in Nigerian High Courts: Lawal and Others v. Younan and Others Re-examined", *Journal of Islamic and Comparative Law*, 3: 27, 1969.

Kermode, D.G. "Parliamentary Control of the Executive in Nigeria", *Nigerian Journal of Economic and Social Studies*, 10: 261, 1968.

Kirk-Greene, A.H.M. "Administrative Training in Africa: the Northern Nigerian Experience and Beyond", *International Review of Administrative Sciences*, 35: 19, 1969.

Lloyd, P.C. "Divorce Among the Yoruba", *American Anthropologist*, 70: 67, 1968.

Madauci, I., Isa, Y. and Daura, B. *Mansa Customs*, Zaria 1968.

Marasinghe, M.L. "Monogamy, Polygamy and Bigamy", *Journal of Islamic and Comparative Law*, 2: 54, 1968.

Markov, W. and Sebald, P. "The Treaty Between Germany and the Sultan of Gwandu", *Journal of the Historical Society of Nigeria*, 4(1): 141, 1967.

Muller, J.C. "Preferential Marriage Among the Rukuba of Benue-Plateau State, Nigeria", *American Anthropologist*, 71: 1057, 1969.

Netting, R.McC. "Women's Weapons: The Politics of Domesticity Among the Kofyar", *American Anthropologist*, 71: 1037, 1969.

Nienhaus, M. "Die Verwaltungsreformen in Nordnigeria", *Internationales Afrika Forum*, 5: 439, 1969.

Nigerian Press Law, Lagos 1969.

Obilade, A.O. "Reform of Customary Court Systems in Nigeria under the Military Government", *Journal of African Law*, 13: 28, 1969. *The same* in *Nigerian Law Journal*, 3: 141, 1969.

Ogunbiyi, I.A. "The Position of Muslim Women as Stated by Uthman b. Fudi", *ODU*, N.S. (2): 43, 1969.

Ojo, A.O. "Law Making in Nigeria", *Lagos Notes and Records*, 2(1): 15, 1968.

Ojo, A.O. "Judicial Approach to Customary Law", *Journal of Islamic and Comparative Law*, 3: 44, 1969.

Okogwu, L.E. *The Legal Status of the Aliens in Nigeria*, Bern 1969.

Orojo, J.O. *A Guide to Insurance Claims*, London 1969.

Orojo, J.O. *A Guide to the Conduct and Etiquette of Legal Practitioners*, London 1969.

Phillips, A. "The Significance of Nigeria's Income Tax Relief Incentive", *Nigerian Journal of Economic and Social Studies*, 11: 143, 1969.

Phillips, A. "Nigeria's Experience with Income Tax Exemption", *Nigerian Journal of Economic and Social Studies*, 10: 33, 1968.

Phillips, A. "Nigeria's Companies Income Tax", *Nigerian Journal of Economic and Social Studies*, 10: 321, 1968.

Phillips, A. "Nigerian Industrial Tax Incentives: Import Duties Relief and the Approved User Scheme", *Nigerian Journal of Economic and Social Studies*, 9: 315, 1967.

Sangree, W.H. "Going Home to Mother: Traditional Marriage among the Irigwe of Benue-Plateau State, Nigeria", *American Anthropologist*, 71: 1046, 1969.

Symposium on Human Rights in Nigeria, Lagos 1968.

Tamuno, T.N. "The Role of the Legislative Council in the Administration of Lagos 1886–1913", *Journal of the Historical Society of Nigeria*, 4(4): 555, 1969.

Taylor, M.C. "The Relationship between Income Tax Administration and Income Tax Policy in Nigeria", *Nigerian Journal of Economic and Social Studies*, 8: 203, 1967.

Teriba, O. "The 1967–1969 Banking Amendments in Nigeria", *Nigerian Journal of Economic and Social Studies*, 11: 43, 1969.

Zabel, S.C. "Hyde v. Hyde in Africa: A Comparative Study of the Law of Marriage in Sudan and Nigeria", *Utah Law Review*, (1): 22, 1969.
Zabel, S.C. "The Legislative History of the Gold Coast and Nigerian Marriage Ordinances", *Journal of African Law*, 13: 64, 1969; 13: 158, 1969.

REPUBLIQUE CENTRAFRICAINE — CENTRAL AFRICAN REPUBLIC

Gon, F. "L'organisation de la justice administrative en République centrafricaine", *Revue juridique et politique, Indépendance et coopération*, 23: 929, 1969.
Gon, F. "L'organisation judiciaire centrafricaine en matière civile", *Revue juridique et politique, Indépendance et coopération*, 23: 543, 1969.
Potolot, J. "L'organisation judiciaire de la République centrafricaine en matière pénale", *Revue juridique et politique, Indépendance et coopération*, 23: 737, 1969.

REPUBLIQUE VOLTAIQUE — VOLTA REPUBLIC

Hochet, J. "Inadaptation sociale et délinquance juvénile en Haute Volta", *Recherches voltaïques*, 9: 1, 1968.
Pageard, R. "Le droit privé des Mossi — Tradition et évolution". *Recherches voltaïques*, 10: 1, 1969.
Zongo, F.-X. "L'organisation judiciaire voltaïque en matière pénale", *Revue juridique et politique, Indépendance et coopération*, 23: 779, 1969.

RHODESIA — RHODESIE

Baron, L.S. "The Rhodesian Saga", *Zambia Law Journal*, 1(1): 36, 1969.
Boothby, P. "The Deflected Blow: Aberratio Ictus", *Rhodesian Law Journal*, 8: 19, 1968.
Brookfield, F.M. "The Courts, Kelsen and the Rhodesian Revolution", *University of Toronto Law Journal*, 19: 326, 1969.
Bruckner, P. "Sydrhodesia of FN.", *Nordisk Tidsskrift for International Ret og Jus Gentium*, 239, 1967.
Christie, R.H. "Banker and Customer: Some Recent Developments", *Rhodesian Law Journal*, 8: 40, 1968.
Christie, R.H. "Practical Jurisprudence in Rhodesia", *Comparative and International Law Journal of Southern Africa*, 2: 3, 1969; 2: 206, 1969.
Devine, D.J. "Does South Africa Recognize Rhodesian Independence?", *South African Law Journal*, 86: 438, 1969.
Devine, D.J. "Rhodesia and the United Nations: The Lawfulness of International Concern — A Qualification", *Comparative and International Law Journal of Southern Africa*, 2: 454, 1969.
Eekelaar, J.M. "Rhodesia: The Abdication of Constitutionalism", *Modern Law Review*, 32: 19, 1969.
Green, L.C. "Rhodesian Independence: Legal or Illegal?", *Alberta Law Review*, 6: 37, 1968.
Green, L.C. "Southern Rhodesian Independence", *Archiv des Völkerrechts*, 14: 155, 1969.
Hahlo, H.R. "The Privy Council and the Gentle Revolution", *South African Law Journal*, 86: 419, 1969.
Harris, P.B. "The Failure of a 'Constitution': The Whaley Report, Rhodesia 1968", *International Affairs*, 45: 234, 1969.
Jaffey, A.J.E. "The Rhodesian Constitutional Cases", *Rhodesian Law Journal*, 8: 138, 1969.
Lang, A.J.G. "The Validity of Municipal Legislation and Ignorance of the Law", *Rhodesian Law Journal*, 8: 172, 1968.
McDougal, M.S. Marshall, C.B. and Reisman, W.M. "Arrogance of International Lawyers", *International Lawyer*, 2: 591, 1968; 2: 729, 1968; 3: 435, 1969.
Mittlebeeler, E.V. "Race and Jury in Rhodesia", *Howard Law Journal*, 15: 181, 1969.

Molteno, D.B. "The Rhodesian Crisis and the Courts", *Comparative and International Law Journal of Southern Africa*, 2: 254, 1969; 2: 404, 1969.
Powell, J.T. "U.S. Television and Southern Rhodesia: In issues of Basic Rights", *Federal Communications Bar Journal*, –: 122, 1969.
Silberberg, H. "The Economics of Standard Contracts", *Rhodesian Law Journal*, 8: 89, 1968.
Silberberg, H. "Problems of Individual Flat Ownership", *Rhodesian Law Journal*, 8: 161, 1968.
Spafford, D.H. "Death Duties", *Rhodesian Law Journal*, 8: 56, 1968.
Van Wyk, A.J. "Rhodesia Constitutional Proposals", *Africa Institute Bulletin*, 7: 19, 1969.

RWANDA — RWANDA

Gatwa, T. "Le régime disciplinaire des magistrats rwandais", *Revue juridique et politique, Indépendance et coopération*, 23: 1179, 1969.
Gatwa, T. "L'organisation judiciaire de la République rwandaise en matière pénale", *Revue juridique et politique, Indépendance et coopération*, 23: 823, 1969.
Gravel, P.B. "The Transfer of Cows in Gisaka (Rwanda)", *American Anthropologist*, 69: 322, 1967.
Maquet, J. "Institutionalisation féodale des relations de dépendance dans quatre cultures interlacustres", *Cahiers d'études africaines*, 9: 402, 1969.
Vidal, C. "Le Rwanda des anthropologues ou le fétichisme de la vache", *Cahiers d'études africaines*, 9(3): 35, 1969.

SENEGAL — SENEGAL

Aurillac, M. "La cour suprême du Sénégal", *Revue juridique et politique, Indépendance et coopération*, 23: 65, 1969.
Bilbao, R. "Statuts civils et nationalité", *Revue sénégalaise de droit*, (5): 28, 1969.
Bono, S. "L'ordinamento costituzionale del Senegal secondo la revisione della Costituzione del 20 giugno 1967", *Rassegna parlamentare*, 10: 205, 1968.
Bourel, P. "La formation du contrat en droit sénégalais: réflexions sur la modernité du Code des obligations civiles et commerciales", *Revue sénégalaise de droit*, (6): 33, 1969.
Diarra, M. "Rôle constitutionnel de la Cour suprême du Sénégal", *Revue juridique et politique, Indépendance et coopération*, 23: 1004, 1969.
Diop, A. "Les relations entre le pouvoir exécutif et le pouvoir judiciaire au Sénégal", *Revue juridique et politique, Indépendance et coopération*, 23: 1035, 1969.
Diop, A. "L'organisation judiciaire sénégalaise en matière administrative", *Revue juridique et politique, Indépendance et coopération*, 23: 940, 1969.
Gautron, J.C. "Réflexions sur l'autonomie du droit public sénégalais", *Annales africaines*, 29, 1969.
Idowu, H.O. "Assimilation in 19th Century Senegal", *Cahiers d'études africaines*, 9: 194, 1969.
Issa-Sayegh, J. "Arrêts de la Cour d'Appel de Dakar", *Annales africaines*, 101, 1969.
Lavroff, D.G. "Cadre constitutionnel et réalité politique de la République du Sénégal", *Afrika Spectrum*, 4(1): 5, 1969.
Legier, H.J. "Institutions municipales et politique coloniale: les Communes du Sénégal", *Revue française d'histoire d'outremer*, 54: 414, 1968.
Mademba-Sy, S. "La Cour de discipline budgétaire du Sénégal: panorama doctrinal et jurisprudentiel", *Revue sénégalaise de droit*, (5): 5, 1969.
Masseron, J.-P. "Les établissements publics au Sénégal", *Bulletin de l'Institut international d'administration publique*, 11: 74, 1969.
Mollion, J. "La célébration du mariage des étrangers au Sénégal", *Revue sénégalaise de droit*, (6): 55, 1969.
O'Brien, D.C. "Le talibé mouride: étude d'un cas de dépendance sociale", *Cahiers d'études africaines*, 9: 502, 1969.
Pasquier, R. "A propos de l'émancipation des esclaves au Sénégal en 1848", *Revue française d'histoire d'outremer*, 54: 188, 1967.

Raybaud, L.C. "L'administration du Sénégal du 1781 à 1784", *Annales africaines*, –: 173, 1969.
Stamm, A. "La linger, reine des Serer", *Penant*, **79**: 87, 1969.
Sy, S.M. "La révision constitutionnelle du 26 février 1970", *Annales africaines*, –: 9, 1969.

SIERRA LEONE — SIERRA LEONE

The African Law Reports — Sierra Leone 1964–1966, Dobbs Ferry 1969.
Cole, C.O.E. "The Administration of the Law", *Freetown: A Symposium*, 166.
Omu, F.I.A. "The 'New Era' and the Abortive Press Law of 1857", *Sierra Leone Studies*, **(23)**: 2, 1968.

SOMALIA — SOMALIE

Contini, P. *The Somali Republic: An Experiment in Legal Integration*, London 1969.
Pettoello Mantovani, L. *Fasi processuali e processo penale somalo*, Padova 1969.

SOUTH AFRICA — AFRIQUE DU SUD

Adler, C. "Magic, Witchcraft and Medicine", *Lex et Scientia*, **5**: 157, 1968.
Amerasinghe, C.F. "The Concept of Animus Iniurandi", *South African Law Journal*, **86**: 299, 1969.
Amerasinghe, A.R.B. "Adultery as an Injuria in South African and Ceylon Law", *Acta juridica*, 111, 1968.
Apartheid and Racial Discrimination in Southern Africa, New York 1968.
Avins, A. "Racial Separation and Public Accommodations: Some Comparative Notes Between South African and American Law", *South African Law Journal*, **86**: 53, 1969.
Barlow, T.B. and Emmett, M.D. "The Books of an Insolvent Company", *South African Law Journal*, **86**: 444, 1969.
Barlow, T.B. and Emmett, E. *Principles of South African Company Law*, Cape Town 1969.
Barrie, G.N. "Die Bevoegdheid van die Howe om Wette van die Parlement te Toets", *Tydskrif vir Hedendaagse Romeins-Hollands Reg*, **32**: 209, 1969.
Beinart, B. "Fideicommissum and Modus", *Acta juridica*, 157, 1968.
Beuthin, R.C. "The Range of a Company's Interests", *South African Law Journal*, **86**: 155, 1969.
Bisset and Smith's Digest of South African Case Law, Cape Town 1968.
Botha, D.J.J. "Taxation by Local Authorities in South Africa", *South African Journal of Economics*, **37**: 393, 1969.
Carey, J. "United Nations Scrutiny of South African Prisons", *Les droits de l'homme*, **1**: 531, 1968.
Cilliers, H.S. and Benade, M.L. *Maatskappyereg*, Durban 1968.
Coaker, J.F. *Wille and Millin's Mercantile Law of South Africa*, Johannesburg 1967.
Cohen, D. *Amler's Precedents of Pleadings*, Durban 1967.
Copeling, A. "The Nature and Object of Copyright", *Comparative and International Law Journal of Southern Africa*, **2**: 242, 1969.
Copeling, A.J.C. *Copyright Law in South Africa*, Cape Town 1969.
Davenport, R. "African Townsmen? South African Urban Areas Legislation", *African Affairs*, **68**: 95, 1969.
Devine, D.J. "Does South Africa Recognise Rhodesian Independence?", *South African Law Journal*, **86**: 438, 1969.
De Vos, W. "Die Condictio Indebiti van Eksekuteurs, Skuldeisers en bevoordeeldes in die hedendaagse praktyk", *Acta juridica*, 220, 1968.
Diemont, M.A. "Law Teachers and the Law", *Acta juridica*, 1, 1968.
Dugard, C.J.R. "South-West Africa and the Supremacy of the South African Parliament", *South African Law Journal*, **86**: 194, 1969.
El Chafei, B. "Crise des droits de l'homme en Afrique du Sud", *Revue "Al Qanoun Wal Iqtisad"*, **39**: 727, 1969.

Elliott, R.C. and Banwell, E. *The South African Notary*, Cape Town 1969.

Erosion of the Rule of Law in South Africa, Geneva 1968.

Evans, S. *New Management Committees in Local Government*, Cape Town 1969.

Findlay, G. "A Proper Basis for Water Rights", *Tydskrif vir Hedendaagse Romeins-Hollands Reg*, **32**: 338, 1969.

Germishuizen, W.A. "A Factual and Legal Survey of the Republic of Malagasy's Role as Trading Partner in Southern Africa", *Comparative and International Law Journal of Southern Africa*, **2**: 118, 1969.

Gerntholtz, R.O.P. "Are Medical Methods Patentable?", *Tydskrif vir Hedendaagse Romeins-Hollands Reg*, **32**: 242, 1969.

Gilmour, D.R. "United Nations and Apartheid — Certain Procedural Aspects of the Problem", *Netherlands International Law Review*, **16**: 12, 1969.

Goodman, I. *Judges I Have Known*, Cape Town 1969.

Gordon, G. and Getz, W.S. *The South African Law of Insurance*, Cape Town 1969.

Gordon, R. "A Plea for the Acceptance of Bantu Law by Our Courts", *Responsa Meridiana*, **2**: 31, 1969.

Gross, F.A. *Who Hangs the Hangman?*, Cape Town 1967.

Hahlo, H.R. *Company Law through the Cases*, Cape Town 1969.

Hahlo, H. and Kahn E. *The South African Law of Husband and Wife*, Cape Town 1969.

Henning, P. "Thoughts on Administrative Law", *Comparative and International Law Journal of Southern Africa*, **2**: 86, 1969.

Heyl, J.W.S. "Oordrag aan Gesamentlike Boedels", *Tydskrif vir Hedendaagse Romeins-Hollands Reg*, **32**: 226, 1969.

Heyne, J.F. "Republic of South Africa v. Sea-Polluters and Others", *Comparative and International Law Journal of Southern Africa*, **2**: 290, 1969.

Hiemstra, V.G. *Suid-Afrikaanse Strafproces*, Durban 1967.

Honoré, A.M. "Honoré's Views on Trust Law — A Reply", *Tydskrif vir Hedendaagse Romeins-Hollands Reg*, **32**: 126, 1969.

Hoppenstein, A.S. "The Formation, Presentation and Resistance of Third Party Claims", *Tydskrif vir Hedendaagse Romeins-Hollands Reg*, **32**: 153, 1969.

Joubert, D.J. "Contracts Between Doctors and Patients", *South African Law Journal*, **86**: 290, 1969.

Joubert, D.J. "Die Onherroeplike Volmag", *Tydskrif vir Hedendaagse Romeins-Hollands Reg*, **32**: 263, 1969.

Joubert, D.J. "Die Waarborg van Volmagsbestaan", *Tydskrif vir Hedendaagse Romeins-Hollands Reg*, **32**: 109, 1969.

Kerr, A.J. "The Courts and the Law", *South African Law Journal*, **86**: 179, 1969.

Kerr, A.J. *The Law of Lease*, Durban 1969.

Klopper, C.F. "Artikel 36 van Wet n° 62 van 1955", *Tydskrif vir Hedendaagse Romeins-Hollands Reg*, **32**: 50, 1969.

Krogh, D.C. "Taxation in a Developing Economy", *South African Journal of Economics*, **37**: 285, 1969.

Kuper, A. "The Work of Customary Courts: Some Facts and Speculations", *African Studies*, **28**: 37, 1969.

Levine, R.D. "A Comparison Between Anglo-American and South African Proxy Voting Provisions", *Comparative and International Law Journal of South Africa*, **2**: 363, 1969.

Maister, P. "Judicial Attitudes to Race in South Africa", *Responsa Meridiana*, **2**: 1, 1969.

Malpica de Lamadrid, L. "Sudafrica, el Comité olimpico internacional y la posicion de Mexico", *Revista de Ciencias juridicas*, **(13)**: 73, 1969.

Morris, E. *Technique in Litigation*, Cape Town 1969.

Morsbach, H. and G. "Attitudes Towards Capital Punishment in South Africa", *British Journal of Criminology*, 394, 1967.

Mostert, D.F. *Die Romeins-Hollands Reg in Oënskou*, Pretoria 1969.

Mostert, D.F. "Vitwinning by die Koopkontrak in die Suid-Afrikaanse Reg", *Acta juridica*, 5, 1968.

Mouton, D.J. "Resale Price Maintenance in the Republic of South Africa", *Antitrust Bulletin*, **14**: 981, 1969.

Olivier, N.J.J. *Die Privaatreg van die Suid-Afrikaanse Bantoe*, Durban 1969.

Penny, P. "The Valuation of Land for Subdivision and the Law", *South African Law Journal*, **86**: 205, 1969; **86**: 325, 1969.

Randell, G.H., Bax, K.C. and Van Niekerk, J.P. *The South African Attorney's Handbook*, Durban 1968.

Reinsma, M. " 'Adverse User' of 'Adverse Possession' ", *Tydskrif vir Hedendaagse Romeins-Hollands Reg*, **32**: 293, 1969.

Rogers, C.L. *Hockly's Students' Guide to the Insolvency Law of South Africa*, Cape Town 1969.

Roome, K.D.S. "Discrimination in By-Laws", *South African Law Journal*, **86**: 319, 1969.

Sadie, J.L. "Company Taxation", *South African Journal of Economics*, **37**: 345, 1969.

Schaeffer, M. "The Industrial Laws in the United Kingdom and in South Africa: A Comparative Study", *Comparative and International Law Journal of Southern Africa*, **2**: 24, 1969.

Schaeffer, M. and Heyne, J.F. *Nywerheidsreg in Suid-Afrika*, Pretoria 1968.

Shrand, D. *What Every Taxpayer Should Know About Income Tax*, Cape Town 1969.

Silke, A.S. *Silke on South African Income Tax*, Cape Town 1969.

South Africa and the Rule of Law, Pretoria 1968.

"Southern Africa", *Review of the International Commission of Jurists*, **3**: 19, 1969.

Spiro, E. "Non-compliance With Order of Court", *South African Law Journal*, **86**: 65, 1969.

Spiro, E. " 'Person' in the Income Tax Act", *Tydskrif vir Hedendaagse Romeins-Hollands Reg*, **32**: 1, 1969.

Strauss, S.A. *Die Suid-Afrikaanse Geneeskundige Reg*, Pretoria 1967.

Strauss, S.A. Strydom, M.J. and Van Der Walt, J.C. *Die Suid-Afrikaanse Persreg*, Pretoria 1968.

Stuart, K.W. and Klopper, W. *The Newspaperman's Guide to the Law*, Johannesburg 1968.

Suttner, R.S. "The Legal Status of African Women in South Africa: A Review Article", *African Social Research*, **8**: 620, 1969.

Suttner, R.S. "The Study of Bantu Law in South Africa", *Acta juridica*, 147, 1968.

Swift's Law of Criminal Procedure, Durban 1969.

Thompson, M. "The Ethics of Capital Punishment", *Codicillus*, **10(1)**: 4, 1969.

Trial of Andries Botha, Pretoria 1969.

The Trial of Dinuzulu, Pretoria 1969.

Trotter, G.J. "Personal Income Tax", *South African Journal of Economics*, **37**: 306, 1969.

Tselentis, M. and Friedman, J.H. "Criminal Attempt: A Reappraisal", *Responsa Meridiana*, **2**: 59, 1969.

Uys, J.F. "The Continuation of Civil Proceedings in a Foreign Country", *Comparative and International Law Journal of Southern Africa*, **2**: 99, 1969.

van der Merwe, H.R. "Die aard en betekenis van die gemeenskaplike boedel", *Responsa Meridiana*, **2(1)**: 17, 1969.

van der Merwe, N.J. and Rowland, C.J. *Die Suid-Afrikaanse Erfreg*, Pretoria 1969.

Van Der Walt, J.C. "Die Grondslag van Deliktuele Aanspreklikheid", *Tydskrif vir Hedendaagse Romeins-Hollands Reg*, **32**: 319, 1969.

Van Niekerk, A.F. "The Interim Report of the Commission of Inquiry into Fiscal and Monetary Policy in South Africa", *Comparative and International Law Journal of South Africa*, **(2)**: 108, 1969.

Van Niekerk, B.V.D. "Hanged by the Neck Until You Are Dead", *South African Law Journal*, **86**: 457, 1969.

Van Niekerk, B.V.D. " 'Render unto Caesar . . .' A Study of the Sunday Observance Laws in South Africa", *South African Law Journal*, **86**: 27, 1969.

Van Waasdijk, T. "Some Thoughts on Indirect Tax Effects in South Africa", *South African Journal of Economics*, **37**: 372, 1969.

Van Winsen, L. De V., Thomas, J.D. and Cilliers, A.C. *The Civil Practice of Superior Courts in South Africa*, Cape Town 1967.

Verloren Van Themaat, R. "Legal Education for the Bantu of South Africa", *Comparative and International Law Journal of Southern Africa*, 2: 73, 1969.

Verloren Van Themaat, R., Coete, P.M. and Mapena, I.O.H.M. "Ontwikkelinge i. v. m. die Reg en Regspleging van die Bantoe-Oorsig vir 1967 en 1968", *Tydskrif vir Hedendaagse Romeins-Hollands Reg*, 32: 134, 1969; 32: 362, 1969.

Visagie, G.G. *Regspleging en Reg aan die Kaap van 1652 tot 1806*, Kaapstad 1969.

Welsh, D. "The State President's Powers under the Bantu Administration Act", *Acta juridica*, 81, 1968.

Wiechers, M. *Verloren van Themaat Staatsreg*, Durban 1967.

Williams, R.C. "Pacta successoria", *Responsa Meridiana*, 2: 45, 1969.

Zajtay, I. and Hosten, W.J. "The Permanence of Roman Law Concepts in the Continental Legal Systems and in South African Law", *Comparative and International Law Journal of Southern Africa*, 2: 181, 1969.

SOUTH WEST AFRICA/NAMIBIA — NAMIBIA/SUD-OUEST AFRICAIN

"Apartheid in South West Africa", *Bulletin of the International Commission of Jurists*, (30): 26, 1967.

"El 'apartheid' en Africa sud occidental", *Revista juridica veracruzana*, 19(2): 25, 1968.

Dugard, C.J.R. "South West Africa and the Supremacy of the South African Parliament", *South African Law Journal*, 86: 194, 1969.

Gross, E.A. *Ethiopia and Liberia vs. South Africa; the South West Africa Cases*, Los Angeles 1968.

"South West Africa Cases. Report of the Committee and Background Materials", *Asian African Legal Consultative Committee. Reports*, 9: 3, 1967.

"South West Africa Cases. Study Prepared by the Secretariat of the Committee for its Consideration at the Ninth Session", *Asian African Legal Consultative Committee. Reports*, 9: 23, 1967.

Van Wyk, J.T. "The United Nations, South West Africa and the Law", *Comparative and International Law Journal of Southern Africa*, 2: 48, 1969.

SUDAN — SOUDAN

Deng, F.M. "Future of Customary Law in Sudan", *Malaya Law Review*, 11: 268, 1969.

El-Agraa, A.M. "The Sudan and the Arab Customs Union: A Conflict", *Eastern Africa Economic Review*, 1(2): 39, 1969.

Henin, "Marriage Patterns and Trends in the Nomadic and Settled Populations of the Sudan", *Africa*, 39: 238, 1969.

Holt, P.M. "Four Funji Land-Charters", *Sudan Notes and Records*, 50: 1, 1969.

Sharma, B.S. "Local Government and Community Development in the Sudan", *Journal of Administration Overseas*, 8: 46, 1969.

Sudan Law Reports (*Civil Cases*), *Vol.1, 1900–1931*, Dobbs Ferry 1969.

Zabel, S.C. "Historical Sketch on the Legislative Process in the Early Condominium Period of the Sudan from 1899 to 1912", *Journal of Islamic and Comparative Law*, 2: 45, 1968.

Zabel, S.C. "Hyde v. Hyde in Africa: A Comparative Study of the Law of Marriage in Sudan and Nigeria", *Utah Law Review*, (1): 22, 1969.

SWAZILAND — SWAZILAND

Crawford, J.R. "The History and Nature of the Judicial System of Botswana, Lesotho and Swaziland — Introduction and the Superior Courts", *South African Law Journal*, 86: 476, 1969.

Dening, B.H. "Local Government Trends in Swaziland", *Journal of Administration Overseas*, 8: 197, 1969.

TANZANIA — TANZANIE

Carey, K. "The Possession of Suspect Property", *Eastern Africa Law Review*, **2**: 358, 1969.

Grohs, G. "Traditionalismus und Sozialismus im tansanischen Strafrecht", *Verfassung und Recht in Uebersee*, **2**: 449, 1969.

Grohs, G. "The Resettlement of Offenders Act, 1969", *Eastern Africa Law Review*, **2**: 247, 1969.

Gulliver, P.H. "Dispute Settlement without Courts: The Ndendenli of Southern Tanzania", *Law in Culture and Society*, 24.

Hardwick, S. "Local Government Elections in a One-Party State", *Journal of Administration Overseas*, **8**: 124, 1969.

Harries, L. "Language Policy in Tanzania", *Africa*, **39**: 275, 1969.

Jain, S.C. "Nationalization in Tanzania: Some Legal Aspects", *Africa Quarterly*, **9**: 141, 1969.

James, R.W. "Horizontal Ownership and the Tenant Purchase Scheme", *Eastern Africa Law Review*, **2**: 355, 1969.

Kassam, F.M. "Legal Aid and the Law Student", *Journal of the Denning Law Society*, **2(2)**: 179, 1969.

Kieran, J.A. "The Origins of the Zanzibar Guarantee Treaty of 1862", *Canadian Journal of African Studies*, **2**: 147, 1968.

Lee, E.C. *Local Taxation in Tanganyika*, Berkeley 1969.

Maquet, J. "Institutionalisation féodale des relations de dépendance dans quatre cultures interlacustres", *Cahiers d'études africaines*, **9**: 402, 1969.

Martin, R. "Teaching Law to Non-Lawyers in Tanzania", *East African Law Journal*, **5**: 214, 1969.

Mutharika, A.P.T. "Is there An Obligation Under International Law to Deport a Stateless Person?", *Eastern Africa Law Review*, **2**: 339, 1969.

Omori, M. "Dynamics in Bachiga Rural Life — A Preliminary Analysis of the Dispute Cases at Buhara", *Africa Kenkyu*, **8**: 27, 1969.

Picciotto, S. and Whitford, W.C. "The Impact of Tanzania Hire-Purchase Act, 1966", *Eastern Africa Law Review*, **2**: 11, 1969.

Roe, A.R. "The Future of the Company in Tanzania Development", *Journal of Modern African Studies*, **7**: 47, 1969.

Sawyer, G.F.A. "Reflections on the Internal Conflicts of Laws in Tanzania — An Outline", *Afrika Spectrum*, **4(3)**: 23, 1969.

Sawyer, G.F.A. "Discriminatory Restrictions on Private Dispositions of Land in Tanganyika: A Second Look", *Journal of African Law*, **13**: 2, 1969.

Schröder, D. "Tansania — eine Heranforderung an die europäische Verfassungslehre", *Afrika Spectrum*, **4(1)**: 31, 1969.

Sonius, H. "Problèmes de l'organisation judiciaire au Tanganyika", *L'organisation judiciaire en Afrique noire*, 259.

Von Sperber, K.W. "Das Verhältnis von Partei und Staat in Tansania seit 1961", *Internationales Afrika Forum*, **5**: 434, 1969.

Wada, S. "Territorial Expansion of the Iraqw — Land Tenure and the Locality Group" *Kyoto University African Studies*, **(4)**: 115, 1969.

TCHAD — TCHAD

Adler, A. "Essai sur la signification des relations de dépendance personnelle dans l'ancien système politique des Mundang au Tchad", *Cahiers d'études africaines*, **9**: 441, 1969.

Brahim Seid, J. "Le rôle de la Cour suprême au Tchad", *Revue juridique et politique, Indépendance et coopération*, **23**: 1011, 1969.

Brahim Seid, J. "L'organisation judiciaire du Tchad en matière civile", *Revue juridique et politique, Indépendance et coopération*, **23**: 601, 1969.

Brahim Seid, J. "L'organisation judiciaire du Tchad en matière administrative", *Revue juridique et politique, Indépendance et coopération*, **23**: 952, 1969.

TOGO — TOGO

Segbeaya, L. "L'organisation judiciaire du Togo en matière civile", *Revue juridique et politique, Indépendance et coopération*, **23**: 605, 1969.

TUNISIE — TUNISIA

Abdesselem, M. "L'organisation de la procédure civile contentieuse selon le code tunisien de 1959", *Revue juridique et politique, Indépendance et coopération*, **23**: 613, 1969.

Abdesselem, M. "Le rôle d'une Cour suprême dans l'évolution du droit privé en Tunisie", *Revue juridique et politique, Indépendance et coopération*, **23**: 1012, 1969.

Benamor, A. "Le Conseil supérieur de la Magistrature en Tunisie", *Revue juridique et politique, Indépendance et coopération*, **23**: 1049, 1969.

Benamor, A. "L'organisation judiciaire tunisienne en matière civile", *Revue juridique et politique, Indépendance et coopération*, **23**: 625, 1969.

Benamor, A. "L'organisation judiciaire tunisienne en matière pénale", *Revue juridique et politique, Indépendance et coopération*, **23**: 843, 1969.

Benattar, R. "Evolution récente du droit international privé tunisien en matière de divorce", *Revue critique de droit international privé*, **38**: 17, 1969.

Ben Slama, H. "La sélection des magistrats en Tunisie", *Revue juridique et politique, Indépendance et coopération*, **23**: 1189, 1969.

Boudhiba, A. "Alcuni aspetti della delinquenza minorile in Tunisia", *Quaderni di Criminologia Clinica*, **11**: 399, 1969.

Boudhiba, A. "Quelques aspects de la délinquance juvénile en Tunisie", *Revue tunisienne des sciences sociales*, **(19)**: 67, 1969.

Dubois, A. "Association de la Tunisie et du Maroc à la Communauté", *Revue du Marché Commun*, 355, 1969.

Lucchini, L. "L'administration tunisienne", *Bulletin de l'Institut international d'administration publique*, **12**: 67, 1969.

Mennens, E. "Associatieovereenkomsten tussen de E.E.G. en Tunisië en Marokko", *Sociaal-Economische Wetgeving*, **17**: 562, 1969.

Zghal, A. "Système de parenté et système coopératif dans les campagnes tunisiennes", *Civilisations*, **19**: 483, 1969.

UGANDA — OUGANDA

Ali, P. "Ideological Commitment and the Judiciary", *Transition*, **7(5)**: 47, 1968.

Ali, P. "The 1967 Republican Constitution of Uganda", *Transition*, **7(3)**: 11, 1968.

Due, J.F. "The Uganda Sales Tax On Importation and Manufacture", *Eastern Africa Economic Review*, **1(1)**: 1, 1969.

Fallers, L.A. *Law Without Precedent: Legal Ideas in Action in the Courts of Colonial Busoga*, Chicago 1969

Kasfir, N. "The Uganda Constituent Assembly Debate", *Transition*, **7(2)**: 52, 1967.

Maquet, J. "Institutionalisation féodale des relations de dépendance dans quatre cultures interlacustres", *Cahiers d'études africaines*, **9**: 402, 1969.

Moore, S.F. "Descent and Legal Position", *Law in Culture and Society*, 374.

ULTRAMAR PORTUGUES — PORTUGUESE TERRITORIES

Wilensky, A.H. *Tendencias de la legislacion ultramarina portuguesa en Africa*, Braga 1968.

UNITED ARAB REPUBLIC — REPUBLIQUE ARABE UNIE

Ahmed, F. "The Concept of Public Corporation and Its Significance to the U.A.R. High Dam", *Cahiers africains d'administration publique*, **(3A)**: 47, 1968.

Bibliography   407

Al Quaysi, R. "Torts in the Conflict of Laws", *Revue Al-Ulum Al-Quanuniya Wal-Iqtisadiya*, **10**: 581, 1968.

Behnam, R. "Délits de mise en danger: République Arabe Unie", *Revue internationale de droit pénal*, **40**: 381, 1969.

Doherty, K.B. "Rhetoric and Reality: A Study of Contemporary Official Egyptian Attitudes Towards the International Legal Order, *American Journal of International Law*, **62**: 335, 1968.

El-Azzouni, M.K. "The Development of Inspection, Control and Follow-up Administration in the U.A.R.", *Cahiers africains d'administration publique*, **(2B)**: 36, 1967.

El-Azzouni, M.K. "Powers of the Inspectorate and the Initiative of the Central Inspection, Control and Follow-Up Administration and its Freedom of Action", *Cahiers africains d'administration publique*, **(2B)**: 48, 1967.

Eldin, A.A.G. "Quelques aspects du code pénal militaire", *Revue Al-Ulum Al-Qanuniya Wal-Iqtisadiya*, **11(A)**: 151, 1969.

El-Kalyoubi, S. "Régime juridique des inventions en R.A.U.", *Revue Al Qanoun Wal Iqtisad*, **39**: 205, 1969.

El-Marsafawi, H. "Division du procès pénal en deux phases", *Revue internationale de droit pénal*, **40**: 477, 1969.

El-Mikayis, A.W. "Internationales und interreligiöses Personen-, Familien- und Erbrecht in der Vereinigten Arabischen Republik", *Rabels Zeitschrift für ausländisches und internationales Privatrecht*, **33**: 517, 1969.

El-Outeifi, G. "Le fondement juridique de la justification de la diffamation en cas de publication relative aux faits et instructions criminels (in Arabic)", *Revue Al-Qanoun Wal-Iqtisad*, **39**: 611, 1969.

Khalil, M.S. *Le dirigisme économique et les contrats: étude de droit comparé*, Paris 1967.

Mostafa, M. "Les nouvelles tendances du projet de code pénal de la R.A.U.", *Proche Orient, Etudes juridiques*, **45**, 1968.

Riad, F.A.-M. "Le conflit de compétence en matière de nationalité en R.A.U.", *Proche Orient, Etudes juridiques*, **51**, 1968.

Saad, W. "Structural Changes and Socialist Transformation in Agriculture of the U.A.R.", *Egypte Contemporaine*, **60(337)**: 103, 1969.

Salama, M.M. "Les infractions des fonctionnaires contre l'administration publique à la lumière de la méthode téléologique" (in Arabic), *Revue Al-Qanoun Wal-Iqtisad*, **39**: 120, 1969.

Seif, R. "La procédure d'injonction de paiement dans le droit judiciaire privé de la R.A.U.", *Proche Orient, Etudes juridiques*, **–**: **9**, 1967.

Shanab, M.L. "L'exercise du droit de rétention", *Revue Al-Ulum Al-Qanuniya Wal-Iqtisadyia*, **10**: 437, 1968.

Shirata, I. "Cadre juridique pour l'encouragement et le contrôle des investissements privés étrangers", *Revue égyptienne de droit international*, **24**: 139, 1968.

Wade, S. "Quelques réflexions sur la réforme agraire en Egypte", *L'Afrique et l'Asie*, **(79)**: 31, 1967.

Ziadeh, F.J. *Lawyers, the Rule of Law and Liberalism in Modern Egypt*, Stanford 1968.

ZAMBIA — ZAMBIE

Baron, L.S. "The Liso Case", *Zambia Law Journal*, **1(1)**: 92, 1969.

Collingwood, J.J.R. "D.P.P. v. Chirwa", *Zambia Law Journal*, **1(1)**: 106, 1969.

Collingwood, J.J.R. "Should Zambia Retain a Trial Within a Trial?", *Zambia Law Journal*, **1(2)**: 31, 1969.

Gluckman, M. "Concepts in the Comparative Study of Private Law", *Law in Culture and Society*, 349.

Gupta, C.P. "The Patel Currency Case", *Zambia Law Journal*, **1(2)**: 49, 1969.

Harvey, C.R.M. "Observations on the 1969 Zambian Budget and the Administrative Constraint on Further Tax Reform", *Zambia Law Journal*, **1(2)**: 37, 1969.

Holleman, J.F. *Shona Customary Law*, Manchester 1969.

Krishnamurthy, B.S. "The Thomson Treaties and Johnston's Certificate of Claim", *African Social Research*, (8): 588, 1969.

Menary, W.J. "When is a Member not a Member?", *Zambia Law Journal*, 1(1): 87, 1969.

Mutharika, A.P.T. "Thixton's Case: A Brief Comment", *Zambia Law Journal*, 1(1): 99, 1969.

"The People v. Chisata", *Zambia Law Journal*, 1(2): 57, 1969.

Werbner, R.P. "Constitutional Ambiguities and the British Administration of Royal Careers among the Bemba of Zambia", *Law in Culture and Society*, 245.

Zafer, M.R. "Kachasu's Case", *Zambia Law Journal*, 1(2): 44, 1969.

GENERAL INDEX